MW00978806

Professional Selling: A Relationship Process

Mary Ann Oberhaus
Orange Coast College

Sharon A. Ratliffe
Golden West College

Vernon R. Stauble
California State Polytechnic University

Professional Selling: A Relationship Process

The Dryden Press

Harcourt Brace Jovanovich College Publishers

Fort Worth Philadelphia San Diego New York Orlando Austin San Antonio
Toronto Montreal London Sydney Tokyo

Editor in Chief	Robert A. Pawlik
Acquisitions Editor	Lyn Keeney Hastert
Developmental Editor	Glenn E. Martin
Project Editor	Sheila M. Spahn
Production Manager	Alison J. Howell
Book Designer	David A. Day
Photo Permissions Editor	Sandra Lord
Literary Permissions Editor	Sheila Shutter

Address for Editorial Correspondence
The Dryden Press, 301 Commerce Street, Suite 3700, Fort Worth, TX 76102

Address for Orders
The Dryden Press, 6277 Sea Harbor Drive, Orlando, FL 32887
1-800-782-4479, or 1-800-433-0001 (in Florida)

ISBN: 0-03-032769-5

Library of Congress Catalogue Number: 92-075903

Printed in the United States of America

3 4 5 6 7 8 9 0 1 2 036 9 8 7 6 5 4 3 2 1

The Dryden Press
Harcourt Brace Jovanovich

The Dryden Press Series in Marketing

Assael
Marketing: Principles and Strategy
Second Edition

Bateson
Managing Services Marketing: Text and Readings
Second Edition

Blackwell, Blackwell, and Talarzyk
Contemporary Cases in Consumer Behavior
Fourth Edition

Boone and Kurtz
Contemporary Marketing
Seventh Edition

Churchill
Basic Marketing Research
Second Edition

Churchill
Marketing Research: Methodological Foundations
Fifth Edition

Czinkota and Ronkainen
International Marketing
Third Edition

Dunn, Barban, Krugman, and Reid
Advertising: Its Role in Modern Marketing
Seventh Edition

Engel, Blackwell, and Miniard
Consumer Behavior
Seventh Edition

Futrell
Sales Management
Third Edition

Ghosh
Retail Management

Hutt and Speh
Business Marketing Management: A Strategic View of Industrial and Organizational Markets
Fourth Edition

Ingram and LaForge
Sales Management: Analysis and Decision Making
Second Edition

Kurtz and Boone
Marketing
Third Edition

Murphy and Cunningham
Advertising and Marketing Communications Management: Cases and Applications

Oberhaus, Ratliffe, and Stauble
Professional Selling: A Relationship Process

Park and Zaltman
Marketing Management

Patti and Frazer
Advertising: A Decision-Making Approach

Rachman
Marketing Today
Second Edition

Rogers, Gamans, and Grassi
Retailing: New Perspectives
Second Edition

Rosenbloom
Marketing Channels: A Management View
Fourth Edition

Schellinck and Maddox
Marketing Research: A Computer-Assisted Approach

Schnaars
MICROSIM
Marketing simulation available for IBM PC and Apple

Sellars
Role Playing: The Principles of Selling
Second Edition

Shimp
Promotion Management and Marketing Communications
Third Edition

Talarzyk
Cases and Exercises in Marketing

Terpstra and Sarathy
International Marketing
Fifth Edition

Tootelian and Gaedeke
Cases and Classics in Marketing Management

Weitz and Wensley
Readings in Strategic Marketing Analysis, Planning, and Implementation

Zikmund
Exploring Marketing Research
Fourth Edition

Preface

With increasing domestic and international opportunities, companies are looking for new and creative ways to serve customers better. The globalization of markets and rapid changes in technology are influencing the ways firms access and deliver information as well as redirecting the manner in which salespeople relate to their customers. Companies are recognizing that professionalism is synonymous with competence. Such competence is realized when a salesperson is able to operate both effectively and appropriately at all levels of account procurement and management.

In a March 1988 issue of *Sales and Marketing Management*, Arthur Bragg cited in his article, "Personal Selling Goes to College," that:

> Colleges and universities are being encouraged by corporations to offer classes that equip learners with job-related skills. Also, sales executives tend to prefer courses—if only because each time a learner decides not to become a sales person, it saves some company the high cost of recruiting and training an eventual dropout.
>
> Personal selling courses, say academics in the field, are attracting more interest among marketing students and even among nonbusiness students, who usually take the courses to improve their communication skills.

Also in 1988, we began to merge the two disciplines of professional selling and communications into a partnership that meets the needs of both the academic and business community. This book is the product of those efforts.

In the proposal that we mailed to nearly twenty publishers five years ago when we created our title, *Professional Selling: A Relationship Process*, we could find no text on the market that used a similar description. Since then, at least five books with current copyright dates have emerged with almost identical titles. We are both encouraged and excited that many other academics and sales professionals embrace our philosophy of relationship selling.

OUR PHILOSOPHY

Gone are the days when all that was needed for personal selling was an abundance of product information with an ability to outtalk the buyer. Today's sales professionals not only need to have superior product knowledge but they also must demonstrate communication skills that will endure long after the product data becomes obsolete. If they are to obtain and maintain a competitive edge, they must be able to establish relationships that yield repeat business. Thus, sales communication is systemic to building partnerships in the buying-selling process.

The content of this book offers an innovative and challenging approach to professional selling because it provides learners with a systematic structure for learning skills which implement effective principles of selling. This approach is also unique because it merges two disciplines—professional selling and communication. The text treats professional selling as a relationship process. Thus, the road map for achieving competence is carved in the integration of communication skills with the steps of the selling process.

TEXT AND CHAPTER PEDAGOGY: SPECIAL FEATURES AND INNOVATIONS

Each chapter of the book presents an internal consistency for competency-based skill development by including: 1) behavioral learning objectives, and 2) modules to develop these objectives, consisting of a **SKILL BUILDER** and one or more **TRY THIS** exercises. Students may use these to apply the skills in a buyer-seller situation. Charts and graphs are designed to enhance and explain selling theory.

A chapter outline, key terms, a chapter summary, and review and discussion questions are included in the format of each chapter. Case problems have been carefully designed to promote students' critical thinking skills. Lastly, each chapter contains an **"On the International Front"** box that emphasizes the relevance of international sales to personal selling. Where appropriate, **"On the Ethical Side"** boxes are added to serve as a vehicle for heightening awareness of the mandate for ethical selling practices. The twenty people profiled in this text were selected for their relational selling philosophy and practices as competent sales professionals.

Supplemental Material Resources

To enhance the Skill Builder and Try This exercises, a **VIDEOTAPE** produced exclusively for this textbook will be provided free to adopters. Additionally, the **INSTRUCTOR'S MANUAL** and **Video Instructor's Manual** provide directions for demonstrating skills in the classroom with peers and skill assessment forms on which to provide feedback.

The Competency-Based Format

While the skill focus of each chapter of the book develops hierarchically upon previous chapters, each chapter is written with a separate integrity so that the instructor may change the order to accommodate his or her teaching preferences or use a chapter as a self-contained module for seminar or training purposes.

There are at least five major advantages to this competency-based format. First, this approach provides an opportunity to individualize instruction by allowing learners to acquire sales communication skills at their own rate and to repeat skill demonstrations as necessary. As a result, all users can master learning objectives. Second, this format meets accountability needs by focusing the user's efforts toward learning objectives rather than competing with other classmates. Third, this format reduces uncertainty among learners about what is required in order to succeed. Fourth, when this approach is used across multiple sections of a professional selling course, it eliminates most of the inconsistency that often exists among instructors. Finally, this format provides a means of pre- and post-assessment which can facilitate the placement of learners at levels of instruction that match their abilities.

ORGANIZATION OF THE TEXT

The twenty chapters contained in *Professional Selling: A Relationship Process* are divided into five parts:

- "Twenty-first Century Sales Horizons" discusses the importance and perspectives of professional selling and illustrates the elements of a competency-based learning system in a relational communication selling environment. It also examines the ethical, legal, and cultural issues in personal selling.

- "The Salesperson and the Profession" covers understanding the self and developing a positive sales image. Knowing one's industry, company, products, and competition is also a focus of this section.

- "Anatomy of the Selling Process" covers the entire sales call from opening the interview to postsale activities and contains the heart of the presentational system. Relational selling strategies, practices, and techniques are offered with heavy emphasis on developing sales communication competency through practicing Skill Builders and Try This exercises.

- "Staying Alive—Methods of Maintaining a Professional Sales Career" discusses telemarketing, technology, communication systems, and sales management as they apply to personal selling. Further emphasis is given to career search and management with a continued focus on skills that are important to building sales competency.

INSTRUCTIONAL RESOURCE PACKAGE

All of the skills presented in the textbook and the supplemental materials have been class tested and field tested by the authors in classrooms as well as in business or seminar environments. All components of the developed package have been designed and created by the authors to provide an integrated learning system linked to the textbook. This comprehensive teaching and learning resource package is designed to fit the needs of all users: the instructor or trainer and the student or salesperson.

- ***Instructor's Manual***, written by Carolyn Shiery of Orange Coast College and Western National Property Management, contains teaching ideas, transparency masters, answers to end-of-chapter questions, and comments on cases. Most important, pre- and post-assessment forms to accompany the Skill Builders are presented as well as additional skill-building exercises and feedback forms for sales presentation analyses. The Instructor's Manual is designed to be "user-friendly" for both instructor and student.

- ***Test Bank***, containing 1,500 questions of a multiple-choice and true-false variety. Prepared by Rita Mix and Blaise Waguespack, Jr, both of the Marketing Department of the University of North Texas, the Test Bank is available for both IBM and Apple MacIntosh PCs. These questions are derived from the various components of the chapters and test for both individual chapter comprehension and collective competency as the student moves through the course.

- ***A professionally produced video*** highlights the skill-building components of the text and offers the instructor additional opportunity for discussion and role-playing scenarios. This video will be provided free to adopters through their local Dryden representative.

- ***Video Instructor's Manual***, developed and written by Mary Ann Oberhaus and Sharon Ratliffe, contains detailed analysis of the video. Specific instructions and suggestions are given for using the video as a training and skill-building instrument. Models of student self-analysis of a presentation are provided, as well as guidelines for the student to follow in writing a self-analysis of a videotape sales presentation.

- ***Additional VHS Videotapes*** of the selling principles and examples of techniques discussed in the text will be available to adopters.

ACKNOWLEDGMENTS

This text is not only the culmination of years of experience and research; it also was made possible by contributions from many people.

The expertise and creative contributions of Carolyn Shiery, Manager of Training for Western National Property Management, Inc., and instructor at Orange Coast College, in writing the Instructor's Manual and assisting with the training video were major contributions to this instructional package, and we are genuinely appreciative. The contribution of the initial draft by David Hudson, Golden West College, on buying climate, nonverbal communication, and using visuals effectively is also appreciated. We also wish to thank our colleagues who have provided generous support and encouragement, including Pat Hopkins, Chuck Taylor, and Ed Klewer at California State Polytechnic University; Steve Welborn and Frank Marvasti at the University of Redlands; and Don Schall and Queen Hamilton at San Bernardino Valley College.

We are grateful for the guidance of the original Dryden team, who steered us through the first two drafts of the manuscript. In addition, Laura Coaty, a former Dryden Sales Representative and now Saunders' Product Manager for physical sciences, supported us throughout the development of the original manuscript. To our current Acquisitions Editor, Lyn Keeney Hastert, and Developmental Editor, Glenn E. Martin, we extend our sincerest gratitude for generating a renewal of energy and enthusiasm in the final stages of the work. We are moved by their insight, sensitivity, and commitment to excellence. The partnership we have formed with them and the Dryden production staff, epitomizes the relationship process. We wish to thank all of the book team—Dee Salisbury, Sheila M. Spahn, Alison J. Howell, David A. Day, Sheila Shutter, and Sandra Lord—for their creativity and commitment to the integrity of the book; and we would also like to extend our thanks to Kathy Mangus, HBJ's receptionist, for her cheerfulness and helpfulness.

The quality of this work is, in part, the result of the extensive constructive feedback and interaction with reviewers at three critical stages in the development of this manuscript, including:

Kay Keck, University of Georgia
Bill Witherspoon, Triton College
Charles Treas, University of Mississippi
Kathy Feichter, Stark Technical College
Rick Shield, California Polytechnic University
Robert Piacenza, Madison Area Technical College
C. Gus Petrides, Manhattan Community College
M. R. Bowers, University of Alabama
Philip W. Mahin, West Virginia University
Joann Driggers, Mt. San Antonio College
Ben T. Schiek, Western Illinois University
H. Reed Muller, Salisbury State University
Robert E. Thompson, Indiana State University
Alan Zinser, Mattatuck Community College
Ned J. Cooney, University of Colorado, Boulder
Alicia Lupinacci, Tarrant County Junior College
David Good, Central Missouri State University
John Lanasa, Duquesne University

Finally, the importance of class-testing instructional packages cannot be underestimated. The enthusiasm and candor with which the students at Orange Coast College and California State Polytechnic University, Pomona, class-tested the first draft of this manuscript were invaluable, as were their suggestions for improvement when working with the Skill Builder and Try This exercises.

DEDICATION

It is to these students, our colleagues, and our friends and sales professionals who served as models for the relationship process that we dedicate this project.

Mary Ann Oberhaus
S. A. Ratliffe
V. R. Stauble

Contents

Professional Selling: A Relationship Process

PART THREE: FROM PROSPECT TO CLIENT

PART FOUR: ANATOMY OF THE SELLING PROCESS

PART 1

Twenty-first Century Sales Horizons

Chapter One:
Professional Selling: Its Importance and Perspectives

Chapter Two:
Professional Selling Through Relational Communication

Chapter Three:
Ethical, Legal, and Cultural Issues in Professional Selling

Design for the Relational Selling Process

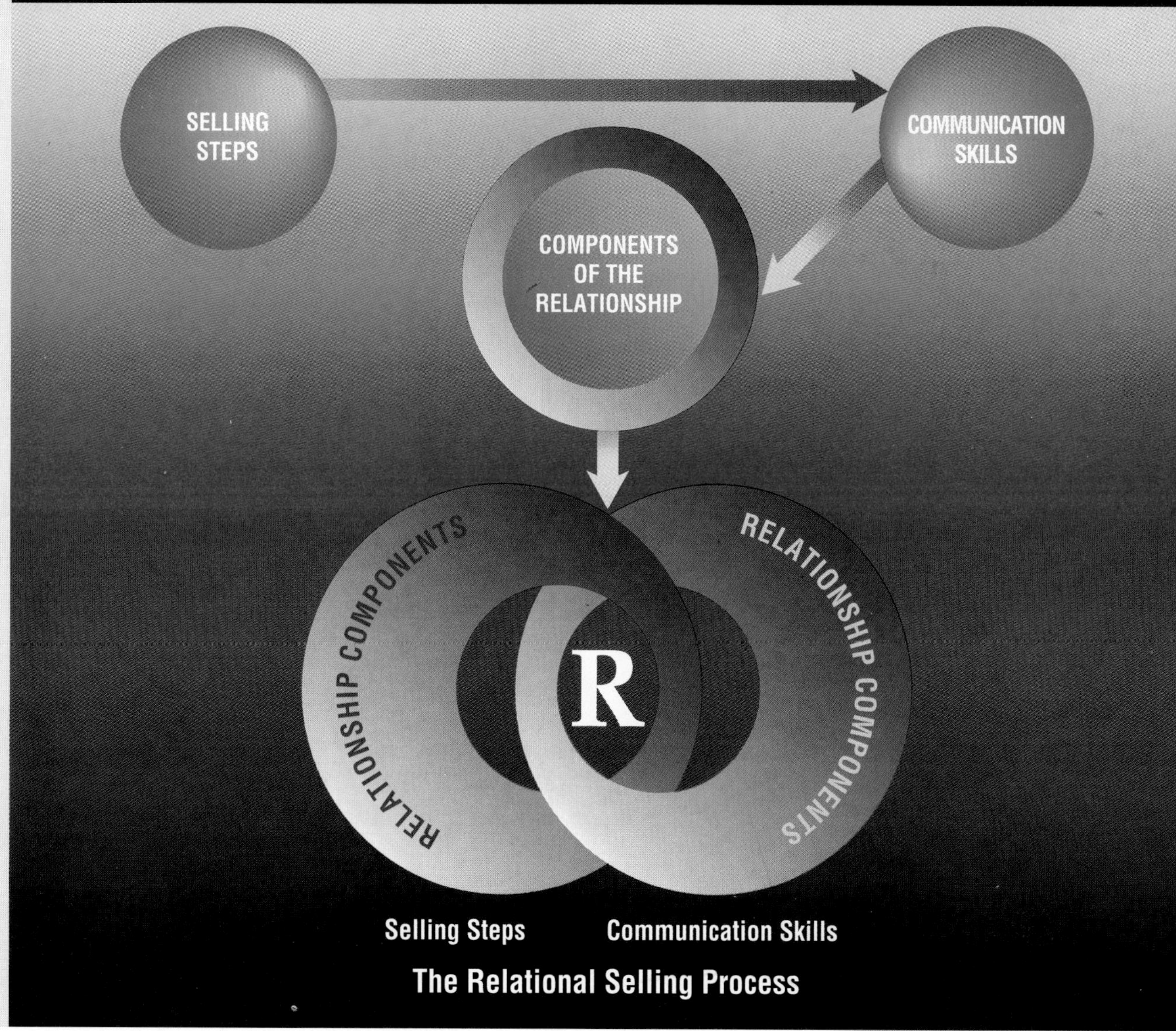

CHAPTER

1

Professional Selling: Its Importance and Perspectives

Knowledge Objectives

In this chapter, you will learn:

1. Why professional selling is such an exciting career choice
2. The part selling plays in the shift to a global market economy
3. How personal selling has evolved through the twentieth century
4. How personal selling fits into the broader marketing umbrella
5. The stages involved in the personal selling process

Consider This

Always changing, sales is still the engine of American business.

Martin Everett, General Editor
Sales & Marketing Management

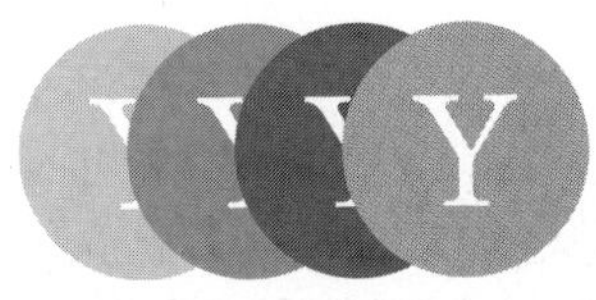

ou are now entering the world of personal selling. It is an exciting, dynamic world where the opportunities to combine personal and financial rewards abound. It is a professional world, and yet at the same time one of the most underrated and misunderstood of all professional worlds—at least during the past several decades. Yesterday's back-slapping, sleazy, joke-telling huckster contributed to those misconceptions, although this type of salesperson now has all but disappeared. Instead, today's consumer is finding a new generation of sales professionals—highly trained and groomed with the characteristics of honesty, trustworthiness, and competence.

On the Ethical Side Guidelines for Setting the Ethical Tone

There is no single answer to the question of what is ethical in each sales situation because different salespeople may take different positions, depending on their particular sense of ethics. A sense of ethics is instilled in each of us by the fundamental customs of our society.

Of course, there are gray areas, where salespeople need guidelines from their managers in dealing with questionable practices. Top management of companies such as IBM, NCR, and AT&T have policies that set the ethical tone, representing a blend of principles and values ingrained in and widely shared by their sales forces, as the cornerstone of their relationships with customers, suppliers, stockholders, and employees.

- IBM's three basic beliefs highlight respect for the dignity of the individual, offering the best customer service in the world, and excellence.
- NCR's mission statement recognizes belief in conducting business activities with integrity and respect and building mutually beneficial and enduring relationships with customers and suppliers.
- AT&T's value system emphasizes universal service, fairness in handling personnel matters, and a commitment to relationships among departments.

Other ways used by companies to keep the sales force on the straight and narrow path include:

1. Developing and circulating a sales ethics policy
2. Setting the proper moral climate
3. Setting realistic sales goals
4. Instituting controls when needed
5. Encouraging salespeople to ask for help when they face an ethically troublesome sale
6. Resisting prospectively shady deals
7. Keeping perspective—"Following the path of least resistance is what makes people and rivers crooked"

Ethical standards go beyond a company policy and value system as guidelines in selling situations. A closer look reveals that the individual salesperson must take control of the situation and determine what is right and wrong. It is the salesperson's responsibility to possess the background and values that are needed to avoid engaging in unethical behavior. Salespeople who exemplify the highest standards of ethical practices become valued in the development of long-term relationships.

Source: Glenn Carroll and David Vogel, *Strategy and Organization: A West Coast Perspective* (Marshfield, Mass.: Pitman Publishing,1984), p. 60; Arthur Thompson and A. J. Strickland, *Strategic Management* (Irwin, 1990), p. 50; and *Sales and Marketing Magazine* (October 11, 1976), p. 42.

Today's sales practitioners are professionals dedicated to customer relations, who view selling as both a discipline to be learned and an art to be performed.

Sales Professional Spotlight

When Jack Ayer retired from professional baseball in 1988, he was concerned that he would be unable to find a career that would give him the same satisfaction as professional athletics. He thrived on the competition and the pressure to perform night after night. "I really enjoyed the competition, and my success was directly related to my performance," he says. After researching many career opportunities, Jack decided that a career in sales would make the best use of his talent and personality.

After receiving his B.A. degree, Jack accepted a position with a large pharmaceutical company, Marion Merrell Dow. "Initially I was a little nervous; I felt inadequate and unprepared because of my limited business experience," Jack says. "I soon realized that the attributes required to be successful in athletics were also essential in sales." Jack was productive from the beginning, winning two sales awards in 2 years for performing among the top 10 percent of salespeople in the company. He used his success as a springboard to a more challenging position selling surgical supplies for Johnson & Johnson.

In his present position with Johnson & Johnson, Jack is responsible for selling products to surgeons. According to Jack, "It is a real challenge uncovering the different needs of individual surgeons. I spend much of my time preparing for each call I make. I try hard to find out all I can about each of my customers. I want to know the kind of surgical procedures they undertake, the hospitals they use, and any other relevant personal information that will be valuable in preparing me to best serve my prospects. I use all the information I can gather to personalize my call to each client's particular needs."

Jack believes that persistence and active listening are the most important qualities needed for success in sales. Active listening is when the listener not only hears what is being said but tries to understand why the person is saying it. "By using active listening, a salesperson can better understand his or her customers' needs," Jack says. "Only then is the salesperson able to tailor-make the presentation to meet those needs. Then you have to realize that rarely is a sale made on the first call. You must be persistent and keep going back asking for an order."

Jack recommends selling as a career because it provides freedom for growth and achievement based on individual effort. It also is an opportunity to help other people solve problems and accomplish goals. As Jack's experience demonstrates, selling is one of the best outlets for creativity and initiative available to enterprising young people.

This chapter is devoted to three main aspects of career sales training: (1) helping the student understand why professional selling is such an exciting career, (2) describing the conceptual framework of marketing, and (3) providing a schematic of the seven steps in the selling process.

Professional Selling As a Career Choice

In business there is an axiom that "nothing happens until someone sells something." Marketing professor H. Reed Muller of Salisbury State University in Maryland emphasizes that point:

> The personal selling component accounts for the typical organization's "cash flow." Without this cash flow, generated by sales personnel, an organization can't survive. Most people don't realize the critical nature of personal selling, and the profession's image suffers accordingly.

That same principle reaches into our personal and social activities as well. In fact, selling permeates all of our lives today. Broadly defined, **selling** is a process of defining needs and persuading potential customers to respond favorably to an idea that will result in mutual satisfaction for both the buyer and the seller. It is a dynamic and interpersonal process in which the buyer and the seller participate in reaching the purchasing decision. This definition is illustrated in the following incident:

A rich man went to a jewelry store to purchase a diamond. A salesclerk showed him a number of stones, one of which he seemed to like. However, after some consideration, he started to leave, saying he would not decide at that time. The owner of the store, who had overheard most of the sales conversation, stopped him as he was leaving the store.

"Excuse me," he said to the departing customer, "but would you give me just 5 minutes to show you that stone again?"

"I have decided not to buy it today," replied the customer.

"Ah, yes," said the merchant. "I have not asked you to buy. I have only asked you to let me show it to you again. Will you grant me that pleasure?"

"Well, yes. I do not mind looking at it again, as it was indeed a wonderful stone," replied the man.

The merchant took the stone from the case, holding it up where the sunshine turned it into a flashing gem of fire and brilliance. He began to talk about it as one speaks of things that are dear and precious.

Finally the buyer said, "I believe I will buy that stone today, after all."

When the purchase had been completed, the rich man turned again to the merchant and said, "Sir, I have been wondering just why I changed my mind after first deciding not to buy that diamond. Why did I buy it from you when I refused to buy it from your salesman?"

"Well, sir," answered the merchant, "I think I can explain it. You see, my salesperson knows as much about that stone as I do—its size, weight, coloring, and price, but there is a difference. I love that gem. If I could put into the hearts of my salesmen the same feeling for my jewels that I have, they would sell many more than they do. Really, sir, I did not sell you that stone—we bought it together."[1]

If we recognize and understand the significance of the phrase "we bought it together," we accept selling as an interpersonal process. Thus, we can readily see as a corollary the way that personal selling works with family, friends, or any "significant other" in building and maintaining a relationship. Similarly, when interviewing for any job or position, it is interpersonal skills that help convince the recruiter that an individual is the best person for that job. Fundamentally, we are usually selling ourselves—our ideas, our values, our products, or our services—to someone else.

There are six perspectives that make professional selling so appealing: personal rewards; financial rewards; career opportunities; characteristics, requirements, and responsibilities that are typical of the sales profession; changes in the task; and kinds of selling careers. We will look at each of these in some detail.

Personal Rewards

Personal satisfaction and *psychic income* are often used synonymously when discussing the rewards of being a professional salesperson. Psychic income is a measure of one's degree of satisfaction relative to having made someone else's life better, as well as improving one's own growth and development. As psychic income intensifies, the pleasure of living one's passion is realized.

Among the many personal rewards of a career in sales are these:

- Freedom to be on your own, moving around and meeting new people every day.
- Flexibility in allocating the use of your time and feeling as if you are your own boss.
- Financial independence and security through sales incentives that are based on performance rather than on seniority.
- Psychic income through personal satisfaction in having improved the quality of your customers' lives by helping them make sound buying decisions.
- Job satisfaction and recognition by the firm for achieving top performance—Personal selling has such a visible effect on the company's success that the sales professional's contributions rarely go unrecognized.
- Increased self-confidence in proving that you can hold your own in a highly competitive environment.
- Opportunity for advancement in your company.

Financial Rewards

Studies show that selling is one of the better paid careers. It is not uncommon for salespeople to earn more than their managers or even a vice president of the corporation. The compensation plans and financial rewards of personal selling vary considerably, however, as shown in Figure 1.1, which reports industry averages. Each group can yield well over $100,000 annually. For further clarification, the following definitions are provided by *Sales & Marketing Management* for each of the industry titles:

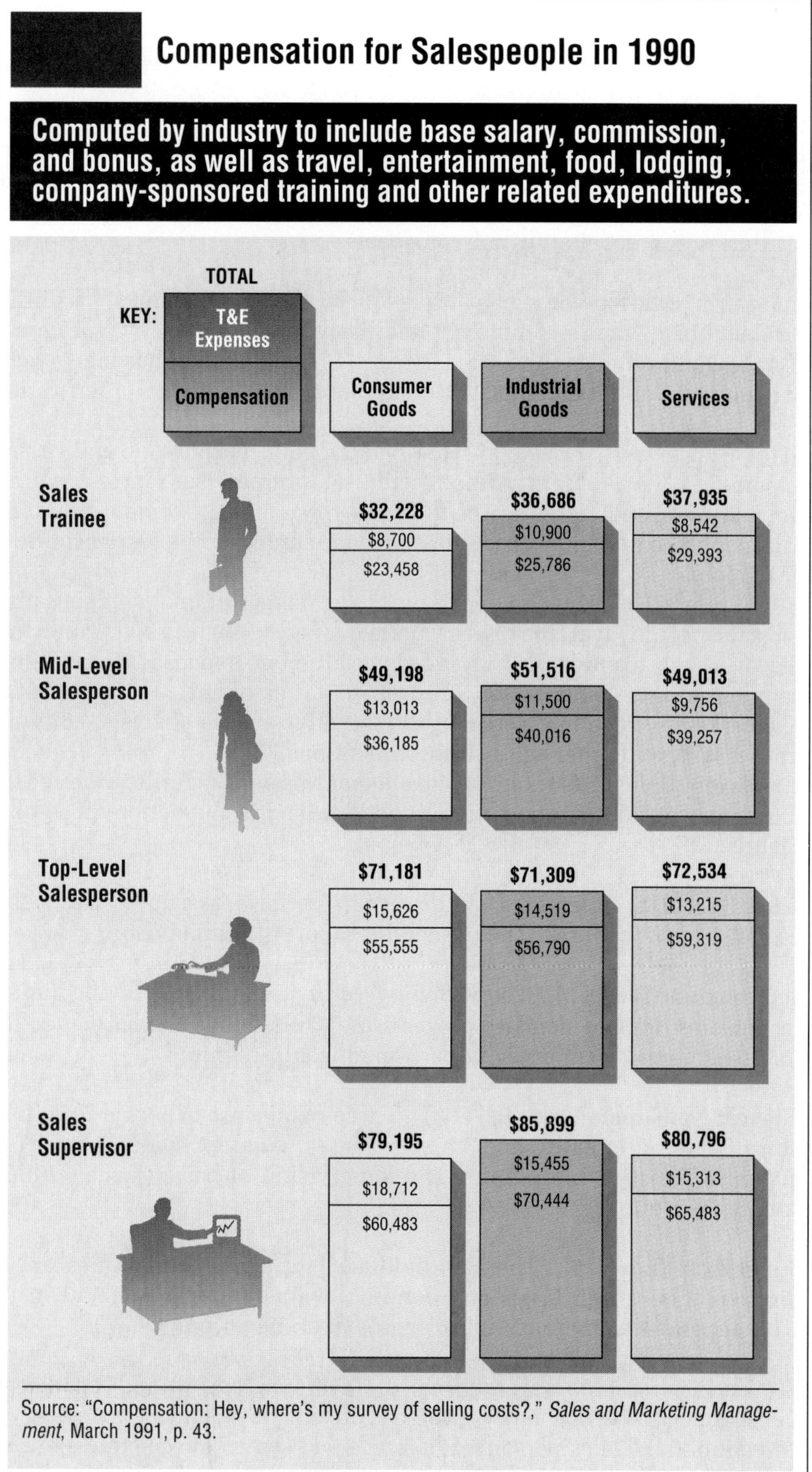

Source: "Compensation: Hey, where's my survey of selling costs?," *Sales and Marketing Management*, March 1991, p. 43.

Figure 1.1

Sales Trainee Anyone at an entry level who is learning about the company's product, services, and policies in preparation for a regular assignment.

Middle-Level Salesperson A salesperson with selling experience ranging from a beginner, who primarily contacts already established customers and accounts, to more experienced field sales personnel who have a broad knowledge of products and services and are selling in established territories and developing new prospects.

Top-Level Salesperson A salesperson at the highest level of selling responsibility who is completely familiar with the company's products, services, and policies. A salesperson at this level usually has many years of experience and is assigned to a company's major accounts or territories.

Sales Supervisor A veteran salesperson who, because of ability and experience, leads others. Although the sales supervisor's primary functions are to direct activities of the sales force and, in some cases, train salespeople, certain key accounts may be included in the responsibilities of the job.

Figure 1.2 presents an overview of the average annual compensation for salespeople over the 5-year period from 1986 to 1990. Note that the overview excludes travel and entertainment expenses. In addition, compensation is shown for sales-support personnel, which includes telemarketers, customer service representatives, sales analysts, administrative staff, and other sales-support positions.

Again, *Sales & Marketing Management* provides clarification for the four levels of sales-support personnel described in the bottom portion of Figure 1.2:

Basic (Level 1) Members of this group perform assigned tasks using established procedures. They generally report to a supervisor.

Intermediate (Level 2) These employees perform tasks involving limited responsibilities and standard procedures. While some originality is called for, evaluation by supervisory personnel is still required.

Highest Nonsupervisory (Level 3) These people are expected to initiate considerable originality and, in some cases, conduct evaluations. They may also assist in the training and supervision of basic (level 1) sales-support personnel.

Supervisor (Level 4) These individuals' major responsibilities are to direct others, assign tasks, and conduct evaluations. They also consult with superiors in more complex phases of assigned projects.

Further research suggests that the changing educational profiles of salespeople influence entry-level earnings. For instance, in 1977, 59 percent of field sales personnel had received some college education. By 1987, however, that figure had risen to 82 percent.[2] College graduates

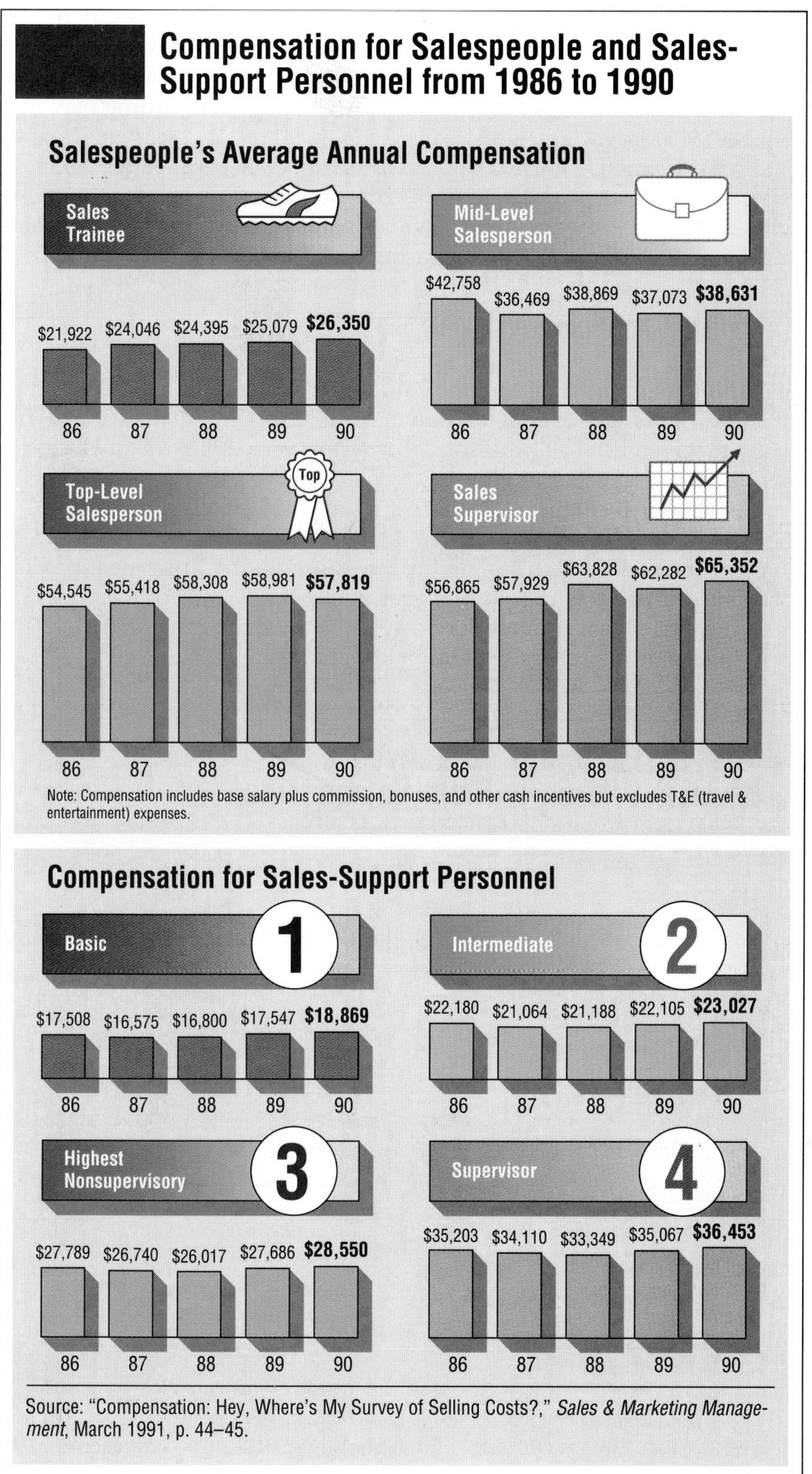
Compensation for Salespeople and Sales-Support Personnel from 1986 to 1990
Salespeople's Average Annual Compensation
Sales Trainee
$21,922 $24,046 $24,395 $25,079 $26,350
86 87 88 89 90
Mid-Level Salesperson
$42,758 $36,469 $38,869 $37,073 $38,631
86 87 88 89 90
Top-Level Salesperson
Top
$54,545 $55,418 $58,308 $58,981 $57,819
86 87 88 89 90
Sales Supervisor
$56,865 $57,929 $63,828 $62,282 $65,352
86 87 88 89 90
Note: Compensation includes base salary plus commission, bonuses, and other cash incentives but excludes T&E (travel & entertainment) expenses.
Compensation for Sales-Support Personnel
Basic 1
$17,508 $16,575 $16,800 $17,547 $18,869
86 87 88 89 90
Intermediate 2
$22,180 $21,064 $21,188 $22,105 $23,027
86 87 88 89 90
Highest Nonsupervisory 3
$27,789 $26,740 $26,017 $27,686 $28,550
86 87 88 89 90
Supervisor 4
$35,203 $34,110 $33,349 $35,067 $36,453
86 87 88 89 90
Source: "Compensation: Hey, Where's My Survey of Selling Costs?," Sales & Marketing Management, March 1991, p. 44–45.

Figure 1.2

with no specialized training who enter selling careers can expect to start at about $26,000 a year, frequently with a bonus in addition to that. This usually puts them ahead of their peers in other areas of business. Salespeople who have advanced degrees or technical training may earn $40,000 or more in their first year.[3]

Other financial rewards appear in the form of perquisites, generally referred to as "perks." Table 1.1 shows how industry honors its salespeople with numerous rewards over and beyond the traditional insurance benefits, retirement, and profit-sharing programs.

Career Opportunities

According to employment outlook studies conducted by the U.S. Bureau of Labor Statistics, overall employment in the United States will rise about 19 percent to 133 million jobs by the year 2000. Meanwhile, the labor force is expected to grow by 18 percent.

As shown in Figure 1.3, marketing and sales jobs are projected to increase by 30 percent. Forecasters also see a significant increase in the demand for services while jobs in goods-producing areas decline. The labor bureau projects that by the year 2000, nearly four of five jobs will be in industries that provide services, such as banking, insurance, health care, information processing, and management consulting.

Table 1.1

Perks and Incentives Offered to Field Salespeople

Type of Perk	Industry (Percent Offering)				
	Manufacturing	*Wholesaling*	*Retail*	*Finance*	*Service*
Entertainment expense account	60	63	53	41	54
Telephone credit card	52	43	37	24	38
Company car	46	32	32	24	23
Incentive travel	45	56	43	50	55
Company credit card	38	20	11	31	28
Merchandise	36	59	43	25	39
Frequent flyer program	28	15	16	10	21
Paid leave	25	13	29	25	35
Paid parking	16	18	11	28	29
Discounts on products	10	27	32	17	15
Car phone	13	12	5	7	11
Low-interest loans	7	7	11	14	10
Personal computer for home use	5	2	5	7	9
Health club membership	4	0	5	3	6
Country club membership	4	1	0	3	2

Source: National Institute of Business Management, 1988 Sales Compensation Survey, *Sales & Marketing Management*, February 20, 1989, pp. 24, 26.

Figure 1.3

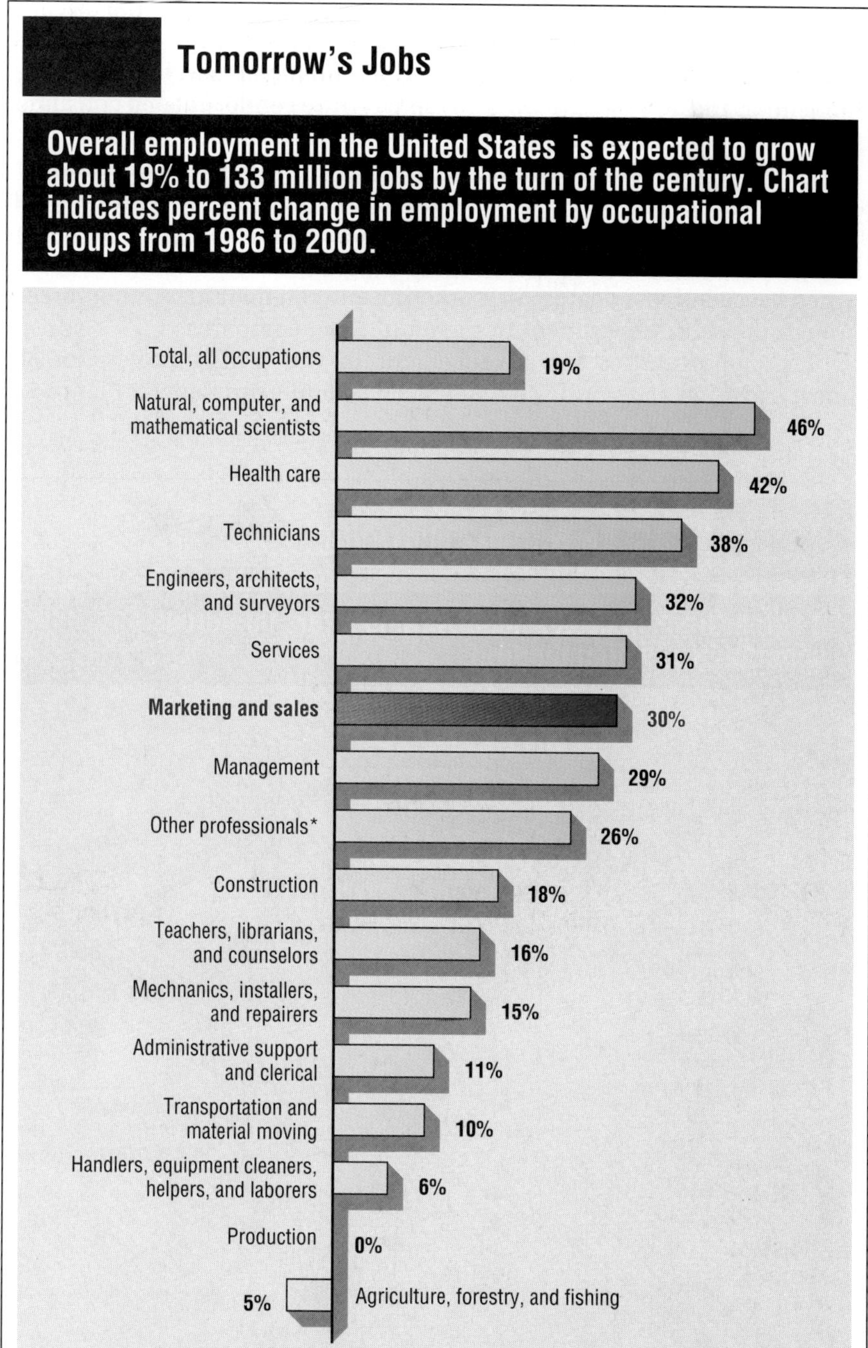

Source: Linda Williams, "A job hunter's crystal ball," *Los Angeles Times*, special section, "Southern California Job Market," September 17, 1989.

In addition, women now account for nearly 20 percent of the nation's sales force and have significant presence in industries such as housewares, apparel, and food products. In banking, financial services, utilities, publishing, and advertising—where there is little gender-related consumer bias—women equal or surpass their male counterparts in numbers.[4]

Personal selling is the closest and strongest link between the salesperson and the end user of the firm's product or service. In several informal studies conducted by the marketing departments of 4-year campuses throughout the western states, over 60 percent of the graduates who earned baccalaureate degrees in marketing entered their marketing careers through the sales department of the employing company.

The opportunities for advancement in the selling profession are almost as varied as the titles by which salespeople are known. Figure 1.4

Figure 1.4

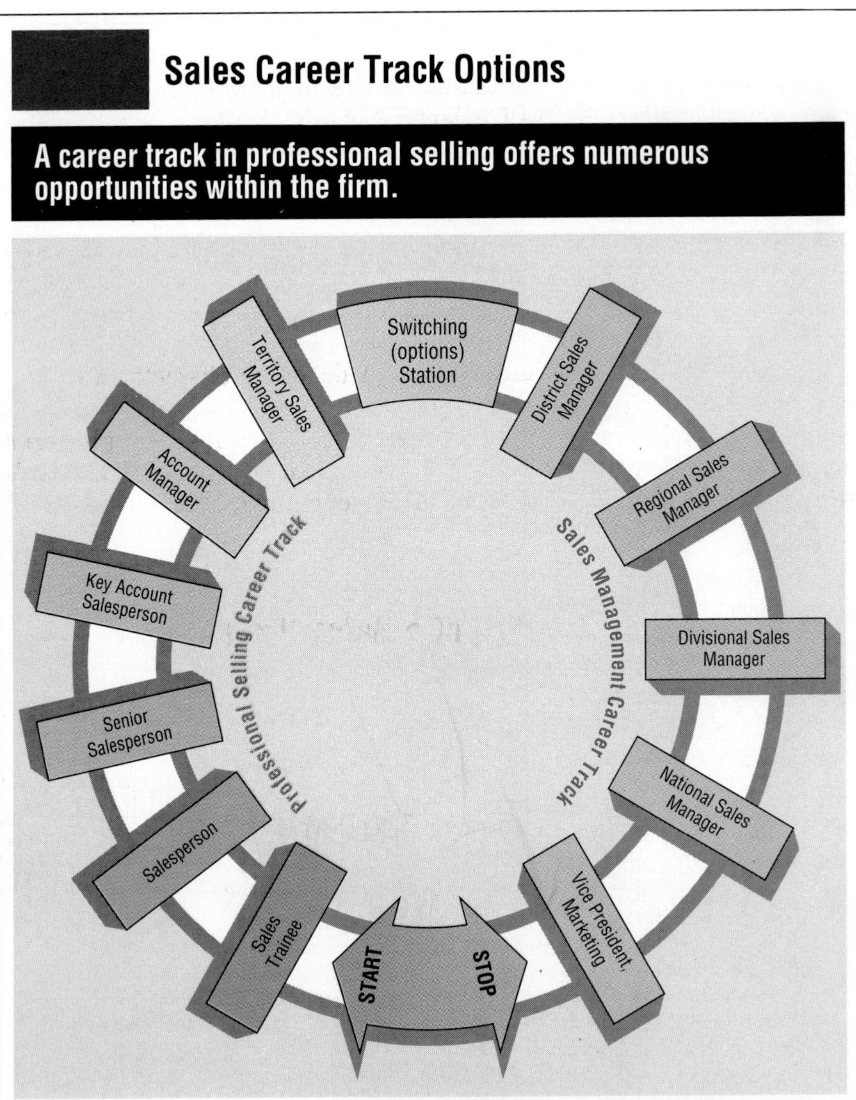

focuses on the salesperson's career track options. Each "box" may be considered a lifetime career cycle choice. Proportional sets of rewards and benefits are available at both the personal and financial levels. David Good of Central Missouri State University refers to this relationship as the risk-reward concept. That is, "As risk increases, so does the amount of reward in sales."

Characteristics, Requirements, and Responsibilities

Listening ability, persuasiveness, and industriousness are common characteristics among today's sales professionals. Willy Loman, the traveling salesman character created by Arthur Miller in *Death of a Salesman*, was built on hustle and charm. And just as in that play, Willy Loman is one of a dying breed who will find himself out of place among this emerging group of sales professionals.

One such professional is Catherine Hogan, who at 28 years of age was account manager for Bell Atlantic Network Service, Inc., in Silver Springs, Maryland. When asked to relate the advice that has brought her success, she replied: "Go beyond what the world prescribes for you. Be strong enough to lance the dragon but soft enough to wear silk." Her ambition is "to direct a sales force that's on the 'leading edge,' even though that may be the 'bleeding edge,' too."[5] This kind of tenacity is described by sales managers as hardworking, persevering, dedicated, and stable.

Tables 1.2 and 1.3 identify the most desirable characteristics of a sales professional for the current decade. Employers continue to stress the need to have both technical and interpersonal skills. One requirement that all industries appear to have in common is that their personnel have enthusiasm, adaptability to change, and strong communication skills.[6]

Table 1.2

Characteristics of a Sales Professional for the Nineties

- Having personal integrity
- Being an excellent listener
- Being goal directed
- Having self-confidence
- Being decisive
- Having intellectual curiosity
- Being speedy and accurate
- Being an effective communicator
- Having perseverance and patience in building a relationship
- Being a self-starter
- Being able to juggle responsibilities (personal and professional)
- Having a sense of humor
- Being culturally sensitive
- Being a team player as well as a strategy planner and implementor

Table 1.3

Qualifications of Successful Salespeople

Lack of any one of these five traits may result in failure, but possessing them may not guarantee success. The first-line contact with customers must be dedicated to enhancing the company's image and reputation. Customers form their ideas of the company from its salespeople.

- *Empathy*—Feeling as the customer does, sensing reactions, and adapting when necessary.
- *Ego-driven*—The desire and personal need to make the sale. Managers want people who are self-motivated.
- *Positive mental toughness*—Optimism and enlightened enthusiasm; having the power to attract wealth, health, and happiness; constantly seeking growth. Some experts claim selling is 5% ability and 95% attitude.
- *Personality dynamics and attitude traits*—Interest, tact, emotional stability, determination, persistence, dominance, self-reliance, appearance, speaking abilities, and consideration.
- *Honesty*—Personal integrity, high productivity, loyalty, commitment, dependability, trainability, and the ability to negotiate and make sound decisions.

The two most significant changes occurring in professional selling, as we approach the next century, are the changing nature of the tasks performed by the salesperson and the shift in selling philosophy. This philosophy has progressed with a shift in focus from a sales-driven to a customer-driven to a relationship-driven perspective. This change will be thoroughly explored in Chapter 2.

How the Task Is Changing

A key issue affecting the role of salespeople and their productivity is the amount of time the average salesperson spends not selling. Nonselling activities include administrative tasks, internal meetings, training, travel, and report writing. In the last 10 years, the weekly time spent not selling has grown from 12.6 to 15.0 hours per week, resulting in an additional 120 nonselling hours per year.[7] Such an increase dramatically affects the amount of time actually spent in face-to-face selling, which, in turn, forces the salesperson and the sales manager to determine which customers get priority and how each customer can best be served.

Another key issue in the sales professional's evolving role is the changed conditions, or pressure points, under which salespeople operate. Because of the enormous number of leveraged buyouts and foreign acquisitions of major chains that occurred in the eighties, more buying power is now in the hands of fewer people. As a result, for example, retailers are using this power to reduce their own costs by shifting their in-store labor burden to manufacturers. Sophisticated computerized

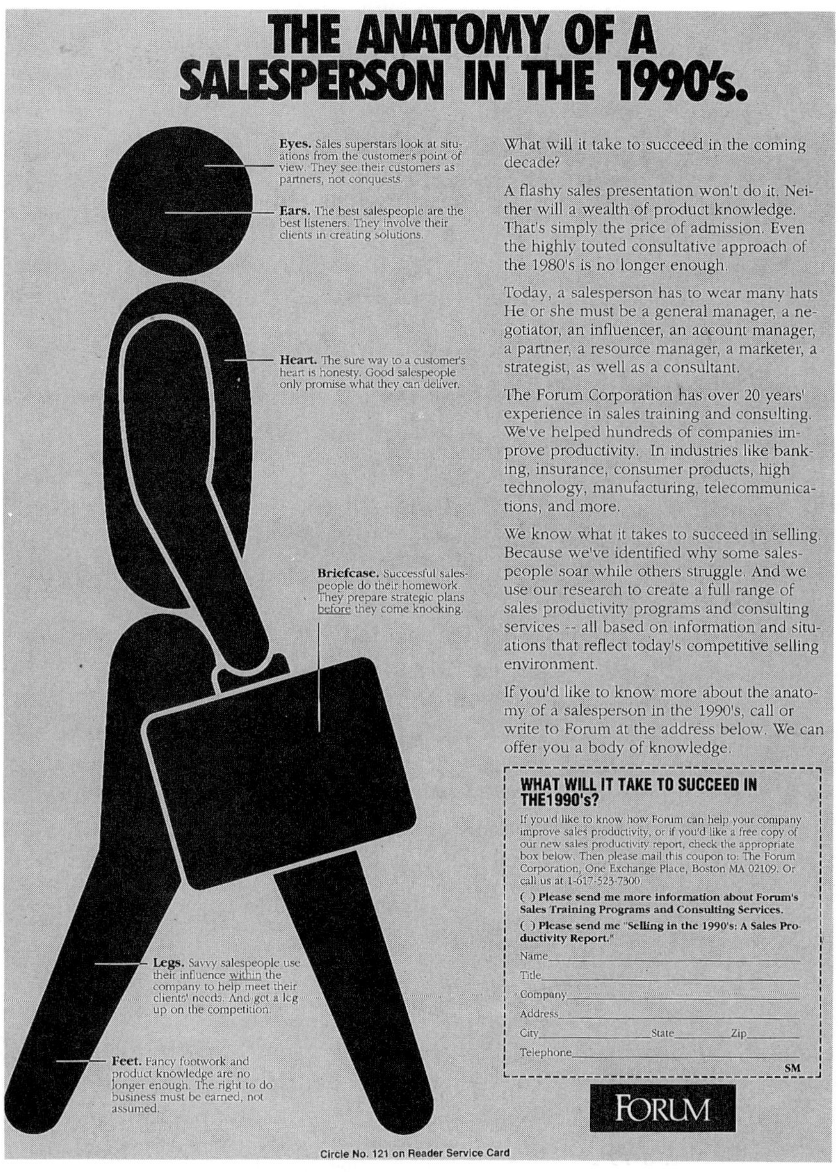

scanner data now provide the retailers with better and more timely information on product movement than can be obtained from the manufacturer's representative. In other words, the retailer is using this information to throw out slow-moving merchandise, to question whether a new product helps the store or the manufacturer, to build personal computer models on product profitability, and to automate areas such as shelf management. Thus, the salesperson is dealing with a better informed, more sophisticated, and more influential buyer. Because of these trends, salespeople must develop competence in areas such as quantitative analysis. For example, if a buyer in one store says that the product is doing poorly and the sales representative knows that the product is doing well in the competitor's stores, the sales representative must know how to analyze the information and advise the buyer on what might be going wrong. Selling is more information-intense today than it was even 5 years ago.

Obviously, as companies become increasingly enmeshed in information issues, they become more involved with computer technology. This area is so significant to the emerging sales professional that a section of Chapter 18 focuses on the influence of the computer on the sales force.

Kinds of Selling Careers

In-store Retail Selling

Retailing encompasses all those activities involved in the sale of products and services to the ultimate consumer. There are nearly two million retail outlets in the United States. In 1990, consumers spent over $1.5 trillion on goods and services purchased from retailers.

Retail organizations include specialty shops, department stores, supermarkets, discount houses, mass merchandisers, catalogue showrooms, superstores, hyperstores, and convenience stores. Like manufacturers and wholesalers, retailers develop marketing strategies to meet their organizational goals and objectives.

A retail strategy consists of several elements: types of products carried, customer service, target customers, pricing, promotion, distribution, location, and store atmosphere. These components combine to make up the *retail image*—the customer's perception of the store and the shopping experience it provides.[8] The store's salespeople serve as a vital link in projecting the image desired by the organization. If the store does not have a grasp of its customers' needs and perceptions, then even its best efforts will fail. In a *Business Week* cover story, consultant Carol A. Farmer discusses customer-driven companies that are current leaders and suggests that "putting a piano player in the atrium because it works for Nordstrom and putting a senior citizen greeter at the front door because it works for Wal-Mart" is not the answer for everyone.[9] Farmer mentions these two organizations because of their enormous success during the 1980s. Both Nordstrom and Wal-Mart have made a significant impact by forcing their competition to implement customer-driven strategies.

Nonstore Retail Selling

Another approach that is gaining popularity as a means of reaching the ultimate consumer is computer-generated television home shopping. Here, a "video rep" presents the products and services to the buyer, who electronically consummates the sale without ever leaving the comfort of home. Television's "Home Shopping Club" is an example of nonstore retail selling.

Inside Selling

The inside salesperson generally is involved in telemarketing. As personal selling costs continue to rise, many firms are building telemarketing programs to help reduce these expenses and to help the outside salesperson accomplish sales objectives. A good telemarketing program may follow one of two courses or a combination of both: serving as a stand-alone program to move the firm's products or services or supplementing the activities of the outside sales force. Four typical activities are performed by an inside salesperson:

1. Prospecting for and qualifying new accounts—Sometimes generating leads for the outside salesperson will yield a percentage or commission if the field representative closes the sale.
2. Seeking repeat purchases from existing accounts that are seen as marginal or are located in remote areas of the salesperson's territory.
3. Disseminating current marketing developments, such as promotional programs that could enhance the customer's sales, or sales promotion for the customer's personal use.
4. Developing a "hotline" that provides immediate technical assistance to existing customers.

Outside Selling

The outside salesperson interacts face to face with prospects and customers. This person generally initiates the appointment and goes into the field. For this reason, outside salespeople are often called field salespeople.

Sales-support personnel are rarely involved in soliciting the order. Their function is to disseminate information and perform other activities designed to stimulate sales. Two popular categories of support salespeople are missionary or detail salespeople and technical support salespeople.

Missionary salespeople generally work for a manufacturer, a manufacturer's representative, or a broker. This is particularly true in the grocery industry. They operate in a manner similar to a religious missionary in that their focus is on "spreading the word," with the hope of converting the listener into a customer.

Another kind of missionary support person is the *detailer*, often found in the pharmaceutical industry. The detailer's job may be to support the sales effort by calling on physicians. The objective is to provide information regarding the capabilities and benefits of certain drugs. In turn, the detailer hopes that the physician will prescribe the company's product.

Technical support salespeople usually assist in installing equipment, training the customer's employees, performing follow-up services of a technical nature, and working on design and specification processes. These people may sell in tandem as a part of the sales team, with one member responsible for identifying the prospect's needs, recommending the appropriate product or service, and securing the order. Sometimes called *sales engineers*, they usually work in the heavy equipment, machinery, and chemical fields.

Two types of new business salespeople are pioneers and order-getters. These people add new customers or introduce new products to the marketplace.

Pioneers devote their time to new product introductions, new customers, or both. They are frequently found in the sale of business franchises and fly throughout the country and the world seeking new franchises. They may also be found in consumer and industrial firms, where new accounts are turned over to another salesperson once the pioneer has established the buyer-seller relationship.

Order-getters, or order generators, are sales representatives who actively seek orders in a highly competitive environment. Unlike pioneers, who move on to new customers as soon as possible, order-getters may serve existing customers on an ongoing basis. Sometimes an order-getter will establish a relationship with a customer by selling a single product from the line, then gradually add other items from the line in subsequent sales calls.

The responsibility of these salespeople is opposite that of new business representatives. Their task is to maintain relationships with existing customers. While creative selling skills are less important to the personnel in this category, reliability and competence in assuring customer convenience are critical to their performance.

Order-takers are among those salespeople who specialize in maintaining existing business. Route salespeople who work an established customer base, taking routine reorders of stock items, are examples of order-takers.

Direct-to-Consumer Selling

Another category, *direct-to-consumer* salespeople, may be identified with such companies as Mary Kay Cosmetics, Tupperware, Avon, and Amway. In addition to working for these well-known companies, direct-to-consumer salespeople are often found in intangible goods areas such as insurance and financial services.

Combination Sales

Another broad category of sales work employs the person who performs multiple types of sales jobs within the framework of a single position. For instance, Georgiana Kennedy is a former unit manager for the Package Soap and Detergent Sales Department of Procter & Gamble. Her job blends responsibilities for acquiring new business, maintaining and stimulating existing business, and performing sales support activities. These activities include merchandising and in-store promotion at the retail store level. She also calls on managers of chain stores to handle existing business and to seek new business.

College graduates frequently begin their careers in a combination sales job. Firms like Procter & Gamble, Carnation, Campbell Soup, and Pepsi recruit heavily on college campuses. These firms often will include combination jobs as a part of the person's experience in a career sales track.

In searching for a position in sales, it is appropriate to have knowledge of the firm's objectives, including how the firm views professional selling within its system. This understanding is facilitated by investigating sales and the broader marketing perspective and by tracing the evolution of personal selling throughout the twentieth century.

Sales and the Broader Marketing Perspective

The United States within the Global Economy

Today's business and industrial environment has changed dramatically from that of the turn of the century, when companies enjoyed the luxury of focusing on the product. At that time, few products were available and competition existed primarily among firms in the United States rather than worldwide. Today's firms no longer rely solely on domestic markets but must compete effectively in global markets. Because of this vast increase in the availability of products and the spread to markets outside the United States, domestic companies are now faced with competition from around the world.

The 1980s saw this expansion of trade with European and Pacific Rim countries. The nineties will bring even more countries into the world trade explosion. By the year 2000, virtually every business enterprise will be inseparably linked to the global economy.[10]

With these developments has come increasing world reliance on the U.S. economy. This implies that the United States will find itself positioned as only one link in the marketing chain, rather than as the basis for the chain itself. United States firms must find more effective ways to market their goods and services to maintain the pivotal role and the competitive edge in international economic relations. Management activities must shift from short-term, instant dollar gratification with profit goals to long-term marketing planning based on the development of meaningful and sustained relationships.

Success will then require long-term thinking toward cultivating those markets. Success will also require that salespeople continue to gain knowledge, assertiveness, and patience as efforts toward trade expansion continue. This knowledge of cultures, languages, and business customs will be explored in Chapter 3.

The main objective of this section is to show how U.S. businesses and industries are responding to the world market challenge. A related objective is to show how today's sales professionals are serving as a vital link to aid the organization as it accomplishes its goals.

During this century, American businesses have operated within one of two frameworks: the production-oriented concept and the marketing-oriented concept. We will discuss each and show the progression from one to the other.

Production-Oriented Concept and Selling

Basing their operations on the *production-oriented concept,* firms operate on the premise that if a quality product can be made, the product will sell itself.[11] The essence of this concept is embedded in a statement purportedly made over a century ago by the poet Ralph Waldo Emerson:

> If a man writes a better book, preaches a better sermon, or makes a better mousetrap than his neighbor, though he builds his house in the woods, the world will make a beaten path to his door.[12]

Over the years this statement became a philosophy under which American businesses operated. Eventually Emerson's statement was shortened to "Build a better mousetrap and the whole world will beat a path to your door." Along with this production-oriented philosophy came the manufacturers' practice of dictating how many units would be built, where they would be sold, and for how much.

This era, which is now referred to as the Product Era, lasted until about 1920. Henry Ford, who developed the mass-assembly-line process into a workable reality, was the leading automobile manufacturer of the day. In his classic statement, "You can have any color of car you want so long as it's black," Ford demonstrated the kind of thinking that permeated

On the International Front Setting Up an International Sales Force

A major task of the international sales manager is to set up and maintain a well-trained sales force when pursuing international opportunities. This process is often more difficult and time-consuming than selecting salespeople for domestic sales because of the many special requirements.

A variety of alternatives are considered when setting up a sales force or conducting selling activities in the international arena:

Direct Sales Force Companies may set up their own direct sales force in the foreign country, armed with an understanding of the local culture and business conditions. This approach provides for a high degree of sales control and support.

Long-Distance Selling Long-distance selling involves handling the international sales transactions from the United States. Personal contact is made only at the contractual stage.

Intermediaries The use of intermediaries (independent distributors and dealers) involves local nationals with an established network of local business contacts. This approach calls for acquiring independent firms to sell, service, and support the company's product line, preferably on an exclusive basis. Although this is a cost-effective means, it may result in minimal loyalty and lack of service support provisions, eventually downgrading the company's image in the foreign market. Companies incurring dissatisfaction with distributors' efforts, such as Coca-Cola Corporation, realized that they could better exploit their foreign market potential by acquiring foreign distributors to sell their products internationally.

Agents/Brokers These "finders" seek out foreign buyers without taking ownership of the products. They are usually paid strictly on a commission basis.

Affiliate Partnership Some countries have laws that do not permit foreign companies to establish autonomous sales forces. Hence, an affiliate partnership with a local company in the market area, sharing similar interests and complementary strengths, may prove valuable in responding to the expectations of the foreign country.

When entering a foreign market, a definite drawback is not having the initial representation of a strong sales force. Therefore, deciding to enter the potentially profitable foreign market requires special insights and abilities while exercising great care in the selection of sales representatives.

Source: *A Basic Guide to Exporting* (Washington, DC: U.S. Department of Commerce, 1989); Eugene M. Johnson, David L. Kurtz, and Eberhard E. Scheuring, *Sales Management: Concepts, Practices, and Cases* (New York: McGraw-Hill, 1986), pp. 508–512.

American manufacturing practices. While Ford wanted to make a car every American family could afford, he had little regard for the consumers' wants or needs. He felt that he knew what was best for them in transportation.

As technology improved and businesses were able to mass produce more products than they were able to sell in their immediate markets, companies started to hire salespeople to create a market where perhaps none existed before. In addition to being production oriented, companies adopted a business theory assuming that most customers would resist buying nonessential products and services but that, through creative advertising and personal selling, customer resistance could be overcome.

As a result, these companies frequently engaged in high-pressure selling techniques that were sales driven. *Sales driven* implies a unilateral process in which the salesperson acts as the chief authority, almost coercing the customer into a buying decision. The intent was that the salesperson's needs would be met by increasing company profits through sales volume.

Sales training generally meant product training, emphasizing how the product worked and operated. Sales presentations were built around what the company thought was best for the customers, not what the customers perceived were their wants or needs. Typically, a company required its sales force to memorize a canned sales pitch to be used with every customer. As a result of the constant pressure to make a profit through sales, the salesperson's method of operation became authoritative, dogmatic, overbearing, and mechanical.

The basic characteristics of the personal selling behaviors promoted by product-oriented firms are summarized in Table 1.4. Basically, production-

Table 1.4

A Functional Comparison of the Salesperson's Approach when Using the Sales-driven and Customer-driven Concepts

Sales-driven Concept	Customer-driven Concept
1. Selling philosophy (makes sales)	1. Buying philosophy (makes customers)
2. Linear communication (one-way)	2. Circular communication (two-way)
3. Monologue	3. Dialogue
4. High pressured (often creates tension and fear)	4. Low pressured (builds trust and understanding)
5. Aggressive, defensive	5. Assertive, supportive
6. Inflexible	6. Adaptable, spontaneous
7. Short-term relationship	7. Long-term relationship
8. Talking and persuading	8. Listening and responding
9. Creates needs (telling)	9. Discovers customer-disclosed needs (listening)
10. Memorized or canned pitches	10. Spontaneous, customer-responsive presentations
11. Presents information	11. Absorbs and synthesizes information
12. Problem creator	12. Problem solver
13. Impersonal	13. Interpersonal
14. All customers viewed the same	14. Each customer viewed as unique
15. Deceptive strategies	15. Open agendas, problem orientation
16. Win-lose, competitive attitude	16. Win-win, cooperative attitude
17. Profits through sales volume	17. Profits through customer satisfaction

oriented firms viewed selling as impersonal. Notice how selling was defined in these two sales textbooks:

> Selling is the process of *inducing* and assisting a prospective customer to buy goods or services or to act favorably on an idea that has *commercial significance* for the *seller*.[13]
>
> . . . the act of persuading another person to do something when you do not have, or cannot exert, the direct power to force the person to do it.[14]

It is important to note that many firms still subscribe to a production-oriented philosophy with sales-driven practices. Companies that typically have a one-call selling cycle follow these principles. These companies may sell products such as magazines, solar heaters, insulation, time-share plans, and health club memberships.

Marketing-Oriented Concept and Selling

Since the 1950s, enormous changes in our society have influenced the way we market our goods and services. Some of these conditions that have encouraged companies to change to a marketing-oriented philosophy are listed in Table 1.5.

A marketing-oriented concept means that the firm tries to produce what customers need instead of getting customers to buy what the company has produced.[15] Well-known and highly respected management consultant Peter F. Drucker underscores the importance of marketing in his book *The Practice of Management:*

> If we want to know what a business is, we have to start with its purpose. And its purpose must lie outside the business itself. In fact,

Table 1.5

Factors That Influenced the Development of a Marketing-oriented Philosophy

Since the fifties, enormous changes have taken place in the way we market goods and services. A variety of conditions have influenced these changes.

- Shift from a shortage of goods and services (during the war years) to an abundance of goods and services
- Development of high-tech communication systems such as telecommunications (satellite delivery) and computers that provide the consumer with immediate information
- Movement from an industrial age to an information age and a highly sophisticated consumer
- Increased competition in the domestic and international arenas
- Change in negotiation philosophy from win–lose to win–win

> it must lie in society since a business enterprise is an organ of society. There is one valid definition of business purpose: to create a customer.[16]

Professors J. P. Guiltinan and G. W. Paul explain how an organization "creates" a customer in this manner:

> Essentially, "creating" a customer means identifying needs in the marketplace, finding out which needs the organization can profitably serve, and developing an offering to convert potential buyers into customers. Marketing managers are responsible for most of the activities necessary to create the customers the organization wants. These activities include:
>
> - Identifying customer needs
> - Designing products and services that meet those needs
> - Communicating information about those products and services to prospective buyers
> - Making the products or services available at times and places that meet customers' needs
> - Pricing the products to reflect costs, competition, and customers' ability to buy
> - Providing for the necessary service and follow-up to ensure customer satisfaction after the purchase.[17]

In those companies that have adopted the marketing-oriented approach, the philosophy toward selling and the view of the sales force's role take on the following characteristics:

- Members of the sales force are seen as marketing and customer analysts. They are received as problem solvers whose function is to report back to the company or sales manager what the customers perceive as needs.
- Sales training programs focus on teaching salespeople how to structure sales presentations to include customer participation throughout the interview, using appropriate skills for both initiating and responding to communication between buyer and seller.
- The primary focus of the sales interview is to establish rapport through an exchange process, the goal of which is to initiate and maintain a long-term relationship.
- The salesperson's efforts are directed toward earning profits through satisfying customer needs rather than earning profits through sales volume.

These characteristics establish a basis for the *customer-driven* approach that was more specifically outlined in Table 1.4. The customer-driven approach is an extension of the marketing-oriented concept and implies a process that focuses on identifying and satisfying buyers' needs and building a relationship that results in repeat business.

The second version of the selling process that has emerged in our marketing-oriented organizations is the *relationship-driven* process. This process is based on a reciprocal interaction between customer and salesperson that enables them to meet each other's needs, predominantly through the use of sales communication skills. Figure 1.5 summarizes the development of the selling process as it relates to both a production-oriented and marketing-oriented company.

The focus of this discussion is to link the salesperson and customer more closely together by integrating professional selling techniques with communication skills. We will stress the relationship-driven process of the marketing concept.

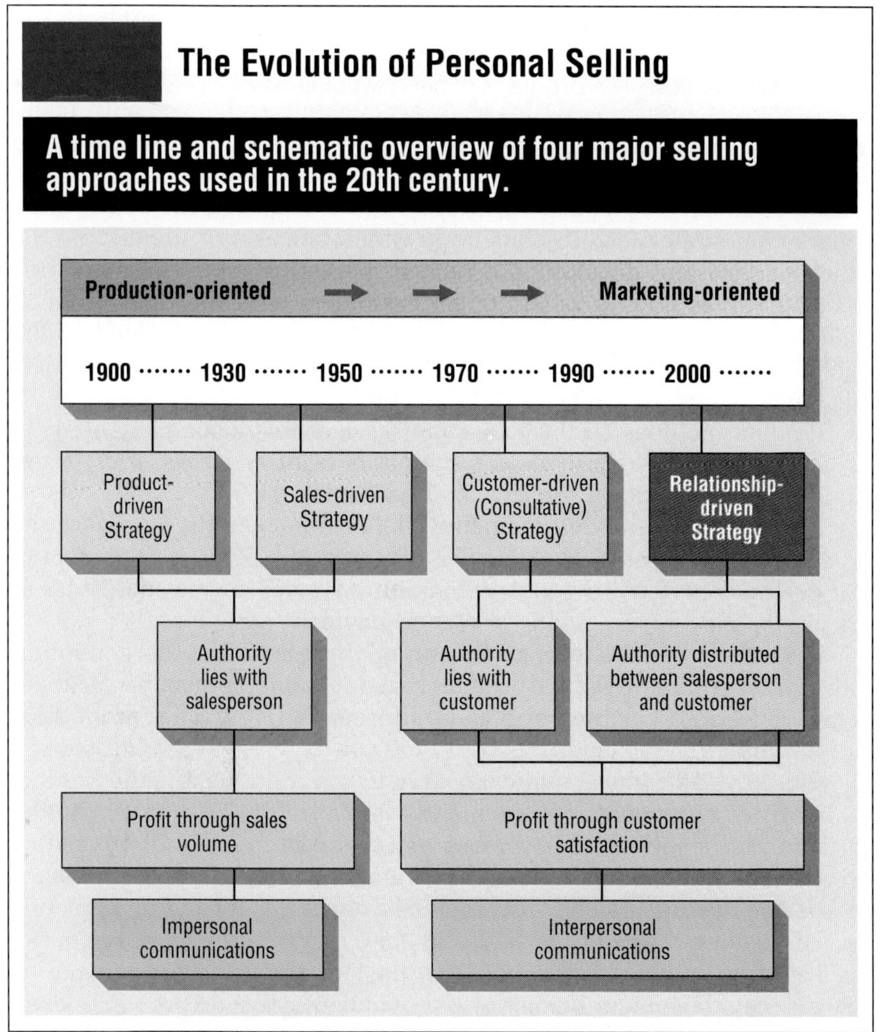

Figure 1.5

The Marketing Concept

Gaining acceptance for the marketing concept may be the biggest challenge facing the firm. Conflict occurs when some departments in a firm operate from the framework of the marketing concept and others follow the production-oriented concept. Conducting operations from the broad marketing concept that focuses attention on customers is the foundation of professionalism in sales.

Traditionally, the marketing department in a firm would develop a marketing strategy and the sales department was responsible for executing it. In contrast to this linear approach, modern firms are more process oriented because the sales organization is becoming more involved in working with marketing from the beginning to develop plans that respond to continuous growth and change. Subsequently, the approach is changing, from that of a company that uses the marketing concept to that of a company in which the systemic motivating force for the entire firm's existence is marketing. Marketing is becoming tied more closely to top management.

Marketing management is the analysis, planning, implementation, and control of programs designed to bring about exchanges with target customers for the purpose of personal or mutual gain. It relies heavily on the adaptation and coordination of product, price, promotion, and place to achieve effective response.[18] One basic task of management is to develop a marketing strategy for the business, which consists of identifying the target markets and developing a related marketing mix. The marketing mix determines how to satisfy target customers with the right product, available at the right price and at the right place and promoted in the right way. Extensive dimensions and elements are combined to satisfy this target group, as depicted in Figure 1.6.

Product includes all the goods and services that a company offers to its target market. This covers areas such as features, accessories, sizes, brand name, warranties, services, and packaging.

Price includes the dollar amount that customers must spend for the product. It also involves the perceived value of the offer and the amount that customers are willing to pay. In addition, price covers such areas as discounts, allowances, credit terms, and payment periods.

Promotion, or mass selling, includes all those activities that communicate to the customer what the product is about and influence the customer to buy. Promotion involves personal selling, advertising, sales promotion, and publicity.

Place includes the activities that are involved in making the product available to the consumer. It frequently is referred to as the distribution variable. Place includes such areas as channel types, kinds of market exposure, middlemen, inventory and warehousing, and transportation.

In sum, the integrated efforts invite the development and implementation of all these business activities as they relate to the achievement of the firm's marketing objectives. In fact, the success of the entire planning process may depend on the performance and effectiveness of the interaction between salespeople and customers.

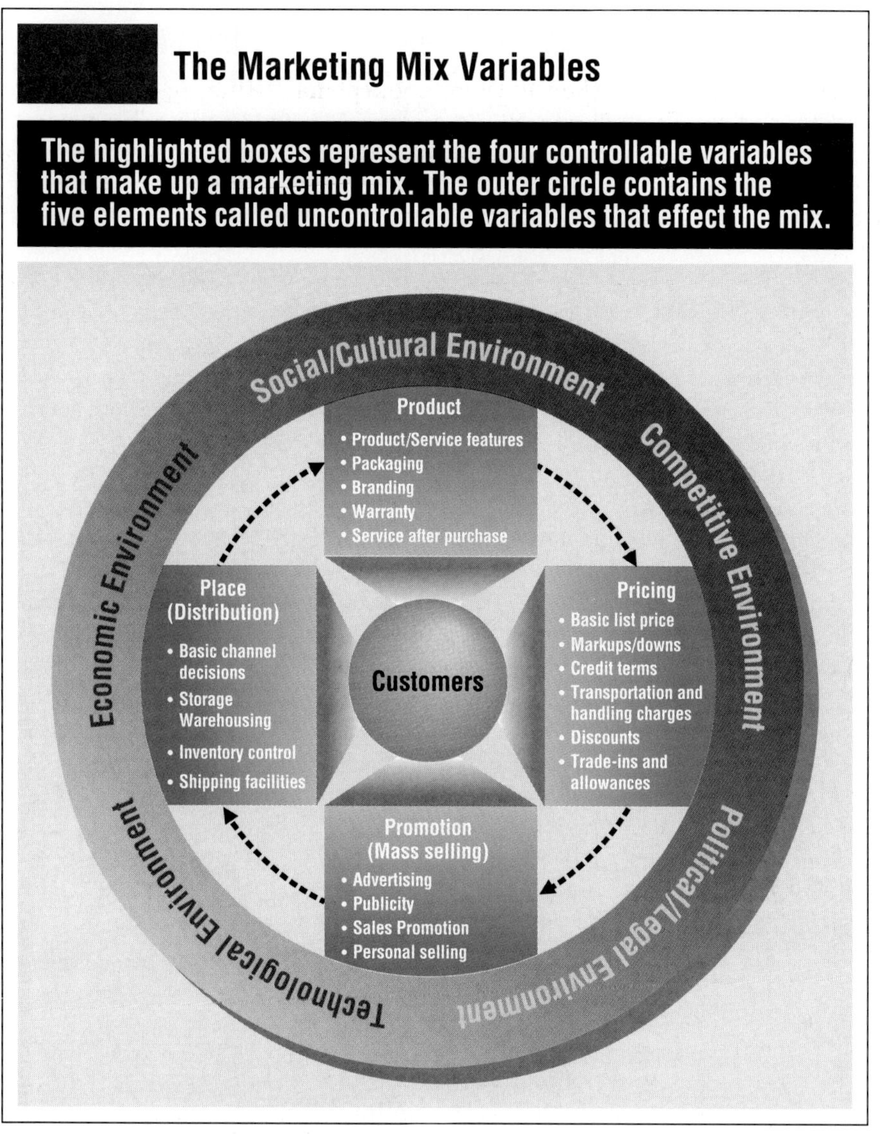

Figure 1.6

Personal Selling and the Promotion Variable

The promotion variable includes activities that affect consumer demand through communication. How the promotion manager communicates depends on the blend of techniques selected. In general, promotion refers to creating demand through stimulating activities. Its purposes are to communicate, convince, and compete.

Figure 1.7 identifies the four elements contained in the promotion variable: advertising, sales promotion, publicity, and personal selling.

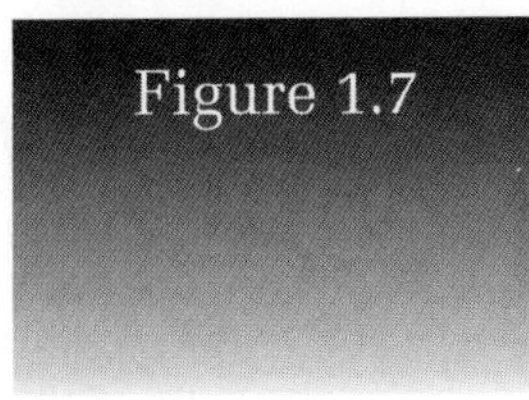

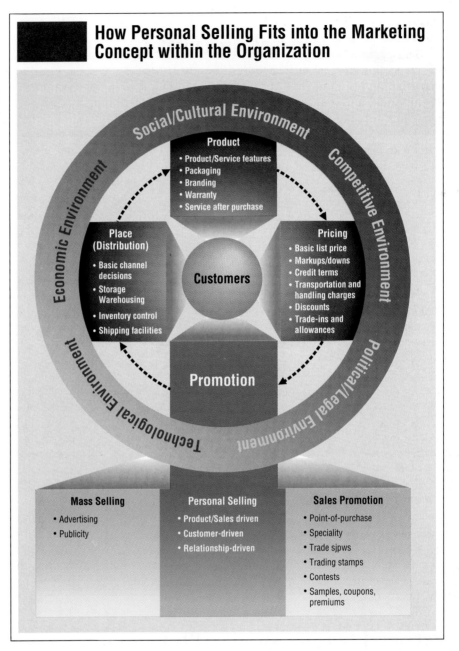

How Personal Selling Fits into the Marketing Concept within the Organization

Advertising is any paid form of nonpersonal communication of ideas, goods, or services used by individuals, business firms, and nonprofit organizations, the purpose of which is to inform and persuade members of a particular audience.[19] Advertising is designed for use with mass media—television, radio, magazines, newspapers, billboards, and direct mail. Those individuals and firms concerned with mass consumption and geographically dispersed markets find that advertising is particularly useful in sending the same message to a large audience.

Sales promotion involves those marketing activities that stimulate awareness, interest, or purchase by ultimate consumers or others in the channel. Sales promotion is usually designed to complement other promotional methods. Examples of sales promotion are trade shows and exhibitions, specialty advertising items, in-store demonstrations, point-of-purchase displays, and coupons. These nonrecurrent selling efforts are used on an occasional basis to enhance the effectiveness of the advertising and personal selling objectives.

Publicity is any unpaid form of nonpersonal communication that stimulates demand for a person, product, organization, or cause. It is free and favorable information that is delivered through television, radio, magazines, newspapers, or any other source that is not paid for by one identified sponsor. Publicity is a vehicle used by the firm for dealing with its various audiences—suppliers, clients, stockholders, the government, employees, and the general public.

Personal selling is the company's most expensive promotional tool. The fact that nearly nine million people were employed in field sales in the late 1980s attests to its significance. While the average firm's advertising expenses represent anywhere from 1 to 3 percent of total sales, personal selling expenses often equal 10 to 15 percent.[20]

Louis E. Boone and David L. Kurtz, marketing educators, define personal selling as "an interpersonal process involving a seller's promotional presentation conducted on a person-to-person basis with the prospective buyer."[21] They tie promotional strategy to the process of communication. Thus, they expand the variable to include marketing communications, "those messages that deal with buyer-seller relationships."[22]

Cutting-edge marketers and sales professionals recognize the significance of adopting a marketing communication approach to their overall marketing management objectives. The constant attention they must pay to getting and keeping the competitive edge promotes the development of repeat business through ethical standards, practices, and communication with their customers. This integrity sets the tone of the relationship process. The communication perspective and the selling process will be explored in Chapter 2.

The Personal Selling Process

As Figure 1.8 illustrates, personal selling is a process that follows a series of seven steps: (1) precall preparation, (2) preapproach, (3) approach, (4) presentation, (5) managing resistance, (6) closing the sale, and (7) postsale activities. It is important to see how each of these steps interacts with the others and how each step influences the others. Successful sales interviews are built on prior planning; therefore, thorough preparation must be completed before the salesperson and prospective buyer meet.

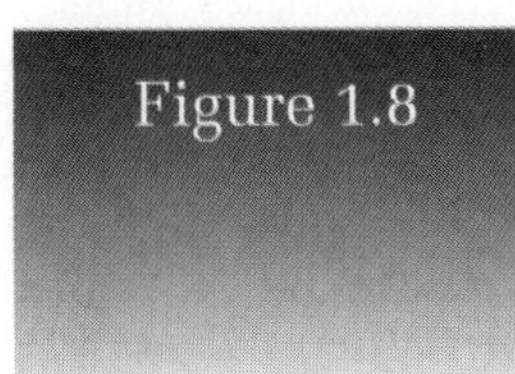
Figure 1.8

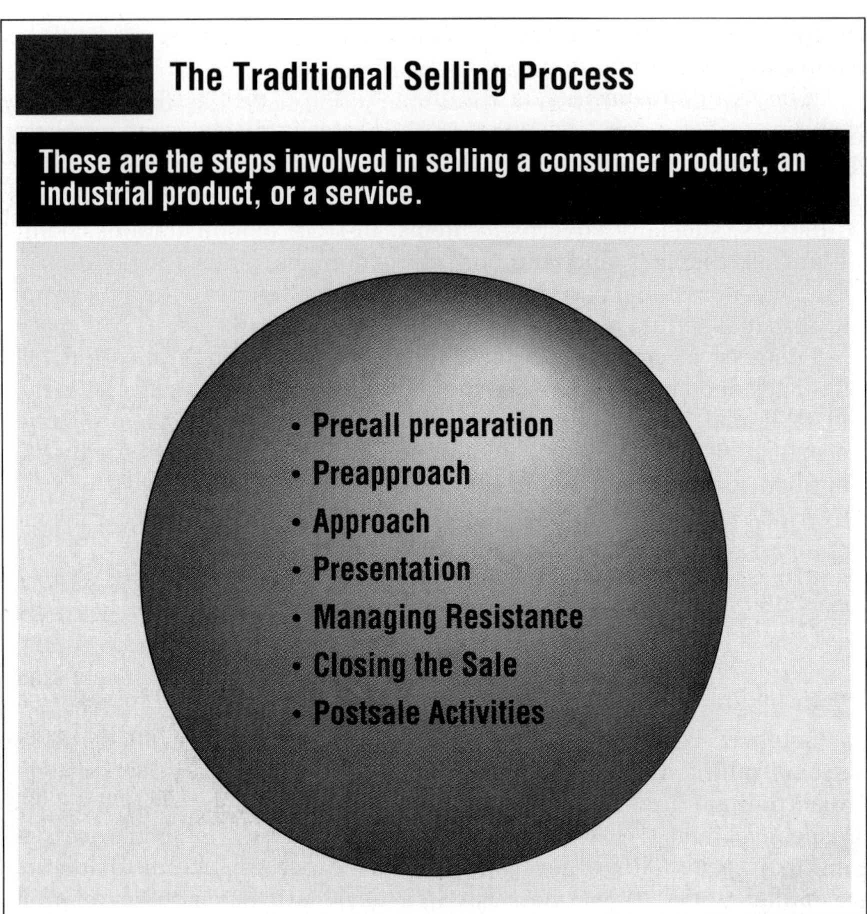

The Traditional Selling Process
These are the steps involved in selling a consumer product, an industrial product, or a service.
• Precall preparation
• Preapproach
• Approach
• Presentation
• Managing Resistance
• Closing the Sale
• Postsale Activities

Precall Preparation

In the first stage, salespeople prepare themselves physically, emotionally, and mentally to meet the sales challenge. Grooming oneself physically means eating, resting, and exercising properly—not just dressing appropriately for the sales job. Developing a positive sales image involves thinking and feeling positively about one's life and the role professional selling plays in it. This includes developing self-confidence, self-esteem, and self-worth.

Precall preparation also refers to the outside work that salespeople do to learn about the company they work for and the products or services they represent. In addition, information must be gathered on competitors, and all salespeople should understand as much as possible about the customers they serve.

Preapproach

In personal selling the term *prospect* is used to represent a qualified potential buyer. This term was created to differentiate between "suspects" (people to whom the product is targeted) and people who are qualified as potential end users of the product.

The term *prospecting* is assigned to those methods and systems that are used for locating prospects. Chapter 7 discusses this process extensively.

A second component of the preapproach stage is the planning phase, in which the salesperson maps out the strategies that will be used to satisfy the prospect's needs.

Approach

This phase of the selling process usually starts with buyer-seller interaction. This may include setting an appointment and talking with the prospect over the phone, as well as the face-to-face conversation of a sales call.

In the approach stage, the salesperson's primary concerns are about opening the sales interview appropriately, getting the prospect's interest, and building rapport based on mutual respect and trust. Another element that is critical at this stage, if the next step is to be successful, is the salesperson's ability to determine the buyer's needs and motives for making a purchasing decision.

Presentation

The sales interaction is an ongoing process. Rapport building continues throughout the sales call, and probing for buying needs may be necessary throughout the interview. During this phase of the interaction, the salesperson discusses the product with the prospect in terms that will satisfy the needs that previously have been uncovered. At this point, the salesperson may conduct an actual demonstration, present printed support material, or use audiovisual aids to enhance the presentation.

Managing Resistance

At some time during the sales interaction, objections or resistance is likely to occur. Salespeople must always be ready to negotiate to a win-win solution. Resistance can provide the seller with feedback that will allow adjustment of the message and even a change of strategies.

Closing the Sale

Recognizing buying signals, inserting trial closes, and asking for the order are the significant functions covered in the closing stage. Understanding the techniques and methods used to gain commitment increases the salesperson's chance of completing the interaction successfully. Taking leave of the interview in a way that is appropriate to maintain rapport is another component of this phase.

Postsale Activities

Relationship management is a goal in the final phase of the personal selling process. Depending on the selling context, what salespeople do after the sale may be just as important as what they do during the actual negotiation. Activities such as sending thank you notes, making sure that the customer receives prompt delivery and excellent service, and identifying a callback schedule all help to facilitate a long-term relationship and repeat business.

At this point, it is clear that the personal selling process is cyclical—what the salesperson does before, during, and after the sale influences the possibility of generating new prospects and additional business.

Summary

Professional selling remains one of the most dynamic career choices in business today. Not only does it provide an opportunity to "live one's passion," but it offers lucrative financial rewards and enriched psychic income.

Career opportunities abound for the person who is self-motivated, willing to make changes, and seeking personal challenges. The two major classifications of selling are retail sales and field sales. While the interpersonal skills required for success are the same for both kinds of selling, the salesperson's tasks vary considerably.

Profiles of the sales professional for the nineties include strong interpersonal skills and competence in technical skills. One of the most effective tools for building interpersonal competence is developing effective interpersonal communication skills.

This chapter has offered perceptions and concepts of selling appropriate to the twenty-first century. Highlighted was the importance of the "V.I.P." who presides in many types of sales assignments. The importance of information must be considered in assessing abilities and opportunities, thus ensuring permanent and mutually profitable relationships. In the final analysis, the professional salesperson undertakes steps in the selling process and accomplishes an exchange transaction through communication. Both of these areas will be explored in Chapter 2.

One of the keys to professional selling is the salesperson's ability to adapt to a variety of customers and selling situations that have become more worldly in every sense of the word. The treatment of personal selling as it involves particular instances of firms servicing customers on an intercultural and global level will be examined further in Chapter 3.

Concurrent with the progression of a firm's selling approach from a production-oriented to a marketing-oriented concept, one finds the evolution of professional selling moving from a sales-driven to a customer-driven or relationship-driven process of satisfying customers' needs. Developing a marketing strategy consists of identifying the appropriate target markets and developing marketing mixes to fit those markets. The marketing mix consists of the four variables of product, price, promotion, and place. Personal selling, which is a part of the promotion variable, commands a large portion of the promotional expenditures in the quest for continued growth and increased long-term relationships. Appropriate responses to change require a clear understanding of alternative options available as change takes place.

All personal selling systems have seven basic components. These elements or steps are: (1) precall preparation, (2) preapproach, (3) approach, (4) presentation, (5) managing resistance, (6) closing the sale, and (7) postsale activities. While these steps are common to all selling systems, the skills available for implementing these steps have improved considerably as more effective ways of moving goods and services have been developed.

Key Terms

Advertising Any paid form of nonpersonal communication of ideas, goods, or services used by individuals, business firms, and nonprofit organizations, the purpose of which is to inform and persuade members of a particular audience

Customer-driven One of two extensions of the market-oriented system; implies a process in which the focus is on identifying and satisfying buyers' needs and building a relationship that results in repeat business

Psychic income A measure of one's degree of satisfaction relative to having made someone else's life better, as well as improving one's own growth and development

Publicity Any unpaid form of personal communication that stimulates demand for a person, product, organization, or cause

Relationship-driven A reciprocal process between customer and salesperson that enables them to meet each other's needs

Sales-driven Implies a unilateral process in which the salesperson acts as the chief authority, almost coercing the customer into a buying decision

Selling The process of defining needs and persuading potential customers to respond favorably to an idea that will result in mutual satisfaction for both buyer and seller

Review Questions

1. How does the expression "live your passion" apply to a professional selling career?
2. List three reasons for choosing professional selling as a career.
3. What is meant by the term *career path*? What are the various positions to which a salesperson may be promoted within a company?
4. Describe the differences between order-takers and order-getters. Give examples of industries or products that would be likely to employ either or both kinds of salespeople.
5. Why are salespeople made, not born?
6. Identify and explain five characteristics of the sales professional of this decade.
7. Describe the changes that have taken place among salespeople during the past 15 years.
8. What is the difference between the production-oriented concept and the marketing-oriented concept?
9. Define the marketing concept. What are the four variables of the marketing mix?
10. Why is personal selling considered the company's "most expensive promotional tool"?

Questions for Discussion

1. Describe what you believe the personal philosophy of a professional salesperson should embrace.
2. What conditions of the selling job make the salesperson more susceptible to unethical behavior?
3. Discuss the impact of the global market on personal selling.

4. Discuss the role of personal selling as it relates to a firm's marketing effort.
5. Discuss the four elements of a firm's marketing mix.
6. Cite examples of how a specific company has developed a marketing mix to compete successfully.
7. What type of coordination is required between a firm's sales force and its advertising department to achieve a coordinated selling effort?
8. How can sales representatives be an important feedback element in the firm's efforts to obtain market information?
9. In managing the promotional efforts, what typical objectives does a firm's management desire? How are the promotional objectives related to marketing objectives?

Getting Started in Sales

Case 1.1

Mary Dickens is in her last quarter at Iowa State University. She is a marketing major with a career emphasis in professional selling. Mary has been active in many school organizations, including the sales organization of Pi Sigma Epsilon and the Marketing Club.

"I want to become a manufacturer's representative for a cosmetics firm," Mary said to her marketing advisor. "What I really want to know is how to get started in seeking out a career in this sales profession." A professor replied that she should get some sales experience by first going to work in the cosmetics department of a retail store.

Mary's advisor replied that without a doubt, Mary would learn a lot about the cosmetics business that would be useful to her as a sales representative. However, the professor offered another course of action for Mary. "How about getting a job selling for a cosmetics manufacturer instead? There are some manufacturers who hire salespeople to work for them, selling direct to retailers. You will get better training from the manufacturer and the pay is much better. Is pay important for you?"

Mary thought for a moment. "Money is always important but I am more concerned about training and growth potential," she said. She was told by a college recruiter that the starting salary in the cosmetics industry would be about $1,000 per month for a 3- to 6-month training period. After this, the method of compensation would be straight commission, with earnings of about $30,000 in the second year and $50,000 or more in later years. Mary was encouraged by the possibility of being promoted to sales manager with the proper training, if she were successful in sales, and eventually reaching a point where she could move up the ranks to vice president of marketing.

1. What advice would you give Mary about how she should acquire sales experience?
2. How would selling for a retailer help Mary gain experience in preparing for a position as a manufacturer's representative? Is it worth making less money to gain this experience?
3. What questions should Mary ask of the manufacturer before making a decision?

Case 1.2

The Friendly Working Relationship

Superior Sports, Inc., is a successful sports equipment manufacturer that has been in business for 5 years. It manufactures high-tech training equipment designed specifically for competitive athletes. The firm has achieved excellent market success because it responds quickly to technological advances.

An important factor in the company's success has been Leslie Kingdom, a recognized world-class athlete and a very successful salesman in the sporting goods industry. When he was hired by Superior, he brought along a large number of excellent customers with whom he had developed a friendly working relationship over the years.

The personal relationship Leslie has with his customers is based on sincerity, interpersonal understanding, and trust. He establishes and maintains good working relationships with his customers through lengthy social conversations, believing that relationships are formed slowly and carefully. His customers respect his suggestions and advice as worthwhile and dependable. Leslie takes the time to understand the customer's needs when presenting the product's quality and its uses, and never tries to sell unnecessary equipment or extras just for profit.

Recently, however, Superior's management has put enormous pressure on Leslie to sell more and increase profits to cover the escalating costs of research and development. His managers have persuaded Leslie to emphasize unnecessary frills and demand a higher price. Although the equipment Superior has developed is better than any other on the market, the firm has been able to sell the equipment at prices only slightly higher than those of far lower quality machines. The company believes that the relationship Leslie has with his buyers is good enough that, should he tell them frills are needed and important, they will buy the equipment and be willing to pay even more for it.

Management has emphasized to Leslie that if he doesn't use a different approach with his customers, profits may be reduced, forcing Superior to cut back on its long-term strategies. Leslie doesn't agree and states that the long-term relationship could be jeopardized by any approach less than straightforward, high-quality information.

1. Discuss management's point of view.
2. What is your opinion of the approach Leslie is currently using?
3. Which direction would you take if you were the salesperson?

Notes

1. Frederic A. Russell, Frank H. Beach, and Richard H. Buskirk, *Selling Principles and Practices*, 11th ed. (New York: McGraw-Hill, 1982), p. 57.
2. W. O'Connell, "A 10-Year Report on Sales Force Productivity," *Sales & Marketing Management*, December 1988, p. 34.
3. M. Everett, "Selling's New Breed: Smart and Feisty," *Sales & Marketing Management*, October 1989, p. 52.
4. H. Mackay, "Humanize Your Selling Strategy," *Harvard Business Review*, March/April 1989, p. 44.
5. Everett, "Selling's New Breed," p. 52.
6. "Southern California Job Market," *Los Angeles Times*, Special Section, September 17, 1989, p. 5.
7. O'Connell, "A 10-Year Report on Sales Force Productivity, p. 35.
8. Louis E. Boone and David L. Kurtz, *Contemporary Marketing*, 6th ed. (Hinsdale, IL: The Dryden Press, 1989), p. 470.
9. Stephen Phillips and Amy Dunking, "King Customer," *Business Week*, March 12, 1990, p. 91.
10. Jo McClenahan, "Thinking Globally," *Industry Week*, August 21, 1989, pp. 12–13.
11. Boone and Kurtz, *Contemporary Marketing*, pp. 8–9.
12. L. E. Boone and L. Kurtz, *Contemporary Marketing*, 7th ed. (Fort Worth: The Dryden Press, 1992), p. 9.
13. Ferdinand M. Mauser, *Selling: A Self-Management Approach* (New York: Harcourt Brace Jovanovich, 1977), p. 8.
14. Frederic Russell, Frank H. Beach, and Richard H. Buskirk, *Textbook of Salesmanship*, 10th ed. (New York: McGraw-Hill, 1978), p. 3.
15. E. J. McCarthy and W. D. Perreault, Jr., *Basic Marketing*, 9th ed., (Homewood, IL: Irwin, 1987), p. 28.
16. Peter F. Drucker, *The Practice of Management* (New York: Harper and Row, 1954), p. 37. Adapted from Boone and Kurtz, *Contemporary Marketing*, p. 5.
17. J. P. Guiltinan and G. W. Paul, *Marketing Management* (New York: McGraw-Hill, 1985), pp. 3–4. Adapted from Boone and Kurtz, *Contemporary Marketing*, p. 5.
18. S. W. Dunn and A. M. Barban, *Advertising: Its Role in Modern Marketing* (Hinsdale, IL: The Dryden Press, 1989).
19. Boone and Kurtz, *Contemporary Marketing*, 7th ed., p. 556.
20. Ibid.
21. Ibid., p. 543.
22. Ibid., p. 536.

CHAPTER

2

Professional Selling through Relational Communication

Knowledge Objectives
In this chapter, you will learn:

1. The differences and similarities between the traditional and consultative selling models
2. The nature of relationships and their critical role in the selling process
3. The nature of communication and how its characteristics and components affect the intensity and depth of a relationship
4. The elements of a competence-based learning system
5. How communication skills can be used to build a buyer-seller relationship that leads to sales communication competence

Consider This

We're in the relationship business . . . we don't want to do anything to jeopardize that relationship.

James Tobin, Vice President,
Consumer Affairs
American Express

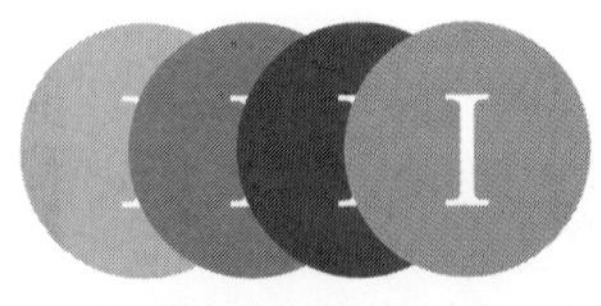

n Chapter 1 we traced the history of personal selling as it has changed from a production-oriented marketing concept with product-driven and sales-driven strategies to a marketing-oriented concept using customer-driven and relationship-driven selling strategies. Continuing this discussion of the evolution of personal selling, Chapter 2 focuses on the two selling models depicted in Figure 2.1 and the various selling strategies described under each model.

Our main objective in this chapter is to establish a basis for professional selling as a relational process. A second objective is to lay the foundation for developing professional selling competence through the

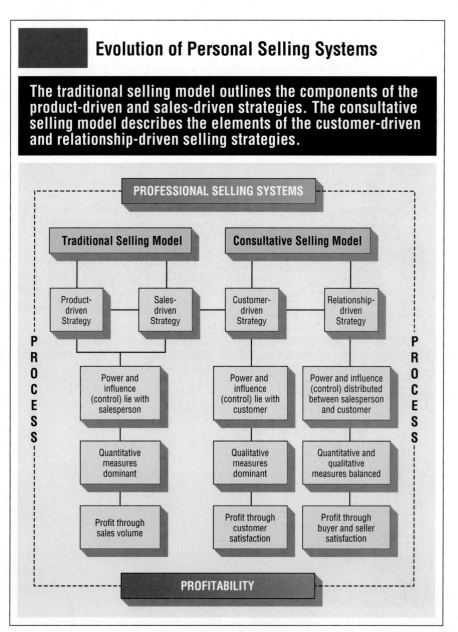

Evolution of Personal Selling Systems

The traditional selling model outlines the components of the product-driven and sales-driven strategies. The consultative selling model describes the elements of the customer-driven and relationship-driven selling strategies.

PROFESSIONAL SELLING SYSTEMS

PROCESS

Traditional Selling Model		Consultative Selling Model	
Product-driven Strategy	Sales-driven Strategy	Customer-driven Strategy	Relationship-driven Strategy
Power and influence (control) lie with salesperson		Power and influence (control) lie with customer	Power and influence (control) distributed between salesperson and customer
Quantitative measures dominant		Qualitative measures dominant	Quantitative and qualitative measures balanced
Profit through sales volume		Profit through customer satisfaction	Profit through buyer and seller satisfaction

PROFITABILITY

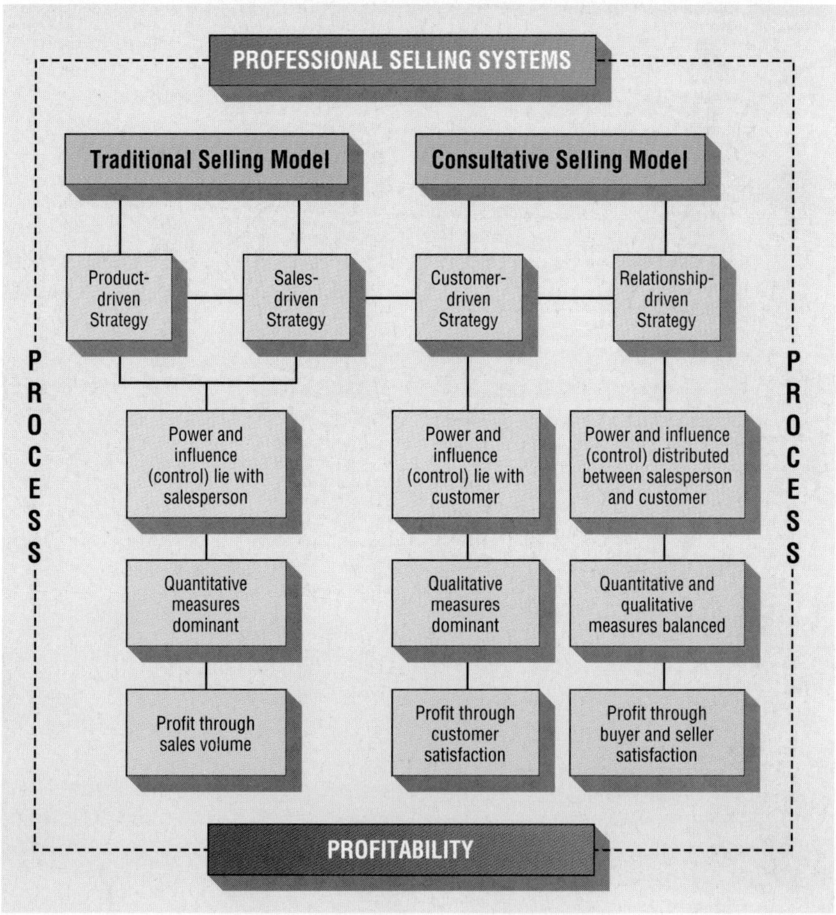

Sales Professional Spotlight

Although Monica Myers has been in professional selling for only 2 years, her efforts at personalizing her selling style have not gone unnoticed. Monica was featured in the July 1990 issue of *Sales & Marketing Management* magazine for outstanding achievement in sales.

Monica is a sales representative for Stuart Pharmaceuticals. Positions in the pharmaceutical sales industry are extremely competitive and difficult to obtain. Most companies require at least 2 years of prior sales experience and a 4-year university degree, both of which Monica has accomplished. Her prior sales experience consisted of 2 years of merchandising with Campbell's Soup and Carnation. These experiences provided Monica the opportunity to familiarize herself with marketing and sales practices applied in the corporate world.

"My first exposure to the pharmaceutical industry came when I was assigned a project in a professional selling class. Pursuing what I thought was a logical idea, since I had some interest in pharmaceutical work, I immediately began researching all the companies that might have openings. I started by going to a pharmacy and asking the pharmacist to recommend the pharmaceutical company he preferred most. The card of the sales representative from Stuart Pharmaceuticals was all I needed to proceed. I contacted the sales representative from Stuart and expressed an interest in an interview. At the end of the interview, I had made up my mind that Stuart Pharmaceuticals was the company that I wanted to sell for." It was at Stuart Pharmaceuticals that Monica launched her first big sales career move, allowing her to work in the industry and territory of her choice.

Six months of intensive product training and field sales training is the usual introductory rigor. "I was a relatively good student in college, but the training I received during the first 6 months with Stuart Pharmaceuticals was more than demanding. Training is never-ending in the medical profession. New clinical information is continually being introduced that must be updated. The work itself is a challenge. I strive to be a team player and use communication skills and selling techniques to accomplish the end result—customer satisfaction."

Monica has excelled to become one of the top sales representatives in her region. Many professionals who read the article featuring Monica in *Sales & Marketing Management* offered an enthusiastic "thumbs up" for her frank and honest insights. "Gaining a medical doctor's trust is a difficult thing to accomplish. The doctors may listen to what you have to say, but whether or not they believe you enough to recommend and prescribe the product to a patient is a major concern. When asking a doctor questions, my purpose is to determine his or her buying needs."

Monica tries hard to be creative and make her job exciting. Her fresh approach is well received by most of the doctors she serves. "The doctors I call on see representatives on a daily basis, and it becomes vital for me to differentiate myself from the others. I must be sensitive to the doctor's time constraints and the frequent interruptions of the nurses and staff."

Monica stresses the importance of establishing an interpersonal association that is influenced by the knowledge and skill she brings to the selling situation. "My efforts are directed toward building long-term relationships through consultative selling. Relationship building is everything in professional selling," she says.

application of interpersonal communication skills. The goal of this chapter is to help develop competence in establishing and maintaining a relationship in the context of sales through the appropriate use of sales communication skills.

Professional Selling Systems

This section covers the two categories of selling systems: the traditional model and the consultative model. Figure 2.1 shows the general framework of the various types of selling systems that are operational today.

Key Elements

As Figure 2.1 shows, three key elements are common to both the traditional and the consultative selling models: profitability, quantitative and qualitative determinants, and power and influence.

Profitability

Every organization that is responsible for reporting income operates on the premise that it will turn a profit—even the nearly one million nonprofit organizations whose principal objective is something other than returning profit to their owners. These organizations, which employ 10 percent of the American work force, earn an estimated $300 billion in revenues each year.[1] It is also safe to assume that any business that incorporates the promotional part of the marketing mix into its operational activities intends to earn and increase profits by generating revenue through the sale of its goods and services.

For the salesperson, that means increasing profits by optimizing one's level of performance. This translates into developing competence in both interpersonal communication skills and sales strategy flexibility, which will yield repeat business.

Quantitative and Qualitative Determinants

Applying *quantitative* measures, as used in a traditional selling system, requires that everything the salesperson does be assigned a numerical or dollar value. For example, quotas may include the number of calls made by the hour, day, week, or month. Quotas may also require that a certain number of presentations be made per day. Sales volume may be reached through total number of units sold or total dollar volume of each order. The sales interview may be organized into a precise number of steps with a prescribed number of closing attempts and a structured method of responding to all objections. When taken to extremes, this heavily measured set of activities and results often creates stress, aggressiveness, defensiveness, and burnout among the sales force. As a result of this pressure, the salesperson may feel forced to develop brief, impersonal relationships with customers. These activities may evoke a similar response from prospects and customers who are the recipients of such pressures.

In the consultative selling model, salespeople continue to use quantitative measures to attain their targeted sales volume. Qualitative measures, however, become increasingly important. *Qualitative determinants* refers to the nature of the relationship between the customer and the salesperson. While quotas and sales volume remain quantifiable, the selling strategies become those in which salespeople seek to profit through an exchange process that involves developing authentic relationships for the purpose of mutually satisfying needs. In this model the relationship-driven selling strategies optimize the balance of qualitative and quantitative measures.

Equipped with the interpersonal communication skills and basic selling competence that the relational process requires, salespeople achieve their greatest potential for maneuverability in the sales interaction. With this competence they acquire the flexibility to operate effectively in both the traditional and consultative models.

Power and Influence

In an interpersonal relationship, such as that between a buyer and a seller, *power* is the ability to influence the other person in that relationship to accomplish preferred results.[2] More than 30 years ago Paul Hersey and Kenneth Blanchard, experts in organizational behavior and leadership training, identified two kinds of power—*position* and *personal*. Their definitions are useful in describing the control element shown in Figure 2.1:

> An individual who is able to influence the behavior of another because of his position in the organization has *position* power, while an individual who derives his influence from his personality and behavior has *personal* power. Some people are endowed with both types of power. Still others seem to have no power at all.[3]

Generally speaking, the selling strategy used in the interaction dictates whether the salesperson or the prospect has the most power. While it isn't as clear-cut or simple as this may sound, the respective power of the buyer and the seller is distributed in the following manner.

Traditional Selling Model Where the selling strategies are product- or sales-driven, the salesperson exercises the strongest influence over the buyer's behavior. Taken to extremes, this may manifest itself in aggressive,

On the Ethical Side Identifying with the Client

Clients are generally very positive about their ethical stances. They have spent their lives establishing their moral positions, and the salesperson who is truly customer oriented will soon be able to discover what these moral positions are.

Each salesperson is an individual and, as such, has also established personal moral positions. But it is purely ethical to examine those moral positions that the salesperson and the customer have in common. In fact, it is to the advantage of their relationship if they do. The common ground between the two can nourish agreement on sales-related items as well.

hostile, and high-pressure tactics that intimidate the buyer into making a purchase. On the other hand, if the prospect contacts the salesperson because of a perceived need for the product, the prospect may relinquish power to expedite the buying decision.

Consultative Selling Model If the basic selling strategy is customer-driven, power and influence typically rest with the prospect or customer. Taken to extremes, the salesperson may use passive behavior and wait for the customer to initiate the order. The cliché that "the customer is always right," if taken literally, is an example of giving up power and influence to the buyer.

When the selling strategy used by the salesperson is predominantly relationship-driven, then power and influence are shared between the prospect or customer and the salesperson.

Power and influence may shift according to the selling situation and the projected short-term and long-term outcome of the relationship. For example:

1. The salesperson initiates the sales call. The prospect may need the product or service but is unaware of the need or that such a product or service exists. The product or service is highly competitive with others.
2. The salesperson initiates the sales call. The prospect may or may not need the product or service and is unaware of the need. The product or service is superior to any other available.
3. The salesperson responds to the prospect's call. The salesperson's product or service may be either superior or similar to others on the market.

The likelihood of a balance of power existing between the prospect and the salesperson is greatest in the first case. The salesperson may have more influence and control in the second selling situation, and the prospect may have greater power in the third case.

Finally, it is important to remember that in both the traditional and the consultative models, the stages in the selling process are similar. The steps that the salesperson takes by selecting a specific selling strategy are adjusted to accommodate the situation as it compares to the three conditions just discussed.

The Nature of Relationships

Businesses and related sales organizations recognize that associations formed between their sales forces and customers greatly influence the propensity of the customer to make repeat purchases from them, rather than to seek out the competition.

Frederick W. Smith, founder and chairman of Federal Express, acutely understands the importance of relationships. In just 17 years, Federal Express grew from a fledgling enterprise beset by stalled negotiations and related adversity to a company with an impressive $7 billion in sales worldwide. By 1990, Federal Express employed over 80,000 "quality-focused" people, of which 1,300 are sales professionals. Bill Razzouk, vice president of U.S. sales for Federal Express, gives this account of his company's philosophy in maintaining a relationship edge:

> Our mission is to create a satisfied customer at the end of each transaction. To achieve that mission we need to understand the customer's business first, speak his language and learn about his needs, goals, and objectives. . . . Every employee at Federal Express, must be sales-oriented, and each manager must be an outstanding individual salesperson. . . . Our officers need to understand sales and need to spend a given number of days each quarter with salespeople in the trenches. They benefit from what our salespeople have to say and learn about what our customers want and need. As a result, our officers develop a greater customer sensitivity and we all gain by working together on better programs that more closely meet our customers' requirements. . . . Everybody is 100% committed and everybody has a lot of fun. We spend as much time in this company talking about customers as we do about operations.[4]

This kind of dedication to its customers has made Federal Express a global expressway for the exchange of ideas and services. This exchange is promoted from the highest level within the company. In the 182-page Manager's Guide, Smith writes, "Federal Express, from its inception, has put its people first both because it is right to do so and because it is good business as well. Our corporate philosophy is succinctly stated: People—Service—Profits (P-S-P)."[5]

More and more companies are experiencing success as they begin to treat their sales forces as the link that binds the customer to their company profits. As they focus their efforts on long-term objectives and profitability, they are training their salespeople to respond to the necessity for building long-term relationships. The two goals go hand in hand. Harvey B. Mackay, chief executive officer of Mackay Envelope Corporation and author of the bestseller *Swim with the Sharks*, says,

> People don't care how much you know until they know how much you care. . . . Knowing your customer means knowing what your customer really wants. Maybe it is your product, but maybe there's something else, too: recognition, respect, reliability, concern, service, a feeling of self-importance, friendship, help—things all of us care more about as human beings than we care about malls or envelopes.[6]

Mary Kay Ash, who founded Mary Kay Cosmetics in 1964, directs a relationship-based company that had retail sales of $800 million in 1989. Her belief in sustaining customer loyalty is so strong that she talks about it in terms of love. She says, "The role of love in management is to care about other people and to have them care about each other. And that's what we do in our company."[7]

What Influences People in Forming Relationships

According to marketing communication proponents, people enter relationships fundamentally to satisfy basic needs. The extent to which a person establishes an interpersonal association may depend on eight relationship determinants:

1. *Appearance*—This factor refers to the influence that physical attractiveness has in forming first impressions of another person.
2. *Similarity*—Individuals are drawn to each other when they share common interests or goals.
3. *Complementarity*—People may be attracted to others who fulfill a particular need that they have at that particular time in their lives.
4. *Reciprocity*—This refers to the interpersonal attraction one has toward another in a mutual exchange—a return in kind for something given.
5. *Competence*—Interpersonal attraction is influenced by the knowledge and skillfulness that a person brings to the situation.
6. *Disclosure*—Disclosure includes the degree to which we are involved with someone else and the breadth and depth of our association.
7. *Proximity*—The sheer chance of physical location determines, to a large degree, those to whom we are attracted. On the whole, proximity allows us to gather more information about others and to benefit from a relationship with them.
8. *Exchange*—In differentiating exchange from reciprocity, a person must determine whether working with another is a "good deal" or a "wasted effort." It suggests that we seek people who can give

us personal rewards that are equal to or greater than the costs we face in dealing with them. In economics, this is called the exchange theory.[8]

These components of interpersonal attraction influence us in our social and professional lives. In a selling context, most people do not have a choice when it comes to selecting their co-workers or their customers. Yet these eight determinants may influence the depth and extent to which they initiate and nurture their interpersonal associations.

Relationship Management

Factors such as competition, global marketing, shifting cultural demographics, and ethnic influences add to the complexity of how and why we form relationships. As we noted in Chapter 1, we live in an information age and a service-oriented economy. Therefore, sales trainers and sales managers are rethinking and reforming their selling strategies to meet these new demands through relationship management.

For the past 30 years, Learning International, a Times Mirror company headquartered in Stamford, Connecticut, has trained more than three million people in thousands of organizations, including 85 percent of the *Fortune* 500 companies.[9] President John J. Franco was asked to respond to the statement that "customers are becoming skeptical or even cynical." He responded,

> Absolutely. That's exactly why average salespeople find it more difficult to develop long-term relationships.Well-trained salespeople are able to form an alliance with the customer even though they may have to discourage the use of their own product in the interest of maintaining a high level of trust. Gaining trust and rapport over the long term is time consuming; however, it is the only way to achieve consistent sales success.[10]

Franco's response directly supports a relationship approach to sales. In practice, this attitude gives salespeople a "relationship edge" in obtaining customer satisfaction. Notice that in Figure 2.2, "Dedication to Customer" ranks second highest among the key factors that satisfy customers. That "perceived credibility of the organization and the salesperson, as well as the salesperson's ability to solve business problems and function as a business partner," is an integral part of all sales and organizational relationships.

The Communication Process

Inherent to the success of the relationship-oriented sales professional are two key elements: technical skills and communication skills. Technical skills cover areas such as obtaining and sharing product knowledge about one's own company, the prospect's company, and the competition; being

Figure 2.2

The Six Key Factors That Satisfy Customers

Over the past 20 years Learning International has sponsored extensive research projects. A recent study questioned 210 buyers from *Fortune* 1300 and Canadian 450 firms to determine the key factors that satisfy customers. The six factors, along with their contribution to overall satisfaction, are listed below.

1. **Business expertise and image (29 percent):**
   This factor includes the business stability of the company and the expertise of the salesperson.
2. **Dedication to customer (25 percent):**
   The items included describe the perceived credibility of the organization and the salesperson, as well as the salesperson's ability to solve business problems and function as a business partner.
3. **Account sensitivity and guidance (23 percent):**
   This factor includes a salesperson who is sensitive to pricing and budget needs.
4. **Product performance and quality (10 percent):**
   The product or service should be of consistent quality, perform as anticipated, and allow customers the flexibility to purchase only the specific features desired.
5. **Service department excellence (9 percent):**
   Items listed under this factor deal exclusively with customer service's interpersonal skill, reliability, and overall competence in helping the customer.
6. **Confirmation of capabilities (4 percent):**
   This factor encompasses the abilities of both the sales organization and the salesperson to provide customer references.

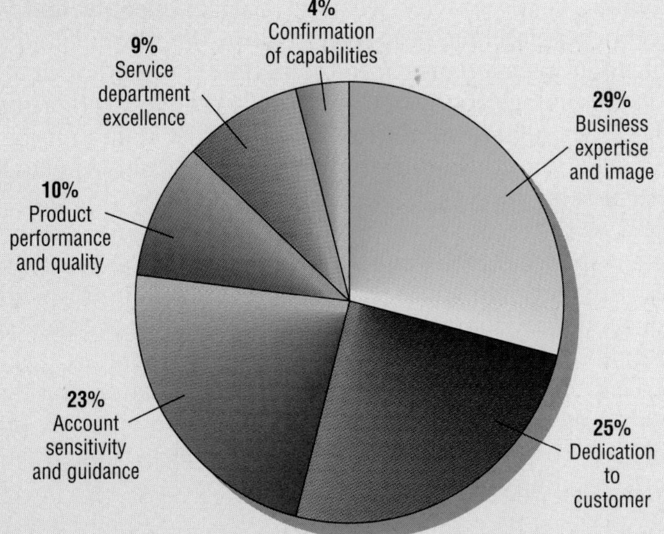

Source: Adapted from *Profiles in Customer Loyalty* with permission of Learning International, a sales and management training company headquartered in Stanford, CT.

able to demonstrate one's product effectively and appropriately; and providing the customer with training, support, and follow-up services when needed.

Communication skills give the organization life and make the salesperson the lifeline from the company to the customer. To understand a sales relationship and sales communciation competence, we must understand the communication process.

Its Nature—What It Is

Communication—the essential process used by all salespeople to plan, implement, and control their selling activities—is not easy. In the communication process, symbols such as words or gestures comprise messages. Thus, understanding first rests on a common meaning or frame of reference for the symbols.

When sending a message, a salesperson may have clearly in mind the meaning of the symbols selected. If the customer who is receiving the message attributes a different meaning, however, the message will not be understood accurately. The process is complicated even more because the meanings held by the salesperson and customer may change over time.

When a salesperson sends a message to a customer who then responds to that salesperson, one transaction has taken place. Communication may be made up of one or many such transactions and may include gestures or nonverbal symbols only. For instance, when someone says "Good morning" to you and you nod in return, a transaction has occurred. Nonverbal communication is so critical to the salesperson in relationship-driven strategies that we devote half of Chapter 10 to the subject.

Most sales communication experiences must involve numerous transactions for understanding to occur. Usually, the buyer and seller need to interact several times and modify the message until understanding is reached. This process may break down if either person stops trying to understand or assumes prematurely that the other person understands.

William C. Mason, Jr., is a well-known and successful representative for New England Life Insurance. Over the past 20 years he has developed an expertise in financial planning and pension fund programs. Mason's success hinges to a great extent on his use of effective communication practices to achieve clarity and understanding with his clients:

> In the absence of extraordinary circumstances, in order to effectively communicate, it is critical to lay down a common frame of reference, insofar as possible, and to include within that framework a common objective. In a sales situation that means (1) understanding the prospect's needs and environment, (2) being able to communicate to him that you so understand, and (3) serving his needs because serving the prospect's needs is the only legitimate objective in a sales meeting.
>
> If the client's needs reign supreme in the mind of the salesperson, and if the salesperson communicates clearly, taking care to establish

> objectives that will facilitate the meeting of client needs in a way that the client can comprehend, the communication process flows freely and easily; thus, even a simple statement becomes an invitation to reciprocate the delivery of important and even delicate information.[11]

This testimony points out that salespeople communicate *with* their customers, not *to* them. A true communication experience requires that both the buyer and the seller are involved until they both understand one another.

In this section we examine those aspects of the process of exchanging symbols that relate to sales communication. To achieve this goal, we examine a model of sales communication, followed by a discussion of six elements that affect the process. The ability to communicate in this model is determined by competence in using mutually understood symbols. If both the salesperson and the customer give mutual meaning to the words and have similar frames of reference, effective communication and mutual understanding will develop.[12]

A Model of the Communication Process

The foundation for a model of sales communication is a circle, as shown in Figure 2.3. This circle is appropriate because communication is a continuous two-way process between the salesperson and the prospect. The flow does not go just from one person to another but returns to the point of origin. The messages may be altered as a result of the flow from one point to the other.

When a salesperson and a customer communicate orally, one person at a time functions mainly as a sender of information while the other person functions mainly as a receiver. However, as the salesperson provides the customer with information (sending), the buyer's action is also observed (receiving), and the salesperson thinks about what to say next (interpreting). At the same time, the customer listens and observes the salesperson's behavior (receiving). The customer also gestures, smiles, makes eye contact, shows agreement by saying such things as "Yes, I see" and "uh-huh," and shifts posture (sending). The customer thinks about what the salesperson is saying and about how to respond (interpreting). While each communicator takes turns talking, both individuals are sending, interpreting, and receiving information at the same time.

When two people interact, they exchange information. The information is referred to as a message, or feedback. When a salesperson or a customer functions mainly by talking and acting, this person is sending a message. The message usually includes spoken words, which represent the verbal message. The nonverbal message includes mainly the sender's action and voice. When a salesperson or customer functions mainly as a receiver, the message is called feedback. Feedback is the receiver's response to another person's verbal and nonverbal messages. These four elements—two communicators and two kinds of information—are the main parts of the communication process.[13]

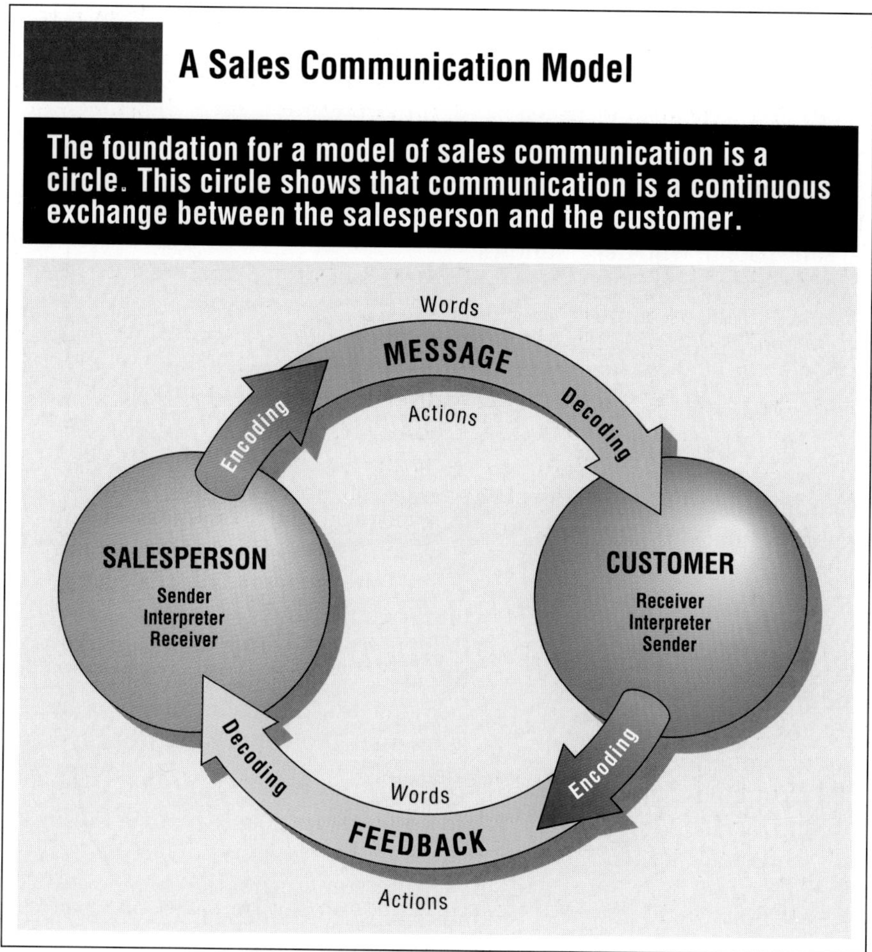

Figure 2.3

Characteristics and Influencing Elements

Several additional factors influence the ways these four basic elements interact in the communication process. Six factors are especially important in the sales context:

1. *The language skills of each communicator*—These skills include both encoding and decoding. Encoding is the process of putting ideas and feelings into words and actions. Encoding is affected by how much vocabulary a person can use to put the message together and how skillful one is in using that vocabulary. Vocabulary also includes a person's grasp of "trade language," that is, the terms, symbols, and jargon that are commonly used in a specific industry. Decoding is the process of understanding the words and actions received from another communicator. In Figure 2.3, both the salesperson and the customer engage in a mutual exchange process of encoding and decoding.

On the International Front Developing Relationships

Attitudes toward the development of personal relationships vary widely from country to country. Professional salespeople who develop an understanding of those nationalities that value relationships may function more effectively in developing successful, long-term relationships.

In many parts of the world, much more is involved in the selling function than just selling products and services. In many countries, personal relationships are more important than company reputations and products. Many foreign buyers take a long-term view of the selling relationship, which is usually based on trust.

Developing relationships may take a long time in some parts of the world, quite different from in the United States where the pace is rapid. "Too fast and too much" on the initial contact could lead to forcing the relationship, which can be a big mistake. Activities involving socializing and small talk are welcomed and appreciated before jumping into discussions related to the product or service.

The process may start with a getting-acquainted interlude involving personal rapport and social conversation. Some examples of cultural distinctiveness toward developing relationships in certain countries are as follows:

- In Latin America and the Middle East, solid sales opportunities usually follow a strong personal relationship. Building relationships is a long, slow process.
- In Africa, it is important to get to know co-workers as individuals before getting down to business. Friendship comes first. Discussions usually begin with general talk that can go on for some time.
- Belgians, on the other hand, are likely to get down to business right away and are unusually conservative and efficient in their approach to business meetings.

A slow-paced approach in developing relationships with foreign buyers usually takes more time, sometimes weeks or months. This time gives the salesperson and the prospect more time to learn about each other and build a base of trust. Learning the first steps leads to the most lasting relationships, which are crucial to the selling process.

Source: Adapted from M. Katherine Glover, "Do's & Taboos: Cultural Aspects of International Business," *Business America*, August 13, 1990, p. 3.

Bilingual considerations—The United States is a culturally diverse nation, and in many parts of the country a salesperson may be serving a territory where a language other than English is spoken. It is important for the salesperson to know that when a person is learning English as a second language, recoding is involved. Recoding is the process of encoding and decoding messages in one's native language before doing so in a second language. For example, a person whose primary language is Spanish may first encode a message in the native language and then recode it in English before stating or writing the message.

When functioning as a receiver, this person may first decode the message in Spanish and then recode it in English. When Americans are operating abroad in international sales, they tend to be patient with non-native speakers of English. When they are working at home, however, where English is the primary language, they often lack that patience. Extra time and effort are required to understand a message in a second language, especially when the message contains an unfamiliar business or trade vocabulary.

2. *The context of the communication*—The context includes the time and place of the communication. For example, the communication that takes place over lunch in the company cafeteria with other members of the sales staff is very different from the communication that takes place over lunch with a client or customer, in the client's office, or during a golf game with a customer.
3. *The purpose each person has for communicating*—The purpose is the reason or goal a person has for communicating with others. Skilled communicators are able to relate their purpose to the context and the persons with whom they communicate. For example, you may want to persuade your sales manager that you are the best person for a particular account. When asking a customer questions, your purpose may be to determine the person's buying needs. Learning may be the major purpose when practicing selling skills in the classroom.
4. *The cultural background of the communicator*—A culture is a common set of beliefs, attitudes, values, behaviors, and language shared by a group of people. Every major culture also includes subcultures. A subculture is a group of people who have values, interests, or experiences in common. Subcultures may be based on factors such as ethnic background (Asian Americans, African Americans, and Hispanic Americans), occupation (electricians, dentists, engineers), or religion (Catholics, Buddhists, Baptists).

   Developing cultural sensitivity as a salesperson is important in building a "relationship edge" in our competitive environment. For example, American salespeople frequently exchange business cards upon first meeting their prospects. They usually set the card aside immediately and continue with their conversation. Japanese businesspeople consider immediately setting the card aside to be rude behavior. Instead, they "present" their business cards with both hands and expect the customer or other salesperson to study it at length. To do otherwise is considered distasteful and disrespectful.
5. *The feelings and beliefs each communicator has about communicating*—Some people enjoy the experience of communicating more than others. For example, one communicator may enjoy conducting sales meetings more than making cold calls. Another communicator may enjoy telling jokes and stories but may not want to discuss opinions. A salesperson may feel nervous when meeting a prospect for the first time but may enjoy talking with established clients.

6. *Noise factors involved in the communication process*—Noise is anything that interrupts the achievement of communication goals between the parties. Noise can occur at every stage of the communication process. Whereas the previous five factors are positive influences in the process, noise is viewed as negative because it disrupts the sales interview.

   Three types of noise can interrupt communication. *Environmental noise* includes those elements outside the receiver that make hearing and seeing difficult. For instance, standing next to a paper shredder in operation while trying to demonstrate the benefits of a copy machine will make it difficult for the buyer to hear what the salesperson has to say. Having the customer frequently interrupted by phone calls distracts both the customer and the salesperson during the sales interview. Poor lighting, extreme room temperature, or a cluttered work space may impede communication flow.

   Physical noise involves internal biological factors in the communication that block accurate message exchange. Hearing loss, illness, and hunger pangs are examples.

   Psychological noises are internal factors that interrupt a person's ability to process a message. For example, if the customer just came from a meeting with the boss and was reprimanded for overrunning the budget, the ability to concentrate may be limited. Fear of spending more money may make another purchasing decision impossible at that moment. A salesperson who is under intense pressure to meet increased quotas may not be thinking clearly because of the anxiety involved in trying to meet those demands. Psychological noise also occurs in the buyer when there is no interest in the product or there is resentment toward the approach taken by the salesperson.

Interpersonal Communication Defined in a Sales Context

Interpersonal communication in a sales context can be defined in terms of both the situation in which it occurs and the way the buyer and seller are communicating with each other—the quality of interaction between individuals.[14] When communication is defined in terms of the situation, almost any interaction between two people qualifies as interpersonal. However, a purchasing agent who phones the inside salesperson to reorder a load of aluminum stripping that is purchased routinely is likely to be communicating in an impersonal rather an interpersonal manner. The situation alone does not guarantee that the communication between two people is interpersonal.

Three significant factors may distinguish impersonal from interpersonal communication. First, when communicating impersonally, two people perceive each other in terms of obvious labels or categories, such as sales manager, salesperson, prospect, purchasing agent, old man, African American woman, and so on. When communicating interpersonally, however, the people involved perceive beyond the labels. They see each other's specific personal characteristics.

Second, impersonal communication is based primarily on socially established rules and socially accepted topics. When first meeting a prospect (after setting an appointment), greetings, name and business card exchange, company history, and weather are suitable topics of conversation, as with any stranger. In contrast, interpersonal communication moves away from generally accepted rules and topics to communication that is more specifically tailored to the unique characteristics and experiences of the persons involved.

The third characteristic that distinguishes impersonal from interpersonal communication is the amount of information two people have about each other. When a salesperson and a prospect meet for the first time, they know only what they can assume from the situation in which they meet—the clothes they wear, the other possessions they may have with them or surrounding them in their work environment. As communication moves from impersonal to interpersonal, they learn more about each other and use that information in developing their relationship.

Sales Communication

Learning Systems International (LSI) is a consulting firm that develops selling systems and provides sales training programs worldwide. Dominique Cerofini is an account representative and one of LSI's top three sales professionals. He is exceptional in building new accounts and maintaining long-term relationships with his clients.

The following conversation occurred when Dominique called on Nora Cheung, training director for Allied Industries, Inc. Allied is a multinational *Fortune* 1000 company with over 80,000 employees worldwide. Despite its large industry market share, the company is experiencing a high turnover among its sales force.

The purpose of this dialogue is to illustrate how sales communication becomes transactional as both the sales representative and the prospect participate in a mutual exchange process.[15]

Sales Rep: Good morning, Ms. Cheung. As always, I appreciate having the opportunity to meet with you today.

Prospect: Likewise, Dominique. Although my time is limited today, I do want to share with you what motivated me to keep our appointment. Dominique, I have a serious concern about our pattern of losing our top salespeople.

Sales Rep: Am I to understand that the purpose of our visit this morning should cover two areas? One, what your perceptions are of the reasons why you're experiencing high turnover, and two, how Learning Systems International can help solve your turnover problems and make a significant difference in your bottom-line results. Is that right?

Prospect: Yes. And naturally, we're committed to profitability so I'd be interested in something that improves our bottom line.

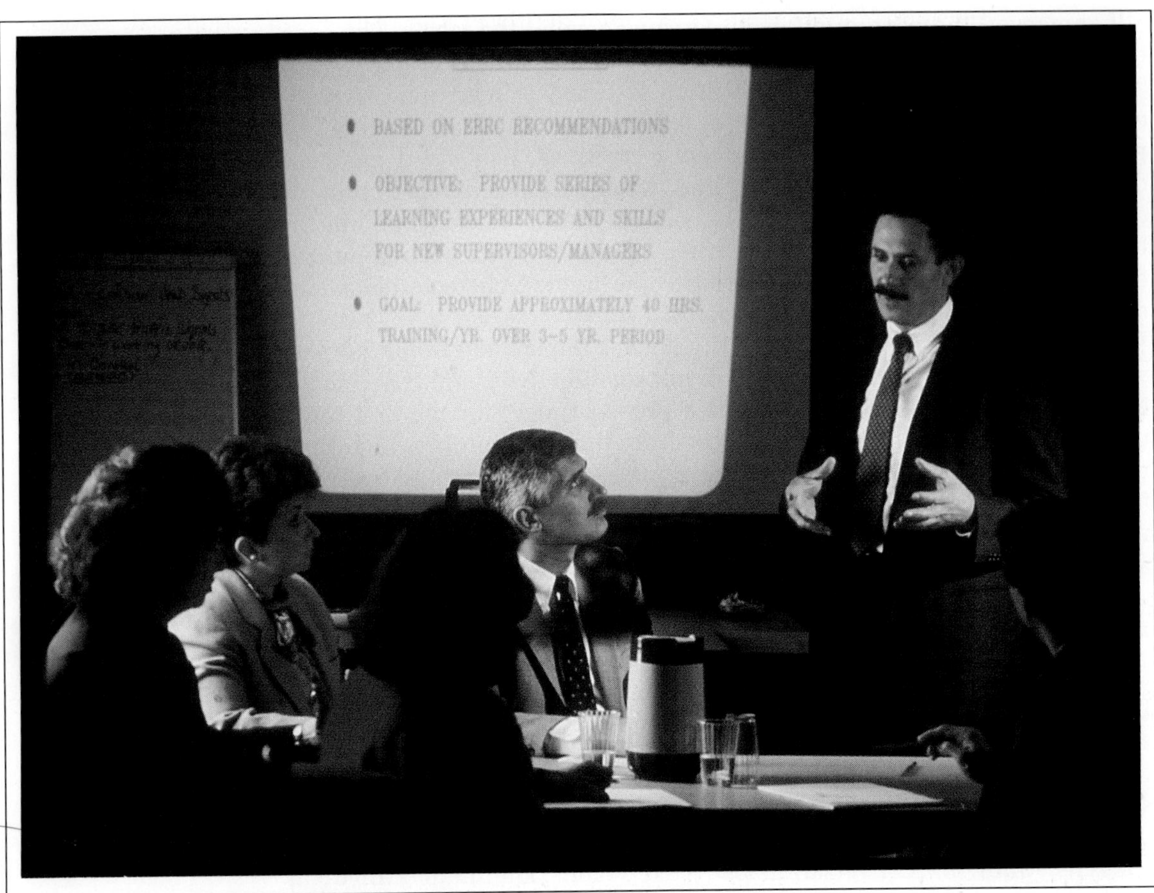

Sales Rep: Ms. Cheung, what outcomes do you most expect to receive from a sales training program?

Prospect: Well, in addition to increasing sales, I'd like to find some kind of training that addresses the reasons for our turnover.

Sales Rep: I'd like you to elaborate more on the turnover issue.

Prospect: Okay. For the past 8 years we have lost an average of 35 percent of our sales force each year. And that loss is split almost evenly between our domestic and international sales forces.

Sales Rep: Oh. I see. [Nods, giving a nonverbal response.]

Prospect: We recruit and hire the brightest young reps we can find on our college campuses. They come to Allied full of enthusiasm and energy. We give them the best product training available. They learn the industry inside and out, backwards and forwards. Then we turn them loose in the field and they charge into it full steam. But after maybe 7 or 8 months the wind goes out of their sails and they start muttering things like "selling isn't my thing." Within another 3 months they leave. My guess is that they lose their confidence—their fear of people and rejection increases, and they develop a sort of psychological paralysis.

Sales Rep: I see.

Prospect: My frustration is that many of them have potential. Another real concern is the thousands of dollars that we lose each year to training costs that are never recovered because they leave within 2 years.

Sales Rep: Your concern about turnover is really valid—it's a major problem in selling today. And I can understand your frustration in losing people who show the kind of potential you're describing.

Prospect: It is. And I'm at the point where I want to get to the bottom of this now and start recovering both our people and profit losses.

Sales Rep: Ms. Cheung, would you mind if I jotted down some notes? I think these ideas are important, and I want to be sure that they're included in my proposal.

Prospect: Go right ahead. And please call me Nora. [And so the interview continues until all issues are thoroughly addressed and an agreement is reached that satisfies both parties.][16]

As a process, sales communication is a continual cycle of mutual influence.[17] Everything about the participants—their values, experiences, attitudes, beliefs, and needs—influences the communicative choices they make. As Nora Cheung and Dominique Cerofini communicate, they are each affected by the interaction, which further alters what is said and how it is said. This, in turn, affects the kind of relationship that they will develop.

Sales communication involves more than the simple transmission of information about a product from a salesperson to a customer. In fact, the customer is an active participant who is always reacting in some way to the information being received from the salesperson. The preceding dialogue makes this clear. It is a misconception to assume that a salesperson does something to a customer during a sales interview to make the customer purchase a product or service. For example, as the salesperson is presenting information about a product, the customer is also responding in many ways, such as by asking questions, resisting efforts to close a sale, and smiling or frowning. All of these responses occur simultaneously. Similarly, at the same time that the salesperson is providing information about a product or service, the salesperson is also listening to how the customer responds and is thinking about what is being said to decide what to say next and how to say it.

This simultaneous transmission, reception, and interpretation of messages by both the salesperson and the customer involves transactional communication. In a sales interview, *transactional communication* occurs when both the salesperson and customer send, receive, and interpret information at the same time. When viewed transactionally, both the salesperson and the customer are active participants in a dynamic communication process.

Although the salesperson will probably take the responsibility for initiating the relationship, the salesperson and the customer depend on and influence each other to a large extent. The salesperson relies on the customer to express interest in and, ultimately, to purchase the product or service presented. On the other hand, the customer depends on the salesperson for assistance in defining problems, providing products and services that will solve them, and servicing the account. If the relationship were not reciprocal and the participants were not mutually interdependent, then the salesperson and the customer could each satisfy his or her own needs without the other's assistance. There would be no need for either participant to be involved in the relationship. Therefore, because the mutual dependence does exist, *sales communication* can be described as the process by which the salesperson and the customer create and manage a relationship by interacting with each other for the purpose of mutual need satisfaction.

Figure 2.4 shows this linking of communication skills with the basic selling steps that form the sales communication process.

Figure 2.4

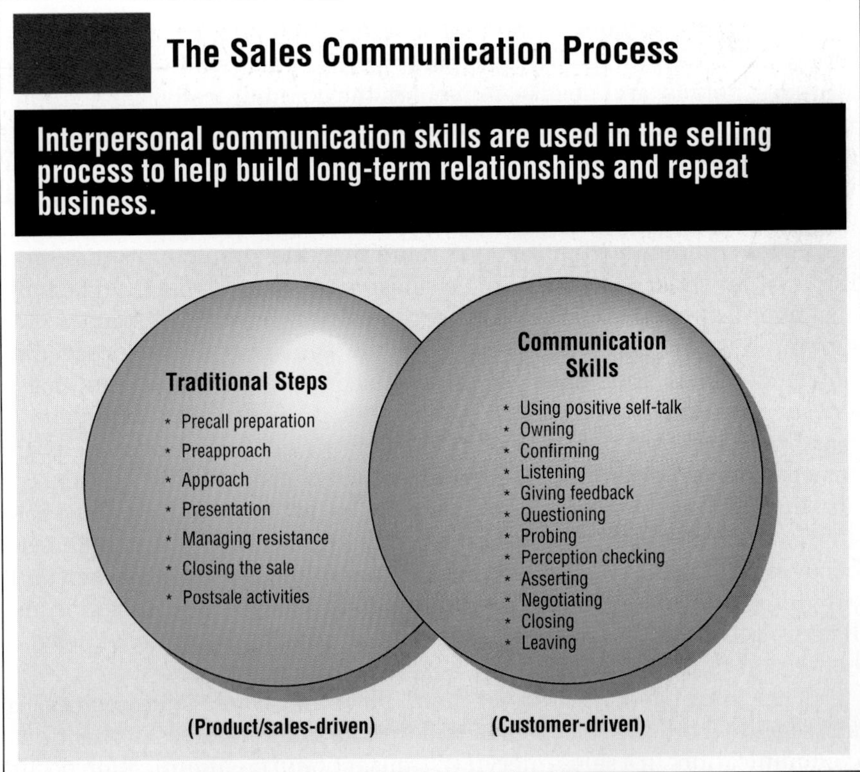

The Sales Communication Process
Interpersonal communication skills are used in the selling process to help build long-term relationships and repeat business.
Traditional Steps
* Precall preparation
* Preapproach
* Approach
* Presentation
* Managing resistance
* Closing the sale
* Postsale activities
Communication Skills
* Using positive self-talk
* Owning
* Confirming
* Listening
* Giving feedback
* Questioning
* Probing
* Perception checking
* Asserting
* Negotiating
* Closing
* Leaving
(Product/sales-driven)
(Customer-driven)

The Relational Selling Process

The relationship-driven selling strategy is a refinement and an extension of the consultative model. Relationship-driven salespeople see selling as an exchange process in which the buyer and seller are equal participants. To talk about an important relationship with a customer involves discussing the dimensions that define that relationship. Because a relationship is as dynamic as the people involved in it, a salesperson can choose to change and maintain it in ways that continue to help both the salesperson and the customer to meet each other's needs in mutually satisfying ways.

To become more aware of how these needs are met in professional relationships, we need to examine the following dimensions of a relationship: time, intimacy, affinity and control.[18] Figure 2.5 shows these four components and how they interface with the traditional steps and communication skills to form the relational selling process.

Time refers to how long a person has known another and how much time they have spent together. The importance that salespeople place on

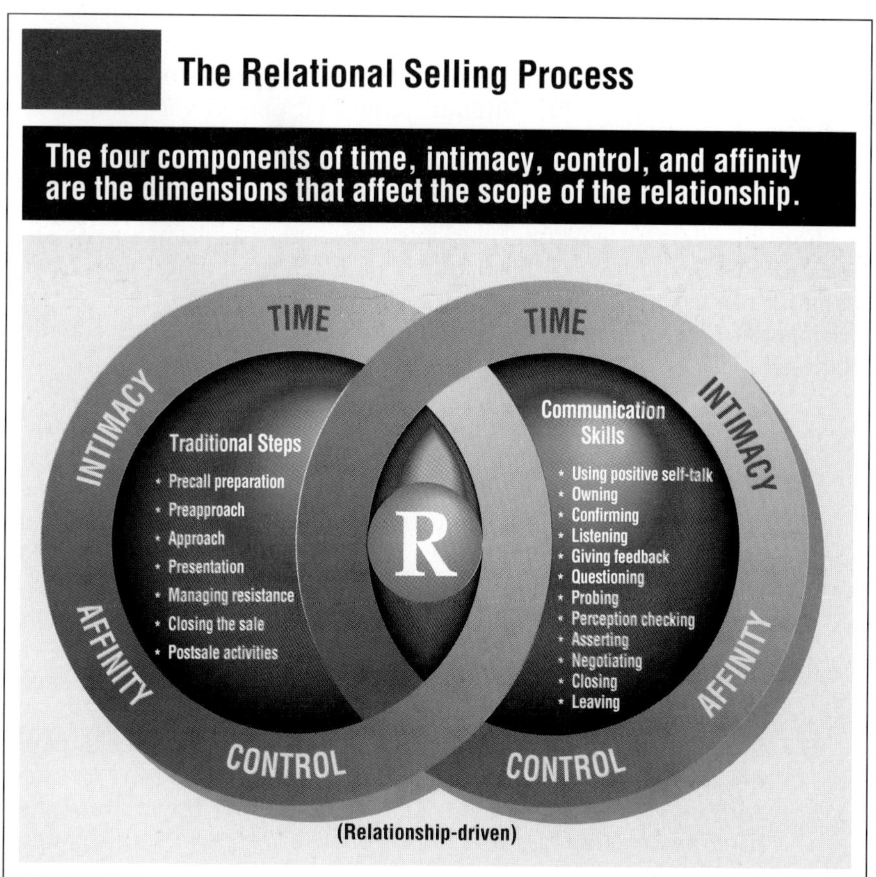

Figure 2.5

a particular relationship may be influenced by the amount of time they are willing to spend with the buyer.

According to the principles of effective time management, salespeople should spend 60 percent of their selling time obtaining and servicing their "A" or high-volume accounts. Yet many salespeople, especially beginners, tend to focus on their "C" or low-volume accounts, claiming they are friendlier and easier to work with. Subsequently, they perceive that their relationships with those customers are more solid and more productive. This is probably true because time affects the quality of the relationship. A drawback is that these relationships are not as financially profitable, and the salesperson should reassess the time spent with each account. The length of the selling cycle is also a consideration in determining the amount of time that one spends with a customer (for example, a one-call selling cycle versus a ten-call selling cycle spread over 18 months). Typically, the amount of time a salesperson spends with a buyer should be in direct proportion to the size of the account.

Intimacy refers to the closeness of one's contact with another person on intellectual, emotional, and physical levels. Close interpersonal relationships can differ significantly from one to another. For example, a salesperson may have a strong intellectual bond but little emotional or physical closeness with some buyers, yet share a strong emotional or physical bond (plays golf or tennis regularly) with other customers.

Affinity is the degree to which salespeople and their customers like or appreciate one another. It is possible for a salesperson to work with a customer over a long period without liking that person very much. Yet the salesperson may appreciate the customer's openness and honesty. Affinity is created in the relationship by behaving in nurturing and supportive ways.

Control refers to who makes decisions in the relationship. It also refers to who influences conversational patterns by talking most often, changing topics most often, and interrupting the other person. Three possible patterns of control distinguish the various types of buyer-seller relationships:

A. *Complementary pattern*—In this pattern, control is distributed unequally; one person takes control and the other goes along. This pattern can be very stable as long as both individuals agree to it. Consider a Kodak sales representative introducing a client to the new Kodak Datashow HR system, which puts IBM PC images on a big screen with an overhead projector. This is a revolutionary idea in combining two high-tech fields, and most customers would willingly defer to the sales representative—at least until they are knowledgeable enough to be able to discuss how the system might fit their needs.

B. *Symmetrical pattern*—In this pattern, two individuals make decisions equally and neither person dominates the conversation. Although equally balancing the needs of both buyer and seller in every decision requires considerable time and talk, this pattern is a goal of competent sales professionals.

C. *Parallel pattern*—In this pattern, one person assumes control for specific aspects of a relationship, and the other person takes charge in other areas. Shared responsibility exists with this pattern, but total equality does not. To continue with our Kodak example, the purchasing decision may involve multiple-buying influences, and because of the complexity of the system, the salesperson may serve as the technical representative at all buying levels while the purchasing agent provides the necessary data, conditions, and opportunities for the salesperson to make the presentation at each level.

To characterize how the relationship-driven strategy is an extension of the consultative selling system, let us review the dimensions that affect the scope of the relationship.

> It is important for the salesperson to examine and revise the amount of time that is spent with a customer, as well as the way in which it is spent.
>
> Salespeople can define and change the amount of intimacy they experience by becoming more or less close through increasing or decreasing their intellectual, emotional, or physical communication.
>
> The degree of affinity that both the salesperson and the buyer experience can be altered by increasing or decreasing their expressions of appreciation for one another. It is also possible to increase the degree of mutual liking by agreeing to change one's behavior.
>
> Salespeople can identify and adjust the type of control that exists in their relationships by exploring what kinds of decision making will meet their mutual needs most effectively.

Add to the dimensions outlined in the sales communication strategies and the steps in the selling process, and we have the framework into which we can fit the major component called *competence*. It is by developing competence, employing high ethical standards, and practicing cultural sensitivity that a salesperson becomes a sales professional.

Sales Communication Competence

Dr. Kenneth Blanchard, an internationally known management consultant and co-author of *The One-Minute Manager*, brings clarity to the meaning of competence in the following paragraphs:

> Competence is a function of knowledge and skills, which can be gained from education, training and experience. A business school graduate can be assumed to have a certain level of competence by virtue of having gained the appropriate number of credits for graduation. An individual with 10 years of marketing experience with a consumer package goods company can be expected to have a fairly strong level of competence in marketing.

> Competence is not just another word for ability. People often use the word "ability" to mean potential. They talk about "natural" ability to describe why some people seem to be able to learn certain skills so easily. Competence, on the other hand, can be developed with appropriate direction and support. It's not something you are born with. It's learned.[19]

Developing communication competence involves four components. It involves the ability to:

1. Develop a wide range of communication skills that includes but reaches beyond the current habitual ways of communicating
2. Evaluate sales situations in which communication is intended
3. Choose from the wide range of available skills those believed to be most appropriate for the specific sales situation
4. Evaluate the communication to determine what, if any, changes might be made in another, similar sales situation

In other words, using communication skills appropriately requires that both people have a range of skills that can be used effectively and that one make decisions about how to use them appropriately in specific sales contexts.

Several factors are involved in the ability to decide how to communicate appropriately in a specific sales situation:

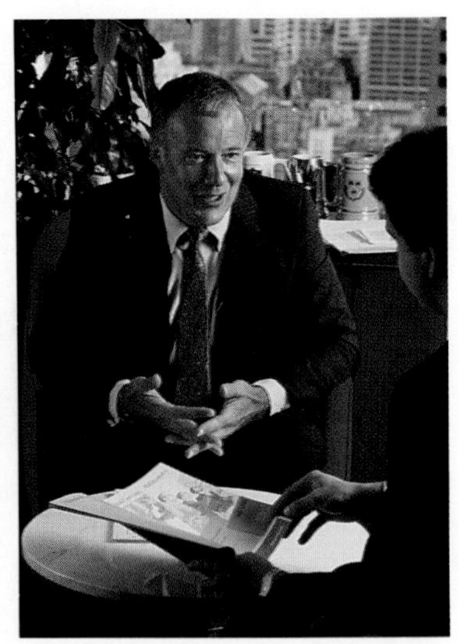

1. *The context*—The time and place influence most decisions about how to communicate. If one meets a potential customer at a party, it may be appropriate to tell a joke. If the first meeting is in the customer's office, however, and the customer obviously has broken away from a project for the meeting, telling a joke may be inappropriate.
2. *The salesperson's goal*—The purpose for communicating also influences how the communication is conducted. If the purpose is to learn about the customer's company, initiating and responding skills may be used to elicit information from the customer, and the salesperson may function mainly as a receiver. If the purpose is to describe a new line of products, the salesperson may use presentational skills and function mainly as a sender.
3. *The other person*—Information the salesperson has about the other person and the relationship between them will aid in selecting which skills to use for achieving appropriateness. Even when meeting a new customer, factors such as age, gender, status, and cultural background have an impact on the communication that takes place. When initiating a relationship with a new customer, the roles as salesperson and customer will be distinctly apparent. After a relationship has been established, however, the formal roles may be less evident and the two people will function more as a team, working to solve problems in the context of the customer's workplace.

The degree to which one can use communication skills in appropriate ways will depend on two main factors: the diligence with which one is able to apply the skills in the context of one's company and actual sales environment, and one's critical analysis of the ways one applies the skills, using the reporting procedures provided in this learning system.

The Four Stages in Learning Communication Skills

The design of the learning system presented in this section is based on the four stages involved in learning sales communication skills: awareness, awkwardness, skillfulness, and integration.

Awareness

The first stage involves becoming knowledgeable about skills through reading textbooks and participating in discussions with classmates and co-workers. When one begins to apply skills in practice demonstrations and actual sales interviews, one becomes aware of the steps or components and how the skills differ from the ways one typically communicates.

Awkwardness

When one begins using a skill, it may feel awkward. What is said and how it is said may even appear awkward to others. The degree of awkwardness experienced may be related to how similar the skill is to one's own habitual communication style. In this stage, using the skill usually requires obvious effort and concentration. The communication may seem contrived or scripted. The discomfort felt will probably be similar to the feelings experienced when playing a sport, using a keyboard, or riding a bicycle for the first time.

Skillfulness

As a skill is practiced, awkwardness is overcome and skillfulness takes its place. Skillfulness is the result of conscious effort and requires thinking, planning, and practice. A major purpose of this learning system is to provide the materials and methods for becoming a skillful sales communicator. While skillfulness involves communication effectiveness, the final stage in learning a skill involves communication appropriateness.

Integration

After repeated practice in the classroom or laboratory setting, one may begin to use the skill in sales interviews with customers. At this stage, the skill becomes habitual or integrated into the range of available communication behavior. As the skill becomes a part of one's own communication style, its repeated use will alleviate some of the stiffness and prescriptiveness. Once a skill becomes integrated into the range of available communication behaviors, one can use the skill in decisions about the appropriateness of the communication in sales interviews.

Sales professionals become more competent as they become able to use more skills at their highest level of effectiveness. With this competence comes the responsibility of the salesperson to perform at the highest level of ethical standards. In Chapter 3 we will define ethics and what ethical behavior means to the salesperson, the customer, and both of their organizations.

Summary

An understanding of the professional selling systems is of primary value to the salesperson. The two overarching selling models—traditional and consultative—are comprised of three major components: profitability, quantitative and qualitative determinants, and power and influence relationships between the salesperson and the customer. From these the various other selling strategies (those that are product-, sales-, customer-, and relationship-driven) are derived.

The facilitator for these systems and strategies is, of course, good communication, which we have defined as the process by which salespeople plan, implement, and control their selling activities. In the sales setting, the communication process is a dynamic transactional negotation toward mutual understanding. This viewpoint is achieved by seeing communication as a continuum from impersonal to interpersonal relations, based on an examination of three factors in human behavior:

1. People first see each other as roles or titles (impersonal).
2. People develop sets of unique conversational and social roles (quasi-personal).
3. People share information about themselves with each other (interpersonal).

The salesperson is thus wise to develop a wide range of communication skills, evaluate the skills that may be needed for a particular sales context, select the appropriate skills, and evaluate their effectiveness afterward. Each of these steps offers insight into the meaning of selling as a relational process.

Key Terms

Affinity The degree to which salespeople and their customers like or appreciate each other

Consultative Selling Model Selling strategies that are customer-driven

Context of Communication The time and place in which the communication takes place

Control Refers to who makes decisions in the relationship

Culture The beliefs, attitudes, values, behaviors, and language shared by a group of people

Decoding The process of making order and sense from the words and actions of another communicator

Encoding The process of putting ideas and feelings into words and actions

Environmental Noise Disruptive elements outside the receiver that make hearing and understanding difficult

Feedback Receiver's response to another person's verbal and nonverbal communication

Intimacy The closeness of one's contact with another person on intellectual, emotional, and physical levels

Nonverbal Message Body language and other physical actions intended for communication

Power Ability to influence another person to accomplish the preferred results

Profitability Earning and increasing profits by generating revenue through goods and services

Qualitative Determinants Derived from the nature of the relationship between the customer and the salesperson, and gauged by how well their needs are mutually satisfied

Quantitative Determinants Assigning a numerical or dollar value to everything a salesperson does

Relationship Determinants The eight factors by which one establishes an interpersonal relationship: appearance, similarity, complementarity, reciprocity, competence, disclosure, proximity, and exchange

Subculture A group of people within a culture who hold values, interests, and experiences in common

Traditional Selling Model Selling strategies that are product- or sales-driven

Verbal Message Any verbal utterance intended for the purpose of communication

Review Questions

1. What are the eight basic components in all selling systems?
2. What are the differences between quantitative and qualitative determinants in a selling system?
3. Identify the eight determinants that influence people in forming relationships.
4. Why is the communication process model depicted as a circle?
5. What elements make up the communication process? Explain each.
6. What are the six characteristics that influence the way a salesperson and a customer interact in the communication process?

7. What kinds of noise can disrupt the flow of communication in a selling context?
8. Define interpersonal communication and how it relates to professional selling.
9. What are the three characteristics that distinguish impersonal from interpersonal communication?
10. What four stages are involved in developing sales communication competency?

Questions for Discussion

1. Describe how profitability and quantitative and qualitative determinants influence the relationship process.
2. Describe how the eight determinants of interpersonal attraction influenced someone with whom you have established either a social or professional relationship.
3. What is communication and what is its significance to relationship management?
4. How does nonverbal feedback enter into the communication process? Is it possible for an individual to understand another individual without nonverbal feedback? What impact does nonverbal communication have in a sales context?
5. Discuss how sales communication is a mutual exchange process.
6. Describe a selling situation in which communication moved from impersonal to interpersonal.
7. Defend the statement, "As a process, sales communication is a continual cycle of mutual influence."
8. Under what conditions would the traditional selling system and the consultative selling system be appropriate?
9. The focus of contemporary sales training programs is on the relationship-driven strategy. Why?
10. What is involved in developing sales communication competence?

The Importance of the Right Language

Case 2.1

John Merino sells construction materials and compounds to contractors, general construction workers, and specialists such as plumbers and electricians. Many of his products must be combined and incorporated with other products. Construction workers sometimes find these procedures overly technical and frustrating.

John has an excellent education and has a tendency to express himself with big words that can be frustrating and intimidating to buyers. He believes that using big words gives him a professional image. He also likes to wear fashionable suits when working in the store and when calling on customers.

John's sales manager recently went with him on a call because John is behind on his quota. They met with Don Wood, the owner of a large plumbing company that specializes in installing plumbing materials for new office buildings. Don arrived at the meeting wearing blue jeans, a T-shirt, and work boots. John was dressed in a fashionable three-piece suit and wore highly polished black shoes. The sales manager heard John use these two statements during the course of a conversation with the prospect:

> With this particular premerge compound, photodecomposition will occur unless incorporated.
>
> The efficacy of hydrochloric acid is indisputable, but corrosive residue is incompatible with any alternative other than a permanent metallic substance.

Although Don Wood has been in business for 18 years and is extremely knowledgeable in his trade, he found it difficult to understand John's sales presentation. When the presentation was completed, Don looked at John with frustration and said, "Could you please repeat that again in plain and simple English?"

1. Considering the background of Don Wood in this specific communication situation, do you agree with John's approach?
2. What advice should the sales manager give John to help him improve his communication and sales image?
3. How would a more experienced salesperson change the phrases to be more effective in communicating with buyers in the construction industry?

Case 2.2

Having Knowledge of Language and Customs

Selling internationally involves buyers and sellers from many different countries, each operating under different customs and rules regarding communication.

Disagreement was raised following receipt of a shipment of beef products shipped from the United States to Spain. With a limited knowledge of English, the buyer, Sr. Garcia, placed an order for 1,000 pounds of beef from Hanson's Meat Company. In the past, Hanson's, a major supplier from Nebraska, had dealt only with buyers from the United States. In an effort to expand sales, they decided to seek international market opportunities. Lacking knowledge of foreign customs and language, they pursued their first overseas venture and hastily accepted Sr. Garcia's order.

Sr. Garcia owns a chain of specialty catering services and restaurants located throughout Spain. He is well known and highly respected in Europe for gourmet meals that require a certain quality of beef. According to Sr. Garcia, the order did not meet his expectations, and the American company did not understand exactly what he wanted.

The conflict occurred when Sr. Garcia said the standard of the beef received was of a rather low quality, and the grade was unacceptable for his particular needs. According to Sr. Garcia, it was lower in grade than expected, and he demanded that the order be returned to Nebraska at the supplier's expense. He offered a compromise, expressing willingness to accept the beef at a substantial discount.

The American supplier refused to accept any compromise and insisted that the importer should have clearly specified in English any requirements different from customary U.S. standards. According to Hanson's Meat Company, "when products are ordered from our company, they are shipped according to customary U.S. standards unless specified differently."

1. A communication breakdown exists here. How could this dispute have been avoided?
2. Using the relational process, how would you go about resolving this situation?
3. What is the significance of this case in terms of American companies doing business internationally?

Notes

1. L. E. Boone and D. L. Kurtz, *Contemporary Marketing*, 6th ed. (Chicago, IL: The Dryden Press, 1989), p. 15. Adapted from Jay Finegan, "Tax Advantages," *INC.*, August 1987, p. 23.
2. David H. Holt, *Management: Principles and Practices*, 2nd ed. (Englewood Cliffs, NJ: Prentice-Hall, 1990), p. 323.
3. Paul Hersey and Kenneth H. Blanchard, *Management of Organizational Behavior*, 2nd ed. (Englewood Cliffs, NJ: Prentice-Hall, 1972), p. 32.
4. Gerhard Gschwandtner, "Secrets of Sales Success at Federal Express," *Personal Selling Power*, January/February 1990 (Vol. 10, No. 1), p. 15.
5. Ibid.
6. Harvey B. Mackay, *Swim with the Sharks* (New York: Ivy Books, 1988), p. 26.
7. L. B. Gschwandtner, "Mother of Thousands—Mary Kay," *Personal Selling Power*, January/February 1990 (Vol. 10, No. 1), p. 65.
8. Larry R. Smeltzer and John L. Waltman, *Managerial Communication: A Strategic Approach* (New York: John Wiley and Sons, 1984), p. 2.
9. Advertorial, "Sales Training for the Next Generation," *Personal Selling Power*, January/February 1990 (Vol. 10, No. 1), p. 54.
10. Ibid., p. 56.
11. William C. Mason, Jr., "Self-Analysis," Video Sales Presentation II, November 1989, p. 5.
12. Paul Hersey, "A Look at Situational Selling in Action," in *Selling: A Behavioral Science Approach* (Englewood Cliffs, NJ: Prentice-Hall, 1988), p. 120.
13. Sharon A. Ratliffe and David D. Hudson, *Communication for Everyday Living* (Englewood Cliffs, NJ: Prentice-Hall, 1989), p. 11.
14. Sharon A. Ratliffe and David D. Hudson, *Skill-Building for Interpersonal Competence* (New York: Holt, Rinehart & Winston, 1988), p. 1.
15. Hersey, "A Look at Situational Selling in Action," p. 121.
16. Hersey, *Selling: A Behavioral Approach*, pp. 122–128.
17. Lynne Kelly, Linda C. Lederman, and Gerald M. Phillips, *Communicating in the Workplace: A Guide to Business and Professional Speaking* (New York: Harper & Row, 1989), p. 5.
18. Ratliffe and Hudson, *Skill-Building for Interpersonal Competence*, p. 257.
19. Kenneth Blanchard, "Competence and Commitment Determine Management Style," *Personal Selling Power*, January/February 1990 (Vol. 10, No. 1), p. 44.

CHAPTER

3

Ethical, Legal, and Cultural Issues in Professional Selling

Knowledge Objectives

In this chapter, you will learn:

1. The importance of ethical practices for professional salespeople
2. To identify ethical conduct as it relates to the salesperson as an individual, to prospects and customers, and to the company
3. Major laws that affect personal selling activities
4. The importance of understanding culture in selling
5. The nature of U.S. subcultures and the variety of targets for the salesperson
6. To recognize the legal aspects of ethics

Consider This

Almost all our faults are more pardonable than the methods we resort to to hide them.

François de La Rochefoucauld

An independent sales representative sold heavy industrial equipment. He went to a purchaser's construction site, observed his operations, then told the president of the company that his proposed equipment would "keep up with any other machine then being used and that it would work well in cooperation with the customer's other machines and equipment." The customer informed the rep that he was not personally knowledgeable about the kind of equipment the rep was selling and that he needed time to study the rep's report. Several weeks later, he bought the equipment based on the rep's recommendations.

After a few months he sued the rep's company, claiming that the equipment didn't perform according to the representations in the sales literature sent prior to the execution of the contract and to statements made by the rep at the time of the sale. The equipment manufacturer defended itself by arguing that the statements were made by the rep, in good faith, with no intent to deceive the purchaser.

The court ruled in favor of the customer, finding that the rep's statements were predictions of how the equipment would perform; this made them more than mere sales talk. The rep was held responsible for knowing the capabilities of the equipment he was selling, so his assertions were deemed to be statements of fact, not opinions. Furthermore, the court stated that it was unfair that a knowledgeable salesperson should take advantage of a naive purchaser.[1]

any salespeople are unaware that they assume ethical and legal obligations each time they approach a prospect or customer. Frequently, they may engage in "sales puffery," or opinions, and exaggerate the capabilities of their products or services just to close the sale. They fail to realize that there are legal constraints urging them to behave ethically. Furthermore, professional salespeople must also concern themselves with cultural factors that affect selling situations.

This chapter focuses on some of these issues and the challenges that confront salespeople. The chapter is divided into four sections. The first contains an examination of the ethical issues. The second section presents an overview of professional salespeople's responsibilities to themselves, to prospects and customers, and to the company. In the third section, a basic knowledge of the law is presented because consideration of the law is involved in all sales transactions. Finally, an examination of cultural settings offers approaches to meet the demands of cultural differences that have an impact on the selling situation.

Ethics and the Salesperson

A salesperson falling below quota pushed an increased order onto a customer without concern for the potential overstocking of merchandise. The salesperson achieved quota despite the risk of long-term customer dissatisfaction. Similar cases reveal salespeople offering a kickback from a commission and gifts to the decision makers for purchases to close the sale.

These situations illustrate the kind of ethical confrontations salespeople often encounter when they are involved in sales transactions. Salespeople usually have alternatives when faced with an ethical decision. The situation becomes more difficult, however, when there is not a single acceptable ethical action agreeable to everyone involved.

Furthermore, if no laws are violated, is it unethical to offer the client a bribe? Should the decisions of a salesperson be based on the law or on personal values and ethical standards? Moreover, what is the proper thing to do in developing a long-term, trusting relationship with the client? It is the sales professional's standards of right and wrong that determine the guidelines for decisions and behavior as they relate to selling situations. Overall, the complicating factor is that what is considered right by one person, company, or country may be considered wrong by another. Hence, the ethical and legal problems associated with bribery can be quite confusing and involved.

The Importance of Ethical Conduct

Ethical conduct is receiving more attention today because of the increased number of government regulations, which may result in fines, penalties, and damage to a company's public image. Overall, it is simply good practice to behave ethically in building and maintaining the relationships essential for success in professional selling. The ethical issue gets further complicated, however, because what is unethical in one culture is not necessarily so in another.

A Definition of Ethics

Ethics are defined as "the study of standards of conduct and moral judgment" or "the system or code of morals of a particular person . . . group, profession, etc."[2] Ethics are the rules of conduct and practices of a particular society, which are used to determine what is good or bad, acceptable or unacceptable.

Consequently, although a code of conduct can provide useful operating guidelines for ethical decision making, that code may not adequately address the circumstances involved in many sales situations, such as those designed to appeal to the general public, the media, customers, employees of the government, and other interests. Such codes assume that sales professionals are willing and able to conduct activities consistent with broader social values.

Mark Frankel, an author specializing in the topic of ethics, states:

> Not all the planks of a professional association's code of ethics are meant to be taken in the same spirit. Some are merely costumes the profession puts on to impress outsiders. Some are preachments to be honored but not necessarily obeyed. Some are guides, but permissive ones. Some are tactical moves in controversies with outside groups. Some are seriously intended.[3]

The question of what is ethical in a given situation forces the salesperson to make a choice. W. D. Roundtree, a recognized authority on the topic of ethics in personal selling, addresses the dilemma:

> Ethical standards are set by society and not by individuals. Thus, society evaluates an individual's behavior as ethical or unethical. The problem is that society lacks commonly accepted standards of

> behavior. Determination of what is right and what is wrong is an extremely difficult task. What is considered ethical conduct varies from country to country, from industry to industry, from situation to situation, and even from person to person.[4]

From a professional salesperson's perspective, adopting a code of ethics helps to gain the public's trust, confidence, and respect. One such code is that of Avon Products, Inc., as presented in Exhibit 3.1.

Exhibit 3.1

Avon Products, Inc., Code of Ethics

Avon Products, Inc.

a member of the Direct Selling Association

and a subscriber to its nationally recognized Code of Ethics, is proud to endorse and support these standards that ethical independent salespeople should follow

President
Avon Products, Inc.

President
Direct Selling Association

The Standards That Ethical Independent Salespeople Should Follow

Offers should be clear, so that consumers may know exactly what is being offered and the extent of the commitment they are considering.

A description of the goods and quantity purchased, and the price and terms of payment, should be clearly stated on the order form, together with any additional charges.

Contracts or receipts used should conform to applicable laws or regulations.

Any guarantee or warranty stated by the sales representative should be consistent with, and at least as protective as, that of the manufacturer or supplier of the product sold.

Any description of after-sale service should be accurate and clear.

Any receipt or contract copy should show the name of the sales representative, and his or her address or the name, address and telephone number of the firm whose product is sold.

All salespersons should immediately identify themselves to a prospective customer and should truthfully indicate the purpose of their approach to the consumer, identifying the company or product brands represented.

Salespersons should not create confusion in the mind of the consumer, abuse the trust of the consumer, or exploit the lack of experience or knowledge of the consumer.

A salesperson should not imply that a prospective customer has been "specially selected" to receive some reputed benefit or that any offer is special or limited as to time when such is not the case.

Salespersons should respect the privacy of consumers by making every effort to make calls at a time that will suit their convenience and wishes. Selling contacts should not be intrusive and the right of the consumer to terminate a sales interview should be scrupulously respected.

All references to testimonials and endorsements should be truthful, currently applicable and authorized by the person or organization giving same.

If product comparisons are made, they should be fair and based on facts which have been substantiated.

A salesperson should refrain from disparagement of other products or firms.

A salesperson should not attempt to induce the consumer to cancel a contract he has made with another salesperson.

A more in-depth version of a code of ethics that also embraces topics important to professional salespeople is highlighted in Exhibit 3.2. The code of the American Marketing Association recognizes the significance of the professional conduct of salespeople as well as their responsibilities to society and to other members of their profession. For example:

1. It acknowledges their accountability to society as well as to the organization for which they work.
2. It pledges efforts to ensure that all presentations of goods, services, and concepts are to be made honestly and clearly.
3. It strives to improve marketing knowledge and practice to better serve society.
4. It supports free consumer choice in circumstances that are legal and consistent with generally accepted community standards.
5. It pledges that salespeople will use the highest professional standards in their work in their competitive activity.
6. It acknowledges the right of the American Marketing Association, through established procedure, to withdraw a salesperson's membership if that person is found to be in violation of ethical standards of professional conduct.

Some Standards of Conduct

Sales professionals' responsibilities fall into three categories: responsibilities to oneself, to the prospect or customer, and to the company represented.

Exhibit 3.2

American Marketing Association Code of Ethics

Members of the American Marketing Association (AMA) are committed to ethical professional conduct. They have joined together in subscribing to this Code of Ethics embracing the following topics:

Responsibilities of the Marketer

Marketers must accept responsibility for the consequences of their activities and make every effort to ensure that their decisions, recommendations, and actions function to identify, serve, and satisfy all relevant publics: customers, organizations, and society.

Marketers' professional conduct must be guided by:

1. The basic rule of professional ethics: not knowingly to do harm;
2. The adherence to all applicable laws and regulations;
3. The accurate representation of their education, training, and experience; and
4. The active support, practice, and promotion of this Code of Ethics.

Honesty and Fairness

Marketers shall uphold and advance the integrity, honor, and dignity of the marketing profession by:

1. Being honest in serving consumers, clients, employees, suppliers, distributors, and the public;
2. Not knowingly participating in conflict of interest without prior notice to all parties involved; and
3. Establishing equitable fee schedules including the payment or receipt of usual, customary, and/or legal compensation for marketing exchanges.

Rights and Duties of Parties in the Marketing Exchange Process

Participants in the marketing exchange process should be able to expect that:

1. Products and services offered are safe and fit for their intended uses;
2. Communications about offered products and services are not deceptive;
3. All parties intend to discharge their obligations, financial and otherwise, in good faith; and
4. Appropriate internal methods exist for equitable adjustment and/or redress of grievances concerning purchases.

It is understood that the above would include, *but it is not limited to,* the following responsibilities of the marketers:

In the area of product development and management,

- ☐ Disclosure of all substantial risk associated with product or service usage;
- ☐ Identification of any product component substitution that might materially change the product or impact on the buyer's purchase decision;
- ☐ Identification of extra-cost added features.

In the area of promotions,

- ☐ Avoidance of false and misleading advertising;
- ☐ Rejection of high-pressure manipulations or misleading sales tactics;
- ☐ Avoidance of sales promotions that use deception or manipulation.

In the area of distribution,

- ☐ Not manipulating the availability of a product for purpose of exploitation;
- ☐ Not using coercion in the marketing channel;
- ☐ Not exerting undue influence over the reseller's choice to handle a product.

In the area of pricing,

- ☐ Not engaging in price fixing;
- ☐ Not practicing predatory pricing;
- ☐ Disclosing the full price associated with any purchase.

In the area of marketing research,

- ☐ Prohibiting selling or fundraising under the guise of conducting research;
- ☐ Maintaining research integrity by avoiding misrepresentation and omission of pertinent research data;
- ☐ Treating outside clients and suppliers fairly.

Organizational Relationships

Marketers should be aware of how their behavior may influence or impact on the behavior of others in organizational relationships. They should not demand, encourage, or apply coercion to obtain unethical behavior in their relationships with others, such as employees, suppliers, or customers. Marketers should:

1. Apply confidentiality and anonymity in professional relationships with regard to privileged information;
2. Meet their obligations and responsibilities in contracts and mutual agreements in a timely manner;
3. Avoid taking the work of others, in whole, or in part, and represent this work as their own or directly benefit from it without compensation or consent of the originator or owner;
4. Avoid manipulation to take advantage of situations to maximize personal welfare in a way that unfairly deprives or damages their organization or others.

Any AMA member found to be in violation of any provision of this Code of Ethics may have his or her Association membership suspended or revoked.

Source: Reprinted with permission from "AMA Adopts New Code of Ethics," *Marketing News* (September 11, 1987), pp. 1, 10, published by the American Marketing Association.

Ethical Conduct toward Self

Professional salespersons take full responsibility for their actions under all circumstances. Passing responsibility for conduct off to others is considered unacceptable. This responsibility for conduct recognizes the need to establish ethical values and to develop an understanding of responsibilities to oneself and others.

Hence, salespeople must be ethical with themselves before they can be ethical with others. This ethical behavior will lead them to long-term success and lifetime opportunities.

Ethical Conduct toward Prospects and Customers

Areas of conflcit arising between the salesperson and the customer may involve bribery, gratuities, entertainment, mispresentation, and reciprocity.

Bribery

A bribe is an effort to buy the sale from a customer by extending a kickback or by giving an elaborate gift. In most situations, bribes are unacceptable and illegal.

Ethical considerations about bribery are more ambiguous in international settings because bribes are acceptable in certain countries. The following situations provoke diversity of opinion concerning bribery:

The Sam P. Wallace Company, a specialty construction company, paid the chairman of the Trinidad and Tobago Racing Commission 5 percent of the project cost to obtain the contract to build the grandstand and buildings for a new luxury horse racing track.[5] The chairman of the racing commission requested the payment to bind the agreement. Was this a bribe? Of course, this action was a bribe, which is illegal under the Foreign Corrupt Practices Act of 1977. But was this action considered unethical? This case of bribery is definitely considered unethical because a payoff was offered, thereby contributing to the cost of the contract.

International cases have cited further situations whereby customs officers of many foreign countries are given a sum of money as an incentive to speed the processing of required documentation at the port of entry. It is customary in certain countries to extend a monetary incentive for services provided, such as for customs clearance. It is vital to determine, however, how much of a "monetary incentive" is acceptable and how much of a limit or expectation proves acceptable or unacceptable.

We may agree that this practice conducted in this foreign country is acceptable because there is no law prohibiting it. In the United States, tipping a customs official is unethical because the action is considered bribery. In the United States, a bribe is illegal by law as well as ethically inappropriate. Should the U.S. firm approve of its representative bribing a foreign customs officer to gain favored treatment? If the firm failed to establish a certain set of standards for its international transactions—standards that allow for a certain amount of otherwise unethical behavior, such as modest incentives—the company would probably be unable to compete or succeed abroad.

On the Ethical Side When Does a Gift Become a Bribe?

It is acceptable simply to say that there is no place in selling for bribery because of its unethical and illegal nature. Questions may arise, however, relating to the varying perspectives on this critical issue of when a gift becomes a bribe.

In the United States it is perfectly acceptable for a person to take a customer out to lunch or dinner. Also acceptable is the payment of a commission, which is the receipt of money for services rendered. Further customs of influencing, such as offering a free trial, are also considered acceptable. If money is given with the purpose of inducing favorable treatment, however, then such gifts become bribes and are considered illegal. Does giving a gift before a deal is reached make the gift a bribe? This offering may appear unacceptable because it was extended as a means of gaining something in return that would not have been assumed voluntarily.

Is it then acceptable when a gift is offered after a business agreement is made? Such a gift appears to be less questionable when extended after the agreement has been concluded. Often gifts are given as a symbol of thoughtfulness or consideration and as an attempt to make friends ("bonding"). Also, the occasion for giving, such as special holidays, might be considered.

The difference between bribery and gift giving is not a straightforward or simple issue; there are many questions regarding what form the gift takes, when it is extended, why it is offered, and what is really implied by giving it. In responding to such situations, guidelines for gift giving might include the following:

1. Determine your motive and sincerity. Gifts are extended for the purpose of expressing appreciation for services rendered and acknowledging a positive working relationship.
2. Extend the gift after the consummation of a sale to avoid any implication of a potential bribe, which could bruise the relationship.
3. Do not accept a gift from a customer when special considerations may be expected afterwards. Be fair in your treatment of all customers.
4. Know the policies and practices of your company and customers in terms of what is acceptable.

Although some companies have policies that prevent a client from accepting or extending gifts in selling situations, the professional salesperson must consider personal definitions of what is right and wrong in conforming to local laws, customs, and personal ethics.

The main reason for the condemnation of bribery, whether on a domestic or an international level, is that it is unfair to offer special incentives or payments to influence a decision that should have been based on merit.

A gratuity, although not far removed from a bribe, is considered more acceptable and is extended more openly. A gift is something that rewards the customer and is of personal benefit. A gift becomes a bribe when it is given to unduly influence or corrupt the buyer.

Among many industrial buyers, gift giving is considered ethical and acceptable as long as the decision maker considers first the interest of the firm. In essence, providing small gifts to purchasing agents enhances cordial working relationships between the buyer and the seller. However, if the salesperson offers a gift in the form of a payment to a purchasing agent in exchange for business, and the gift is intended to entice the agent to act against normal duties, a bribe has taken place.

Furthermore, the Internal Revenue Service carefully scrutinizes gift giving. The limit of $25 contained in the corporate income tax code serves as a benchmark for a reasonable gift. A gift of $50 was considered enough above the benchmark to be significant.[6]

It is important to become familiar with the guidelines for gift giving listed in Table 3.1.

Entertainment

Entertaining prospects and customers is a common practice in many industries, although at times it can fall under the same category as bribes and gift giving if it is an attempt to influence the buyer. Using entertainment with the hope that the prospect will feel obligated to buy products is unacceptable.

In the United States, entertaining clients is considered an acceptable practice. On the international scene, the Japanese spend more time entertaining than Americans do, sometimes taking the prospective business associate out at night to drink until dawn. Usually, this entertaining is done by a low-level member of the firm who is not the key decision maker. In Spain, the business lunch is one of the most important moments in a business meeting, sometimes stretching from 2:30 to 5:00 p.m.

Other forms of entertaining can be far more effective than lunches and dinners. For example, a sporting goods representative might offer tickets to a ball game to the prospect and his family. Again, all of this should be done without any intent to influence the buying decision.

Table 3.1

Guidelines for Gift Giving

1. Determine your motive and level of sincerity. Gifts are for the purpose of expressing appreciation to your customer and serve as a tangible way of acknowledging a mutually rewarding relationship.
2. Wait until the sale is consummated so that there is no thought in the customer's mind that a bribe is being offered that could discolor your relationship.
3. Check on your company's policies and practices as well as those of your customer. Many firms have a dollar limit on what is considered acceptable.
4. Refuse gifts from customers when even the slightest doubt exists about the buyer's motive (for example, wanting lower prices, trade-in allowances, or special order considerations). Refusing such gifts helps you to treat all customers fairly.

Misrepresentation

Misrepresentation involves interpreting facts loosely and in favor of the salesperson's point of view. Professional salespeople should not give false data or withhold information that might otherwise influence the prospect to think differently.

The most important consideration in avoiding misrepresentation is honesty, which provides the foundation for building a reputation and a long-term relationship with the client. Such behavior is usually reciprocated by customers.

Reciprocity

Reciprocity refers to the practice of doing business with prospects if they will do the same in return. This reciprocal agreement must be based on reasonable prices and value. It is an acceptable practice as long as it does not interfere with each party's right to choose and does not consist of any predetermined expectation.

Ethical Conduct toward the Company

Salespeople's obligations also extend to their companies. Ethical considerations in this category relate to expense accounts, sales calls, moonlighting, and time accountability.

Expense Accounts

Accurate statements of legitimate sales expenses are required when submitting expense accounts because most salespeople are reimbursed by the company for expenses incurred in the course of their work. Travel expenses, entertaining, and other expenses are often difficult to verify, and salespeople can be tempted to engage in "creative" deception by padding expense accounts. Salespeople must avoid inflating and falsifying expense accounts. These practices may result in a salesperson being fired.

Sales Calls

The temptation to pad daily sales call reports always exists. A real call has not been made until the interview has occurred. A complete product demonstration on a security alarm device is not the same as a brief glimpse of the product given to the security guard at the door as one leaves the building.

Moonlighting

Some salespeople try to do two jobs at once by selling for two companies. Handling another product line while taking time away from an employer is a case of "kiting." This effort cheats both employers of the full effort for which the salesperson is being compensated. This type of involvement is considered unacceptable and unethical.

Time Accountability

One of the most difficult areas to assess and measure in all work situations, but particularly in field sales, is the issue of an employee's performance and use of time. Numerous articles have been written that cast the person who steals time as the greatest perpetrator of theft within the firm. For example, a person who works on a straight commission basis and takes excessive lunch breaks or spends 60 percent of selling time with "C" accounts is, in effect, stealing profits from the company. Another person who may be paid a salary plus commission, and who spends too much time at home or on the golf course entertaining clients, may be guilty of failing to sustain the sales-support staff whose jobs depend on making sales.

Toward Professionalism

Ethical action is often directed by the norms and beliefs defined by the company's leadership. A norm is a standard of conduct that is typical of a certain group. For instance, a norm may appear in the company's code: The salesperson must not accept personal gifts with a monetary value of more than $25 in total from any business associate. Ultimately, the salesperson may have to rely on personal judgment to resolve the ethical aspects of the decision. This decision is often dependent on the integrity and experience of the decision maker. Thus, salespeople must maintain their values steadfastly and focus on what they believe is right.[7] Exhibit 3.3 recalls a test of such integrity as presented by a company's top officer.

Nonetheless, honesty is always the best policy in selling. Once customers know a salesperson is dishonest or untruthful, they will hesitate to deal with that salesperson again. Professional salespeople are honest and committed to serving customers' needs and problems because they realize that honesty is essential in developing a long-term relationship with the customer.

Ethical versus Legal Standards

An ethical standard is an outgrowth of the customs and behavior of a society, but a legal standard is enforced by statute of law. The ethical standard need not be a legal standard of conduct and can extend beyond what is spelled out in the law. To many, what is legal is what is ethical. Although laws and ethics are related, they do not mean the same thing, however. Generally, ethics precede law. In the case of a gratuity, even if no laws are violated, offering a gift can still be considered unethical.

One government official charged with regulation in the insurance industry notes, "Ethical behavior begins where the law leaves off. Being ethical means obeying the spirit not just the letter of the law."[8] Furthermore, "laws cannot be so pervasive as to reach every corner of human activity; a society needs ethical standards so that individuals and busi-

Maintaining Your Integrity

Exhibit 3.3

Alan Lesk, senior vice president, sales and merchandising for Maidenform, recounts his most unforgettable sales call:

It was my first call as a district manager in Washington, D.C., in 1970. One of the major department stores there was not doing a lot for business with Maidenform, and we were looking to get some more penetration in the market. Surprisingly, the sale took only two sales calls.

The first person I approached was a buyer. He was completely uncooperative. On the way out of the store, I popped my head into his boss's office and we set up a meeting with some higher level executives later in the week.

So there I was, a young kid facing a committee of nine tough executives, and I had to make my presentation. I was in the middle of my pitch when the executive vice president stopped me. He told me this was going to be a big problem, about $500,000, and asked me point-blank, how much of a rebate I was willing to give him to do business with the store, over and above the normal things like co-op ad money. He was actually asking me for money under the table!

I had to make a decision fast. I stood up and said, "If this is what it takes to do business here, I don't want anything to do with it." I then turned to walk out the door, and the guy started cracking up. I guess he was just testing me to see what lengths I'd go to in order to get my sales program into the store.

This one incident taught me some very important things: You can't compromise your integrity, and you can't let people intimidate you. But most important, don't lose your sense of humor. Needless to say, we got the program into the store, and today, we do more than $2 million worth of business a year with it.

Source: Reprinted from "Strange Tales of Sales," *Sales & Marketing Management*, June 3, 1985, p. 46.

nesses can be free to make decisions on sensitive issues affecting their own interests and those of others."[9]

Several types of activities used by salespeople may be illegal. As already stated, bribery is unacceptable from both an ethical and a legal point of view in the United States. It is essential that professional salespeople be aware of the legal aspects of their jobs because one error can cost the company millions of dollars and a loss of reputation.

One activity that may elicit discussion on the virtues of ethics versus legal standards is that of donations to charity. A cigarette manufacturer declared that all profits from sales transactions to a specific dealer would be donated to a charity. However, the sales contract was obtained through bribery. Does the end (the contribution to charity) justify the means (bribery)? Most of us would agree that charitable giving is good and commendable. But an ethical dilemma is faced here. What is it?

Legal Issues Facing the Salesperson

Many laws regulating selling activities exist to protect consumers. Sales representatives who lack legal guidance could violate regulations and be held personally liable. Companies must therefore train salespeople properly to avoid such violations.

It is beyond the scope of this text to deal with all the laws that pertain to professional selling; however, some of the primary laws that are of special concern to most American salespeople will be discussed. Key antitrust legislation affecting salespeople is presented in Exhibit 3.4.

Exhibit 3.4

Antitrust Legislation Affecting American Salespeople

Sherman Act (1890)

The Sherman Act was passed to protect the public from monopolistic practices that hinder competition. The courts decided that a group of sellers who sought to fix prices adversely affected competition.

Clayton Act (1914)

The Clayton Act was an amendment to the Sherman Act. It contains provisions that are intended to restrain business people from circumventing the Sherman Act by engaging in such practices or exclusive dealing contracts and tying agreements that substantially affect competitors' opportunities to compete. This act also made price discrimination illegal under some conditions. Price discrimination is a monopolistic practice that involves supplying some buyers at one price and other buyers at another price under similar circumstances.

Federal Trade Commission Act (1914)

A companion law to the Clayton Act, the Federal Trade Commission Act is responsible for enforcing the Robinson-Patman Act. Violators may receive fines of up to triple the damages if indicted and prosecuted. Because all individuals within the company, including sales managers, field salespersons, and chief operating officers, may be personally liable for failing to act within the law, companies have given special attention to training salespeople and other executives in this area of the law.

Robinson-Patman Act (1936)

The Robinson-Patman Act is also an amendment to the Clayton Act. It was designed to close the loopholes discovered in the preceding two laws. This law forbids price discrimination in interstate commerce and prohibits unfair business practices that may reduce competition. Many of the unfair business practices that are defined in this act occur when salespeople are selling to the trade, including both wholesalers and retailers.

Sales implications and guidelines are provided to help both salespeople and managers avoid costly mistakes. Following these guidelines reduces the potential for costly misrepresentations and breach-of-warranty lawsuits:

1. Thoroughly prepare for sales presentations and interviews. Know the technical specifications of the product, and review all promotional literature to be sure that no claims are made that cannot be substantiated.
2. Study all design changes and revisions in the product's operating manual so that you will know the product's capabilities well.
3. Before making the sale, educate the customer thoroughly by revealing full details about the product or service. This is particularly critical if the prospect is unsophisticated in the product area and will generally rely entirely on the technical expertise that is provided.
4. Be operationally familiar with federal and state laws affecting warranties and guarantees.
5. Avoid distorting the truth by relying on emotional appeals or using forceful and manipulative tactics to close the sale.
6. Do not offer opinions on what results may be expected from the product or service unless your company has tested the product or service and has statistical evidence to support what it will do.
7. Be as accurate as possible when describing performance capabilities of the product or service. Refrain from speculating about what it will or will not do.
8. Avoid making exaggerated statements about product safety. These remarks may be interpreted as warranties that could lead to product liability.
9. Do not circumvent authority when discussing prices and company policies. Statements made by the salesperson can bind a company in a court of law.
10. Avoid making damaging statements about your competitor's products or services. Inaccurate, misleading, or slanderous statements about a competitor's reputation may ruin a potential business relationship.

Additional areas where the law directly affects salespeople are business slander, business libel, product disparagement, and unfair competition.[10] Business slander occurs when an unfair or untrue oral statement is made about a competitor to a third party (such as a customer) and can be construed as damaging that competitor's business reputation or the personal reputation of an individual within that company. Business libel is constituted by unfair and untrue statements in writing communicated to customers. It can be found in letters, sales literature, advertisements, or company brochures. Product disparagement is represented by false or deceptive comparisons or distorted claims concerning a competitor's products, services, or property. Unfair competition includes statements made by the salesperson that reflect on a competitor's product in a way that misrepresents its characteristics or qualities.

These four methods of business defamation are considered "unfair and deceptive acts and practices" in the Federal Trade Commission Act. Some instances where sales language has caused a company trouble are:

- Accusing competitors of engaging in illegal or unfair business practices
- Saying that a competitor fails to live up to its contractual obligations and responsibilities when the allegation is untrue (for example, saying that the competitor ships defective goods and is always being sued)
- Making false statements that a principal executive of the competition was incompetent, of immoral character, unreliable, or dishonest
- Stating that a product is custom made when this is untrue
- Making statements that a product was "proved" when there is insufficient scientific and empirical evidence to substantiate this claim
- Stating falsely that a product is fireproof and flame resistant
- Passing off certain company personnel as experts when they are not
- Awarding a dealer's staff for sales of a company's product or service without the consent of the dealer[11]

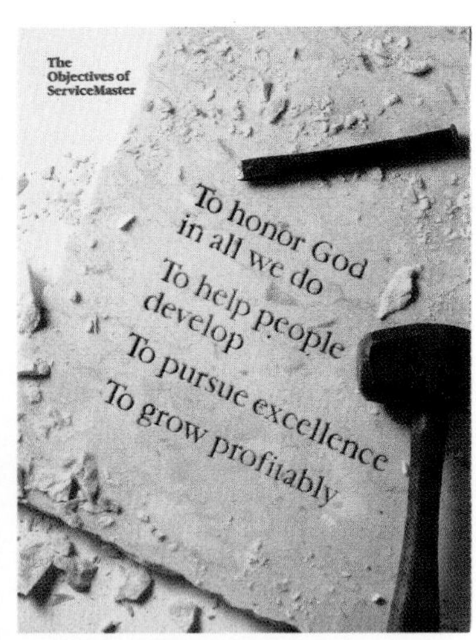

"At ServiceMaster, *corporate culture* exerts a powerful force for ethical behavior. These are the four official goals displayed at the company's headquarters in Illinois. Employees honor these values while performing their jobs as mundane polishing floors and cleaning carpets for customers. ServiceMaster achieves extraordinary responsiveness and quality because every manager worries not only about its customer's employees too. Not surprisingly, ServiceMaster is one of the most admired companies in the United States."

With reference to engaging in exaggerated statements, there is often a slight and subtle difference between sales puffery and statements of fact. "Generally, the less knowledgeable the customer, the greater the chances the court will interpret a statement as actionable."[12] For example, if a salesperson says, "Our repair service is outstanding; it can't be beat," the statement is usually viewed as an opinion. The customer will usually discount its reliability, and the standard defense used by attorneys is that it is unreasonable to take these kinds of remarks at face value. However, when a salesperson makes a claim or promise of a factual nature relative to the product's capacity to perform (that is, results that will be achieved, profits or savings that will be realized), the law treats these claims or comments as statements of fact.

In addition to these regulations, other significant laws that pose restrictions and legal guidelines in domestic selling include the Uniform Commercial Code and cooling-off laws. Also highlighted is the Foreign Corrupt Practices Act, which should be understood as the U.S. domestic market being expanded to global proportions.

Uniform Commercial Code

The Uniform Commercial Code (UCC) covers many aspects of selling, including the need for written contracts, warranties, delivery agreements, and commissions. A brief description follows of these primary areas that directly affect the relationship between the buyer and seller as governed by the UCC:

1. *Definition of a sale*—The UCC clearly states that salespeople have the authority to legally obligate the company they represent.
2. *Warranties and guarantees*—The code describes warranties as either "express" or "implied." Express warranties are those described by the express, or specific, language of the seller. Implied warranties are those legal obligations imposed by law upon the seller that are not described in express language.
3. *Salesperson and reseller*—In the event the salesperson has a customer who is a reseller (someone who buys to sell to another), the salesperson must be aware of the obligations the supplying company has to the reseller. For example, in the case of a warranty statement, if the salesperson is a middleman representing a manufacturer's product, the middleman must make certain that the buyer (in this case, the reseller) understands that the manufacturer is providing this warranty.
4. *Financing of sales*—Salespeople who work for firms that are directly involved in either financing products or services or in arranging such financing from outside sources must be aware of the legal aspects of making these credit arrangements.
5. *Product consignment*—On some occasions, goods are sold on consignment. In cases where goods are delivered to the buyer but title remains with the seller, the responsibility rests with the salesperson to be familiar with the rights of the company (for example, if goods have a limited life span, depreciation may occur with the passing of time).[13]

Cooling-off Laws

Almost all states have laws regulating solicitation and door-to-door selling because these are characterized as high-pressure selling. The cooling-off law that applies to solicitation and door-to-door selling for purchases of $25 or more provides buyers 3 days to think over their decision. Consequently, if the buyer decides that the purchase is not acceptable, the contract can be voided.

Additionally, the salesperson must provide the buyer with information pertaining to the following terms and conditions: (1) the number of days before the contract is binding, (2) the procedure to legally cancel the agreement, and (3) any penalties that may be involved with the cancellation.

Foreign Corrupt Practices Act

This act limits payment of fees to obtain a foreign contract. At a glance, this act of payment appears to be one of bribery; as discussed previously, however, on the international scene bribery is not a straightforward issue. According to the Foreign Corrupt Practices Act of 1977, bribery—which may take the form of gifts or even cash—is "the use of interstate commerce to offer, pay, promise to pay, or authorize giving anything of value to influence an act or decision by a foreign government, politician, or political party to assist in obtaining, retaining, or directing business to any person."

Although at present the law is ambiguous, new conditions of the law specifically permit payments to officials to facilitate business transactions. The difficulty in determining the legality or acceptability of a bribe has added to the many frustrations and challenges for salespeople dealing with cultural differences. Professional salespeople have realized that, in some situations, this is part of the game that must be played when selling internationally.

The following section addresses the cultural diversity of the global market. The professional salesperson is challenged by the increasing sophistication of the sales environment and is confronted with the need to acquire knowledge from different cutural perspectives.

Cultural Perspectives in Professional Selling

The president of a drill company was planning his first international business trip to Saudi Arabia, where he saw the greatest overseas opportunity for his products. He had found that one of the best ways to show cultural sensitivity was to give the right gift to a potential client, and his good taste had always served him well in the United States. Following the lead of presidents and secretaries of state, he decided that gifts chosen to take to Saudi Arabia should be typically American. He therefore selected a case of his favorite bourbon. Having learned from a 1969 Commerce Department brochure, "Doing Business in the Gulf," that Arabs show intense concern for their families, he also chose a gift for his potential client's wife—a tasteful gold bracelet from Tiffany. He decided to present both gifts in person.

Upon his return from the business trip, he told members of his executive staff what had happened. "You should have seen his face when I gave him the bourbon; he was completely speechless. And he's always been so talkative on the phone." After several days of negotiations, not having seen his client's wife at all, he had finally asked if the client were trying to keep her all to himself. Shown the gift intended for his wife, the client again was speechless. Too sensitive to pursue the matter further, the executive had given the gift to the client. He mentioned that he hoped to meet the wife on his next trip to Saudi Arabia.

Before returning home, the executive had tried to break the client's increasingly stony silence. He complimented the client on his favorite camel on a number of occasions. "I told him how much I admired the strong, reliable animal. You know, to please him. But he did not smile! He looked at me a long time and petted the camel. Finally, he handed me the camel and walked briskly away."

The executive did not express concern that he has not heard from his Saudi Arabian client. "A man just does not give away his favorite camel lightly. There is a real bond between us. He will call me in time."

Key rules to be learned from this example are as follows:

1. Do not rely on your own taste in selecting appropriate gifts.
2. Do not bring a gift to an Arab's wife; in fact, do not ask about her at all. Bringing gifts to the children, however, is quite acceptable.
3. In Arab countries, do not admire an object openly. The owner may feel obligated to give it to you.
4. Do not bring liquor to an Arab's home. For many Arabs, alcohol is forbidden by religious law.[14]

Culture and Its Characteristics

Culture is a set of traditional beliefs and values that are shared in a given society. Professional salespeople should continually search for these values, even though they may be embedded in a particular culture, described in Exhibit 3.5.

As a general rule, when playing in someone else's ballpark, you had better know the rules. Successful American companies, such as Procter & Gamble, General Motors, and Exxon, have recognized this need for their employees to gain cross-cultural understanding. As professional salespeople continue to cultivate relationships on a global scale, cultural sensitivity and adaptation serve as keys to viable long-term relationships.

Exhibit 3.5

An Example of Cultural Values

Arabs have developed a value for qualities of character such as generosity, fellowship, and a certain ability to spend:

"Even when it is inconvenient, one is under a compulsion to accept another's hospitality. Just as an Arab is more than willing to extend hospitality to others, he expects them to be hospitable to him also. For example, when an Arab businessman goes to the United States and calls on an American executive he expects considerable hospitality. If the American says "I'm free for lunch next Wednesday" or "I'll be free for thirty minutes in the office tomorrow," he might just have done himself a bad turn. To an Arab hospitality should be immediate."

(Adapted from Almeney, Adnan, "International Communication and the MNC Executive," Vol. 9, No. 4, Winter 1974, p. 23)

Key topics such as time and patience, personal space, customs and manners, agreements, and friendship patterns will provide a starting point in acquiring the knowledge necessary to establish sales relationships with people in different cultures.

Time and Patience

In many parts of the world, time is perceived as being more flexible than it is to people in the United States. Promptness is considered very important in making appointments in the United States. In some countries, however, setting appointments to the hour may not be proper because people come late to appointments or may not come at all.

Americans tend to value time highly—both work time and leisure time—because "time is money." They often feel that things need to be settled and completed as soon as possible and that they have no time to waste or spare. People in the former Soviet republics, in contrast, have formal classroom training in bargaining and chess. They are patient and careful before making a move, often taking extra time just to gain an advantage in the process of negotiation.[15]

Patience and flexibility are two main qualities that professional salespeople must have when working internationally. Selling in China takes a lot of patience because of the many legal restrictions. The same is true in Greece and Italy. A document that may take a day to obtain in the United States could take a week in Italy. In Spain, being patient is a prerequisite to consummating a sale. Furthermore, negotiations are conducted at a slower pace than would be expected in the United States. Considerations related to negotiating will be discussed in Chapter 13.

This call for patience should be taken seriously: In many countries, Americans are seen to be in a rush—in other words, unfriendly, arrogant, and untrustworthy. Almost everywhere, we must learn to wait patiently and never to push for deadlines. Count on things taking a long time, the definition of "a long time" being at least twice as long as you would imagine.

Personal Space

Personal space also has implications in selling situations. Latin Americans are comfortable with just a few inches of space between salesperson and client. Asians, on the other hand, prefer substantial conversational distance and no physical contact. For Americans, a comfortable distance is somewhere between those extremes. An American can unwittingly give the impression of crowding to an Asian and of running away to a Latin American.[16]

Customs and Manners

Imagine a salesperson in the United States who came late to an appointment, refused to discuss prices, and looked out the window while making the presentation. That person certainly would not get the sale. Indeed, that person should be asked to leave. It is no exaggeration to say that Americans behave this inappropriately abroad in terms of the codes of conduct in many foreign cultures. An American trying to make a good

Sales Professional Spotlight

Santiago Echevarria is president and chief executive officer of Intermart, Inc., an international business management and consulting firm that develops business strategies and negotiates business contracts for major U.S. companies in Australia, Canada, Europe, the Far East, the Middle East, and Latin America.

His accomplishments have included increasing U.S. foreign subsidiary sales from $14 million to $80 million within 2 years and increasing sales from $25 million to $70 million within 3 years for 11 wholly owned, foreign high-tech subsidiaries. Other accomplishments include negotiating franchising agreements and developing joint ventures, from the initial research and partner identification stage to the contract signing stage.

Born in Spain, Mr. Echevarria moved to Mexico as a young child. Even though the Spanish language spoken in both countries is quite similar, broad cultural differences do exist. At a very young age he learned the need and importance of adapting to Mexico's different culture and life-style.

While growing up in Mexico, Mr. Echevarria was interested in the way business was conducted in the United States. This interest prompted him to study English and seek out business opportunities with Mexican subsidiaries of American corporations, such as Container Corporation of America, Samsonite Corporation, and the Southland Corporation (7-Eleven). His first opportunity to come to the United States came in 1974, when the Southland Corporation invited him to develop its international markets.

With over 20 years of experience, Mr. Echevarria enjoys developing different business concepts and selling the technology required for the start-up of these ventures in different countries. This type of sales requires adapting to specific government regulations and market needs, which differ from country to country.

"I have never attempted to sell technology in a country unless I am fully convinced that all the parties involved will mutually gain from the relationship," he says. He stresses the acceptance of different methods and procedures, and preparation in effective communication to survive in the global marketplace.

Mr. Echevarria speaks two languages fluently and is able to conduct negotiations in five languages. He continually studies cultural environments when representing U.S. and foreign corporations on the international scene. According to Mr. Echevarria, "To be a successful salesperson in the international marketplace, one must respect and appreciate the distinctive ways in which sales practices are conducted in those countries. Salespeople cannot succeed internationally if they are destined to conduct sales following U.S. procedures and practices." He advises everyone interested in international sales to be willing to study and understand foreign cultures, and be prepared to adapt to various facets of cultural differences existing in those countries.

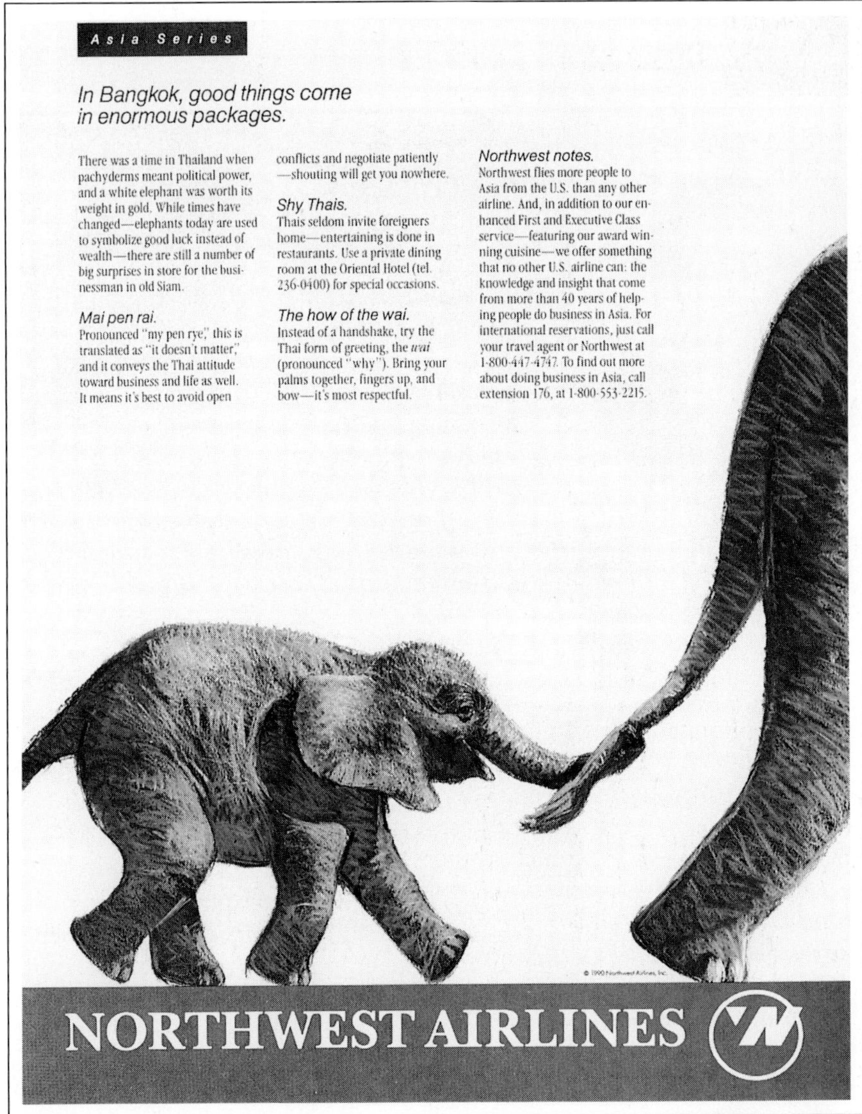

impression may innocently sit with legs crossed, exposing the sole of a shoe to the customer. This is insulting to traditionalists in the Arab world and parts of Asia. The salesperson may pass over a catalogue, price list, or contract with the left hand—the toilet hand in many countries. Perhaps with great sincerity, the salesperson might peer deeply into the eyes of a customer, unaware that this staring is considered hostile or insane in Japan. Even worse would be to touch an Asian customer on the arm or shoulder (a technique encouraged in the United States), or, equally bad, to retreat in horror when hugged and kissed by an Arab or Latin American.[17] Several additional customs relevant to selling in China are presented in Exhibit 3.6.

Customs in China

Exhibit 3.6

Some of the business customs relevant to sale transactions when doing business in China include:

- Greet by the last or surname of the person. For example, Mr. Chen Chi Ming should be addressed as Mr. Chen. Unless the person tells you to call him by some other name, never address the person by first name.
- Present business cards at the business meeting. Presentation of cards may not be reciprocated. It is good to have one side printed in English and the other side in Chinese. (Japanese salespeople expect their prospects to use both when receiving cards and to examine them attentively.)
- Chinese businesspeople invite competitive bids, and Chinese negotiators usually ask foreign firms to quote a price first.
- Do not discuss politics, and never speak lightly of political leaders.

Source: Franklin Ho and Vernon Stauble, "Tactical Practices Directing China's Trade Development," *Cal Poly Scholar*, Spring 1990.

The understanding of customs and manners is especially important in selling situations, particularly in negotiation. Negotiators from a particular culture must take into consideration negotiation etiquette related to proper social customs. Good manners might include refraining from negotiating over lunch or dinner.

Consider the reaction of a salesperson from the United States if a Finnish counterpart were to propose continuing negotiations in the sauna. Many foreign customs may seem trivial or even humorous. Nonetheless, the failure to recognize good manners in negotiation can reduce the opportunity to reach an agreement.

Agreements

The meaning of an agreement varies among cultures, making it difficult to know what is being arranged. Salespeople from the United States consider the signing of a contract to be the end of the negotiation process. In the Arab world, however, a man's word may be more binding than many written agreements, and insistence on a contract may be insulting. Even so, the Arab or other foreign businessperson might not fulfill an "agreement," because a Westerner can mistakenly hear commitment when only politeness was intended.[18]

Friendship Patterns

Dealings with the Chinese are prime examples of how business relationships can be subsumed under the notion of friendship. And how do you seal a deal that will last in Japan? The answer lies in entering into a relationship and not a contract.[19]

In the United States, a proposed contract becomes the determining factor for an interested prospect. Friendship often replaces the legal or contractual system for ensuring that business and other obligations are honored. In countries without a well-established and easily enforceable commercial code, many people insist on doing business only with friends. For example, in the Middle East, "the caliber of the executive team from the standpoint of its personal acceptability (or lack of it) to a prospective customer can be crucial in winning or losing an opportunity, hence the need for tailoring the team to the assignment."[20]

Contracts clearly do not have the same meaning in other parts of the world as they do in the United States, because interpersonal understanding and bonds are often major considerations. It is important that the professional salesperson establish a reputation as being worthy and dependable in the long run. A personal relationship and trust are developed carefully and sincerely over time. Furthermore, business is often not discussed until after several meetings, and in any one meeting business is discussed only after lengthy social conversation. The American must learn to sit on the catalogue until the relationship has been established.[21]

In sum, in many parts of the world friendships are formed slowly and carefully because they imply long-term relationships. As noted earlier, friendships replace the legal and contractual system for ensuring this relationship.

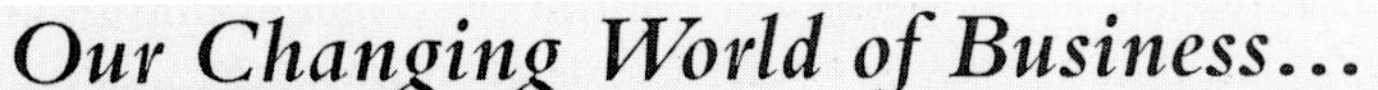

On the International Front Dealing with Foreign Cultures

Salespeople in the international arena are likely to encounter a diverse set of cultural differences when conducting sales practices in foreign countries. The following differences with reference to attitudes toward punctuality, greetings, and exchange of business cards should be kept in mind when conducting selling activities in different cultural settings.

Punctuality. In many parts of the world, time is viewed differently than in the United States. Asians, for instance, tend not to be punctual, but it is essential to arrive early in Hong Kong. Europeans generally observe strict punctuality for appointments and social occasions. Romanians, Japanese, and Germans are very punctual, while many of the Latin American countries have a more relaxed attitude toward time. Latin Americans are often late but expect Americans to be on time. The Japanese consider it rude to be late for a business meeting, but it is acceptable to be late for a social occasion. In the Middle East, long waits for appointments are typical. In Africa, lateness in starting meetings is a part of life. In Middle Eastern and African cultures, being in a hurry may be viewed with suspicion and distrust.

Greetings. Traditional greetings may be a handshake, bow, hug, kiss, or placing the hands in a praying position. The handshake is the most acceptable form of greeting in most cultures. Italians use handshakes for greetings and goodbyes. Combining the handshake with a bow is acceptable when Americans and Japanese interact. The Japanese bow symbolizes respect and humility. In the Middle East it is appropriate to use only the right hand when greeting or touching. A kiss on both cheeks when greeting symbolizes a friendly relationship in some parts of the Middle East and Europe. In Thailand, greetings are extended by placing both hands in a prayer position at the chin and bowing slightly. The higher the hands, the greater the respect.

Exchange of Business Cards. The American tradition of accepting a business card and putting it immediately in a desk drawer or pocket is considered very rude in some cultures. In Japan and Korea it is proper to accept the card with both hands and carefully admire it. This action symbolizes respect. Salespeople working in Japan should use business cards with their name and title in Japanese and also in their own language. In the Middle East, business cards are essential and should be presented on the first meeting.

Sources: M. Katherine Glover, "Do's & Taboos: Cultural Aspects of International Business," *Business America,* August 13, 1990, pp. 3–4; and Robert Moran, "How to Understand Your Partner's Cultural Baggage," *International Management,* September 1983, pp. 50–51.

Increasing Importance of Women's Roles

Adding to the complexity of going international is the increasing importance of women's roles. Women often operate under a different set of rules. Rules for women in selling situations are listed in Exhibit 3.7.

Exhibit 3.7

Five Rules for Women in International Sales

Rule 1: Know that you are crossing traditional barriers.

In many countries, this adds to the confusion the foreigner may already be feeling working with an American. Greta McKinney, a woman who sells computers and related equipment in the Middle East and Asia, says: "Remember, business abroad is always based on trust and on knowing who you are dealing with."

Rule 2: Consider asking the foreign man whether he has done business with a woman before.

The foreigner may admit he doesn't know quite how to work with a woman. You can tell him to use the same approach he would when doing business with a man. In some situations a woman can use the foreigner's discomfort and confusion to her advantage. One woman in Korea found the men there so insecure working with her that she had the upper hand; they gave her whatever she wanted.

Rule 3: Be prepared to handle sexual overtures with the same composure you would in the United States.

You must be in control. Never let the situation get out of hand. Remind your foreign colleague or customer that you are there for business, but avoid an emotional outburst or anger.

Rule 4: Have faith in yourself.

When you hear "Women can't do business in . . . ," try to find out what the obstacles, and the opportunities, really are. Andrea Shah of Digital Equipment Corporation says: "The woman who has successfully dealt with the male corporate culture in the U.S.A. probably has developed the right instincts to help her deal with the barriers of a foreign culture. She has already experienced working in a foreign environment and brings special skills to the international assignment."

Rule 5: You are a pioneer and a model.

It will be up to you to educate your organization. As Nancy Adler points out, few organizations have any history of expatriate or traveling women managers; when your colleagues have problems with you in this role, go about the task of altering perceptions and behavior patterns. Your behavior and performance will set a precedent for other women to follow you in international sales.

Source: Lennie Copeland and Lewis Griggs, *Going International* (New York: Random House, 1985), p. 224.

Subcultures

The term *subculture* is used to recognize group variations that exist within a culture. Subculture is best defined as "Any group within a society that preserves the principal characteristics of that society's culture but provides values and beliefs distinguishable as its own."[22]

The American market actually consists of several distinct subcultures, in spite of the notion that the United States is a "melting pot." The distinctions that have been used to classify subcultures include socioeconomic group (upper class, lower class); ethnic, racial, and nationality group (African Americans, Hispanics, Irish, Chinese, Native Americans); geographic area (South, Midwest); age (adolescents, the elderly); community type (rural, urban); religious organization (Jewish, Muslim); political entities (conservatives, radicals); and gender.

Furthermore, influences on preference and behavior tend to be strongest when the numbers increase geographically, as with the Mexican population in the southwestern states (California, Arizona, New Mexico, Colorado, and Texas), the Cuban population in Florida, or the Vietnamese population in southern California.

A subculture has a unique identity and provides for the maintenance of relationships with others within the same subculture. A subculture also offers a patterned network of communication, as will be discussed in the next section. Subcultures in the United States and their implications on consumer and buyer behavior will be discussed in greater depth in Chapter 8, providing insights for the professional salesperson.

Influence of Culture on Communication Processes

Culture is the foundation upon which all social interactions rest. Emphasis on culture also concerns the manner in which communication occurs and how it affects the sales situation.

There is no selling without communication, the tool of understanding and persuasion. In international sales, the power of communication is often blunted by ignorance. The risk of misunderstanding is great and time is wasted on "pitches" that are meaningless to the prospective client. Even when both sides seem to speak the same language, intercultural communications are full of pitfalls. For instance, in the United States, to "table" a subject means to postpone it indefinitely. An American trying to negotiate a contract in England might be irritated when the British persist in discussing a subject that has been tabled. In Britain, however, to "table" means to put on the agenda for present discussion. Of course, the communication problem is greatly multiplied when trying to sell to someone who is speaking a second language or using an interpreter. Even the simplest words can be confounding: In Japanese "yes" often means "no" and in China "no" often means "yes." Direct translations may produce unwanted nuances because words also have subjective meanings.[23]

Furthermore, communication can be classified as more verbal in some cultures than in others. Countries that use actual words to convey the main information when communicating are those in North America and northern Europe (such as Switzerland, Germany, and the Scandinavian countries). Those countries that are primarily nonverbal include Japan, France, Spain, Italy, Asia, Africa, and many of the Middle-Eastern Arab nations. Culturalizing nonverbal cues and behavior will be explored further in Chapter 8.

Summary

No direct relationship exists between the law and ethical behavior, and at times action is simply left to interpretation. Consequently, relying totally on the law as a guide to acting along ethical lines proves inadequate and inefficient. A basic requirement, however, is to know and respect the law, which may vary from country to country.

Ethical codes are a vital resource for salespeople. Such codes consist of beliefs and norms to follow, generally expressing a sense of obligation to customers, the company the salesperson works for, and society. Efforts must be undertaken to reduce conflict and strengthen long-term relationships.

Many decisions regarding ethical behavior become individualized when considering one's responsibility to the customer and the firm; making these decisions can often be difficult for the professional salesperson, especially in international settings. Overall, striving to maintain

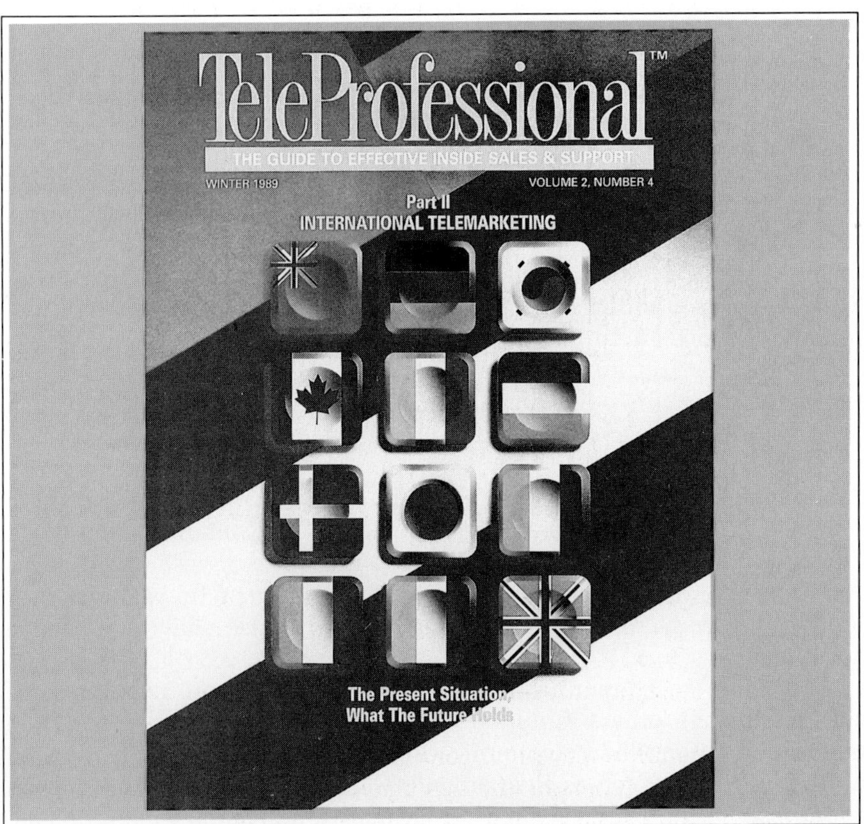

ethical standards is simply the proper thing to do in gaining long-term relationships.

Furthermore, the increase in international interactions today forces salespeople to learn to communicate within a greater variety of cultures. To effectively establish a sales relationship, the salesperson must understand the many intra- and intercultural variations that can affect the selling situation, including different perspectives on time and patience, personal space, customs and manners, agreements, and friendship patterns. To meet this challenge successfully, the professional salesperson must adapt to those differences in the sales environment.

Key Terms

Cooling-off Law Provides buyers in certain states with a specified period within which to void sales contracts; applies particularly to door-to-door and high-pressure sales

Entertainment Providing meals, shows, or other pleasurable benefits in the hope that the prospective customer will be kindly disposed to do business with the host salesperson's company

Ethics Principles of conduct governing an individual or group; a set of moral principles or values

Foreign Corrupt Practices Act Limits payment of fees for obtaining foreign contracts

Gratuity A gift that rewards and is of personal benefit to the customer; to qualify as a gratuity, the gift must not unduly influence or corrupt the buyer

Libel Unfair or untrue statements about a company or an individual communicated in writing to a third party

Misrepresentation Providing loosely interpreted or false data for the purpose of obtaining business

Reciprocity The practice of doing business with prospects to convince them to do the same in return

Slander Unfair or untrue oral statements made about another (for instance, a competitor) to a third party (such as a customer) that damage the business or personal reputation of that company or a person within that company

Uniform Commercial Code (UCC) Governs such aspects of selling as the need for written contracts, warranties, delivery agreements, and commissions

1. Provide a definition of ethics and explain what a code of ethics might include.
2. The text identifies 5 areas of conflict involving ethics that may arise between the salesperson and customer. Compare and contrast these five areas, indicating the ethical issue basic to each area.

3. What ethical responsibilities exist for salespersons with regard to relationships with their companies?
4. What is business slander? In what ways can sales language create legal difficulties?
5. What is the Uniform Commercial Code? How does it affect the buyer-seller relationship?
6. What is culture? What are the key characteristics about which a salesperson should be knowledgeable? Why?
7. In what ways are cultures and subcultures different? The same?

Questions for Discussion

1. Discuss the question, "What factors should be taken into consideration when a salesperson faces an ethical decision?"
2. The chapter suggests that sales professionals' responsibilities fall into three categories: responsibilities to oneself, to the prospect or customers, and to the company represented. Discuss what ethical obligations exist in each category and what differences and similarities exist across categories.
3. Compare and contrast ethical with legal standards.
4. Discuss the ethical implications of "cooling-off laws."
5. Discuss the Foreign Corrupt Practices Act as it relates to the assertion, "What is unethical in one culture is not necessarily so in another."
6. Discuss how a salesperson in the international market can best meet the challenge of acquiring knowledge from different cultural perspectives.
7. Discuss how salespersons might best respond when they inadvertently violate a social custom of an international customer.
8. Discuss how culture influences the communication process.

Preparing for the Bid

Case 3.1

A manufacturer of industrial equipment was seeking a large order of raw materials, inviting bids from about ten major suppliers in a very competitive arena. Glenco, Inc., was determined to win this contract because it has been underbid on several previous contracts. "This time we are going to go about this the right way," said the sales manager.

Before submitting the bid, the sales manager of Glenco sent one of the company's top salespeople, Bill Bauer, to contact the purchasing agent and obtain as much information as he could to help prepare the bid. Bill had learned how vital the lowest bid was in winning the contract.

During the discussion with the purchasing agent pertaining to the manufacturer's particular needs, Bill began probing for insights about the other bids to gain a competitive advantage. Although the purchasing agent was reluctant to discuss information on other bids, he did indicate that all the bids were in, pointing to a stack of files on his desk.

Shortly thereafter, the purchasing agent asked to be excused for 5 minutes while he ran a quick errand down the hallway. He requested that Bill wait for him in the office. As the purchasing agent departed, Bill quickly removed the list of competitive bids, looked at all of them, and noted the lowest one.

Upon submitting the bid several days later, Bill Bauer was successful in gaining the contract with the industrial equipment manufacturer, placing a bid that was $200 below the lowest bid.

1. Is it possible that the purchasing agent intended for Bill to see the competitive bids? And, if so, was Bill right in the way he handled this situation?
2. Was the manner in which Bill Bauer acquired this information considered unethical?
3. What might have been a more desirable approach for Bill to have taken?

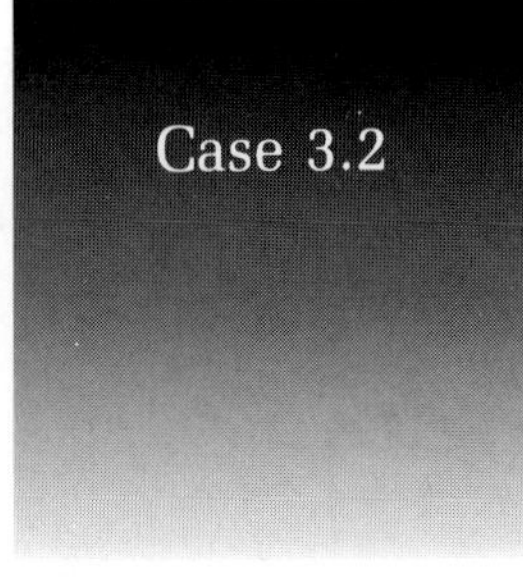

Caught between Disclosure and the Law

Jack Kerns is a real estate salesperson representing a southern manufacturer that desperately needs to sell a piece of coastal property. If the property sells, the manufacturer will gain the funds needed to save it from bankruptcy, which would put 200 people out of work.

Jack recently learned that severe flooding has occurred on the property in the past and, to the best of his knowledge, the property is probably useless. Jack continues to promote the property with much vigor because the law of that state does not require that problems be disclosed to potential buyers.

Jack's philosophy is that the law is his guide, and he supports the sale to a small southern developer with limited resources who is financially unable to conduct a thorough investigation of the property. Consequently, this buyer will probably suffer tremendous financial losses in the future.

Jack faces several concerns: It may be simply unethical to conceal the full truth about the land for sale, yet if he tells the prospect the truth Jack could lose the sale and commission. When the buyer realizes the problems with the property after the sale is consummated, however, Jack's reputation will be in danger. Another concern is the substantial reduction in commission should a discounted price be offered due to the potential risks.

The owners of the land are pressuring Jack to stand firm on the original asking price and not to admit to any occurrences of flooding. Their plea is that a considerable sum of money is needed to save the jobs of 200 employees. As Jack sees it, the dilemma lies with the sellers. He also believes that the law is on his side and consideration for disclosure is not required or deemed necessary.

1. What are the long-run implications of going ahead with the sellers' demands?
2. What might be a more desirable approach for Jack to take?
3. Would Jack be behaving ethically should he support the purchase of such property?

Notes

1. S. M. Sack, "Legal Puffery: Truth or Consequence," *Sales & Marketing Management*, November 1985, pp. 59–60.
2. *Webster's New World Dictionary*, 3rd college ed., (New York: Simon & Schuster, 1988), p. 466.
3. Mark S. Frankel, *Professional Codes: Why, How, and with What Impact?* (Washington, D.C.: Kluwer Academic Publishers, 1989), pp. 109–115.
4. W. D. Roundtree, *Ethical Aspects of Personal Selling* (Boone, NC: Appalachian State University, 1976), p. 2.
5. "Robert Buckner Had a Painful Choice to Make after Learning Sam P. Wallace Co. Paid a Bribe," *The Wall Street Journal*, May 1983, p. 52, in Gene R. Lacznick and Patrick W. Murphy, *Marketing Ethics* (, MA: Lexington Books, 1987), p. 91.
6. Frederick Travich, John Swan, and David Rink, "Industrial Buyer Evaluation of the Ethics of Salesperson's Gift-Giving, Value of the Gift and Customer vs Prospect Status," *Journal of Personal Selling and Sales Management* (V.1. IX, Summer 1989): 31–37.
7. Jeffrey P. Davidson, "Integrity: The Primary Sales Tool," *Personal Selling Power*, November/December 1986, p. 22.
8. W. Creighton, "Roundup," *The Haftford Courant*, October 16, 1985, p. C-1.
9. Leonard Silk, *Does Morality Have a Place in the Boardroom?* (Chicago: Western Publishing Co., 1989), pp. 11–13.
10. R. B. Marks, *Personal Selling: An Interactive Approach* (Needham Heights, MA: Allyn & Bacon, 1991), p. 578.
11. Sack, "Legal Puffery: Truth or Consequence," pp. 59–60.
12. Ibid.
13. G. Manning and B. L. Reece, *Selling Today: A Personal Approach*, 4th ed. (Needham Heights, MA: Allyn & Bacon, 1990), p. 506.
14. Kathleen K. Reardon, "It's the Thought That Counts," *Harvard Business Review*, September/October 1984, pp. 136–141.
15. Sak Onkvisit and John J. Shaw, *International Marketing* (Columbus, OH: Merrill Publishers, 1989), p. 232.
16. Ibid., p. 233.
17. L. Copeland, "Sales Customs," *Business America*, June 1984, p. 6.
18. Ibid., p. 8.
19. David L. Jones, "The Art of the Deal," *Business Month*, November 1989, p. 93.
20. M. E. Metcalfe, "Islam, Social Attitudes," in Del I. Hawkins, Rodger J. Best, and Kenneth A. Coney, *Consumer Behavior* (Homewood, IL: Irwin Publishers, 1989), p. 64.
21. L. Copeland, "Foreign Markets: Not for the Amateur," *Business Marketing*, July 1984, p. 116; see also D. Ford, "Buyer/Seller Relationships in International Industrial Markets," *Industrial Marketing Management*, 2nd quarter, 1984, pp. 101–112; and J. L. Graham, "Cross-Cultural Marketing Negotiations," *Marketing Science*, Spring 1985, pp. 130–145.
22. C. Glenn Walters and Blaise J. Bergiel, *Consumer Behavior* (Cincinnati: South-Western Publishing, 1989), p. 253.
23. L. Copeland, "Cross-Cultural Contact," *Business America*, June 1984, p. 4.

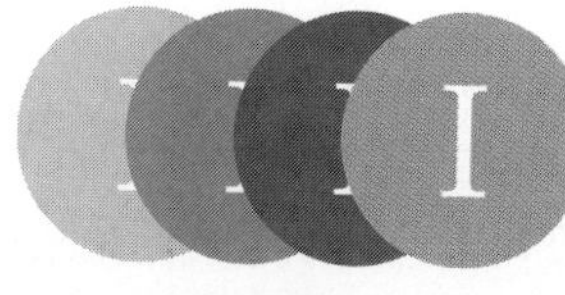

In a September 1988 article in *Sales & Marketing Management*, senior editor Arthur Bragg summarizes a study in which top executives and consultants were asked whether salespeople are successful because of inborn characteristics or because of training.[1] While the persons in the interview did not agree on the way the characteristics might be acquired, there was consensus that important benchmarks of success for the salesperson include such characteristics as stability, self-sufficiency, self-confidence, goal directedness, decisiveness, self-motivation, intellectual curiosity, and accuracy.

These characteristics are developed and nurtured to a great extent by the sales image that the salesperson carries into the work environment. A *sales image* includes the salesperson's perceptions of self in the selling role. This chapter focuses on the importance of developing and communicating a positive sales image.

The relationship process begins with the salesperson. To develop and maintain a healthy interpersonal relationship with customers, salespeople must know themselves and have relatively high self-esteem. How they think and feel about themselves and how they perceive their world are all areas involved in constructing a positive sales image. Salespeople can use communication skills to build and maintain a positive self-image.

This chapter is divided into four sections that examine the sales image. The first section focuses on methods of increasing self-awareness

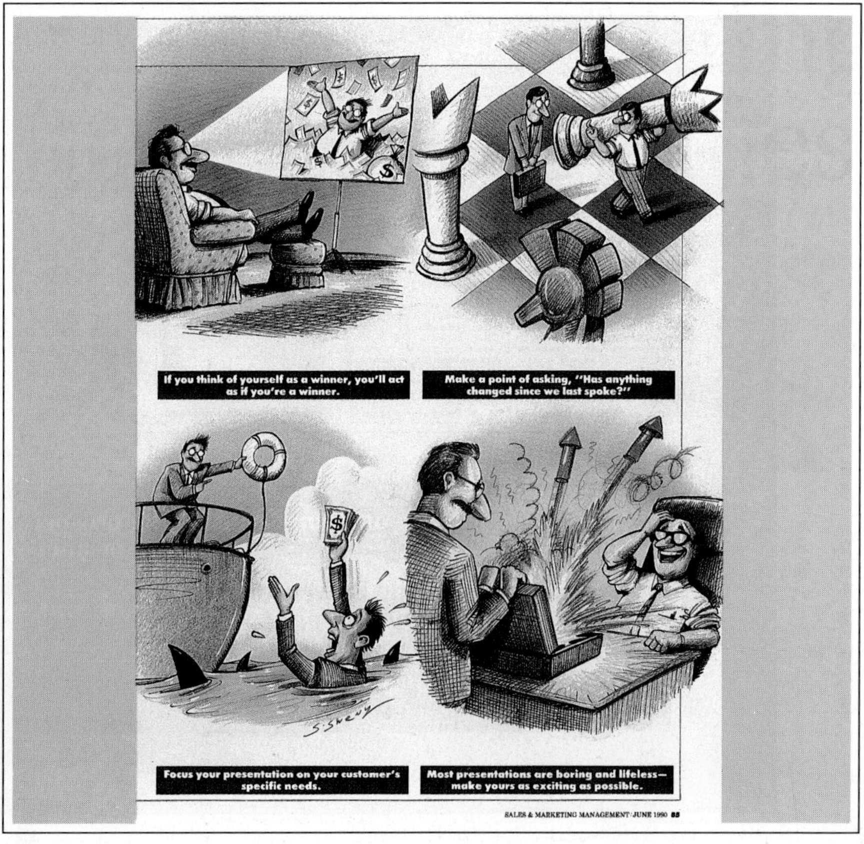

Sales Professional Spotlight

Suzanne Labat serves as a role model for many associates in retail sales, having held executive positions with top specialty retailers in the nation, such as Neiman Marcus and Saks Fifth Avenue. She has been recognized as one of the most successful and respected sales representatives and managers in the fashion industry.

Suzanne has a business degree from the University of Texas with an emphasis in marketing. During college, she worked as a salesperson for two clothing boutiques and achieved top sales in both stores. "I have always had an idea of the career I wanted to pursue. At a very young age I became interested in fashion, and I have always enjoyed being around people and helping them make buying decisions. Retail has allowed me the best of both worlds." Despite being told that the retail sales business wasn't for her, she never lost faith in herself and her passion for the fashion industry.

The retail industry is constantly changing. Changes occur in trends and styles, designers, management, and customers' wants and needs. Suzanne recognizes the importance of keeping current in staying ahead of the competition. However, she stresses, "Your integrity and your positive sales image must never change. Be true to yourself and your customer. You must believe in yourself and know what you stand for. You will lose respect if you compromise yourself."

It is important to be consistent when dealing with a customer, offering the same enthusiastic service every time. Enthusiasm is contagious. An enthusiastic salesperson transfers the same enthusiasm to other sales associates, to management, and, most importantly, to the customer. Furthermore, it is imperative that a salesperson perform "self-awareness" techniques on a regular basis. In other words, examine the roots of your unhappiness. Whether the problem is personal or professional, seek direction from within, and don't allow yesterday's problem to have a negative effect on today's performance.

When managers hire a salesperson, they must make sure the applicant has three traits: a positive attitude, flexibility, and trustworthiness. All of these traits can be acquired when individuals recognize what they stand for and continually work to improve themselves. To acquire a positive self-image, salespeople must take pride in what they do and in the company they represent. "I have always had great pride in the fact that Saks Fifth Avenue and Neiman Marcus stand for the best in fashion. They are leaders in fashion with a reputation of high quality and excellent service," Suzanne says.

Success in selling and a positive self-image go hand in hand. Experience reveals that individuals with a good self-image tend to be more successful in sales positions. "Don't be intimidated by an aggressive salesperson or a demanding customer. In general, assertive salespeople are goal oriented, but not at the expense of customer satisfaction. Therefore, always strive toward being assertive, by listening to the prospect's needs and trying your very best to fulfill them. Let down your guard sometimes and don't pretend to know everything. Customers will in turn let their guard down, and shift from the defensive response of 'I am just looking' to 'I am looking for . . . ,'" she says.

Managers must further establish clear and consistent standards and expectations, and must recognize and praise good performance. Salespeople should be encouraged to communicate their needs to management, and everyone in the company should work together to create a positive working environment and shopping atmosphere.

and self-acceptance to develop a realistic and positive sales image. Because human beings are always feeling, thinking, and acting, the second section of this chapter deals with understanding and expressing feelings appropriately within the context of the salesperson's role. And because thoughts are closely linked to feelings, the next section focuses on replacing irrational with more rational thinking to nurture emotions conducive to sales effectiveness. The final section deals with setting goals for self-improvement in professional selling. It includes methods of identifying specific new behaviors that can be practiced to increase sales effectiveness by developing a more positive sales image.

Developing a Realistic and Positive Sales Image

A sales image, or self-perception related to the role of salesperson, is part of a total *self-concept* that includes all the self-perceptions a person has. A self-concept includes likes, dislikes, talents, values, attitudes, beliefs, and emotions. It also embraces thoughts about physical features and how these features affect and are affected by the various roles a person takes during daily life. Aspects of self-concept vary in their importance to the different roles a person takes daily, such as student, parent, spouse, lover, and salesperson.

As you read this section, concentrate on the perceptions of self that might affect the role of salesperson. While we recognize that a salesperson's self-concept is multidimensional, we will focus on only the part of self-concept that emphasizes a person's role in professional selling. We will use the term "sales image" to focus on this single component. Achieving and maintaining a positive sales image is the core of interpersonal effectiveness in the sales relationship process.

While one's sales image is relatively consistent on a day-to-day basis, perceptions of self tend to change over longer periods. The self-image a person has can become outdated if the person does not consciously update the sales image as these changes occur. This sales image may change considerably between the time one starts to use the learning materials presented in this text and the time this course or training program is completed. An important way of keeping the self-image current is to talk about one's self-perceptions with another person. The words the salesperson selects to talk about personal characteristics and to describe self-behavior help to sharpen the individual's perceptions. In addition, the feedback received from others may affect this sales image.

Characteristics of a Sales Image

As is characteristic of the total self-concept, a person's sales image is characterized by subjectivity and resistance to change. A healthy sales image must be flexible to break through the resistance.

1. *One's sales image is subjective*—No matter how hard salespeople try to be objective, their descriptions of themselves will tend to be subjective. For example, the way they see themselves may not match observable facts because they will view themselves as they would like to be rather than as they actually feel, think, and act. If they have changed recently, their perceptions of themselves may be outdated. They may also have an image of themselves that is based on how other salespeople, their sales managers, or their customers perceive them. Those perceptions may not be consistent with their own. Another source of a subjective sales image may stem from their continual efforts to improve. As a result, they may view themselves presently as positive, simply because they are eager to replace current emotions, thoughts, and behaviors with those they would consider an improvement.
2. *One's sales image resists change*—Even though sales professionals may readily accept the notion that realistic sales images change over time, they probably will resist revising their sales images. Salespeople might resist revising a favorable sales image, for example, by clinging to the memory of an especially effective long-term relationship with a customer that has resulted in large profits for their companies. Even though recent customer relations and levels of productivity are not consistent with the special success to which salespeople cling, they might insist that they are still successful even though their recent records do not support this perception.

   Even if a new sales image might be more favorable than the old one, there is still a tendency to resist change. There are dramatic cases of salespeople who, because of personal characteristics in their youth or in other roles in their lives, have outmoded sales images. The sales trainee may recall an acute case of adolescent acne so vividly that a shy, reserved image is projected, based on the notion that others will not want to talk with a person whose face is blemished. In fact, only the memory of that physical condition remains; the trainee's complexion is clear. Similarly, the salesperson who is recently divorced and views the marriage as a personal failure may permit these views to carry over into the role as salesperson. Preoccupation with being divorced (or another "personal failure") may cause a salesperson to disregard actual signs of success in the selling role.[2]

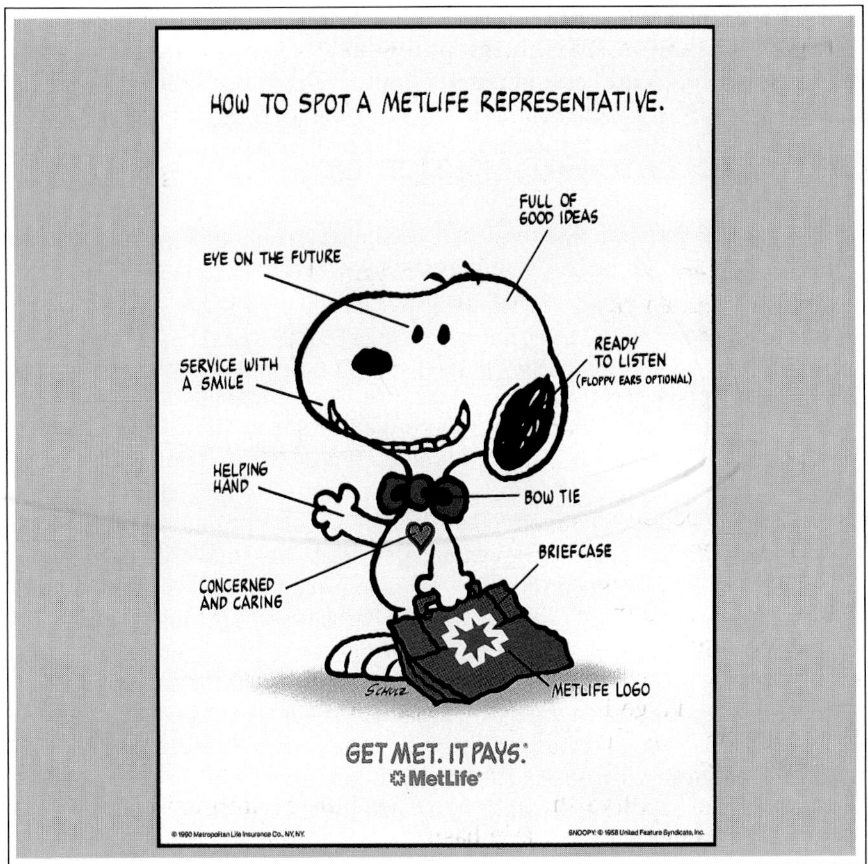

3. *One's sales image will be flexible if it is healthy*—While a salesperson's sales image remains relatively constant over short periods, it will change in important ways as one becomes more skilled and experienced as a salesperson. One's sales image also changes somewhat when interacting with different customers in different situations. The ability to adjust one's sales image to different contexts facilitates appropriate communication.

Four Components of a Sales Image

A sales image includes four important components, or processes, that are continually operating as an integrated system. Understanding each of these components contributes to increased sales effectiveness and personal satisfaction. These components are self-awareness, self-acceptance, self-actualization, and self-disclosure.

Self-awareness

Georgia Noble, executive director of Self-Esteem Seminars in Culver City, California, explains self-awareness in this manner:

> After substantial research, we know losers mentally rehearse their past defeats, while winners review past victories. Just before the crucial sales call, the successful salesperson mentally reviews why she will get the contract, while the losers busy themselves with inventories of why their product or service isn't right for the customer. This thought process is silent, but it is nonetheless pervasive and powerful.[3]

Self-awareness is the process of bringing to a conscious level all of the information about the self that is associated with one's sales image. The information must be at a conscious level for a salesperson to periodically update the sales image and bring self-perceptions in line with actual behavior.

Self-acceptance

A second component of sales image, self-acceptance, involves the degree to which a person likes and is satisfied with the self in the role of salesperson. For example, a salesperson could assign all of the perceptions included in a sales image into two categories: those perceptions that are satisfactory and need to be reinforced and those that could be changed or improved. Self-acceptance involves both categories of descriptions, knowing that change is a dynamic part of a successful sales career.

A simple tool that helps Carol Price, a trainer with CareerTrack Seminars in Florida, achieve and maintain self-acceptance is repeating affirmations or positive thoughts. Her version of affirmations is saying these four statements on a daily basis:

- I am competent.
- I am creative.
- I deserve respect.
- I own this day.[4]

Self-actualization

Self-actualization is the process of selecting specific aspects of one's sales image that one wants to change and then setting personal goals and devising a plan for accomplishing them. The exercises in this chapter are designed to help the salesperson set goals and make plans for changing behavior. For instance, Sheila Porter, a representative for Revlon, may want to increase her use of rapport-building skills when she first meets a customer. She can use the skill builders in Chapters 8 and 9 to change her behavior. When she is satisfied with the changes, she will probably be more self-accepting, resulting in a more positive sales image.

Self-disclosure

The fourth component of one's sales image is self-disclosure, which involves verbally communicating information about self to another person.

By talking about one's sales image to a classmate, friend, or fellow salesperson, a person usually increases self-awareness. Receiving feedback from people who are respected usually results in a more positive sales image. Many sales organizations offer mentor programs to formally provide constructive relationships that promote appropriate self-disclosure related to the work setting, and thus promote improved sales performance.

Acceptance by others usually increases a person's self-acceptance and results in personal motivation to engage in further self-actualization. Setting new goals for personal improvement often results. When these goals are addressed, more positive feelings about one's sales image usually develop, along with increased enthusiasm for self-disclosure and a willingness to be vulnerable. The four components of a sales image are interrelated in these ways and can be managed to increase both professional effectiveness and personal satisfaction.

One way to understand self-disclosure is by using the Johari window to examine the openness of specific sales relationships.The four-quadrant window shown in Figure 4.1 provides a grid that can be used to chart the dynamics of any conversation between two people:

1. The "Open" square contains information that both the salesperson and the customer know about each other. Such observable information may include names, titles, and settings of conversations or sales interviews. This quadrant grows as the relationship develops.
2. The "Blind" area contains information that one person is unaware of but that the other person knows. This information may include undisclosed attitudes, beliefs, values, plans, and needs.

Figure 4.1

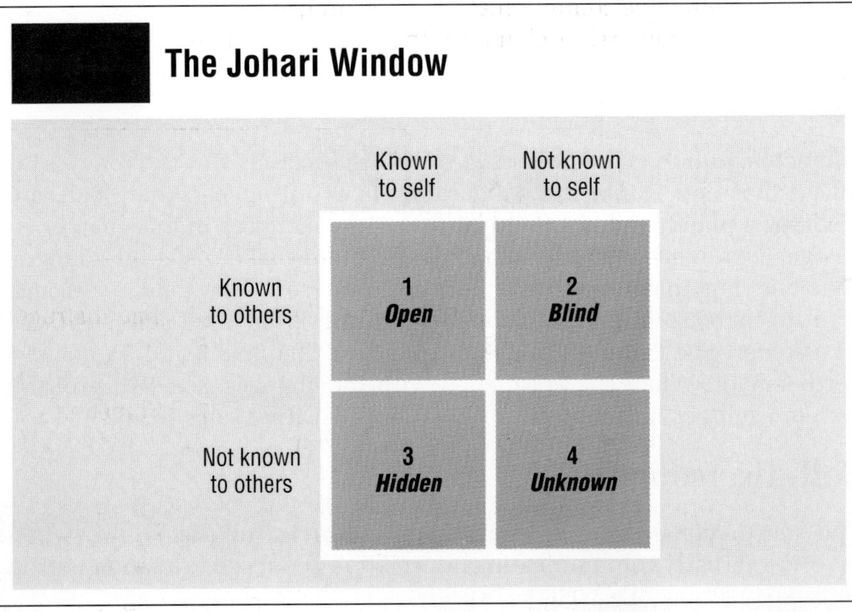

3. The "Hidden" square contains information that one person knows but is not willing to disclose to the other, such as hidden agendas and observations about the buyer's situation.
4. The "Unknown" area represents information that is unknown to both persons and all others who may be involved (for example, the outcome of a meeting).

The relative sizes of the quadrants in a salesperson's Johari window change for each situation. Factors that influence these changes include the participants' moods, the subjects they are discussing, and their overall relationship with each other. By visualizing the quadrants changing constantly in proportion to the amount of information disclosed or shared, salespeople are able to judge the strength of their position in the selling situation. This, in turn, helps them to select the appropriate selling strategies.

It is important to emphasize that it is virtually impossible to engage in interpersonal communication of any depth if the salesperson and the customer have little open area. In other words, the relationship is limited by the individual who is less open. Therefore, it is important that salespeople continually strive to maintain a positive self-image so that their willingness to risk, trust, and be vulnerable creates a climate for openness and intimacy in which the relationship can grow. *Try This* Exercise 4.1 provides an opportunity for you to practice using the Johari window in analyzing your self-disclosure patterns.

Emotions and Sales Image

Having a positive affective orientation or feeling about one's roles in life is one of the three elements that appear to have the greatest impact on developing effective communication, according to Virginia Richmond and James McCroskey, researchers in the area of communication apprehension.[5]

Try This 4.1

Plot a Johari window for the following people with whom you interact. Be as specific as you can:

1. Your roommate or officemate (if you have one)
2. Your favorite customer or co-worker
3. Your least favorite customer or co-worker
4. Your best friend
5. The instructor of this course
6. A customer or person you recently met for the first time
7. Someone whom you know but who does not know you

It is important to note that the sizes of the various quadrants of the window depend on the amount of self-disclosure that has occurred between you.

San Francisco State University marketing professor Rich Nelson believes that some salespeople have the gift of self-motivation. He also warns, however, "Salespeople need to realize that selling means failing time after time, being constantly rejected." He notes that "selling is one of the few professions where a successful individual also may fail eight out of ten times."[6]

Fran Tarkenton, whose track record in business is as successful as it was in his football career, shares this story on dealing with rejection:

> One of the biggest challenges I faced playing college football was in my sophomore year at the University of Georgia in Athens. I was a third-string quarterback. Ahead of me were two excellent quarterbacks, both of them magnificent players. I knew that the coaches were going to hold me out, but I was determined not to sit out. I wanted to be in the game. I did not want to spend the season on the sidelines. I did well in training camp, but the word was that I had no chance of getting into the arena. Our first game was held in Austin, Texas, against the University of Texas. Before we left, I remember riding around in Athens after practice, steaming at how they really could not do this to me. We went to Austin and during the first half, we didn't make a first down. We got midway through the third quarter and we still hadn't made a first down. Texas punted to us and we got the ball on the five-yard line. During the entire game I had gone up to our coach, Wally Butts, tugging at his shirt, pleading, "Put me in, put me in, put me in." But Wally didn't pay attention to my begging. When they punted to us on the five-yard line, I ran on the field. Nobody told me to go in. I got halfway on the field and nobody called me out and nobody came to get me. The quarterback saw me run on the field and thought that somebody sent me in, so he just left. Suddenly I found myself in the huddle on the five-yard line against the University of Texas and I took our team on a drive of 95 yards and we scored. True story. I've never told this story before in any interview, but I've never forgotten the lesson: If you've got a deep, burning desire inside, you'll make your own opportunity. You just go ahead and run with it.[7]

Salespeople can use the four components of their sales image in ways that promote a positive sales image. They can also surround themselves with people whose feedback and skills they respect. However, for salespeople to manage rejection and failure so that they continue to be motivated and feel positive about themselves requires knowledge about human emotions and skills for expressing them. As a result, they will achieve a more positive affective orientation toward their sales communication and their role as sales professionals.

The Four Components of Emotion

Just as logs provide the fuel for a wood-burning stove, a salesperson's emotions are a personal energy source. Experiencing an emotion also involves thinking and acting, as vividly described by Fran Tarkenton in the preceding story.

Social scientists tend to agree that emotion consists of physiological changes, nonverbal manifestations, cognitive interpretations, and verbal expression. What are these components, and how do they relate to a positive sales image?

Physiological Changes

When a salesperson experiences emotion, changes occur in internal bodily functions such as temperature, breathing, blood circulation, and muscle tension. These functions are ongoing. For example, a person's temperature can increase or decrease. One's rate of breathing and heartbeat or pulse can become faster or slower. One's muscle condition will vary from tense to relaxed. When changes occur toward the extreme ends of the high-low, fast-slow, and tense-relaxed ranges, then a person is likely to become aware of them.

An awareness of these internal changes is useful. For example, Abbott Abrasives manufacturing representative Carlos Hernandez may notice that his stomach and neck muscles tense up, his breathing rate increases, and he feels flushed when making cold calls, but not when he makes appointments in advance with customers. He has learned from these physiological changes that he prefers to schedule sales interviews.

Nonverbal Manifestations

If several logs are put on a fire in a wood-burning stove and the door is closed, the fire will probably roar and the heat will be felt in the room. The new logs inside the stove create an observable reaction outside the stove. Similarly, when physiological changes occur inside a person's body, these changes are often manifested in nonverbal behaviors. A rising temperature may be observable in redness of the neck and face. Tense neck muscles may result in a change in tone of voice.

Because the nonverbal manifestations are external, other people may notice them. As shown in Chapter 8, observing nonverbal behavior is an important way to identify how another person may be feeling. Facial expressions, gestures, posture, and the distance placed between one person and another may be evidence of the emotions one is experiencing.

Cognitive Interpretations

The human body contains a limited number of systems and functions. Therefore, the types of possible physiological changes in these functions are also limited. If Carlos Hernandez experiences extensive physiological changes when making cold calls (such as tense neck muscles or sighing), he may label them as "fear." Another salesperson may experience similar physiological changes but call them "excitement," depending on the context and the salesperson's attitude toward the changes.

The labels we attach to physiological changes and their nonverbal manifestations are referred to as cognitive interpretations. They involve what one thinks about what is happening to oneself and are an integral part of emotions. As is discussed in the third section of this chapter, one's thought processes are the keystone to managing one's emotions in ways that will nurture a positive sales image.

Verbal Expression

A person's ability to put emotions into words is verbal expression, the final component of emotion. When salespeople express their emotions to other people, they do so by using a feeling statement, which is an essential part of effective communication. Notice the differences between these statements:

- "I thought I'd stop by to see how the new X802 is working for you." (not a feeling statement)
- "I thought I'd stop by to see how the new X802 is working for you, and I'm pleased you have time to talk with me. I'm excited to hear how things are going." (feeling statement)
- "I thought I'd stop by to see how the new X802 is working for you, and I'm pleased you have time to talk with me. I'm a little embarrassed because I didn't call first." (feeling statement)
- "I thought I'd stop by to see how the new X802 is working for you, and I'm pleased you have time to talk with me. I feel a little disappointed because I haven't heard from you since we installed it." (feeling statement)

Notice how the addition of a feeling statement, as well as each different feeling statement, significantly alters the message. Refer to *Try This* Exercise 4.2 for additional practice.

Try This 4.2

Using the four components of an emotion (physiological changes, verbal manifestations, cognitive interpretations, and verbal expression), describe how you were thinking and feeling in each of these situations:

1. When you were preparing to make a videotaped sales presentation in this class, and you were scheduled for the following morning
2. When you walked up to the front of the room with the class watching, the instructor standing behind the camera, and your "buyer" waiting to be approached by you
3. When you first introduced yourself to your prospect and you realized that you had forgotten both your business cards and the combination lock on your attaché case
4. When you were pulling into your prospect's (or campus) parking lot and you realized that your month's quota (or course grade) depended on your performance in this interview

Managing Emotions

The energy kindled by one's emotions usually does not begin to dissipate until they are expressed. In addition to clarifying one's communications and adding to the genuineness of one's relationships with customers and co-workers, expressing one's emotions can also contribute to one's physical and mental health. Emotions that are suppressed may intensify and last longer than they would if expressed. Emotions that are extreme in intensity and duration are referred to as *debilitative emotions* because they may inhibit salespeople from functioning as effectively as they would like to.

Any emotion may be debilitative. For example, Rachael Ostrom, a manufacturer's representative for Dynamic Tool and Dye, may feel ecstatic as a result of a large order from an important customer. She may still have difficulty concentrating on other sales calls and the needs of other customers 2 or 3 days after the agreement. Her excitement over the large order may be debilitative; it keeps her from functioning in productive ways.

In contrast, she may feel angry that a longstanding customer has placed a substantial order with a competitor without contacting her first. She may avoid calling the customer, and when she tries to turn her attention to other accounts, her anger may intervene; thus, she avoids work entirely. This intense anger that lasts a relatively long time is as debilitative as the excitement experienced in the first example.

It is inaccurate to categorically classify an emotion as positive or negative, debilitative or facilitative. Any emotion can last long enough and be intense enough that one does not function effectively when under its influence. Similarly, any emotion can be a *facilitative emotion* by contributing to one's effective performance. Whether an emotion is facilitative or debilitative must be interpreted in each context.

Therapeutic hypnotist and motivational author Matt Oeschsli uses this "purging technique" to convert a debilitative emotion into a facilitative feeling:

1. *Identify the thought:* If you find yourself hesitating before making that cold call, name the specific fear. Failure? Rejection? Incompetence?
2. *Interrupt it:* Now visualize a candle flame. Take a deep breath. That triggers a physiological relaxation response. It's impossible to think two thoughts at once, so as you visualize, you'll find your fear receding.
3. *Eject it:* Now, as you exhale, imagine that you're breathing out the negative thought. Watch the candle flame flicker and blow out.
4. *Replace it:* Repeat an appropriate affirmation, such as, "I am a cold-calling machine!"[8]

When salespeople recognize that their emotions are interfering with the way they want to function, then they can make choices that will help them use their emotions productively. To do so, they must first understand the role their thinking plays in managing emotions.

The Role of Thinking in Shaping Emotions

To manage their emotions effectively, salespeople need to reduce the debilitative elements while enhancing the facilitative aspects of their emotions. Psychologists Albert Ellis and Robert Harper have developed a rational-emotive approach based on the principle that one can change one's feelings by revising unproductive thinking.[9]

People often assume that other people or events cause their feelings. "It [or they, you, he, she] makes me feel . . . " is a typical way to begin a feeling statement. A salesperson may say, "Cold calls make me feel anxious" or "Cold calls make me excited." The activating event (cold calls) is connected to the emotion (anxiety or excitement), which is the consequence of the activating event. A causal relationship leads to this type of thinking, and the salesperson seemingly has little control over the resulting feelings.

Ellis and Harper argue, however, that it is not the *event* (cold calls) but the way the salesperson *thinks* about the event that results in the type of emotion that is experienced. They point out that one salesperson feels anxious while another in the same circumstance experiences excitement, supporting the theory that their thinking about the event causes the resulting emotion.[10] For example:

Activating Event	Thinking	Emotion (Consequence)
Cold call	"I'm not as prepared as I should be."	Anxiety
Cold call	"Being spontaneous is a challenge."	Excitement

If this theory is correct, salespeople can manage their emotions by monitoring their thinking, or self-talk, and thereby regain control over how they feel.

Rational and Irrational Thinking

We think in at least two significant ways: rationally and irrationally. *Rational thinking* results in logical conclusions and promotes facilitative emotions. In contrast, *irrational thinking* leads to illogical conclusions and nurtures debilitative emotions. Understanding seven common types of irrational thinking, or myths, will help salespeople to manage their emotions.

The Myth of Perfection

Salespeople who subscribe to this myth believe that the competent salesperson must manage every situation with skill and confidence. It is unrealistic and illogical to assume that any single salesperson has all the answers to every customer's needs in every sales interview. In fact, the salesperson who is able to create a façade of perfection often intimidates customers.

While customers value competence, perfection is usually viewed with awe and can become a distancing factor because most people feel uneasy around those who seem never to make a mistake. In addition, if salespeople set up perfection as the standard for measuring their self-acceptance, they will usually fall short of their goal. The results will be reduced self-acceptance and increased pressure on themselves to measure up to unobtainable expectations.

The alternative to the myth of perfection is to readily admit mistakes and continually set goals for self-improvement. Customers and associates will be more willing to identify with salespeople if they do so.

The Myth of Approval

This form of irrational thinking involves the notion that it is essential, not merely desirable, to be liked by one's fellow workers and customers. When approval becomes essential, then salespeople begin to compromise their needs and ideals to obtain respect. For example, a salesperson in such a situation may cut corners on company policy or procedures to meet a customer's needs for products or services. In so doing, the salesperson's behavior may verge on dishonesty. Or a salesperson may reduce the cost of products and services to a customer so drastically that the sales commission is almost nonexistent. The result may be lowered self-respect. While it is important to earn the respect of one's associates, it is also important not to sacrifice one's own needs and principles in the process.

The Myth of Shoulds

Salespeople's inability to separate reality from ideals, or what should be, is a source of stress and dissatisfaction. They may wish that their companies had more efficient methods of keeping them current on available inventory or that their high-volume customers made decisions more quickly. The fact is, the world in which they work is no more perfect than they are as individuals living in it. Salespeople who always want the sales environment to be something other than what it is may be perceived as chronic complainers. Furthermore, this preoccupation with being critical may prevent them from creating solutions to unsatisfactory conditions over which they actually have some control. As a result, others may perceive them as part of the problem and respond defensively toward them.

The Myth of Overgeneralization

This form of irrational thinking occurs when salespeople base their reasoning on a limited amount of information or when they draw exaggerated conclusions. For example, observe the following series of statements:

- "I don't know how to explain the drive ratio on the new LX100." (fact)
- "I'm so stupid!" (overgeneralization based on limited information)
- "I'm never going to be a successful salesman!" (overgeneralization in the form of exaggerated conclusion)

Such overgeneralizations often cause a salesperson to be self-critical in front of others, who then feel awkward. In addition, the salesperson may feel frustrated with the self-image and may actually begin to believe the overgeneralizations.

The example might be revised into a more accurate and logical series of statements as follows:

- "I don't know how to explain the drive ratio on the new LX100." (fact)
- "I feel embarrased and overwhelmed by the amount of new data I need to accurately inform customers. Being successful is an unending challenge!" (more realistic, logical conclusion)

This revised statement may result in empathy from associates, and the salesperson may then feel challenged rather than frustrated. Mild embarassment may still be present, but not the self-image of being stupid.

The Myth of Causation

When salespeople subscribe to this myth, they believe that they cause other people's emotions. As a result, they may not express their honest thoughts and emotions directly, fearing that their associates will feel hurt or angry. As we discussed earlier regarding the components of an emotion, individuals respond differently to activating events, and their reactions are determined by their own perceptions. One is not in control of other people.

The myth of causation is a source of miscommunication in sales interviews. When people withhold thoughts and emotions, their needs often go unmet because other people must guess about them. When their needs go unmet, feelings of frustration often build to the debilitative level; they may become resentful or hostile or begin to feel sorry for themselves. As a result, they may use defense-arousing behaviors. If their associates learn that these people tend to withhold their perceptions and let their frustrations build into aggressive behavior, the associates may be rightfully suspicious of their statements. Trust breaks down, and others are less willing to risk being honest with them at this point.

The Myth of Helplessness

This fallacy in thinking results when salespeople believe that their satisfaction is determined by forces beyond their control. Consequently, they may view themselves as victims. For example, the following statements may be an indication of this type of irrational thinking:

- "Selling is a man's profession. I might as well resign myself to the fact that, as a woman, I can't make it in sales."
- "I can't object to having my territory increased because my supervisor will fire me. I'm not able to give effective service to my present customers, but I'll just have to live with the increase."
- "My sales manager told me to be more outgoing. I'm just not an extrovert and there's nothing I can do about it."

Notice that each of these statements either directly contains or indirectly implies the notion of "can't." If salespeople genuinely believe they cannot do something, they probably will not do it. Using "can't" and subscribing to the myth of helplessness often result in a negative *self-fulfilling prophecy*, in which expectations of an event make the predicted outcome more likely to occur than it would have if the expectations had been different.

In fact, circumstances seldom exist that cannot be altered in some way. Salespeople can reverse this type of irrational thinking by replacing "can't" with "won't" or "don't know how to." When they use "won't," they face the realization that they are making a choice. For example, if Mary Jorgensen believes she will succeed as a woman in sales, she will tell her supervisor and he will react favorably to information about the size of her territory, and maybe Mary will experiment with new, more outgoing behaviors. Because the myth of helplessness usually comes into focus regarding future events, there is at least a 50-50 chance that the outcome will be favorable.

If Mary decides that "can't" is a substitute for "don't know how to," then by revising "can't" she may begin to learn how to behave differently. When she revises her language, she takes control by attempting to seek solutions. By admitting that change is possible, she takes the first step in altering unsatisfactory situations and moving toward her goals.

The Myth of Catastrophic Failure

This myth involves the assumption that the worst will happen and, as a result, the salesperson will fail. The fear of failure tends to immobilize salespeople. They are unable to perceive possible alternatives that might be more favorable. One way to think more rationally is to describe the worst alternative and consider whether you could live with the consequences if those consequences actually occurred. For example:

- "If I propose this system, my customer will laugh and think it's ridiculous." (Assess the consequences by asking yourself, "What's the worst that would happen if my customer laughed? If I *don't* share the system, what will happen?")
- "Even if I ask to be promoted, I won't be." (Consider the question, "What will be the impact on me and my job if I don't get the promotion? How will I view myself if I don't ask for it? What's so bad about asking and being refused?")
- "If I explain my position, my customer and I will argue." (Probe further with questions such as, "What would be so bad about an argument? If I conceal my views, how will that affect our working relationship?")

The fear of failing is often worse than actual failure would be. In addition, failure usually does not occur as frequently as it is anticipated.

Skill Builder — Using Facilitative Emotions to Overcome Irrational Beliefs

Irrational thinking stimulates debilitative, self-defeating feelings such as extreme fear and anger. Conversely, you can nurture self-motivating emotions such as enthusiasm and excitement by thinking more rationally. The approach recommended by Ellis and Harper includes four systematic steps.

1. *Monitor your emotional reaction.* The first step involves identifying debilitative emotions. You may do this by listening to your internal physiological changes, such as tightness in your muscles, hot or cold sensations, or increased pulse rate. Nonverbal behaviors also may be signs of strong emotion. For example, you may notice (or someone else may tell you) that your voice seems raised or that you are unusually quiet.
2. *Describe the activating event.* Once a person has identified the debilitative emotion, the next step is to identify

the event or events associated with the emotion. The event that activated the emotion may be obvious: a customer ordered materials from a competitor after making a verbal commitment to you. Sometimes, however, the event is obscure and may actually consist of a series of incidents that would not stimulate a debilitative emotion had they occurred as unrelated events. For example, in the process of preparing a presentation for a customer, you are interrupted several times, and the last phone call triggers a strong emotional reaction. When you recognize debilitative emotions, you should observe the situation, the people involved, and the topic of conversation. These may be cues to what activates your emotions.

3. *Record your self-talk.* Once you have identifed your emotions and the events that activate them, the next step is to identify the thinking that links them. Here is an example of records one salesperson kept of his self-talk.

   Todd observed a tightness in his throat and felt butterflies in his stomach when he was asked questions about the new models in his company's line of cellular telephones (activating event). He felt embarrassed (emotion). Todd recorded this self-talk:

   - "I should know the answers to his questions."
   - "If he hadn't asked me that question, the agreement would be in the bag."
   - "He'll never buy anything from me—I'm incompetent."
   - "If I tell him I don't know the answer, he'll laugh me out of the room."

   Listening to your self-talk requires patience because you may have difficulty at first in matching your thoughts and emotions with the activating events. You will improve with practice.

4. *Dispute your irrational thoughts.* The final step in this system involves using the explanation of the seven myths to revise irrational into more rational thoughts.

   Here's how Todd completed this step. He disputed his thoughts in this way:

   - "I wish I knew all the answers. Because the model is new, it is unrealistic for me to know all the questions that will be raised and have answers prepared. I can tell him I'll have the answer later today or tomorrow morning."
   - "I may be right. The agreement may have been completed if he hadn't thought of that question, and it still can be. I can have an answer for him soon. On the other hand, maybe we weren't that close to consummating an agreement—and it might not happen even when I do answer all of his questions."
   - "I am competent. My sales record on the old models is among the top ten in the company. He may not buy anything from me if I tell him honestly that I don't know the answer. Judging from my past record, however, someone else will."
   - "He may laugh if I'm honest because he may believe I should have the answers. The rate of development of these new models is so fast that it is laughable. I won't like it, but I can survive if he laughs."

Source: Adaptation from A. Ellis and R. Harper, *A New Guide to Rational Living* (North Hollywood, CA: Wilshire Books, 1977).

A Rational-Emotive Approach to Managing Emotions

Salespeople can use the Skill Builder to reduce the intensity and duration of their debilitative emotions, but they may not be able to eliminate them. It also may be difficult for them to really believe more rational alternatives to their irrational thinking. If they can *act* consistently with the more rational thoughts, however, their thinking can become self-fulfilling prophecies and they will have developed a system for coping with strong emotions. Table 4.1 provides guidelines that will help salespeople express their emotions.

According to William Howell, professor of interpersonal and intercultural communication at the University of Minnesota, emotion is a major component of the motivational complex.[11] Salespeople's ability to use this rational-emotive approach to increase the facilitative dimensions of their emotions is the key to developing self-motivation in professional selling.

Setting Goals for Self-Improvement

In the second and third sections of this chapter, the primary emphasis has been on the salesperson's emotions and thoughts. The final section

Table 4.1

Guidelines for Expressing Emotions

Share your emotions when they occur.
At the time you are experiencing the emotion, your physiological sensations are usually manifested in nonverbal behaviors that are observable by others. Your expression of emotion will seem most genuine when your nonverbal behavior is consistent with your feeling statements.

Share your emotions with the person directly involved.
It may be helpful to share your emotions with an involved person. You will experience more emotional release if you communicate your emotions to the person involved in the activating events. In addition, that person is likely to be experiencing emotion also.

Express your emotions clearly by reporting their intensity.
People frequently either overstate or understate their emotions. If an associate has broken an agreement, ask yourself if you feel mildly angry or extremely angry. Perhaps "annoyed" would be a more appropriate choice of words for mild anger while "livid" could clearly communicate intense anger.

Take responsibility for your emotions by avoiding the myth of causation.
Because the link between the activating event and the emotions you experience is your cognitive interpretations, it is inaccurate to report, "You make me feel angry." It is more accurate to indicate, "When you tell me you will meet me on Friday and then don't keep the appointment, I feel angry."

focuses on behavior. Setting goals for self-improvement in the role of salesperson primarily involves the ability to use *behavioral description*, which is verbal language that breaks into distinct steps (operationalizes) what the salesperson or others say and do. Behavioral description is factual in that multiple observers of the same behaviors will be able to verify described observations. More important, observers will be able to identify which behaviors they want to practice if the behaviors are stated clearly in behaviorally descriptive language.

Goals for improvement are usually worded in general, abstract language. Salespeople, like most individuals, often fail to achieve goals because they do not know how to operationalize them with specific behavioral description. A sales communication goal is a statement that includes behavioral descriptions of speaking and listening behaviors that salespeople want to learn to use effectively. For example, contrast the following goal statement with the behavioral descriptions that follow it. Then notice the behavioral descriptions that enable sales professionals to practice and incorporate new behaviors into their sales communication styles.

Goal Statement: I want to *take charge* of the opening of a sales interview with a new customer.

Behavioral Description:

1. I will smile and extend my hand when I first meet a customer.
2. I will offer a verbal greeting, using the customer's name.
3. I will be observant of the surroundings and comment on them in a complimentary way.
4. I will review my prospecting notes before the interview and make a positive comment about one aspect of the customer's personal business record or the company's record.
5. I will be prepared to state my purpose for requesting the interview and will do so within the first minute of the interview.

These statements operationalize what the salesperson must do to take charge of the opening of a sales interview with a new customer. The statements provide a personalized regimen for taking charge, similar to the way fitness centers provide programs to meet their members' individual needs. Just as a person may select a training program for competitive athletics or a workout program for getting in shape and keeping physically fit, there are many ways to write behavior descriptions to operationalize a goal for personal improvement. It is important that salespeople operationalize their goals in ways that complement their personal sales communication style.

One of the most vital skills that salespeople can develop for operating in a relationship-driven environment is their ability to create individualized programs for self-improvement. Table 4.2 outlines steps to help salespeople design personal improvement programs for themselves. In addition, Denis Waitley, a superstar in the field of motivation and achievement, shares his insight into self-improvement in Exhibit 4.1.

Table 4.2

Guidelines for Designing a Personal Improvement Program

- Identify one goal to work on at a time.
- Observe the sales communication behaviors of one or more persons who already have accomplished your goal (social comparison).
- Describe three to five specific behaviors that you will practice to operationalize your goal.
- Identify specifically when, where, and with whom you will practice the behaviors.
- Record your progress regularly (for instance, daily or weekly) as appropriate.
- Modify your goal as necessary.

A competent salesperson persists in self-actualizing through personal goal setting. Achieving one's goals will be a major source of the motivation needed to cope with the high level of rejection inherent in the selling profession.

Summary

Increasing sales effectiveness involves examining the personal characteristics and skills that one would like to develop. A person's sales image includes four integrated processes: self-awareness, self-acceptance, self-actualization, and self-disclosure. A salesperson, like all human beings,

Exhibit 4.1

Dr. Denis Waitley's Tips for Achieving Consistent Success

1. Never wait for others to create your success.
2. Don't try to go it alone.
3. As you achieve goals, raise your limits.
4. Surround yourself with fresh ideas and interesting people.
5. Beware of delusions of grandeur.
6. Remain loyal to friends, family, and the people responsible for helping you succeed.
7. Self-pity has no place in a successful person's life.
8. Make a commitment to your dreams and accept your vulnerability.

Commitment to strength and acceptance of vulnerability are two major consistent success keys. Continue to invest in your health, in your fitness, as well as your primary tasks that have made you successful. Relentlessly strip away negative habits and eagerly seek self-renewal. Remain faithful to your family, to your value system and to your dreams.

Source: G. and L. B. Gschwandtner, "Profile of Dr. Denis Waitley: The Great Balancing Act—How to Achieve Consistent Success," *Personal Selling Power,* July/August 1989, pp. 8–11.

is always feeling, thinking, and acting. Expressing feelings approximately as they relate to one's role as a salesperson involves understanding how thoughts link emotions with the events to which they are related.

Understanding and expressing emotions involve a salesperson's ability to identify the four components of internal physiological changes, external behavior manifestations of those changes, cognitive interpretations, and verbal expressions. Furthermore, managing emotions in facilitative ways requires rational thinking. The alternative is to generate emotions at a debilitative level, which inhibits effective functioning.

Understanding the various myths of irrational thinking is necessary when using a rational-emotive approach to manage emotions. This approach involves identifying emotions, noting the activating event, recording irrational thoughts, and disputing those irrational thoughts to exchange them for more rational thinking. As a result, a salesperson will tend to increase facilitative dimensions of emotions, thereby achieving higher levels of self-motivation.

When salespeople understand their sales images, including the ways that they think and feel, then they can focus on behavior to set goals for self-improvement in professional selling.

Key Terms

Debilitative Emotions Emotions of extreme intensity and duration, to the point that they prevent salespeople from functioning as they would like

Emotion Consists of four components that directly influence a positive sales image: physiological changes, nonverbal manifestations, cognitive interpretations, and verbal expressions

Facilitative Emotions Those emotions, regardless of intensity or duration, that contribute to one's effective performance

Feeling Statement An expression of empathy by one person to another

Irrational Thinking Thinking that is muddled, leads to illogical conclusions, and promotes debilitative emotions

Johari Window A grid by which one can chart the dynamics of any conversation between people

Operationalize Verbal language that breaks into distinct steps what others say and do.

Rational Thinking Thinking that results in logical conclusions and promotes facilitative emotions

Self-Acceptance The degree to which a person likes and is satisfied with self in the role of salesperson

Self-Actualization The process of selecting specific aspects of one's sales image that need changing, setting personal goals, and devising a plan to accomplish them

Self-Awareness The process of bringing all the information about self that is associated with one's sales image to a conscious level

Self-Disclosure Verbally communicating information about oneself to another

Review Questions

1. What is meant by having a positive sales image?
2. Describe the three characteristics of a sales image and how each might affect sales performance.
3. Identify the four components of a sales image and explain how they interact.
4. Describe the Johari window and how it can be used to improve sales performance.
5. List the four components of emotion and how they affect a person's sales image.
6. What are the differences between debilitative and facilitative emotions?
7. Distinguish between rational and irrational thinking.
8. What are the seven myths of irrational thinking described by Ellis and Harper?
9. Describe the four steps recommended to help one think more rationally.
10. Explain the steps in setting goals for self-improvement.

Questions for Discussion

1. Why is a person's sales image a critical factor in developing a relationship strategy?
2. What is meant by the statement, "One's sales image will be flexible if it is healthy"? How does the meaning of that statement apply to the relationship process?
3. Discuss the four components of a sales image. Use personal examples to explain each component.
4. Use the Johari window as a guide to examine the level of self-disclosure in a relationship with a friend, a co-worker, and a family member.
5. Review the four components of an emotion. Identify an emotion you have felt recently and describe how the four components apply. Discuss which components you are most aware of. Why might some components be more obvious than others?
6. Discuss the relationship among activating events, thoughts, and emotions according to Ellis and Harper.
7. Explain the relationships that exist among facilitative and debilitative emotions and rational and irrational thinking. Use examples from personal experience.
8. Select one of the seven myths of irrational thinking. How can the four steps in the rational-emotive approach be used to turn irrational into more rational thinking to manage one's emotions?

9. What are the advantages in using behavioral description to operationalize personal goals and sales goals?
10. Identify one personal or sales goal and write three to five behavioral descriptions following the model presented in the text. Make a commitment to implement these behaviors. One week later, share your progress with the class.

Changing an Image with Resistance

Case 4.1

Bruce has been a stock broker selling stocks and bonds for a well-known brokerage firm for nearly 10 years. Due to volatile market conditions, he was forced to expand into other investment offerings, serving more as a financial advisor than a stock broker.

Bruce's new assignment was to solicit new accounts for a variety of investments other than stocks. He acquired the names of about 50 elderly people from a file he had collected of senior citizens in a very high tax bracket. About 1 year ago he had contacted them to propose stock purchases. Many of these potential investors kept their money in secure bank accounts bearing low interest rates and were unwilling to take the kinds of risks inherent with the stock market.

Although Bruce attempted to secure an appointment to present conservative investment packages yielding higher interest rates than the banks and tax-free interest-bearing alternatives, he encountered enormous resistance. A major problem was that he was known and respected as a stock broker to many of these investors. Furthermore, these elderly people were not willing to place their funds in any perceived risk-taking opportunities.

Bruce's image to these people was as a stock broker. He clearly emphasized that as a financial advisor his job was not to sell stocks but to discuss investment opportunities in general, recognizing their concern for security. Many of the prospects declined an appointment with Bruce, suggesting that they felt more comfortable with their present investments at the banks and savings and loan associations.

1. How can Bruce handle the resistance raised by these prospects?
2. What can Bruce do to change this image he has in the investment field?
3. How can a salesperson gain credibility in a new assignment?

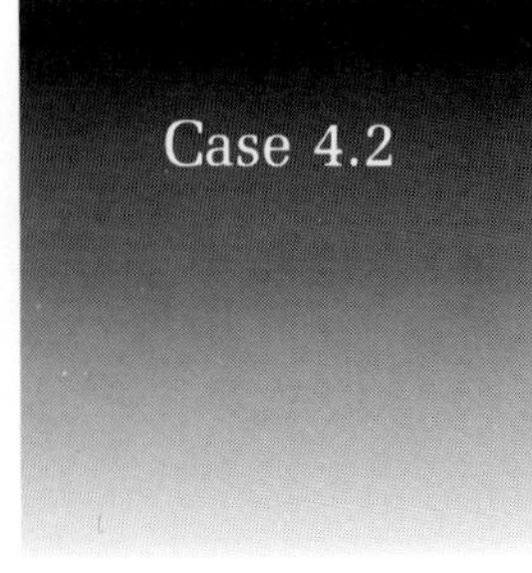

The Effects of Irrational Thinking

Juliette Chateau is a representative for Citi-Comp Metered Mailing Corporation (CCMMC). She is proud to be a member of the Citi-Comp sales team and has a distinguished sales record. In the past she has enjoyed representing CCMMC because it dominated the market with a highly respected product line. Furthermore, she enjoyed working in a predominantly male industry. Recently, however, Citi-Comp raised its prices, making it among the most expensive firms in the business.

At the same time prices increased, the size of Juliette's territory was expanded and more competitors entered the market. Juliette's salary is based on a modest guarantee plus a program of substantial commissions and bonuses.

In addition, her new sales manager, Gene Albright, has been pressuring her by increasing her quota and pushing her to increase her sales on their most competitive postage meter, the one with the greatest price increase. After attending a recent sales meeting in which Albright threatened to cut her guarantee if she did not perform, Juliette processed the following thoughts:

- "Selling is really a man's world. I might as well resign myself to the fact that, as a woman, I can't make it in sales."
- "I can't object to having my territory increased because my supervisor will fire me. I'm not able to give effective service to my present customers, but I'll just have to live with the increase."
- "My sales manager just doesn't understand me. He told me to be more outgoing. I'm just not an extrovert, and there's nothing I can do about it."
- "I can't justify the new increase in our prices, and I can't see how I can look my customers in the eye and tell them with a straight face. I'll just have to give up my commission to remain competitive."
- "Just because I'm a woman and have consistently sold over quota, Albright expects more out of me. I should have reminded him that I've given up countless weekends to keep my customers satisfied."
- "I should spend Sunday on paperwork even though I've already worked 6 days this week. At least he can't accuse me of being incompetent."

1. Revise Juliette's unproductive thinking by changing her irrational statements to rational statements.
2. Suggest how Juliette can convert her debilitative emotions into facilitative feelings.
3. How will Juliette's new rational thoughts create facilitative emotions?

Notes

1. Arthur Bragg, "Are Good Salespeople Born or Made?," *Sales & Marketing Management*, September 1988, pp. 74–78.
2. Ibid., p. 77.
3. Robert McGarvey, "Who's Hot," *Entrepreneurial Women*, June 1991, p. 44.
4. Ibid.
5. V. P. Richmond and J. C. McCroskey, *Communication: Apprehension, Avoidance, and Effectiveness* (Scottsdale, AZ: Gorsuch Scarisbrick Publishers, 1985), pp. 67–70.
6. Bragg, "Are Good Salespeople Born or Made?," pp. 74–78.
7. Gerhard Gschwandtner, "Fran Tarkenton: Knowledgeware's $60 Million Champion," *Personal Selling Power*, May/June 1991, p. 14.
8. Lynne Sanford, "The Sales Arsenal," *Success*, May 1991, p. 38.
9. A. Ellis and R. Harper, *A New Guide to Rational Living* (North Hollywood, CA: Wilshire Books, 1977).
10. Ibid.
11. W. S. Howell, "Coping with Internal Monologue," in J. Stewart, ed., *Bridges Not Walls: A Book about Interpersonal Communication*, 4th ed. (New York: Random House, 1986), pp. 112–123.

CHAPTER 5

Know Your Industry, Company, Products, and Competition

Knowledge Objectives

In this chapter, you will learn:

1. The importance of being knowledgeable
2. What is important to know about your industry, company, products, and competition
3. How knowledge is being used in various personal selling strategies
4. The role and relationship of product features, advantages, and benefits in personal selling
5. Sources that are available to help salespeople acquire the information they need

Consider This

An honest heart being the first blessing, a knowing head is the second.

Thomas Jefferson

s we stated in Chapter 2, becoming a competent salesperson involves both knowledge and skills. As seen in Chapter 4, having knowledge about oneself and one's prospect is essential in learning professional selling. Additionally, during this precall preparation stage the salesperson must acquire information about the industry, company, products, and competition. The first section of this chapter discusses why having sales knowledge is important; the next four sections cover what, where, and how salespeople gather information in these specific areas. The last section identifies sources of sales information, both within and outside the company.

On the Ethical Side — Proper Behavior in the Face of Competition

In the 1990s, professional salespeople sometimes find themselves confronted with competitive salespeople who are not ethical in their approach. Sometimes the reason for the lack of ethics in the competitor's approach is poor training; at other times, it may be something even worse: greed. In either case, truly professional salespeople will respond positively, asserting their own ethical stance through their behavior.

One thing to remember when confronted with unethical behavior is that similar behavior (such as an attack on the competition or the competitor's product) may belittle your standing in the eyes of the customer. Your purpose is to persuade the customer to buy your product; since persuasion involves presenting a logical sales approach, it is advisable to avoid committing the following logical fallacies when counteracting negative ethics in the competition.

1. *Hasty Generalization:* This most often occurs when one uses a generalized statement that has little evidence to support it or is based on evidence that is biased.*
2. *Ad Hominem:* This occurs when one launches an attack on the competitor personally, rather then dealing with the issues at hand.*
3. *Red Herring:* This happens when one focuses attention on an irrelevant issue (feature, benefit) rather than dealing with the real issue.
4. *Either . . . Or:* This occurs when the salesperson convinces the customer that there are only two alternatives in an issue, when in fact there are many.
5. *False Analogy:* This is leading the customer to think that because two things are alike in some areas, they are alike in other, unrelated areas as well.
6. *Oversimplification:* This happens when a salesperson omits relevant considerations about a product or service.

When the professional salesperson is able to spot which of these, or other, fallacies was the instrument of the competition's attack, the damage can be overcome by supplying the correct information. This is a *positive* action and can help to overcome erroneous buying objections.

* In all likelihood, it is one of these first two fallacies that the competition has used to attack you or your product.

A Strong Emphasis on Sales Knowledge

High-tech electronic delivery and communication systems make information instantly accessible to consumers all over the world. Add to that global distribution of newspapers, magazines, and all print media, and the result is a highly sophisticated, knowledgeable, yet sometimes confused customer.

In response to the confusion often resulting from information overload, firms are spending millions of dollars to make themselves heard above the others—to be *the* one among many. Thus, they are equipping their sales forces with the latest procedures and innovative techniques, including technological know-how. In both domestic and international markets, the driving force behind this preparation has been an emphasis on productivity, which means increasing sales.

Sales Knowledge Is Important

Would you take an automobile to a mechanic who lacks adequate auto repair knowledge? Or hire a trial attorney or seek out an orthodontist who has insufficient knowledge or training? How often are we dissatisfied with the salesperson at the retail store? When buying a home, would the purchaser consult a real estate agent who is unfamiliar with the area in which the purchaser wants to live or who doesn't know anything about the related market values or mortgage interest rates?

What should the salesperson know? *As much as possible!* Although it is impossible for anyone to know everything about anything, the salesperson must have a thorough understanding of the facts and benefits to continue serving customers' needs. Successful selling is based on delivering facts and benefits and on responding to the demands of the changing marketplace.

The relational selling process has two main objectives: relationships and results. Just as sensitivity contributes to the relationship, knowledge helps to create the results.

Knowledge Builds Credibility and Confidence

Credibility is a key ingredient in all selling relationships. Acquiring extensive knowledge and being able to match it with the customer's needs encourages credibility. Credibility inspires the buyer's confidence in the salesperson, which stimulates self-confidence in the seller. Furthermore, having extensive sales knowledge prepares salespeople to answer questions confidently and respond to any resistance that may be raised by prospects. "Knowledge is power"—especially when it is offered as proof and support. Testimony based on facts boosts the salesperson's believability. Believability and credibility are the two basic elements of reliability, which is a fundamental component of relational selling.

Know Your Industry

The more salespeople know about the industry they serve, the greater will be their ability to meet the needs of their customers. Many industrial and consumer goods buyers are too busy to stay informed about what is available. Frequently, they rely on salespeople to keep them informed in an honest and ethical manner. Those salespeople who do can claim a competitive edge in building repeat business. For example, detail salespeople, such as those selling pharmaceuticals, use knowledge of their industry to keep physicians informed on new drugs and procedures.

Exhibit 5.1

Know Your Industry

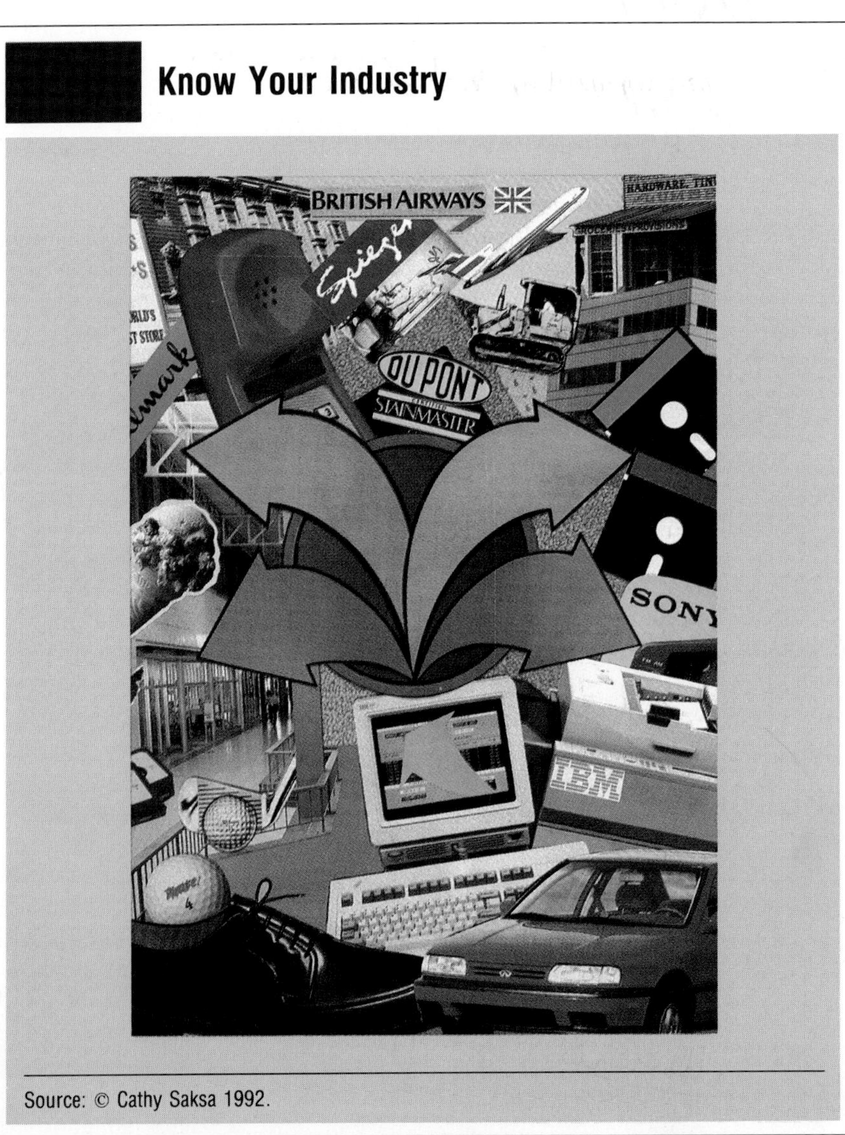

Source: © Cathy Saksa 1992.

Sales Professional Spotlight

Mike Davari, president and owner of Carpet House, one of the leading floor covering retailers in southern California, recalls when owning his own store seemed only a dream. It was after successfully completing a university marketing research project that he first felt he had the potential for establishing his own operation. Mike realized his dream in 1987 when he established his own retail store.

In his early years Mike worked for one of the largest carpet retailers in the United States. After his first month he was recognized by the president as the top salesperson for the entire store. His performance in sales was unmatched, and he was recognized as the leading salesperson every month for 5 years, an accomplishment never before achieved in the industry.

Mike always set high limits for himself and worked hard to achieve them. He was always determined to achieve the number one position in sales volume for his company. Furthermore, he insisted on learning everything he could about the industry and was anxious to gain experience in all operational levels of the company. His job entailed working in the manager's office, at the front desk and the order desk, and even in the stock room. This enabled him to gain an understanding of the company and the industry's procedures and functions.

Mike believes in knowing everything he can about his products and competition. He explains, "It is important to know the lines of products the competitors carry, their prices, terms, installation charges." Knowing your product and competition can better prepare you to solve the client's needs and problems. Every sale can be considered a solution to a problem.

Mike further expresses a desire to extend excellent service from the moment the clients enter the store until they are enjoying the comforts of fine carpeting in their home. "Never criticize or knock your competitors," he strongly emphasizes. His philosophy is to "always be honest, trustworthy, and confident."

Building customer loyalty is vital for success in sales. Mike stresses that success in sales often results from repeat business and referrals. "The best form of advertising is a satisfied customer, and the worst advertising is a dissatisfied customer. A happy customer will tell another and an unhappy customer will tell ten others."

Furthermore, he believes, "In most selling situations there are so many products available at competitive prices that the customer commits to a purchase decision because of the relationship established with the salesperson. I firmly believe that a bond is created between the customer and salesperson in most selling situations."

In Chapter 1 we talked about market segments and the marketing mix variables of product, price, place, and promotion. Sales professionals frequently act as marketing consultants to the customers they serve. By so doing, they can not only identify the markets their customers are currently serving but guide them into new markets that they may be overlooking. Exhibit 5.2 illustrates how a company may direct its sales force to customize its approach by changing the distribution (place) channel.

Understanding the uncontrollable variables will give salespeople additional tools to help them offer their customers marketing direction. These variables include the economic, technological, cultural-social, competitive, political-legal, and ethical environments, which are constantly changing and over which we have little control. Clearly, knowing about these environments is important on both the domestic and international levels. For instance, a change in competitive action from foreign suppliers may cause a person's sales to fall short of sales potential. In some industries, such as the U.S. automobile industry, the key forces are foreign competitors. The companies that have prospered over the years are those that have anticipated and responded to the dynamic changes occurring in the broader (macromarketing) environment.

Often we think of international sales (both importing and exporting) as being available only to giant multinational corporations. This is not true today. Regarding exporting, a survey conducted for the Small Business Administration targeting the European Economic Community (EEC) revealed some interesting statistics:

- 37 percent of companies with fewer than 500 employees are exporting overseas.
- A quarter of all exporting companies—more than 16,000 firms—employ fewer than 100 people.
- Among the small companies currently exporting, 56 percent said their export sales had increased over the previous year, and 41 percent said their export sales had grown more quickly than domestic sales.[1]

Most businesspeople are aware that by 1994 or 1995 many internal trade barriers will be eliminated from the 12 EEC nations. This means that restrictions on free movement of goods, services, and people in these countries will be replaced by a single set of regulations and directives coordinated by the EEC Commission headquartered in Brussels, Belgium. Accordingly, these uniform EEC standards will "streamline the sale of billions of dollars of products ranging from forklifts to toys to medical devices."[2] For small American companies, this will offer an opportunity to sell billions of dollars of products to a single market that includes Denmark, Sweden, Spain, Italy, Greece, France, Portugal, Germany, and the United Kingdom. Exhibit 5.3 reports such a victory of sales abroad in an "American entrepreneurial dream" story.

Matching Your Sales Force to Multiple Channels

Exhibit 5.2

As markets fragment, different customers inevitably seek alternate channels of distribution. A firm's sales force, used to one standard selling approach for the entire market, must then begin to customize its approach—and its skills—by distribution channel.

Consider, for instance, a firm that produces and sells software for accounting applications—where the software fits small-, medium-, or large-sized business needs.

This firm may have begun by selling its software through two distinct channels of distribution: VARs [value-added resellers] and chain computer retailers. Over time, its products will also show up in other channels, including bookstores, electronics superstores, warehouse clubs, "software only" retailers, office stationers, catalog/mail order houses, and the computer departments of national department stores. Each of these channels serves different customer segments by company size, level of computer literacy, price sensitivity, after-sale service requirements, and application complexity.

As the firm sells to these multiple channels, it must develop different skills in the reps who call on them. For instance, for channels that are heavily retail-oriented, reps need to know how to assist the stores in merchandising software via displays, point-of-sale price specials, customer handouts, and other retail sales techniques.

With channels selling wholesale or industrial accounts (such as office stationers), reps may need to assist with direct mail promotions, vertical marketing programs, and sales leads.

For channels selling hardware and software network applications (such as VARs), the sales rep may need to acquire extensive technical knowledge and the skills to help the VAR with key account presentations or written sales proposals.

For specialized channels such as warehouse clubs or mail order companies, the rep may need program selling skills for bulk packaged and priced product (for the warehouse club) or knowledge of how to position and price the product for sale by catalog (for the mail order firm).

Inevitably, if channels have very distinct needs from the sales force, reorganizing the rep structure by channels may make sense. Certainly, selling to national or regional computer stores or bookstore chains is quite different from selling to independent VARs or local office stationers. Channel variety, therefore, often dictates specialized trade-class selling within the sales force.

Source: Allan J. Magrath, "Differentiating Yourself Via Distribution," *Sales & Marketing Management*, March 1991, p. 56.

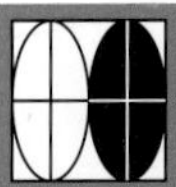

On the International Front — Competitive Audit of a Foreign Market

A company moving into the international market must evaluate its competitive environment in estimating its market potential. The following questions form part of a competitive audit:

Basic Information

1. Which competitive products are sold in country X?
2. What are the market shares of competitive products?
3. How do competitive products compare with our own in reputation, features, and other attributes?
4. What support facilities (production, warehousing, sales branches, and so on) do competitors have in country X?
5. What problems do competitors face?
6. What relationships do competitors have with the local government? Do they enjoy special preferences?

Market Information

1. What distribution channels are used by competitors?
2. How do competitors' prices compare with our own?
3. What credit terms, commissions, and other compensation are extended by competitors to their channel members?
4. What promotion programs are used by competitors? How successful are they?
5. How good are competitors' postsale services?

Market Supply Information: How do competitive products get into the market?

1. If they are imported:
   a. Who are the importers?
   b. How do importers operate?
   c. What credit, pricing, and other terms are extended to importers by foreign suppliers?
   d. How long has each importer worked with a foreign supplier? Is the importer satisfied with the supplier?
2. If they are produced locally:
   a. Who are the producers?
   b. Are the producers entirely locally owned, or is there foreign participation?
   c. What advantages do local manufacturers have over importing competitors?

Source: Franklin R. Root, *Entry Strategies for International Markets* (Lexington, MA: Lexington Books, 1987), pp. 42–44.

Understanding Professional Buyers

Every industry has fundamental characteristics that involve techniques and procedures common to that industry as a whole. It is the responsibility of salespeople to learn how their industries think and operate, and what the buyer expects from the individual salesperson. For example, salespeople who represent industrial and commercial products work with

A Guide to Selling Abroad for the Small Company

Exhibit 5.3

In the European Economic Community (EEC), small American companies are marketing in a bigger and bigger way.

Beginner's Luck

Too often, the specter of exporting sends small American businesses running for cover. But exporting to the EEC may be easier than one might think. For example, James Clem of James Clem Corporation of Chicago first got involved in the European market on a suburban Chicago golf course.

Clem's company manufactures Claymax, a patented concoction of sodium bentonite glued to a fabric base, which allows it to be rolled out and laid down like a carpet.

Claymax is a barrier to water seepage and is used as a liner for building foundations and freshwater ponds. More important, it can also be used to replace the meter-thick layers of clay that the U.S. Environmental Protection Agency mandates in all landfills to prevent toxic wastes from seeping into groundwater.

Like many great business deals, however, Clem's silver lining was wrapped in a very large gray cloud.

Sherri Sorenson, Clem's wife and business partner, recalls, "Sales were so slow we could barely pay our gas bills. We eventually realized that all the orders we were getting were for freshwater applications. They were staying away from landfills—our biggest potential market—because they were afraid of product liability claims. By the summer of 1986, we were desperate. We couldn't sell direct in North America because of our contract with the chemical company, and we were only doing a little business in the United Kingdom because we didn't really know how to sell anywhere else."

Which brings us back to the golf course.

"I got invited to a golf outing," Clem explains. "It was the first and last time I ever played golf. I was talking about the product, asking everybody how I could get distributors abroad. On the eleventh hole, a woman told me to call the Commerce Department.

"The guy who answered the phone was a trade specialist named Dick Marsh," Clem recalls. "When I told him my problem, he said, 'Sir, that's my job.'"

Through a little-publicized effort begun in 1982, the Commerce Department offers several programs—either free or at minimal cost—to help small and medium-sized companies sell their goods and services overseas. As part of this effort, the Commerce Department employs more than 1,300 trade professionals and support staffers in 68 domestic offices and 122 locations abroad.

Clem placed one phone call, and Dick Marsh in effect became his company's pro bono export consultant. He worked out a strategy to get Claymax exported to Europe, helping at every stage of the process—addressing concerns about paperwork, red tape, payment, packaging, shipping, even lining up experts who spoke the necessary foreign languages.

First, Marsh had Clem and Sorenson put together a sales brochure in three languages, along with some sample packages of Claymax. Next, he advised them to attend a trade show for the water resources industry in Amsterdam. The idea was to network at the show and then stay in Europe for 2 weeks to get to know the lay of the land, meeting with all the American commercial counselors they could during that time.

Commercial counselors are Commerce Department trade experts based abroad. They provide American companies with on-the-spot information and direct access to more than 95 percent of the world market for American exports. In addition, they also help line up distributors for American companies.

Striking a Match

Even though that first trip didn't result in any immediate business, it still turned out to be an important confidence builder for Sorenson. "I was an artist before I went into business," she explains, "a person who always wore blue jeans and had etching ink under her fingernails. But once I got over there, I realized it was just like a business trip to L.A.—maybe a little more exotic."

In April 1987, Sorenson suggested that they put that confidence to the test by attending a Commerce Department Matchmaker event in Milan. The Matchmaker program introduces small and medium-sized American companies to potential agents, distributors, and licensing partners abroad. The Commerce Department does all the background work: finding and screening contacts, scheduling meetings, and handling the logistics.

Matchmaker veteran Alexander McMahon, of Lukens Medical Corporation, is a true believer in the program. "Matchmakers is one of the best ways a small company has to develop trading partners abroad," he says. "For a big company, selling overseas is basically an internal job. You're introducing new products to wholly owned subsidiaries or joint venture partners of your company. Big companies have matchmakers on their payroll; small companies need an organization like Matchmakers."

Clem thought the Matchmaker idea was great but wasn't very excited about Italy as a prospective market. "To me, it was the land of red wine and boccie," he says. "The trip was going to cost us about $4,000—airfare, hotels, food, and expenses—and here we were, barely alive."

But Sorenson eventually prevailed, which was fortunate because Matchmakers turned out to be Clem Corporation's deliverance.

Why? Because Italy just happens to have one of the biggest toxic waste problems in Europe, which naturally meant that Claymax was viewed as something of a Holy Grail in the landfill business. The result: Clem and Sorenson came back with an initial $50,000 order from an enthusiastic Italian distributor, followed over the course of the next 12 months by an additional $400,000 in sales. Today that distributor is Clem Corporation's biggest dealer, accounting for $1.5 million in sales in 1989 alone.

"It was almost like a dating service," says Clem, referring to the Matchmaker event. "Sherri had one-on-one meetings every hour from eight in the morning to six at night. In 3 days, she met with 30 Italian companies that had a strong interest in our product. We eventually narrowed it down to three companies, then to the one we wanted to negotiate a contract with."

Marsh and his counterparts at the Illinois Department of Commerce and Community Affairs continue to assist Clem, providing the kind of support that most companies pay big bucks for.

"It's amazing to me that the federal and state programs we used are still among the best-kept secrets in the business world," says Clem. "And to think I found out about them on a golf course!"

Source: Adapted and reprinted from Daniel M. Rosen, EC '92: A Guide for the Small Company, *Sales & Marketing Management*, September 1990, pp. 98, 100.

professional buyers called purchasing agents. For years, salespeople relied on long-standing, personal ties where prices were the key point of negotiation. Today's purchasing agent is looking for salespeople who

> have thorough knowledge of what their customers are producing, someone who can offer some powerful insights into helping them make things better, faster, and cheaper. In short, purchasing agents want a salesperson who can act as a bridge between all the various departments at both companies, rather than just concentrating on a one-to-one relationship with a particular agent.[3]

Additional expectations of salespeople are described by purchasing agents in Exhibit 5.4. These comments ring true regardless of whether a person sells industrial, commercial, or consumer products and services. Consequently, sales professionals who demonstrate that they have researched their industry, have studied their customers' industry, and understand their customers' problems will help build the mutual trust, respect, and credibility upon which a long-term relationship is based.

Know Your Company

The following statement is taken from Procter & Gamble's sales training brochure:

> No matter where a consumer buys a P & G product, a sales representative was usually there first. P & G products are sold to retailers by wholesalers, distributors, and agents, as well as by the company's own sales force. The ultimate success of P & G depends, in an important way, on the skill and resourcefulness these people bring to their job. When a P & G representative walks into a customer's place of business—whether he's calling on an individual store or

Exhibit 5.4

"Do Your Homework"

Want the lowdown on what purchasing agents are thinking when a salesperson asks for a few minutes of their time? Suffice it to say that it's not all hearts and flowers, but a glimpse at some of the comments from purchasing agents may just encourage your sales reps to be prepared and stay focused on the topic at hand.

- "My time is short. I get maybe twenty calls a day. Walking in without an appointment isn't a big plus."
- "Do your homework. Am I the one you want to see? At this company, I buy axles for our trucks. Don't call me with your line of office supplies."
- "Read our annual reports, read anything you can about us. Follow the trades. Know ahead of time what we're up against in the market, what we're trying to do. If I offer to show you around, jump at the chance. Or better yet, ask me yourself."
- "Know your product inside and out. Or at least know how and where to get answers for me—fast. Be ready to set up a meeting between your engineering people and ours."
- "With our new computers, it takes no time for me to pull up the facts of our past relationship and the current market conditions. Use this to help us improve our relationship and solve our problems rather than looking at it as a negative."
- "I don't want to change suppliers just for the heck of it. You have to have something really better or cheaper."
- "I may like you, but the old-boy network isn't going to cut it today. I don't plan to stick around forever if something better comes along, and neither do you. The link is company to company and how you can help us. Don't fight it."
- "I'm trying all the time to trim our supplier base. Don't tell me how much you appreciate my business. Just tell me if you can deliver the product."

Source: Edith Cohen, "A View from the Other Side," *Sales & Marketing Management*, June 1990, p. 112.

the headquarters of a large chain of stores—he or she not only represents P & G but, in a very real sense, is P & G. To the customer, the sales representative is the direct source of knowledge about P & G's products, its policies, and its character.

Procter & Gamble has a reputation for providing its sales force with ongoing and long-term training. Many people who enter the selling profession, however, will not have the luxury of the highly structured, formalized sales training found among most *Fortune* 500 companies. Some firms will provide a manual listing product assortments, product lines, prices, and terms. Other companies will give their new salespeople a "black bag," a map of the territory, and an order book and call these supplies "training." Regardless of the depth or length of company training, the prospect and customer expect the salesperson to have a thorough knowledge of the company's history, size, and standing; its organization and personnel; billing, credit, and finances; and related policies and procedures.

History

How old is your company? Who started it? How large is it? Where does it stand in the industry? What percentage of the market does it have in its respective product lines?

Policies and philosophies are often passed down from the company's founders and origins. Probably every marketing class in every business school in the country has studied and idealized, at least in part, International Business Machines (IBM) as the brightest paragon of American business. Since 1924, when Thomas J. Watson, Sr., changed its name from Computing-Tabulating-Recording Company, IBM has dominated its markets. By the 1950s, IBM controlled 95 percent of the punch-card machine business.[4] By the late 1960s a top mainframe, the System/360, had gained IBM 70 percent of the computer market. Launched in August 1981, the IBM personal computer immediately captured 75 percent of the corporate market.[5] In 1991, however, after enjoying almost monopolistic success and with 373,000 employees, "Big Blue" was forced to change because of falling profits and decreasing market share. But given the track record of IBM, its salespeople can revel in a history rich with long-term success. This reputation makes sharing the company's history with prospects a task filled with pride and confidence.

How does a small firm or a young company compete with the IBMs of its industry? One way is to build on the strengths and credentials of its members. For example, a salesperson for a 2-year-old computer software company might emphasize that all of its programmers have Master's degrees in computer information systems and that its team of six represents over 100 years of programming experience. It is important to recognize that, historically, big is not always better.

Organizational Structure

One of the first tasks salespeople should complete upon beginning their employment is to familiarize themselves with all the departments in their companies. Often, successfully servicing the customer's needs is the joint responsibility of several departments.

The most important people for salespeople to know within their own organization are not necessarily the company officers but rather the support staff in each of the departments that assist in processing customers' orders and maintaining accounts. This also requires knowing the routine that every customer order must follow and who is responsible for each step in processing the order. These people may include departmental secretaries, billing and filing clerks, transportation or shipping and receiving staff, and customer service coordinators.

Pricing and Distribution Policies

Salespeople must know their companies' policies and procedures on pricing and distribution. Admitting ignorance of these policies is unlikely to inspire customers' confidence and trust in the salesperson. This lack of knowledge reflects inadequate preparation.

Policies must also be known so that salespeople can avoid making promises to customers that their companies cannot or will not satisfy. Such commitments might include how to handle a customer billing complaint or what to do in the event of a shipping error. In such situations, action should be taken to deliver immediate satisfaction to the customer. Salespeople are advised to learn about pricing and credit terms, shipping procedures, and distribution policies.

Pricing

Generally, salespeople do not participate in establishing the company's pricing structure. Any flexibility in pricing available to the salesperson, however, should be specified in a statement of policy. Exhibit 5.5 depicts a hypothetical policy statement using actual policies. This statement, developed by Robert Haas, industrial marketing specialist, covers discounts, problems with damaged goods, payment charges, and returns and replacement.

Discounting and Price Incentives

When discounts are available, the salesperson should know what discounts can be offered. Typical types of discounting offered to buyers are as follows:

1. Cash—a percent discount if the buyer pays within a shortened period. A typical cash discount might be "2/10, net 30," indicating that the buyer can subtract 2 percent from the bill for payment within 10 days or pay the full amount at the end of 30 days from receipt of the invoice.

Exhibit 5.5

Return and Replacement Policy—Haas Engineering

Merchandise may not be returned without written authorization, and shipment must be made freight prepaid. Where factory defects are found in current merchandise, then following the authorized return of merchandise, Haas Engineering will make replacement without charge if claim is justified. Return shipment will be made freight prepaid. In addition, credit will be issued to cover the incoming freight cost incurred on returned shipment of defective merchandise. Authorized returns of salable merchandise, other than shipments made in error, will be subject to a 20% restocking charge.

2. Trade—a payment offered to channel members for carrying the product. For example, a publisher with a list price of $15 for a book might grant the bookstore and wholesaler trade discounts of 30 percent and 20 percent, respectively. The wholesaler's purchase price would be figured as follows:

$15.00	list price
−4.50	(.30 × $15.00 for the 30% retail discount)
$10.50	
−2.10	(.20 × $10.50 for the 20% wholesale discount)
$ 8.40	purchase price to the wholesaler

   These trade discounts are based on the operating expenses of the wholesaler and retailer.
3. Quantity—an incentive given to encourage customers to buy in large volumes.
4. Rebate—a cash payment offered to the buyer at the end of a designated period that is based on sales volume during that period. This incentive encourages the buyer to increase purchases with a single supplier. Under a typical rebate system, a customer whose purchases total between $10,000 and $25,000 may receive a 2-percent cash rebate; from $25,000 to $50,000, the rebate may be 4 percent; if the purchase is from $50,000 to $100,000, the rebate may be 6 percent; and so on.[6]
5. Seasonal discount—a reduction of the basic list price when the demand has declined because of a change in climatic or holiday conditions. Many companies have a policy of offering their customers seasonal discounts during off-season sales periods, with the objective of balancing sales patterns.
6. Credit terms—allowing buyers to pay at a later date for goods received today. This is a common practice in negotiating. In such instances, it is important to know when credit can be granted and the extent of the credit limit. Extending credit is one of the most common methods Japanese suppliers use to gain a competitive advantage.

Shipping

How is merchandise delivered? Is a common carrier used? Is there an extra charge for this? How are damages in shipping handled? How are price changes handled? Applying postagreement price increases after shipment without prior notification is detrimental to a long-term relationship. When prices may fluctuate because of drastically changing conditions, an escalator clause should be provided, allowing the seller to raise the price of the shipment under contract if costs increase before delivery. This method is becoming common in international sales transactions.

Distribution

What channels of distribution are currently used for each product line? What are the current selling methods? What are the sales policies and terms (for example, is an escalator clause included in the agreement)? Are different costs incurred in serving different types (sizes, locations) of buyers?

Salespeople must know the distribution policies for their products and through what channels the products are distributed. This includes the extent of protection and flexibility in coverage that the company gives to the channel member or members.

Related Policies and Procedures

Production Methods and Facilities

Does the company have up-to-date production methods? Is the equipment efficient? Is it expensive? When was the last time the salesperson walked through the production department? The salesperson should understand the process that the product goes through in the production facility. The salesperson may also need knowledge of plant capacity, production schedules, and other relevant data. Many companies require that their new salespeople spend time in the production facility, which gives them firsthand insight into the operational side of the business.

Salespeople should also spend time in the warehouse to gain product knowledge. This time can also be used to develop a good working relationship with the organization's personnel. Interdepartmental relationships are a prerequisite to expediting successful sales transactions.

Knowledge of the manufacturing process may provide the salesperson with solid information when responding to quality-conscious buyers. For example, sometimes clothing buyers express interest in the dying and weaving processes used. The care and standards undertaken in the manufacturing process can be significant features. Emphasizing testing procedures often can prove valuable. For customized products, hand workmanship is often stressed.

Socially Responsible Activities

Does your company participate in programs that are beneficial to society and the community? Salespeople should be aware of programs that are important to the public and promote them widely. Generally, a company wishes to communicate its concerns and support efforts toward environmental and social issues to gain a favorable image and build goodwill.

When offerings are relatively equal among competitors, a prospect is inclined to patronize a company that supports causes beneficial to society.

Know Your Product and Service

Product Information

Competent salespeople want to know how their products are made, how they interface with related products, what services are provided for the products they offer, and, most importantly, how their products satisfy their customers' needs. In fact, research consistently shows that the most effective salespeople have extensive knowledge about their products.[7] Little respect is paid to those salespeople who do not understand the technical aspects of their products or how they enhance their customer's operation. Exhibit 5.6 illustrates the importance placed on product information by one company.

Listed below are four categories of information that salespeople may want to know about their products and services:

1. *Materials*—Where was the product grown, mined, manufactured, or assembled? What does it contain? What quality control procedures are involved?
2. *Design*—Who designed the product? How was it made? What engineering data, if any, are important to know? What are the unique product features?
3. *Application*—How is the product or service used? How do other customers use it? Who handles the installation and training? How does it work or operate?
4. *Guarantees and Warranties*—Who assumes responsibility: Is there a manufacturer's warranty or a retailer guarantee? How is the customer protected against a defective product? What is the company's return policy?

Service Support

Good service support is an expectation in most selling transactions, and the company with a strong service program can gain a competitive edge. It is important that salespeople *not* promise services that their companies cannot deliver. In many industries service provisions help to differentiate a company from its competition. This is particularly true in foreign markets. In fact, international sales of technical products need service capability to give the company credibility with foreign buyers.

Buyers may ask:

- Does the company service its products?
- Is the service department local?
- Is there a charge for this service?
- What does company service include?
- How long will service take?
- Under what conditions are the services available?

Buyers want to know what services are available should something go wrong. Support services should be studied and a description of them integrated into the sales presentation, adding to overall customer satisfaction by meeting these needs. The availability of excellent service facilities is of vital importance to many buyers. Service, technical assistance, and other product support activities, such as training personnel to use the equipment, are particularly important in industrial sales.

Exhibit 5.6

Adding Information Power to the Sales Force's Punch

Scott Walker sounds like your typical software salesperson: "Let me tell you about this new software," he says enthusiastically. "It's quite exciting. It has very, very advanced mechanisms that enable you to go in in a very user-friendly way to examine the information, organize it, and ask questions."

Despite appearances, though, Walker is not a software vendor. He's a software buyer, director of business planning and analysis for the Golden Cat Corp. of South Bend, Ind. The software he is so excited about is called SalesPartner, part of a general information service program offered by Information Resources, Inc., of Chicago.

SalesPartner and similar database software are examples of SFA at its best—when it not only automates a traditional paper function, but improves it beyond previous capabilities. And it is only the tip of the information iceberg. Companies like Dow Jones News Retrieval, Nexis, and Dialog are literally putting libraries at salespeople's beck and call.

Marketers have long recognized that information is power and have long relied on industry reports, such as SAMI, in their planning and selling. SAMI is a supermarket industry report that measures warehouse withdrawals.

Computers (and cash register scanners) have made these reports more sophisticated, more accurate, and more quickly available. What companies like Nielsen and IRI Resources have done is develop creative and user-friendly ways to make this information meaningful and much more usable.

What IRI has done, with software it calls DataServer, is surround those bare bone facts with several additional and important layers of information. Let Golden Cat Corp.'s Walker explain:

"DataServer integrates the sales information with powerful, action-oriented merchandising information. It will tell you what feature ads the stores are running, what displays are taking place in the stores, what pricing is happening, what couponing is happening, what kind of distribution you have on the product.

"With this information, you can attribute margin efficiencies and effectiveness to each individual marketing and sales vehicle. That's an incredibly powerful tool for managing the business and allocating funding in a way that generates incremental sales and profitability."

Golden Cat is the largest producer of cat box filler (it manufactures the Kitty Litter brand) in the nation, with about 40 percent of the $500 million (at retail) market.

It works exclusively through food brokers supervised by six district and six regional managers. (The districts and regions coincide.) The industry—like the consumer package goods business, in general—is very competitive, and this kind of information is considered key to maintaining and improving market share.

"We went through a process internally where we agonized," Walker recalls. "Not everybody understood the merits of placing technology in the hands of the sales force directly. It was a job of explaining to people what regional managers would use this equipment for and why it was not merely a matter of 'selling the product.' You had to be closer to the information."

The explaining apparently went well, because senior management did more than just okay the purchase of new computers for regional managers. It also authorized adding new applications to the company's mainframe "that allow better tracking of sales histories, shipment histories and orders," as well as communications software that linked the regional offices with the mainframe.

But what gets Walker really excited is new IRI software called SalesPartner.

"It tells you in the English language what conditions are in the marketplace, conditions in the account, what the opportunities are. It even tells you the kind of information that is important to convey to the account, about what's going on and what should be done.

"It scans the information in the IRI database and based on a wide array of logic actually comes back and helps you build a story to take to the account. It looks for business-building opportunities in terms of new distribution, better merchandising, and how to highlight to the account the profit and sales contributions of your items versus the competition.

"More important, it's all available via a direct link to IRI's computers in Chicago. So we don't have to store, maintain, and update the information on individual PCs."

Companies like Nexis, Dialog, and Dow Jones News Retrieval have vast libraries that salespeople can call up to get anything from current news straight off the wire services to a decade-old story from the trade press. For example, Larry Joyce, an account executive with IBM in New York City, is hooked up to Dow Jones News Retrieval.

"When I turn my PC on at work in the morning, the first thing I do is check Dow Jones News Retrieval to get the headlines about the companies I'm interested in," he says. His computer is programmed to scan for news about his clients.

Dow Jones provides general news, government and regulatory agency news, economic and stock market news, as well as a full line of trade publications written for dozens of industries from accounting and acquisitions to truck lines and utilities.

"Customers want us to know what's going on in their business," Joyce says. "They want us to provide solutions.

"This is a tough economic climate, and it helps to know a lot about your customers and industry. I think it's critical to success.

"The fact is there's a lot of data sales people could and would use if it were easier to get," Joyce says. "This makes it easy."

Source: Excerpted from advertisement, *Sales & Marketing Management*, March 1991.

Additional service support offerings may include delivery, installation, maintenance, guarantees, and related elements. The following related elements are worth considering:

- Product performance-enhancing services—These may include aid in selection, adjustments to make the product work properly, altering the product to fit a special need, and instruction in optimal use.
- Prolonging the product life by stocking parts over a long period—If this year's Ford is to be produced only until July 15, how many extra front left fenders should be produced to provide spares for the next 5 years?
- Risk reduction by offering return privileges and warranty—Under what conditions will a paper manufacturer, for example, accept rejects or grant allowances for paper that is lighter in weight than promised?
- Reduction of purchase effort—The company may offer phone and mail-order privileges, provide parking facilities, take orders at trade shows, and so on.
- Reduction of capital required—This can be accomplished through credit terms, selling on consignment, floor-plan financing of inventory for retailers, and several years' contractual financing of retailers' furniture and fixtures.
- Efficiency-increasing services—The manufacturer can do accounting for the manufacturer's representatives; the wholesaler may perform inventory control for the retailer; and the retailer can provide restaurant and nursery facilities for the consumers' convenience.

- Sales-increasing services for the reseller—These include training retail salespeople, providing specialists' advice in local advertising, and controlling floor traffic through layout.
- Meeting customers' intangible need to feel important—Courtesy, prompt attention, and friendliness in handling complaints are means of accomplishing this, as well as asking for opinions about possible new products and services.[8]

Converting Product Knowledge into Benefits

As salespeople acquire product knowledge, they will be learning about their product on three levels: features, advantages, and benefits.

- Feature—A feature is a *fact* about the product or service. It is generally an observable property or attribute and may involve the buyer's sense of touch, taste, sight, hearing, or smell.
- Advantage—The advantage explains the *function* of the feature, a performance characteristic that has buyer appeal.
- Benefit—A benefit is the *satisfaction* that the buyer derives from a particular advantage or feature. It is an emotional or rational sense of value that the buyer receives from the product or service.

The challenge for the salesperson is to convert his knowledge into benefits. Ultimately, focusing on the benefit is more likely to complete an exchange transaction than stressing product features or advantages.

The FAB model will be developed thoroughly in Chapter 12. Because it is the core of the presentational system for the relational process, we introduce it briefly now so that you can think about it as we move through the seven basic selling steps. Figure 5.1 effectively illustrates how the FAB approach may prepare salespeople to address customer benefits.

Know Your Competition

Competition is the cornerstone of the American free enterprise system and the force behind improving product quality, services, and price limits. It is also the springboard from which personal selling has evolved into the relationship process.

It is almost inevitable that salespeople will encounter competition on both domestic and international levels, giving buyers still greater choice. And as choices continue to multiply, salespeople *must* know the features, advantages, and benefits that distinguish their products from the competition's. In fact, all items listed in the "Know Your Company" section of this chapter also apply to a competitor's company. Table 5.1 depicts how one corporation provides comparison with the competitor when submitting a written proposal to a prospect.

Being knowledgeable about the competition helps salespeople to make accurate comparisons between their products and those of the competitors. After identifying the criteria to be used for comparison,

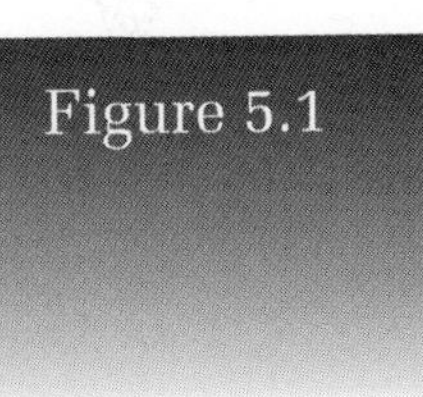

Figure 5.1

Selling Product Benefits

MacGregor recently advertised its Tourney golf clubs in a manner that effectively showed the clubs' *features*, *advantages*, and *benefits*. A portion of this advertisement illustrates how products should be sold in terms of customer benefits.

Feature	Advantage	Benefit
Compact woodhead model	Smaller head provides golfer with more confidence on controlling club	More *confidence* results in smoother swing for more control
Shallow-faced fairway woods	Ball leaves club above high point of 9" roll	Gets ball into air *easier*
12-degree lofted driver	Extra loft makes it easier to get ball into air off tee	Gives more *consistency* and *control* with driver
All edge grain maple laminate	Hardest surface of maple is positioned toward the face	More *durability* in face area
Sole weighted blade	Lower center of gravity	Imparts *more spin* to get ball into air *easier* and *quicker*
Wider effective hitting area	Allows ball to fly well if hit off center	*Straighter, longer shots* on off center hits
Offset blade	Forces hands to lead clubhead into the shot	Makes it *easier* for golfer to hit through shot

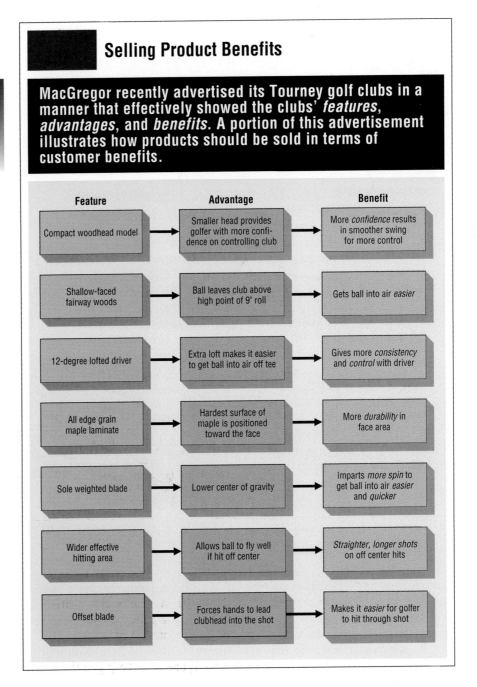

salespeople must determine the sources for obtaining such information. Sources of sales information will be discussed later in this chapter.

Management also has a responsibility to know the competitive environment and its impact on the company's present operations and future plans. There is also a responsibility to exchange competitive information with the company's salespeople. Here are some of the questions that management should ask:

Table 5.1

Comparison of Product Features

Feature	Present Copier	Proposed System
Speed		
Rated speed	10 per minute	40 per minute
Warm-up	None	None
First copy	15 seconds	8 seconds
Flexibility—Copy on:		
Plain cut-sheet bond paper	No	Yes
Digital letterhead	No	Yes
Gummed labels	No	Yes
Transparencies	No	Yes
Colored stock	No	Yes
Copying bound volumes	Only for volumes up to 1 inch thick	Yes, books of any thickness
Copying on both sides of paper	No	Yes
Capacities		
Paper tray capacity	625 8½ × 11 copies per roll	2,000 sheets
Toner capacity	16,000 copies	16,000 copies
Productivity*	10 copies per minute; manual feeding and manual sorting	40 copies per minute; automatically feeds originals and sorts finished copies

* Productivity refers to personnel who have increased their output by doing unproductive chores (copying, sorting, changing originals) much more rapidly and then returned to their more productive duties.

- What kind of competition is our company apt to confront?
- What is known about the size of the competitors' companies?
- What is the availability (actual or potential) of competing and substitute products?
- How do our company's prices compare with those in the rest of the industry?
- How does our product quality compare?
- Who is the competition now? Who will be the competition 5 years from now?
- What are the strategies, objectives, and goals of major competitors?
- How important is a specific market to each competitor, and what is the level of its commitment to that market?
- What are our competitors' relative strengths and limitations?
- What weaknesses make the competition vulnerable?

- What changes are competitors likely to make in their future strategies?
- What effects will the competitors' strategies have on the industry, the market, and our strategy?[9]

Ethical and Legal Concerns Relating to the Competition

You and a salesperson from a competitive international firm are waiting in the lobby. Upon leaving the room, the competitor leaves his briefcase open, exposing information that appears to be confidential. Would you review it? This concern is proposed to emphasize the fact that salespeople faced with increased competition are exposed to opportunities encouraging them to become more aggressive to survive.

The ethical and legal aspects of selling are discussed specifically in Chapter 3, but the topic is mentioned again here to emphasize that salespeople must be knowledgeable about ethical and legal concerns.

Discussing the competition with a prospect can be a touchy subject, especially when a salesperson wants to become aggressive under intensive competitive pressures. The focus should be kept on the sales interaction relative to the company's products. Recognize that each company's product may have strengths and limitations.

Criticizing or discrediting a competitor may encourage the prospect to seek out more information on the competition. At the same time, however, this gives the prospect cause to question the salesperson's integrity. The salesperson should always be able to substantiate statements made about competitors. The salesperson and the company could be liable for false and defamatory statements about a competitor's offerings.

Some guidelines may be helpful for salespeople in addressing the questions and issues surrounding competing products:

1. In most cases, do not refer to the competition during the sales presentation. This will shift the focus of attention to competing products, which is usually not desirable. Always respond to direct questions, but do not initiate the topic.
2. Never discuss the competition unless you have your facts straight. Your credibility will suffer if inaccurate statements are made. If you do not know the answer to a specific question, simply say, "I don't know." It is also best to avoid generalizations about the competition.
3. Avoid criticizing the competition. You may be called on to make direct comparisons between competing products. In these situations, stick to the facts, and avoid emotional comments regarding apparent or actual weaknesses. Prospects tend to become suspicious of salespeople who initiate strong criticism of the competition. Your critical comments might be viewed as an attempt to divert attention from shortcomings in your own product.[10]

Legal issues involving a salesperson's activities with the competition could stem from an act such as "bugging" the competitor's office or making untrue statements about a competitor's product. Lawsuits have also resulted from a salesperson's carelessness when referring to a competitor in a sales presentation. Exhibit 5.7 serves as a reminder to salespeople to watch their words.

Develop a Positive Attitude toward the Competition

The attitude that salespeople display toward their competitors will have a major effect on the rapport they are building with a prospect. Therefore, the professional salesperson should strive to maintain a good relationship with the prospect, always taking care not to be offensive. Prospects typically resent critical and judgmental remarks about the competition. It is acceptable for a customer to make a negative comment about the competition; however, it is important that the salesperson not participate in the criticism. Overall, consideration and honesty are greatly appreciated and respected among professionals.

Is there an ethical yardstick for salespeople to turn to when referring to and dealing with competition? "Let your conscience be your guide" seems to be the theme. On the legal side, would you wish to participate in illegal conduct, such as defamatory statements about a competitor's product, that could lead to a felony conviction and even a jail sentence? Let the law be your guide.

Sources of Sales Information

The sources from which information can be secured are extensive and fairly easy to acquire. Successful companies distribute pertinent information to their salespeople regularly to keep them abreast of new

Exhibit 5.7

Legally Referring to the Competition

1. Review promotional literature to ensure that references to competition are accurate.
2. Avoid repeating unconfirmed trade gossip, particularly about a competitor's financial condition.
3. Avoid statements that impair the reputation of a business or individual.
4. Avoid making unfair or inaccurate comparisons about a competitor's products.

Source: Steven Mitchell Sack, "Watch the Words," *Sales & Marketing Management*, July 1985, pp. 56–58.

developments. Information is easily accessible today, and staying ahead in one's industry demands mastering information technology, which will be explored in Chapter 17.

Prime sources of information available to salespeople are divided between internal sources (those within the company) and external sources.

Sources within the Company

Information is available from a wide variety of company sources: sales and service manuals, sales meetings, company literature (including handbooks, publications, and bulletins), advertising, and sales and product training programs. The typical content of sales training programs, based on a survey of 152 companies, is shown in Table 5.2.

Additional informational support can be acquired from the sales manager, salespeople, service, warehouse, and research and testing labs.

Sources outside the Company

External sources can provide the professional salesperson with tremendous amounts of data. One major group of sources is the literature and professional magazines published by trade associations. Similar types of information can be acquired from the newspapers, television, trade associations, and business magazines. Many business publications, such as *Business Week, Fortune, The Economist, The Wall Street Journal,* and the *Financial Times,* are standard information sources worldwide.

In deciding which international publications to use, an exporter must apply the general principles of marketing communications strategy. Coverage and circulation information is available from Standard Rate and Data. This organization provides a complete list of international publications in the International Section of *The Business Publication,* and audit information similar to that on the U.S. market is provided for the United Kingdom, Italy, France, Austria, Switzerland, Germany,

Table 5.2

Topics Covered in Sales Training Programs

Topic	Percent of Training Time
Product Information	42%
Market-Industry Information	17
Company Information	13
Selling Techniques	24
Other Topics	4
	100%

Source: David S. Hopkins, *Training the Sales Force: A Progress Report* (New York: The Conference Board, 1984), p. 1.

Mexico, and Canada. Outside of these areas, the exporter must rely on the assistance of publishers or local representatives.[11]

Additional information sources include customer feedback, libraries, educational institutions, trade association offices, conferences and seminars, factory tours, labels and tags on products and their containers, brochures, exhibitions, and trade shows and fairs.

A good source for international activity is government-sponsored tours and trade shows. Participation in trade shows depends largely on the type of business relationship the company wants to develop with a particular country. A company looking only for one-time or short-term involvement may find the investment worthwhile.[12]

Information about competitors' products may also be obtained from competitive sales literature and advertising, trade association magazines, trade shows, sales conventions, claims of competitive salespeople, and customers' experiences with competitive products. Additional data that should be obtained on the competition are listed in Exhibit 5.8.

Exhibit 5.8

Data to Be Gathered on Competitors

Names and addresses
Products manufactured—SIC
Principal officers and executives (organization)
Geographical coverage
Total sales over past 5 years (and earnings)
Net worth
Inventory (such as in process, finished goods)
Plant and warehouse size
Number of salesmen, distributors, employees
Number and location of branches
Share of market
Selling methods
Competitive practices (such as allowances, terms, discounts)
Advertising and promotion methods, plans, and apparent results
What your and their customers think of them
Quality, performance, and reliability of products
Shipment lead time
Promptness of deliveries
Field service capability
Costs: production, distribution, and service
Research and development capability
Strengths and weaknesses of competitive products
Operating advantages and disadvantages of products
Guarantees and warranties

Source: Cochrane Chase and Kenneth L. Barasch, *Marketing Problem Solver*, (Radnor, PA: Chilton Book Company, 1977), p. 12.

Summary

Salespeople must be thoroughly familiar with industry, company, product, and competitive information to be prepared for the demands and expectations of the sales situation. Professional selling is most effective when the salesperson develops a measure of confidence in the eyes of the prospect.

The salesperson must be well informed of industry trends and developments. The professional should understand economic trends and how the industry relates to the overall economy. To benefit fully from company knowledge, the salesperson must acquire information about the company's standing in the industry, the history of the company's organization and personnel, pricing and distribution policies, and socially responsible activities.

Product knowledge is important, particularly in industrial settings because of the technical requirements. The most common product information the salesperson should learn to meet customers' demands and expectations is knowledge of the materials, design, application, and guarantees and warranties. Converting product knowledge into customer benefits involves three levels: features, advantages, and benefits. This FAB approach becomes the core of the presentational system upon which the relational selling process is built.

A challenging task for salespeople is to determine their product differences and competitive advantages. It pays to study major competitors, competitive offerings, and ethical and legal concerns regarding competitive activity. A good sales presentation, tailored to stress the selling points of product or service in terms of resulting benefits, is the way to beat competition.

Finally, salespeople can gather information from various sources within and outside the company. Sales professionals must regularly obtain information that is important to the customer. Learning about their industry, company, products, and competition is a continuous activity—the process never ends.

Key Terms

Advantage A term used to describe the function of a feature

Benefit Satisfaction the buyer derives from a particular advantage or feature

Feature A benefit fact related to a product or service

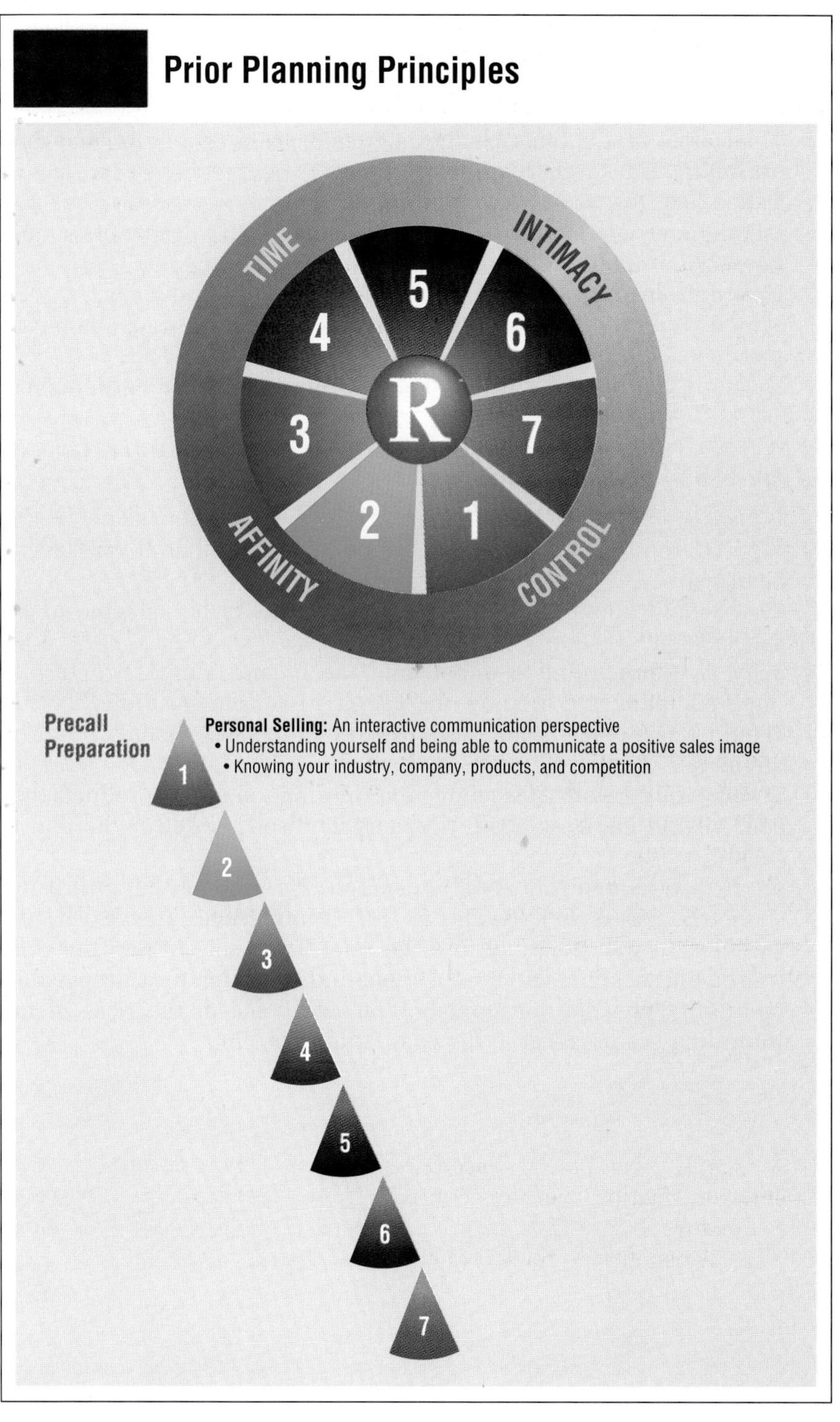
Prior Planning Principles
TIME
INTIMACY
AFFINITY
CONTROL
R
5
4
6
3
7
2
1
Precall Preparation
Personal Selling: An interactive communication perspective
• Understanding yourself and being able to communicate a positive sales image
• Knowing your industry, company, products, and competition
1
2
3
4
5
6
7

Review Questions

1. How does product knowledge benefit the salesperson?
2. The lack of product knowledge exposes the salesperson to what risks during the sales transaction?
3. Define features, advantages, and benefits.
4. List the four most important types of information salespeople should know about their company.
5. How do salespeople generally acquire their sales knowledge?
6. Why do buyers expect salespeople to know the features of competing products?
7. Give at least three reasons to avoid criticizing the competition.

Discussion Questions

1. Why is product knowledge more important today than it was several years ago?
2. How would knowing the history of an industry be valuable to the salesperson?
3. Why is it important to understand the organizational structure of one's company and to know the people in various positions?
4. Would a customer be interested in how the salesperson's products are made? Why or why not?
5. Where would retail salespeople find information on the products they sell? Would knowing about the merchandise they sell be helpful to them?
6. A prospect is unaware about a competitor's product that will better serve the customer's needs. If this information is revealed, the salesperson will probably lose the sale. If the salesperson does not inform the customer and the customer finds out later, the salesperson's credibility may be questioned. What are some of the risks of not informing the prospect of the competitor's product?

Is the Customer Always Right?

Case 5.1

The Empire Shoe Store trains its salespeople to respect company policy, stipulating that the customer is always right. More specifically, every shoe is sold with a 100% guaranteed money-back refund if a customer is dissatisfied with a purchase for any reason.

Empire is proud of its loyal clientele and few customer complaints. All the salespeople undergo extensive training in proper fitting procedures to ensure the best possible fit for the customer. Also, as part of an overall performance evaluation, management keeps track of the number of shoes returned per month. The salesperson earns no commission on a returned shoe transaction.

In one instance, James Paul was faced with a dilemma after taking necessary steps to suggest the right size for a particular prospect's needs. He made a concerted effort to advise the prospect of the appropriate fitting shoe, stating that proper fit is essential for good health and comfort. He concluded that a tight fit would be painful after wearing the shoe for several hours. Nonetheless, the prospect refused to listen to James' recommendation and decided that the larger size was unattractive, favoring the smaller pair simply for aesthetic reasons.

"It is ridiculous to wear shoes that do not fit properly," James remarked abruptly. James then refused to conclude the sales transaction based on the prospect's unacceptable choice because he felt certain that the sale would result in dissatisfaction, eventually having a negative effect on his evaluation for the month.

1. With respect to company policy, would it be appropriate to conclude that the customer is right in this instance?
2. If the prospect chooses to purchase the smaller sized shoes and later returns them claiming dissatisfaction, what should James do?
3. What might be a more desirable approach for James to take in persuading the prospect to select the appropriate size?

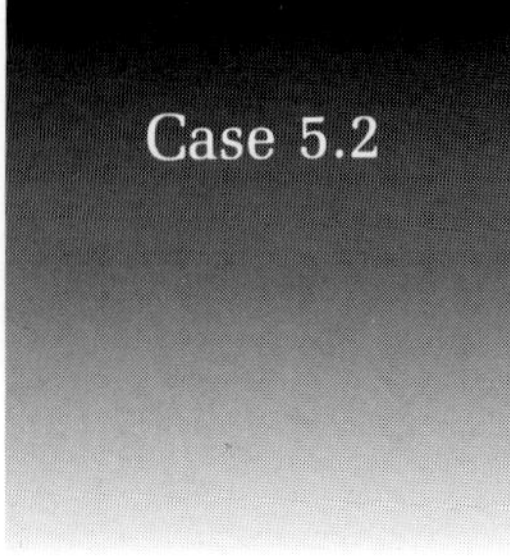

Japanese Marketing as an Interactive System

A visit to a major consumer electronics firm in Japan revealed that the Japanese had a very strong tradition of innovating and developing products that were more functional and conveniently in tune with people's lifestyles than certain other countries. The Japanese products were also aesthetically appealing.

In comparing the Japanese company with American firms in the same industry, senior executives with experience working in the United States stated that the Japanese did more in-depth studies of consumers' needs through a combination of formal research and frequent contacts between managers and consumers. From these findings they developed a guiding principle, or umbrella concept, covering the product range and presented it to the customers in a unique manner.

Engineers and sales people also interacted frequently to discuss new products. When a product failed, it was not through lack of internal discussions, but because the company's product development had gotten behind the competition.

Furthermore, in comparing the Japanese sales activities with those of American firms, the executives felt that the selling activities of American firms were based on learning and following the sales manual, where the Japanese trained their salespeople to go beyond the manual and develop real empathy with the customers. Partnership with customers was also an important part of the Japanese philosophy, embodied in such phrases as "we are in the same boat," "we have grown together," and "your problem is our problem." This philosophy was based on mutual trust and the idea that it took a long time to develop mature relationships.

1. Discuss the methods used by the Japanese company as applied to sales activities.
2. Express your support of or disfavor toward the following statements:
   a. Japanese companies are more likely to direct their efforts toward 'developing interaction among company members.
   b. Shared information is extremely beneficial in response to innovation.
   c. Innovation and attention to customers' needs lead to a steady stream of new products.
3. How important are the practices of the Japanese company in staying competitive?

Source: Nigel Campbell, *Japanese Marketing as an Interactive System* (Lyon, France: International Marketing and Purchasing Group Conference, 1986).

Notes

1. Daniel M. Rosen, "EC '92: A Guide for the Small Company," *Sales & Marketing Management*, September 1990, p. 96.
2. Ibid.
3. Edith Cohen, "A View from the Other Side," *Sales & Marketing Management*, June 1990, p. 108.
4. John A. Byrne, Deidre A. Depke, and John W. Verity, "IBM—As Markets and Technology Change, Can Big Blue Remake Its Culture?," *Business Week*, June 17, 1991, p. 28.
5. Ibid., pp. 28–29.
6. Robert W. Haas, *Industrial Marketing Management*, 4th ed., (Mass: PWS-Kent, 1989), p. 134.
7. Harish Sujan, Mita Sujan, and James R. Bettman, "Knowledge Structure Differences between More Effective and Less Effective Salespeople," *Journal of Marketing Research*, February 1988, pp. 81–86.
8. Thomas Stroh, *Managing the Sales Function* (New York: McGraw-Hill Book Company, 1978), p. 90.
9. Michael G. Allen, "Strategic Planning with a Competitive Focus," *The McKinsey Quarterly*, Autumn 1978, p. 6.
10. Gernal Manning and Barry Reece, *Selling Today*, 4th ed. (Boston: Allyn & Bacon, 1990), p. 139.
11. Michael R. Czinkota and Ilkka A. Ronkainen, *International Marketing* (Chicago: The Dryden Press, 1988), p. 257.
12. Ibid., p. 258.

ased on the relational selling model, the next four chapters cover areas that are related to the preapproach step in the selling process. The topics covered are identifying prospects, understanding buyer behavior and the buying process, creating a positive buying climate, and listening effectively for selling success.

This chapter is devoted to prospecting and is divided into five sections. The first section discusses the importance and benefits of prospecting and distinguishes between *suspects* and *prospects*. The second explains criteria for qualifying prospects, while the third section describes methods for finding qualified potential buyers. In the fourth section we will recommend some of the most popular sources salespeople use for locating information about their prospects. The final section contains ideas and procedures for managing prospect information.

The Importance of Prospecting

Prospecting is one of the least understood areas of selling. Prospecting is a task that is often neglected because, although it takes place early in the selling cycle, the results occur late in the cycle. Quite often, a salesperson's prospecting efforts may produce little or no evident gain. In spite of the obstacles, however, prospecting continues to yield the "gold" every salesperson is searching for.

Paul Meyer, president of Success Motivation Institute in Waco, Texas, stresses the importance of prospecting:

> Develop a prospecting consciousness—a prospecting awareness; it is the key to your success in professional selling. Prospecting is to successful selling what breathing is to living. There are prospects by the millions if you open your eyes and see them.[1]

Exhibit 6.1 lends additional support for the importance of prospecting, as demonstrated by Thomas Ortel during his 25 years of experience in selling insurance.

Prospecting Defined

Prospecting is a systematized process for identifying and locating potential customers. Companies such as IBM, Burroughs, Hewlett-Packard, Xerox, Cannon, and Ricoh seldom wait for buyers to ask to purchase their machines. In most cases, the salesperson seeks out buyers. Unlike field salespeople who initiate the contact, retail salespeople generally rely on potential buyers to seek them out. Thus, methods for retail prospecting are limited to procedures that accommodate the retail or ultimate consumer.

When looking at an entire target market for a product or service, each person within that market is a *suspect*. A *lead* is any person or organization that could benefit from buying the product or service. A *prospect* is a qualified potential buyer who has the ability and authority to complete

Exhibit 6.1

Prospecting Strength through Numbers

Thomas E. Ortel has been successfully selling life insurance for almost twenty-five years with John Hancock Insurance Company as a regular member of the Million Dollar Round Table. Ortel has found through experience that the key to success in selling is having an abundant supply of prospects to call on. His approach to prospecting begins with an attitude that prospecting must be done consistently, systematically, and religiously, realizing that the salesperson can take advantage of the law of averages, assuming enough leads are generated. Ortel routinely spends each Monday morning reviewing prospects he's generated from his three basic sources: new members of the community identified through Welcome Wagon, referrals from satisfied customers, and replies from direct mailings. Ortel knows that this prospecting time is absolutely essential to each week's sales productivity. Ortel says, "For most people, prospecting is not fun, but it is necessary. It's one of the main things that separates the successes from the failures in the life insurance business."

Source: Thomas E. Ortel, "Prospecting: Safety in Numbers," *Life Association News*, September 1986, pp. 139–140.

the transaction. Qualifying is the act of identifying legitimate buyers based on, but not limited to, four general criteria:

1. Benefit from buying the product or service—Buyer receives some additional utility.
2. Eligibility to buy—Buyer meets a minimum level of projected sales volume, size requirements, and so on.
3. Ability to pay—Buyer is able to finance the purchase.
4. Authority to buy—Buyer is a key account influence in the buying process.

For example, a small company that develops and sells software programs for accounting systems could say that anyone who has a legitimate business and who keeps records and pays taxes and salaries is a suspect for purchasing an accounting software program. It is unrealistic, however, to assume that all businesses will buy software packages. Using the above guidelines, the company's salesperson may establish the following criteria:

1. Benefit—One utility received is the money prospects will save by automating their accounting systems.
2. Eligibility—The prospect must own or lease IBM-compatible computer hardware and must have annual revenue of \$15–75 million.
3. Ability—The company must have a solid credit rating and be able to meet monthly billing fees of X dollars.
4. Authority—The prospect must be either the key influence or final decision maker or both.

Of course, other conditions may be added to these criteria by the salesperson's company. Nevertheless, it is usually the salesperson's responsibility to separate suspects from prospects.

Benefits to the Overall Sales Effort

Prospecting is important to the overall sales effort because existing customers must be replaced periodically. Most estimates of annual customer turnover fall in the range of 10–25 percent. This means that a significant portion of the firm's customers cease to buy its products every year.[2]

The loss of customers can be attributed to a wide variety of reasons:

- A customer may go out of business.
- A customer's business may be acquired by a larger firm that buys from a different source.
- The buyer the salesperson has been selling to may transfer, retire, or resign.
- A customer may move out of the salesperson's territory.
- A customer may die, become ill, or have an accident.
- A customer may have only a one-time need for the product or service.
- A customer may be lost to a competing salesperson.[3]

As a continuing part of the sales effort, salespeople must be ready to replace lost accounts with others and continue to prospect for new buyers. Otherwise, their companies' sales will decline over time. Joe Girard, a popular sales consultant, calls this process of continually finding people and firms the ferris wheel of selling. Imagine a ferris wheel at an amusement park with a line of people waiting to get on. The operator will stop the wheel periodically to let some riders off and other riders on. In this way, the ferris wheel is always fully occupied.

Unlike the person in the ferris wheel line who is already holding a ticket, a salesperson often must approach many potential "riders" before any "tickets" are sold. The extent of one's contacts depends on the industry, company, products, and competitiveness. For example, in the insurance industry it may take 100 suspects to obtain 50 prospects, leading to 25 sales presentations and finally resulting in 12 sales.[4] Consequently, only about one of nine suspects becomes a customer.

In the high-tech industries, prospecting can be even more demanding. For instance, in the computer business, 125 phone calls may result in 25 interviews leading to five demonstrations and one sale.[5]

Qualifying Prospects

Not all prospects are the same. A principal step in developing a prospecting system is to establish qualifying criteria before the salesperson makes the first sales call. The objective for establishing these criteria is to allow salespeople to get the most out of their selling time. As a result, they will be calling on the people and organizations who show the most potential for buying, rather than wasting their time on those who probably will not buy.

Proper qualification of prospects involves obtaining a positive response to four basic questions:

1. **Does the prospect have a need or want?** If the salesperson determines that the prospect can gain benefits and use the product or service to his or her advantage, then a need or want exists. (Determining the extent of needs is addressed in Chapter 7.) Once again, the benefits must add some additional utility—the quality or property of being useful.
2. **Does the prospect have the authority or influence to buy?** Identifying and talking with the person who is responsible for making or influencing the buying decision is an essential step in the "authority" criterion. For example, for household purchases in the United States, the wife may be influential over the husband in many buying decisions. On the other hand, decisions regarding expensive products may be made jointly, involving both husband and wife.

   In the industrial setting, the production people or engineers may be instrumental in the purchase of tools, supplies, or equipment. In computer sales, the salesperson may have to see several decision makers individually or make a presentation before a group of executives. Sometimes a team, such as a buying committee, may be responsible for purchasing.

   Finding the individual with the buying power isn't always an easy task. Although the purchasing agent may place the order, someone else may have decision-making authority. It is important that salespeople not overlook the influence of those people who may be involved in the buying process, even though they may not have buying authority.
3. **Can the prospect afford to buy?** In addition to having a need, the prospect must have the ability to pay. A qualified potential buyer must have sufficient income. Similarly, businesses must demonstrate that they have good credit and are good risks for making their payments. Sources of credit information are mentioned later in this chapter.
4. **Can the prospect be approached favorably?** Some suspects have a need for the product or service, could afford to buy, have the authority to purchase, but still do not qualify. They are not approachable or accessible to the salesperson. Young salespeople may have difficulty approaching people in upper management or older clients. Prospects are more easily approached when they share similar backgrounds and interests with the salesperson. Therefore, as indicated in Chapter 5, it is vital to obtain the required knowledge in preparing for the sales interview. Being thoroughly prepared may help the salesperson feel more eligible to move through perceived barriers, such as differences in age, culture, and position.

Additional Criteria for Qualifying Prospects

Six additional questions are important in developing appropriate criteria to help salespeople match their prospects with their products:

1. What is the size of the prospect's business?
2. What type of business is it? Can one tell by the name?
3. How important are the size and location of the prospect's facilities to buying the salesperson's product and service?
4. What is the potential sales volume that can be generated from this prospect?
5. Into which of the following categories does this prospect fit?
    a. Present customer (Is there additional order potential?)
    b. Old or former customer who hasn't purchased recently (Has anyone approached the customer lately?)
    c. Lost customer (What is the reason for the loss?)
    d. New prospect
6. Based on potential account volume, how would all prospects be ranked or grouped?
    a. "A" (high-volume) Accounts—These include both existing and potential customers who are or will be the best customers of the firm.
    b. "B" (medium-volume) Accounts—These are typically existing customers who are not the "best" customers but have the potential to be. These customers usually have several sources from whom they buy.
    c. "C" (low-volume) Accounts—These are existing or new accounts that do not or are not likely to buy a large enough quantity of merchandise to make their business profitable to the company.

    Ranking customers by volume of business generated can help the salesperson to focus on important accounts and minimize time spent with less important ones. The following example proposes a method of ranking accounts with reference to the distribution of sales volume generated[6]:

- "A" accounts = 65% of sales volume from 15% of customers
- "B" accounts = 20% of sales volume from 20% of customers
- "C" accounts = 15% of sales volume from 65% of customers

Prospecting Methods

There are numerous methods for locating prospects. The appropriate method should be selected carefully to match the market toward which the product or service is targeted. Dorothy Leeds, a sales consultant, suggests painting a mental picture of the ideal prospect. This means

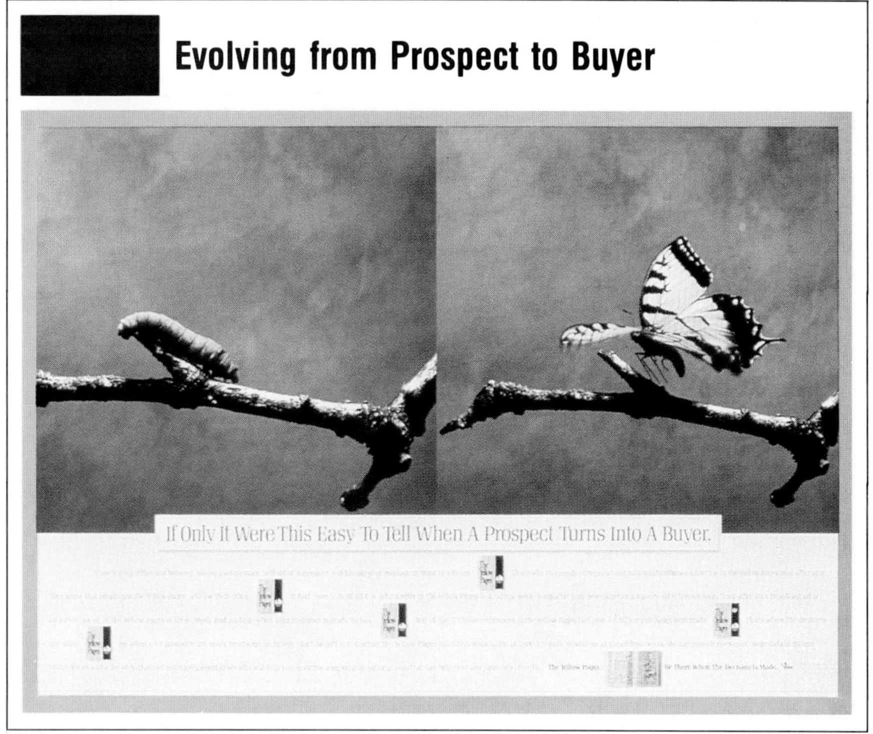

If Only It Were This Easy To Tell When A Prospect Turns Into A Buyer.

Exhibit 6.2

Evolving from Prospect to Buyer

selecting or describing this person according to the four qualifying criteria. This portrait then serves "as a standard against which you measure all potential customers and clients."[7] Once this portrait is clearly in mind, the next step is developing a plan to locate these prospects. This section describes popular prospecting methods used by salespeople working in the industrial, consumer, and service industries (Figure 6.1).

- Endless Chain—This method is based on the idea that from each interview, a salesperson will secure the names of additional prospects for future interviews. The salesperson may secure two or more names of people who possess similar qualifications, resulting in an exponential growth in the prospect pool. This method is most effective when the prospect is a satisfied user. It is especially effective when selling intangibles such as insurance or financial services.
- Referral—This includes any identification of a suspect by a third party. A referred lead may be the best kind of prospect because a basis of friendliness and mutual interest has been established between the salesperson and the referred prospect through the salesperson's customer. A prospect to whom the salesperson is referred will usually listen out of deference to the friend or associate who made the referral.

  A referral paves the way for a sales interview by having the customer initiate a telephone call, a letter of introduction, or a

Figure 6.1

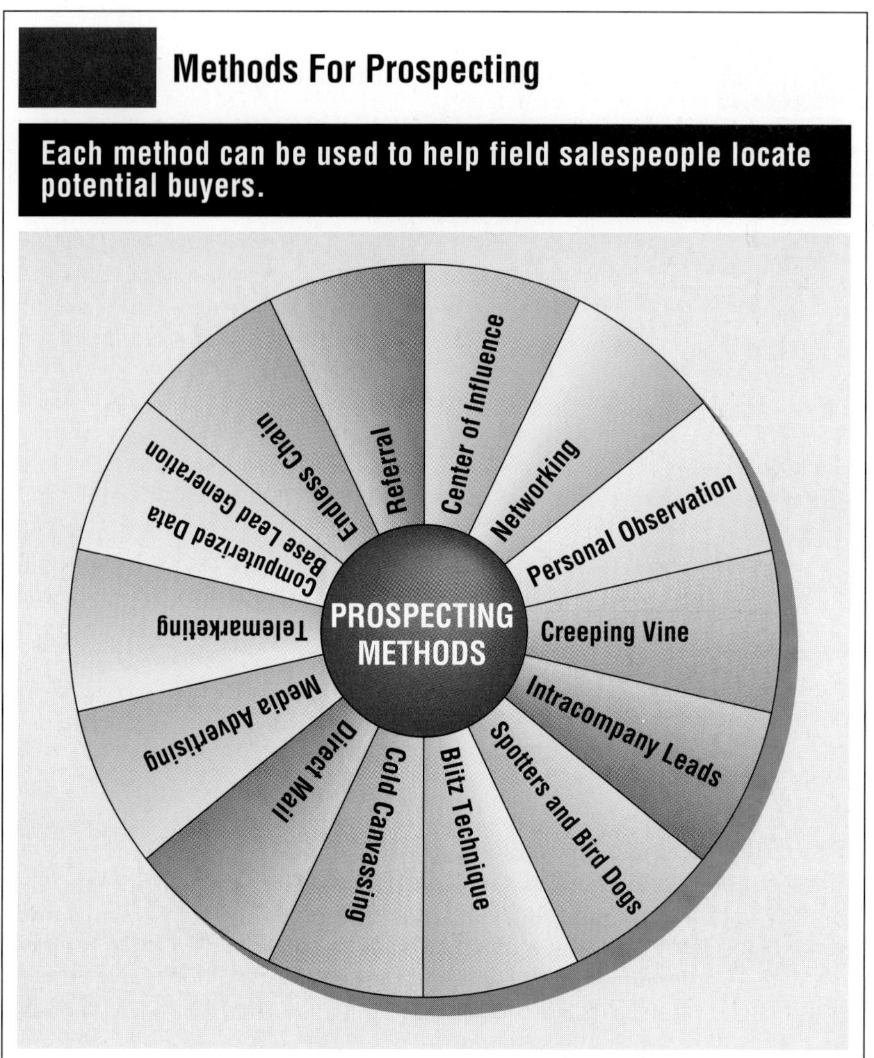

personal introduction. Referral selling is used widely in industrial sales and when reaching the key decision maker may be extremely difficult.

- Center of Influence—Using the center of influence approach, the salesperson cultivates relationships with several influential people in the community who are in a position to refer leads and are willing to do so. Influential people have prestige, which the prospect transfers to the salesperson. Bankers and key executives are helpful in this respect. Noncompeting sources of leads also include community leaders who have business, cultural, political, and religious influence.
- Networking—Networking is the process of making and using contacts. It involves connecting people with people based on their business and social contacts. Affiliation with civic, religious, professional, fraternal, or other national organizations (such as

Sales Professional Spotlight

When the stock market crashed in 1987, Tal Wilson was a successful sales manager for Sears, Roebuck and Company who yearned to get back into personal selling. Though the market decline would have blinded most people to a career opportunity in the full-service brokerage industry, it gave Tal the chance to satisfy his longings.

Tal had been one of Sears' top salespeople before his promotion to management. He is the first to credit his success in selling to prospecting. "When I started selling for Sears, prospecting meant standing closer to the aisle than the other salespeople," he says. Tal became a top producer because of his unique prospecting strategies in an industry that rarely used this sales cultivation method.

Tal kept records of all large transactions, and when walk-in business was slow he would call previous customers to see if their purchases were still satisfactory. These customers would often ask about features or instructions that were not clear; at the end of each call, Tal would ask if and when additional features would be needed, and request the name of someone else whom he might help. According to Tal, "Asking for a referral has always seemed like a natural conclusion to a sale. Customers always seem willing to share their good buying decisions with others."

Tal put his referral strategy to good use when, after the market debacle in 1987, he moved to Dean Witter, Inc., as an account executive. In 1988, the average account executive opened 63 accounts; Tal, through referrals, opened 194. In 1990 the average account executive opened 57 accounts; Tal opened 174. Tal is certain that he will more than double the company's average again in 1991.

Tal shares the simple key to getting referrals from satisfied clients with salespeople entering the brokerage business. He tells them, "I am sure this practice of asking current clients for referrals would work well in all types of selling." He says that high-quality clients will usually give high-quality referrals: "It takes just as much time to construct a large portfolio as a small one. And because time management is always a main concern for salespeople, we must constantly reevaluate our productivity levels."

Tal's success with new accounts also stems from his visibility in the community. He serves on two hospital boards, is presently the treasurer of the local branch of the American Red Cross, and is president of a local golf club. "My volunteer activity with the community sends me many referrals," he says. He strongly believes in supporting the community, which reflects on his personal integrity.

Tal is a superior salesperson because he believes in himself, his service, and his company. He conveys this feeling to his clients and prospects through his appearance, conviction, and commitment to his career. Tal stresses that "if you are not enthusiastic in what you are doing, you will never convince the prospect to buy, much less give you a referral."

the Lions, Rotary, Kiwanis, and chambers of commerce) are used to develop a reference point for expanding social contacts.

Networking organizations are especially popular among women in business and among small companies. The American Society for Training and Development is particularly popular in a wide range of professions and businesses.

Successful networkers suggest the following guidelines for developing meaningful contacts:

1. Meet as many people as possible. Networking can take place at a service club meeting, such as the chamber of commerce, or at a trade show, church social, or special function such as the opening of a gallery.
2. Customarily, salespeople should tell others what they do for a living. Networking is low-cost advertising.
3. Trying to do business or close the sale is inappropriate and impractical. Select a date to meet the new contact later.
4. Salespeople should edit their contacts and follow up. They should separate productive from nonproductive contacts and follow up on the productive ones by phone, letter, or personal visit.[8]

David Dworski is the head of Dworski and Associates, a Santa Monica, California, consulting firm. Dworski likens networking to "social selling."[9] In Exhibit 6.3, he discusses how salespeople should behave when networking at a party.

- Personal Observation—Personal observation involves recognizing leads under all circumstances in all situations. It requires being aware of the total environment in which the salesperson operates. For example, many salespeople travel a great deal. Contacts made in airports, in flight, or in transit may develop into leads.

  Sales professionals tend to consider their surroundings as reservoirs for future business. Sporting events, concerts, and community functions all provide additional opportunities for exchanging business cards to initiate networking. Current customers should be monitored for reordering or uncovering a need or want that they have not yet realized. Salespeople must also be careful when removing former prospects from their lists. Needs and conditions may change or improve their prospect status. Sometimes former prospects have problems with their current suppliers and are open to receiving new sources. In Table 6.1, note that all seven areas where insurance agents secure their prospects include sources for making use of personal observation.
- Creeping Vine—Sometimes referred to as "back-door" or "progressive" prospecting, the creeping vine method requires that the salesperson start the search in an indirect manner. Sometimes it may be extremely difficult, for whatever reasons, to make direct contact with the key buying influence or decision maker, so the salesperson goes through the "back door" and works through the

The Seven Deadly Sins of Socializing

Exhibit 6.3

If the business meal is the 100-yard dash of salesmanship, the party is its triathalon. In a room full of potential clients and/or competitors, the opportunities are vast and the risks all too real. Play a party right, and the next day a salesperson might just find a huge stack of orders on his or her desk. Play it wrong, and there might not even *be* a desk.

The trick is to avoid committing any of the Seven Deadly Sins of working a party. They are:

1. **Failing to set a goal.** Before stepping through the door, a salesperson should know who's going to be there, who he wants to meet, and have made arrangements to be introduced. The salesperson who doesn't do this will have nothing better to do than sample the hors d'oeuvres and in the long run will have accomplished nothing.
2. **Finding someone you know and clinging to that person throughout the evening.** This just isn't profitable in terms of building business. If you're there to work the room, work it. Tell salespeople to imagine they're the host instead of a guest. Tell them to circulate, introduce themselves, and introduce other guests to each other.
3. **Hiding in a corner, hoping the world will come to you.** It generally won't. The best place to station oneself is just to the left of the door inside the room. It's a proven fact that people tend to drift to their left as they enter. When they do, be ready to intercept. And be sure to say hello.
4. **Passing the very people you're there to meet, like ships in the night.** If planned introductions fail to materialize, salespeople should introduce themselves. A simple technique is to get close, wait for an opportune moment, then put out your hand. Tell them you've been looking forward to meeting them. Tell them you've admired their company, or a certain product, or the way they've marketed it. Most people are flattered to have their work recognized, and that will start the conversational ball rolling. You don't have to push hard, but you do have to break that inertia.
5. **Being inattentive.** In their desire to circulate, some people keep their eyes wandering around the room, obviously looking for the next target of opportunity. Instead, they need to focus on the person they're talking to, not beyond his or her shoulder. To do anything else is unnerving, impolite, and counterproductive. When the conversation is over, that's the time to say goodbye and start circulating again.
6. **Overstaying one's welcome.** Good salespeople (like all good guests) know when to leave. You don't necessarily have to be the first to leave, but you should never be the last.
7. **Failing to follow up.** This is perhaps the deadliest of the seven sins of socializing. If you make a promise to call on Monday, do it! If a certain article or report discussed over the crab canapé has been promised, it must be sent! Otherwise, the credibility a salesperson has worked so hard to establish is lost, and the whole encounter will have been a wash.

Source: David Dworski, "Social Selling," *Sales & Marketing Management*, December 1990, p. 46.

Table 6.1

Where Successful Agents Secure Their Prospects

Source	Percent
Old general acquaintances	35
Old associates	4
Recommended or introduced	39
Office leads	11
Newspapers and lists	4
Advertising and circulars	2
Cold-canvass	5

Source: Guardian Life Insurance Company of America. *The Guardian Training Program for Successful Selling,* sec. 3, "Prospecting," p. 3.

channels. For example, contacts in an industrial setting may include mechanics, engineers, assistant supervisors, clerks, superintendents, and buyers' secretaries.

- Intracompany Leads—These leads are found within a salesperson's own company by examining sales records, responses from promotional activities, records of walk-in prospects, and referrals from other departments and divisions. For instance, credit departments can provide information on inactive accounts and credit bureau rating reports on noncustomer accounts. They may also subscribe to a credit rating service that gives information about newly formed companies. The salesperson should request this information on a regular basis because credit department personnel may not think of turning over such names to the sales department.

  Another excellent source of intracompany leads is the company's service department records. These records should indicate calls made to service old equipment for which a new replacement may mean savings to the customer. Service personnel may not be trained to report such possibilities to the sales department.
- Spotters and Bird Dogs—"Spotters" are junior salespeople assigned to search out prospects and contact the regular sales force on hot leads, usually by canvassing an area. "Bird dogs" are people who can furnish information about new developments and new prospects in the community. Bird dogs are usually cultivated by salespeople, not by their companies. Examples include security guards, hair stylists and barbers, and elevator operators.
- Blitz Technique—The blitz technique involves saturating a particular region or group in as short a time as possible. A "blitz team" may be assigned to an area temporarily. This approach is a modification of cold canvassing.
- Cold Canvassing—When using a cold call method, the salesperson calls on every person or organization in a certain category within

the territory. The salesperson has no background information or personal contact before approaching the individual. Based on the law of averages, this approach assumes that if enough people or organizations are contacted, a percentage will turn out to be prospects.

- Direct Mail—Direct mail prospecting is used effectively where many prospects exist for a product or service. This approach often consists of mailing consumer coupons or inserting information cards in magazines and trade journals. The idea is to entice readers to request more information about the product or service. It usually consists of a response card that is returned by the interested party, as shown in Exhibit 6.4.
- Media Advertising—Media advertising and, more specifically, advertising-generated inquiries, have become increasingly popular. To use this method, the salesperson's firm runs an advertisement that includes a toll-free telephone number or a tear-out inquiry form. Some companies combine the toll-free number with computerized telecommunication systems as a way of providing better customer service.

The value of "teleservicing" is illustrated in the following excerpt from an article on customer service in the insurance industry reported in the magazine *TeleProfessional*:

> According to many published articles:
>
> - 96% of dissatisfied customers will never complain, but 60–90% of those will change companies and recommend others do the same.
> - Satisfied customers result in positive referrals and increased profits.
> - The cost of attracting new customers is five times higher than servicing your current customer base.
> - Companies spend thousands of dollars on advertising, marketing, and technology, but they are losing their most valuable resource, their customers.
>
> When you consider the above facts, it shouldn't come as a surprise to find companies looking for new and effective ways to service their clients.
>
> Missouri-based Kansas City Life Insurance Company is no exception. Finding ways to provide better service to their customers is an ongoing and major goal of the company. One group of policy owners that the company is especially concerned about serving is their "orphans." (An "orphan" is an insurance industry term used to describe policy holders whose original agent/agency is no longer associated with the company. The home office and a strategically-placed local agency usually take care of their service requests.)
>
> In the past, the company has used traditional methods such as the mail to try and stay in touch with these customers.

Exhibit 6.4

Sample Response Cards

The Ultimate Incentive.
Ask for More Information and Win a Free Vacation.

Please send me Inter-Continental Hotel's Ultimate Incentive brochures on the following destinations:

☐ Abidjan ☐ Geneva ☐ Nairobi
☐ Abu Dhabi ☐ Glasgow ☐ New Orleans
☐ Al Ain ☐ Helsinki ☐ New Delhi
☐ Amman ☐ Lisbon ☐ New York
☐ Amsterdam ☐ London ☐ Paris
☐ Athens ☐ Luxembourg ☐ Rio de Janeiro
☐ Bangkok ☐ Madrid ☐ Rome
☐ Cairo ☐ Manila ☐ San Francisco
☐ Cancun ☐ Manzanillo ☐ Seoul
☐ Cannes ☐ Maui ☐ Sydney
☐ Caracas ☐ Miami ☐ Tokyo
☐ Chicago ☐ Mombasa ☐ Toronto
☐ Dubai ☐ Munich ☐ Vienna
☐ Edinburgh ☐ Muscat ☐ Washington, D.C.

Name ______________________ Phone (____) ______________

Title/Position ______________________ Company ______________

Address ______________________ City ________ State ______ Zip ______

For our next incentive trip we are considering: Location ________ Month __ Year __

☐ Please enter my name in the drawing for the Cancun vacation spectacular.

Ask for more information and win a free meeting!

Return this card to receive free information on the Inter-Continental hotel locations of your choice and our new Meetings and Conferences Portfolio. We'll also enter you in our "Meeting Spectacular Sweepstakes" drawing for a chance to win a free meeting including airfare at the North American Inter-Continental Hotel of your choice.

Please send me more information on the Inter-Continental Hotels located in the following destinations:

North America

☐ Chicago ☐ Los Angeles ☐ Maui ☐ Miami ☐ Montreal
☐ New Orleans ☐ New York ☐ San Francisco ☐ Toronto ☐ Washington, DC

I would also like to receive information on Inter-Continental Hotels located in:

☐ Latin America ☐ Europe ☐ Pacific/Asia ☐ Middle East/Africa

In addition, please send me:

☐ **The new Meetings and Conferences Portfolio.** Contains information on Inter-Continental's unique programs and services, including two all-inclusive meeting packages, along with detailed facts about Inter-Continental Hotels throughout North America.

Name ______________________ Phone ______________________

Title ______________________ Organization ______________________

Address ______________________ City ________ State ________ Zip ________

I will next be planning a conference in: City ________ Month ________ Year ________ # of Attendees ________

☐ Please have a sales representative contact me.

☐ Please enter my name in the "Meeting Spectacular Sweepstakes" drawing.

If I win the free meeting, I would like to hold it at the Inter-Continental in ______________ (city).

Preferred month/year______/______.

> The approach was reactive, with the standard urge being, "If you have any questions or problems, please call our 800-number."
>
> In an effort to provide better service to their policy owners, Kansas City Life decided to test a proactive approach. Instead of waiting for their policy owners to call, they decided to call them. They further decided that if they were going to test the effectiveness of teleservicing, they should also compare the results with those of direct mail.[10]

- Telemarketing—Telemarketing is a telecommunication system allowing for person-to-person interaction between the suspect and the salesperson. Inside salespeople frequently are assigned to prospects by phone. Telemarketing procedures have changed drastically in the past decade. We will discuss these changes in Chapter 17, which deals with developing telemarketing programs and telecommunication technology.

  Mike Zibrun, president of S. Michael Associates, Ltd., in Chicago, is a consultant, trainer, and seminar leader for the Customer Service Institute's "Competitive Telemarketing" course. His view of three classic approaches in business-to-business telemarketing prospecting is worth repeating:

> While one may initially picture telesales as simply using the phone to dial for business opportunity, there are subtleties which distinctly separate them and their impact. From my experience, I believe that we can now witness three distinct calling options in B-B [Business-to-Business] telesales: Blitz programs; Production programs; and Relational programs.
>
> Blitz programs are the result of a user mindset that believes that occasional canvassing is the best way to uncover business opportunity. And, although if carefully crafted, a blitz approach can be very helpful for a firm's short term interests, most blitzes are not well planned. They are often marked by poor targeting, "one-shot" contact, untrained talent on the phone, noncommittal management and a poor offer structure. Not surprisingly, the results are often only a shadow of what could have been.
>
> Production programs rely on fairly strict scripting of what can be said and how it must be said, relentless quotas for completed calls per hour (and perhaps sales per hour), shallow product/service application knowledge and a segregation of the contact list that usually best matches the specific offer with the most appropriate audience. The shortfall in this approach is not in the sales that occur (which in successful programs can be significant) but rather in all of the other opportunity that is inadvertently bypassed in favor of quantity production requirements.
>
> Relational selling is based on the best of what your field representative and your customer service representative add

to the sales equation. Relational, or consultative, selling relies on activity guidelines to meet minimal expectations per calling day, yet optimizes the conversation to uncover additional present day opportunities, as well as future potential. The end result of a successful program is in discovering and acquiring additional business that would have been given to another vendor by default.

When carefully and constructively applied, each of the approaches mentioned can be viable and should result in incremental opportunity. However, my experience curve in working with B-B firms who are in telebusiness for the long haul, leads me to believe that maximizing business opportunity with each account occurs because of a developing relationship, vendor confidence and account attention. This is the basis of relational "selling" and much different from the "traditional" view of "telemarketing."[11]

Source: Courtesy of CompuServe, Incorporated.

- Computerized Data Base Lead Generation—It may be possible to purchase a computerized data base from a company, such as Dun's Marketing Services, that specializes in collecting information about companies. The data base is used to match product features and benefits with the needs of potential customers. Another popular service available in many college libraries is Dialog. If a salesperson's company subscribes to Dialog's services, searches through the data may be possible with one's own personal computer hooked up to the service with a modem.

  Each year since 1984, *Sales & Marketing Management* has published a "Directory of PC-Based Sales and Marketing Applications Software." Originally a listing of 83 software packages covering 13 different categories, the directory now identifies more than 600 packages spanning more than 37 individual subject areas.[12] Information about software includes title, vendor, functions, and cost, as well as necessary hardware and available training and telephone assistance.[13]

Secondary Sources of Prospecting Information

A *secondary source* is a repository of information that is available publicly. Journals, magazines, newspapers, public records, indices, directories, and associations provide salespeople with a wide range of prospect potential.

Professional journals that are fundamental for the sales professional include *Journal of Personal Selling*, *Journal of Marketing*, *Journal of Market Research*, and *Journal of Consumer Behavior*. Newspapers such as the *Wall Street Journal* and the *Christian Science Monitor* are leaders in reporting new product and service developments, mergers, and acquisitions. Sales professionals recognize these publications as sources for potential buyers. Weekly sources of business news for salespeople include magazines such as *Barron's* and *Business Week*. For more consolidated sources of data, salespeople may refer to:

- *Business Periodicals Index*—Indexes contents of over 150 business and financial publications
- *F & S Index of Corporations and Industries*—Indexes business and financial news from over 5,000 publications
- *Reader's Guide to Periodical Literature*—Indexes contents of over 200 U.S. consumer and nontechnical publications
- *Wall Street Journal Index*—Indexes all articles printed in the *Wall Street Journal*

Directories are publications that list or describe information about specific people or companies. Probably the most commonly known directory is the telephone directory—both the white and yellow pages.

Many directories list information by standard industrial classification (SIC) code. These were developed by the U.S. government and use a seven-digit number to classify industries according to their type of economic activity. The first two digits represent the major industry category, and the following digits divide the industry into more specific categories (Exhibit 6.5).

Information USA, Inc., in Chevy Chase, Maryland, publishes the *Federal Data Base Finder*, a directory of free and fee-based data bases and files available for a fee from the federal government. Other directories frequently used by salespeople are the *Dun and Bradstreet Directory*, *Moody's Industrial Manual*, and *The Thomas Register of American Manufacturers*.

There are over 2,000 professional associations serving different prospect groups. Professionally prepared lists of their members are sold by list brokers. Lists of subscribers to publications cover all activities and fields from boating, skiing, camping, and fishing to coin collecting, antiques, theater, and gourmet dining. Four other easily attainable secondary sources are:

1. Voter registration lists—These can be obtained from precinct captains.
2. License applications—Examples are business license permits and boat, automobile, and recreational vehicle registrations.
3. New construction applications—Contractors and builders are useful sources for finding prospects.
4. Lists of recorded warranties—These indicate the ages of products for possible replacement opportunities.

Managing Prospect Information

Establishing a "Tickler File"

Prior planning is the touchstone of selling success. In the beginning of any worthwhile venture, preparation requires considerable care and

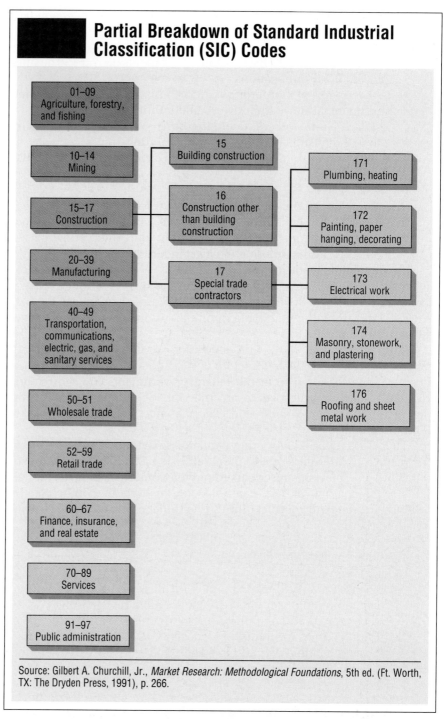

Partial Breakdown of Standard Industrial Classification (SIC) Codes

- 01–09 Agriculture, forestry, and fishing
- 10–14 Mining
- 15–17 Construction
  - 15 Building construction
  - 16 Construction other than building construction
  - 17 Special trade contractors
    - 171 Plumbing, heating
    - 172 Painting, paper hanging, decorating
    - 173 Electrical work
    - 174 Masonry, stonework, and plastering
    - 176 Roofing and sheet metal work
- 20–39 Manufacturing
- 40–49 Transportation, communications, electric, gas, and sanitary services
- 50–51 Wholesale trade
- 52–59 Retail trade
- 60–67 Finance, insurance, and real estate
- 70–89 Services
- 91–97 Public administration

Source: Gilbert A. Churchill, Jr., *Market Research: Methodological Foundations*, 5th ed. (Ft. Worth, TX: The Dryden Press, 1991), p. 266.

attention. To keep track of prospect information, the salesperson should develop a procedure for recording this information systematically. The filing procedure can vary, from a simple 3-inch × 5-inch prospect card file to prospecting software packages that use personal computers to organize and forecast sales volume potential.

If the company's sales force does not use computers, then the salesperson can initiate a simple system called a *tickler file* by following these guidelines:

1. Buy 500 or more 3-inch × 5-inch cards, a card box, and a set of color-coded dividers that contain weekly, monthly, and blank tabs.
2. To set up the box, place a tab for the present month in front. Insert a set of weekly dividers behind each month.
3. Write on each 3-inch × 5-inch card all the information available on the prospect. Figure 6.2 shows a sample prospect card.
4. When setting appointments, place these cards behind the month and week when the prospect will be called on.
5. As the weeks and months go by, the dividers and the prospect cards should be moving toward the front of the box.
6. The present week and month should always be in front. Prospects that have not been contacted yet should be filed in a separate section in the back of the box—waiting for the salesperson to schedule an appointment.[14]

For salespeople in an industry that requires special attention to detail, Figure 6.3 offers a useful illustration of how information may be grouped into a meaningful and useful account profile.

Developing Prospecting Quotas

In addition to keeping extensive records on each prospect and customer, many companies have developed a lead management model to help them determine how many customers they need to meet sales/profit objectives. Mark Evans, vice president of Bricker-Evans, a marketing communications firm in the Silicon Valley area of California, describes "modeling" as constructing an entire scenario of what is projected to happen in developing suspects, leads, prospects, and closes for your program before you commit and implement them.[15]

Evans proposes that the starting point is a company goal of 100 new customers, 20 percent of whom come from responses to advertising and 80 percent from direct mail. His findings revealed that 15 percent of all leads become suspects, 60 percent of the suspects become prospects, and 10 percent of the prospects become customers. From that information he constructed this model:

> By taking the number of closes (new customers/accounts) from both advertising and direct mail and dividing them by the percentages of suspects, prospects, and closes, we can determine our objectives. In this case, we need 2,222 advertising leads [20 ÷ 0.15 ÷ 0.60 ÷ 0.10] and 8,888 direct mail leads [80 ÷ 0.15 ÷ 0.60 ÷ 0.10]. At an estimated 1.5% response, we need 592,533 [8,888 ÷ 0.015] direct mailings.[16]

Figure 6.2

Prospect Record

FRONT

Prospect to contract

Dates to Call

Salesperson

Name

Occupation

Address

Phone

Phone

Hobby/Interest

Credit

Source

Now Owns

Make

Model

Year

Value

Owes

Family

Wife

Children

Motives

BACK

Contract Record

Best Time ______ Secretary ______ Other ______

DATE	CONTRACT Phone/Person/Letter	RESULTS/COMMENTS

With these figures, a budget can be defined. At $0.98 for a direct mailing, the direct mail budget should be $580,683. When the company's average number of leads per ad (45) is divided into the number of leads needed (2,222), the number of ads required is calculated to be 49. At an average cost per ad of $5,000, the ad budget is $245,000.

Figure 6.3

Account Profile

Current Account Information

1. Account name:
2. Account address:
3. Phone
4. Type of business:
5. Number of years in business:
6. Estimated sales volume (total):
   Estimated annual purchases from us:
7. Sales potential this year:
   What do you feel will be our greatest obstacle to achieving this goal:
8. Have we had problems with this account?
   If so, what has been the nature of the problems (delivery, billing errors, quality, postsale service, other) and how have they been resolved?
9. Other suppliers:
10. Years of repeat business:
11. What is the key determinant in their buying decision (quality, quick shipment, discounts, price postsale service)?
12. In what areas of our performance do you feel we can do a better job?
13. Do you feel that this account now requires a visit of visits from executives of our company?
14. Does the customer have plans for expansion?
15. Does the customer plan on becoming part of a merger or acquiring other companies?
16. Does the customer plan on adding new products to the existing line?
17. Have you read a Dun & Bradstreet report on this account?
18. What is the account's credit rating?

Buying Decision Information

19. Buyer's influence in purchasing decision:
20. Key influence in decision:
21. Other people involved in final decision:
22. Length of buying decision:
23. Do they use a buying committee?
24. Meeting day of buying committee:
25. Types of sales presentations least and most preferred:

Buyer/Customer Demographics

26. Name: Nickname:
    Title:
27. Secretary:
28. Social style:
29. Home address:

Figure 6.3
Continued

Account Profile

30. Home telephone:
31. Birthdate and birthplace:
    Hometown:
32. Height: Weight:
    Outstanding physical characteristics:
    (Examples: balding, great condition, arthritis.)

Education

33. High school and year:
    College:
    Graduated when: Degrees:
34. College honors: Adv. degrees:
35. College fraternity or sorority:
    Sports:
36. Extracurricular college activities:
37. If customer didn't attend college, is he/she sensitive about it?
    What did they do instead?
38. Military service: Discharge rank:
    Attitude toward being in the service:

Family

39. Marital status: Spouse's name:
40. Spouse's education:
41. Spouse's interests/activities/affiliations:
42. Wedding anniversary:
43. Children's names and ages:
    If divorced does client have custody?
44. Children's education:
45. Children's interests (hobbies, problems):

Business Background

46. Previous employment (most recent first):
    Company:
    Location:
    Dates: Title:

    Company:
    Location:
    Dates: Title:

    Company:
    Location:
    Dates: Title:
47. Previous position at present company:
    Dates: Title:
48. Any "status" symbols in office?

Figure 6.3
Continued

Account Profile

49. Professional or trade associations:
    Office or honors in them:
50. Any mentors?
51. What business relationship does he/she have with others in company?
52. Is it a good relationship: Why?
53. What other people in our company know the customer?
54. Type of connection: Nature of relationship:
55. What is client's attitude toward his/her company?
56. What is client's long-range business objectives?
57. What is client's immediate business objective?
58. What is of greatest concern to customer at this time: the welfare of the company or personal welfare?
59. Does customer think of the present or the future?
    Why?
60. Kind of car(s)?
61. Conversational interests:
62. Whom does the customer seem anxious to impress?
63. What adjectives would you use to describe customer?
64. What accomplishments is the client proud of?
65. What do you feel is customer's long-range personal objective?
66. What do you feel is customer's immediate personal goal?

The Customer and You

67. What moral or ethical considerations are involved when you work with client?
68. Does client feel any obligation to you, your company, or your competition?
    If so, what?
69. Does the proposal you plan to make require customer to change a habit or take an action that is contrary to custom?
70. Is client primarily concerned about the opinion of others?
71. Or very self-centered? Highly ethical?
72. What are the key problems with your proposal as customer sees them?
73. What are the priorities of the client's management?
    Any conflicts between client and management?
74. Can you help with these problems? How?
75. Does your competition have better answers to the above questions that you have?

On the International Front — Prospecting in a Foreign Country

Small companies seeking overseas prospects can learn from Jeff Ake, international sales manager of Electronic Liquid Fillers, Inc. (ELF). Ake obtained many of his leads from foreign-based English-language magazines that cover the industry. He then faxed or mailed letters to about 400 prospects, announcing ELF's search for sales representatives in the Pacific Rim. The 100 who responded received a second fax or letter announcing Ake's visit and requesting detailed descriptions of their businesses. Appointments were then confirmed with the qualified prospects. The trip cost $19,000 and generated $2 million in sales.

In another case, a fast-food operation was reviewing the potential in the Latin America market. The corporation realized that a large amount of data was available on the economies of Latin American countries, much of which could be obtained at practically no cost through the country's embassy or consulate office in the United States.

Although the secondary data were available at a substantially reduced cost, much of the information was inaccurate or outdated. In many countries, the most recent data may be several years old or may have been inflated to attract foreign investment. Using such poor-quality data sources is of little or no value to the foreign market opportunity.

Another corporation describes its use of international sources:

> Identifying potential in a new foreign market is a real problem for us. Well over half of our information comes from the U.S. Department of Commerce. Their materials are comprehensive, basic and make you aware of the trends. Of course, like information from other sources, it has to be filtered and used cautiously.
>
> In developing countries, statistics are not available or reliable, so there is more dependency on the Department of Commerce. In many cases, there will be a significant divergence in the potential implied by the U.S. Department of Commerce figures versus competitive activity information. Information from competitors is more credible but at the same time more difficult to come by.

An enormous amount of information is available from various sources. Reservations about the scarcity of reliable data suggest the need to develop an effective market information system evaluated for accuracy, timeliness, and comparability.

Sources: S. Tamer Cavusgil, "International Marketing Research: Insights into Company Practices," in *Research in Marketing*, vol. 7, J.N. Sheth, ed. (Greenwich, CT: JAI Press, 1984), pp. 261–268; T.L., "Selling Overseas: The Pacific Rim on a Shoestring," *Inc.*, June 1991, p. 122.

A major underlying question for management is whether it is profitable to develop 100 new customers for $825,682, or $8,256 per customer. This model offers management a framework that serves as a guide in making a decision about prospecting goals for the sales force to follow.

Summary

Prospecting is the continuous process of gathering names of potential buyers that are likely to be interested in the salesperson's product or service. Prospecting consists of two levels: differentiating between a suspect and a prospect and identifying benefits related to the overall sales effort.

To determine which individuals should be contacted, a salesperson must qualify a prospect in at least four basic areas: 1) benefits received by both the buyer and the seller; 2) eligibility of the potential buyer; 3) ability of the person or company to pay; and 4) the authority of the individual to make the buying decision. Additional criteria for determining who a salesperson should contact may be set by ranking the prospects into "A-B-C" account volume potential.

The most common methods of prospecting are the endless chain, referral, center of influence, networking, personal observation, the creeping vine, intracompany leads, spotters and bird dogs, the blitz technique, cold canvassing, direct mail, media advertising, telemarketing, and computerized data base lead generation. In addition, secondary sources for gathering information include journals, magazines, newspapers, public records, indices, and directories.

Every salesperson should have a system for managing prospect information. Failing to do this could cost you time and sales efficiency. Not all sales forces have computer capabilities. A simple system for managing prospects is known as a "tickler file."

In sum, prospecting is the lifeblood of the salesperson's long-term success. It is a cyclical process of identifying, qualifying, and managing that operates concurrently with the regular sales interview and presentation activities.

Key Terms

Center of Influence Influential person in the community who is in a position to, and willing to, provide referred leads

Endless Chain Prospecting concept based on the idea that the salesperson will obtain names of additional prospects at each interview for future sales calls

Lead Person or organization that could benefit from buying a particular product or service

Networking Process of making and using contacts

Personal Observation Recognizing and singling out leads in any circumstance or situation

Prospect A *qualified* potential buyer who has the means and authority to complete the transaction

Qualifying Act of identifying legitimate buyers

Referral Any identification of a suspect by a third party

Standard Industrial Classification (SIC) Codes Codes developed by the U.S. government to group industries according to types of economic activities

Suspect Each person within a target market for a product or service

Telemarketing Person-to-person interaction between salesperson and suspect via telecommunications systems

Review Questions

1. Briefly identify the following:
   a. Sales lead
   b. Prospect
   c. Qualified prospect
2. What is required for a lead to become a prospect?
3. Explain how the endless chain referral prospecting method works. How effective is this method of prospecting?
4. What is a referral? How do you get referrals?
5. What is a center of influence?
6. Name several directories that might be helpful sources of prospects for a particular industry. Where would you go to acquire these directories?
7. How does a networking system serve the salesperson? How might a real estate salesperson use networking to identify prospects?
8. What qualifications must an individual have to become a prospect?
9. What is meant by the ferris wheel of selling? How does this relate to prospecting?

Discussion Questions

1. Discuss the steps a salesperson should go through in qualifying a prospect. How can the salesperson's company help?
2. Assume you are a salesperson for a company selling high-priced snow skis and related equipment. How would you go about prospecting?
3. Evaluate the qualifying criteria identified in this chapter. Under what conditions would one criterion be considered more valuable and important than others?
4. Your mother has decided to become a door-to-door salesperson for a water purifier system that fits under the sink. She asks you for advice on prospecting. What would you tell her?
5. As a sales representative for a roofing materials company, describe the methods you would use for considering prime prospects.
6. Discuss the importance of using the local newspaper to discover prospects.
7. Describe the best prospects for buying (a) a Ricoh copier machine; (b) a commercial building. What factors would you identify in qualifying leads?
8. The company you represent carries a full line of word-processing equipment and small business computers. How would you develop a list of business, government, and educational accounts? What information would you collect to screen your prospect list?

Prospecting for New Accounts

Case 6.1

Simmons Corporation has sold commercial furniture and office decor through a network of distributors for 10 years. Although considered a small company, Simmons' sales have grown at a consistent rate since the company began advertising in trade publications. This advertising seemed appropriate and less costly in gaining widespread exposure. In the past Simmons had relied solely on the distributors' salespeople.

Simmons has considered taking the list of present accounts and researching every one of its customers' competitors in those areas. If an insurance company is a good customer, then Simmons would contact all other insurance companies in that area. If a real estate company is a good customer, then all other local real estate companies would be contacted. The company is confident that it can keep accounts once it has sold to them, but initially it will have to win the business away from existing firms. The problem is that Simmons has few existing accounts.

Another traditional method Simmons considered was using the telephone directory. The company could hire people to sit down with the yellow pages and randomly call businesses that might need office furniture or exciting new decor. Contacting commercial developers and owners of buildings for lease also seemed to be a viable avenue, although quite time consuming and costly.

Management at Simmons believes that by using trade magazines the company can reach thousands of people at a minimal cost and then screen select the choice prospects. Management further suggests that this method could maintain the present customer count and add a few new customers. "New customers will automatically contact us once they read about us in the trade magazines," management has stated. In seeking out new accounts through widespread advertising, however, the company may gain exposure in territories where distributors are unavailable.

The market is growing, and Simmons feels that it can gain potential opportunities by soliciting new businesses opening in the area. Management is convinced that the company should not limit generating sales leads to its distributors' salespeople. In considering prospecting alternatives, management is somewhat in doubt about how to best develop a new-account prospecting method and at the same time keep costs down.

1. Should Simmons rely solely on advertising in trade publications?
2. Are distributors' salespeople considered a more acceptable method of acquiring sales leads?
3. How should Simmons develop a list of qualified prospects to call on?

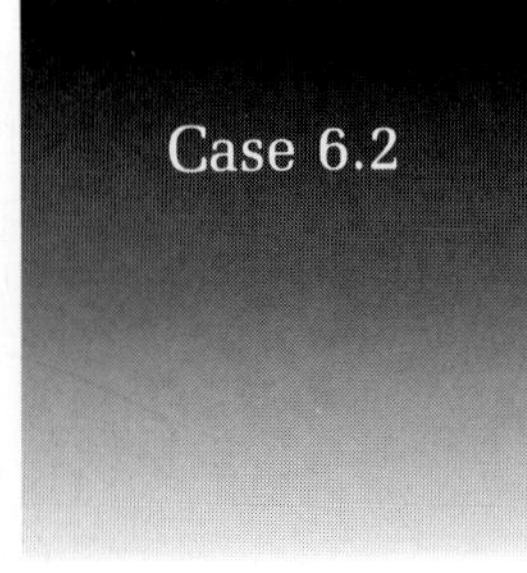

Wasting Time in Prospecting

Tom Hanes has been working as a sales representative for a Japanese line of sporting goods for nearly a year. He sells a variety of sporting goods ranging from fishing gear to an extensive line of bicycle equipment and parts designed for all ages and levels. Tom is paid strictly on commission and is operating on his own with minimal training and experience.

The only learning material that Tom was provided by the company was a handbook on selling, which contained a section on prospecting methods as applied in general sales situations. Having reviewed the entire text thoroughly, Tom was determined to apply as many methods as possible. These methods included telephone solicitation, cold canvassing, a variety of mailing lists, letters attempting to secure appointments, and some leads from friends and acquaintances. Highly ambitious, Tom spent many hours and many full working days knocking on doors.

Following through on the prospecting methods studied, it was apparent that most of Tom's time was spent prospecting instead of selling. An acquaintance of Tom's, a successful insurance salesman, suggested to Tom that his time was being wasted by pursuing any method other than the endless chain and the center of influence. Tom was not convinced that the endless chain and the center of influence could be applied to sell sporting goods, and he continued applying many of the other traditional methods of prospecting.

After 6 months of hard work and long hours, Tom has grown disappointed because he cannot find enough prospective buyers to warrant all the time and effort he has allocated to this new exciting career.

1. Where is Tom lacking in his efforts toward prospecting?
2. Why would the endless chain or the center of influence be acceptable or inappropriate in selling sporting goods?
3. What prospecting methods would you suggest to Tom to increase his selling potential?

Notes

1. Paul J. Meyer, "The Nature of the Game Is Prospecting," sales training materials for distributors of SMI International, Inc., Waco, TX.
2. David L. Kurtz, H. Robert Dodge, and Jay E. Klompmaker, *Professional Selling*, 5th ed. (Texas: Business Publications, Inc., 1988), p. 119.
3. H. Webster Johnson and A. J. Faria, *Creative Selling*, 4th ed. (Illinois: South-Western Publishing Co., 1987), p. 168.
4. "The New Supersalesman: Wired for Success," *Business Week*, January 6, 1973, p. 45.
5. Vincent L. Zirpoli, "You Can't 'Control' the Prospect, so Manage the Presale Activities to Increase Performance," *Marketing News*, March 16, 1984, p. 1.
6. R. E. Anderson, J. F. Hair, and A. J. Bush, *Professional Sales Management* (New York: McGraw-Hill Book Company, 1988), p. 331.
7. Dorothy Leeds, "To Find Golden Opportunities . . . Pan for Prospects," *Personal Selling Power*, November/December 1990, p. 26.

8. Steve Fishman, "The Art of Networking," *Success*, July/August 1985, p. 41.
9. David Dworski, "Social Selling," *Sales & Marketing Management*, December 1990, p. 46.
10. Annette Burke, "Teleservicing Takes on Direct Mail," *TeleProfessional*, September/October 1990, pp. 31–32.
11. Mike Zibrun, "Following the Blue Highways . . . to Maximize Customer Opportunity," *TeleProfessional*, September/October 1990, pp. 20–21.
12. Richard Kern, "Man Bytes Editor," *Sales & Marketing Management*, December 1990, p. 5.
13. Ibid., p. 69.
14. David H. Sandler, "Prospecting . . . for Profit," *Personal Selling Power*, September 1990, p. 40.
15. M. Evans, "Lead Management Is in a Rut," *Sales & Marketing Management*, November 1988, p. 10.
16. Ibid.

Understanding buying behavior and the buying process is an extension of precall preparation and the preapproach. While studying the customer is a continuous activity of all sales professionals, it is especially helpful to the person who is entering a sales position for the first time. Think of the information presented in this chapter as a professional athlete thinks of a total training program. The hours spent viewing videotapes or scouting the competition help the athlete to prepare the best game strategy. Understanding the forces that motivate and influence a buyer's behavior prepare the salesperson to discover the buyer's needs (Chapter 12) and prepare a presentation strategy (Chapters 13 and 14) that fits those needs. Understanding consumer behavior contributes to achieving the competitive edge in selling.

Consumer behavior is a complex process. Much of what is known about today's consumer has been learned from the behavioral sciences, such as anthropology, psychology, and sociology. Behavioral concepts that relate closely to professional selling are explored in this chapter.

In defining consumer behavior, we borrow from James Engel, Roger Blackwell, and Paul Miniard, well-known consumer behavior authors: "CONSUMER BEHAVIOR . . . [is] those actions directly involved in obtaining, consuming, and disposing of products and services, including the decision processes that precede and follow these actions."[1] Accordingly, the chapter is divided into four sections. The first section focuses on the nature of buying behavior and the buying decision process. In the second section, we explore culture, social class, and other environmental influences that shape buying behavior. Individual differences also help to shape the consumer's buying behavior. Thus, the third section addresses the areas of attitude, personality, and life-style through the study of VALS, a value and life-style classification system developed by Stanford Research International. Another component that contributes to the decision process is psychological influence. Therefore, the last section concentrates on two specific areas of psychological influence: Maslow's hierarchy of needs and Schutz's model of social needs.

Consumer Behavior: To Buy or Not to Buy

If product knowledge is all that was needed to make a sale, the buyer could simply read the product labels, brochures, and printed material without any help from the salesperson. As stressed in Chapter 4, however, people do not make purchasing decisions based only on features. They actually buy the advantages and benefits resulting from a feature, such as the satisfaction of added utility provided by a particular feature. Consequently, skilled salespeople recognize that they must direct their attention to the needs and motives of the prospect. They must act as facilitators to help the buyer reach a purchasing decision that is the best possible choice for that individual's perceived level of satisfaction.

Just as salespeople go through the process of prospecting to help them choose qualified potential buyers, consumers go through a series of critical thinking steps called a *buying decision process* to help them

Sales Professional Spotlight

Laz Mascarenhas and Troy Getty are top sales representatives of Business Computer Specialists (BCS), a small, growing computer service company serving the needs of a variety of industries, such as accounting, construction, manufacturing, mortgage, real estate, health care, government, education, restaurant, and leisure firms.

Laz and Troy speak glowingly of BCS's mission to provide state-of-the-art equipment and excellent service, especially with respect to the company's size and resource capabilities. "The real strength of our quality program is the result of our understanding our clients' requirements and recommending the appropriate software to meet individual needs. We have always maintained the highest level of professionalism among our staff. Our salespeople are recognized in the industry for their skill and experience, dedicated to meeting customers' needs and demands."

The salespeople at BCS perform an important function as problem solvers. They start by asking questions about the application and environment, such as, "Is the system sufficiently flexible in terms of equipment and software to respond to unforeseeable changes?" The firm's present and future requirements are determined, and then a software package specifically suited to its current procedures is recommended.

A crucial point in software selection is determining the specifications the software must meet to fulfill the client's objectives. "We are also committed to making sure that the firm's expectations are met by comparing price and performance." Once the software has been selected, BCS recommends whatever hardware the client needs to provide for its computer environment, which sometimes requires physical facility changes. This determination is shared by BCS and the client company's staff.

BCS's commitment to clients does not stop when the agreement is signed. A close working relationship is developed with the clients, one in which BCS is sensitive to the pressures the clients face during the installation phase. Adapting to an entirely new system can bring about even more pressure. BCS's assistance in the conversion to new equipment and software helps reduce that pressure. The client recognizes the value of well-trained and highly skilled sales representatives and appreciates the training they provide for user personnel; this often includes the expertise to support the installation.

Laz and Troy know that the approach they take to their selling job focuses on cultivating strong, lasting business relationships with their clients. Organizations faced with growth may require regular upgrading of equipment. In the final analysis, BCS—through dedicated sales representatives like Laz and Troy—strives to maintain an absolute commitment to produce the best possible services and products, while at the same time maintaining a cost-competitive market position. The process starts with understanding and evaluating the prospect's needs.

choose products and services. This buying decision process contains five phases of problem-solving activity:

1. Need recognition
2. Search for information
3. Alternative evaluation
4. Purchase
5. Outcome or postpurchase response

Figure 7.1 illustrates this decision process integrated with a complete overview of the influences on consumer decision-making behavior.

Table 7.1 diagnoses the decision-making process from a broad marketing perspective. Some of the responses to the questions listed there may be gathered by the marketing or other department of the company and passed on to the sales force. A relational selling philosophy, however, involves the salesperson seeking answers to these questions through daily activities and then feeding the information to the firm.

When the buyer engages in an extensive search for information before making an initial purchase decision, and then follows up with extensive alternative evaluation, the buyer is involved in what Engel, Blackwell, and Miniard call extended problem solving. If this is viewed as one end of a continuum, then the opposite end is described as limited problem solving.[2] Table 7.2 describes the characteristics of the extended and limited problem-solving approaches to the buying decision process.

Figure 7.1

A Complete Overview Model of Consumer Decision-Making Behavior and the Influences on It

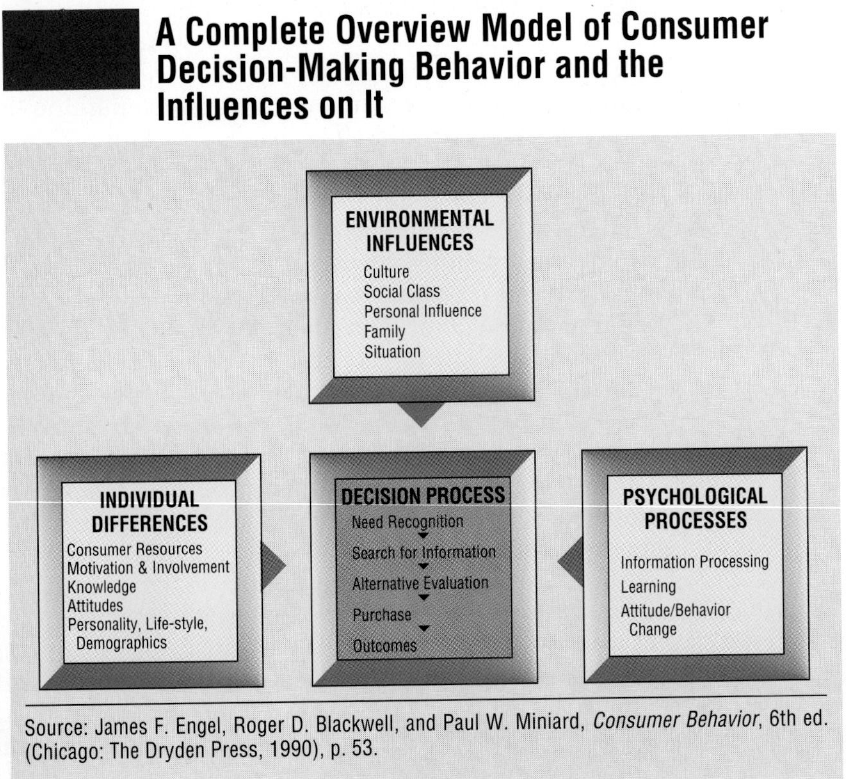

Source: James F. Engel, Roger D. Blackwell, and Paul W. Miniard, *Consumer Behavior*, 6th ed. (Chicago: The Dryden Press, 1990), p. 53.

Diagnosing the Consumer Decision-Making Process

Table 7.1

Need Recognition

1. What needs are satisfied by product purchase and usage? (i.e., What *benefits* are consumers seeking?)
2. Are these needs dormant or are they presently perceived as felt needs by prospective buyers?
3. How involved with the product are most prospective buyers in the target market segment?

Search for Information

1. What product- and brand-related information is stored in memory?
2. Is the consumer motivated to turn to external sources to find information about available alternatives and their characteristics?
3. What specific information sources are used most frequently when search is undertaken?
4. What product features or attributes are the focus of search when it is undertaken?

Alternative Evaluation

1. To what extent do consumers engage in alternative evaluation and comparison?
2. Which product and/or brand alternatives are included in the evaluation process?
3. Which product evaluative criteria (product attributes) are used to compare various alternatives?
   a. Which are most salient in the evaluation?
   b. How complex is the evaluation (i.e., using a single attribute as opposed to several in combination)?
4. What kind of decision rule is used to determine the best choice?
   a. Which are most salient in the evaluation?
   b. How complex is the evaluation?
5. What are the outcomes of evaluation regarding each of the candidate purchase alternatives?
   a. What is believed to be true about the characteristics and features of each?
   b. Are they perceived to be different in important ways, or are they seen as essentially the same?
   c. What attitudes are held regarding the purchase and use of each?
   d. What purchasing intentions are expressed, and when will these intentions most likely be consummated by purchase and use?

Purchase

1. Will the consumer expend time and energy to shop until the preferred alternative is found?
2. Is additional decision-process behavior needed to discover the preferred outlet for purchase?
3. What are the preferred modes of purchase (i.e., retail store, in the home, or in other ways)?

Postpurchase Response

1. What degree of satisfaction or dissatisfaction is expressed with respect to previously used alternatives in the product or service category?
2. What reasons are given for satisfaction or dissatisfaction?
3. Has perceived satisfaction or dissatisfaction been shared with other people to help them in their buying behavior?
4. Have consumers made attempts to achieve redress for dissatisfaction?
5. Is there an intention to repurchase any of the alternatives?
   a. If no, why not?
   b. If yes, does intention reflect brand loyalty or inertia?

Source: James F. Engel, Roger D. Blackwell, and Paul W. Miniard, *Consumer Behavior*, 6th ed. (Chicago: The Dryden Press, 1990), p. 473.

Table 7.2

Characteristics of Decision-Process Behavior

Extended Problem Solving	Limited Problem Solving
Need Recognition	
1. High involvement and perceived risk.	1. Low involvement and perceived risk.
Search for Information	
1. Strong motivation to search.	1. Low motivation to search.
2. Multiple sources used including media, friends, and point-of-sale communication.	2. Exposure to advertising is passive, and information processing is not deep.
3. Information processed actively and rigorously.	3. Point-of-sale comparison likely.
Alternative Evaluation	
1. Rigorous evaluation process.	1. Nonrigorous evaluation process.
2. Multiple evaluative criteria used, with some more salient than others.	2. Limited number of criteria, focus on most salient.
3. Alternatives perceived as significantly different.	3. Alternatives perceived as essentially similar.
4. Compensatory strategy where weakness on given attributes can be offset by others.	4. Noncompensatory strategy, eliminating alternatives perceived to fall short on salient attribute(s).
5. Beliefs, attitudes, and intentions strongly held.	5. Beliefs, attitudes, and intentions not strongly held.
	6. Purchase and trial can be a primary means of evaluation.
Purchase	
1. Will shop many outlets if needed.	1. Not motivated to shop extensively.
2. Choice of outlet may require a decision process.	2. Often prefer self-service.
3. Point-of-sale negotiation and communication often needed.	3. Choice often prompted by display and point-of-sale incentives.
Postpurchase Response	
1. Doubts can motivate need for postsale reassurance.	1. Satisfaction motivates repurchase because of inertia, not loyalty.
2. Satisfaction is crucial and loyalty is the outcome.	2. Main consequence of dissatisfaction is brand switching.
3. Motivated to seek redress if there is dissatisfaction.	

Source: James F. Engel, Roger D. Blackwell, and Paul W. Miniard, *Consumer Behavior,* 6th ed. (Chicago: The Dryden Press, 1990), p. 474.

In Chapter 1 we outlined the basic steps involved in the professional selling process. These steps are again presented in Figure 7.2 to illustrate how the buying decision process is incorporated in the selling process. This figure reaffirms the essence of relational selling. The salesperson has a responsibility to guide the buyer toward a purchasing decision. The buyer and the seller must be involved in mutually shared activities to achieve a win-win exchange.

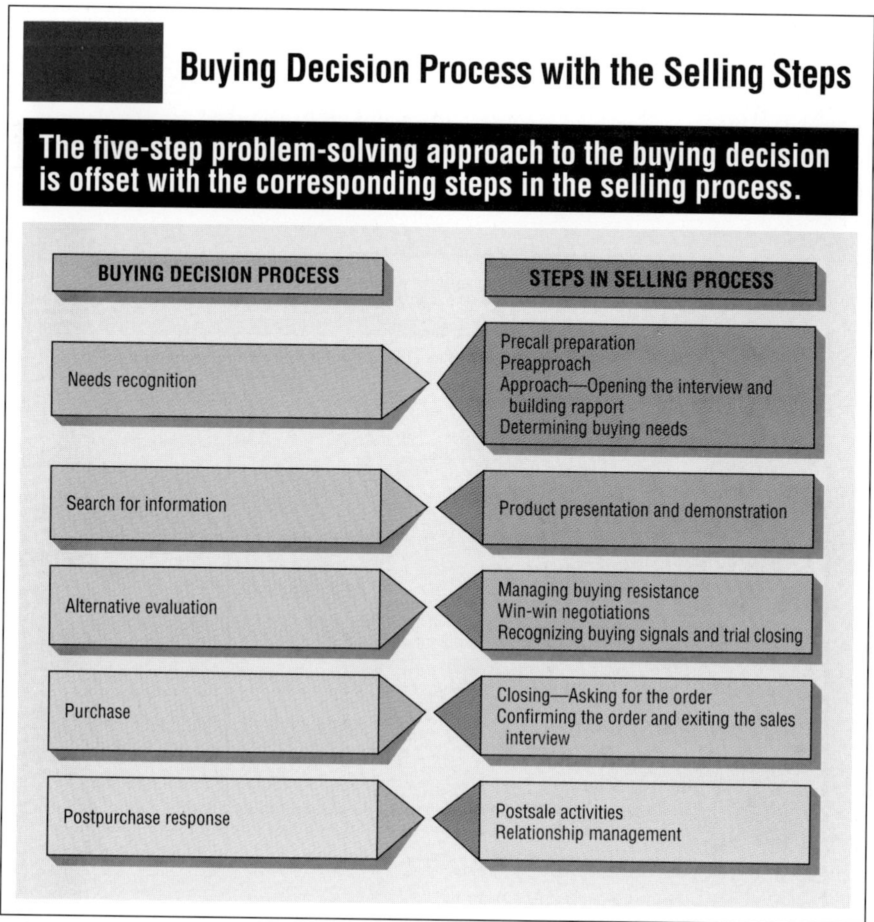

Figure 7.2

Three major components affect the buying decision process: 1) environmental influences, 2) individual differences, and 3) psychological processes. The next sections focus on each of the types of influences that may affect the buying decision.

Environmental Influences That Shape Buying Behavior

As seen in Chapter 1, America has been evolving from a mass consumer market to many segmented target markets. As this evolution occurs, the balance of power shifts from marketers to consumers. Martha Farnsworth Riche, national editor of *American Demographics* magazine, says, "As consumers become more diverse, they become more independent."[3] She reasons that their independence comes from an increasing number of choices. Because of technological advances, consumers have more control over when, where, and how they buy. Salespeople are being forced by the impact of technology to study consumers and the influence that choice plays in their buying behavior.

Exhibit 7.1

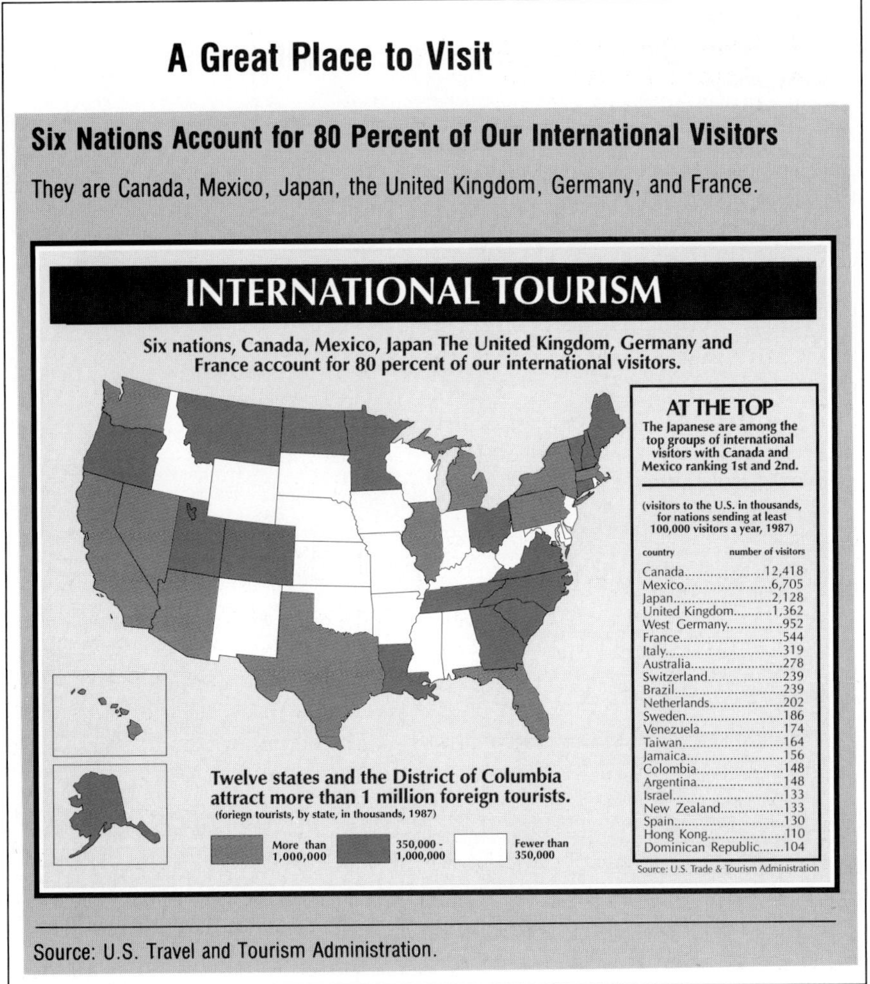
A Great Place to Visit
Six Nations Account for 80 Percent of Our International Visitors
They are Canada, Mexico, Japan, the United Kingdom, Germany, and France.
INTERNATIONAL TOURISM
Six nations, Canada, Mexico, Japan The United Kingdom, Germany and France account for 80 percent of our international visitors.
AT THE TOP
The Japanese are among the top groups of international visitors with Canada and Mexico ranking 1st and 2nd.
(visitors to the U.S. in thousands, for nations sending at least 100,000 visitors a year, 1987)
Twelve states and the District of Columbia attract more than 1 million foreign tourists.
(foriegn tourists, by state, in thousands, 1987)
More than 1,000,000
350,000 - 1,000,000
Fewer than 350,000
Source: U.S. Trade & Tourism Administration
Source: U.S. Travel and Tourism Administration.

country	number of visitors
Canada	12,418
Mexico	6,705
Japan	2,128
United Kingdom	1,362
West Germany	952
France	544
Italy	319
Australia	278
Switzerland	239
Brazil	239
Netherlands	202
Sweden	186
Venezuela	174
Taiwan	164
Jamaica	156
Colombia	148
Argentina	148
Israel	133
New Zealand	133
Spain	130
Hong Kong	110
Dominican Republic	104

Other underlying determinants that affect buying behavior include a variety of environmental influences, such as culture, personal influence, family, and social class situations.

Culture

Culture is one of the most basic influences on a buyer's needs, wants, and behavior. Understanding culture is a challenging undertaking as it encompasses the knowledge, values, beliefs, and customs of a society.

Culture is a set of meaningful symbols that help people communicate as members of society. Culture provides individuals with a sense of identity and a notion of what is acceptable behavior within their society. Some of the most significant attitudes and behaviors influenced by culture are[4]:

- Sense of self and space
- Communication and language
- Dress and appearance
- Food and feeding habits
- Time and time consciousness
- Relationships (family, organization, government)
- Values and norms
- Beliefs and attitudes
- Mental process and learning
- Work habits and practices

Culture is learned and shared by people belonging to a particular group. This learned behavior is passed on from generation to generation. It is a principal factor that permits us to live together in a society by providing ready-made solutions to common problems, helping us to predict the behavior of others, and permitting others to know what to expect of us.

In general, culture influences consumers through the manner in which they acquire and use goods and services. Therefore, the salesperson should adapt selling efforts to cultural differences (such as different values) and constantly monitor changes in both the domestic and international markets. This effort is difficult and challenging because people tend not to notice cultural differences even when they are in the midst of a particular cultural setting. Some of the dominant American cultural values are summarized in Table 7.3.

Thomas Miller and Bickley Townsend of the New York-based Roper Organization suggest that businesses can bridge the gap between consumer attitudes and behavior by analyzing the data collected by demographers and consumer behavior researchers. *Demography* is "the statistical science dealing with the distribution, density, and vital statistics" (such as income, age, and education) of human populations.[5] Miller and Townsend cite the following as an example of this gap:

> A growing majority of Americans claim to be environmentalists, but few do much to help solve environmental problems, and most are not willing to pay significantly more for "green goods." Most Americans favor laws to regulate environmental issues. . . . Voting behavior will overshadow consumer behavior in the buying of "green" products.[6]

For salespeople, this may mean adjusting their prospecting mixes—the methods used to locate prospects and the criteria used to qualify their potential buyers.

Cultural and ethnic diversity are intriguing and popular topics. Marketers are obsessed with figuring out how these demographic trends will affect buying patterns. Exhibit 7.2 illustrates the extent of the marketers' attempts to identify these groups in American markets.

Ethnic diversity is only one facet of culture. Other elements of culture may be encompassed by subcultures. As discussed in Chapter 3, a *subculture* is a distinct cultural group that exists as an identifiable segment

Table 7.3

A Summary of Some American Cultural Values

	Value	General Features	Relevance to Consumer Behavior and Marketing Management
1.	Achievement and success	Hard work is good; success flows from hard work.	Acts as a justification for acquisition of goods ("You deserve it").
2.	Activity	Keeping busy is healthy and natural.	Stimulates interest in products that are time-savers and enhance leisure-time activities.
3.	Efficiency and practicality	Admiration of things that solve problems (e.g., save time and effort).	Stimulates purchase of products that function well and save time.
4.	Progress	People can improve themselves; tomorrow should be better.	Stimulates desire for new products that fulfill unsatisfied needs; acceptance of products that claim to be "new" or "improved."
5.	Material comfort	"The good life."	Fosters acceptance of convenience and luxury products that make life more enjoyable.
6.	Individualism	Being one's self (e.g., self-reliance, self-interest, and self-esteem).	Stimulates acceptance of customized or unique products that enable a person to "express his or her own personality."
7.	Freedom	Freedom of choice.	Fosters interest in wide product lines and differentiated products.
8.	External conformity	Uniformity of observable behavior; desire to be accepted.	Stimulates interest in products that are used or owned by others in the same social group.
9.	Humanitarian-ism	Caring for others, particularly the underdog.	Stimulates patronage of firms that compete with market leaders.
10.	Youthfulness	A state of mind that stresses being young at heart or appearing young.	Stimulates acceptance of products that provide the illusion of maintaining or fostering youth.

Source: Leon G. Schiffman and Leslie Kanuck, *Consumer Behavior*, 2nd ed. (Englewood Cliffs, NJ: Prentice-Hall, 1983), p. 420.

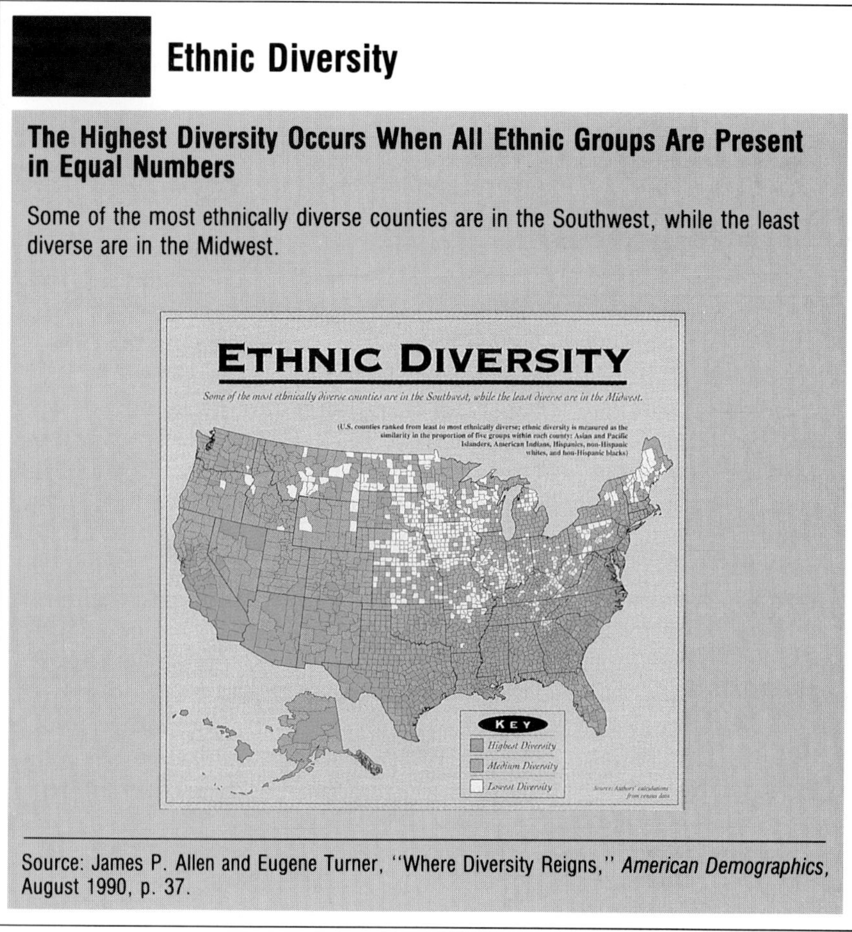
Ethnic Diversity
The Highest Diversity Occurs When All Ethnic Groups Are Present in Equal Numbers
Some of the most ethnically diverse counties are in the Southwest, while the least diverse are in the Midwest.
ETHNIC DIVERSITY
Some of the most ethnically diverse counties are in the Southwest, while the least diverse are in the Midwest.
(U.S. counties ranked from least to most ethnically diverse; ethnic diversity is measured as the similarity in the proportion of five groups within each county: Asian and Pacific Islanders, American Indians, Hispanics, non-Hispanic whites, and non-Hispanic blacks)
KEY
Highest Diversity
Medium Diversity
Lowest Diversity
Source: Authors' calculations from census data

Exhibit 7.2

Source: James P. Allen and Eugene Turner, "Where Diversity Reigns," *American Demographics*, August 1990, p. 37.

within a larger, more complex society. We will examine subcultural categories based on nationality, race, and age.

Subculture Based on Nationality

American business is at a point where it must adapt itself, because of its global perspective, to a world that is dominated by Asian business rather than the typical European business environment that has prevailed in the past. Increasingly, our trade is across the Pacific Ocean rather than the Atlantic. This shift in the world market can be seen at home as well. There are numerous subcultures based on nationality in the United States, such as Hispanics (consisting of Mexican Americans, Puerto Ricans, and Cubans), Scandinavians, Italians, Poles, Irish, Japanese, Chinese, and Vietnamese. Of particular interest are the upwardly mobile Hispanics—a rapidly growing but little noticed market.

William O'Hare, director of policy studies at the Population Reference Bureau in Washington, D.C., reports, "The mainstream media usually portray America's Hispanics as a group of impoverished, newly arrived

On the International Front Adapting to Foreign Buyers

Despite the growing global reliance on the English language, purchasing agents and other decision makers may not always understand all the details of product descriptions or specifications written in English. A company can gain a favorable initial reaction by having its product brochures translated into the buyer's language. Many European companies are known especially for producing brochures and publications in the languages of prospect countries. Singer Corporation, for example, provides its salespeople with instruction books printed in more than 50 languages. Some books consist entirely of pictures. In many cases, more than a basic translation of the manual is needed.

Computer software developers must also translate the product's screens, commands, and currency functions to suit the cultural business requirements. One reason Japanese computer makers still have difficulty breaking into the U.S. market is the problems encountered in exporting software written in Japanese. Apple lost its market share in Japan because it had only a U.S. model available in Japan, with little software adapted to the Japanese language. To overcome the problem, the Apple IIe now comes in 18 national versions, each keyboard displaying a different alphabet. Supporting documentation and training materials also must be translated. In the translation process, however, the quality and functionality of the product and service must never be compromised.

For many businesses entering the international market, quality has been a vague concept. Worldwide standards are now being established for all industries, from banking to resin manufacturing, to provide a universal framework for managing quality control. The ISO 9000 is an example of such a tool to ensure cross-cultural quality. This quality assurance program requires a process of internal auditing and managment review and the establishment of a quality system with defined procedures, work instructions, and complete documentation. Competitiveness in international sales may increase as a result of implementing this basic quality control program.

A global sales strategy must match products and services to the language and practices of each market. Preparation for entry into a foreign market is enhanced by understanding and learning as much as possible about the company's requirements and the practices and standards of that industry.

Sources: Kimberly K. Hockman, "The Last Barrier to the European Market," *The Wall Street Journal*, October 7, 1991; Edward R. Koepfler, "Strategic Options for Global Market Players," *Marketing 91/92* (The Dushking Publishing Group, 1991), p. 208; Sak Onkvisit and John J. Shaw, *International Marketing* (Columbus, OH: Merrill Publishing Company, 1989), pp. 227–228.

immigrants from Mexico or Central America."[7] A significant percentage of the Hispanic community has moved into affluence since 1970, however. O'Hare's study shows that the number of households with annual incomes of $50,000 or more (in 1988 dollars) increased 234 percent between 1972 and 1988. By 1988, more than 2.6 million Hispanics were included in these 638,000 affluent households. O'Hare also noted that:

- Hispanics tend to achieve affluence by having multiple pay checks.
- Hispanic households tend to be larger than white households.

- Affluent Hispanics are more likely than affluent whites to be young adults, and they are less likely to be aged 65 years or older. Of all affluent Hispanics, 54 percent are aged 25–44 years, compared with only 40 percent of affluent whites.
- Almost half (48 percent) of affluent white householders have at least a 4-year college degree, compared with only 29 percent of affluent Hispanic householders.
- Affluent Hispanics are heavily concentrated in large western cities (those with populations of one million or more). Within these metropolitan areas, about 40 percent of Hispanics, compared to 25 percent of whites, tend to live in the central city.[8]

Additional characteristics of the increasingly important Hispanic-American market are described in Table 7.4.

One unique feature of the Hispanic culture is its use of the Spanish language. It is an enduring characteristic of this subculture and has many subtle variations. In all, 23 percent of Hispanics speak only Spanish, and another 20 percent speak just enough English to get by. This means that salespeople must target their presentations to this segment with some concern for the Spanish language and the slang that exists among the varied subcategories of Hispanics.

Subculture Based on Race

The major racial subcultures in the United States are white, African American, Asian, and Native American. Because African Americans

Table 7.4

Characteristics of the Hispanic-American Market

Exhibit high brand loyalty
Trust well-known or familiar brands
Likely to buy what their parents bought
Buy brands perceived to be more prestigious
Prefer fresh to frozen or prepared items
Buy brands advertised by their ethnic group stores
Prefer to shop at smaller stores
Dislike impersonal stores
Tend not to be impulse buyers
New product adoption inhibited by difficulty with English
Are less confident shoppers
Are price-oriented, careful shoppers
Are more negative about marketing practices and government intervention in business

Sources: Adapted from Wayne D. Hoyer and Rohit Deshpande, "Cross-Cultural Influences on Buyer Behavior: The Impact of Hispanic Ethnicity," *AMA 1982*, pp. 89–92; Robert E. Wilkes and Humberto Valencia, "Shopping Orientation of Mexican-Americans," *AMA 1984*, pp. 26–31; Danny N. Bellenger and Humberto Valencia, "Understanding the Hispanic Market." *Business Horizons*, May–June 1982, pp. 47–50; and Peter L. Benzinger, "Hispanics: A Profitable Consumer Segment," *Marketing Review*, 41 (December 1985–January 1986), pp. 19–20.

constitute the largest racial minority in the United States at this time, increased effort is being made to understand the characteristics of the buying behavior and preferences among these consumers.

Traditionally, African Americans have been characterized in terms of their motivation to strive for middle-class values. Such values are reflected in their patterns of material goods consumption, particularly regarding "conspicuous consumables." Notably, this group possesses strong brand preferences. Some of the motivation for the buying behavior of this racial subculture is highlighted in Table 7.5.

Subculture Based on Age

The phrase *the graying of America* is indicative of an aging population. The older half of our age structure is growing faster than the younger half. According to Thomas Exter, research director of *American Demographics*, these statistics are noteworthy:

> Between now and the year 2020, the number of people aged 50 or older will increase by 74 percent, while the number of those under age 50 will grow a mere one percent. . . . If you define the older market as people aged 50 and older, then one American in four is a member. By 2020, over one-third of the population will belong to this group.[9]

Table 7.5

Understanding African-American Consumers' Brand Preferences

Consumer Traits	Possible Motivations
Purchase popular or leading brands	A strong desire to impress others Buy the "best" to reduce perceived risk Feel better about one's self
Brand loyal	Avoid perceived risk Reduce the time spent searching for product information
Less likely to buy private-label or generic products	Reduce perceived risk Avoid feeling that they have "settled" for second best

Sources: Kelvin A. Wall, "Positioning Your Brand in the Black Market," *Advertising Age*, June 18, 1973, p. 71; Robert B. Settle, John H. Faricy, and Richard W. Mizerski, "Racial Differences in Consumer Locus of Control," in Fred C. Allvine, ed., *1971 Combined Proceedings* (Chicago: American Marketing Association, 1972), pp. 629–633; Raymond A. Bauer, Scott M. Cunningham, and Lawrence H. Wortzel, "The Marketing Dilemma of Negroes," *Journal of Marketing*, July 1965, p. 4; and Alphonzia Wellington, "Traditional Brand Loyalty," *Advertising Age*, May 18, 1981, p. S-2.

Exhibit 7.3

Pick a Future

PICK A FUTURE

There could be 121 million Americans aged 50 or older by 2020, or 105 million. It all depends on how rapidly mortality rates fall in the next 30 years. If your business banks on the mature market, you need to decide which scenario is more likely before you can project the size of your market 30, 20, or even 10 years down the road.

(Projections of the population aged 50 and older by sex and age in 2000–2020, and percent change by decade; slow-growth scenario assumes continued rate of decline in mortality as experienced in the 1980s; high-growth scenario assumes rates of decline in mortality as experienced in the 1970s.)

Source: "Projections of the Population of the United States, by Age, Sex, and Race: 1988 to 2080," **Current Population Reports,** *Series P. 25, No. 1018, Bureau of the Census, 1989.*

Source: Thomas Exter, "How Big Will the Older Market Be?" *American Demographics,* June 1990, p. 32.

Exter further suggests that those predictions depend on current trends in mortality rates and the progress we may make against specific diseases, primarily heart disease, cancer, and stroke. For example, at the peak of the Baby Boom's retirement years, there may be as many as 58 million elderly or as few as 48 million, according to the U.S. Census Bureau.[10]

Salespeople are beginning to recognize the market potential of elderly consumers and their new approaches to life. Older consumers seem to derive great satisfaction from social involvement and physical activity. In terms of buying activity, they are more apt to pay cash and avoid using credit cards for installment purchases. This subculture has several specific segments:

- *Preretirement Segment (50–64 years)*—This group consists of the most active and affluent consumers of this subculture. Most are still working and many are in their peak earning years.

- *Early Retirees (65–74 years)*—Also an active group, these people have more time to engage in activities such as travel, continuing education, hobbies, sports, physical fitness, and volunteer work.
- *Less Active (75 years and older)*—This group is more likely to need health care products and services. Its members are independent but less active than younger consumers over 50. This is the fastest growing 50-and-over segment, however, and by the year 2000 it will represent half of this subculture.

Personal Influence

Over 50 years ago Herbert Hyman introduced the term *reference group.*[11] It has been defined as "a person or group of people that significantly influences an individual's behavior."[12] In a buying situation, the prospect may look toward, and identify with, a certain individual or group when forming an attitude or opinion about which product or service to purchase.

Reference group influence is used by salespeople in determining prospects' needs, attitudes, and values. By studying a buyer's reference group, a salesperson can learn a great deal about that prospect's consumption patterns. One task for the salesperson is to determine what sort of reference group influence exists or can be developed. A second task is to determine the degree of difference the reference group will tolerate in product, brand, store, services, and method of purchase. For example, if a person belongs to a ski club, the brand of skis, ski equipment, apparel, and even "mountains to conquer" that the individual chooses may be determined by the opinions frequently voiced by the club's members.

Family

In consumer behavior vocabulary, the following definitions are important if salespeople are to investigate how family influences affect their prospects' buying behavior:

- *Family*—a group of two or more persons related by blood, marriage, or adoption who reside together.
- *Nuclear Family*—the immediate group of father, mother, and children living together.
- *Extended Family*—the nuclear family and other relatives, such as grandparents, uncles, aunts, cousins, and in-laws.
- *Household*—all persons, both related and unrelated, who occupy a housing unit. The household is becoming an important unit of analysis for salespeople because of the growth in nontraditional and nonfamily households. Most nonfamily households consist of people living alone.[13]

The family is often referred to as a *buying center* that reflects the activities and influences of the family members. Family purchase decisions involve at least five identifiable roles. It is normal for these roles to be assumed by any or all members within the household. For members to assume various roles in different buying decisions is quite normal. Engel, Blackwell, and Miniard provide a clear explanation of each role:

1. *Gatekeeper* Initiator of family thinking about buying products and the gathering of information to aid the decision.
2. *Influencer* Individual whose opinions are sought concerning criteria the family should use in purchases and which products or brands most likely fit these evaluative criteria.
3. *Decider* The person with the financial authority and/or power to choose how the family's money will be spent and the products or brands that will be chosen.
4. *Buyer* The person who acts as purchasing agent: who visits the store, calls the supplier, writes the check, brings the products into the home.
5. *User* The person or persons who use the product.[14]

Salespeople need to communicate with the fulfiller of each role. It is also important to note that these roles apply to buyers of consumer products and services rather than buyers of industrial products. In industry, the organization serves as the buying center.

Social Class

Social class is a major source of group influence because buying is frequently directed by class structures. In the United States, social class is measured as a combination of occupation, income, education, wealth, and other variables. Table 7.6 describes seven American social classes

Table 7.6

Characteristics of Seven Major American Social Classes

Upper uppers (less than 1 percent)
Upper uppers are the social elite who live on inherited wealth and have well-known family backgrounds. They give large sums to charity, run debutante balls, own more than one home, and send their children to the finest schools. They are a market for jewelry, antiques, homes, and vacations. They often buy and dress conservatively rather than showing off their wealth. While small in number, upper uppers serve as a reference group for others to the extent that their consumption decisions trickle down and are imitated by the other social classes.

Lower uppers (about 2 percent)
Lower uppers have earned high income or wealth through exceptional ability in the professions or business. They usually begin in the middle class. They tend to be active in social and civic affairs and buy for themselves and their children the symbols of status, such as expensive homes, schools, yachts, swimming pools, and automobiles. They include the new rich who consume conspicuously to impress those below them. They want to be accepted in the upper-upper stratum, a status more likely to be achieved by their children than by themselves.

Table 7.6
Continued

Upper middles (12 percent)
Upper middles possess neither family status nor unusual wealth. They are primarily concerned with "career." They have attained positions as professionals, independent businesspersons, and corporate managers. They believe in education and want their children to develop professional or administrative skills so that they will not drop into a lower stratum. Members of this class like to deal in ideas and "high culture." They are joiners and highly civic-minded. They are the quality market for good homes, clothes, furniture, and appliances. They seek to run a gracious home, entertaining friends and clients.

Middle class (32 percent)
The middle class is made up of average-pay white- and blue-collar workers who live on "the better side of town" and try to "do the proper things." To keep up with the trends, they often buy products that are popular. Twenty-five percent own imported cars, and most are concerned with fashion, seeking the better brand names. Better living means owning a nice home in a nice neighborhood with good schools. The middle class believes in spending more money on worthwhile experiences for their children and aiming them toward a college education.

Working class (38 percent)
The working class consists of average-pay blue-collar workers and those who lead a "working class life style," whatever their income, school background, or job. The working class depends heavily on relatives for economic and emotional support, for tips on job opportunities, for advice on purchases, and for assistance in times of trouble. The working class maintains sharper sex role divisions and stereotyping. Car preferences include standard size and larger cars, rejecting domestic and foreign compacts.

Upper lowers (9 percent)
Upper lowers are working (are not on welfare), although their living standard is just above poverty. They perform unskilled work for very poor pay although they strive toward a higher class. Often, upper lowers are educationally deficient. Although they fall near the poverty line financially, they manage to "present a picture of self-discipline" and "maintain some effort at cleanliness."

Lower lowers (7 percent)
Lower lowers are on welfare, visibly poverty stricken, and usually out of work or have "the dirtiest jobs." Often they are not interested in finding a job and are permanently dependent on public aid or charity for income. Their homes, clothes, and possessions are "dirty," "raggedy," and "broken-down."

Sources: See Richard P. Coleman, "The Continuing Significance of Social Class to Marketing," *Journal of Consumer Research,* December 1983, pp. 265–280; and Richard P. Coleman and Lee P. Rainwater, *Social Standing in America: New Dimension of Class* (New York: Basic Books, 1978).

identified by social scientists. Figure 7.3 provides a sampling of how individuals are grouped according to income-distribution. This example is useful for salespeople as an analytical tool in helping them identify their prospect base for buyers of consumer products and services.

Situational Factors

No single theory can totally explain why consumers behave as they do. Not only are people different from each other, but they also act differently

Figure 7.3

Just the Facts

Upscale householders are most likely to be married and well educated, but middle-income households are just as likely to have children.

Selected characteristics of households by income groups	*total*	*less than $25,000*	*$25,000 to $49,999*	*$50,000 and over*
Total households *(in thousands)*	92,830	42,569	30,927	19,332
Percent of all households	100.0%	45.9%	33.3%	20.8%
Median household income*	$27,200	$12,900	$35,500	$66,300
Family households	70.9%	56.9%	79.1%	88.7%
Married couples	56.1%	36.6%	66.9%	82.0%
Female-headed families	11.7%	17.5%	8.5%	4.1%
With children under 18	36.1%	29.2%	41.6%	42.7%
One person in household	24.5%	39.5%	15.4%	5.9%
Two or three persons in household	49.8%	44.2%	54.6%	54.6%
Four or more persons in household	25.7%	16.4%	30.0%	39.5%
Median age of householder	49	51	41	42
Percent high school graduates	75.8%	61.0%	85.1%	93.3%
Percent with four or more years of college	22.3%	9.7%	23.7%	47.5%
Black	11.4%	16.4%	8.2%	5.4%
Hispanic	7.1%	8.7%	6.6%	4.4%

* *Income figures from the 1989 Current Population Survey are for 1988.*

Source: *American Demographics'* tabulation of the U.S. Census Bureau's March 1989 Current Population Survey

under different conditions. Accordingly, situational factors can be viewed as conditions particular to a specific time and place that influence how an individual reacts at that given moment. Some specific situational factors that may influence the prospect's choice are:

- *Physical surroundings*, such as decor, lighting, sounds, weather, humidity, altitude, distraction, and other visible objects or merchandise surrounding the stimulus object.
- *Social surroundings*, including interpersonal interactions involving the persons present, their characteristics, and their roles.
- *Specific conditions* induced by alcohol, cigarettes, caffeine, or medication taken for pain or colds.
- *Task definition*, which includes a requirement or reason to shop. For example, a person shopping for a household product as a birthday gift for a friend poses a different situation than a person shopping for a household product for personal use.
- *Previous events*, such as a fight with a spouse, a speeding ticket, problems at work, or winning the lottery.

- *Antecedent state,* including the temporary moods or conditions that affect a buyer, such as anxiety, fatigue, excitement, or having cash on hand.[15]

Other situational influences cover three main areas:

- *Communication*—The consumer may be exposed to personal or nonpersonal communications. Personal communication involves interactions the buyer might have with salespeople and other consumers. Nonpersonal communications refer to a wide range of stimuli, such as advertising media, consumer television programs and seminars, and publications such as *Consumer Reports.* This exposure may influence the kind of presentation strategy the salesperson uses. This choice is also guided by whether the sales communication is interpersonal or impersonal.
- *Purchase*—A purchasing situation refers to where the buyer acquires products or services. For instance, the price of a single soft drink at a major sporting event sometimes equals the price of a six-pack at a supermarket. A consumer's decision to buy at a retail store may be influenced by elements in the store's environment such as layout and design, music, colors, displays, crowding and density of both merchandise and shoppers, and the kind of service given by salespeople.
- *Use*—This refers to product consumption, or how the buyer intends to use the product or service. Social surroundings may influence use. During the past 10 years, the group Mothers Against Drunk Driving has exerted considerable pressure on breweries to alter their sponsorship of college and fraternity functions. Exhibit 7.4 illustrates the concern of all national sororities to be socially responsible to their members by discouraging alcohol abuse.

  The time at which use occurs is another element affecting buying behavior. Food consumption is highly dependent on times of day. The type of restaurant open and the menu offered varies considerably from morning to evening. The fast-food chains that were originally open for lunches and dinners are now competing heavily for the "on-the-move" breakfast crowd.

Individual Differences

Individual difference is a broad category of buying influences that continue to challenge both marketers and salespeople. As previously shown in Figure 7.1 (page 206), these differences may be grouped into six categories: consumer resources, motivation and involvement, knowledge, attitudes, personality, life-style, and demographics. Each element provides salespeople with extended knowledge about the consumers they serve.

Exhibit 7.4

National Presidents Show Concern

In October 1990, the presidents of the National Panhellenic Conference organizations agreed unanimously to the following position statement, which is binding on all college chapters.

Position Statement on Alcohol

Because of our concern for the health and well-being of our members, the presidents of all 26 National Panhellenic Conference (NPC) groups have agreed to the following:

1. **that we are opposed to the misuse of alcohol;**
2. **that all college chapters, all individual members, and all guests must abide by federal, state/provincial, local, college/university laws and regulations;**
3. **that it is inadvisable to host a party involving alcohol when the majority of guests attending are under the legal drinking age;**
4. **that no college chapter funds may be used to purchase alcohol. (Co-sponsors of social events are potentially liable regardless of how the expenses are shared.)**

Each NPC group has an alcohol policy and is expected to abide by it. In addition, the presidents expect their chapters to respect the regulations of any NPC co-sponsoring group.

We hope that this agreement will give college chapters the courage and ability to initiate discussion and formulate a Panhellenic stand on the subject of alcohol.

ALPHA CHI OMEGA	DELTA ZETA
ALPHA DELTA PI	GAMMA PHI BETA
ALPHA EPSILON PHI	KAPPA ALPHA THETA
ALPHA GAMMA DELTA	KAPPA DELTA
ALPHA OMICRON PI	KAPPA KAPPA GAMMA
ALPHA PHI	PHI MU
ALPHA SIGMA ALPHA	PHI SIGMA SIGMA
ALPHA SIGMA TAU	PI BETA PHI
ALPHA XI DELTA	SIGMA DELTA TAU
CHI OMEGA	SIGMA KAPPA
DELTA DELTA DELTA	SIGMA SIGMA SIGMA
DELTA GAMMA	THETA PHI ALPHA
DELTA PHI EPSILON	ZETA TAU ALPHA

Source: *The Kappa Alpha Theta Magazine,* Summer 1991, p. 15.

VALS and the Nine American Life-styles

One of the most popular tools for psychographic research is the Values and Lifestyle (VALS) program developed by Arnold Mitchell at Stanford Research International, an applied research organization in Menlo Park, California. Mitchell, as founding director, and associate director Marie Spengler launched the VALS program in May 1978 with 39 corporate sponsors.[16]

The VALS typologies consist of four categories of consumer groups that are subdivided into a total of nine life-styles. Table 7.7 provides the

Table 7.7

VALS Life-style Segmentation

Percentage of Population (Age 18 and Over)	Consumer Type	Values and Life-styles	Demographics	Buying Patterns
		Need-Driven Consumers		
4%	Survivors	Struggle for survival Distrustful Socially misfitted Rules by appetites	Poverty-level income Little education Many minority members Many live in city slums	Price dominant Focused on basics Buy for immediate needs
7	Sustainers	Concern with safety, security Insecure, compulsive Dependent, following Streetwise, determination to get ahead	Low income Low education Much unemployment Live in country as well as cities	Price important Want warranty Cautious buyers
		Outer-Directed Consumers		
35	Belongers	Conforming, conventional Unexperimental Traditional, formal Nostalgic	Low to middle income Low to average education Blue-collar jobs Tend toward noncity living	Family Home Fads Middle and lower mass markets
10	Emulators	Ambitious, show-off Status conscious Upwardly mobile Macho, competitive	Good to excellent income Youngish Highly urban Traditionally male, but changing	Conspicuous consumption "In" items Imitative Popular fashion

Table 7.7
Continued

22	Achievers	Achievement, success, fame Materialism Leadership, efficiency Comfort	Excellent incomes Leaders in business, politics, etc. Good education Suburban and city living	Give evidence of success Top of the line Luxury and gift markets "New and improved" products
		Inner-Directed Consumers		
5	I-Am-Me	Fiercely individualistic Dramatic, impulsive Experimental Volatile	Young Many single Student or starting job Affluent backgrounds	Display one's taste Experimental fads Source of far-out fads Clique buying
7	Experiential	Drive to direct experience Active, participative Person-centered Artistic	Bimodal incomes Mostly under 40 Many young families Good education	Process over product Vigorous, outdoor sports "Making" home pursuits Crafts and introspection
8	Societally Conscious	Societal responsibility Simple living Smallness of scale Inner growth	Bimodal low and high incomes Excellent education Diverse ages and places of residence Largely white	Conservation emphasis Simplicity Frugality Environmental concerns
		Combined Inner- and Outer-Directed Group		
2	Integrated	Psychological maturity Sense of fittingness Tolerant, self-actualizing World perspective	Good to excellent incomes Bimodal in age Excellent education Diverse jobs and residential patterns	Varied self-expression Esthetically oriented Ecologically aware One-of-a-kind items

Source: From Arnold Mitchell, *Nine American Lifestyles: Who We Are and Where We Are Going* (New York: Macmillan, 1983). Copyright © 1983 by Arnold Mitchell.

VALS consumer typology, a brief description of its values and life-styles, and demographic information and buying patterns.

Many marketing organizations and advertising agencies use this information as a guide in preparing their advertising messages to reach a targeted group. Having access to this kind of information can help salespeople tailor their presentations to emphasize the specific advantages and benefits of the product that hold appeal to the prospect's typology.

For example, one heavily targeted group in the 1980s was the yuppies, a subset of the Baby Boomers. These young, upwardly mobile professionals were often *emulators* while struggling to be *achievers* in their choices of products and services.

Psychological Processes

The third major area of influence affecting buying behavior is the buyer's psychological processes, which include information processing, learning, and attitude and behavior change. This section will focus on two levels: attitude and behavior change as they apply to consumer motivation, and how these changes affect the salesperson's approach.

Attitude and Behavior Change

People buy products and services and enter into relationships to satisfy basic needs. This may be especially apparent in relationships between customers and salespeople. (This concept will be developed more thoroughly in Chapter 11, which focuses on identifying buyers' needs, one of the basic selling steps.)

One comprehensive theory of needs is presented in the work of Abraham Maslow. He conceptualized a hierarchy of five basic human needs, each of which must be satisfied before the next one receives our attention.[17] Figure 7.4 presents that hierarchy, with the first or lower level being the most fundamental. This basic concern is *physiological*, including the satisfaction of such fundamental needs as water, air, food, and sleep. The second level is *safety and security*, mainly involving protection from

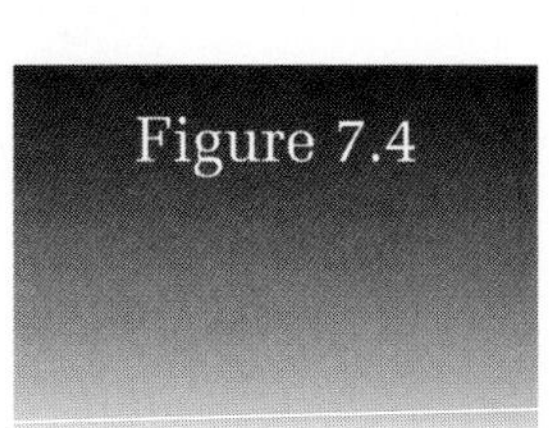

Figure 7.4

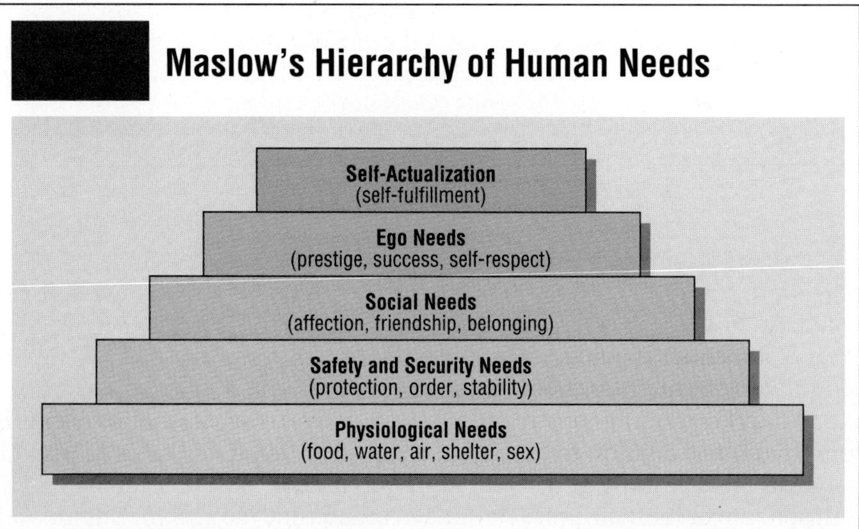

anything that could endanger a person's life. *Social* needs include the longing for love, affection, and belonging. The fourth level, *esteem* or ego needs, reflects a person's desire to feel a sense of respect from others. This also may include a desire for achievement, independence, and self-confidence. When individuals reach the fifth level, *self-actualization*, they seek to satisfy their desire to grow or to achieve everything that they feel capable of becoming.

The top three levels of Maslow's hierarchy probably have the greatest relevance in personal selling relationships. Social needs involve relating to others for the purpose of defining self-images. Psychologist Will Schutz distinguishes three social needs that people attempt to meet through communicating with others: inclusion, control, and affection.[18] Most outside salespeople, and probably the prospects who become their long-term customers, have strong social needs. Therefore, it will be helpful to examine each of these needs as Schutz describes them:

- *Inclusion*—This need involves the desire to affiliate with other people to obtain a sense of belonging and acceptance from others. Therefore, in addition to accomplishing tasks and accomplishing the work of their respective companies, most salespeople and their customers also want to feel accepted or included by the people with whom they associate in their work environment. The establishment of a long-term relationship between salesperson and customer is a way for both of them to meet their needs for inclusion in the working environment.
- *Control*—The desire to influence others is a second type of social need. While control needs vary among individuals, each of us has some desire to lead, exert authority, or possess power. Salespeople and their customers may have selected their professions because they enjoy the opportunity to take independent leadership and make things happen.
- *Affection*—The desire to exchange feelings of warmth and caring with other people is the third social need described by Schutz. Perhaps no other type of relationship has as much potential for personal rejection and superficial manipulation as does the relationship between salesperson and customer. Demonstrations of affection—through the use of sincere compliments and customer referrals, for example—can be an antidote to rejection and superficiality.

Beyond the social needs, which are classified on the third level in Maslow's hierarchy of human needs, are self-esteem needs. Self-esteem, a component of self-acceptance, is a measure of how much people like themselves. Both salespeople and customers want to view themselves as worthwhile, valuable people. To the degree that each is able to meet the other's social needs, they will tend to view themselves as valued, and a long-term relationship involving repeat business is likely to develop.

The highest need in Maslow's hierarchy is self-actualization, or the desire to maximize our potential for becoming the best people we can be.

Exhibit 7.5

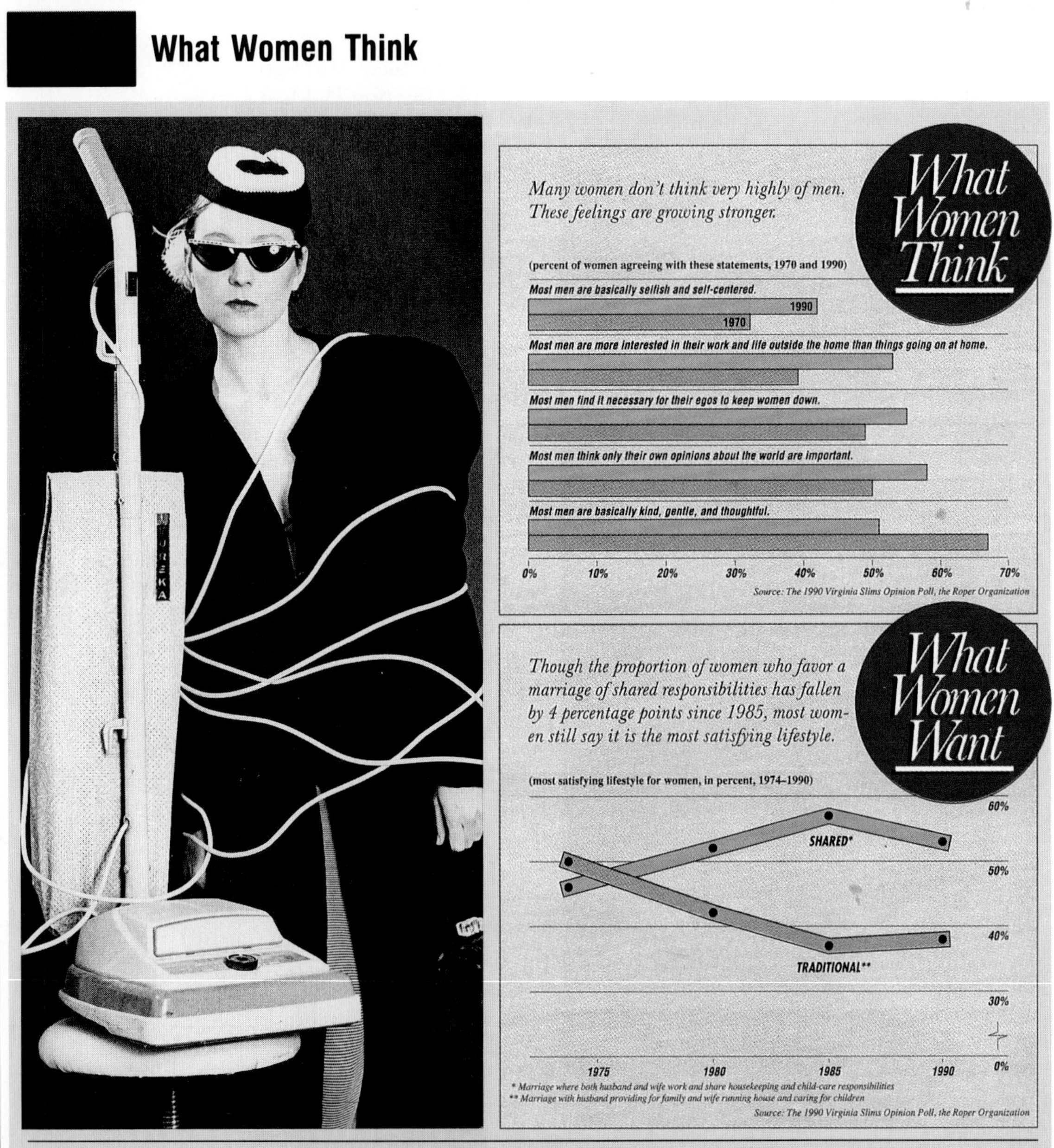

Source: Bickley Townsend and Kathleen O'Neil, "Women Get Mad." Reprinted with permission © *American Demographics*, August 1990, p. 28 and by permission of Philip Morris Incorporated. Photo © Jon Gipe.

It is perhaps at this level that the interaction of task and interpersonal needs is most obviously integrated. The salesperson and customer are mutually interdependent, facilitating each other's needs for self-actualization in their professional roles. In practical and simplified terms, the customer has the problems that need to be analyzed and the salesperson has the solutions. If relationships exist because they meet the needs of the individuals who participate in them, then the relationship between the salesperson and the customer has the potential for being a perfect match.

Summary

Success in selling begins with understanding people. Understanding the forces that motivate and influence a person's buying behavior helps the salesperson to discover the buyer's needs and prepare a presentation strategy that appeals to those needs.

Like selling, buying is a process. Buyers of consumer products and services and industrial products are engaged in a process that includes five problem-solving activities: need recognition, search for information, alternative evaluation, purchase, and outcome or postpurchase response.

Surrounding the buying decision process are three major areas of influence that affect the individual's buying behavior. These elements are environmental influences, individual differences, and psychological processes. Environmental influences include culture, subcultures, and social classes in our society and their affect on buying behaviors. Personal, family, and situational influences are also environmental factors.

The second component contributing to the purchase decision process is individual differences, such as consumer resources, motivation and involvement, knowledge, attitudes, personality, and life-styles. This component involves the nine values and life-style typologies used in the VALS program. Each typology has a characteristic buying behavior.

Finally, the third factor influencing buying behavior is the buyer's psychological processes, which may be viewed from two perspectives: Maslow's hierarchy of needs and Schutz's structure of social needs. Overall, the more understanding salespeople have about consumer behavior and the buying process, the more effectively they can adapt to the buying situation. This adaptability allows them to build selling strategies that tailor the product's advantages and benefits to the buyer's perceived set of conditions that influence all buying behavior.

Key Terms

Extended Family The nuclear family and other relatives

Family A group of two or more persons related by blood, marriage, or adoption

Household All persons, related or not, who occupy a housing unit
Nuclear Family The immediate group of father, mother, and children living together
Values and Lifestyles (VALS) Program Consumer typology as categorized by psychographic research

Review Questions

1. List and explain the five stages of the buying decision process.
2. How is buying behavior shaped by environmental influences?
3. How do individual differences shape buying behavior?
4. List and explain the interaction among the needs in Maslow's hierarchy.
5. Explain Schutz's social needs theory and how it relates to a sales relationship.

Discussion Questions

1. What is the importance to the salesperson of buying behavior and the buying decision process?
2. Consider a major purchase you have made recently. Apply the five-step problem-solving format to the process you went through in deciding to make the purchase.
3. What environmental influences shape your buying behavior when you are in the role of student?
4. Examine each of the individual differences presented in this chapter. Explain how they influence your buying behavior. Then compare and contrast how they affect the buying behavior of another member of your family.
5. Discuss psychological influences on buying behavior by identifying which basic needs in Maslow's hierarchy you satisfied in making a recent major purchase.
6. Discuss who a buyer and a salesperson might mutually satisfy their needs for inclusion, control, and affection through a sales relationship.
7. Form a group with four classmates. Viewing yourselves as student consumers, discuss how a campus club or bookstore might use Maslow's hierarchy to plan a sales presentation urging you to use its services or products.

Knowing Market Characteristics

Case 7.1

Antonio Fernandez accepted a position as a sales representative with a small, growing insurance firm serving Los Angeles and the surrounding area. He was hired primarily because of his knowledge of the Hispanic culture and his ability to speak Spanish.

Although he had not been very successful in sales, he was encouraged by the tremendous growth of the Hispanic population and the potential insurance needs of this group. Antonio was determined to specialize in selling life insurance to the Hispanic community.

It was apparent that the potential for sales existed; however, it was still necessary to seek out specific market characteristics with reference to demographic profiles, such as income, age, occupation, and so on.

Antonio's research efforts clearly indicated that Hispanics do not represent one large market, but rather several subcultures with many differences, such as choice preferences in products and life-style. He did, however, observe some similarities, including the Spanish language.

Realizing the significant differences among the Hispanic population, the insurance firm felt that the many submarkets demanded too much special attention, making it too time consuming for Antonio. "Maybe we should just develop one approach and sales presentation for all Spanish-speaking people, and not waste time and money tailoring presentations to the characteristics and needs of specific submarkets," suggested the sales manager.

Antonio is convinced of the great potential in serving the Hispanic market and is confident that he can become a top seller for the insurance company. Although he believes that the sales manager will not give him the needed support, he is still determined to pursue this opportunity on his own.

1. Is it worth convincing the sales manager of the potential of the Hispanic market?
2. What advantages do you feel result from gathering information about varied markets and their distinctive needs?
3. Evaluate the following statement: "Markets are markets. It doesn't really matter if your customers are Hispanic or not because buyers engage in about the same type of purchasing behavior."

Case 7.2

Finding Out Customer's Needs

St. Moritz Exquisite, a 10-year old Swiss manufacturer of cosmetics and facial beauty creams, is launching a line of perfumes for the first time. Perfumes represent a significant departure from its beauty items, with the expectation of enhancing its reputation in its expanding foreign markets.

Since its inception, this Swiss company has earned a reputation of quality and reasonable prices. Its products have always aimed toward middle-income buyers, particularly women in the 30 to 50 age bracket.

St. Moritz's management has developed a new strategy with its perfumes aiming at the higher-income buyers in the same 30 to 50 age bracket. With prices higher than the industry average, their line of perfumes will respond to the exquisite image of the discriminating buyer.

St. Moritz plans to distribute its perfumes selectively in large well-known department stores. Although this method of distribution is not uncommon for many cosmetics and beauty items, the competitiveness of the perfume industry has led the distributor to favor small perfumeries and specialty gift shops, since supported by a limited promotional budget.

The sole distributor in the west United States does not have a track record of dealing with small shops, much less high-income, up-scale buyers. The manufacturer has convinced the distributor that the profit potential is great for its limited line of fragrances, recognizing its success with other beauty items.

1. What are the benefits of perfumes that are important to serving buyers' needs?
2. How would the retail salesperson go about encouraging the buyer to select the St. Moritz fragrance?
3. What factors should the distributor keep in mind in making the decision to carry the St. Moritz line of perfumes?

Notes

1. James F. Engel, Roger D. Blackwell, and Paul W. Miniard, *Consumer Behavior*, 6th ed. (Chicago: The Dryden Press, 1990), p. 3.
2. Ibid, p. 52.
3. Joe Schwartz, "Focus on Diversity: The 1990 American Demographics Conference," *American Demographics*, August 1990, p. 19.
4. Phillip R. Harris and Robert T. Moran, *Managing Cultural Differences* (Houston: Gulf Publishing Company, 1987), pp. 190–195. Cited in James F. Engel, Roger D. Blackwell, and Paul W. Miniard, *Consumer Behavior*, 6th ed. (Chicago: The Dryden Press, 1990), p. 63.
5. *Webster's New World Dictionary*, 3rd College Edition (New York: Simon & Schuster, Inc., 1988), p. 367.
6. Schwartz, "Focus on Diversity," pp. 21–22.
7. William O'Hare, "The Rise of Hispanic Affluence," *American Demographics*, August 1990, p. 40.
8. Ibid., p. 42.
9. Thomas Exter, "How Big Will the Older Market Be?," *American Demographics*, June 1990, p. 30.
10. Ibid., p. 32.
11. Herbert Hyman, "The Psychology of Status," *Archives of Psychology*, 38 (1942).
12. William O. Bearden and Michael J. Etzel, "Reference Group Influence on Product and Brand Purchase Decision," *Journal of Consumer Research*, 9 (September 1982), p. 184.
13. Engel, Blackwell, and Miniard, *Consumer Behavior*, p. 170.
14. Ibid., p. 174.
15. Russell Belk, "Situational Variables and Consumer Behavior," *Journal of Consumer Research*, 2 (December 1975), pp. 157–164.
16. Arnold Mitchell, *The Nine American Lifestyles: Who We Are and Where We Are Going*, (New York: Macmillan Publishing Company, 1983), p. x.
17. Abraham H. Maslow, *Toward a Psychology of Being* (New York: Van Nostrand Reinhold, 1968).
18. Will Schutz, *The Interpersonal Underworld* (Palo Alto, CA: Science and Behavior Books, 1966).

CHAPTER

8

Creating a Positive Buying–Selling Climate

Knowledge Objectives

In this chapter, you will learn:

1. The nature and elements of an organizational culture and climate
2. The characteristics of an effective buying climate in a sales communication relationship
3. The function of the communication climate in developing relationships with customers
4. To distinguish between confirming and disconfirming messages in a buying–selling climate
5. To identify a framework for interaction using a dimensional sales model

Consider This

You can't create a sales culture with words alone.

James F. Lewin, senior vice president
Security Pacific National Bank

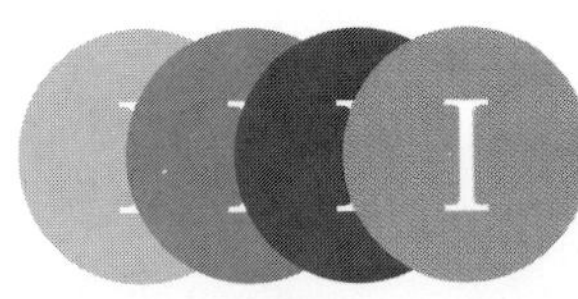

n Chapter 2, professional selling was introduced as a relationship-driven process, the success of which is measured in terms of profitability, both quantitatively and qualitatively. Communication was also presented in that chapter as the process by which salespeople plan, implement, and control their selling activities. Communication is the vehicle by which relationships are moved from short term to long term, and often from an impersonal to a more interpersonal level.

In addition to knowing the company, products, competition, customers, and buying process, sales professionals seek to create a buying–selling environment that will enhance the relational process. In this chapter we will continue the development of these preapproach activities by discussing how communication influences the development and maintenance of a positive buying–selling climate. We will explore this climate in terms of the organizational, communication, and buying–selling environments.

Organizational Structure, Climate, and Culture

Organizations, like fingerprints, are unique. This uniqueness prompts sales managers to look at three facets of their organizations: structure, climate, and culture.

Structure consists of the arrangement or interrelation of all the parts of the organization. This arrangement depends on the mission of the organization—whether it has been established to provide goods or services.

Organizational climate is the human environment in which employees accomplish their tasks. It includes the general atmosphere of supportiveness or defensiveness in the company. A study of managers suggests that a supportive climate usually occurs in organizations where there is mutual trust and confidence, where superiors exhibit a willingness to help subordinates with job and personal matters, where managers are approachable and honest about company policies and procedures, and where managers are willing to give credit to subordinates' accomplishments and ideas.[1]

The relationship and activities of the organization's structure and climate combine to produce its culture. A business *culture* is defined as the "shared language, events, symbols, rituals, and value systems of its members, working together in a system affected by its environment. Organizational culture evolves from past members' behavior and is reconstituted by current members."[2] Communication has been identified as the most significant component for building and maintaining strong organizational cultures:

> The companies and organizations that do the best job thinking through what they are all about, deciding how and to whom these central messages should be communicated and executing the communication plan in a quality way, invariably build a strong sense of esprit within their own organization and among the many constituents they serve.[3]

In other words, it is listening and talking that make up the communication in the system.

Organizational structure, climate, and culture influence salespeoples' perceptions of the buying situation and conditions, which in turn influence their behavior. For instance, in a company where speed is valued over quality, salespeople are likely to perceive many situations as requiring fast, but not necessarily accurate, results. This affects their daily work habits and the way they communicate with others inside and outside the company in their internal and external environment. For example, if the firm has rigid quotas to meet that are constantly increasing, the sales force may feel pressured to spend as little time as possible with a customer and may often resort to pressure tactics to close the sale. Salespeople may also ignore follow-up activities that are important for servicing the account and maintaining the relationship.

In this chapter we provide a framework within which salespeople can build a supportive climate for meaningful, long-term relationships. To achieve this goal, we must examine the nature of a sales communication climate.

The Nature of a Sales Communication Climate

When meteorologists describe climatic conditions, they refer to the predominant pattern of elements, such as the degree of humidity in a specific geographical area. Daily weather occurrences, such as rainfall or changes in barometric pressure, are a part of the climate only to the degree that they contribute to the predominant pattern. Climates often play a significant role in people's decisions about where to live.

When people relate to one another, a communication climate develops. *Communication climate* refers to the quality of personal relationships among people, such as between salespeople and customers.[4] The organizational climate of a company may be a major reason a job applicant joins the sales force.

Each relationship between a salesperson and a customer also has a climate. In fact, the sales rep may have to resist the tendency to give the most service to those customers with whom the feeling is that of being personally accepted and supported. As is true of communication in all organizations, groups, and one-to-one relationships, the desirable sales communication climate is typically linked with conditions hospitable to growth, productivity, need satisfaction, and rapport.

A climate is to a relationship what a personality is to an individual: It is the emotional tone of the relationship. There is no specific formula or single factor that promotes successful relationships between salespeople and their customers, just as there appears to be no single meteorological climate that appeals to all people. However, there are characteristics common to high-quality relationships that can be attributed to the climate. The climate usually is a major factor in customers' decisions to participate in developing a long-term professional selling relationship with individual

Thirteen Steps To Develop Your Own Sales Culture

According to sales consultant Barbara Sanfilippo who heads her own firm by the same name in Oakland, California, developing a sales and service culture is an evolutionary process that can take four to five years or longer. If top management is committed and supportive to implementing the 13 steps outlined below, you have an excellent chance of being successful.

1. **Mission Statement**

   Where are you leading your troops? Develop a mission statement with input from all managers and employees. Send out a memo from the president with the mission attached and hold a series of kick-off meetings to discuss each department and each individual's contribution. Every employee should be asked to sign a personal pledge of commitment.

2. **Customer Service**

   Make it easy for your customers to complain. Provide comment cards, hot-line numbers, and mystery shoppings as regular parts of your culture. Hire enthusiastic and professional sales and customer service representatives from a retail store or another service industry.

3. **Job Descriptions**

   Update job descriptions and performance evaluations to reflect the skills and behavior you want. Require sales managers to hold regular sales meetings, reinforce product knowledge, set goals, track performance, coach, recognize, reward, and create a customer service attitude.

4. **Measurement**

   A sales management tracking system recognizes managers and employees who make a contribution. Ideally, customer contact employees should each receive their own tracking report each month showing individual sales accomplishments. These reports can be a valuable coaching tool for your sales managers.

5. **Communicate Results**

   Set up charts everywhere at all levels and post referrals, sales, dollars, productivity and complaints. Make sure individual and team results are in your company paper or in a special sales flyer. Since achievement is the number one motivator, post results to boost your staff's morale and stimulate healthy competition.

6. **Goal Setting**

   Instill a feeling of ownership and accountability among all bank employees. Ask your employees what they feel they can do to increase sales and customer satisfaction. Establish referral, cross-sell, dollar, retention, or fee income goals according to your bank's needs. All employees should sign off, in writing, on their personal goals. These goals should then become part of their performance evaluation.

7. **Training**

   Training should begin with sales and sales management skills for your managers and assistant managers. All customer contact employees from officers to tellers need sales and customer service training. The support and administrative employees would also benefit from a customer service seminar.

8. **Product Knowledge**

   Reinforce product knowledge in challenging and fun ways. Consider a product knowledge team game like "Jeopardy" with questions having a specific point value. Offer a "product-of-the-month" quiz that rewards employees for proficiency in a particular product. Develop a product knowledge certification program that certifies employees for their knowledge of a particular product.

9. **Incentive Programs**

You should have an "ongoing" program to reward both sales and service. Ideally, cash can be paid for both individual and team results. The trend now is to pay for results above a specific minimum or according to profitability. Achievement clubs are also a popular method to stimulate and reward performers. With an achievement club, you set a minimum entry level and everyone who achieves the goal becomes a club member.

10. **Meetings**

Communicate results at branch or department meetings by beginning with the team goal and personal results. Encourage all employees to talk about their sales or service success stories. Keep the meeting alive with interactive exercises and role play. Recruit guest speakers from other areas of the bank or from the retail industry. Props and music can add a little spice.

11. **Newsletters**

A newsletter is one of the most easy, inexpensive and effective ways to motivate and recognize employees. Publish score cards, individual results, team results, sales and service stories and tips. Publish the names of CSRs with a 2.0 or higher cross-sell ratio, all tellers with 25 monthly referrals, all branches achieving 100% of goals and all managers with loan and deposit goals of 90% or greater.

12. **Non-Performers**

It's no longer true that when you work for a bank you are guaranteed a job for life. Do not accept mediocrity. Non-performers must be terminated to continually upgrade the quality of your personnel. Always offer your employees training, measurement, incentives and your support. Some employees will successfully make transitions and others will ask for new assignment. There will always be others who will not function well in the transition.

13. **Management Involvement**

Although most top quality sales organizations in the U.S. have a senior sales and marketing director reporting to the president, banks often select a junior sales or business development coordinator who reports to a senior loan or operations executive. This is ludicrous. Every bank president should have a senior-level sales director on his or her management team whose sole purpose is to develop a sales and service culture, train, motivate and improve customer service. All sales support areas should report through the sales function. Banking is a profit business and sales must take its rightful place on the senior management committee's agenda.

Source: Barbara Sanfilippo, "Thirteen Steps to Develop Your Own Sales Culture," *Personal Selling Power*, April 1989.

On the Ethical Side: Communicating and Enforcing Ethical Behavior

For an organization to display consistently high ethical standards, its leadership must be openly and unequivocally committed to ethical conduct. In companies that strive to make high ethical standards a reality, top management communicates its commitment in a code of ethics, in speeches and publications, in policies concerning the consequences of unethical behavior, in the actions of top executives, and in the actions taken to ensure compliance.

All managers are expected to stress ethical conduct with their subordinates and involve themselves in the process of monitoring compliance with the code of ethics. In exercising ethical leadership, managers can do several concrete things, including the following:

- They can take a strong stand on ethical behavior and establish a tradition of integrity, setting an example by their own behavior.
- Managers and employees need to be educated about what is ethical and what is not. Gray areas should be pointed out and discussed. Discussions with reference to ethical issues should be encouraged.

Overall, management must secure the support of key personnel and use the full force of the organization to uphold ethical standards and behavior. The stronger the corporate climate, the stronger its direction should be toward serving customers and markets.

Source: Adapted from "Corporate Ethics: A Prime Asset," *The Business Roundtable*, February 1988, pp. 4–10.

salespeople and their companies. We will examine both the characteristics and functions of an effective sales communication climate.

Characteristics of an Effective Sales Communication Climate

The success of sales professionals depends on the motivation, satisfaction, and success of those being served. Just as students must ultimately do their own learning, so customers ultimately make their own buying decisions. The principal role of both the professor and the salesperson is to create a communication climate in which their clientele is motivated to engage in high-quality relationships conducive to their mutual success.

According to educators John Roueche and George Baker, five sets of characteristics are common to most effective school organizations. These are order, purpose, and coherence; efficiency and objectivity; student-centeredness; optimism and high expectations; and organizational health.[5] Each set of characteristics is translated here into the context of a supportive buying climate in a sales interview.

1. *Order, Purpose, and Coherence*—A climate characterized by order, purpose, and coherence communicates the impression that the organization operates with a sense of direction that occurs by intent and action rather than out of habit. There is a master plan shared by all members of the community that includes common goals and objectives to facilitate coherent mutual action. Achievement and effort are recognized and rewarded.

   A shared sense of direction is essential to a salesperson–customer relationship. Through the mutual problem-solving skills developed while using this textbook, salespeople will be able to work with their customers to facilitate a master plan for meeting the customers' needs. When there is mutual agreement on the goals and objectives that will guide a salesperson's work with a customer, the relationship becomes a means of achieving tangible success. For example, rewards—such as genuine compliments, references, or referrals—will be more easily given and received because they will more likely be mutually recognized as sanctioned by the plan.
2. *Efficiency and Objectivity*—Growing out of the mutually shared master plan, the buying–selling environment becomes efficient and objective. Salespeople control the environment to help their customers succeed in accomplishing clearly identified goals and objectives.

   Salespeople can contribute to a meaningful communication climate by using the information in Chapters 5 and 6 to conduct their precall planning activities in ways that facilitate efficient sales interviews. When salespeople are prepared for an interview, most of the time they spend with a customer can be focused on tasks that will contribute to their shared goals and objectives. They can mutually develop procedures for monitoring progress toward their goals and objectives, and determine assessment techniques based on specific, observable, and objective (not subjective or judgmental) measures. For example, in preparing for a first sales call, identifying that the salesperson will determine the customer's reasons for buying and leave the product for a 2-week trial demonstration is more objective than assuming that the sales rep will make the first call and "sell the customer everything he can."

   Finally, salespeople can learn to use failure to constructively redirect their goals and activities. Feelings of personal rejection and incompetence often accompany tendencies to personalize failure. These feelings detract from efficiency and a productive sales communication climate.
3. *Customer-Centeredness*—Customer-centeredness involves adapting the sales strategy and environment to respond to individual customer needs. Customer-centeredness involves a high level of interaction between customer and salesperson. In fact, achievement increases when salespeople demonstrate "high interpersonal skills."[6]

Sales Professional Spotlight

Craig Franz is acclaimed as one of the top producers in the insurance industry, an industry where relatively few succeed. Working for an independent insurance agency representing large corporations, such as The Hartford, Aetna, and Fireman's Fund, he notes that success in his field is commonly perceived as depending on the relationship developed between the salesperson and the client.

He learned his first lesson in sales from his grandfather, who has played a major role in his sales success. He relates this story told to him by his grandfather many years ago: "An associate in his office was selling life insurance to a client. The associate had two acceptable policies to offer the client, although one offered a little more coverage at a lower commission. The associate asked my grandfather whether he should sell the client the better policy or the one that earned the higher commission. 'You just take care of your client, and the commission will take care of itself,' my grandfather responded to his associate."

Craig strongly believes that the final decision to buy is more often based on the relationship and service support provided to the client, as well as a competitive price. Few clients discriminate among the nationally ranked insurance companies, believing that the large companies are equally good and their prices are somewhat similar. He emphasizes that "every time I have failed to sell a new client it has been because of the relationship that client has with their present agent."

Furthermore, because success in this industry comes from renewal business, this relationship effort is vital. As Craig points out, "One thing that attracted me to selling insurance is the renewal business. In fact, it is more important for me to keep an account when the insurance renews than it is to write a new account. The effort that goes into finding the prospect, doing the paperwork, preparing the quote, negotiating with insurance companies, and presenting the results to the client is far greater than simply updating and renewing an existing client's coverage." The relationship and service support thus become even more critical factors in selling insurance.

There is also some truth to equating hard work with success. The agent must locate prospects and help them make buying decisions based on needs for specific insurance coverage and protection. "My objective is to get the client to make the decision to do business with me before I get to the stage of closing the sale. It is vital to do a good job prequalifying the prospect, preparing for the client, educating the client, and developing a good buying climate. I try hard to make clients feel as if everything I do is for their best interest. I am honest, sincere, and simply myself. The more honest and sincere I am up front, the more comfortable I will make the client feel," Craig says.

An important phase in the relationship-building process is getting the client to feel comfortable with the support staff. This is critical because the support staff handles clients on a daily basis while the salespeople are in the field. "To build confidence with the client, I often take my assistant with me on service calls to meet the clients personally. This helps to develop a strong personal relationship with our clients that may never have been accomplished otherwise."

Craig's approach to winning the confidence of his prospects is to act less as a salesman and more as a consultant. His philosophy is further embedded in the belief that his clients deserve to be treated as he would want to be treated, and the relationship with his client becomes a vital factor in his business.

Although the customer may not always be right, the main function of salespeople is to respond to the individual needs of their customers in a way that is mutually satisfying. When customers believe that their individual needs are being addressed by the salesperson, they will personally feel valued. As a result, they will more readily make and keep appointments with the sales rep, interact openly and responsively, and participate in achieving the goals and objectives they have established.

The sales communication skills discussed throughout this textbook are customer-centered. The skills developed in this chapter will help the salesperson establish a positive communication climate and discover the customer's reasons for buying in ways that encourage the customer to feel valued. When salespeople manage the climate in these ways, customers are likely to appreciate their customer-centered and relationship-oriented approach.

4. *Optimism and High Expectations*—A fourth major variable identified by Roueche and Baker is a degree of optimism or a conviction that success is inevitable. In successful educational environments, teachers often express a belief that they are responsible for promoting the inevitability of success. Students gain a positive attitude and a sense of control over the learning tasks and activities. An atmosphere of high expectation for students' academic development often accompanies this optimism.

   The salesperson's ability to provide direction by developing a long-term plan and a problem-solving system that meet the customer's needs is a strong foundation on which to build an atmosphere of optimism. Another important factor is acceptance and pride in oneself and one's role as a salesperson, as discussed in Chapter 4. Skills for managing the sales communication climate that address the customer's reasons for buying will be taught in Chapter 11 to help promote an atmosphere of genuine optimism.

In turn, this atmosphere will often generate high professional expectations between the customer and the salesperson.

5. *Organizational Health*—Organizations have personalities, just as the individuals who work in them do. The healthy organization has managerial characteristics such as strong leadership, accountability, commitment to organizational excellence through in-service training and evaluation, and community involvement.

The individual salesperson's efforts are an extension of the salesperson's company. Behavior with customers is a reflection on the company; the personality and behavior of the company reflect on the individual's sales image and on how customers perceive the salesperson. If a person has genuine pride in the company, the customers may come to share that pride in being affiliated with both the salesperson and the company. A strong, positive company image and the sales professional's personal image promote a healthy communication climate among salespeople, their customers, and their sales associates.

From the work of Roueche and Baker, we can conclude that a communication climate is a complex combination of factors. These factors include a sense of *mutual purpose* understood and subscribed to by the people involved and *efficiency* achieved by spending time primarily on tasks that relate to the achievement of goals, with objective means of monitoring success. Furthermore, relationships are *customer-centered* and permeated by a strong sense of *optimism* that generates high expectations for achievement. Finally, the organization and its employees are viewed as *healthy* because they demonstrate leadership, accountability, and commitment to excellence and take part in their community.

The Function of Climate in Developing Relationships

Communication climates are often shaped more by the way people feel toward one another than by the tasks they perform.[7] Research in human relations consistently demonstrates that when relations are poor, task achievement is minimal. In other words, positive working relationships motivate people to be productive.[8] The primary function of the communication climate in a selling relationship, then, is to generate a positive working relationship that stimulates progress toward meeting the customer's needs in such a way that the salesperson's needs are also met.

Sales managers, other departments within the organization, and its salespeople share responsibility for developing a communication climate built on trust and respect. Marketing programs that are trumpeted to salespeople as "The Trade Deal You've Always Wanted" or "The Real Deal of the Century" are usually off target when dealing with sales.

Exaggeration, hype, and sweeping generalities are discounted by professional salespeople. What they seek and use in developing a positive climate are the types of information described in Chapter 5: objective information on market share, product and category trends, analysis of these trends, consumer response to earlier promotions, what concerns went into making a decision, and what the program is expected to accomplish.

After examining the characteristics and functions of a sales climate, it becomes clear that genuine communication generates a buying–selling climate that will improve one's relationships with customers. Genuine communication is the type of exchange that demonstrates that one person values another.

Communication Elements That Affect the Buying Climate

Messages that express feelings of value toward others have been labeled by scholars as *confirming messages*. Conversely, *disconfirming messages* are those that either fail to express value or explicitly show a lack of concern toward others.[9] As mentioned earlier, the nature of the sales communication or buying–selling climate is determined by the degree to which the salesperson and customer see themselves as valued by each other. While verbal messages definitely contribute to the tone of the relationship, the buying climate is frequently shaped by nonverbal messages. Smiles or frowns, distance or closeness, direct or evasive eye contact, and tone of voice provide cues about people's feelings toward each other. Nonverbal communication is a powerful way of conveying attitudes.[10] (Chapter 10 will explore nonverbal communication in depth.)

Disconfirming Messages

Professors E. Sieburg and C. Larson, in a paper presented to the International Communication Association, describe seven types of disconfirming messages that ignore other people or their ideas. These are impervious, interrupting, irrelevant, tangential, impersonal, ambiguous, or incongruous messages.

- *Impervious Messages*—These responses do not acknowledge the other person's attempt to communicate. Failure to return a phone call, answer a customer's letter of complaint, or respond to a customer's suggestion are examples of impervious responses that a salesperson might make to a customer's communication.
- *Interrupting Messages*—These responses are likely to occur when both customer and salesperson are eager to contribute to the interaction and one person interrupts the other. The indirect message of an interruption is "What you have to say is not as important as what I have to say" or "I'm not interested in what you have to say."
- *Irrelevant Messages*—These responses are unrelated to what one person has just told the other. For example, a salesperson might

make a cold call on a customer and open the conversation with, "I want to talk with you about your promise to order a container of paper." The customer replies, "I'm really glad you dropped by. Why has our bill for last month's supplies increased by 5 percent?"

- *Tangential Messages*—These responses recognize the other person's message but use the acknowledgment to redirect the conversation. Tangential responses may be "shifts," which are abrupt changes in the conversation, or "drifts," which provide brief comments on what the other person says and then slowly move the conversation in another direction. A customer may say, "I'd like to schedule a meeting with you to project our objectives into the next 5-year period." The salesperson might respond with, "Sure, but right now I'm mainly interested in the printout on your productivity for last month." This is an example of a tangential shift. On the other hand, the salesperson might reply with a tangential drift by stating, "Oh yes, these projections will increase volume. By the way, do you have the printout on your productivity for last month ready for me yet?"
- *Impersonal Messages*—These responses are superficial reactions that provide an intellectualized, overly general, or clichéd answer instead of addressing the person's feelings and ideas on a direct, personal level. If the customer disclosed, "Production is down by 10 percent this month and this is the third month in a row that we've had a decrease in production," the salesperson might respond with, "Times are hard for everybody right now."
- *Ambiguous Messages*—These messages are difficult to understand because they often contain more than one meaning. They usually are stated in abstract language that obscures meaning. The customer might state, "I'd like to see the statistics you told me about that verify the success of your new Z-3000 model." The salesperson replies with, "Yes, I'll have to remember to look into that and get back to you."
- *Incongruous Messages*—These contain two messages that seem to contradict each other. Often a verbal message provides one response while the nonverbal message indicates a second, contradictory response. The customer asserts, "There's no reason for you to be angry with me because our budget allocations have been cut." The salesperson replies slowly through clenched teeth, "I'm not angry."

Confirming Messages

Unlike the preceding messages, which will probably lead to an ineffective relationship, confirming messages encourage others to feel positive about themselves. Confirming messages have not been researched as extensively as their negative counterparts. Professors Sieburg and Larson asked members of the International Communication Association to describe the behaviors of people with whom they most and least enjoyed communicating. The following five types of response were considered most confirming, in rank order:

1. *Direct acknowledgment*, or the recognition of a person's communication followed by a direct verbal response
2. The *expression of positive feeling* about what a person has just said
3. A *clarifying response*, in which one person asks another to expand on what has been said
4. An *agreeing response*, by which one person reinforces or affirms what another has already said
5. A *supportive response* offering comfort, understanding, or reassurance[11]

In a more recent essay, authors K. Cissna and E. Sieburg classify confirming behaviors into three clusters: recognition, acknowledgment, and endorsement.[12]

1. *Recognition Cluster*—Recognition is expressed by making frequent eye contact, touching, speaking directly to the customer, and giving the customer an opportunity to respond without having to interrupt or break into the conversation forcefully.
2. *Acknowledgment Cluster*—A relevant, direct response to the customer's communication demonstrates acknowledgment. Praise and agreement are not required. According to Cissna and Sieburg, "To hear, attend, and take note of the other and to acknowledge the other by responding directly is probably the most valued form of confirmation—and possibly the most rare. It means that the other's expression is furthered, facilitated, and encouraged."[13] They are referring to the use of active listening skills, which are presented in the Skill Builder.
3. *Endorsement Cluster*—Responses that validate the other person's feelings as appropriate constitute endorsement. This cluster includes any response that accepts the other person without judgment.

Neither the disconfirming nor the confirming behaviors are listed exhaustively. Both lists highlight the differences between a confirming style, which tends to acknowledge, accept, and support others, and a disconfirming style, which denies and undermines another person's sense of worth.

Disconfirming responses are often used unintentionally or because a person lacks skill in using confirming responses. Salespeople may use an occasional disconfirming response and probably will not destroy a relationship with their customers. However, the use of even one disconfirming message may result in customers questioning their trust in the salesperson.

The salesperson will benefit from consciously practicing confirming responses. Table 8.1 demonstrates both disconfirming and confirming responses. "Try This" exercise 8.1 provides an opportunity to practice changing a disconfirming message into a confirming message.

Skill Builder 8.1 Active Listening

Effective listening requires energy and concentration. *Active listening* is a three-part skill that involves responding to the customer with feedback that includes verbal and nonverbal attending behaviors, paraphrasing statements, and verification questions.

1. *Attending Behaviors* help you to focus your attention on what the customer is saying rather than on yourself.
   A. Nonverbal: SOFTENS Technique
      Smiling and **S**quarely facing the customer so that you are more accessible. Your facial expression will affect the tone of your voice.
      Open posture will help you give your undivided attention to the prospect. Keep your feet flat on the floor as opposed to crossing your legs.
      Forward lean. Leaning slightly forward from the chair in which you are seated helps show the prospect that you are interested in communicating and that you want to relate as an equal.
      Touching by shaking hands. A warm, firm handshake helps the salesperson extend warmth and caring.
      Eye contact is a way of indicating that your attention is focused on the prospect or customer. It also helps you concentrate on what is being said and communicates that you are interested in listening to what the buyer has to say.
      Nodding when appropriate lets the prospect know that you are attentive to what is being said. It may also encourage the prospect to continue talking.
      Space. Americans relate most comfortably in sales at a distance of 4–5 feet. If you want to move closer so that you may share information with the prospect, ask for permission to do so.
   B. Verbal: Include brief comments that are supportive of what the customer is saying:

"Uh-huh"	"Okay"	"Yes"
"I see"	"What else?"	"Oh"
"Really"	"Right"	"How interesting"

2. *Paraphrasing* involves briefly summarizing in your own words the customer's ideas and feelings. A restatement of what you hear the customer saying, along with your paraphrase of what you observe and hear as the customer's emotions, will provide the customer with clarification of stated and unstated thoughts and feelings. Use nonverbal communication that matches your emotions to create a supportive climate. This nonjudgmental manner will encourage the customer to respond with honesty and openness. For example:

Customer: I've looked *everywhere* for a gourmet potato chip that people won't find at other restaurants.

Salesperson: What I'm hearing you say is that you want a potato chip that will be in keeping with your upscale image, *and* it sounds to me like you're tired of the search. (paraphrase)
Am I correct? (verification)

3. *Verification Questions* are used to check the accuracy of your paraphrase:
   "How accurate is this?" "Did I hear you correctly?"
   "Is that so?" "Is this true?"
   "Is there something important that I missed?"

Table 8.1

Disconfirming and Confirming Responses

Irrelevant Message

Customer: I want to talk with you about the shipment that's a week overdue.
Salesperson's disconfirming response: I'll be happy to. Have you ordered for next month yet?
Revised confirming message: I feel that it is important that we find out why the shipment is late, so we can prevent it from happening again.
Types of response: Direct acknowledgment, agreeing response, and supportive response

Impersonal Message

Customer: Production is down by 10 percent this month.
Salesperson's disconfirming response: Too bad. Oh well, you aren't the first one that's happened to.
Revised confirming message: I'm sorry to hear that. I'm sure that things will get better if we give it special attention.
Types of response: Direct acknowledgment, expression of positive feelings, supportive response

Ambiguous Message

Customer: I'd like to see the statistics that verify the success of your new X-100 model.
Salesperson's disconfirming response: Yes, I'll have to see that those get dropped by sometime.
Revised confirming message: Sure, I'll bring them by tomorrow. I think you'll be impressed by them.
Types of response: Direct acknowledgment, expression of positive feelings, and supportive response.

Try This 8.1

1. Identify a recent experience during which you felt disconfirmed by someone's communication with you.
2. Practice responding to the disconfirming message with one or more of the following confirming response styles:
   a. Direct acknowledgment
   b. Expression of positive feelings
   c. Asking for clarification
   d. Agreeing with all or part of the comment
   e. Offering support
3. How does responding to a disconfirming message with a confirming response affect the interpersonal climate? What might be the effects in a sales relationship or buying climate?

A Framework for Interaction in the Buying–Selling Climate

Organizations have been described from the perspectives of structure, climate, and culture. Relationships may be also viewed in three dimensions: as goals, structure, and rules.[14] In a relational selling system, salespeople's communications both reflect and determine each of the three dimensions in relationships with customers.

Goals

Relationships form because of a goal or outcome that each person wishes to achieve. In sales, that goal may be short term—to sell, as in product-driven and sales-driven systems—or long term—to build repeat business, as in customer-driven and relationship-driven systems. Other outcomes or expectations in building a supportive buying climate may be to learn about the prospect's environment, to identify the customer's buying needs, to secure information about the customer's buying procedures, to help the customer solve a problem, to show appreciation to the customer for business and continued support, or to change the customer's attitude or behavior.

Structure

Relationships in the buying climate are distinguished by the structure of their communication—how talk is organized and coordinated. The structure of a relationship is based on two continuums: dominance/submission and warmth/hostility. The dominance/submission continuum represents how much control the salesperson and the customer have over each other. The warmth/hostility continuum reflects how much affection or love each person gives and receives.[15] Figure 8.1 displays the general characteristics found when the two continuums are combined to form four quadrants.

The element of control is described in Chapter 2 as a distinguishing feature of the relationship-driven selling system. It includes three structural factors: the complementary, symmetrical, and parallel relationships. These properties may be applied to the two structural continuums as well.

1. *Complementary Relationship*—The relationship between behaviors is complementary—one person's behavior complements, or reciprocates, the other's. For example, dominance in the salesperson tends to provoke its opposite (subordinance) from the customer, and submission tends to provoke its opposite (control).

Figure 8.1

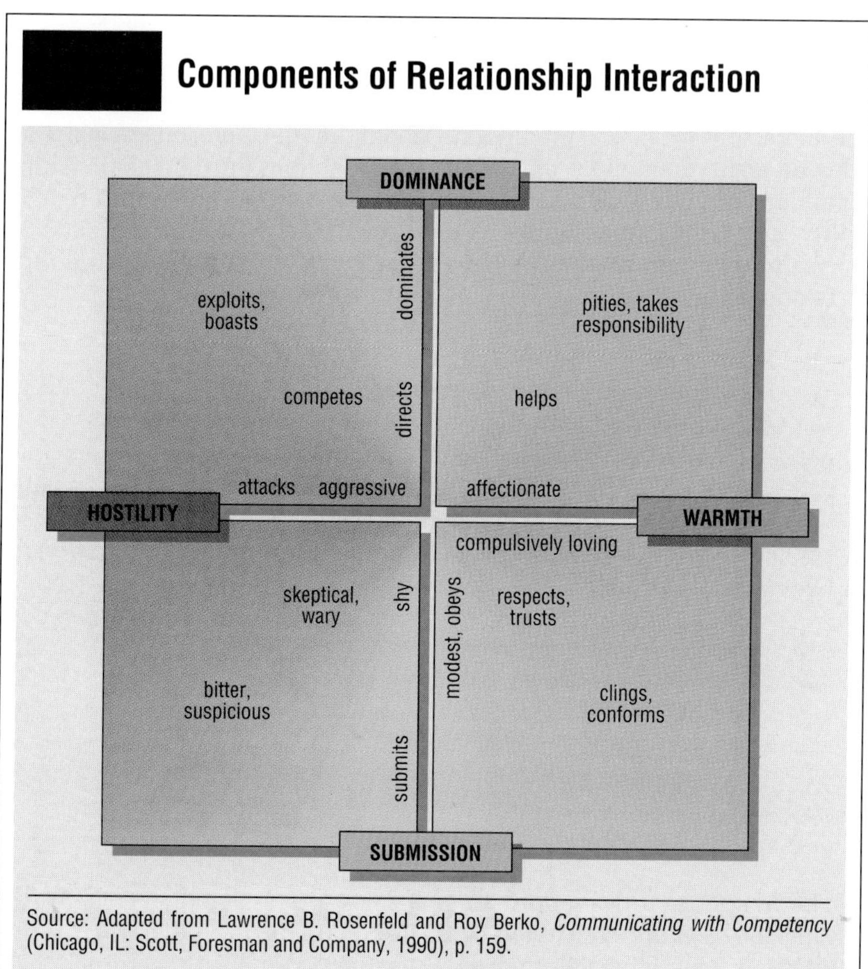

Source: Adapted from Lawrence B. Rosenfeld and Roy Berko, *Communicating with Competency* (Chicago, IL: Scott, Foresman and Company, 1990), p. 159.

2. *Symmetrical Relationship*—This suggests balance: Both buyer and seller contribute to the relationship. Unlike dominant and submissive behaviors, which tend to provoke their opposites, warm behaviors tend to evoke warmth, and hostile behaviors tend to evoke hostility. For example, a sales manager's dominant-hostile message, "I've been on the job here twice the time you have and have worked these accounts for just as long, so do the job the way I say to do it," is likely to receive this kind of a hostile-submissive response from the salesperson: "All right, all right! But just because you've been here a long time doesn't make you a genius!"
3. *Parallel Relationship*—This relational structure combines complementary and symmetrical aspects. The salesperson may be dominant and the customer submissive at times; at other times they will reverse roles. Sometimes both salesperson and customer are dominant; at other times they are both submissive. In general, this is the most flexible structure because the contributions to the relationship vary depending on the situation.[16]

Rules

For a person to make predictions about another person's behavior, rules or regulations must exist that govern actions in the relationship. Communication experts agree that rules organize the world, add predictability, and reduce uncertainty. In studies conducted in various parts of the world, five universal rules have been uncovered that help structure all relationships[17]:

1. Respect another's privacy.
2. Look the other person in the eye during conversations.
3. Do not divulge something that is said in confidence.
4. Do not criticize another person publicly.
5. Seek to repay debts, favors, or compliments, no matter how small.

Seven definite rules help structure specific personal, professional, and work relationships:

1. Stand up for another person in that person's absence.
2. Share news of success with another person.
3. Show emotional support.
4. Trust and confide in each other.
5. Volunteer your help in time of need.
6. Strive to make another person happy when with that person.
7. Do not nag another person.

Both sets of rules apply to the sales professional. Typically, a salesperson is more concerned with task-maintenance rules than with intimacy as it pertains to a spouse. Rules may also exist regarding what topics should be discussed. Sex, politics, and religion are high-risk topics, especially during the first sales call or early in a relationship. As rapport is built and the relationship grows, more rules will need to be negotiated. For example, the degree of formality may change or how the task is completed may be altered. The more the relationship reflects the salesperson's and the customer's individual characteristics, the more specific the rules for the interaction must be. These rules ideally facilitate the mutual exchange process in the relationship-driven strategy.

The Dimensional Sales Behavior Model for Interaction

To clearly understand relational structure and the framework for interaction in the buying–selling climate, we must discuss the *dimensional sales behavior model.* This model applies the principles of dominance/submission and warmth/hostility to salespeople and customers. In 1968 two clinical psychologists, V. R. Buzzota and Robert E. Lefton, with their associate Manuel Sherberg, designed a model of behavior that focused on developing salespeoples' interpersonal skills to increase personal growth and sales. Their work is based on two principles of behavior, dominance/submission and warmth/hostility, that have been validated by behavioral scientists and adapted to fit the sales profession.[18]

Principle No. 1: Every Person Tends to Be Either Warm or Hostile

In this principle, *tends* is the operative word; behavior cannot be described in absolute terms. The intention is that a salesperson is *inclined* to be either warm or hostile, not is *always* or *invariably* warm or hostile.

Warmth

> Warmth is regard for others. It involves awareness of the worth and dignity of other people, and sensitivity to their needs. It implies that the gratification of one's own needs is bound up with the gratification of other people's needs.
>
> The warm person is characteristically interested in and responsive to others. He is frequently outgoing and good-humored, although warm persons are sometimes shy and retiring. He is optimistic and willing to place confidence in others. The warm person is certain that his self-interest is entwined with that of other people, so competititon must always take place in a framework of mutually respected rules.[19]

Hostility

> Hostility is lack of regard for others, the attitude that other people matter less than oneself, and therefore deserve less care. It implies indifference to others, insensitivity to their needs and ideas, resis-

tance to collaboration, and, in some cases, outright animosity. Hostile people are often cold and manipulative.

Hostility is self-seeking behavior. It has its roots in egoism, the frequently unconscious doctrine that self-interest should be the final goal of one's actions. Hostile people often disdain others. Not surprisingly, they frequently provoke dislike in others, and then complain that they are surrounded by unfriendly people. The hostile man's view of the world is self-fulfilling; he stimulates hostility in others which in turn reinforces his own hostility, enabling him to say, "I told you so."[20]

Principle No. 2: Every Person Tends to Be Either Dominant or Submissive

Again, the descriptions that follow are not absolutes; pure dominance and pure submission are seldom found in life. What is true is that each of us *tends* to be predominantly one or the other.

Dominance

Dominance is the drive to take control in face-to-face situations. It includes a cluster of traits: initiative, forcefulness, and independence. It implies leadership in personal encounters, control of situations, and a wish to be paramount.

Dominance is an *active* trait found in people who believe they can mold, control, and master situations. Whatever his real worth, the dominant person *thinks* he has something valuable to contribute to others, and he acts on that belief. He is invariably ambitious, with a strong desire for personal independence.[21]

Submission

Submission is the disposition to let others take the lead in personal encounters. It includes traits like dependence, unassertiveness, and passiveness. It implies willingness to be controlled, avoidance of personal confrontations, and compliance with other people's wishes.

In brief, submissive people would rather be led than lead. They feel tense or uneasy when called upon to take charge; they prefer the secure knowledge that someone else is responsible for things. Submissive people, often characterized by self-doubt, are sometimes slow to assert themselves in their own behalf.[22]

Table 8.2 briefly summarizes these four typologies and how salespeople of each type relate to themselves and other people.

Figure 8.2 depicts the fact that both dimensions exist simultaneously in the behavior of every salesperson. Buzzota, Lefton, and Sherberg identify these four possible quadrants as combinations of traits that may be found in all salespeople. They consistently emphasize four points:

Table 8.2

How Salespeople Relate to Themselves and Other People

Relationship	Sales-driven (Q1)	Product-driven (Q2)	Customer-driven (Q3)	Relationship-driven (Q4)
To self	Largely unaware that other people see them as manipulative and overbearing; have strong need to be on top, where they can enhance their self-esteem and assert their independence; fearful of any signs of personal weakness or failure; see selves as forceful leaders in a world comprised largely of submissive followers	Consider self realist whose bleak outlook is justified by the facts; but they are sometimes defensive about their submissiveness; their lack of forcefulness sometimes bothers them; seek well-ordered, predictable existence; greatest concern is with endurance in a threatening world	Try to ignore hostility in self and others by laughing it off, rationalizing it, or minimizing it; persist in believing that world is basically warm and accepting, and that things are sure to work out right in the end	Flexible, open, growth-oriented; objective about self; able to admit weaknesses and accept strengths; want to use talents to go as far and as fast as they can; but their ambition is tempered by their concern and respect for others
To others	Frequently insensitive to others' needs and feelings; often clash with other forceful people; get along best with docile people; with people who are assertive, they are usually shrewd and manipulative; with those who are submissive, they are aggressive and overbearing; many of their relationships marked by tension and muted antagonism	Often look down on others, and are regarded as cold; generally aloof, uncommunicative, distant; have few close friends; these usually reflect their own outlook; are especially careful not to get involved with aggressive people; cannot understand people who manifest deep concern for others; basically "loners"	View everyone as sincere, dependable, decent; very willing to trust and rely upon others; sometimes exploited by more aggressive people, who regard them as pushovers; generally well-liked, but not always highly respected	Good relationships with others; rarely appear as threat to others, yet are assertive and forceful; exercise dominance without seeming hostile; display candor and respect for other people's ideas; refuse to manipulate or exploit

Source: Adapted from V. R. Buzzota, R. E. Lefton, and M. Sherberg, *Effective Selling through Psychology* (New York: Wiley Interscience, 1972), p. 99.

1. All salespeople who fit one of the types are not identical.
2. Everyone in each of the four categories is different.
3. There are as many distinctions as there are salespeople.
4. In general, every salesperson can be classified *basically* in one of the four groups.

Figure 8.2

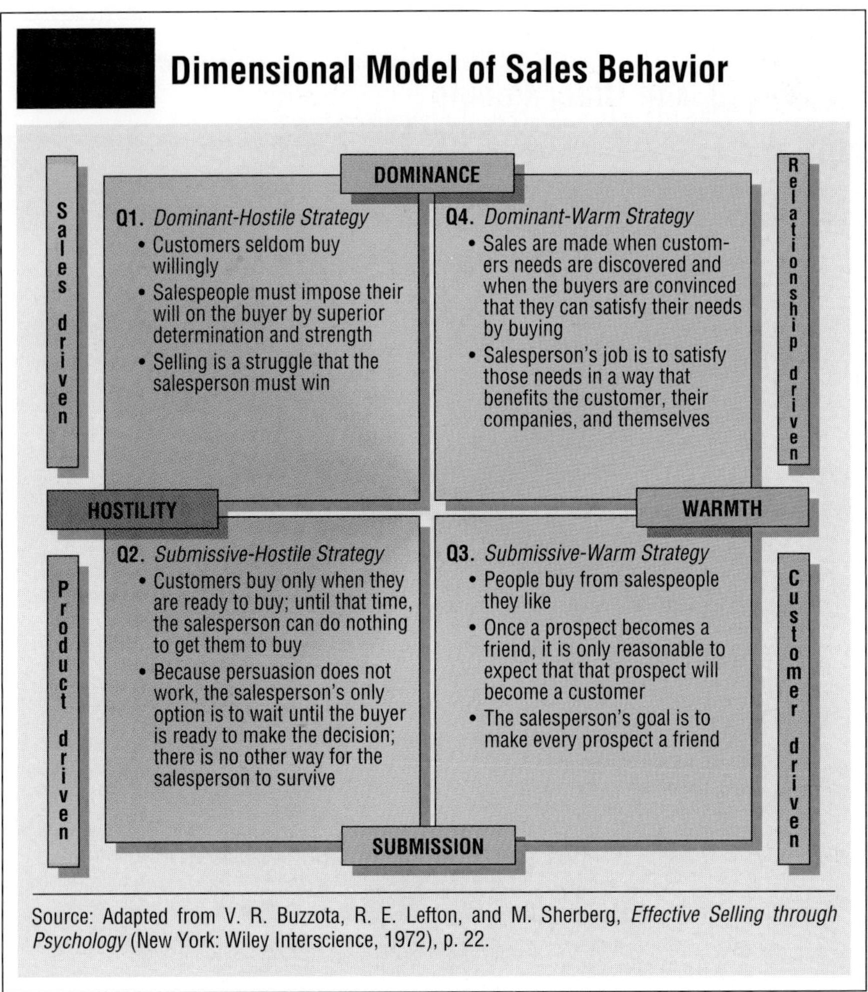

Dimensional Model of Sales Behavior
DOMINANCE
Q1. Dominant-Hostile Strategy
• Customers seldom buy willingly
• Salespeople must impose their will on the buyer by superior determination and strength
• Selling is a struggle that the salesperson must win
Q4. Dominant-Warm Strategy
• Sales are made when customers needs are discovered and when the buyers are convinced that they can satisfy their needs by buying
• Salesperson's job is to satisfy those needs in a way that benefits the customer, their companies, and themselves
HOSTILITY
WARMTH
Q2. Submissive-Hostile Strategy
• Customers buy only when they are ready to buy; until that time, the salesperson can do nothing to get them to buy
• Because persuasion does not work, the salesperson's only option is to wait until the buyer is ready to make the decision; there is no other way for the salesperson to survive
Q3. Submissive-Warm Strategy
• People buy from salespeople they like
• Once a prospect becomes a friend, it is only reasonable to expect that that prospect will become a customer
• The salesperson's goal is to make every prospect a friend
SUBMISSION
Sales driven
Product driven
Relationship driven
Customer driven

Source: Adapted from V. R. Buzzota, R. E. Lefton, and M. Sherberg, *Effective Selling through Psychology* (New York: Wiley Interscience, 1972), p. 22.

Also, in Figure 8.2, a related selling strategy is assigned to each quadrant. Just as salespeople differ in each quadrant, so the degree of extremism varies in the related selling strategies. To review the strategies, refer back to Chapter 2. "Try This" exercise 8.2 provides an opportunity to relate the typologies and control properties to the world at large.

We have already discussed how parallel relationships provide the most flexibility in the structure of a communication climate. In studying Table 8.3 on salesperson-customer interaction, a paradigm emerges from which the following corollary can be drawn: The more closely the salesperson and the customer operate within the dominant/warm, fourth quadrant (Q4), the more likely it is that the purest state of the relational selling process will be experienced.

Try This 8.2

Select a (sales) relationship that is important to you. Using Figures 8.1 and 8.2 as guides, indicate the extent to which you and the other person are dominant, submissive, hostile, and warm. Use a five-point scale to mark your responses:

1	2	3	4	5
Almost never				Almost always

____ 1. I am dominant.
____ 2. The other person is dominant.
____ 3. I am submissive.
____ 4. The other person is submissive.
____ 5. I am hostile.
____ 6. The other person is hostile.
____ 7. I am warm.
____ 8. The other person is warm.

Using the terms *complementary*, *symmetrical*, and *parallel*, describe your relationship. What might be the effects in a sales relationship?

Variations in Behavior and the Buying Climate

Each of the typologies has been described in its purest or most intense form. We have also stressed that most salespeople exhibit behavior that is a combination or mixture of all four quadrants. Buzzota, Lefton, and Sherberg suggest that there are five reasons why selling behavior is rarely found in the pure, undiluted form:

1. A specific interaction between a salesperson and a customer can be located at any point in the quadrant. There are an infinite number of such points within each quadrant, indicating different intensities and qualities of behavior.
2. Behavior is often related to situations and to other people in these situations, and situations and people or customers change.
3. Salespeople may shift to secondary quadrants as an automatic or unconscious reaction to frustration or pressure.
4. Salespeople may shift to mask strategies as a deliberate or conscious reaction to frustration or pressure.
5. Secondary strategies may become quasi-permanent.[23]

It is important to understand that the dimensional sales behavior model is a typology of useful caricatures and is not intended to stereotype salespeople with behaviors that are carved in stone. It is merely a device to help learners organize and comprehend their own experiences in the real world of selling, either as salespeople or as customers. This discussion

Table 8.3

Salesperson–Customer Interaction

Salesperson Type	Interaction	Q1 Customer (Dominant-Hostile)	Q2 Customer (Submissive-Hostile)	Q3 Customer (Submissive-Warm)	Q4 Customer (Dominant-Warm)
Q1 salesperson (dominant-hostile)	Sales relationship	Rapport readily established; businesslike; competitive; presentation is argumentative, a contest	Little rapport; salesperson dominates and dictates; customer tensely withdraws	Rapport established easily; salesperson dominates and dictates; customer, slightly uncomfortable, complies	Salesperson struggles to dictate and dominate; customer struggles to gain information and understanding
	Regard	High mutual regard; each views other as formidable	Low mutual regard; salesperson is disdainful, customer fearful	Mixed regard, salesperson disdains customer's weakness; customer admires salesperson	Mixed; salesperson respects customer's businesslike approach; customer admires salesperson's forcefulness but feels suspicious of him
	Sales result	Average	Below average; customer postpones commitment	Above average	Average
Q2 salesperson (submissive-hostile)	Sales relationship	Little rapport; customer in control from outset; tries to get information, but salesperson, intimidated, withdraws	Little rapport; both withdrawn; low interaction; not much said or done	Salesperson aloof while customer tries to interact; inconsequential conversation; little business gets done	Customer tries to gain information and understanding; salesperson remains aloof
	Regard	Low mutual regard	Neutral regard	Salesperson neutral toward customer; customer positive toward salesperson	Low mutual regard
	Sales result	Below average	Average; salesperson primarily order-taker	Average; customer is eager to be nice helpful guy	Below average
Q3 salesperson (submissive-warm)	Sales relationship	Customer peeved by salesperson's meandering, unbusinesslike approach; dominates interview; salesperson oblivious to customer's impatience	Salesperson meanders; customer aloof and occasionally sarcastic; very unbusinesslike and unrestricted interview	Excellent rapport soon established; mutual admiration society; business secondary to personal relationship	Customer increasingly restive as salesperson meanders and ignores business; customer tries to keep salesperson on track

Table 8.3
Continued

	Regard	Customer disdainful; salesperson has high regard for customer	Customer neutral; salesperson has high regard for customer	High mutual regard	Salesperson has high regard for customer; customer has mixed regard for salesperson
	Sales result	Below average	Average; salesperson primarily order-taker	Above average	Average
Q4 salesperson (dominant-warm)	Sales relationship	Businesslike climate; salesperson flexible; aware of customer's needs for esteem and independence; customer responds by meeting questions realistically	Rapport established easily after slow start; salesperson acts as a constructive, nonthreatening guide to decision-making	Salesperson controls customer's meandering but still responds to social needs; guides customer gently but firmly	Excellent rapport; both function as partners in problem-solving; atmosphere constructive and sales-oriented
	Regard	High mutual regard	High mutual regard	High mutual regard	High mutual regard
	Sales result	Above average	Above average	Above average	Above average

Source: V. R. Buzzota, R. E. Lefton, and M. Sherberg, *Effective Selling Through Psychology*, (New York: Wiley Interscience 1972), pp. 145–46.

is also intended to identify the interdependence of behavior in the communication climate and to link the organization with the communication and buying–selling climates. Flexibility and a positive self-image are once again integral parts of the success that salespeople may have in operating within their own firms and in cooperating with customers and their organizations.

Summary

The relational selling process may best be understood with regard to three perspectives: organization, communication, and the buying–selling environment. Each of these categories interacts with the others to develop and maintain a climate conducive to positive sales experiences.

Three elements are necessary for an organization to function: structure, climate, and culture. Structure is the individual segments of the organization that interrelate to produce the organization as a whole. The climate of the organization is the human environment in which employees do their work, with an atmosphere ranging from supportive to defensive. A supportive climate is one where mutual trust and confidence exist, where superiors are willing to help subordinates with job and personal matters, and where managers are approachable and honest about company policies and procedures and willing to give credit to subordinates for their accomplishments and ideas. Organizational culture—the shared language, events, symbols, rituals, and value systems of the organization's members—results from the evolution of past members' behavior, shored up and reconfirmed by the behavior of current members.

Communication is a necessary function of life, particularly the life of an organization. The three major categories of the relational selling process are interactive: Without communication, there is no organization; without communication, the buying–selling environment is lost. Thus, the communication climate is the fulcrum of the relational process. As such, it has sometimes been thought of as the emotional tone of an organization or a relationship between salesperson and customer. It is from this latter perspective that the climate surrounding communication is explored.

The climate is a major factor in determining whether the individuals involved in a selling relationship are willing to work toward long-term involvement. Roueche and Baker's characteristics of effective organizational climates (order, purpose, and coherence; efficiency and objectivity; customer-centeredness; optimism and high expectations; and organizational health) point out the necessity of good communication as these characteristics are used to describe the effective sales organization. The primary function of the communication climate in a selling relationship is to generate positive working relationships that satisfy both the customer's and the salesperson's needs. The positive nature of this relationship begins in the salesperson's firm.

The buying–selling environment is made up of two communication elements: confirming and disconfirming messages. Disconfirming messages are those that fail to express that other people are valued, and they can be a particularly destructive force in a selling relationship. Seven types of disconfirming messages are impervious, interruptive, irrelevant, tangential, impersonal, ambiguous, and incongruous. By contrast, confirming messages demonstrate to others that they *are* valued by the sender. There are five types of confirming messages: direct acknowledgment, expression of positive feeling, clarifying response, agreeing response, and supportive response. Cissna and Sieburg have classified confirming behaviors into three clusters: recognition, acknowledgment, and endorsement. These messages may sometimes be used to offset the negative impact of disconfirming messages. In this way, the potential cycle of defensiveness can be either halted or reversed.

The buying–selling climate may be viewed three-dimensionally in terms of goals, structures, and rules. Structure is the interrelating dimension, and its relationships include complementary, symmetrical, and parallel forms. From these, Buzzota, Lefton, and Sherberg have constructed a dimensional sales behavior model that includes four quadrants based on the principles that everyone tends to be either warm or hostile and dominant or submissive. The more a salesperson and customer operate within the dominant/warm fourth quadrant, the more likely they will be to experience the true spirit of the relationship-driven selling process.

Key Terms

Complementary Relationship A relationship in which one person's behavior complements (or reciprocates) the other's

Confirming Message A message that expresses feelings of value toward others

Culture Shared language, events, symbols, rituals, and value systems of a group of people; organizational culture evolves from past members' behavior and is reconfirmed by current members

Disconfirming Message A message that expresses feelings of lack of value toward others

Organizational Climate Human environment in which employees accomplish their tasks

Parallel Relationship A combination of complementary and symmetrical relationships

Structure Arrangement or interrelation of all parts of an organization

Symmetrical Relationship A balanced relationship in which both buyers and sellers contribute to the relationship

Review Questions

1. Compare and contrast organizational structure, climate, and culture. In what ways are they different? Interrelated?
2. Describe the role of a salesperson's communications in creating the climate within an organization.
3. Identify and explain the six characteristics of effective organizations described by Roueche and Baker.
4. Explain the primary function of a communication climate in a selling relationship.
5. Explain the difference between confirming and disconfirming messages. How are the two types related?
6. Explain disconfirming messages in terms of the recognition, acknowledgment, and endorsement clusters.
7. Explain confirming messages in terms of the recognition, acknowledgment, and endorsement clusters.

8. On what two principles of behavior is the dimensional sales behavior model of interaction based? How do the two principles interact in the model?
9. Why do Buzzota, Lefton, and Sherberg maintain that the behavior of a salesperson is usually a combination or mixture of all four quadrants of their model?

Discussion Questions

1. In a group of three to five persons, describe the organizational structure of an organization that you currently work for or have worked for in the past.
2. Select an organization with which you are familiar and use Roueche and Baker's five characteristics of effective organizations to assess the effectiveness of this organization.
3. In what ways can salespeople have a positive effect on the communication climate within their organization?
4. Identify the types of disconfirming messages to which you react most negatively. How might you change your reaction? In what ways would your change in behavior be more (or less) productive for you and your relationship with another person?
5. How might confirming and disconfirming messages affect the trust level between customer and salesperson?
6. Select a sales relationship that is important to you and describe it in terms of goals, structure, and rules.
7. What skills and principles can a salesperson use to direct the sales relationship toward the fourth (dominant/warm) quadrant of Buzzota, Lefton, and Sherberg's model?
8. A supervisor for an office with an inside sales staff has a toll-free number for customers to use. One employee, who sits near the supervisor but reports to someone else, severely abuses the toll-free number by encouraging members of her family, who live in another state, to call her every day. The supervisor answers her phone at times and is aware that this is going on, but the employee's supervisor doesn't have a clue. What should the supervisor do?
9. You are the senior account rep for a consumer product line. Your divisional sales manager invited a group of his salespeople out to a celebratory lunch after showing a significant increase in quarterly sales. At the end of the lunch, each of you chipped in $10. Your manager collected the money and then paid the bill on his charge card. Later on you made a very disturbing discovery: You found out that he had submitted the bill from the lunch on his expense account. What should you do about it? What impact does his behavior have on your view of your company's climate?

The Grow-Rite Seed Company

Case 8.1

The Grow-Rite Seed Company, located in South Dakota, started doing business in 1975 through a small mail-order catalog specializing in seeds and garden supplies. The company has recently been acclaimed for having the largest mail order garden catalog in the United States, mainly due to a philosophy perpetuated by the company's founder, David Logan. He has always believed that a business should be run with a defined set of values and attitudes.

The company has established a 24-hour customer service department to answer all customer questions that its telephone operators are unable to answer. These telephone operators are not just order takers; they are trained to assist customers in purchasing the right type of seeds for the appropriate need and season. The operators are further trained to treat all customers with personal and courteous service. Their objective is to inform the customers of the product's availability and shipment schedules, in addition to making them feel comfortable with their purchases, regardless of the size of the order.

Research and testing are continuous efforts. The growers maintain the company's reputation of providing the highest quality seeds. Durable tools and gardening supplies are also available for every type of user, from weekend gardeners to professional landscapers. Special effort has been made to locate hard-to-find items, such as seed planters and special tools for kneeling and support when bending.

David Logan strongly believes that if you sell quality merchandise at a reasonable price and treat your customers with respect, you will gain satisfied customers who will return and also tell others. The company also extends a 100-percent money-back guarantee to its customers on all items listed in the catalog, if the customer is dissatisfied with a purchase for any reason. The bottom line for the Grow-Rite Seed Company is to please the customer.

1. What are the shared values and beliefs of the Grow-Rite Seed Company that underlie its corporate culture?
2. How do you think being located in South Dakota has influenced Grow-Rite's culture?
3. What specific attributes of the company do you think customers appreciate and respect?

Case 8.2

A Declining Reputation

Tony Gross has been the sales manager of Men's Exclusive, one of a small specialty chain of eight clothing stores located in suburban shopping centers in large cities. The shop has been successful since its opening in 1964, mainly due to the store's loyal clientele and its excellent reputation of offering quality merchandise at reasonable prices.

Tony's philosophy has been oriented toward customer service. He has stressed that it is important for the sales staff to stand behind the products the store sells and strive to maintain a loyal clientele. He has further emphasized providing friendly, warm, and helpful service to the customers, even if it meant going out of the way to do so. Recently, Tony was ordered by his physician to curtail his 65-hour work week to a maximum of 25 hours. He immediately recommended that the senior salesman, Bill Brown, be assigned the position of sales manager.

An evaluation conducted during the first quarter after Bill took over showed that business had dropped significantly. Also, the number of customer complaints about the sales staff had increased. The complaints consisted of inattentiveness to customers, inability to handle product-knowledge questions, and overall lack of service orientation. A customer arriving at the store would often have difficulty finding a sales clerk. In some instances, the salespeople would ignore the customers. This poor service had been unheard of under Tony's leadership.

Since Bill has been promoted to sales manager, he takes frequent breaks, fails to reprimand employees who are late for work, and has proved insensitive to customers' needs. His reasoning is that because the pay scale of the sales staff is lower than the industry's average, performance expectations must also be lower. According to Bill, it is worthwhile to tolerate some inadequacies among the sales staff, considering the difficulty of getting people to work for minimal pay.

Bill is not aware of the long-term effects of losing the chain's loyal clientele to dissatisfaction. Eventually, this poor service and customer dissatisfaction may result in future sales losses through adverse publicity. The problems are creating an unfavorable image for the store. Its reputation is becoming tarnished and profits are declining. Although serious changes are taking place, Bill continues to believe that the reputation of Men's Exclusive is so solid that nothing could affect it.

1. Can a store's reputation and image be affected by unfavorable customer reactions?
2. Suggest ways for Bill to change the expectation level of the salespeople and increase customer satisfaction.
3. Losing a loyal client deserves serious attention. Discuss this statement.

Notes

1. Cal W. Downs and Michael D. Hazen, "A Factor Analytic Study of Communication Satisfaction," *Journal of Business Communication*, 14 (Spring 1977), p. 144.
2. David H. Holt, *Management Principles and Practices*, 2nd ed. (Englewood Cliffs, NJ: Prentice-Hall, 1990), p. 318.
3. Sylvia Shimmin, "The Future of Work," in K. D. Duncan, M. M. Gruneberg, and D. Wills, eds., *Changes in Working Life* (New York: John Wiley and Sons, 1980), p. 5.
4. R. B. Adler, *Communicating at Work: Principles and Practices for Business and the Professions*, 2nd ed. (New York: Random House, 1983), p. 103.
5. John Roueche and George Baker, *Profiling Excellence in America's Schools* (Arlington, VA: American Association of School Administrators, 1986), pp. 24–34.
6. D. Aspy and F. Roebuck, "From Humane Ideas to Human Technology and Back Again Many Times," *Education*, 95 (Winter 1974), pp. 63–72.
7. R. B. Adler, L. B. Rosenfeld, and N. Towne, *Interplay*, 3rd ed. (New York: Holt, Rinehart & Winston, 1986), p. 237.
8. "Positive Personnel Practices," *Quality Circles: Participant's Manual* (Prospect Heights, IL: Waveland Press, 1982), p. 59.
9. V. DiSalvo, D. C. Larsen, and W. J. Seiler, "Communication Skills Needed by Persons in Business Organizations," *Communication Education*, 25 (1976), pp. 269–275.
10. K. L. Villard and L. J. Whipple, *Beginnings in Relational Communication* (New York: John Wiley and Sons, 1976), p. 125.
11. E. Sieburg and C. Larson, "Dimensions of Interpersonal Response," paper presented to the International Communication Association, Phoenix, AZ., 1971.
12. K. N. L. Cissna and E. Sieburg, "Patterns of Interactional Confirmation and Disconfirmation," in J. Steward, ed., *Bridges Not Walls*, 4th ed. (New York: Random House), 1986.
13. Ibid.
14. Lawrence B. Rosenfeld and Roy M. Berko, *Communicating with Competency* (Chicago, IL: Scott, Foresman and Company, 1990), pp. 157–165.
15. Ibid., pp. 158–165.
16. Ibid.
17. For a summary of the series of investigations, including comparisons of the rules for different types of relationships in different parts of the world, see: Michael Argyle and Monika Henderson, "The Rules of Relationships," in Steve Duc and Daniel Perlman, eds., *Understanding Personal Relationships* (Beverely Hills, CA: Sage, 1985), pp. 63–84.
18. V. R. Buzzota, R. E. Lefton, and M. Sherberg, *Effective Selling through Psychology* (New York: Wiley Interscience, 1972), pp. 17–18.
19. Ibid.
20. Ibid.
21. Ibid.
22. Ibid.
23. Ibid., p. 102.

Listening: The Key to Effective Selling

Knowledge Objectives

In this chapter, you will learn:

1. The importance of listening during the professional selling process
2. The primary factors influencing the listening process
3. The various levels of listening—discriminative, comprehensive, therapeutic, critical, and appreciative
4. The distinction between the seven different styles of feedback—advising, judging, analyzing, questioning, supporting, active listening, and giving relational feedback

Consider This

The effects of really good listening can be dramatic. These effects include the satisfied customer who will come back, the contented employee who will stay with the company, the manager who has the trust of his staff, and the salesman who tops his quota. Good listeners are valued highly by the people they work with.

John L. DiGaetani*

* "The Business of Listening," *Business Horizons*, 23 (October 1980), p. 42.

istening is a powerful force that influences how people behave toward each other. In the age of data collection and information exchange, it is not surprising that listening receives unprecedented attention in American business enterprises. The paradox is that, while listening is the number one communication problem, it also may hold the primary solution to most communication breakdowns.

People need listening skills at all levels within an organization. Individuals must listen to their supervisors, peers, fellow employees, customers, vendors, stockholders, community leaders, professional educational groups, labor unions and leaders, government officials, and communication media.[1]

Listening skill determines productivity in the workplace. Lyman K. Steil, president of Communication Development, Inc., estimates that American businesses lose billions of dollars each year because of poor listening skills:

> With more than 100 million workers in this country, a simple $10 mistake by each of them, as a result of poor listening, would add up to a cost of a billion dollars. And most people make numerous listening mistakes every week.
>
> Because of listening mistakes, letters have to be retyped, appointments rescheduled, shipments rerouted. Productivity is affected and profits suffer.[2]

Tests have shown that after a 10-minute oral presentation, the average listener hears, receives, comprehends, and retains only about 50 percent of any given message. After 48 hours, untrained listeners remember only about 25 percent of what they heard.[3]

American employees spend a significant amount of time listening. Paul Rankin, an early pioneer in listening research, determined that adults spend 42 percent of their communication time listening, in contrast to 32 percent speaking, 15 percent reading, and 11 percent writing.[4] Later sources have documented an increase in the communication time spent in listening to 53 percent.

The goal of this chapter is threefold: (1) to define listening as an integral part of the sales communication process, (2) to describe the levels of listening and their impact on the professional selling process, and (3) to assist the reader in achieving effective listening skills for use in the selling context.

The chapter is divided into three sections. The first section discusses the listening environment, particularly in a "listening-intense" organization. The second section describes the levels of listening that salespeople use. The focus of the third section is on interpersonal listening in a sales context, with particular emphasis on giving and receiving feedback.

The Listening Environment

Listening goes beyond hearing. *Hearing* is "the physiological process during which sounds are received through the ears as sensory data and

Sales Professional Spotlight

A recognized leader from the beginning of her sales career, Karen Cerwin is a real estate professional with a proven track record. Ever since her association (beginning in 1984) with Coldwell Banker-Sky Ridge Realty in Lake Arrowhead, California, she has been the company's top producer. In 1990 she ranked among the top 1 percent of all real estate professionals in the United States, with a total sales volume exceeding $30 million. That same year she was acclaimed the Number Five Top-Producing Sales Associate in gross commission income out of 43,000 Coldwell Banker residential sales associates.

Total dedication and commitment to client satisfaction explain Karen's phenomenal track record. She feels strongly that her clients should not have to settle for anything less than excellent service from beginning to end. She stresses commitment to excellence in every transaction as the only way to do business.

Understanding her clients and their needs is what Karen does best. She delivers knowledge and awareness of properties that fit buyers' requirements and needs. Therefore, she must continually study the ever-changing market conditions and offer valuable advice to help her clients obtain maximum value. She recognizes that buying or selling a home can be one of the most important financial and emotional decisions her clients will make in their lifetime.

"Personal attention to every client is the only way I do business," says Karen. She is also respected by clients for taking the time to listen. That means being aware and sensitive to many clues, both verbal and nonverbal, and being in tune with all the actions and feelings expressed by the prospect. A weakness among many salespeople is becoming too deeply involved in what they are trying to sell and failing to focus on what the prospect is saying.

Furthermore, Karen is committed to helping the client make a beautiful life-style become an affordable reality and making the purchasing decision a pleasant experience. She claims that "the opportunity to help others realize their dreams is most fulfilling." Most importantly, she treats every client as her friend and neighbor and builds friendships on honesty, integrity, and trust.

Knowledge and expertise, together with the ability to really listen and understand her clients' needs, comprise Karen's winning edge. She possesses a rare ability to listen and understand buyers' needs. Continually searching for innovative ways to better serve her clients, Karen is a true professional dedicated to a career in real estate sales.

then transmitted to the brain. Hearing is reception."[5] *Listening* is a complex process "which involves concentrating on what has been received as sensory data, and providing a response."[6] More simply stated, listening is the counterpart of talking in the communication process.

Listening specialists Florence Wolff, Nadine Marsnik, William Tacey, and Ralph Nichols agree that:

> Listening is a magnetic, enriching, and rewarding experience. We are drawn magnetically to those who will lend an ear. We are enriched when we take the time to listen to those who need an ear. We are rewarded and we prosper by learning and personally growing as we use our ears.[7]

Building a supportive listening environment may be difficult. Factors that can become obstacles include time pressures, interruptions, previous encounters, message sending, ongoing relationships, and perceptions.[8] Any business can provide a solid listening environment, however, by "(1) providing a forum for listening; (2) creating a physical location for listening; (3) encouraging feedback and reinforcement; (4) providing listening training; (5) giving employees frequent opportunities for listening; and (6) adopting the positive attitude that listening is valuable."[9]

The Importance of Listening

Although salespeople want their customers to believe that they are good listeners, most are not. Many sales are lost and many buyer-seller relationships are disrupted—and some are destroyed—by poor listening habits. Competition in our culture rewards self-expression. Even if we have nothing to express, we try to compensate for our lack of knowledge with fast talking. This is especially true when fear of losing a sale or self-doubt are the chief motivators. Some people, while appearing to listen, are inwardly preparing their next remark to astound the prospect as soon as they get the floor. Listening experts Edmond Addeo and Robert Burger explain that people are poor listeners because their egos interfere:

> The reason that no one listens, usually, is that our egos get in the way, in the sense that we're mentally formulating what *we're* going to say when the other person gets through speaking. Instead of digesting the other person's information, we are most often busy thinking only of how best we can *impress* him with our next statement. The result is what we call *Egospeak*.[10]

Listening is such a key ingredient of personal selling success that it is considered part of the preapproach step in the relational process. Listening is a learned behavior. As with all communication skills, learning to listen requires frequent practice. Learning to listen effectively is not difficult—just unusual.

In 1957 Ralph Nichols, a pioneer and expert in listening, coauthored what was possibly the first book on listening analysis. The following

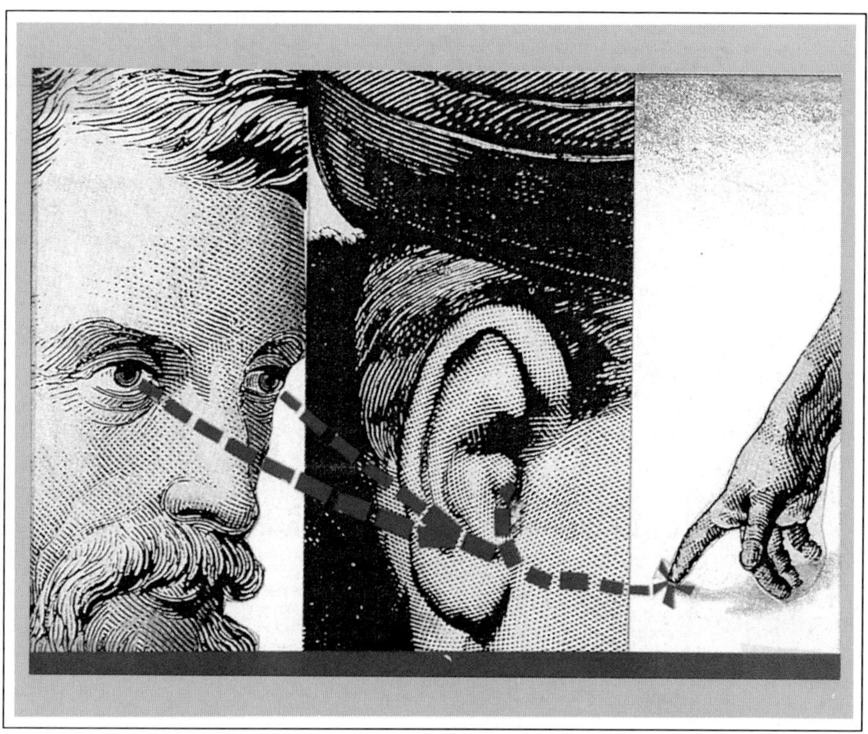

Reprinted with permission from *USAir Magazine,* Pace Communications, Inc., Greensboro, North Carolina.

excerpt is the introduction to an entire chapter he and coauthor Leonard Stevens wrote to illustrate the critical effects of listening in a selling context.

> *The Salesman: Fast Talker or Fast Listener?*
>
> "It's one of our occupational diseases that's hard to cure once you're stricken," said a man to me not long ago.
>
> The disease: talking too much. The occupation: salesman.
>
> For many of us, the word "salesman" brings to mind an image of a nattily dressed individual who talks as though he had been "vaccinated with a phonograph needle." He sells iceboxes to Eskimos; and if you don't beware, he will sell you something you don't want.
>
> The personality accounting for this image is disappearing from the scene, but many a salesman clings to the notion that one of his most valuable attributes is the ability to verbalize. He may recommend the "low-pressure sell," but we still find him cultivating his voice for purposes of oral persuasion. Books on how to talk are well read in the sales field, and adult-education courses on public speaking are almost certain to be well populated with salesmen. Deep inside many people who live by selling lies the conjecture that glibness has magic.

> High-pressure salesmanship, however, is rapidly giving way to low-pressure methods in the selling of both industrial and consumer goods. Today's salesman is likely to center his attention upon the "customer-problem approach" of vending his wares.
>
> To put his approach to work, the skill of listening becomes a valuable tool for the salesman, while vocal agility is less important. *How* a salesman talks becomes relatively unimportant because *what* he says, when it is guided by his listening, gives power to the spoken word.[11]

Nichols and Stevens' discussion reinforces the importance of listening in building and maintaining positive customer relationships.

A classic example of what happens when communication breaks down is found in the celebrated case of Morton Thiokol, originally the sole supplier of booster rockets to the National Aeronautics and Space Administration (NASA). Early on, when Morton Thiokol's relationship with NASA was working well, the company was using "client-oriented" (consultative) selling strategies. Its salespeople were "listeners, strategists and problem-solvers who possess as much knowledge of their clients' business as they do their own."[12] But in time, according to federal investigators, numerous pressures "caused each side to stop communicating with the other," setting the stage for the space shuttle tragedy that occurred in 1986.[13]

Companies such as IBM, Apple Computer Corporation, Campbell Soup Company, and Union Carbide are encouraging supportive listening environments through their relationship-driven training programs, which allow salespeople to practice effective listening skills.

While effective listening can be learned, it is more than just an acquired skill. It requires a total commitment to self that is influenced by one's attitude toward life. It requires an attitude of *wanting* to receive a message, not creating your own "noise" through biases or physical or environmental distractions. For example, if a salesperson perceives that all fat people are dull and lazy and is prejudiced by race and gender, those biases will distort the salesperson's ability to receive messages openly and nonjudgmentally. As seen in Chapter 8, active listening requires attending behaviors that include nonverbal expressions of attentiveness. And, as may be recalled, one cannot keep from communicating nonverbally. Thus, if this salesperson is attempting to actively listen to an obese, Hispanic woman, biases will probably be reflected through nonverbal behavior patterns. In Chapter 4 we discussed developing a positive sales image and said that the healthier a person is physically, mentally, and emotionally, the more receptive a person is to using communication skills unencumbered by bias.

Mary Lou Dobbs, founder and president of Seminar Associates, includes listening as one of the modules for her *Five-Step Customer Care Course*: "Listening is not just a question of technique, but of attitudes like commitment, caring and compassion."[14] She recalls one of her favorite stories:

Are You Listening?

Exhibit 9.1

When a salesperson's reaction to what the customer is telling him is, "Uh, huh . . . uh, huh . . . uh, huh," is it a sign of interest? Agreement? In the opinion of Chris Rice, a senior product manager at Learning International (and formerly a sales manager), it's neither. "The guy simply isn't listening," says Rice.

Teaching salespeople, who tend to be talkers rather than listeners, to listen so that they get a complete picture of customer needs is a major part of Learning International's client-oriented training package. Another of the company's programs, Interactive Listening for Salespeople, is devoted entirely to that skill. Salespeople are told:

- Listening involves a dialogue, a mutual exchange of ideas, opinions, and information with the customer. Keeping up a dialogue also demonstrates respect for the customer.
- Nonverbal behavior, such as making eye contact and changing facial expressions, can telegraph strong signals of interest. Customers, like most of us, are good at reading nonverbal signals.
- One way to demonstrate to the customer that he's being heeded is to clarify and confirm what he says, even when the listener is sure he understands.
- A salesperson is in real trouble when the customer shows any of these signs: he stops talking, he fidgets with his pen, or he starts doodling on his desk pad. They're sure indications that *he's* the one who isn't listening anymore.

Source: Arthur Bragg, "Turning Salespeople into Partners," *Sales & Marketing Management*, August 1986, p. 83.

I once got a referral from a good customer, but failed to write the correct telephone number into my notebook. Instead of calling my customer, I looked up the name in the phone book, called the prospect and made an appointment. When I arrived at the place, I began to have some doubts since it was a trailer office. I was greeted by a friendly, beer-bellied prospect wearing a huge belt buckle. On the wall, I noticed a calendar printed by my customer's firm, so I mentally confirmed that they had an ongoing business relationship. I was amazed to learn that this new prospect owned half the property in the valley and several successful businesses. I earned his trust and sold a large amount of insurance. After the policies were delivered, I stopped by my first client's office to thank him for the referral. To my surprise, he had never heard about this wealthy gentleman. I looked up the wrong number in the phone book and called on the wrong prospect! But I had learned that compassion for your prospect, regardless of the surroundings, always leads to new business.[15]

Factors Influencing the Listening Process

People are poor listeners for many reasons. Four factors that influence the listening process are biological reasons, negative self-concept, failure to understand that meaning is within the listener, and time pressures. In Table 9.1, sales consultants Anthony Alessandra, Phillip Wexler, and Jerry Deen present a long list of irritating listening habits and show how each is specifically inconsistent with good listening.

Table 9.1

Guidelines to Good Listening

Four Steps to Being a Good Listener

A. Listen to the Client
   1. Let the client talk.
   2. Listen for client's psychological needs.

B. Reduce and Circumvent "Noise"
   1. Listen attentively.
   2. Minimize the impact of distractions.

C. Organize the Message You Hear
   1. Take notes.
   2. Listen to everything.
   3. Identify main and supportive points in the client's message.
   4. Support and reinforce any of your client's statements that lead toward the solution of the identified problem.
   5. Listen "between" the words.

D. Check Your Listening

Irritating Listening Habits

Poor listening habits irritate customers and tend to erect barriers to effectively exchanging information. The letter and number for each guideline appear after any example that is inconsistent with that guideline.

1. He does all the talking; I go in with a problem and never get a chance to open my mouth. (A.1, A.2)
2. He interrupts me when I talk. (A.1, A.2)
3. He never looks at me when I talk. I'm not sure he's listening. (B.1)
4. He continually toys with a pencil, paper, or some other item while I'm talking; I wonder if he's listening. (B.1, B.2)
5. His poker face keeps me guessing whether he understands me or is even listening to me. (C.4, D)
6. He never smiles—I'm afraid to talk to him. (C.4)
7. He changes what I say by putting words into my mouth that I didn't mean. (C.1, C.3, C.4)
8. He puts me on the defensive when I ask a question. (C.2, D)
9. Occasionally he asks a question about what I have just told him that shows he wasn't listening. (B.1, B.2)
10. He argues with everything I say—even before I have a chance to finish my case. (A.1)

Table 9.1
Continued

11. Everything I say reminds him of an experience he's either had or heard of. I get frustrated when he interrupts, saying "That reminds me. . . ." (A.1, B.1, C.4)
12. When I am talking, he finishes sentences for me. (A.1)
13. He acts as if he is just waiting for me to finish so he can interject something of his own. (A.1, B.1)
14. All the time I'm talking, he's looking out the window. (B.1)
15. He looks at me as if he is trying to stare me down. (C.4)
16. He looks as if he's appraising me; I begin to wonder if I have a smudge on my face or a tear in my coat. (B.2, C.4)
17. He looks as if he is constantly thinking "No" or questioning the truthfulness or value of what I'm saying. (B.1, C.4)
18. He overdoes showing he's following what I'm saying—too many nods of his head or mm-hm's and uh-huh's. (C.3, C.5)
19. He sits too close to me. (B.2)
20. He frequently looks at his watch or the clock while I am talking. (B.1, B.2)
21. He is completely withdrawn and distant when I'm talking. (B.1, C.4)
22. He acts as if he is doing me a favor in seeing me. (B.2, C.1, C.4)
23. He acts as if he knows it all, frequently relating incidents in which he was the hero. (A.1, B.1)

Source: Anthony J. Alessandra, with Phillip S. Wexler and Jerry D. Deen, *Non-Manipulative Selling* (San Diego, CA: Courseware, Inc., 1979), pp. 77–79.

Biological Reasons

Ralph Nichols cautions that an individual must be careful not to waste the differential between speaking speed and thinking speed. As listeners we can think about 500 words per minute, while the normal speaking rate is 125–150 words per minute. In rapid conversation, people speak 200–250 words per minute. The typical public speaker, newscaster, or lecturer speaks 100–200 words per minute. That leaves as much as 400 words of thinking time available to use for each minute that we are listening.[16] Furthermore, a person's average attention span is limited to 30–45 seconds.[17] Thus, if a salesperson is giving a formal product demonstration to a buying committee of six prospects, there is a strong likelihood that each member of the committee is "tuning in" and "tuning out" throughout the entire presentation. Changing voice pitch or speaking speed, using sales aids, and asking questions can help prospects refocus their attention.

Salespeople are further affected by their physical or psychological state during the listening event. How they feel physically will influence their listening proficiency. If they have a sinus headache, are feeling stressed about meeting promised delivery schedules, or are anxious about reaching a quota, their concentration will be challenged that much more. Auditory acuity may also be reduced as physical deterioration of the hearing mechanism occurs over a person's lifetime.

Negative Self-Concept

How salespeople perceive themselves has a significant effect on how they listen. Individuals who have been told throughout their lives that they have poor listening skills may view themselves as poor listeners. Conditioned at an early age with messages from parents, teachers, and friends, such as "be quiet and listen; why don't you ever listen to me?" or "You haven't heard a word I've said," their negative self-images predominate. Therefore, they conclude that they may as well not expend the effort to improve their listening skills.

Unless people perceive themselves positively, they may be so concerned about doing or saying the wrong thing, or so worried that others may not like them, that they block the message being sent.

Understanding the Intended Meaning

Each discipline and field of specialization has its own internal *jargon*, or specialized vocabulary and idioms used by members within the profession. This jargon and other *"buzz" words* may interfere with salespeople's ability to listen if they are not familiar with the words being used. For instance, salespeople who are manufacturers' representatives for sports apparel need to understand what "OTB" (open-to-buy) and "price points" mean when discussing budget with the retail store buyer.

Inciting words, or symbols serving as emotional triggers, may sound an internal alarm and evoke an emotional response from the customer. Saying "Oh, no problem, trust me" to a customer who has been promised undelivered goods or services by either a competitor or a previous salesperson in the same firm can incite that person to even greater anger. These types of words are the subject of "Try This" Exercise 9.1.

Listening problems may arise from an *inferential message*, one that is assumed and not necessarily based on fact. The salesperson who replied

Try This 9.1 Emotional Triggers in Listening

Identify your red and green flags—words or phrases that incite negative and positive reactions for you—by recording at least three items that set up emotional triggers and affect how you listen to the other person.

Words/Phrases	Positive	Negative
People (salespeople, customers, others)		
______	______	______
______	______	______
______	______	______
Issues (topics)		
______	______	______
______	______	______
______	______	______

"no problem" may be inferring responsibility when, in fact, it has not yet been demonstrated that the salesperson can "deliver." Furthermore, the salesperson is negating or discounting the customer's expression of frustration and disgust.

Yet another listening barrier may occur if the salesperson does not realize that the prospect is incapable of receiving the message being sent, or if the prospect does not give the salesperson feedback to indicate that the message has not been received. Although effective sales communication is a mutual exchange process, the salesperson must be aware of the person with whom the communication is taking place, the nature of the topic, and the environment where the communication is taking place. In addition, the salesperson must also determine whether the terms of the communication and the context in which they are being used will carry the intended meaning of the message to the prospect.

Time Pressures

Time and space have become precious and valued commodities in parts of the country where overcrowding exists and the pace of life is accelerated. Time pressures can also affect the intensity of the sales communication relationship. A salesperson whose territory covers southern California is subjected to endless lanes of traffic inching along the freeways. Even the slightest mishap can cause near-gridlock conditions, frequently reducing the number of sales calls that can be made in a day. Furthermore, these delays often reduce the amount of face-to-face selling time. Thus, the salesperson may feel compelled to talk as quickly as possible and listen only a little to make up for lost time.

Levels of Listening

Clearly, listening is an engaging activity that involves concentration and retention of the message throughout the stages of the sales communication process. In addition to the behaviors of receiving, attending to, and assigning meaning to the aural and visual messages of the customer, the salesperson also engages in other behaviors as the purposes of the listening change.

This section explores how the listening process occurs on various levels, depending on the salesperson's intended purpose. According to communication educators Roy Berko, Andrew Wolvin, and Ray Curtis, individuals function as listeners at five levels: discriminative, comprehensive, therapeutic, critical, and appreciative.[18] Salespeople can improve their listening behaviors as they discover how to function effectively at these various levels.

Discriminative Listening

Discriminative listening is the most basic of the five levels. Individuals listen at this level to distinguish aural and visual differences. The process involves isolating various aspects of the message to identify its distinguishing features before processing the message at any other level. For instance, salespeople selling sophisticated electronic sound systems can better serve their customers' needs if they become proficient in distinguishing the differences in quality among various brands and models. An auto mechanic frequently relies on discriminative listening ability to determine how well an engine is running. In each case the salesperson is perceiving and identifying the sounds in the environment and then adapting the sales message to that environment.

Becoming efficient in this skill also involves developing sensory awareness and understanding of vocal characteristics, such as pitch, inflection, tension, volume, intensity, rate, quality, and tone, as well as nonverbal vocalizations such as "ah."

Salespeople should know that when verbal and vocal characteristics are in conflict, their customers will rely more heavily on the interpretation of vocal expression to infer the salesperson's feelings. Albert Mehrabian illustrates this point by referring to a recorded message or a telephone conversation:

> If the vocal expression contradicts the verbal message, the vocal expression will determine the total impact. The impact will be negative if the words are positive and the vocal expression is negative, or the impact will be positive if the words are negative and the vocal expression is positive.[19]

The ability to discriminate visual cues is a significant function in the listening process. It is so important to the salesperson that a significant portion of Chapter 10 focuses on the topic of nonverbal communication. The greatest impact of the *meaning* of the message may well come from what is communicated through the visual channel.[20] Mehrabian has devised a formula for determining the impact of nonverbal channels in communicating feeling messages. His formula suggests that 38 percent of the meaning of the message comes from the vocal component of the communication, 55 percent from the facial, and 7 percent from the verbal.[21]

Comprehensive Listening

Much of the listening that salespeople do is at the comprehensive level. At this level, their objective is to understand information to retain, recall, and use it at a later time. In Chapter 11 we will discuss probing for buying needs. The information that the salesperson gleans from probing, using comprehensive listening, and what can be done with the responses determine the course of the sales presentation.

Besides listening to customers, sales professionals are expected to learn new skills, procedures, and products through training programs that generally use lecture, discussion, and role-playing techniques. They must also listen to understand briefings, reports, and telephone conversations

On the International Front

International Focus: Valuable Listening

Listening to culturally conditioned responses is essential in selling situations. The following implications of listening may be valuable in foreign settings.

Is a nod of the head by a buyer a sign to get busy with the order book? This nonverbal sign does not necessarily reflect a positive reaction by many foreign buyers. Arabs tend to listen and nod when American buyers talk with them, but, according to Arab communications expert Flora Lewis, this does not mean that they agree. Instead, nodding is merely a sign of politeness and hospitality in the Arab culture.

In Japan, the listener or prospect may make noises of understanding or tentative suggestion, such as "hai" (meaning, literally, "yes") to imply "I am listening." If the listener draws breath between the teeth and makes a remark such as "sah," this means "no." It is also uncommon for an Asian to put the listener in the position of being discredited or corrected. This is one reason why Japanese negotiators never say "no" to a proposal, preferring to use answers such as "we will see," "it will be difficult," and "we will take into consideration. . . ."

In some countries, people use nonverbal communications that give out specific signals when communicating. For example, the "OK" sign, using the index finger and the thumb to form an "O" while extending the rest of the fingers, has different meanings in several countries. In Japan this gesture means money, and nodding the head in agreement while using the sign could mean that money will be extended. In France it means zero, and in Brazil it is an insult to a man and a seductive statement to a woman.

Salespeople dealing with prospects from different countries should listen closely and watch the prospect's face, stance, gestures, hesitation, and other body language.

Source: Steve Hawkins, "How to Understand Your Partner's Cultural Baggage," *International Management,* September 1983, p. 49; and Flora Lewis, "A Brief Analysis of U.S.-Saudi Arabian Relations," *New York Times,* February 27, 1979.

and when attending seminars, conferences, and trade shows. To be an effective comprehensive listener, the sales professional must concentrate on the message strictly to understand, not to make a critical judgment. Comprehensive listening involves three variables: memory, concentration, and vocabulary.

Memory

Memory is an important variable because we often measure comprehensive listening by a person's ability to remember the information that has been presented. Memory specialists Lorayne, Cermak, and Montgomery note several reasons why we do not remember things: we do not pay attention in the first place, have poor organizational methods of storing information, are distracted, or have a lack of caring for people or a lack of motivation to improve our ability to remember.[22]

Concentration

This involves a person's ability to pay attention. According to recent studies, the average attention span has not improved much over the years. Kittie Watson and Larry Smeltzer discovered that "while business students ranked internal distractions and business practitioners ranked environmental distractions as the most serious barrier to effective listening at work, both groups ranked inattentiveness as the third most serious barrier."[23]

Some reasons for poor concentration are misdirection of attention energy, such as external preoccupation and self-consciousness; being too ego-involved with internal distractions, such as hunger, fear of rejection, concern about inappropriate attire, and being "sure" that one "knows" what the customer is going to say and instead focusing on planning a response; and a lack of curiosity or drive. Underlying these four reasons for lack of concentration are not being conditioned to pay attention to various stimuli, lack of self-discipline, lack of self-motivation, and lack of responsibility.

Vocabulary

This variable is important in assigning meaning to the messages we send and receive. Each of us has four functional vocabularies: listening, speaking, reading, and writing. While our listening vocabulary generally ranks as either our largest or second largest functional vocabulary, it is still small; the average adult's personal vocabulary consists of about 20,000 words, compared to an estimated 600,000 to one million words in the English language.[24] Individuals' general vocabularies are as unique as their fingerprints. For salespeople, that uniqueness may make a difference in their success as competent sales communicators.

Therapeutic Listening

Therapeutic listening involves acting as a sounding board, allowing another person to talk through a problem. This level requires empathic listening and is particularly significant to salespeople who use relational selling strategies.

To be an effective therapeutic listener, salespeople must be willing to listen and understand and be capable of caring. In addition, they must have *discretion* (knowing when to refer the prospect or customer to someone else), *honesty* (a sincere, unpretentious interest in the person); *patience* (allowing the customer the time needed to provide adequate expression), and *faith* (belief in the other person's ability to solve the problem). The primary skills involved in therapeutic listening are focusing attention, demonstrating attending behaviors, developing a supportive communication climate, and listening with empathy.[25]

Focusing Attention

An effective therapeutic listener attempts to establish a supportive listening environment that is quiet and provides an atmosphere of privacy.

For instance, if a salesperson is in a customer's office, the saleperson might ask to close the door, hold all phone calls, or discourage interruptions to free the interaction from external distraction. The salesperson would also make a conscious effort to become free from internal distractions by directing all energy to the customer's problem.

Demonstrating Attending Behaviors

Almost any nonverbal behavior that responds directly to the sender (customer) can be identified as an attending behavior. The active listening Skill Builder in Chapter 8 provides a review of attending behaviors, which include touching and silence. Attentive silence, for instance, can have a calming effect on the customer. The individual often interprets it subconsciously as a sign of quiet attention. A brief silence may invite the customer to speak freely.[26]

Developing a Supportive Communication Climate

As a therapeutic listener, a salesperson provides a supportive climate in which the customer or colleague feels free, safe, and comfortable to communicate. By providing a supportive atmosphere, the salesperson says, "I am here and I care about you." The customer knows that the salesperson has interest in and unconditional regard for what is being said. This regard yields a feeling of security and a safeness to self-disclose without the fear or threat of being attacked personally. Creating this supportive listening climate promotes self-exploration and facilitates problem solving for the salesperson. Perhaps the greatest benefit to both salesperson and customer is shared trust and acceptance.

Listening with Empathy

Empathy requires both feeling and thinking with another person by trying to recreate the other person's world or situation as if it were the listener's own world. A second element of empathic listening is identifying with the other's thoughts and feelings by entering the other's frame of reference without losing one's own identity. A third factor is being able to replicate the other's thoughts and feelings by becoming an emotional and rational mirror without foregoing one's own convictions.

Responding Appropriately

Appropriateness is one of the key elements of competence. In developing therapeutic listening competence, a person can learn by first understanding which responses contribute to further self-exploration by the other person. Then it is the responsibility of the salesperson, as an effective listener, to practice furthering these responses.

Critical Listening

This goes beyond the first three levels of listening by adding the dimension of judgment. Critical listening centers on understanding the message and *then* evaluating it. This level of listening is especially useful to customers who are exposed to a persuasive message—"a message designed to influence a change in the listener."[27]

A salesperson often must listen critically to customers, especially when encountering resistance or conflict over the buying decision. Other situations that invite critical listening are evaluating new policies or procedures, weighing the relative merits of solutions proposed in a sales meeting, or deciding whether to use the sales support systems provided by the company.

Appreciative Listening

A salesperson engages in appreciative listening to derive pleasure or sensory stimulation from others' works and experiences. Because this is a highly individualized process, there is no special formula that guarantees something will be appreciated by all salespeople.

It is not necessarily the source of the appreciative listening activity, but rather the person's response to it, that defines appreciative listening. These sources may include "music, the oral style of the speaker, environmental sounds, oral interpretation of literature, theatre, radio, television and film."[28] Some people find an appreciative listening experience by going to the mountains and listening to the silence, while others find enjoyment in the sounds created by the pace of city activities.

Lewis and Nichols recommend three steps to enhance one's ability to listen appreciatively: (1) identify what you like most; (2) verify why you like these things; and (3) observe how these things affect others.[29]

For example, Paiste is a Swiss manufacturer of fine percussion instruments that are sold around the world. The American sales division is 90-percent staffed by either former musicians or those who still play professionally on occasion. Frank Jordan, a sales representative for Paiste America, Inc., helped introduce the company's new line of cymbals at the National Association of Music Merchants' annual trade show. Jack Friederichson, a professional musician with the Los Angeles Philharmonic Orchestra, purchased a set of the Paiste cymbals. Two months later, he sent Frank tickets to a concert under the stars at the Hollywood Bowl, where Frank had the opportunity to listen to Friederichson's masterful performance with the cymbals.

Applying Effective Listening Skills

As listeners, salespeople function in different roles, depending on the situation in which they are placed and the circumstances surrounding the situation. The ways in which they function require that they look at listening from two communication perspectives: intrapersonal and interpersonal. Salespeople listen intrapersonally when they make a genuine effort to listen to themselves. They listen interpersonally in informal conversation with peers, informal and formal sales interviews and presentations, teleconferences and sales meetings, and seminars. The

Try This 9.2 Listening Interpersonally

The next time you are listening interpersonally, do not respond to what the other person says until you follow these three steps:

1. Wait until the other individual *completes* what he or she has to say.
2. *Paraphrase* what you heard the person say.
3. Receive a *positive (affirmative) response.* Use "Is that what you mean?" as your verification question following your paraphrase.

Following a positive response, you may continue the conversation by making appropriate comments. If the other person says that your paraphrase was inaccurate, however, keep practicing until you are correct.

During your conversation, at what level(s) do you find yourself listening: discriminating, comprehensive, therapeutic, critical, or appreciative?

degree of formality of their communication depends on the structure of the communication context itself.

Intrapersonal Listening

Chapter 4 discusses the importance of developing a positive sales image and offers tools with which salespeople can cultivate a positive self-image. One of these tools is using positive *self-talk* by concentrating on productive thoughts and feelings while releasing negative messages.

Another dimension of intrapersonal communication is *self-listening*, which "utilizes an individual's *internal* channels of communication to process the stimuli and to make them more meaningful in the transaction."[30] By listening to themselves, sales professionals create the opportunity to know more about themselves, to listen to who they are, to accept what they learn, and to act on that information.

Interpersonal Listening

Exhibit 9.2 exemplifies the processes of effective listening. Salespeople who are good self-listeners should be able to operate more effectively when listening to others as well. A clear understanding of the self and what motivate one's responses should enable the salesperson to understand and adjust responses while communicating with other people. These responses are called *feedback*, or providing a response to the other person. Listening involves both receiving and giving feedback.

Exhibit 9.2

We listen with our hearts.

When I listen with the heart
I stop playing the game of non-listening.
In other words,
I step inside the other's skin;
I walk in his shoes;
I attempt to see things from his point-of-view;
I establish eye contact;
I give him conscious attention;
I reflect my understanding of his words;
I question;
I attempt to clarify.
Gently,
I draw the other out
as his lips stumble over words,
as his face becomes flushed,
as he turns his face aside.
I make the other feel that
I understand that he is important,
that I am grateful that he trusts me enough
to share deep, personal feelings with me.
I grant him worth.

Source: Loretta Girzaitis, *Listening & Response Ability* (Winona, MN: St. Mary's Press, 1972), p. 42.

- *Receiving Feedback*—Receiving feedback is one of the most effective ways a salesperson has of modifying behavior. Interpersonal communication author Richard Weaver shares these insights on receiving feedback:

> Monitoring feedback is our way of assuring that the message we intended is as closely related as possible to the message received. . . . The cues we receive may cause us to keep talking, restate our ideas, begin to stumble or stammer, or become silent. Whatever the case, we need feedback to gain insight into our own communication and to help us understand the communication behavior of others.[31]

- *Giving Feedback*—When salespeople listen effectively and give appropriate feedback, they show that they are attempting to manage their environment successfully. In doing so, they become active participants rather than passive observers and are able to act in direct response to a particular stimulus.

Listening experts agree that the more feedback there is between the sender and the listener, the more accurate is the listener's interpretation of the message. Subsequently, this increases mutual confidence that the message is being communicated accurately. For salespeople, this means increasing the amount of time allotted for the communication transaction. But then, time is an inherent component of both the traditional and consultative selling strategies. The goal is to develop competence in managing time—to use listening skills effectively and appropriately in each selling and nonselling activity.

To be effective in a sales interview, the salesperson's feedback must be open, honest, constructive, and meaningful to the customer.

Response Styles

For the salesperson, giving feedback is a way of participating in the mutual exchange process of problem solving. There are many ways of responding to customers or others; the most common of these are advising, judging, analyzing, questioning, supporting, active listening, and giving relational feedback.[32]

Advising

This means offering solutions, procedures, or prescriptions for what the customer might do in a specific situation. Most people offer advice when approached with another person's problem. Advising can trigger defense-arousing behaviors that could cost the salesperson a sale. In some instances, however, advising can be a positive factor in problem solving. Before giving advice, three conditions should be met:

1. Be confident that the advice is accurate. Salespeople must avoid the temptation to act as authorities on subjects they know little about. A person coming from an intensive product training session should be careful not to act superior or flaunt newly acquired knowledge with every customer.
2. Be sure that the person seeking advice is honestly ready to accept it. A customer may say "yes, but" to suggestions that are being made, especially if that person has another solution in mind.
3. Be as certain as possible that the person will not point the finger of blame at the advisor if the advice doesn't work out. Regardless of whose fault it is, customers tend to blame salespeople first for any problems that arise. A salesperson may offer advice, but the choice and responsibility for following it belong to the customer.

Judging

Judging involves evaluating a person's ideas, feelings, or behavior by suggesting that they are good or bad, right or wrong. Common judging responses begin with "You know what you should . . . ," "If I were you, I would . . . ," or "One thing you'll want to consider doing is. . . ." Judging responses are quick ways for salespeople to deal with a customer's problems and feelings. They do not always indicate genuine concern. If a prospect perceives that the salesperson is trying to deal with the problem in a quick and easy manner, the salesperson's suggestions will likely be rejected.

Usually, negative judgments are critical and produce defensive behavior. A less negative judgment is called constructive criticism. Salespeople have a greater chance of having their judgments received well when the customer has requested an evaluation and the judgment is genuinely constructive and not made in pejorative language.

Analyzing

For salespeople, analyzing is offering an explanation why they believe a customer thinks, feels, or behaves in a specific manner. Responses that begin with "Your problem is simply . . ." or "You know, the reason you aren't moving the product . . ." are analyzing statements. Analyzing has the same drawbacks as judging responses. These statements may arouse the customer's defenses, turn off the customer, or convey superiority. Four guidelines can help salespeople in deciding how and when to offer an analysis:

1. Offer an analysis or interpreation in a tentative rather than absolute manner.
2. Make sure that the analysis has a reasonable chance of being correct.
3. Be certain that the customer is receptive to the analysis.
4. Determine that the motive for offering an analysis is honestly to help the customer.[33]

Questioning

Questioning is asking for additional, specific information about thoughts, feelings, or behavior to encourage a customer to continue talking. For salespeople, learning to construct open-ended questions that draw out the customer's needs is crucial to interpersonal competence. Open questions that begin with *what, where, when, who,* and *how* are helpful in opening up the customer. *Why* must be used with discretion because it may cause defensiveness. Chapter 11 deals with learning how to develop and use questions effectively.

Supporting

For salespeople, supporting means reassuring, comforting, or calming a customer by suggesting that things may not be as bad as they seem or that the events will pass and more positive experiences will occur. Sometimes a customer needs to be reassured: "You may be assured that I will be here throughout the installation of the equipment, and I'll personally conduct the first training sessions." Reassurance means simply acknowledging the seriousness of the customer's feelings; it does not need to imply agreement. Other times, a customer may be distracted with humor. Again, the appropriateness of the situation should dictate the use of humor; otherwise, the salesperson can trivialize a serious situation. When a customer needs encouragement, sometimes a supporting response is the best choice.

Try This 9.3 Identifying Response Styles

Respond to the following statements using each of the five feedback styles listed below. Assume that the comments were made by a sales colleague of yours, and use owned language in your responses.

Jerry, I'm so frustrated, and I'm worried that my job's on the line if I don't come up with some answers soon. First of all, my ratio of calls for new business is 40 percent instead of the required 60 percent. Secondly, I'm 3 weeks behind in turning in my reports because I've had to spend so much time on customer servicing. And this morning, Jaime (the district manager) accused me of losing my temper with one of my major accounts. He won't believe me when I say that he (the customer) is always complaining. Furthermore, he's rude. I'd sure like to find a way out of the mess I'm in.

Advising response: ____________________
Judging response: ____________________
Analyzing response: ____________________
Questioning response: ____________________
Supporting response: ____________________

Active Listening

As described in the Skill Builder in Chapter 8, active listening is paraphrasing the customer's thoughts and feelings to achieve clarity and understanding. This skill is one of the most powerful tools that a salesperson can use and one of the most helpful ways of responding to a customer's disclosures. Be aware that when customers talk to salespeople about a problem and ask them for help in solving it, they are asking them, above all else, to be attentive listeners—to act as a sounding board (not resounding board), reflecting back the thoughts and feelings being disclosed.

Relational Feedback

Relational feedback can help salespeople respond to their customers by discussing their own experiences and then letting their customers take from those experiences whatever ideas may be useful to them.[34] Responses such as advice, judgment, analysis, and support carry with them the inherent implication that the salesperson knows at least as much about the customer and the customer's future as the customer does. These response styles can place the salesperson in a superior position, somewhat aloof from the customer. Relational feedback, however, enables salespeople to respond by sharing information about themselves, thereby helping to establish an exchange between equals. Skill Builder 9.1 provides an opportunity to practice relational feedback.

Traits of Good Customer Listening

In his latest book, *Thriving on Chaos,* Tom Peters calls for a revolution in the way we do business. He writes:

Skill Builder 9.1 Relational Feedback

Relational feedback builds on active listening. In addition to using attending behavior, paraphrasing, and questioning, relational feedback adds a specific example from your own experience that relates to the other person's comments. If you have had an experience that directly links with the other person's, then you may report your experience. For example, a customer may be explaining frustration with late deliveries. Perhaps your work has been affected by late deliveries as well, and you report your experience. If you have no similar experience, however, then you listen for the person's feelings and relate to these. For example, you might report a time when you have experienced frustration in waiting. It could be an experience waiting for a late plane or standing in freeway traffic. The following example may clarify the use of this skill:

Assume that Nancy Creach, the human resources manager for a large manufacturer of optical lenses, is considering adding more disability insurance and pension plans to the firm's benefit program. She discloses: "Although we have SDI, worker's compensation, and Social Security, I do like your proposal, Jamie. To me, disability insurance is disability insurance . . . get hurt—you get money . . . don't get hurt—and it's money down the drain. I'm especially concerned about the additional premium with our impending strike, and I'd like to think about it. May we defer until next month?"

Jamie, the salesperson, shares a related experience: "Nancy, I'm hearing some hesitation in your voice and appreciate your question. I remember when we were implementing the pension plan for Jeff Smith's firm. He initially wanted to defer implementation but then decided to go ahead. He found that almost immediately employee moral rose and there was corresponding productivity gain. In addition, 2 weeks later he was able to bring Mr. Donaldson on board because he had a pension plan to offer—and you know what that 'acquisition' has meant to Jeff's firm. I'm sharing this with you because I see you in a parallel position, especially because you will begin some of your own head-hunting soon [similar experience]. Can you relate at all to his experience [request for feedback]?"

Notice how the final question requests feedback about the connection you're making between your response and your original disclosure. If you haven't had a similar experience, you might respond with:

"I can't recall any of my clients experiencing exactly what you are right now, especially with the threat of a strike. I do remember, though, a few years back when I was selling residential properties and a young couple, who had fallen heir to nearly two million dollars, decided to buy their dream home near the beach. After showing them a newly listed, under-market-priced, magnificent 'charmer' with an ocean view, they got 'cold feet' and asked to delay making the offer until the following day. As a result, when they phoned the next afternoon, I had to tell them that the house had been sold [similar experience]. What I'm referring to here is the fear that they experienced in making a commitment to that large an investment and a similar kind of fear that you're experiencing in committing your company to that much of an investment program at this time [linking assumptions]. Do you see their feelings as being similar to yours?"

In this case, the common ground established through use of the relational feedback skill is accomplished by focusing on the emotional component. Because emotions are universal, you will rarely, if ever, hear a story from another person to which you cannot relate at the emotional level. Through this skill, you can assist others in self-listening—they may be better able to examine their own situations and take responsibility for them by relating to your similar experience and the emotions you feel. As a result, the two of you can build equality and increase mutual understanding and empathy.

Respond to another person's description of an experience by:

1. Providing attending behavior during the description
2. Paraphrasing the ideas and feelings described in the experience
3. Asking a verification question to determine the accuracy of your paraphrase
4. Briefly reporting an experience of your own that relates directly to the point of the other person's disclosure
5. Stating the similarity you see between your example and the other person's disclosure
6. Asking an open question about the degree of similarity the other person sees between the two examples

---

> Excellent firms don't believe in excellence—only in constant improvement and constant change. . . . The times demand that flexibility and love of change replace our ways of managing. . . . One of the important aspects of flexibility is listening.[35]

Peters identifies three significant traits of good customer listening: listening with intensity, spending time "hanging out" in the marketplace, and taking what is heard seriously and acting quickly.

Listening with Intensity

This means having face-to-face contact with the customer. It may mean not only getting out from behind the desk, but removing the desk altogether. Peters also recommends that companies have a "high roller" contest. Instead of rewarding cost cutting, reward spending—"money and time spent in support of customer listening. Why not give an award to the manager who has logged the most miles and the biggest phone bill on customer calls and visits?"[36]

"Hanging Out"

Peters tells his readers, "Good listeners construct settings so as to minimize 'naive' listening, the undistorted sort."[37] His message to the sales manager is to go into the marketplace to study the latest customer needs and survey the competitive scene.

Japanese management consultant Kenichi Ohmae reports that most successful Japanese consumer-electronics firms "hold regional product conferences with dealers and salesmen to get direct feedback on what improvements they can make in the design and marketing of the product."[38] For example, by watching young Californians on roller skates, an engineer for Sony created the concept of the Sony Walkman, a portable cassette player with headphones.

Take What You Hear Seriously and Act Quickly

According to Peters, "Good listeners provide quick feedback and act on what they hear." He suggests sending to clients abstracts of talks as proof of listening and making changes on the basis of what is heard. He says that "raw listening must be translated more rapidly into product and service ideas essential in today's speeded-up world."[39] Essentially, Peters believes that managers must take feedback from their salespeople quickly, seriously, and without distortion. For Peters, customer listening is more than a marketing, service, and sales job. Effective listening means involving the entire organization in the process.

Summary

Listening in the professional selling process involves eight areas of productivity, and each can be affected by the quality of the listening that takes place. Listening is thus an integral part of the relational sales process.

Listening is distinguished from hearing (a physiological process) in that it is more complex. It involves the interpretation of sensory stimuli and requires a response to these stimuli. The six characteristics of a supportive listening environment are provided in this chapter.

Among the influences—both external and internal—that affect the listening process are four major factors: biological factors, negative self-concept, failing to understand that meaning resides in the listener, and pressures of time.

A useful way of understanding the purpose of listening is offered by the Wolvin–Coakley listening taxonomy that is set forth in this chapter. This taxonomy points to the following five levels of listening: discriminative, comprehensive, therapeutic, critical, and appreciative. All these levels are involved in the selling process to varying degrees.

An important distinction is made in the chapter between two types of listening skills: the interpersonal (by which one listens to others) and the intrapersonal (by which one listens to the self). In addition to promoting the development of listening skills, the chapter points out seven response styles by which the salesperson may offer feedback to the customer: advising, judging, analyzing, questioning, supporting, active listening, and relational feedback. These responses are most often based on what Tom Peters has delineated as three characteristics of effective listening in the sales profession: listening with intensity, spending time "hanging out" in the marketplace, and taking what is heard seriously and acting quickly.

Key Terms

"Buzz" Words Words that are popular in a culture, but have lost their precise meanings through overuse; jargon

Inciting Words Emotionally active words that may evoke a defensive or guarded stance on the part of the listener

Inferential Message A message that is assumed but may not be based on fact

Interpersonal Listening Listening to others
Intrapersonal Listening Listening to one's own inner voice
Jargon Specialized vocabulary and idioms used by members of a certain profession

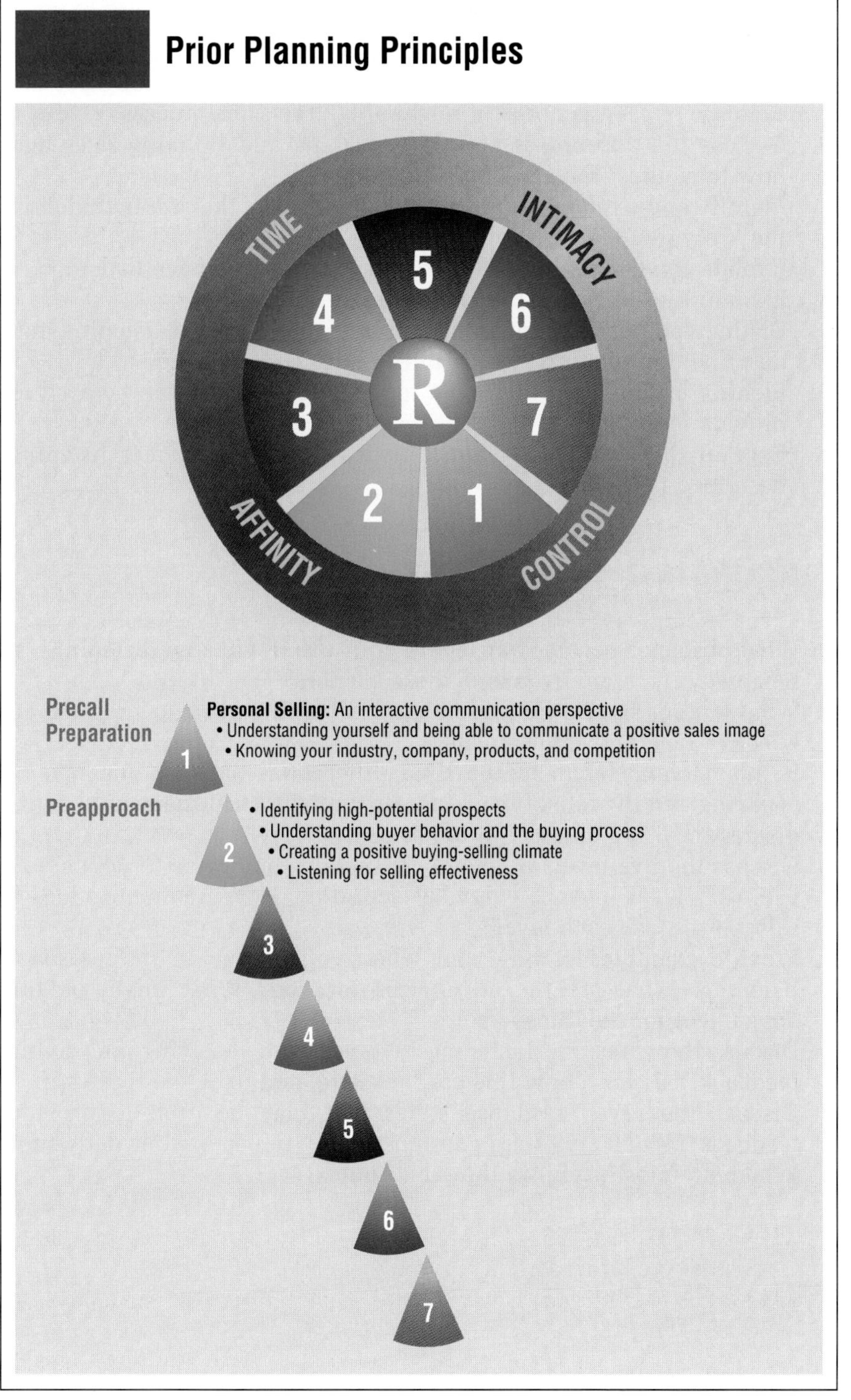

Figure 9.1

Review Questions

1. What areas of productivity can be affected by effective listening, according to L. K. Steil?
2. Distinguish between hearing and listening.
3. What factors may be obstacles to effective listening? How may a productive listening environment be developed?
4. What primary factors influence the listening process? Give an example of each factor as it might affect the sales process.
5. Discuss the differences between speaking and thinking rates and how they affect the sales presentation.
6. Identify and explain the five levels of listening that are included in the Wolvin–Coakley taxonomy.
7. Explain the three variables involved in comprehensive listening.
8. Explain the skills involved in therapeutic listening.
9. Distinguish between intrapersonal and interpersonal listening and describe the function of each in the sales context.
10. Identify and explain the seven response styles that can be used to provide feedback.
11. Explain the significant characteristics of good customer listening described by Tom Peters.

Discussion Questions

1. What obstacles become barriers to your use of effective listening? In what ways can you overcome these barriers?
2. What factors should be present in a sales interview to promote an effective listening environment?
3. Ralph Nichols refers to the time differential between the rate of speaking and the rate of listening. How might a salesperson turn this discrepancy into an asset in the sales interview?
4. Discuss the five levels of listening. Explain the degree to which you use each level in your everyday activities. How frequently does a salesperson use each level?
5. Provide examples of how and when you engage in intrapersonal listening. What are the advantages for you? What might be the advantages for the salesperson?
6. Discuss the concept, "Listening involves both receiving and giving feedback." Discuss how this concept is related to active listening.
7. Discuss the seven response styles that may be used to provide feedback. Which styles are you most likely to use in your daily life? Which are most useful in the sales context?

Listen to Your Prospect's Needs

Case 9.1

John Pace is a successful real estate agent, with commission earnings of over $100,000 a year from Hill Top Realty. The key to his success in sales is to show the client as many homes as possible and hope that one will be suitable. Interestingly enough, he has always found it quite burdensome to take the time to match the customer to the right house.

During a first appointment with a potential buyer, John forms an opinion about what the buyer will want and attempts to push the listings he has for sale. He is apparently more interested in generating high commissions than in listening to the client's needs and wants in buying a home. John seems to always lead the client on a "wild goose chase."

An elderly couple told John that they wanted a traditional house with a large country kitchen, three bedrooms (for their children who visit often) plus a master suite, and a large back yard for a garden and play area for the grandchildren. Realizing the couple's age, he determined that they would probably be too old to keep up a large yard, much less a large house. He formed the opinion that they would be more comfortable in a small home. He repeatedly showed them small houses on small lots, with no concern for the couple's expressed features and desires.

With frustration building between the salesperson and clients, the couple decided to give John one more chance to show them a house that they had seen with a "For Sale" sign posted. As an act of courtesy, they called John and asked him to give them a tour. John remarked that he did not think they would like the house because it had an old-fashioned kitchen and the large yard would be a lot of upkeep.

The couple insisted on seeing this house and convinced John to extend this one last opportunity. He agreed to show it, and as the couple entered this immaculate home, they agreed that it was perfect and made the decision to buy it.

1. Why is it important for salespeople to listen to their prospects' needs?
2. What clues and needs should John listen for that might aid his clients' purchase decisions?
3. Suggest activities using the art of listening that may prove valuable to salespeople.

Something to Learn about Listening

Case 9.2

Peter Downey, a sales representative for Americon Plastics, paid a visit to Jim Plumber, the owner of Fashion Optometrics in Dallas, to set up an appointment for a presentation. He made the call in response to an inquiry from Jim, who had read about new technological advances in eyeglass and sunglass lenses in the trade journals.

Because the demand for the glasses was increasing throughout the United States, Americon Plastics' strategy was to seek distribution through large, reputable retail facilities in the region. Peter was confident that he

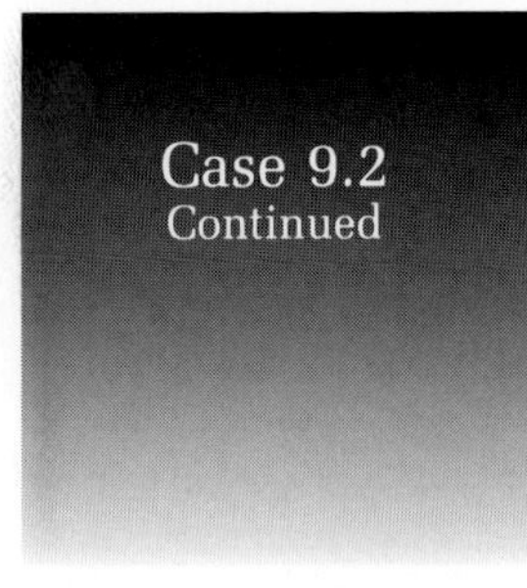

could persuade Fashion Optometrics to carry his line and also handle distribution to the other specialty stores in Texas.

Peter was instructed by the sales manager to prepare well for the presentation because this was the company's first attempt to establish a relationship with a distributor. He started the presentation by mentioning his company's record, its excellent reputation for constructing high-tech eyeglasses, its response to fashion trends, and its production methods and quality control procedures.

The discussion involved the advantages of fashion eyeglasses—better fit, durability, protection. Peter went on and on, discussing the improved vision from fashion glasses, until Jim interrupted him and said, "I want to know more about profit margins, service support, and the marketing program, which includes advertising budget support." Jim continued, "I understand your concern, but first let me tell you about the customers' reactions and what other optometrists have been saying about these glasses."

The buyer stopped Peter abruptly and stated, "I am familiar with your firm and the specifications and production standards of your glasses from reading the trade publications and the promotional material I received from your company several weeks ago." "No problem, then you will love our glasses. Can I take the order?" asked Peter.

"Let me give you a call when I am ready, and maybe you can come back with some answers to my questions," stated the buyer. This response left Peter speechless. "I have some brochures in my briefcase," Peter insisted. The buyer finally got up and said, "I have got an appointment waiting for me, so just leave the materials and I'll call you."

1. Is Peter a good listener?
2. Peter's mistake is obvious. What would you suggest that he say to the buyer right now?
3. What indicates that Peter has something to learn about listening and feedback skills?

Notes

1. Roy M. Berko, Andrew D. Wolvin, and Ray Curtis, *This Business of Communicating*, 4th ed. (Dubuque, IA: Wm. C. Brown, 1990), p. 36. See also: Ernest Parker Mills, *Listening: Key to Communication* (New York: Petrocelli Books, 1974), p. 5; and John L. DiGaetani, "The Business of Listening," *Business Horizons*, October 1980, pp. 40–46.
2. Lyman K. Steil, "Secrets of Being a Better Listener," *U.S. News & World Report*, 88 (May 26, 1980), p. 65.
3. Lyman K. Steil, *Effective Listening* (Reading, MA: Addison-Wesley Publishing Company, 1983), p. 51.
4. Paul T. Rankin, "Listening Ability: Its Importance, Measurement and Development," *Chicago Schools Journal*, 12 (1930), pp. 177–179.
5. Sharon A. Ratliffe and David D. Hudson, *Skill Building for Interpersonal Competence* (New York: Holt, Rinehart & Winston, Inc., 1988), p. 227.
6. Ibid.

7. Florence I. Wolff, Nadine C. Marsnik, William S. Tacey, and Ralph G. Nichols, *Perceptive Listening* (New York: Holt, Rinehart & Winston, 1983), p. 2.
8. Marilyn H. Lewis and N. L. Reinsch, Jr., "Listening in Organizational Environments," *Journal of Business Communication*, 25 (Summer 1988), p. 63.
9. Berko, Wolvin, and Curtis, *This Business of Communicating*, p. 37. See also: Tom Peters, *Thriving on Chaos* (New York: Alfred A. Knopf, 1988), pp. 306–307.
10. Edmond G. Addeo and Robert E. Burger, *Egospeak* (Radnor, PA: Chilton Book Company, 1973), p. xii.
11. Ralph G. Nichols and Leonard Stevens, *Are You Listening?* (New York: McGraw-Hill Book Co., 1957), pp. 164–165.
12. Arthur Bragg, "Turning Salespeople into Partners," *Sales & Marketing Management*, August 1986, p. 82.
13. Ibid.
14. Advertisement, "The Five-Step Customer Care Course—Action Skills to Sales Excellence," *Personal Selling Power*, 9 (November/December 1989), p. 26.
15. Ibid.
16. Andrew Wolvin and Carolyn Gwynn Coakley, *Listening* (Dubuque, IA: Wm. C. Brown, 1988), pp. 207–208.
17. Berko, Wolvin, and Curtis, *This Business of Communicating*, p. 42. See also: Charles T. Brown and Paul W. Keller, *Monologue to Dialogue* (Englewood Cliffs, NJ: Prentice-Hall, 1979), pp. 63–69.
18. Wolvin and Coakley, *Listening*, pp. 135–137.
19. Albert Mehrabian, *Silent Messages* (Belmont, CA: Wadsworth Publishing Company, 1971), p. 56. See also: Wolvin and Coakley, *Listening*, p. 137.
20. Wolvin and Coakley, *Listening*, p. 150.
21. Mehrabian, *Silent Messages*, p. 44.
22. Wolvin and Coakley, *Listening*, p. 191.
23. Kittie Watson and Larry R. Smeltzer, "Barriers to Listening: Comparison between Business Students and Business Practitioners," paper presented at the Fourth Annual International Listening Association Convention, St. Paul, Minnesota, March 4, 1983.
24. Roy M. Berko, Andrew D. Wolvin, and Dasrlyn R. Wolvin, *Communication: A Social and Career Focus*, 1985, pp. 67–68.
25. Wolvin and Coakley, *Listening*, pp. 243–265.
26. Ibid., p. 246. See also: Theodor Reik, *Listening with the Third Ear* (New York: Pyramid Books, 1948), pp. 124, 126.
27. Berko, Wolvin, and Curtis, *This Business of Communicating*, p. 41.
28. Thomas R. Lewis and Ralph G. Nichols, *Speaking and Listening* (Dubuque, IA: Wm. C. Brown, 1965), p. 192.
29. Ibid., p. 193.
30. Richard L. Weaver II, *Understanding Interpersonal Communication*, 5th ed. (Glenview, IL: Scott, Foresman/Little, Brown Higher Education, 1990), p. 148.
31. William C. Schutz, *The Interpersonal Underworld* (Palo Alto, CA: Science and Behavior Books, 1966), p. 13.
32. Ronald B. Adler, Lawrence B. Rosenfeld, and Neil Towne, *Interplay*, 4th ed. (New York: Holt, Rinehart & Winston, Inc., 1989), pp. 187–188.
33. Tom Peters, "Learning to Listen," *Hyatt Magazine*, Spring 1988, p. 16. Adapted from *Thriving on Chaos* (New York: Alfred A. Knopf, 1987), pp. 367–371, 524–532.
34. Ratliffe and Hudson, *Skill Building for Interpersonal Competence*, p. 243.
35. Peters, "Learning to Listen," p. 17.
36. Ibid.
37. Ibid.
38. Ibid.
39. Ibid.

PART 4

Anatomy of the Selling Process

TIME
INTIMACY
AFFINITY
CONTROL
R
TIME
INTIMACY
AFFINITY
CONTROL

CHAPTER 10

Opening the Interview—Developing Verbal and Nonverbal Rapport

Knowledge Objectives

In this chapter, you will learn:

1. The meaning of rapport and its importance in the selling process
2. How to make an appointment and establish sales call objectives
3. The distinction between supportive and defensive climates in building rapport
4. The methods and skills for building rapport through verbal messages
5. The elements of nonverbal messages in building rapport
6. How to build rapport through neuro-linguistic programming

Consider This

It's important to talk to people in their own language. If you do it well, they'll say, "God, he said exactly what I was thinking." And when they begin to respect you, they'll follow you to the death. The *reason* they're following you is not because you're providing some mysterious leadership. It's because you're following them.

Lee Iacocca,* chief executive officer
Chrysler Corporation

**Iacocca: An Autobiography* (New York: Bantam Books, 1984), p. 55.

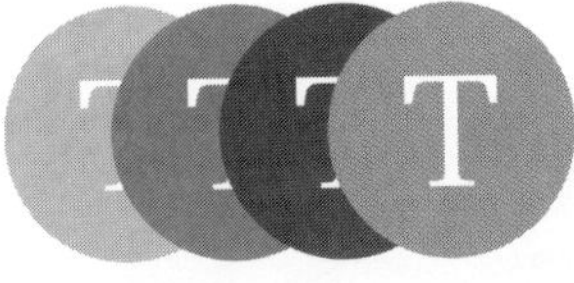

The knowledge and skills that salespeople acquire with prior planning principles (selling steps one and two) prepare them for the next stage, which focuses on meeting the prospect face to face. Step three, the approach, involves five elements: making the appointment, determining sales call objectives, opening the interview, building rapport with both verbal and nonverbal messages, and identifying buying needs.

This chapter focuses on building rapport, including suggestions for opening the interview and developing positive rapport through verbal and nonverbal messages. The first section focuses on how to recognize distinctions between supportive and defensive climates in building customer rapport. Making an appointment and establishing sales call objectives are also discussed. The second section concentrates on opening the sales interview and building rapport through risk taking and intimacy. Included are the seven traditional opening approaches: introductory,

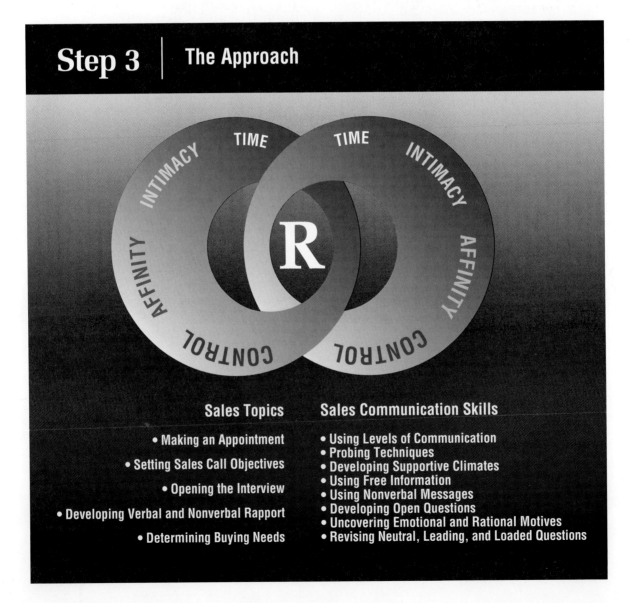

Step 3 | The Approach

TIME
INTIMACY
AFFINITY
CONTROL
R
TIME
INTIMACY
AFFINITY
CONTROL

Sales Topics

- Making an Appointment
- Setting Sales Call Objectives
- Opening the Interview
- Developing Verbal and Nonverbal Rapport
- Determining Buying Needs

Sales Communication Skills

- Using Levels of Communication
- Probing Techniques
- Developing Supportive Climates
- Using Free Information
- Using Nonverbal Messages
- Developing Open Questions
- Uncovering Emotional and Rational Motives
- Revising Neutral, Leading, and Loaded Questions

product, consumer benefit, curiosity, showmanship, referral, and premium. Six consultative communication skills are offered: the use of compliments, open questions, free information, highlighting, follow-up questions, and self-disclosure. The third section focuses on building rapport through nonverbal messages, and the final section offers a view of rapport building through the technique of neuro-linguistic programming.

Distinctions between Supportive and Defensive Climates

For salespeople to establish rapport with their customers there must be mutual trust and respect. G. W. Allport's theory of personality development through social encounter places trust at the center of any satisfying interpersonal relationship.[1] Personal trust is also at the center of Erich Fromm's theories on the art of loving and Martin Buber's ideas about the nature of warm human relationships.[2] Based on his theory of client-centered therapy, Carl Rogers advises people who want to be trusted by other people simply to provide acceptance and a sense of nonthreatening empathy, warmth, and genuiness.[3]

Bobby Patton and Kim Giffin define *interpersonal trust* as "reliance upon the communication behavior (speaking and/or listening) of a person while you are attempting to achieve a desired but uncertain objective in a risky situation."[4] Risk is inherent in a selling relationship for both the salesperson and the customer. The salesperson primarily risks rejection. If the salesperson's main objective is to consummate an agreement, the customer risks making a buying decision that may not be appropriate. Particularly at the beginning of a relationship between salesperson and customer, the risk level is high because the participants' objectives may be unclear and because each person is unknown to the other.

In a study on how industrial salespeople build trust, Swan, Trawick, and Silva found that, on average, 5.6 face-to-face contacts were required before a salesperson was trusted.[5] The study group consisted of purchasing agents who are professional buyers of industrial products. Compared to retail consumers, these buyers tend to be more cautious in their appraisal of a salesperson's trustworthiness.

The Risk-Trust Cycle

In any relationship, a risk-trust cycle develops through the exchange of verbal and nonverbal messages that contribute to the tone of the relationship. As people take risks and find acceptance, they feel valued and a degree of trust emerges. With each risk, a little more trust develops until they are willing to take greater risks. This risk-trust cycle spirals upward toward increasing degrees of openness and spontaneity. When a person takes a risk and is confronted with rejection, however, the risk-trust cycle spirals downward to a lower trust level. The extent of the downward spiraling depends on the degree of rejection, the importance of the information or issue that was communicated, and the intensity of the person's need for acceptance.

Sales Professional Spotlight

Experience and knowledge of many subcultures have equipped Gloria Macias Harrison with the skills and talents to capture the diversity of the Hispanic and local community markets of southern California's Inland Empire. Now, as chief executive officer and copublisher of one of the largest Hispanic newspaper companies in California, the Inland Empire Newspaper chain, she continues to deal with a handful of large accounts and prepares sales representatives to interact more efficiently with their serving markets.

During her years as a graduate student, Gloria was involved in several Hispanic-American organizations and acquired a firsthand familiarity with the Hispanic community. She also earned a Master's degree from the University of California in foreign languages, specializing in Spanish. After graduation, Gloria taught Spanish at a community college and quickly realized that she wanted to achieve other goals that she could not attain in the educational field.

"Our newspaper chain and the Hispanic market are both growing," Gloria says. In the United States, Hispanics comprise one of the largest subcultures. Marketers are becoming more aware of the potential of the Hispanic market. As with all ethnic groups, it has its own language, customs, and traditions. She sums up her preparedness in two words: communication and flexibility.

In establishing confidence with advertisers and customers, her efforts have emphasized interpersonal and intercultural relations. An important aspect of those relations is flexibility, which is vital in avoiding mistakes and misunderstandings in interpersonal and intercultural relations. More importantly, patience is a prerequisite in dealing with Hispanics because selling and negotiating are conducted at a slower pace than in many other cultures. Gloria claims the key to her success is her ability to understand and adapt to the markets being served.

Gloria also speaks several languages. This combination of customs and language knowledge has always been a factor in selling to Hispanic and middle-class markets in California's southland. Most Hispanics speak a mixture of English and Spanish. Realizing that this mixture of languages exists, she effectively uses that mix when it is appropriate and acceptable.

Different cultures also use different types of nonverbal communication. "I tune in to the cultural clues, which vary considerably from culture to culture. I am sensitive to the many unwritten rules that involve touching the client on the arm or shoulder, and the distance one remains from another in face-to-face interactions. Distance is affected by the customs and the relationship of the people involved. In some cases touching is inappropriate with a client of the opposite sex. Individual preferences must definitely be considered," she says.

Furthermore, before conducting business with a client, an amicable relationship must first be established. "I even go to the extent of recognizing the holidays and special occasions as part of the client's customs," she says. Furthermore, "consultative selling is used in developing a favorable relationship with my clients. Clients depend on my advice and recommendations," she says. She emphasizes trust as an important factor in the salesperson-client relationship. This relationship is enriched by the clients' awareness that the salesperson is able to perform and sensitive to their individual needs and expectations.

Salespeople who plan to capitalize on the potential of this fruitful marketplace will lose credibility and a large share of sales if they lack respect for cultural traditions and customs. Gloria advises salespeople to acknowledge those aspects of intercultural interactions that represent important steps toward confronting and adapting to selling situations.

Creating a Supportive Rather than Defensive Climate

In Chapter 8 we discussed three perspectives on climate: organizational, communication, and buying. Because climate is the atmosphere in which all selling activities occur, it is important to extend the discussion and look at how supportive and defensive climates affect the risk-trust cycle in building rapport.

When a salesperson uses defense-arousing statements, the customer feels devalued and attacked and often responds with defensive behavior. Furthermore, defensive behaviors tend to be circular—when the customer responds defensively, the salesperson is likely to reciprocate with defensive behavior. A spiral of mutual distrust builds, negating positive outcomes of previous effective communication.

The question arises: "How can a salesperson break down a customer's defenses?" Certainly not by building a better defense! In research on interpersonal trust, Jack Gibb contrasts two climates that can be established through communication. He refers to an atmosphere as *supportive* when it includes those response styles that help participants feel accepted and more willing to take risks. The contrasting atmosphere, a *defensive* climate, includes response styles that cause participants to feel attacked and concerned with self-protection.[6] Table 10.1 illustrates the six pairs of response styles that Gibb identifies as comprising these two contrasting climates. Let's examine each pair of response styles, placing priority on the style appropriate for generating supportive climates, and identify implications for the salesperson.

1. *Using descriptive (not evaluative) language.* This supportive category involves using descriptive language to report the behaviors of other people. For example, instead of saying to a customer, "You're so disorganized, John; you make me frustrated just watching you," the salesperson might revise these defense-arousing statements to "John, I feel frustrated when I see you digging through the files for a report. I'd like to discuss how we can create a software system to organize your data for quick access." The accusatory "you" is replaced with "I" language, indicating that the salesperson is taking ownership and responsibility for the statements.
2. *Use a problem (not control) orientation.* If the salesperson tries to force customers to perform without allowing them to take part in the decision-making process, the customers may feel devalued and assume that the salesperson has a lack of regard for their needs and interests. In contrast, problem-oriented communication focuses on meeting both people's needs and avoids the "my way/your way" dichotomy. Problem-oriented communication is at the heart of the selling relationship process.
3. *Respond spontaneously (not manipulatively).* Lying to a customer or manipulating with half-truths is one of the quickest ways to turn a supportive into a defense-arousing climate. For example, withholding some conditions of a sales agreement or failing to

Table 10.1

Gibbs' Categories of Contrasting Climates

Supportive Climate	Defensive Climate
Description	Evaluation
Problem Orientation	Control
Spontaneity	Strategy
Empathy	Neutrality
Equality	Superiority
Provisionalism	Certainty

mention hidden costs will quickly turn a customer's willingness to risk into distrust. In contrast, spontaneity involves telling customers all the information they request in a direct, forthright manner. Honesty does not require salespeople to share information that the customer does not request or that does not relate to an agreement. Honesty also does not mean being blunt or cruel in giving criticism, even when it may be openly requested. Usually, salespeople can combine criticism with a genuine compliment, enabling them to be both honest and positive.

4. *Respond with empathy (not indifference).* Indifference, or neutrality, amounts to showing a lack of concern for the customer—a strongly disconfirming message. A salesperson may initiate a lengthy discussion about personal interests while ignoring the spread of work on a customer's desk. A salesperson may interrupt a customer to speak to a third person when a nonverbal acknowledgment of the third person would be equally appropriate. Sincere empathy almost always can be communicated through direct eye contact and restating what the customer is saying without adding criticism or disagreement. In fact, if salespeople use direct nonverbal and listening skills before they offer criticism or disagree, their customers are likely to feel supported because the salesperson has demonstrated that the message was heard and understood, and because the risk has been taken to honestly provide a differing point of view.

   Active listening skills, sometimes called "empathic listening," were presented in the Skill Builder for Chapter 8. Once again, active listening serves at least two functions. First, using the skill helps salespeople verify that they understand their customers' communication. Second, it demonstrates to the customer that the salesperson is interested in and accepting of the customer as a person and respectful of the customer's feelings.

5. *Project feelings of equality (not superiority).* A salesperson who acts superior implies that the customer is inferior, communicating a clearly disconfirming message. In fact, as salesperson may have superior intelligence, talent, skill, and product knowledge, but this does not qualify that person as a superior human being or justify a superior attitude that may take the form of arrogance. An attitude of equality communicates respect for the other person. Direct nonverbal behavior, listening, and open questions used to encourage the customer to communicate openly with the salesperson demonstrate that the customer is viewed with respect and that the salesperson values the contributions to their conversation and relationship.

6. *Strive for provisionalism (not certainty).* Salespeople who behave provisionally demonstrate that they are open minded. "I see no evidence that we should revise our price structure," stated with a tone of finality, constitutes a dogmatic statement. Most customers would respond defensively because their sense of self-worth has been offended. In contrast, this statement demonstrates openness: "Our price structure has been thoroughly researched

and seems reasonable to me. I'd like to hear your thoughts. Perhaps an adjustment might be appropriate in spite of our research." Even if an adjustment is not made, the customer may feel personally supported and more inclined to relate to the salesperson, simply because the opinion has been heard.

There is no guarantee that, if salespeople use supportive response styles regularly, the communication climate in all of their sales relationships will be supportive and all customers will respond with the preferred buying decisions. By using supportive response styles, however, salespeople can be sure that most customers will feel more confirmed and valued than if they use defense-arousing communication. Customers are more likely to take risks because they will feel more trust toward the salesperson and in the relationship. As a consequence of the trusting relationship that salespeople initiate and develop, their customers are more likely to enter into long-term relationships with them that result in repeat business and the buying decisions that they seek.

While the examples cited here involve the prospect or customer and the salesperson, it is important to understand that rapport building often begins before personal contact is made. For most field salespeople, the risk-trust cycle of rapport building begins with the first phone call.

Making the Sales Call Appointment

Buyers generally agree that most individuals prefer to see business-to-business salespeople by appointment only.[7] Professional buyers do not appreciate having their time wasted. Thus, the goal of the salesperson is to develop a persuasive procedure for convincing the prospect to make the initial sales appointment. Often the path to the buyer's door begins with gatekeepers: receptionists, secretaries, and junior salespeople.

Try This 10.1 Developing Supportive Climates

What kind of questions would you ask yourself to determine how to develop a supportive climate for building rapport with a significant person in your life (friend, customer, roommate)? Here is a partial list of questions to consider. Design other questions that would be appropriate for the relationship you are assessing.

1. Do you listen to and empathize with each other?
2. Do you give each other encouragement and support?
3. Do you express your feelings openly and freely?
4. Do you identify, define, and solve problems together?
5. Do you share opinions, thoughts, and ideas without becoming defensive?

As mentioned earlier, the risk-trust cycle develops through the exchange of verbal and nonverbal messages that contribute to the tone of the relationship. When speaking on the telephone, the salesperson should use nonverbal responses heavily weighted toward vocal tone and pitch as well as speaking speed. Because Chapter 17 focuses on telephone techniques and telemarketing programs, the present discussion is limited to what the salesperson must do to initiate the risk-trust cycle.

Two popular approaches to obtaining an appointment are requesting permission to mail product literature and arranging an appointment directly with the secretary.

1. *Requesting permission to mail product literature*—This process has three steps:

   a. Introduce yourself, your company, and the product or service you represent, and obtain the prospect's permission to send product information.
   b. Send the product information and appropriate samples.
   c. After allowing the prospect sufficient time to absorb the information, follow up with a telephone call to schedule a personal appointment.[8]

   This "prenotification" approach obtains a commitment from the prospect on three different occasions. Figure 10.1 contains a model of what the salesperson might say.
2. *Arranging an appointment with the secretary*—This usually involves a department secretary or someone who is trained to screen the buyer's calls. There are five fundamental steps that sales professionals follow to ensure a positive risk-trust cycle:

   a. Treat the person on the other end of the line with dignity, courtesy, and respect.
   b. Use the opportunity to fully introduce yourself, your company, your reason for calling, and a key benefit statement that will catch the listener's attention.[9]
   c. Demonstrate your assertiveness without tentativeness in your voice—lower your voice and speak slowly and clearly.
   d. Thank the secretary for his or her help.
   e. Treat the person with dignity, courtesy and respect.

   Figure 10.2 provides a sample dialogue between a secretary and a salesperson.

There is simply no substitute for good manners, kindness, and courtesy. Integrating these elements so that they are a natural behavioral response secures more appointments and helps open many doors that remain closed when aggressive or defensive tactics are used.

Determining Sales Call Objectives

Respect, a second component of rapport, is something that must be earned. The salesperson who comes to a sales call prepared starts to build that

Figure 10.1

A Telesales Approach to Making a Sales Call Appointment, Part One

Requesting Permission to Mail Product Literature

Good morning, Mr. Halburt, my name is Robin Summers and I'm a sales representative for Acme Widgets. We've recently developed several outstanding pieces of reprographic equipment and customer service concepts that will save you thousands of dollars annually. Several of our current clients have averaged a 15-percent increase in profits by using our new technology. Because you fit the profile of potential users of our equipment and services, I'd like to share with you our latest literature on these products.

Because I prefer not to clutter up your mailbox with something you might discard as junk mail, I wanted to phone you first and obtain your permission to mail the literature. May I send you this information?

Good! I'll mail it this afternoon. I'll place it in a bright yellow folder with our blue and green widget logo on the outside, so you'll easily recognize it. Are there any special instructions or departmental codes that I should put on the envelope to ensure that it will be routed to you as quickly as possible?

I'll phone you within 10 days, after you have had a chance to review the material, to receive your input and respond to any questions you may have. I'm looking forward to our next conversation, Mr. Halburt—and thank you for your courtesy.

respect. One of the salesperson's precall activities is to establish definite objectives for each sales call. Each of these objectives should be realistic, measurable, and as specific as possible.

Three general guidelines may be useful in developing specific and measurable objectives:

1. *Generate sales*—Sell particular products to target customers on designated sales calls.
2. *Expand the market*—Lay the groundwork for developing new business by educating customers and gaining visibility with prospective buyers.
3. *Protect the market*—Learn the strategies and tactics of competitors and protect relationships with present customers.[10]

Table 10.2 provides examples of specific sales call objectives. Note that in each example a time frame is provided, showing when the plan of action will be implemented.

Figure 10.2

A Telesales Approach to Making a Sales Call Appointment, Part Two

Arranging an Appointment through the Secretary

Secretary: (Answers the phone) Good morning, Mr. Crandel's office. How may I help you?

Salesperson: Good morning. My name is Jennifer Campbell from Acme Widgets. I'd like to speak with Mr. Crandel. Is he in?

Secretary: Yes, but he's in conference all morning. Is there anything I can help you with?

Salesperson: (In a positive, assertive, and warm manner) Yes, I believe there is. Are you Mr. Crandel's secretary?

Secretary: Yes. I am.

Salesperson: (Sincerely) Good. And what is your name?

Secretary: I'm Kathy Owens.

Salesperson: I'm pleased to speak with you, Kathy. Again, I'm Jennifer Campbell with Acme Widgets. I'm calling Mr. Crandel to share some of the reprographics equipment technology and customer service concepts that we have recently designed to save companies like yours thousands of dollars annually. We're a 5-year-old company and have a track record of satisfied clients. When would I be most likely to reach Mr. Crandel by phone?

Secretary: I'm not sure that he has or will have a need for your equipment or services.

Salesperson: (Positive, assertive) I understand, Kathy, and I respect the fact that he is very busy. That's why I've developed some specific questions that take about 3 minutes to discuss and determine if our services or equipment will be of benefit to your operation. I'd really like the opportunity to review those questions with Mr. Crandel. Is there any time today or tomorrow that would be convenient for me to get in touch with him?

Secretary: (Pausing, thinking) All right, why don't you try reaching him near the end of the day. Looking at his calendar, I see that he's in meetings until 3:00 p.m. You'd probably be able to catch him around 4:00 p.m. But I warn you (joking), he'll hold you to those 3 minutes.

Salesperson: That's fair—and I'll keep my commitment to you. I'll give him a call at 4:00 then. Thanks very much for your help, Kathy. I really appreciate your courtesy.

Secretary: That's perfectly okay. Good luck.

Salesperson: Thank you. Goodbye for now.

Source: Adapted from Bill Parou, "The Key to Effective Telesales," *Teleprofessional*, March 1991, pp. 29–37.

Determining Your Sales Call Objective

Table 10.2

Before you meet with your prospect, you must decide what you hope to achieve during the sales call. In other words, what is your sales call objective? It should be as specific as possible and measurable. A time frame must be provided showing when the plan of action will be implemented. Following are some examples that will help you develop your own sales call objective.

You Are Selling . . .	Sales Call Objective
A new food product to a grocery store chain buyer	Convince the prospect to buy 20 cases/store of Pep, display the product on the shelf in the diet section of the store, price it $1.79, and accept delivery by next week.
An industrial cleaning solvent to a purchasing agent at a large manufacturer	Convince the prospect to buy a sample quantity of Quick-Cleen for testing, accept delivery by next week, and have the test completed by the end of the month.
A new prescription drug to a doctor	Convince the doctor to accept 50 free samples of Inoxcine today, begin dispensing the samples to his patients, and begin prescribing the medication through his patients' pharmacies immediately.
A new food product to the food and beverage manager of a restaurant	Convince the prospect to buy five cases of Bostonian Frozen Shrimp, accept delivery by Friday, and add the item to the menu immediately.
Meeting room facilities to a sales manager who is planning a sales meeting	Convince the prospect to accompany me to my hotel this week to see the meeting rooms and sample various items on our luncheon menu.
College education to a high school counselor	Convince the prospect to bring 20 students to my campus by the end of the month for a tour, orientation, and lunch.
Construction services to the president of a firm that is planning to build an addition to its plant	Convince the prospect to allow my firm to submit a bid for this construction project on the first of the month.
Radio time to the owner of a clothing store	Convince the prospect to sign a contract for fifty 30-second radio spots to air next month.
A prepackaged tour of Europe to the assistant minister of a large church	Convince the prospect to allow me to make a slide presentation next week to people in the congregation who are interested in such a vacation.

Table 10.2
Continued

A fleet of automobiles to a large food manufacturer	Convince the prospect to accompany me to my dealership this week to test ride the Oldsmobile Cutlass.

Source: David Sellers III, *Role Playing the Principles of Selling* (Chicago, IL: The Dryden Press), 1987, p. 15.

Building Rapport through Verbal Messages

Verbal messages and nonverbal cues serve distinct but complementary purposes. While verbal messages carry meaning about intellectual content, nonverbal cues provide meaning about the relationship between salesperson and customer, including their feelings for and attitude toward each other and the business at hand.

Verbal messages can be used to initiate or reestablish rapport during the opening of the sales interview. As with any conversation, and especially when that conversation is a first meeting between strangers, the opening segment is a search for common interests. The salesperson and customer must at least be interested in discussing the same topics if the interview is to become successful. At best, the salesperson is equipped with communication skills that facilitate the emergence of *common ground*, or areas of mutual interest, between the salesperson and the customer. By establishing rapport, the salesperson also increases the likelihood that the communication will be spontaneous and honest.

In this section we will examine the levels of communication that may exist during the opening of a sales interview and then identify and practice six communication skills that a salesperson can use to establish genuine rapport with the customer. Using these skills will encourage a positive response from the customer.

Levels of Communication during the Opening

Verbal messages occur at different levels. These levels vary in intensity and focus. "How were your sales last quarter?" represents relatively low intensity and provides little focus on the immediate situation or the relationship between salesperson and customer. Little risk is involved and, as a consequence, the contribution made by this statement to the development of mutual trust is insignificant.

Contrast "How were your sales last quarter?" with this opening: "John, I'm genuinely pleased to have the opportunity to be with you today. It's especially exciting for me to take over your account after

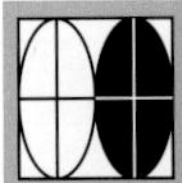

On the International Front

International Focus: Communicating in a Foreign Country

Although selling to foreign buyers is easier if the salesperson speaks their language, it is becoming less imperative that international sales professionals speak languages other than English. A major trend in the international marketplace lies behind this development.

Many industries do not depend on the local language as strongly today as they did just one or two decades ago. English is the world's most widely used language, giving American salespeople a tremendous advantage in international settings. English is spoken throughout Europe and is the second leading language in Asia and Latin America. Americans are fortunate in having English as their native tongue because the ability to speak several foreign languages is becoming less important.

Three-quarters of the world's letters, faxes, and cables and more than half of the world's technical and scientific journals are written in English. Also, 80 percent of all information stored in computers is in English. In many growing and highly sophisticated areas, such as the electronics and aerospace industries, English is the language spoken by most customers.

Consequently, with more and decision makers speaking English in many countries, most firms are selling their products directly to foreign buyers without using local middlemen. In industries where knowledge of the local language is important, however, companies tend to assign sales territories on the basis of language skills. This is particularly important in the traditional industries, such as textile manufacturing, where businesses remain locally oriented and where English may not be spoken well by the purchasing agents.

Purchasing agents and other decision makers may not always understand the nuances and idiosyncracies necessary to communicate effectively in a foreign country. For example, the phrase "How are y'all doing?" might be common in Atlanta business circles but certainly not in New York or Chicago. The same is true abroad, where American English may not be the English—or the language—that professional salespeople speak.

There is no selling without communication, the tool of understanding and persuasion. Lack of understanding leads to distorted impressions, assumptions, and misinterpretations that can jeopardize long-term relationships. It is imperative that the international salesperson adapt to many communication and cultural variations, even though the language barrier seems to be less of an obstacle.

Sources: Christopher T. Linen, "Marketing and the Global Economy," *Direct Marketing,* January 1991, p. 54; Jean-Pierre Jeannet and Hubert D. Hennessey, *International Marketing Management: Strategies and Cases* (Boston, MA: Houghton Mifflin Company, 1988), pp. 437–438; and Edward R. Koepfler, "Strategic Options for Global Market Players," in *Marketing Annual Editions 91/92* (———, CT: The Dushkin Publishing Group, Inc., 199–), p. 206.

hearing the enthusiasm Mike has expressed during his 15 years of working with you." This statement represents a deeper level of communication in that the salesperson is disclosing feelings about the customer, the account, the relationship, and the present situation.

Each level of communication serves important functions and has predictable consequences. "How were your sales last quarter?" is a statement of low intensity that requires little risk on the part of the salesperson. As a consequence, the singular use of a statement such as this will contribute little to the development of a trusting relationship. The second example is a more intense statement that involves the salesperson disclosing emotions about the customer and the immediate situation. When communicated genuinely and at the appropriate time, the second statement will usually contribute to a more trusting relationship. It also represents a higher level of risk taking on the part of the salesperson.

There are five different levels of communication that can occur during a sales interview. The least intense involves low risk and contributes little to building a trusting relationship. The most intense represents the other end of the spectrum; risk is higher, and so is the positive effect on rapport.

Level Five—Light Talk

This level represents a way of starting the conversation. On this level, both salesperson and customer talk in socially acceptable clichés, such as "How are you today?," "How's your season going?," or "Sure has been cold lately, huh?" Note, in the following example of light talk, that little direct information is provided about either the salesperson or the customer.

Hart: Good morning, Mr. Strong. I'm Joyce Hart of Smith Tool.

Strong: Yes, come on in.

Hart: A beautiful day, isn't it?

Strong: Yes, I suppose so.

Hart: Mr. Strong, I appreciate having this opportunity to meet with you.

Strong: That's okay. What's on your mind?

This initial exchange serves an important purpose: If Joyce Hart observes nonverbal cues carefully, she will be able to make assumptions about such factors as Mr. Strong's attitude, attention and energy level, and availability. Mr. Strong's last statement may be a cue that he is ready to move to a more intense level of communication—one that is more focused on the purpose of the sales interview. If the salesperson misses this cue and continues with light talk, the sales interview could end at this point or drag on until the customer becomes irritated.

Level Four—Reporting Facts about Others

At this level, the focus of the interaction becomes more intense in that the salesperson and the customer share their ideas and feelings with each other. The focus, however, is typically on what others have said or done.

Hart: Jerry Smith at IMC Tool and Die asked that I say hello to you when we had lunch yesterday.

Strong: Is Jerry using your 350X system?

Hart: Yes. We installed it a month ago and his first cost-savings report indicated a 5-percent reduction in just 30 days. We're pleased with the results.

Strong: That's interesting, but Jerry has a different operation than we have.

Notice that Ms. Hart and Mr. Strong have expressed feelings of pleasure and interest, bringing the conversation to a level of intensity that was not demonstrated when using light talk. The feelings they have expressed, however, have little to do with the context and purpose of the immediate sales interview or with each other. The topic is Jerry Smith's system.

At level four, the conversation may become more focused and intense than it was at level five and may even reveal common interests, such as a mutual acquaintance. The messages do little to establish mutual rapport, however.

Notice, again, that Mr. Strong has given Ms. Hart an important cue in his last statement in the sample dialogue. If Ms. Hart takes the cue and follows up by shifting the conversation to Mr. Strong's operation, she will move the conversation to the next level, which is more focused on the purpose of this sales interview and has greater potential for directly establishing mutual rapport with Mr. Strong.

Level Three—Sharing Ideas Purposeful to the Sales Interview

At this level, the focus of all messages is on the purpose for the interview between the salesperson and the customer. Light talk of mutual acquaintances or other companies is not part of the conversation unless an experience with another company or customer serves to clarify the purpose of the immediate interview.

Let's pick up the opening conversation between Ms. Hart and Mr. Strong and move it to level three:

Hart: I understand that your system is quite different. In fact, I spent some time yesterday touring your facility and have prepared a schematic drawing that adapts the 350X to your system.

Strong: Oh, you have?

Hart: Yes. I'd like to go over it with you right now so that we can determine what adjustments may be needed to adapt the 350X for your needs.

Strong: Well, I'll be glad to look at it with you, but I must admit that I have some reservations.

At this level, Ms. Hart takes the lead by focusing on the purpose for the sales interview with Mr. Strong. While levels five and four served the purpose of gradually moving into talk about products and services, at this level Ms. Hart reveals the amount and type of her preparation for this interview. Mr. Strong immediately focuses his attention, feels increased goodwill toward Ms. Hart, and seems ready to discuss how the product might meet the needs of his system. These three functions of the interview opening often come together in a focused way when communication occurs at level three.

Level Two—Sharing Feelings Purposeful to the Sales Interview

An opportunity to increase the trust level in a relationship can easily be missed if a salesperson overlooks the verbal and nonverbal cues provided in level three communication that indicate readiness to move the conversation to level two, the sharing of feelings in a purposeful way. Feelings are often communicated indirectly by voice, face, and body cues. The way in which Ms. Hart tells Mr. Strong about her preparation for the interview will affect their rapport. Nonverbal expression that communicates attitudes of enthusiasm, competence, and professionalism will encourage the development of rapport.

In the sample dialogue, Mr. Strong communicates his feelings directly through his verbal message. He expresses his reservations about the appropriateness of the 350X for his system. Let's continue the dialogue with Ms. Hart picking up on those feelings of reservation and discussing them in an open and direct manner.

Hart: Mr. Strong, I shared your doubts. That's why I took the liberty of preparing a schematic to determine if there is an application of the 350X to your program. I'm excited about the results, Mr. Strong. And I think you will be, too. Shall we have a look?

Strong: I can see that you're enthused. As a result, I'm pretty curious about what you've come up with. By the way, may I call you Joyce?

Hart: Of course, Mr. Strong.

Strong: Good. And please call me Ray.

At this point, three things seem clear: (1) feelings of goodwill have been established between Ms. Hart and Mr. Strong, (2) the three general purposes of the opening of a sales interview have been accomplished, and (3) this rapport and achievement of purposes are the result of two-way communication—neither Ms. Hart nor Mr. Strong could have opened the interview successfully without each other's cooperation.

While the opening of the sales interview might well be completed at this point, it is possible to reach a still deeper level of communication, either in the context of the opening or later in the interview.

Level One—Mutual Understanding

Continuing, authentic relationships between salespeople and customers are characterized by moments of mutual understanding that result from open sharing of concerns at both the idea and feeling levels. Let's look in on one of these moments after Ms. Hart and Mr. Strong have examined the schematic Ms. Hart prepared for the interview:

Hart: Well, that's it. What do you think, Ray?

Strong: I'm going to be very direct with you, Joyce. Not only am I impressed with the feasibility of this plan, but I genuinely appreciate the personal interest and time you've given to doing your research and preparing a schematic that will help me improve our system.

Hart: Thank you, Ray. I'm very pleased to hear you say that.

Strong: We'll need to make a few adjustments, but I'm confident that the two of us can work those out.

Hart: So am I, Ray. Shall we identify how the plan needs to be changed?

Moments of mutual understanding may occur at any point in a sales interview. They are most likely to occur when the salesperson and customer have candidly expressed their ideas and feelings about the task at hand. Moments of mutual understanding demonstrate that the salesperson and the customer are a team that functions to solve problems jointly. These moments represent what is meant by "professional selling—a relational process." Skill Builder 10.1 offers an opportunity to practice building rapport by using the five levels of communication.

Traditional Methods for Opening the Interview

Structuring the opening of the interview is as important to one's success as preparing for the presentation. Rapport develops more easily when the buyer feels comfortable and significant, when the physical setting allows for privacy, and when enough time is allowed to create a meaningful dialogue. In addition to moving through the five levels of communication just described, there are seven standard approaches that have gained acceptance over the years for capturing the prospect's attention and moving from light talk to "product talk." These methods are called the introductory, product, customer benefit, curiosity, showmanship, referral, and premium approaches. They are most effective when used in combinations.

- *Introductory*—The introductory approach is the most commonly used and the least effective when used by itself. It opens with the salesperson's name and company and is usually accompanied by a handshake (for example: "Good morning, Mr. Cromwell, I'm Joanna Li with Hawthorne Investment Program"). Giving an effective handshake is critical to this opening.
- *Product*—In the product approach, the salesperson places the product in the hands of the consumer and uses silence as a

Skill Builder 10.1 Opening the Interview: Building Rapport through Levels of Communication

When salespeople learn how to manage the opening of the interview to move conversation expediently, smoothly, and genuinely through the levels of communication, they will use the opening 5 minutes of a sales interview to lay the foundation for mutual success. By modeling effective communication skills, salespeople will enlist the assistance of the customer in focusing attention, initiating rapport, and creating opportunities to discuss products and services that will balance the conversation.

The following dialogue combines the methods of approach and communication skills presented in this chapter into a dialogue that moves the salesperson and the customer through the levels of communication and completes the risk-trust cycle in establishing rapport.

Level Five—Light Talk (Establish a common ground or areas of mutual interest)

Mason: Good afternoon, Mr. Harder. I'm Bill Mason with The New England.

Harder: Yes, come in.

Mason: I couldn't help but notice your impressive display in the reception area [*compliment*]. One of the models was for a project in Kenya; do you also run that plant?

Harder: Yes, we do.

Mason: You know, that's very interesting; I've always wondered about how that was done. . . . Mr. Harder, I want to thank you for the opportunity to meet with you.

Harder: Well, thank you. What's on your mind?

Level Four—Reporting Facts about Others (Focus the conversation on what others have said or done, not on yourself or the buyer)

Mason: As I indicated on the telephone Monday, Vernon Giles and I were working on his employee benefit package and he suggested that I contact you [*referral*]. Vernon and I have had a working relationship for a long time; I not only handle his benefit package, but I also do work for several of his clients [*self-disclosure*].

Harder: Is Vernon using your firm's administration services and investment products?

Mason: Yes, he's been with us for about 3 years. Not only has he saved on administration costs, but investment performance on the pension plan portion has improved significantly, and that has had a direct impact on employee morale, not to mention the increased flexibility [*consumer benefit and using free information*].

Harder: That's very interesting; however, Vernon's situation is very different from ours.

Level Three—Sharing Ideas Purposeful to the Sales Interview (Seller takes risk of relating ideas or concerns to the buyer)

Mason: Yes, it is very different; not only do you have much more diversity among your employees, but your numbers are greater and they're spread out over a large geographical area. That's why my primary purpose is to simply share some information and then see how it applies to you.

Harder: Oh, well . . . fine. I can handle that . . . but don't push, I've had all that I can take today.

Mason: Mr. Harder, I can assure you I have no intention of pushing. Let me show you how we handled a situa-

Continued

tion similar to yours so you can get a feel for how we work, and then we can look specifically at your concerns [*curiosity*].

Harder: Okay, I'd be interested in looking.

Level Two—Sharing Feelings Purposeful to the Sales Interview (Seller takes risk of telling the buyer some feelings about the ideas and concerns)

Mason: Mr. Harder, I hope you can see how our approach provides you with an efficient and effective way of maintaining the goodwill of your employees with a flexible benefit package [*product*]. There are several changes that should be made based on what you've told me [*highlighting*]. I'm really quite excited; I'd like to get some additional information so we can design an approach specifically for your organization.

Harder: I can see your enthusiasm; I think I'd like that.

Mason: That's great; may I ask some more questions and take a few notes? [*follow-up question*]

Harder: Yes.

Mason: How do you feel about . . . [*open questions*].

Level One—Mutual Understanding (Authentic relationships are based on genuineness and honesty; concerns are shared at both the idea and feeling levels)

Harder: I'm going to be very candid with you, Bill. I'm impressed with what you've shown me. Moreover, I really appreciate the personal interest and time you've put into helping me see how I can better meet some of my objectives.

Mason: I'm very glad to hear that, Rich; it means a great deal to me that you feel that way. Let me take the information you've given me and, based on a careful review, I'll come back with some specific recommendations for your consideration . . . [*self-disclosure and highlighting*].

Now that you have followed the salesperson and the customer through the five levels of communication to build rapport in their sales relationship, write a dialogue for *your* product or service that moves through the five levels.

Source: Reprinted with permission from William C. Mason, Jr., Financial Services/Products Representative, New England Life, course material for Marketing 435, California State Polytechnic University, November 29, 1989, pp. 14–15.

response to the action. The salesperson relies on the customer to open the interview by reacting to the item. This may attract the buyer's attention if the product is new, unusual, or unique. It often works well with consumer specialty goods. Frequently, a bit of showmanship or drama is combined with this approach.

- *Customer Benefit*—In the customer benefit approach, the salesperson might open the interview with a statement or question that reflects a primary benefit to that customer of purchasing the product. For example, a sales representative for a company that manufactures pagers might open with "Mr. Geoffrey, would you be willing to pay $17 per sales rep to guarantee that you can contact them at any time during the day?" or "Ms. Hoffman, I'm here to show you how you can save 15 percent on the purchase of our Pagenet pagers."

- *Curiosity*—The curiosity approach requires creativity and solid knowledge of the customer's reaction to surprises. It is safest to use this approach with an established client or one who has previously purchased from the salesperson. For example, the owner of a restaurant who wants to expand into corporate catering might say, "Mr. Simpson, from talking to your employees on their lunch hours, I understand that you are currently looking for a catering service to handle your Christmas party. So, at your employees' request, I arranged this appointment to discuss how Luigi's can help you with this exciting event."
- *Showmanship*—Occasionally, there may be an opportunity to "dare to be different" in gaining the prospect's attention. This approach covers everything from the subtle to the outrageous. One must be careful, however, that the approach does not backfire. It is definitely a high-risk approach.

  A sales manager tells a story about the young advertising account executive who, in his attempt to make a lasting and positive impression, had himself packaged and delivered by United Parcel Service to his client's office. The tactic worked because the client had a sense of humor and because advertising people are generally expected to be creative. In another, more subtle example, the person who was selling pagers in the earlier example may hand the product to the buyer and say, "If I'm one of your sales reps, and I'm in San Diego en route to my next call, you could reach me in 15 seconds." Then the salesperson would execute the paging process within the 15-second time span.
- *Referral*—The referral approach may be used specifically in conjunction with communications at level four, reporting facts about others. It is especially effective in industrial selling, where it is critical to know who has authority to make the significant decisions. The salesperson should also mention the name of someone whom the customer knows and respects. For example, a salesperson for Sensiem radio communication systems might open an interview with "Mr. Hutton, when I talked with Jerry Jeffries at Giffin Rentals last week, he said that you were fraternity brothers and recommended that I contact you. His company uses our system to communicate with its field personnel."
- *Premium*—The premium approach involves offering the buyer free samples or advertising specialties, such as pens, paperweights, notepads, and so forth, in exchange for the buyer's attention. A textbook representative for the accounting book that was adopted at Orange Coast College in Costa Mesa, California, occasionally leaves doughnuts in the division office with her card on the box. Each spring she invites the entire department to lunch at an upscale restaurant overlooking the luxurious yachts and homes of Lido Isle in Newport Beach. To continue with our previous example, the salesperson for Pagenet paging equipment might give the customer a map of southern California with Pagenet's service area shaded.

Try This 10.2 Combining Approaches

Imagine that you are a manufacturer's representative for a line of sports apparel—shorts, tops, t-shirts, and so on. Your customers are specialty retailers such as surf shops and sporting good stores. You have an appointment to see the head buyer of one of the largest and most successful sporting goods retailers in a nearby city.

In preparing for the interview, outline what you will say in the opening stages of the interview to establish rapport. Design seven possible statements you could make, using each of the approaches listed below or a combination of those approaches:

1. Introductory
2. Product
3. Consumer benefit
4. Curiosity
5. Showmanship
6. Referral
7. Premium

Practice what you have written with a classmate or a friend. Ask for feedback on your nonverbal and verbal messages.

Communication Skills for Establishing Rapport

In addition to selecting an approach that is appropriate to the selling situation, the salesperson can use communication skills in the interview to facilitate two-way communication. There are six specific skills a salesperson can use in conjunction with the previous approaches to open a sales interview. These skills encourage the customer to share the responsibility of identifying common ground while focusing attention, initiating rapport, and moving toward a discussion of needs, products, and services. The first three of these communication skills serve mainly to initiate conversation; the other three are primarily listening skills.

The six skills that are useful in opening a sales interview are giving compliments, asking open questions, using free information, highlighting what has been heard, asking follow-up questions, and offering information in the form of self-disclosure.

Giving Compliments

Giving a compliment is a typical way of opening a sales interview. The salesperson's intent must be to express genuine admiration and appreciation. An insincere compliment may discourage further interaction. Even when the compliment is sincere, the customer may feel embarrassed or unsure about how to respond. To avoid this, the compliment should be followed by a question that provides the customer with a topic and a way to respond. For example, a salesperson might give compliments such as these:

"I read in the paper that your new building will be completed this week. I'm really impressed with the way you've been able to stay on your projected time schedule [*compliment*]. What future building plans to you have? [*question to focus customer response*]"

"I really notice the difference in your lighting. The effect is to soften the colors, and the atmosphere seems warmer and more peaceful [*compliment*]. What encouraged you to make the change? [*question to focus customer response*]"

"The other day I was looking at a suit similar in color to the one you're wearing. That shade of blue really complements your coloring [*compliment*]. What have you heard about the colors that will be featured in the new fashions this fall? [*question to focus customer response*]"

Because a genuine compliment is an expression of feelings, this communication skill has the potential to move the conversation directly to level two (sharing feelings purposeful to the sales interview) if the compliment is related to the business at hand. Compliments can be a powerful tool for establishing rapport, especially when followed by a question that assists the customer in responding comfortably.

Asking Open Questions

Notice that the questions following the sample compliments not only provide the customer with a topic about which to respond, but also are phrased in an open manner. An open questions encourages the customer to give expansive answers because it cannot be answered with "yes," "no," or another one-word response. Questions that begin with "what" and "how" tend to elicit extended responses. Questions that begin with "are," "do," "whom," "when," "where," and "which" usually result in answers of "yes," "no," or only a few words.

Open questions that focus on the customer demonstrate genuine interest in the person. A salesperson can use open questions to move the opening of the interview from one communication level to another.

Consider the level five dialogue between Ms. Hart and Mr. Strong that was presented earlier. Mr. Strong asked Ms. Hart, "What's on your mind?" Ms. Hart's response moved the conversation from level five eventually to level two. After reviewing the schematic, Ms. Hart asked, "What do you think?" This open question elicited from Mr. Strong a genuine compliment involving level one disclosure that seemed to solidify their working relationship.

Using Free Information

Because open questions elicit expansive responses, their use by salespeople will draw information from customers. Some of this information will be responses focused on the questions that have been asked. The customer will usually provide some information, however, that is not directly related to the salesperson's questions or the focus of the interaction. Information that goes beyond or is outside the focus of the interaction is referred to as *free information*.

Salesperson: I appreciate your calling to set up this meeting, Mr. Lee. What questions do you have about the services we can provide your company?

Customer: I'm sorry, Charlie. I know I set up this appointment but I'm going to need to cancel. Something has come up and I have to catch a plane [*free information: "I have to catch a plane"*].

Salesperson: Oh, where are you off to? [*using the free information*]

Customer: To Denver—our Aurora plant has a major production problem and I'm being sent in to troubleshoot [*free information: "a major production problem . . . I'm being sent in to troubleshoot"*].

Salesperson: Sounds like a real feather in your cap to have been selected for this job [*using free information as an opportunity to provide a compliment.*] If there's anything I can do to help, Mr. Lee, I'll be working in the office all day tomorrow. Give me a call [*uses free information to offer assistance*].

Although free information is often provided in response to the open questions salespeople ask, their customers may provide information at

Try This 10.3 Using Free Information to Build Rapport

In the following statements, underline the free information provided by the customer. Then highlight that information and ask a follow-up question to expand on a new topic of conversation.

1. **Salesperson:** You seem really enthusiastic about what you're reading. May I ask what it is?
   Customer: Well, Jose, I've been reviewing our quarterly report. It seems that we've picked up over $500,000 in orders this year. What an eye opener!
   Follow-up Question:
2. **Salesperson:** How satisfied are you with your present policy?
   Customer: I don't think this policy is appropriate for me right now. There's only my wife and myself.

Follow-up Question:

____

____

____

____

____

____

____

____

____

____

____

____

____

____

____

____

____

____

____

____

____

any time during the sales interview. When salespeople capitalize on free information to build their relationship with a customer and to move the interview toward the purpose for which it was scheduled, they are demonstrating an effective listening skill.

Highlighting

Highlighting is referring back to something said earlier for the purpose of making it the specific topic of conversation. Salespeople may refer back to something that they said or to something mentioned by the customer. Also, they can either highlight something they heard earlier in the present conversation or restate what they heard in a previous conversation with the customer.

Highlighting not only lets the customer know that the salesperson is interested, it also demonstrates that the salesperson heard and remembered what was said. Highlighting is primarily a listening skill that can refocus the topic or change the communication level of the discussion.

> "Earlier, Ray, you mentioned that you had some reservations about the adaptability of the 350X to your system [*highlighting*]. What specific concerns do you have? [*open question that brings the conversation to levels three and two*].

It is helpful to remind the customer when the original statement was made by using openers such as:

"A moment ago, I heard you say . . ."

"When I called yesterday, I mentioned to you that . . ."

"When we ended our last meeting, you seemed concerned about . . ."

When salespeople use highlighting, it is important that the customer understand what topic they are bringing into focus so that there is no feeling of being caught off guard. These openers provide that type of clarity.

Asking Follow-up Questions

The skill of highlighting is rarely used alone. Once highlighting has been used to focus on a topic of conversation, that topic must be developed. Follow-up questions are a useful tool for developing a topic. They are used to ask for more specific information about something mentioned or discussed previously. If a salesperson's purpose is to clarify information or to request more specific information about a general topic, then open follow-up questions can be especially helpful:

> "You mentioned that IMC Tool and Die has a different operation than yours [*highlighting*]. How does it differ? [*follow-up question*]"
>
> "I've been thinking about your interest in expanding [*highlighting*]. What thoughts do you have about the direction you'd like to take? [*follow-up question*]"

Once again, an astute salesperson can use follow-up questions combined with highlighting to move the conversation to levels of conversation that are more productive in terms of building rapport as well as discussing products and services.

Disclosing Information

Open questions, free information, highlighting, and follow-up questions indicate interest in the customer and encourage the customer to talk about personal interests and concerns. A salesperson can provide balance in two-way conversation by offering personal information within each of the five communication levels.

For example, personal information may qualify as light talk (level five) if one reports weekend activities and how the weather affected them. Level four communication could include talking about a new client whom the salesperson would like to introduce to the customer now being interviewed.

When sharing personal information that is directly related to the purpose and topic of the present conversation and is unknown to the customer, an individual is using the skill of self-disclosure. When used appropriately, this skill moves the conversation to levels three, two, and one. The information offered by Ms. Hart and Mr. Strong to each other during the last three stages of their dialogue qualifies as self-disclosure because it has these three main characteristics:

- Each person talked about individual ideas and feelings. Self-disclosure is much more intense than talking about the weather, facts in the newspaper, or other people.
- Each person shared information related to the purpose and topic of the conversation. Self-disclosure is about one's own ideas, feelings, and perceptions as they relate to oneself, the customer, or one's relationship in the context of the conversation.
- Each person shared information that was new to the other person. If the information is already known, it does not qualify as self-disclosure. In the opening of a sales interview between new acquaintances, nearly everything that meets the first two characteristics also meets this one.

When both people take part in the opening of a sales interview by volunteering information about themselves at levels three, two, and one and use communication skills to encourage each other to talk, genuine rapport is usually established in ways that have an immediate impact on the rest of the sales interview. There is also a positive long-range effect on the establishment of a meaningful sales relationship.

Building Rapport through Nonverbal Messages

Anthropologist Ray Birdwhistle determined that our bodies communicate approximately 65 percent of the total *social* meaning in normal two-person conversation and the words we use transmit the remaining 35 percent.[11] For example, the verbal statement, "I'm sure you'll find our widgets to be very dependable and economical," could be said in a way that conveys genuine interest in the prospect or in a way that communicates indifference, anger, or sarcasm. Changes in vocal tone, facial expression, and body movement can substantially alter the way a customer interprets a salesperson's verbal messages. Nonverbal communication consists of assigning meaning to nonverbal behaviors such as posture, facial expression, gestures, tone of voice, distance or personal space, and appearance. This section focuses on characteristics of nonverbal communication, body language, and congruence of nonverbal behaviors in developing rapport.

Characteristics of Nonverbal Communication

Four important characteristics of nonverbal communication distinguish it from the spoken words a salesperson uses:

1. *Nonverbal Communication Is Inevitable.* When opening an interview, salespeople must be aware that they are sending messages to customers even when they don't intend to. If a customer is aware of the salesperson's presence, it is impossible for the customer not to communicate something personal. Nonverbal behavior is always present and is a continual source of information about individuals and their relationships. Even if one does not *intend* to communicate, one's body transmits a continuous stream of information about oneself. Thus, it is important for a salesperson to consciously use the body to communicate what is to be said. Otherwise a salesperson may create an impression in the customer's mind that contradicts what is being said.
2. *Nonverbal Behavior Primarily Communicates Information about Emotion.* A major component of a salesperson's emotions "involves internal physiological sensations that become externalized as observable nonverbal behavior."[12] For example, Len Van Ly, a sales representative for Bradley Instruments, may introduce himself to a prospect whose name he then promptly forgets. He is embarrassed and, when he becomes aware of his embarrassment, his throat tightens and he feels the blood rising in his neck. As he attempts to recall the customer's name, he stutters or stammers and mispronounces it. The customer may interpret his stammering as embarrassment, insecurity, or lack of confidence. The customer may even interpret his mispronunciation as uncaring, rude, or indifferent.

   Although Len did not want to stammer or mispronounce the customer's name as he spoke, it may be an involuntary response to his internal tension. The adage that actions speak louder than words has a great deal of merit, and salespeople need to be aware of this aspect of communication.
3. *Nonverbal Communication Is Ambiguous.* Nonverbal communication is open to numerous interpretations. Suppose that when Len introduces himself to his prospect, he extends his hand and gives a vise-grip handshake while quickly glancing at the customer with a furrowed brow and speaking in a flat, loud voice. The

PROXEMIC SELLING ZONES

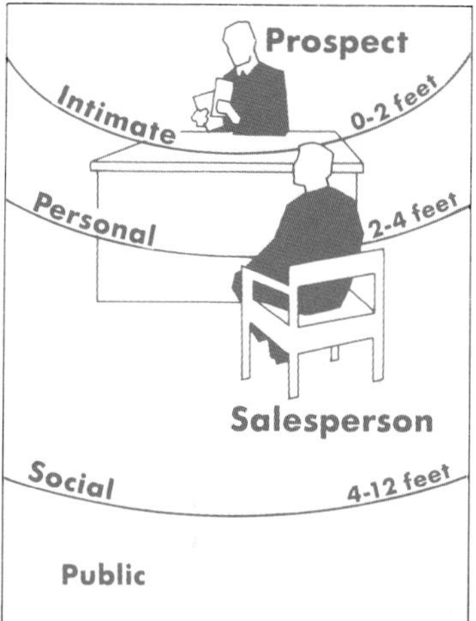

0-2 feet . . . . intimate
2-4 feet . . . . personal
4-12 feet . . . . social
12+ feet . . . . public

1) Sales relationship should begin in the social zone.
2) Selling should be done in the personal zone.
3) Move closer than four feet only by invitation.
4) If you go into the intimate zone, don't stay there for long periods of time. It makes the prospect nervous. □

— *Reprinted with permission. From The Soft Sell Course by Tim Connor. TR Training Associates, 361 W. Eisenhower Pkwy., Ann Arbor, MI 48106. (313) 930-0880.*

prospect might interpret these behaviors as being aggressive or hostile when, in fact, Len may be reacting out of fear. The prospect may respond in a similar way as an unconscious reaction to assumptions about Len's nonverbal behavior. Len must become aware of the *context* in which the prospect's nonverbal behavior occurs when he makes assumptions about it.

4. *Nonverbal Communication Is Culturally Specific*. Nonverbal behavior that is meaningful and appropriate in one cultural group may lack significance or be highly inappropriate in another. For example, among Americans the use of direct eye contact is considered a sign of respect and acknowledgment. In African-American, Japanese, and Hispanic cultures, eye contact is considered a sign of disrespect, especially when interacting with superiors.

Body Language

Body language refers to the role gestures, posture, body orientation, facial expression, voice, touching, clothing, and distance or personal space have in our relationships with others.

Try This 10.4 Nonverbal Messages: Eye Contact

Sit facing a friend or classmate and begin a conversation. Begin by establishing direct eye contact with each other. After a few minutes, stop talking and sit in silence. Meet your partner's eyes and hold the gaze for 5–10 seconds before looking away. Then establish eye contact again. Try not to stare at your partner or overpower the other person with your eyes. Simply try to "be with him or her in silence." If you find yourself feeling awkward or embarrassed about making eye contact, you're probably centered too much on yourself. Focus on your partner's eyes and physical presence. Try to "lose yourself" momentarily in your partner's eyes. After a few minutes, break the silence and discuss your experiences with your partner. Answer the following questions:

1. How did you feel when you established eye contact with your partner? How did your feelings change when you stopped talking and maintained eye contact?
2. How do you usually feel when people don't establish eye contact with you during a conversation? How do you feel when they seem to stare at you?
3. How do you decide how much eye contact is appropriate during a conversation with friends? During a sales interview?
4. How could you use eye contact to build rapport when you meet with customers in a sales interview?
5. What similarities and differences do you identify between your use of eye contact and the use of eye contact by people from other cultural or subcultural groups?

Gestures

Gestures include movements of the hands, arms, legs, and feet. For example, a salesperson shows openness with open hands, uncrossed legs, and arms gently and loosely resting in the lap.

Posture

Posture refers to a person's stance, including the degree of tension. A salesperson who stands with hands on hips and feet slightly spread, or leans forward in a chair in an open position, signals readiness to listen to the buyer.

Body Orientation

Orientation is the degree to which a salesperson's body, feet, and head are turned toward or away from the customer. For example, Sandra Selsia, a representative for Amtex Couriers, exchanged greetings and was invited to be seated. While she was removing her sales aids from her briefcase on the floor, she turned away from the buyer. As she was looking down, facing the briefcase and removing the documents, she asked, "How was your recent trip to London?" This body orientation may give the customer the impression that Sandra is not really interested in the customer's trip.

Facial Expression

A person's mouth, jaw, eyebrows, eyes, and other facial parts can communicate a lot about one's emotions. For instance, when talking with a customer, if Brandon notices the customer looking directly at him, smiling broadly with eyes open wide, he may assume that the customer is pleased about something he has said.

Voice

A salesperson can control variations in vocal patterns, including rate, pitch, tone, and loudness. For example, upward changes in volume and speed generally indicate a change in a positive direction. Enthusiasm and eagerness sometimes emerge from this kind of change. However, so can anger. The salesperson should verify the meaning of the change, particularly if the buyer's vocal rhythm is different from the normal flow.

Vocalics refers to the way salespeople say words, not the specific words they use. For example, consider the range of meanings that can be communicated simply by changing the stress or emphasis placed on the words in the following sentence:

- *Diane* is buying the ring for Larry [*not Brenda or Shirley*].
- Diane is *buying* the ring for Larry [*actually buying, not just thinking about it*].
- Diane is buying the *ring* for Larry [*the ring, and it's a very expensive setting*].
- Diane is buying the ring for *Larry* [*of all people*].

In addition to using stress and emphasis, one's voice communicates through tone, pitch, rate or speed, volume, the number and length of silent pauses, and disfluencies. A *disfluency* is the use of "uh" or "ah" sounds instead of silent pauses while one thinks. For example, "I'm with . . . uhh . . . Pitney Distributors. We're located in . . . ahhh . . . Grand Junction." Disfluencies suggest that the salesperson is uncertain about what is being said. Some customers may question the salesperson's honesty if disfluencies are used excessively when speaking.

Touching

The physical act of touching another person is a powerful way of communicating warmth and interest. One of the ways touch can be used during the opening moments of a sales interview is by shaking the customer's hand.

The most appropriate American business-style handshake is tight enough that it is not interpreted as a sign of weakness but not so firm that it overpowers the customer. In business, the same procedure is used for shaking hands whether the salesperson or customer is a man or a woman. A simple rule of thumb is that the salesperson initiates the handshake. An effective handshake can be a powerful vehicle for transmitting warmth and genuineness and building trust.

Clothing

William Thourlby reports that if a person enters a room with people not met before, they will make ten decisions about that person based solely on appearance. One's appearance, especially during the early stages of the sales interview, is perhaps the single most important nonverbal message one makes about oneself. Table 10.3 identifies these ten appearance-related decisions.[13]

Table 10.3

You Are What You Wear—The Key to Business Success

When you enter a room with people you've never before met, they will make a number of key decisions about you based solely on your appearance. These decisions include:

1. Economic level
2. Educational level
3. Trustworthiness
4. Social position
5. Level of sophistication
6. Economic background
7. Social background
8. Educational background
9. Level of success
10. Moral character

Source: William Thourlby, *You Are What You Wear—The Key to Business Success* (Kansas City, MO: Sheed Andrews and McMeel, 1978), p. 1.

Numerous books have been written on "wardrobe engineering," and numerous consultants make their living as personal shoppers or image consultants, combining the elements of psychology, sociology, fashion, and art into grooming and wardrobe selection. Three guidelines to consider are appropriateness, simplicity, and quality.

Appropriateness means dressing to reflect the image of the salesperson's company and what is acceptable to the customers it serves. It also means taking into consideration the regional variation in dress and grooming standards.

Simplicity translates, for corporate America, into tailored suits and conservative colors for both men and women. The advertising, entertainment, and fashion industries allow for more flamboyant and trendy colors, styles, and designs, but most American businesses still prefer conservative dress. This carries over into grooming as well. Polished shoes, trimmed hair (for both men and women), soft or muted fingernail polish, and unobtrusive earrings for women are the generally accepted standards. It is still considered unacceptable for men to wear an earring in the corporate world.

Quality is important; a salesperson's wardrobe should be considered an investment. While "quality" means different things to different people, sales professionals generally agree that they feel confident in owning two or three good wool suits in basic colors; women supplement these with several silk dresses and blouses. Such clothing should be of high enough quality to hold its newness with repeated dry cleaning.

Distance

Distance is the personal space between a salesperson and a customer. The feelings that a salesperson may have about a customer will influence the use of space. Salespeople will generally stand closer to customers they like and evaluate positively. A salesperson's goals and expectations may also influence physical distance from the customer. For instance, if one's goal is to establish a formal, businesslike relationship with a customer, one might choose to position oneself at an impersonal distance, perhaps standing somewhere beyond 10 feet from the customer. A typically acceptable distance among American businesspeople is between 4 and 5 feet.

Factors related to the physical size of the area in which the sales interview occurs may influence the appropriate distance between customers and salespeople. In large rooms, for example, the distance for comfortable conversation is much less than in smaller physical spaces. People who find themselves in large, open spaces tend to form small, tightly knit conversational units, and people in small spaces will spread out and occupy the entire area.

Congruence

Customers draw conclusions about salespeople based on their verbal and nonverbal behavior. When the verbal statements and nonverbal behavior match so that a clear and consistent message results, a salesperson is communicating congruently. A high degree of congruence occurs when one's nonverbal behavior is perceived to reinforce or emphasize what one is saying. For example, when a salesperson tells a customer that the customer's order will receive special attention by guaranteeing that it will arrive before the first of the month, and at the same time looks directly at the customer and leans slightly forward in the chair, the salesperson's nonverbal behavior reinforces or emphasizes what is being said. A high degree of congruence increases the probability that the customer will see the salesperson as credible, honest, trustworthy, and spontaneous. The alignment of all the different parts of a communication will produce congruence in communication.

When the tone of voice and the stress placed on words contradict what one is saying, there is an incongruence or double message. Incongruence exists when a salesperson's nonverbal behavior is perceived to contradict that person's verbal statements. For example, incongruence probably would be perceived if a salesperson were to frown and roll the eyes while saying, "Your order will be ready on Monday." There is a double message—the nonverbal behavior of frowning and rolling the eyes will probably be perceived as contradicting the verbal statement. When such a contradiction occurs, the customer will usually rely more on the nonverbal message than on the verbal message and, consequently, will probably question the salesperson's honesty and sincerity.

Whether or not the salesperson's verbal statements and nonverbal behaviors are congruent is more than just a matter of intention. The congruence or incongruence of one's message is sometimes beyond one's control. Salespeople cannot be aware of every nuance of their language or behavior. Their nonverbal behavior may be sending unintentional messages to other people. Moreover, they may be unable to achieve the degree of congruence they desire, especially in situations where their emotions run counter to the image they would like to present to others. However, by becoming more aware of their own nonverbal behavior

Try This 10.5 Nonverbal Messages: Posture

Assume various body postures. How do you feel when you assume each one? Does each position allow you to experience different emotions? Can you assume a body posture that makes you feel confident? Insecure? Elated? Depressed? Emotional change involves the body. When you assume a new attitude, the new attitude creates new perceptions, new feelings, and new muscular patterns.

Now try the same exercise with a friend or classmate. Imagine that you are the salesperson and your friend is the customer. How do your feelings differ from when you experimented alone? How did your customer perceive you differently as you changed your posture? You might also experiment with some of the neuro-linguistic programming techniques.

through practicing the skills presented in the Skill Builder and "Try This" boxes, salespeople can increase the congruence of their communication. By increasing the use of nonverbal behavior that reinforces and emphasizes what one says, one's communication will become clearer and more easily understood.

Building Rapport through Neuro-Linguistic Programming

Some salespeople seem to have a natural ability to build rapport by matching customers' behavior and adapting their own personality traits. Learning such skills is a challenging aspect of sales training. Over the past decade, a technique has emerged from the behavioral sciences that helps build rapport between therapists and clients. The technique is called neuro-linguistic programming (NLP). "NLP has been so effective that it is now being taught to salespeople, teachers and others who need to establish and maintain high levels of rapport."[14] The purpose of this section is to introduce NLP and its potential for building rapport between salespeople and their customers.

Buzzotta, Lefton, and Sherberg's description of the interaction among different sales personalities and customer types is discussed in Chapter 8. Their analysis is based on the quadrants formed by intersecting the continuums of dominance/submissiveness and warmth/hostility. While they concluded that the "ideal" quadrant for the relationship-driven salesperson to operate in is the dominant-warm dimension, they concurred that the optimal goal for the salesperson is to be adaptable to all personality types, assuming that the salesperson can identify the personality style of the customer. NLP is a technique enhancing a salesperson's ability to detect personality types by making the salesperson aware of the customer's verbal and nonverbal cues.

Researchers Richard Bandler and John Grinder developed the theory of neuro-linguistic programming after studying outstanding therapists such as Virginia Satir, Milton Erickson, and Fritz Perls. Their research revealed that each of these people appeared to have "an innate ability to 'read' verbal and physical cues from clients and to create desired changes."[15] This same ability to read customers and respond to them with warmth and openness, thus building trust and rapport, is also a characteristic of exceptional salespeople.[16]

According to the NLP theory, people perceive the world through the sorting, processing, and storing of sensory impressions. The basic senses that they use are visual (seeing), auditory (hearing), and kinesthetic (feeling). For instance, a customer who says, "I see what you're saying—I get the picture," is processing information in a visual mode. Another customer may respond in an auditory mode with "I hear what you're saying, and it sounds good so far. Tell me more." Still another customer, who is processing information at a kinesthetic level, might say, "My guts tell me that this will be an exciting experience and that I'll get a real 'rush' from trying it." Nickels, Everett, and Klein report: "People use different sensory systems to understand, communicate and represent their experiences, thoughts and beliefs. In NLP, these sensory systems are called the representational system."[17] Table 10.4 Identifies many of the terms customers use to represent their experiences.

Building Rapport through Matching Techniques

Genie Z. Laborde, a communications consultant and partner in the firm of Grinder, Laborde, and Hill, uses the NLP model in her seminars. In her book *Influencing with Integrity* she states:

> When rapport is not present, it becomes top priority in communication. . . . If rapport is present, proceed toward your outcome. If it is missing, then you can be assured neither of you will gain your outcome until rapport is present. . . . Liking the other person is not a prerequisite for rapport. Mutual confidence in competence for the task at hand is. If credibility cannot be established, consider changing the task.[18]

Laborde suggests that mirroring techniques tend to be effective in gaining rapport if trust in competence has already been established. *Mirroring* is the process of subtly matching another person's nonverbal and vocal behaviors, such as voice tone or tempo or both, breathing, body postures, and rhythms of movement with a different behavior or movement.[19] *Crossover mirroring* is a technique in which the salesperson matches the customer's movement with a different movement. For instance, every time the customer taps a pen on the desk, the salesperson scratches his or her chin. Matching or mirroring must be as subtle as possible so that the customer does not feel mimicked. The same holds true for matching predicates. Figure 10.3 illustrates how NLP works in the rapport cycle of the selling process.

Identifying Representational Systems through Eye Movements

A second way for a salesperson to determine a customer's representational system is to study eye movement. Eye cues are illustrated in Figure 10.4. Thus, a salesperson can gain insight into the customer's thought processes by studying the customer's verbal cues and eye movements.

Eye movements are similar in most customers and usually indicate the following:

- When customers look up and left, they are visualizing something from the past. They are *picturing* it in their minds.
- When customers look up and right, they are *constructing* an image, visualizing what it will eventually look like.
- When customers look down and right, they are either recalling or imagining *feelings*.

Table 10.4

Predicate Words

Predicates are the process words that customers use in their communication to represent their experience (visual, auditory, or kinesthetic). Below are listed some of the more commonly used predicates in the business environment.

Visual	Auditory	Kinesthetic
analyze	announce	active
angle	articulate	affected
appear	audible	bearable
clarity	communicate	charge
cognizant	converse	concrete
conspicuous	discuss	emotional
demonstrate	dissonant	feel
dream	divulge	firm
examine	earshot	flow
focus	enunciate	foundation
foresee	gossip	grasp
glance	hear	grip
hindsight	hush	hanging
horizon	inquire	hassle
idea	interview	heated
illusion	listen	hold
image	mention	hustle
inspect	noise	intuition
look	oral	lukewarm
notice	proclaim	motion
obscure	pronounce	muddled
observe	remark	panicky
obvious	report	pressure
perception	roar	sensitive
perspective	rumor	set
picture	say	shallow
scene	shrill	softly
see	silence	solid
sight	squeal	structured
sketchy	state	support
survey	talk	tension
vague	tell	tied
view	tone	touch
vision	utter	unbearable
watch	vocal	unsettled
witness	voice	whipped

The objective in "matching" predicates is to "match" the language in which the customer speaks, thus creating an atmosphere of rapport and understanding.

Source: William G. Nickels, Robert F. Everett, and Ronald Klein, "Rapport Building for Salespeople: A Neuro-Linguistic Approach," *Journal of Personal Selling and Sales Management,* III (November 1983), p. 2.

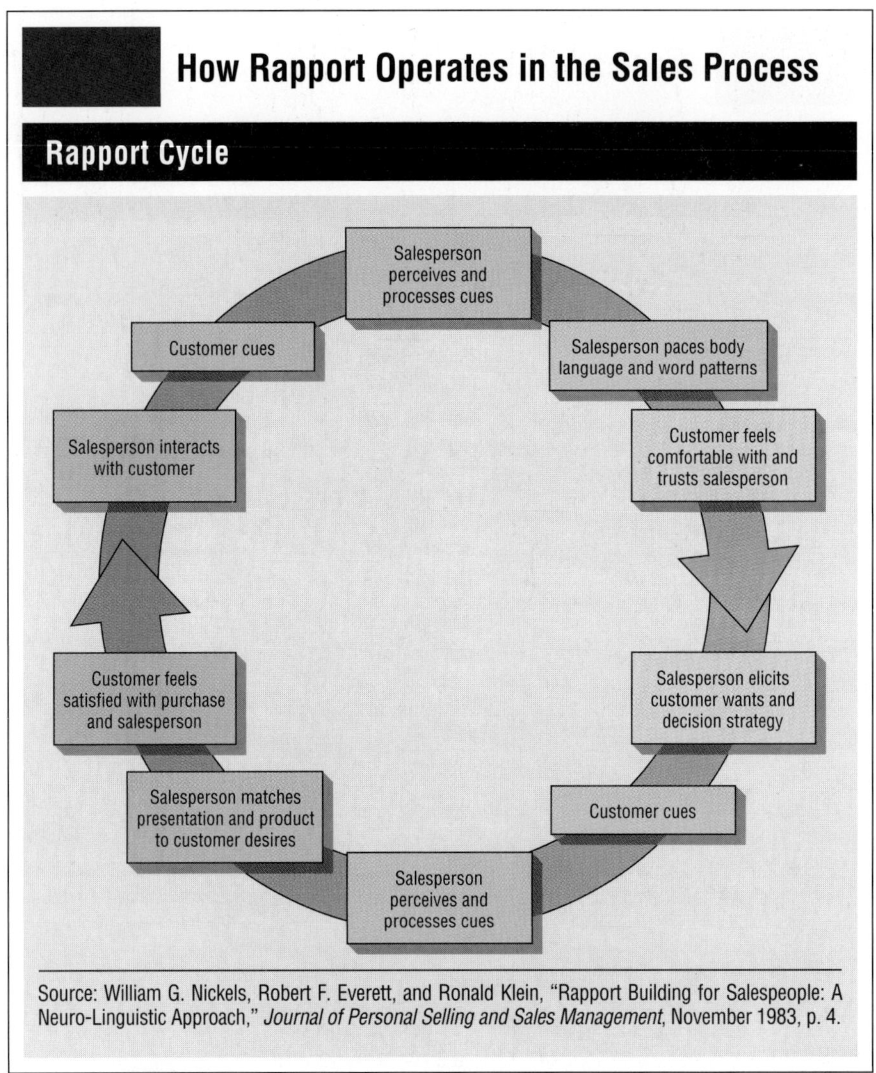

Figure 10.3

How Rapport Operates in the Sales Process

Rapport Cycle

Source: William G. Nickels, Robert F. Everett, and Ronald Klein, "Rapport Building for Salespeople: A Neuro-Linguistic Approach," *Journal of Personal Selling and Sales Management*, November 1983, p. 4.

- When customers look sideways to the left, they are hearing *sounds* from the past.
- When customers look sideways to the right, they are *constructing* a future conversation, thinking of the right words.
- When customers look down and to the left, they are *talking* with themselves in a kind of internal dialogue.

For example, a buyer may be asked to describe what he would want in the optimal copier if he could replace his right now. The buyer looks up and to the right and says, "I can *picture* a state-of-the-art, digital, electronic copier that *shows* a digital read-out of all functions and is covered with all the newest 'whistles and bells.' " Then, looking down and to the right, the buyer continues, "I had a chance to use one like that, and I *felt* a real *excitement* from the speed. It was really *impressive*!"—and, looking left—"I can just *hear* our purchasing department when I ask them for a $28,000 purchase order—'you *said* how much?' "

Basically, sales training in rapport building involves awareness and

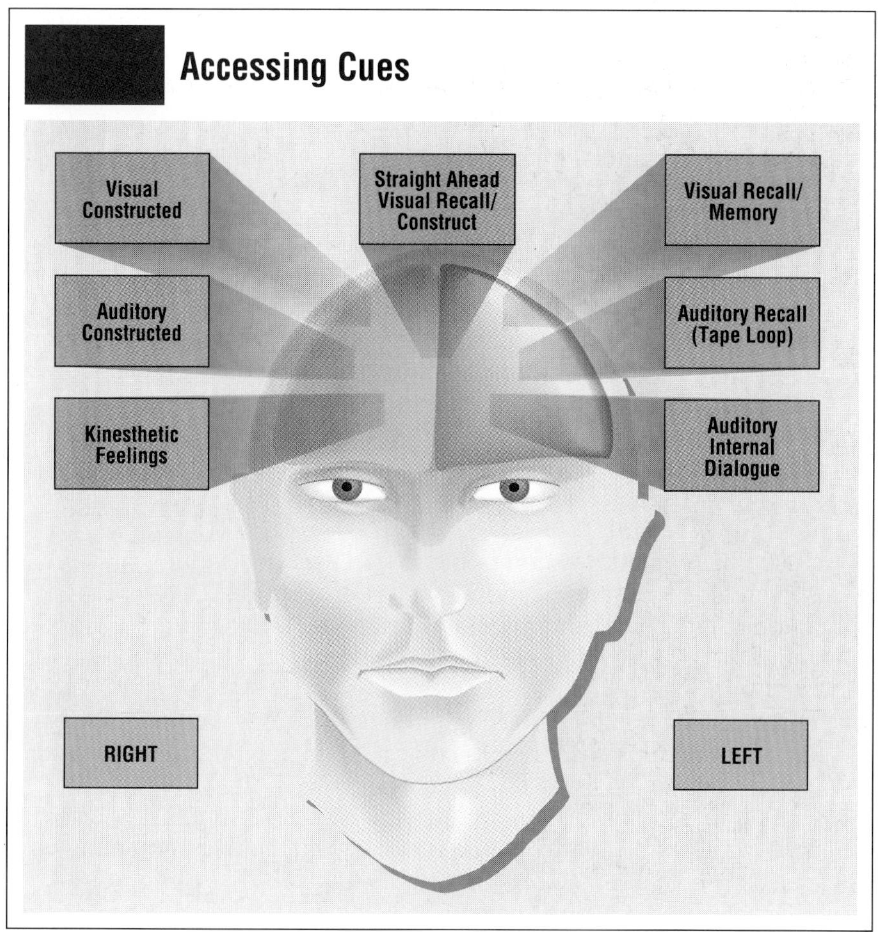

Figure 10.4

practice. Neuro-linguistic programming offers techniques to increase awareness and listening skills, two significant keys to effectiveness in selling and interpersonal relationships in general.

Summary

Rapport in a sales interview comes through developing mutual trust and respect. The development process itself is contingent on the verbal and nonverbal messages given (and interpreted) by the salesperson, especially at the beginning of the interview.

The rapport of the sales interview is influenced by the climate present during the meeting. The climate may be supportive if the participants in the interview demonstrate that they value each other, that trust is prevalent, and that elements of openness and spontaneity are present. A defensive climate, on the other hand, is marked by a lack of valuing each other; a feeling of riskiness; and closed, inflexible behavior stemming from rejection.

Jack Gibbs has provided us with six contrasting pairs of response styles that stem from these two climates. They are descriptive versus evaluative language, problem orientation versus control, spontaneity versus manipulation, empathy versus indifference, equality versus superiority, and provisionalism versus certainty. These should be used in conjunction with the guidelines for setting an appointment and establishing sales call objectives.

Verbal rapport is established through five levels of communication. Moving from low to high risk, the levels are: (5) light talk, (4) reporting facts about others, (3) sharing ideas purposeful to the sales interview, (2) sharing feelings purposeful to the sales interview, and (1) mutual understanding. Because each level of communication is dependent on the prospect's willingness to listen, it is advisable to remember the seven traditional methods for getting the prospect's attention: introductory, product, consumer benefit, curiosity, showmanship, referral, and premium.

In the opening of a sales interview, verbal rapport is established by conversation, and six communications skills have proved useful in this regard: giving compliments, asking open questions, using free information, highlighting what has been said, asking follow-up questions, and performing self-disclosure.

Nonverbal communication is present in every sales interview on all levels. Nonverbal communication consists of posture, facial expression, tone of voice, distance, and overall appearance. Such communication is inevitable, primarily communicates emotions and attitudes, is ambiguous, and is culturally specific.

When verbal and nonverbal communication provide a single message, the communication is described as congruent. Incongruence occurs when verbal and nonverbal messages are contradictory.

One popular technique among those who seek to build rapport with others is the neuro-linguistic programming method of enhancing the salesperson's ability to detect personality types by becoming aware of customers' verbal and nonverbal cues. This technique involves matching prospects' communicative efforts and understanding what various eye movements mean.

Key Terms

Common Ground Area of mutual interest between salesperson and customer

Congruence When verbal statements and nonverbal behavior are perceived to reinforce or emphasize what one is saying

Defensive Climate Climate established by response styles that generate an atmosphere where participants feel they are being attacked

Disfluency Use of stalling words or sounds, such as "uh" or "ah," while thinking

Free Information Information that goes beyond or is outside the focus of the sales interview and that the salesperson can appropriate and use to advantage

Highlighting Referring to something said earlier

Incongruence When nonverbal behavior is perceived as contradicting one's verbal statements

Supportive Climate Climate established by response styles that generate an atmosphere of acceptance

Vocalics The manner in which people say words, as opposed to the actual words being spoken

Review Questions

1. Why is trust central to a sales relationship?
2. How is risk inherent in a selling relationship for those involved?
3. What is a risk-trust cycle? Describe the components and interaction of such a cycle.
4. How does a spiral of mutual trust (or distrust) build?
5. Explain each of Gibb's six pairs of response styles.
6. List the five levels of communication and describe the characteristics of each level.
7. Define and describe the purpose of the seven traditional methods of opening the sales interview.
8. Define and give an example of the five communication skills that can be used to develop rapport in the opening of a sales interview.
9. Give examples of the types of behavior identified as nonverbal communication.
10. Explain the four characteristics of nonverbal communication.
11. Distinguish between congruent and incongruent behavior. Use a specific example to make the contrast clear.
12. Explain the basic techniques of neuro-linguistic programming.

Discussion Questions

1. Describe how the risk-trust cycle operates in one of your friendships and in a sales relationship.
2. Discuss how Gibb's six pairs of response styles have affected the climate in your relationships. Provide specific examples.
3. What is the goal of the opening stage in a sales interview?
4. Explain the five levels of verbal communication, from least to most intense, using examples from your own relationships.
5. Discuss ways of combining two or more of the seven traditional ways of opening an interview.
6. Role-play ways of combining two or more of the five communication skills to open an interview.
7. Discuss the consequences for you when another person's behavior is congruent and incongruent.
8. Discuss the use of neuro-linguistic programming for building rapport in a sales interview.

The County Purchasing Agent

Case 10.1

Jack Spencer arrived promptly for his 9:30 appointment with Tom Perez, the purchasing agent for the county parks and recreation department. Just a few minutes before 10:00 Tom arrived and walked straight to his office to make a phone call, without recognizing Jack's presence.

From the lobby, Jack could hear Tom arranging to meet a friend at the gym during the lunch hour. On several occasions Tom conversed in Spanish as though to attempt a level of secrecy. His telephone conversation

Case 10.1
Continued

continued for nearly 15 minutes, until the receptionist directed Tom's attention to Jack's presence.

Several minutes later, Tom instructed the receptionist to escort Jack into his office. At the same time the receptionist buzzed Tom to inform him of a call waiting from his wife. While discussing a personal matter with her for over 5 minutes, he glanced at his watch on several occasions, expressing the urgent need to leave shortly for an important early luncheon meeting.

Without further delay, Jack immediately started into his presentation, but after just minutes he was interrupted by another salesman. At that point, Tom got up and closed the door, instructing the receptionist to hold all calls.

Within 3 minutes the receptionist entered the office to remind Tom of the luncheon meeting. Getting up to reach for his tennis racquet, he suggested that Jack leave all the brochures and other documentation that he felt would help him with the purchasing decision. "I was hoping to spend more time with you today to discuss these brochures, but the decision is not that urgent," Tom stated. He further remarked, "You really did not expect me to make a decision today, did you?" as he quickly started toward the lobby with his tennis racquet in hand.

1. What nonverbal and verbal communication cues are being sent by Tom Perez?
2. What should Jack have done during the meeting to take control of the situation?
3. What should Jack do now to pursue the sale?

Case 10.2

Emphasizing Nonverbal Communication

Bill Howard, a sales trainer, was recently hired by Tip-Top Textiles to develop a new sales training program for its salespeople, who hope to sell to manufacturers of clothing and household furnishings. This program included exposing the sales staff to face-to-face selling experiences and practicing communication skills.

The salespeople at Tip-Top have never received any formal training. They were given a basic sales manual written by a sales manager 30 years ago and were assigned an experienced salesperson to observe for 1 week. Following this exposure, they were sent into the field to either sink or swim. Although the existing sales force at Tip-Top was able to survive, stronger competition in the marketplace has forced the company to update its methods and techniques.

The training at Tip-Top now involves preparing the salespeople to make presentations using different approaches. The salespeople find it interesting to learn different styles and approaches for presenting the same information. High-pressure selling, which is quite unpopular with the established sales staff, has also been introduced.

The training also includes techniques for improving communication. Bill strongly believed that in most sales situations, how you say the words and express yourself when making the presentation are crucial to your success. "What you really say is secondary," Bill claims. He continually stresses the importance of the nonverbal aspects of a sales presentation.

The company's sales manager has became quite uncertain of this overemphasis on nonverbal communication and is afraid to stress nonverbal techniques in communication. Bill's reputation is based on the practice of nonverbal behavior, and he continues to emphasize its use in training.

1. Do you agree with Bill's claim, "How you say it is more important than what you say"?
2. Suggest ways to train salespeople more effectively by using nonverbal behavior.
3. What clues would a salesperson learn to look for when communication is centered on nonverbal behavior?

Notes

1. G. W. Allport, *Personality and Social Encounter* (Boston, MA: Beacon Press, 1960).
2. Erich Fromm, *The Art of Loving* (London: Allen and Unwin, 1962); and Martin Buber, *I and Thou* (Edinburgh: T & T Clark, 1957).
3. Carl R. Rogers, *On Becoming a Person* (Boston, MA: Houghton Mifflin, 1961).
4. B. R. Patton and K. Giffin, *Interpersonal Communication: Basic Text and Readings* (New York: Harper & Row, 1974), p. 443.
5. John E. Swan, I. Fredrick Trawick, and David W. Silva, "How Industrial Salespeople Gain Customer Trust," *Industrial Marketing Management*, 14 (1985), pp. 203–211.
6. J. Gibb, "Defensive Communication," *Journal of Communication*, II (September 1961), pp. 141–148.
7. R. Hite and J. Bellizzi, "Differences in the Importance of Selling Techniques between Consumer and Industrial Salespeople," *Journal of Personal Selling and Sales Management*, November 1985, pp. 19–30.
8. Marvin A. Jolson, "Prospecting by Telephone Prenotification: An Application of the Foot-in-the-Door Technique," *Journal of Personal Selling and Sales Management*, August 1986, p. 41.
9. Bill Pardu, "The Key to Effective Telesales," *Teleprofessional*, March 1991, p. 28.
10. Philip Kotler, *Marketing Management: Analysis, Planning and Control*, 4th ed. (Englewood Cliffs, NJ: Prentice-Hall, 1980), p. 569.
11. R. Birdwhistle, 1970 as cited in Mark L. Knapp *Nonverbal Communication in Human Interaction*, 2nd ed. (New York: Holt, Rinehart, and Winston, 1978), p. 30.
12. Sharon A. Ratliffe and David D. Hudson, *Skill Building for Interpersonal Competence* (New York: Holt, Rinehart and Winston, 1988), p. 192.
13. William Thourlby, *You Are What You Wear—The Key to Business Success* (Kansas City, MO: Sheed Andrews and McMeel, 1978), p. 1.
14. William G. Nickels, Robert F. Everett, and Ronald Klein, "Rapport Building for Salespeople: A Neuro-Linguistic Approach," *Journal of Personal Selling and Sales Management*, November 1983, p. 1.
15. Ibid.
16. Donald J. Moine, "To Trust, Perchance to Buy," *Psychology Today*, August 1982, pp. 51–54.
17. Nickels, Everett, and Klein, "Rapport Building for Salespeople," p. 2.
18. Genie Z. Laborde, *Influencing with Integrity* (Palo Alto, CA: Syntony, Inc. Publishing Company, 1984), pp. 28–29.
19. Ibid., p. 30.

CHAPTER

11

Probing for Buying Needs

Knowledge Objectives

In this chapter, you will learn:

1. To differentiate between needs and wants
2. To differentiate between personal, organizational, and task needs
3. The two major categories of buying motives—rational and emotional
4. How buyer resolution theory affects the decision process, involving the areas of need, product, price, service, timing, and company
5. How neutral, loaded, and leading questions affect the buyer's responses and influence the sales strategy
6. To be aware of and appreciate effective open-ended questions for determining buying needs
7. To develop an awareness of silence, verbal encouragement, request for clarification and elaboration, and restatement as probing techniques
8. The salesperson's ethical responsibilities when probing

Consider This

Good salespeople get answers to their questions. Great ones probe and clarify each answer until they've solved the mystery.

Dorothy Leeds*

*"How to Ask Questions That Get the Sale," *Personal Selling Power*, October 1991, p. 28.

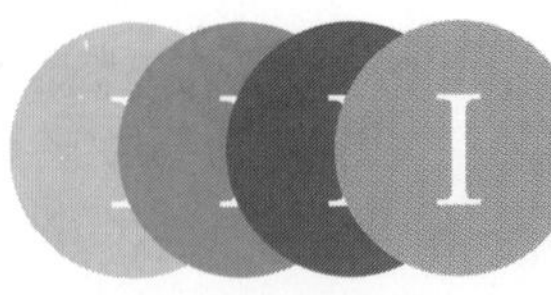

In Chapter 8 we discussed how the communication climate, or the quality of personal relationships between salespeople and their customers, affects customers' buying decisions and their decisions to develop long-term relationships that lead to repeat business. In Chapter 7, buying decision theory was discussed from a marketing perspective. This chapter will apply buying decision theory to the approach phase of the selling process. Thus, we will study the types of needs that motivate a buyer to make a purchase. The purpose is to provide probing techniques for uncovering the buyer's needs so that the salesperson can structure the sales presentation to effectively meet those needs.

The chapter is divided into five sections. In the first of these, we address three fundamental questions: (1) Who is the customer? (2) How does the customer buy? and (3) How can the customer be reached? The second section describes the differences and similarities between rational and emotional motives, and the third focuses on buyer resolution theory, which includes the six major buying decisions that all customers affirm in leading to a purchase: need, product, price, service, timing, and company. The fourth section introduces a systematic procedure for discovering buying needs through the development of open questions and the use of communication skills in probing strategies. The final section focuses on ethical issues and concerns for the salesperson when probing to determine the buyer's needs.

Needs and the Motivational Environment

All individuals are motivated by needs and wants. These needs and wants accumulate within a person, creating a desire to purchase a product or service. *Needs* are the result of a deficit condition, or a lack of something desirable. *Wants* are needs that are learned. For example, a person may need a personal computer or word processor to meet the demands for typewritten papers required of a college student. The type of equipment and software purchased, however, will depend on the wants of the individual. These wants may be influenced by peers, other reference groups, the level of sophistication desired, or the person's level of computer literacy. *Learning* describes the changes that occur in people's behavior as a result of their experiences. Learning specialists say that learning occurs through the interaction of drives, cues, responses, and reinforcements.[1]

A *drive* is a strong internal stimulus that induces action to fulfill a need. A drive becomes a *motive* when it is directed toward the fulfillment of a specific goal. For example, people who live in southern California *need* automobile transportation because of a lack of mass transit systems. The *drive* to get to school, work, or play creates a lucrative and competitive market for the automobile industry. Whether a person buys a Porsche, a Cadillac, a Volvo, or a Toyota depends on that person's *wants* and *motives*.

Through the continual process of acting and learning, individuals acquire beliefs and attitudes. How motivated people act and learn is influenced by their perceptions of a situation. A *belief* is a person's opinion or thought about something. An *attitude* is a person's feelings, tendencies, or point of view toward a product, service, or idea. *Perception* is the "process by which people select, organize, and interpret information to form a meaningful picture of the world."[2] For example, a buyer may hold the opinion that a sports car represents speed, wealth, success, freedom, and independence. The buyer's attitude toward a Ferrari or Lamborghini is that they meet all the criteria believed to be related to sports cars. Thus, a person's perception of people who drive sports cars is that those people are successful, wealthy, and independent—in other words, they are winners. Furthermore, such a person becomes motivated to own or drive a Ferrari because it fits the person's self-image as a winner.

Two people with the same needs and motivation may behave differently based on how they perceive the same situation. Suppose two customers are in the process of buying personal computers. One person may consider a fast-talking computer salesperson to be pretentious and arrogant, while the other individual may see the same salesperson as helpful and intelligent.

Ideally, if a buyer's perceptions create a favorable impression leading to the belief that the salesperson's product best fits the individual's needs, the sale is made. Realistically, however, the prospect may not know about the salesperson, the company, or the product. Thus, it is the salesperson's responsibility to determine the prospect's needs and then provide information that will help the buyer develop positive attitudes and beliefs. On many occasions, salespeople must spend a great deal of time helping to change their buyers' perceptions, attitudes, and beliefs about their products and services.

The Black Box—The Buyer's Mind

In marketing and consumer behavior texts the "black box," as illustrated in Figure 11.1, is sometimes used to explain the buying process. The black box represents a view of the customer's buying behavior, although no one has ever seen a person think or feel. The model shows that a person's mind controls the person's needs, feelings, and thoughts. Marketing professor Joseph Thompson describes the black box in this way:

> It is a master control system that contains abilities, knowledge, skills, needs, motivations, level of aspiration, and so on. . . . All motivation is controlled by the black box—the mind of man. Man is a product of his life style—his environment over time. And at every moment that environment is not only shaping what the individual is, but also affecting the individual's response to stimuli.[3]

According to Thompson, Figure 11.2 represents the businessperson's environment. As a specific example, for the purchasing agent of industrial products this would include various pressures from sources such as business, culture, reference group, and governmental factors, as discussed in Chapter 7. Although all of the pressures described in Figure 11.2 are

Figure 11.1

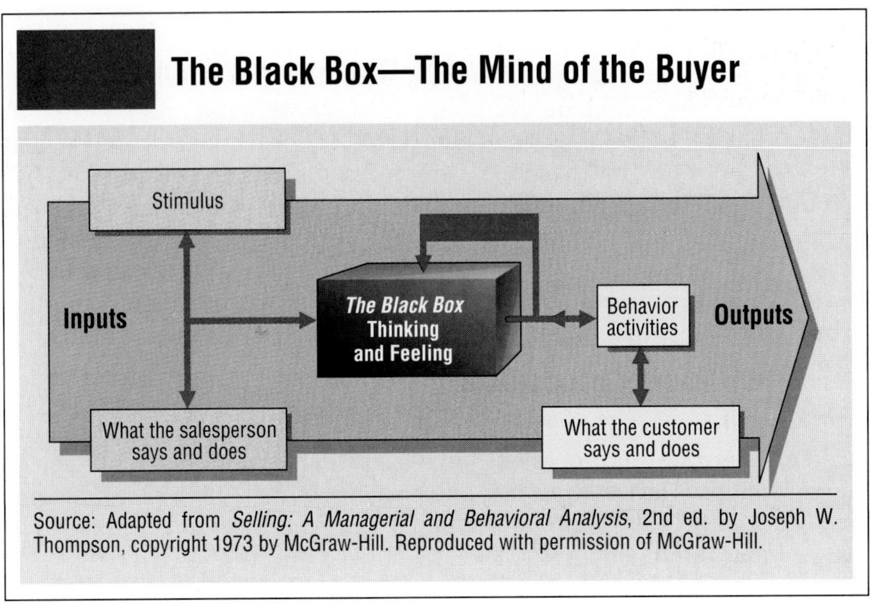

Source: Adapted from *Selling: A Managerial and Behavioral Analysis*, 2nd ed. by Joseph W. Thompson, copyright 1973 by McGraw-Hill. Reproduced with permission of McGraw-Hill.

of interest to the salesperson, we will concentrate on buying needs and motives.

Buying Needs

Three sets of needs are involved in making a buying decision: personal, business, and task needs. *Personal needs* refer to social-affiliative and status needs as described in Maslow's hierarchy in Chapter 7. *Business needs* are requirements by the customer's firm for the salesperson's products or services. For example, an industrial salesperson selling equipment and supplies to a large building contractor identifies the firm's problems and then demonstrates how the product or service will fit the firm's needs.

In most selling situations, however, personal and business needs are interacting variables. Generally speaking, the closer the customer is to using the product, the greater will be that customer's involvement in determining how the product will fill personal (status) needs. The further buyers are from actually using or consuming the product, the less involved they will be with how the product satisfies their needs. For example, people who are buying furniture for their own offices may be very attuned to status emotions when selecting wood or metal or fiberglass, leather or Naugahyde. On the other hand, status or personal needs may not be important to a buyer purchasing furniture for the office staff.

Task needs are all those items and conditions that are required for individuals to perform their work. Things such as staples, notepads, and computers; courses in operating computers; and proficiency in another language are examples of task needs. Personal needs tend to coexist with task needs.

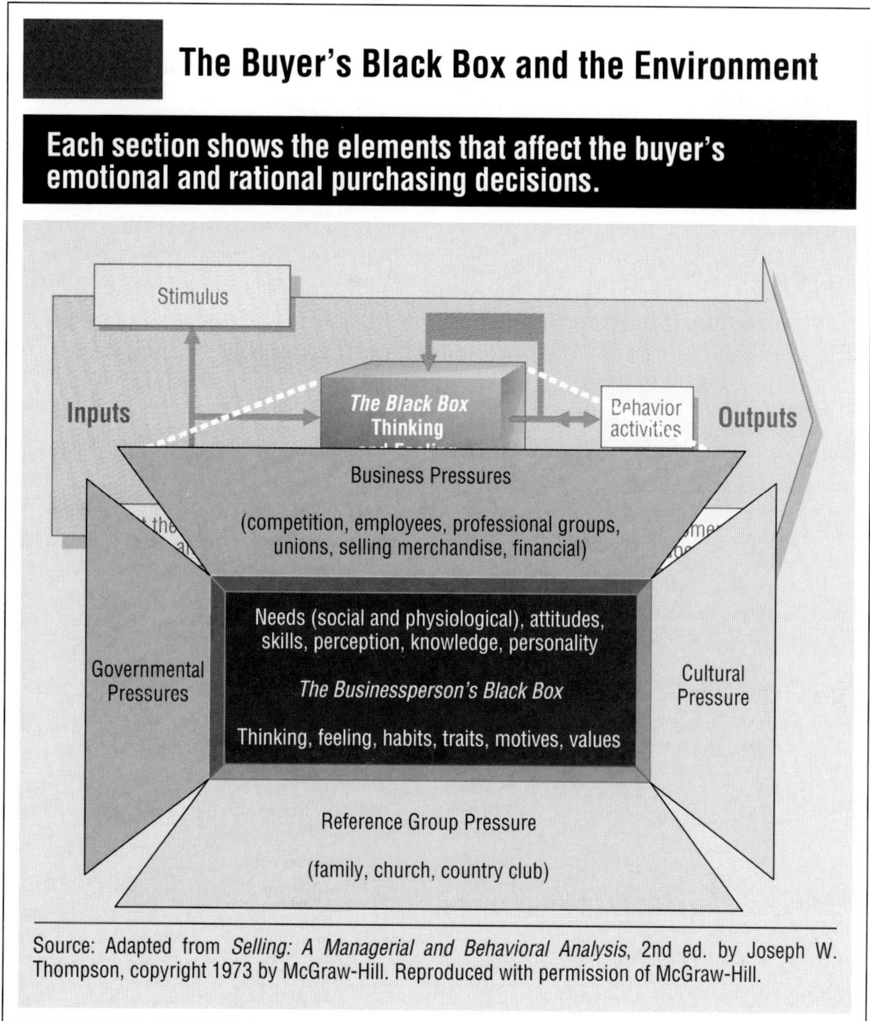

Figure 11.2

The Buyer's Black Box and the Environment

Each section shows the elements that affect the buyer's emotional and rational purchasing decisions.

Source: Adapted from *Selling: A Managerial and Behavioral Analysis,* 2nd ed. by Joseph W. Thompson, copyright 1973 by McGraw-Hill. Reproduced with permission of McGraw-Hill.

Buying Motives

The three levels of customer needs that a salesperson must be aware of can be compared to the steps in peeling an onion. The outer layer of the onion is translucent and somewhat dry. Underneath the top skin, however, is another layer that is thicker in texture and more moist. Under the second layer are a third, a fourth, and so on, until the center of the onion is reached.

Customer needs exist in an arrangement that is similar to a three-layered onion: The external layer, which is visible to the eye, includes the *features* or factual characteristics of the product or service. For example, a salesperson for automobile tires might describe one particular model of tire as providing "more rubber-to-the-road contact." This factual characteristic is a feature.

Beneath the features lies the second need level, which is the *advantage*, or the performance characteristics of a particular feature. For example, a tire that provides "more rubber-to-the-road contact" leads to at least one important area of customer advantage: "better handling."

Beneath the advantages lies the core or heart of a customer's reasons for buying: the *benefit* or satisfaction derived from the advantage of the feature. In other words, the benefit includes the emotional and rational reasons that compel the customer to act. This core level is where a customer's need changes to a want, or a desire for ownership. For example, a customer who sees better handling as desirable may want a tire that provides better handling because the automobile will be a safer place for a new infant to travel. "Safety" would be the benefit, "better handling" would be the advantage, and "more rubber-to-the-road contact" would be the feature.

Marketers have for many years performed extensive research to determine the most powerful and widespread needs influencing how customers behave. Buying needs are based on rational and emotional reasons involving what customers think, how they feel, and how they want to be perceived. These reasons for buying are drives or forces that motivate a customer to act.

Rational Motives

When customers make decisions to purchase a product for rational reasons, they are motivated to do so because of objective and logical information. The vast majority of buying decisions to purchase industrial products are precipitated by rational motives, not emotional ones. In contrast, the vast majority of buying decisions to purchase consumer products are made based on emotional reasons. The best way to prepare for a customer who is motivated by rational needs is to be thoroughly versed in information about the product, one's services, and the competition. Reviewing Chapter 5 will assist in compiling these types of information.

Emotional Motives

Purchases are also made for emotional reasons. These emotional motives may relate to feelings of self-worth and self-fulfillment, as well as a desire to be included in or belong to a personal relationship, a sense of influence or power over the world, and a need to receive affection or care from others.[4] For example, a customer may purchase a particular automobile to increase feelings of uniqueness or to project the image of belonging to a particularly elite group, not because it is considered highly dependable with respect to dealer service. In other words, emotional motives for buying stem more from the customer's feelings than from logical reasons for wanting a particular product.

Whether the product or service is purchased for rational, emotional, or a combination of these reasons depends on the individual customer.

Sales Professional Spotlight

Ella Zanowic is a sales trainer, sales program coordinator, management consultant, and motivational seminar speaker for EZ Success Enterprises in California. She is acclaimed for her motivating, dynamic presentations filled with hard-hitting, down-to-earth information designed to maximize sales potential. Ella's purpose in all her presentations is to influence people to accept new ideas or products and to accomplish their personal career goals.

Ella has been involved in some phase of selling most of her life. Her ventures have included sales and management positions with Zanowic & Associates Real Estate Services; Merrill Lynch Realty; Tarbell Realtors; Wheeler, Steffen & Garrison, Inc.; and Avon Cosmetics, where she earned top producer and recognition awards for designing courses in action selling and developing people skills.

Although most of her clients are in real estate sales, she has found that most of the principles of successful selling are true regardless of what you are selling. Ella considers the importance of discovering the customer's needs and wants as the most neglected phase in selling; statistics reveal that less than 15 percent of salespeople accurately determine the specific needs of the prospect.

Ella states that an easy way to stay ahead of the competition is to become an expert at discovering your customers' wants and needs. Product value is best offered to customers by being able to first identify their needs and wants. This initial step to uncovering the buyer's feelings, needs, and wants includes providing a low-pressure selling environment because the prospect may resist the sales ideas of an overanxious salesperson. "The impatient salesperson who jumps right into the presentation may seem to be unconcerned for prospects' needs, interested only in the financial rewards of making the sale," she says.

Ella supports the contention that everyone has a basic need to feel important. Buyers want to be recognized and demand to be heard. "This desire for attention is present in all of us. Focusing wholehearted attention on the prospect lowers defense barriers and arouses interest in listening to the presentation. By showing customers that they can get what they want, the end result could be a 'win-win' situation for both salesperson and buyer."

When salespeople ask questions of buyers about their specific needs and wants, a sincere interest in the buyer is expressed and communicated. Salespeople should ask open-ended questions to uncover their customers' motives for buying. "Listen intensely and understand completely what the customer is saying verbally and nonverbally. Make every presentation clear in words, pictures, and figures, and encourage feedback. Any misunderstanding could lead to uncertainty and a break in trust."

Ella highlights the discovery portion of the sales process as a chance to develop rapport surrounding the key issues in educating prospects and helping them make the purchase decision. "Educating buyers exposes them to the salesperson's experiences with the buying opportunities in the marketplace. This process keeps buyers' emotions 'on center' and relieves them of some of the stress when making this decision. Tremendous trust and confidence are gained through this educational process."

Ella strongly believes that selling is a "people" business that involves understanding their basic reasons for buying. Professional salespeople should serve the best interests of buyers because they must live with the buying decision. She emphasizes that the key to all the preceding steps in probing for buying needs is to truly care about buyers' interests, share their concerns, and help them solve their problems.

Table 11.1 provides the salesperson with language to describe both rational and emotional reasons for buying.

A customer's reasons for buying are not always stated directly. The customer and salesperson may not even be aware, at least initially, of what these reasons are. This is particularly true of emotional motives. Taking responsibility to identify the customer's reasons for buying is the first step in the problem-solving process. The next two sections in this chapter address important communication skills for identifying a customer's rational and emotional reasons for buying: open questions and probing techniques.

Table 11.1

Terminology Relating to Emotional and Rational Reasons for Buying

acceptance	energy	peace of mind	respect
affordability	esteem	pleasure	safety
assurance	excitement	portability	security
attractiveness	financial gain	power	self-confidence
comfort	freedom	practicality	sensuality
cost-in-use	gratification	pragmatism	status
dependability	happiness	prestige	success
distinctiveness	healthfulness	pride	thrill
durability	individualism	productivity	trust
dynamism	innovativeness	profitability	understandability
economy	intensity	reliability	uniqueness
efficiency	investment	reputability	versatility

Try This 11.1 Emotional and Rational Buying Motives

For each of the products and services listed below, identify at least ten emotional and rational reasons that a customer may have motivating the decision to make a purchase.

1. A personal computer for a:
   a. college student
   b. businesswoman
   c. basketball coach
2. A camcorder and related video equipment for a:
   a. sales trainer in a Fortune 500 company
   b. young married couple with infant twins
   c. local cable television station
3. A chamber of commerce membership for:
   a. a local business enterprise
   b. an orthodontist
   c. a college professor

Using Open Questions to Probe for Buying Needs

There are three main reasons for questioning the customer: to gather information, to assess how a customer thinks or feels, and to verify facts and attitudes discovered by other questions or data sources. Table 11.2 elaborates on these purposes.

As discussed in Chapter 10, open questions encourage the customer to respond in more than one or a few words because they require responses that are more elaborate and in-depth. As a result, open questions provide a valuable tool for identifying customer needs and help the salesperson determine the focus of the sales interview. As long as the salesperson does not interrogate the customer by asking too many questions in succession, open questions will provide a considerable amount of useful information.

Closed questions provide little, if any, free information about the customer and the customer's reasons for buying. In addition, closed questions discourage the type of spontaneous, free-flowing conversation that is critical to the success of the salesperson-customer relationship.

Although open questions do not guarantee that the customer's response will be lengthy and detailed, they do significantly increase the likelihood that the customer's answers will include relevant information. Because one's primary goal in the sales interview is to identify the customer's reasons for buying, a salesperson will want to ask open questions that probe for more detailed responses than closed questions tend to elicit.

Table 11.2

Major Purposes of Questioning

Collect Information

1. Qualify customer as to
   a. Eligibility to purchase
   b. Ability to pay
   c. Authority to purchase
   d. Others involved in purchase decision
   e. Time frame for decision
   f. Special requirements or restrictions
2. Determine customer's wants and needs
3. Discover problems customer has that your product or service could solve
4. Learn which product or service to present if you sell a multiple-product or -service line
5. Ask for the order

Evaluate How a Customer Feels or Thinks

1. Establish rapport with customer
2. Understand customer's personality so you can react properly
3. Determine why customer doesn't want or like something

Confirmation of Facts or Attitude

1. Determine customer's organizational and personal goals with regard to product or service offering
2. Ascertain which benefit of product or service should be stressed
3. Unearth reasons underlying objections and questions
4. Confirm facts and gain agreement on conclusions

Associated Benefit

1. Find additional qualified prospects for your product or service offering

Source: Ronald D. Balsley and E. Patricia Birsner, *Selling—Marketing Personified* (Chicago, IL: The Dryden Press, 1987), p. 62.

Questions that begin with "how," "what," and "in what way" are generally open because they are difficult to answer with only one or a few words. Questions that begin with "why" are also open but should be used less frequently because people are not always aware of the reason why something occurred or why a particular action was taken. In fact, if used in excess, "why" questions may elicit a defensive response from the customer. One should also be aware that open questions can be worded as statements that invite a response—such as "Tell me about . . . ," "Share with me . . . ," or "Discuss your. . . ."

The most appropriate questions or statements to discover a customer's reasons for buying are open and focused enough to provide the customer with direction when the question is answered. In particular, open questions that will be most useful are those that focus on six major buying-

On the Ethical Side Probing—the Ethical Way

The salesperson has many ways to probe for information that will help identify the potential buyer's needs. Some of these methods, however, are ethically suspect. When any question exists about probing techniques, remember Polonius' advice to his son Laertes as the latter was heading off for college: "To thine own self be true: and it must follow as the night the day thou canst not then be false to any man."* In other words, tell the truth; let the prospect know that you are running an inventory to determine how you can help.

Customers generally appreciate the efforts of salespeople who are conscientious enough to help them analyze their situation. An estate analysis, for example, can show the prospect what sort of tax liabilities might face that estate in the event of the prospect's death and how buying insurance to offset those demands can save real, workable dollars for the prospect. Or, if a client has an investment portfolio that is too heavily invested in volatile or no-gain stocks, probing that portfolio can lead to ways of helping the client attain long-term investment goals.

The secret to ethical probing is keeping the client's needs in focus, treating the information as confidential, and using professional knowledge to meet the client's needs.

*William Shakespeare, *Hamlet* I.iii. 78–80.

decision categories: need, product, price, service, timing, and company. The reasons for making buying decisions in each of these areas may be both rational and emotional. Psychologically, a customer must be convinced that each of these six categories has been addressed and satisfied before the final buying decision will be made.

Within the six buying-decision categories, open questions such as those shown below can be used to identify reasons for buying at rational and emotional levels.

1. *Need*—Need applies to how the product or service will be used. Determining need involves asking questions about the customer's interest in adding new products or additional units to the inventory; changing suppliers; or risking unknown products, services, and companies.
   - "I understand you're moving to a new, larger facility, and I'm wondering how the move will affect your reprographics department."
   - "What are your feelings about moving to a facility that's already equipped with state-of-the-art reprographics equipment?"
2. *Product*—Product questions refer to the tangibility or intangibility of a product or service, including characteristics such as composition, structure, and function.
   - "Describe how you expect the equipment to be laid out in your new facility."

- "How will color copying appeal to your advertising department?"

3. *Price*—Questions about price deal with elements such as cost, billing, financing, credit terms, discounts, and markups.
   - "What's been budgeted for your move into the new facility?"
   - "What kind of pressure are you under to stay within your budget?"
4. *Service*—Service questions are directed toward concerns such as delivery follow-up, warranties, guarantees, repair, maintenance, installation, and training.
   - "What are the most important considerations for you in deciding on your servicing and maintenance agreements with new equipment?"
   - "How satisfied have you been with our delivery over the last 5 years?"
5. *Timing*—Questions about timing refer to when a decision will be made, as well as the urgency of acting on the problem at the present time or postponing a decision until later.
   - "What kind of time line are you looking at for starting full-scale production?"
   - "How much stress is your staff currently working under in trying to meet your production needs before you make the move?"
6. *Company*—Questions about the company include factors such as the age, size, financial standing, market share, and rate of growth of the firm, as well as its affiliation with other well-known firms, the status of existing customers, patents held, sound labor relations, and the efficiency of operation.
   - "With your anticipated expansion, what kind of market share are you hoping to gain in the next 3 years?"
   - "What have been your customers' responses to your change in location?"

The open questions listed in each category are also neutral questions, in contrast to loaded or leading questions. *Neutral* questions are objective and unbiased. *Loaded* questions, on the other hand, use judgmental language. *Leading* questions imply that one answer is preferable to another. Both loaded and leading questions are typically closed. Because these types of questions are likely to trigger defensive responses, neutral questions are preferable. The examples listed here provide both loaded and leading questions and then revisions that show how each can be worded in more neutral, open language.

Loaded: "Why are you still using that antique, manual-loading copier?"

Neutral: "What are your reasons for keeping the older, manual-loading copier when you've had to spend so much on labor costs?"

Leading: "You're interested in having this maintenance policy on your new reprographics equipment, aren't you?"

Neutral: "What interest do you have in purchasing a maintenance policy for your new reprographics equipment?"

On the International Front: Using Language and Ambiguity in Probing

In international settings, language becomes directed when probing buyers' needs and expectations. For example, a Korean buyer may ask the American salesperson a question such as, "Why have you included shipping costs on the invoice?" An American buyer may oppose the Korean salesperson's invoice by remarking, "Why have you increased prices 10 percent?" The language becomes even stronger when a problem with the contract is identified.

When confident of the facts, buyers may ask questions to which the seller can only respond "yes" or "no." The American suppliers assures the Korean buyer that the agreement did not include shipping costs being paid by the supplier. In the second case, the buyer was not expecting to pay more because of escalating labor costs in Korea. When language is strong and simple, then the commitment appears considerable. The level of ambiguity is often related to the level of commitment. The less ambiguous a statement is, the greater the speaker's commitment is to the position desired.

Continuing efforts to probe issues reveal further interest and commitment. However, the extent of each party's commitment to the issues must be determined. It is at this time that differences, preferences, and strengths can be identified and satisfied, and buyers and sellers can achieve an agreement.

Source: J. B. McCall and M. B. Warrington, *Marketing by Agreement: A Cross-Cultural Approach to Business Negotiations* (New York: John Wiley & Sons, 1989), pp. 193–198.

Try This 11.2 Revising Loaded and Leading Questions

Identify whether the following questions are closed, leading, loaded with emotionally charged words, or a combination of these. Then revise each question to make it open and neutral.

Example:

Question: Do you really like playing with that poorly strung, cheap tennis racket?

Reason for Revision: Closed and loaded

Possible Revision: What kind of performance are you getting from the racket you've been using?

Question: You do plan to add snowboards to your line this year, don't you?

Reason for Revision: ____________

Possible Revision: ____________

Question: When will you realize that you need to dump that junk you call word processors and get some new equipment?

Reason for Revision: ____________

Possible Revision: ____________

In Chapter 10 we discussed the importance for salespeople of remembering that vocal intonation and the stress placed on a word can change a neutrally worded question into judgmental, loaded language. Note how, by changing the stress pattern in the following question, a neutral question becomes loaded and judgmental.

"*Why* did you buy that copier? [*you know you can't afford it*]"
"Why did *you* buy that copier? [*you should have let him pay for it*]"
"Why did you *buy* that copier? [*you really should have leased it*]"
"Why did you buy *that* copier? [*you should have purchased another model*]"
"Why did you buy that *copier*? [*you should have purchased a laser printer*]"

The Skill Builder for this chapter provides an opportunity to generate open questions that will help uncover reasons for buying, for each of the six buying-decision categories.

Probing Techniques

Open questions can help salespeople identify their customers' reasons for making buying decisions relating to the buying-decision categories. *Probing techniques* help salespeople obtain more specific information. In particular, probing techniques are useful when answers to open questions are brief, incomplete, or vague and superficial. These techniques probe for more information without giving the impression that the customer is being interrogated.

There are several follow-up techniques that salespeople can use to probe for more information when answers to their initial questions are inadequate. These are silence, verbal encouragement, requests for clarification and elaboration, and restatement.[5]

1. *Silence*—When the customer gives an incomplete answer to a question or appears reluctant to provide important details, the salesperson may remain silent for a moment while maintaining eye contact, using supportive facial expressions, and nodding to indicate interest and support. Silence used in this way can often draw the customer out and encourage continued conversation. One must be careful, however, not to use silence for more than a few seconds because it may create discomfort and destroy the supportive climate that has been established with the customer.
2. *Verbal encouragement*—If the customer does not respond after a moment or two of silence, the salesperson may use verbal encouragement, or comments that invite the customer to provide additional information. These comments are usually brief:

   "Go on . . . tell me more about that."
   "What else do you know about your clients?"
   "What happened then?"

3. *Request for clarification and elaboration*—The salesperson may request clarification and elaboration when the customer's reasons

Skill Builder 11.1 Developing Open Questions

Open questions encourage prospects and customers to talk about their problems, needs, goals, and objectives. They are especially useful in drawing out what the prospect or customer hopes, wants, feels, and thinks. Questions that begin with "how," "what," and "in what way" are difficult to answer with only one or a few words and are especially effective in helping the salesperson probe for buying needs.

Using the six buying decisions that all customers affirm before making a purchase, Lacey Boesen, a sales representative for AT&P Work Group Systems, designed a set of open questions that she uses when calling on prospective clients who are considering expanding their businesses.

Need

1. What current communication means or system do you use for writing memos?
2. How often are there waiting lines for use of your peripherals?
3. In what ways do you feel your office efficiency can be improved?

Product

1. How can a work group best be implemented into your department?
2. What locations are available for peripheral storage?
3. How are updated files sent to other employees?

Price

1. What size budget are you committing to your computer expansion?
2. In what ways do you see that our system can be cost effective for you?
3. How important is pricing in this decision?

Service

1. How effective has your past service been?
2. In what ways can it be improved?
3. How fast has response been to equipment breakdown?

Timing

1. What breakdowns in equipment have occurred recently?
2. How involved are you with projects requiring state-of-the-art technology?
3. What kind of pressures are you getting from management and the rest of your staff to streamline your operation?

Company

1. How large are the customers you currently serve?
2. In what ways are your competitors advancing?
3. How important are image, prestige, and reliability to you in deciding on your work group system?

Remember that the most effective open questions are *neutral*—as objective or unbiased as possible. The goal is to create a positive buying climate so that the customer feels safe and free to disclose thoughts and feelings, enabling you to choose an appropriate presentation strategy.

After creating a hypothetical selling situation, design three open questions for each of the six categories of buying decisions. With another person serving as the customer, create a dialogue in which you ask the questions you have just developed. To facilitate your practice of this skill, use the following probing techniques in your sales interview: silence, verbal encouragement, request for clarification, and restatement.

for buying seem vague or superficial. These requests encourage the customer to describe or expand on an answer to the salesperson's primary question:

"I'm interested in hearing more details about that . . ."

"Specifically, what do you mean when you say you're 'downsizing'?"

"I'm interested in hearing some examples of the problem you've identified because I'm not certain I understand precisely what you're saying."

"What examples can you give to help me understand your problem?"

"I'd like to hear more about the different ways you've tried to solve this problem."

"I'm not certain I understand your last point."

4. *Restatement*—When the customer's answer seems irrelevant or the question has not been answered directly, the salesperson can restate or rephrase the initial open question to probe for more complete information. For example, in the following dialogue, the customer does not answer the original question directly, and the salesperson responds using restatement.

Salesperson: How do you like the XK-2180 calculators you purchased from us last year?

Customer: Well, the people over in marketing say they're not very reliable and I've been hearing some complaint that they're too big to carry in a briefcase from job site to job site.

Salesperson: I see. Have *you* used the XK-2180 yet?

If the customer doesn't respond to the question, rephrase it and try again. Any time a customer claims an inability to answer or a desire not to answer the salesperson's question, the salesperson should respect the customer's decision to remain silent. Listen carefully to any reasons given for this response. Then move on and ask a different question.

There are many reasons why customers do not always provide complete, specific, and accurate answers to salespeople's questions.[6] Some of these are:

- The customer may be uncertain about how much detail the salesperson wants. This is most likely to occur when the questions one asks are open but overly broad and unfocused (for instance, "How's business?" or "How are things going?").
- The customer may be uncertain about what type of information the salesperson wants or how much detail is required.
- The customer may not understand the question because of the language or word choice.
- The customer may not have the information the salesperson is requesting because the customer either has a poor memory or has never known the information.

Try This 11.3 Probes That Motivate the Customer to Share

The answers to the open questions below are incomplete or do not elicit a complete enough answer for the salesperson to determine the customer's buying needs. Identify an appropriate strategy that you could use to motivate the customer to provide more specific and complete information.

1. **Salesperson:** How satisfied are you with the new forklift you purchased last fall?
   Customer: It's alright.
   Salesperson: ______________________
   ____
   ____

2. **Salesperson:** What types of customers are you primarily serving this season?
   Customer: It varies.
   Salesperson: ______________________
   ____
   ____

3. **Salesperson:** What do you like about your Suzuki?
   Customer: It's fun!
   Salesperson: ______________________
   ____
   ____

- The customer may think the question is too personal, irrelevant, or not appropriate.
- The customer may be unable to express feelings because of limited language skills, low intelligence, or cultural rules that prohibit openness.
- The customer may think that the salesperson would not understand the answer or that the topic is too technical or personal for the salesperson to understand.

To summarize, in discovering the customer's reasons for buying, the salesperson's first task is to decide if the answer to the initial open question is adequate. If it is not, then the salesperson must decide what additional information is needed and why the customer has provided an incomplete or superficial answer. At this point, the salesperson must decide whether to probe for a more complete answer or ask another primary question. If the decision is made to probe further, the salesperson must decide whether to use silence, respond with verbal encouragement, request elaboration or clarification, or restate the original question.

The use of probing techniques is a skill that differentiates competent from unskilled salespeople. Unskilled salespeople usually do not notice how the customer responds to an open question because they are preoccupied with thinking about the next question to ask. Competent salespeople, on the other hand, listen carefully to what information the customer provides and make decisions about the specific probing techniques that could be used to elicit more complete answers to the questions being asked. When used appropriately, probing techniques help build understanding between the customer and salesperson. They let the customer know that the salesperson is listening and making an effort to understand. Most importantly, these techniques motivate the customer to communicate more completely and honestly about the reasons for buying.

Exhibit 11.1

Types, Purposes, and Uses of Questions during an Interview

Type of Question	Purpose or Use
Probing	Defines key issues, provides "angles" on which to base sales presentations; especially useful when customers can't clearly state goals, objectives, needs, or wants. Probes help you dig deeper into situation—to discover the realities. Probes must be used carefully—may get into sensitive areas that may cause customer to react negatively.
• Silence	Not really a question but a neutral probe. Has the effect of a question because it keeps customers talking. Silence is difficult to face in an interaction—if you remain silent, customer will usually talk to fill the gap. Doesn't bias prospect's responses and seldom causes an unfavorable reaction.
• Encouragement	A neutral probe, also not a question. The salesperson encourages the customer to continue talking by leaning forward, looking interested, nodding agreement, making encouraging sounds. When the prospect appears to be stumped or stops talking, change to a different probe.
• Elaboration	Another neutral probe, but for the purpose of requesting more information along the same line.
• Clarification	Request that customer supply further information on specific subject or situation. Not neutral, so should be alternated with more neutral probes.
• Topic change	A switch to a new topic. Not neutral and can get either positive or negative response. Should also be followed by a neutral probe.
• Directive	A question designed to get factual information. Usually somewhat closed since asked about a limited topic. Helps you find out present state of affairs.
• Verifying:	A question designed to get feedback from customer. Is neutral and nonmanipulative.
Assumptive	States the question so as to simply get affirmation, even though the correct answer is known.
Interpretive	Used to get feedback, correction, or amplification or in an attempt to define problem. Lets the customer correct your thinking.

In addition to the open questions and probing strategies presented here, there are many variations and types of questions that salespeople can use during the sales interview. Exhibit 11.1 identifies several question types, describes the purpose and use of each, and gives examples. Chapters 12 and 13 will introduce a relationship-driven selling system in which

When Used	Example
Throughout approach and recognition steps of sales interview. Some probes are neutral—they don't affect customer's view of situation or of you. Designed to get more information. Others are not neutral and are intended to affect the way customer views situation. Probes should not be used until after rapport is established. May also be used later in the interview, if necessary.	
Silence and encouragement may be used at any point in the interview when customer is or has been talking and you want him or her to continue in same direction.	Sounds like "mmmm" or phrases such as "I see," "That's interesting," "I didn't know that!"
To mix with one or more other probes. If used too extensively, may lock customer into early ideas, limit range of thought, and produce one-sided responses.	"Can you tell me a little more about your financial requirements?"
To ask for clarification of a topic uncovered previously or something to the point but not yet mentioned during interview.	"Could you explain further what you mean by that?" "Can you explain how that will fit in with your expansion plans?"
When previous probes seem to have yielded all possible information.	
To confirm preapproach information, determine likenesses and differences between customer's business and a similar one. To determine facts quickly and set direction for further questioning.	"How many people in your organization are involved in the bottling operation?" "How much casualty insurance do you presently have?"
	"Is the immediate insurance coverage more important than the long-term cost?"
During problem solving or contingency selling, when you are heavily involved in fact finding. May also be used in the close after agreement has been reached.	"Did I understand correctly—is the failure of the caustic to etch the metal the problem?" "Then are we in agreement that you'll take options 1 and 2, with the payments due on February 1, May 1, August 1, and November 1?"

Continued

Exhibit 11.1
Continued

Type of Question	Purpose or Use
• Leading:	Used to check for understanding, get feedback, or answer an unspoken question ("Do I really understand what you are telling me?")
Assumptive	Questioner assumes what answer will be, then asks if that is the case.
Interpretive	Restates what listener understands other person to have said, but in question form.
• Loaded	Contains words with high emotional content to which customer may react negatively. Responses often do not reflect customer's real position. Whether question is considered loaded depends on intent of the questioner, appropriateness of the language, perceptions and background of person being questioned, and situation in which it is asked.
Evaluative	
• Direct	Open-ended questions, often beginning with "what" or "how." Designed to get prospects to talk about their objectives, needs, goals, and problems.
• Indirect	To avoid negative reactions, ask customer to relate reactions to others' situations.
Strategic	To enable you to continue an interview when customer is highly negative. Allows you to get problem out in the open and keep interview productive.
Tactical	To parry or sidestep a difficult question and shift psychological initiative from prospect to yourself. May be open or closed.
Dichotomous	"Either"/"or" questions with choices among alternative possibilities.
Multiple choice	To push customer for a decision. Should be confined to no more than three choices.

When Used	Example
Late in the interview, after gaining a reasonable understanding of customer's position, to confirm rather than force or manipulate. May also be used to settle options and get agreement on a purchase decision.	"Then the total cost of the contract is more important than the unit costs?" "Do I understand that you feel quality control is the major problem?"
Leading questions to avoid:	Opening a call with "If I show you the way to a richer and fuller life in the next five minutes, would you be interested?" or "Would you be willing to agree to a small monthly investment to increase your earnings potential 200 percent?" Later in the interview, asking "Don't you agree that our competitor's approach to this situation is dead wrong?"
To verify a prejudice or when you already can anticipate the answer.	"You don't want your neighbors to think you're a cheapskate, do you?"
To determine customer's objectives and find out what customer hopes, wants, feels, and thinks.	"How do you feel about using word processing in your department?" "What do you think might be the advantages to you of changing over to a fully automated system?" "Most of the people in your other departments have found word processing to be invaluable. Is this true for your department?" "Some of my other customers have found that a fully automated system has saved them thousands of dollars and cut down on the time it takes for milling. Do you think this would be the case in your operation?"
At any time during sales call to determine customer's needs and attitudes underlying negative responses.	"Why do you say that you don't believe we have the experience for close tolerance manufacture, Mrs. Jones?"
When customers ask difficult, sensitive, or nuisance questions or attempt to intimidate you or put you into a defensive position.	"Don't you feel we have an obligation to our customers to try to improve our products?"
To force a hesitant customer to make a choice during the close.	"We can provide you with either a blue or a white background—which would you prefer?" "Do you prefer an open account, or would you rather use a separate purchase order for each transaction?"
During the close, to force customer to make choices.	"Which would you prefer—model 841, model 866, or deluxe model 926?" "Then will you take the entire package, the core proposal, or the core proposal plus the first two options?"

Source: Ronald D. Balsley and E. Patricia Birsner, *Selling—Marketing Personified* (Chicago, IL: The Dryden Press, 1987), pp. 64–67.

salespeople take the responses they have received from these probing strategies, order the responses into major and minor buying points, and develop a strategy built on presenting benefits that will move the customer to a buying decision.

Ethical Issues Relating to Probing Techniques

When using probing techniques, as with any part of the salesperson-customer relationship, it is important to foster trust and rapport. Behaving ethically and responsibly can contribute to a positive sales climate; inappropriate or unethical actions can destroy a trusting relationship. For example:

> Never ask a Japanese person a question that he or she may not be able to answer. Only ask a direct question if you are absolutely positive that it can be responded to adequately. The Japanese often like to know your questions ahead of time in order that they may have sufficient time to consult the group and consider all the alternatives and possibilities. Failure to be prepared can lead to loss of face.[7]

Conducting a sales interview is similar to engaging in other forms of organizational communication or interaction in that ethical behavior is important. In all sales interviews, the salesperson officially represents the firm; thus, that person's conduct reflects on the standards, values, and ethical character of the organization.[8]

Salespeople who ask offensive or improper questions, speak rudely or condescendingly to customers, or through a series of closed questions force buyers into giving "yes" answers for fear of sounding stupid or uncaring, reveal themselves as both tasteless and unethical. Furthermore, such behavior suggests that the company condones unethical sales tactics.

This chapter has presented skills and techniques that, when used appropriately, show openness, caring, and sensitivity to the customers' thoughts and feelings. Consultants Patricia Andrews and John Baird, Jr., describe eight characteristics of an ethical interviewer. These guidelines apply to sales interviews as well. An ethical salesperson:

- Displays concern for the customer and the customer's feelings
- Shows interest in finding out what the customer thinks
- Listens actively and genuinely
- Shows respect for the customer within the communication
- Arranges for enough meeting time so that an "information exchange" can occur
- Understands the law and companies' regulations so that operations occur only within the legal framework
- Is aware of the firm's formal and informal codes of ethics

- Is sensitive to power and authority differences between the salesperson and the customer and attempts to minimize their potentially negative effects

According to Andrews and Baird, behaving ethically as a salesperson in the sales interview is "a matter of knowledge, common sense, good will, and hard work."[9]

Summary

This chapter distinguishes between terms that are often used interchangeably in common language, to accentuate the subtle yet important differences as these terms are applied to relational selling. For instance, wants and needs are different in that needs are the result of a deficit condition or exist because something desirable is lacking. Wants, on the other hand, are needs that are learned. Similarly, human drives are strong internal stimuli that cause one to move toward fulfilling needs, while motives are drives that are harnessed toward the satisfaction of specific goals. In studying these relationships between general and specific categories, we find that three additional factors influence the customer's buying behavior: human beliefs, attitudes, and perceptions.

An analysis of buying needs leads us to see that these factors fall into three distinct categories: (1) personal needs, which may be broken down further into affiliative and status needs (as discussed regarding Maslow's hierarchy); (2) business needs, which are specific requirements by the customer's firm for the salesperson's products or services; and (3) task needs, which are all those items or conditions required for individuals to perform their work.

A useful tool for determining buyers' needs is questioning. Questions allow the salesperson to gather information, assess how a customer thinks or feels, and verify facts and attitudes discovered by other questions or data sources. Questions can be either open, inviting detailed responses, or closed, eliciting answers that give the salesperson little information. Probing techniques may be used to follow up questions when answers are inadequate.

Key Terms

Attitude A person's feelings, tendencies, or point of view
Belief A person's opinion or thought on a particular subject
Drive Strong internal structure that induces action to fulfill needs
Motive A drive directed toward a specific goal
Need The result of a deficit condition or a lack of something desirable
Perception Interpreted data about a particular thing
Want Learned needs

Figure 11.3

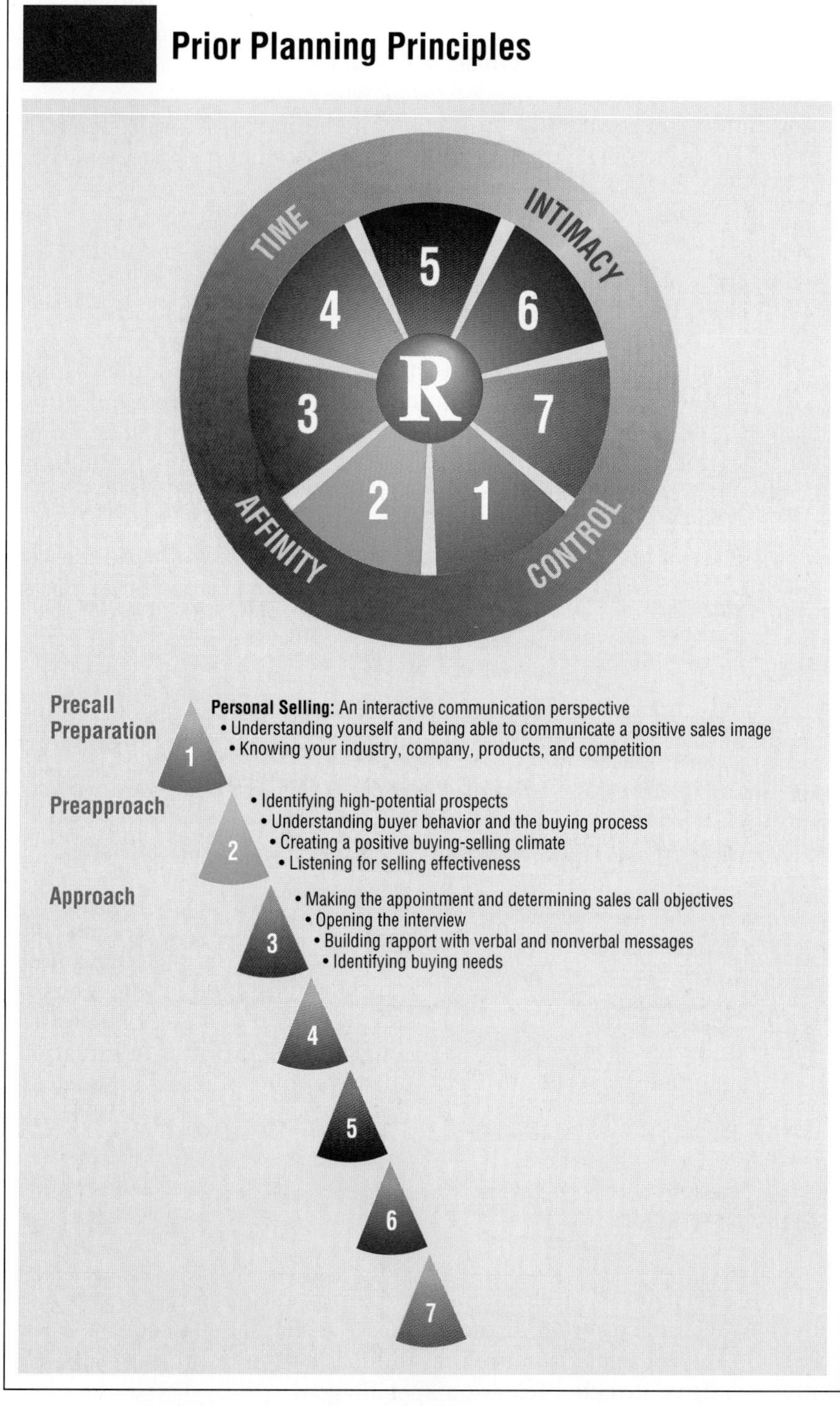
Prior Planning Principles
TIME
INTIMACY
AFFINITY
CONTROL
R
1
2
3
4
5
6
7
Precall Preparation
Personal Selling: An interactive communication perspective
• Understanding yourself and being able to communicate a positive sales image
• Knowing your industry, company, products, and competition
Preapproach
• Identifying high-potential prospects
• Understanding buyer behavior and the buying process
• Creating a positive buying-selling climate
• Listening for selling effectiveness
Approach
• Making the appointment and determining sales call objectives
• Opening the interview
• Building rapport with verbal and nonverbal messages
• Identifying buying needs

Review Questions

1. Distinguish between needs and wants and between drive and motive as they affect motivation.
2. Distinguish among beliefs, attitudes, and perceptions as they affect motivation.
3. Explain three sets of needs involved in a buying decision.
4. Distinguish among features, advantages, and benefits and list three levels of buying motives.
5. Distinguish between rational and emotional reasons for buying and explain how they are interrelated in the buying process.
6. Explain three major reasons for probing.
7. Distinguish between open and closed questions and explain the use of each in probing for needs.
8. Identify and explain each of the six buying-decision categories.
9. Distinguish among neutral, loaded, and leading questions and provide examples of each type.
10. Identify and explain four follow-up techniques salespeople can use to probe for additional information.

Discussion Questions

1. Using the "black box" model of the buyer's mind, discuss buying behavior.
2. Using the analogy of an onion, discuss how the three levels of customers' needs are interrelated.
3. Discuss the advantages and disadvantages of using open questions to probe for buying needs.
4. Discuss examples of open questions that can be used to probe for each of the six buying decision categories at both emotional and rational levels.
5. Discuss how nonverbal communication can turn neutrally worded questions into judgmental, loaded questions.
6. Discuss reasons why customers may not respond to questions adequately.
7. Discuss the ethical issues inherent in the salesperson's use of probing techniques.

Case 11.1

A Question of Price or Service?

David Hardy has been selling new bicycles for the last 11 years. He works for a successful dealership that carries a line of high-quality bicycles and offers extensive warranty coverage, service, and repairs.

David encounters many prospects who shop for bicycles based on price and then hope that repairs are never needed. One Saturday morning a prospect visited his showroom, asking questions about the brands and price ranges of bicycles the store carries. As usual, David responded in an informative and friendly manner and proceeded to uncover the prospect's needs. While conducting this process he realized that the prospect had a certain price in mind, having already determined that bicycles at a dealership are usually more expensive than in department stores. However, the prospect had some reservations about the less expensive bicycles sold in department stores, hence the reason for seeking out information at the dealer.

Further discussions uncovered the prospect's concern for service provisions. Apparently, the prospect had purchased her last bicycle at a bargain price from a large department store with large-volume sales of unknown brands. However, she was faced with the inconvenience of having to wait 3 days for assembly, which also involved an extra charge.

The prospect further complained about another inconvenience: having to take the bicycle back three times to correct an assembly problem, which resulted in an additional week of waiting time. The prospect revealed that the department store was unprepared to offer service and repair, and many bicycle dealers were unwilling to work on her unknown brand.

Stressing the importance of price in the purchase decision, the prospect pointed to the excellent prices advertised by the department stores. It seemed to David that the prospect was again inclined to seek out an inexpensive model and then deal with the problems as they arose. The prospect's decision may have been justified by the motto, "You get what you pay for," hoping to realize savings in the long run.

David proudly informed the prospect of the warranty and service provisions offered by his dealership, then proceeded to quote a price, which he clearly stated would not be as low as that of the large department store.

The prospect stood staring at the bicycle for several minutes, thanked David for his time, and left.

1. If the prospect was inclined to buy the lower priced bicycle at the department store, why was she shopping at David's dealership?
2. Should David's sales appeal focus so extensively on service after the sale?
3. Suggest other appeals that may be important to the prospect.

Getting the Purchasing Agent to Talk

Case 11.2

Peter Milano was the purchasing agent for the county school district. His first call on Monday morning was from Pat Kelly, a sales representative for a paper supply company. The large orders placed by the school district were mostly for copier and typing paper.

Pat knew that Mr. Milano was a man of few words. He never seemed to show any enthusiasm for his work. However, he has been in this position for nearly 20 years and is respected for his shrewd buying decisions. Upon entering Mr. Milano's office, Pat was convinced that the district could benefit from the extended line of other paper supplies and stationery, such as forms, paper clips, and staples, that the supplier also carried. Pat presented Mr. Milano with a price list and the specials of the month. He then proceeded to ask for the order.

Mr. Milano leaned back in his chair and quietly stated, "We have tons of inventory of paper supplies and stationery. Some of this stuff I can't even find as we are in the process of reorganizing the warehouse. In about a month I'll be ready to look at my inventory again."

"Since today is a bad time for you, then it is best I leave," Pat said. Handing Mr. Milano a business card he proceeded to leave the office. "I am interested in giving you a bid on all your paper supplies any time you are ready. Oh! By the way, we also have special educational discounts," Pat concluded.

Mr. Milano nodded and replied with a grunt. As the door closed behind Pat, Mr. Milano mumbled to himself, "I wonder how these companies survive hiring salespeople like Pat."

1. What approach would you suggest to Pat for getting Mr. Milano to relax and talk?
2. Suggest some questions that Pat should have asked in serving the prospect's needs or motives.
3. How much attention should Pat give to the reorganization excuse?

Notes

1. Philip Kotler and Gary Armstrong, *Principles of Marketing*, 4th ed. (Englewood Cliffs, NJ: Prentice Hall, 1989), p. 134.
2. Ibid., p. 132.
3. Joseph W. Thompson, *Selling: A Managerial and Behavioral Science Analysis*, 2nd ed. (New York: McGraw-Hill Book Company, 1973), p. 219.
4. A. H. Maslow, *Toward a Psychology of Being* (New York: Van Nostrand Reinhold, 1968).
5. C. J. Stewart and W. B. Cash, *Interviewing: Principles and Practices*, 2nd ed. (Dubuque, IA: Wm. C. Brown, 1982).
6. R. L. Kahn and C. F. Cannell, *The Dynamics of Interviewing* (New York: John Wiley & Sons, 1964), p. 205.
7. Mitchell F. Deutsch, *Doing Business with the Japanese* (New York: New American Library, 1983), p. 96.
8. Patricia Hayes Andrews and John E. Baird, Jr., *Communication for Business and the Professions*, 4th ed. (Dubuque, IA: Wm. C. Brown Publishers, 1989), p. 167.
9. Ibid.

CHAPTER 12

Preparing the Sales Presentation

Knowledge Objectives

In this chapter, you will learn:

1. The three major selling systems used to develop sales presentations
2. The conceptual basis for developing a fourth system called the relational model
3. How the competitive differential advantage analysis developed
4. To develop and apply a features-advantages-benefits analysis
5. How to arrange buyers' responses to probing questions into major and minor benefits
6. The ethical responsibilities involved in a sales presentation

Consider This

Preparing my attitude for a presentation is as important as the actual product knowledge. . . . When I'm excited about my product, I find I can relate my belief and enthusiasm to the customer. I keep a positive attitude and build relationships with dealers. That way, I know I will always be accepted.

Richard Brune*

*Quoted in a profile by David J. Lill, *Selling: The Profession* (New York: Macmillan Publishing Company, 1989), p. 309.

nce the prospect's needs have been identified, the salesperson is ready to provide information about the product or service. The stage should now be set for discussing ways in which the product or service will satisfy the customer's needs. A positive buying climate has been created; rapport has been initiated and is being maintained. The customer should be ready to welcome new ideas. At this point in the process the salesperson strives to link needs with product or service benefits, advantages, and features to achieve the prospect's commitment and confirm the order.

This chapter contains five sections focusing on how salespeople talk about their products or services, based on the responses they receive to probing questions. The first section examines the various selling system models that are currently being used. This section emphasizes the relational process model as an extension of the consultative selling system. The second section presents the conceptual basis for developing a fourth selling system—the relational sales model. It focuses on the similarities

Sales Topics

- Preparing a Competitive Differential Advantage (CDA) Analysis
- Preparing a Features-Advantages-Benefits (FAB) Analysis
- Selecting and Using Sales Support Materials
- Managing the Interaction

Sales Communication Skills

- Using Perception Checking
- Using the Fab System
- Using Persuasive Communication
- Developing Congruency and Body Language
- Using Win-Win Negotiation

and differences between a salesperson's product or service and that of the competition. The salesperson will learn how to prepare a competitive differential advantage (CDA) analysis that identifies strengths and weaknesses in product, company, source, and personnel.

Learning how to build a sales presentation by preparing a features-advantages-benefits (FAB) analysis, using the information acquired from the CDA analysis, is the focus of the third section. The fourth section discusses how to use the relational presentation system effectively by ordering the selling points into major and minor benefits that are appropriate to each customer's buying needs. Finally, a sales communication presentation example, including a CDA analysis and a FAB analysis, are presented in the last section.

Selling Theories and Presentation Models

A systematic method for approaching the sales interview is an essential ingredient for developing sales competence. All companies today—whether they are production oriented or marketing oriented, *Fortune* 500 status or "mom-and-pop" size—have prescribed methods for presenting their products and services to customers that facilitate a buying decision. Those prescribed methods, or selling theories, fall into three categories: stimulus-response, formula, and needs-satisfaction. Variations on these models depend on such factors as the length of the selling cycle (for instance, the number of sales calls, over a period of weeks or months, required to close the sale), the complexity and technical quality of the product or service, the price of the product or service, and the philosophy of the company toward sales training.

Although each of the three selling theory models will be examined, we will focus on the needs-satisfaction model because it is the basis of the consultative selling process. It is from the consultative selling model that the relational process advanced in this textbook has evolved.

Stimulus-Response Model

Stimulus response has been defined as "any energy or energy change in the physical environment that excites a sense organ."[1] Perhaps a more appropriate application of stimulus to this selling theory is Webster's definition, which describes it as "something that arouses or incites to action or increased action."[2] In any event, stimulus is associated with activating, exciting, or arousing a person to action.

As applied to a selling system, the stimulus-response method signifies that when salespeople concentrate on what to say to their prospects, they will raise a series of points (stimuli) that evoke a favorable action from the prospect. This is typically referred to as a "canned" or memorized sales pitch, in which salespeople are instructed to follow a prepared dialogue. Canned sales pitches are usually associated with high-pressure, forceful, and domineering salespeople. Companies that use this method as a selling model generally use boiler-room telemarketing techniques; their product or service involves a simple decision-making process; and their selling cycle is brief, usually one or two sales calls per prospect. In addition, they typically rely on large numbers of sales calls and play a percentage game for response patterns (for example, 100 calls per day may produce ten leads and close one sale).

As is true with all sales models, there are advantages and disadvantages to the stimulus-response model. Three main advantages are evident: the salesperson has a standardized procedure to follow; the method substantially reduces training time; and little investment is required in the selection, training, and development of salespeople. Frequently described disadvantages of this model are that it treats all customers alike, with no regard for individual differences; there is little or no regard for the customer's viewpoint because the salesperson dominates the interview with a canned pitch; and the model typically depends on closed and leading questions to force the prospect into saying "yes" or "no" (for example, "You do want to save money, don't you?" or "You don't want to miss an opportunity that could mean guaranteed lifetime protection for your family, do you?"). In addition, there is little or no interest in developing a long-term relationship with the customer, and that lack of interest often results in little or no repeat business.

A consequence of using this model is that the career cycle of the sales representative is usually brief, resulting in a high turnover rate among the sales force. The standardized sales pitch prevents the development of an individualized selling style and limits the potential for change and flexibility. Finally, the presentation is sales-driven rather than relationship-driven.

Formula Model

The formula model is a structured or ordered plan for achieving a buying decision. In this model, the salesperson assumes that the customer will follow a systematic process in making the purchasing decision. A popular example of the formula theory is the AIDA selling model, in which the salesperson is trained to capture the prospect's *Attention*, create *Interest*, stimulate *Desire*, and obtain *Action*. The salesperson uses this formula approach as a series of steps to help the prospect reach a buying decision.

The advantages of this model are that it is not complex and can be easily adapted to either consumer or industrial products and services. The disadvantages of using the formula or AIDA model are that the presentation is sales-driven rather than relationship-driven and, as with the stimulus-response model, it tends to encourage the use of gimmicks, canned phrases, and cheap marketing tricks.[3] For example, an insurance salesperson might use this approach to gain the prospect's attention: "Ms. Smith, you will be pleased to know that *my policy will be a real benefit to you* [*canned*]. And I want to assure you that *you are under no obligation to buy* [*canned*]. In fact, *my call will take only a few minutes of your time* [*canned*]." If the buyer hesitates, the salesperson may use a *feel-felt-found* canned response to manage resistance: "I understand how you *feel*, Ms. Smith. Many of my customers *felt* the same way until they had a death in the family, and then they *found* that they couldn't have managed without this policy."

That same insurance salesperson, when meeting resistance, may use a gimmick, such as asking the prospect to step outside and look back in through the window at the family sitting around the table: "Can you imagine what it would be like for them not having you here when they need you?" The formula approach frequently uses prospects' emotions to manipulate them into making a buying decision.

Needs-Satisfaction Model

This consultative approach to personal selling was identified as early as 1925 by psychologist Edward K. Strong, who advanced the needs- or wants-satisfaction approach as a theory of selling.[4] The needs-satisfaction model stresses the importance of finding appeals or selling points by analyzing the product and relating the selling points to the prospect's needs, resulting in customer satisfaction. To use the needs-satisfaction concept of selling, the salesperson must fully understand the customer's point of view. The needs of the customer must be kept in focus.

The needs-satisfaction theory of selling was developed largely to explain the reaction of the consumer. It was concerned mainly with selling consumer goods such as automobiles, insurance, and products sold door to door. Strong published this theory to describe the kind of selling that existed in 1925. While it did recognize the customer as a significant participant in the selling process, it still treated all people alike.[5]

While this needs-satisfaction model is an elementary approach to needs analysis, it has provided a springboard for the development of the consultative model. Today's consultative salespeople hold the view that sales is a *buying* process in which both buyer and seller are *equal* participants. The types of purchases made by most industries and businesses today call for problem-solving and decision-making processes in which the salesperson acts as a facilitator to help the prospect reach a buying decision.

The type of sales model needed to accomplish this is customer- or relationship-driven, rather than product- or sales-driven, and is explained by the expansion of the needs-satisfaction model into the consultative model. Marketing-oriented firms use this selling theory almost exclusively. It is particularly appropriate for buying situations in which subtle differences exist among the customers in a target market.

Some of the advantages of the needs-satisfaction theory are:

- It provides a vehicle whereby the problem-solving process becomes a mutual exchange of ideas and solutions.
- The sales presentation outline is built around spontaneity and dialogue, rather than canned pitches and monologues.
- Probing with open questions is encouraged to determine each prospect's needs, so no two prospects are treated alike.
- Each prospect is considered unique, and the salesperson's goal is to discover each customer's uniqueness and tailor the presentation and recommendations to fit that customer's needs.
- Sales training is extensive and ongoing.
- The goal of the salesperson is to develop rapport and a long-term relationship with the customer.

Sales Professional Spotlight

Mark Sutton, a branch sales manager representing Ricoh products, emphasizes that experience from being in many selling situations is a prerequisite for a successful career in sales. He maintains that every company needs a strong sales force and that the potential for earnings is endless in the field of sales, especially when representing a company with an outstanding reputation and a high-quality line of products. Ricoh is the number one company in office machine sales in Japan.

Mark worked for several companies that sell copiers and other office machines before he joined Ricoh. His progress has been rapid with Ricoh ever since he accepted his first position as a sales representative; he was promoted from that position to account executive, then to vertical market representative, and finally to his current position as branch sales manager.

Mark describes his present assignment managing a sales force as encompassing much more than simply managing and training. Working with each salesperson to prepare for sales presentations is a vital and crucial requirement in the sales process. "A sales representative must prepare both mentally and physically," he says.

"Being in a positive state of mind is essential to being successful in selling situations," he says. He comments on having a positive attitude, much like a professional athlete preparing for a game against a competitor. This must be accomplished on a daily basis. He further recommends being around other positive-energy people as helpful in acquiring the right attitude when preparing for a presentation.

According to Mark, preparing also consists of having the proper information and proof in writing. "An effective salesperson must always be prepared to validate selling points and be capable of substantiating all claims. For each presentation, acquiring extensive knowledge and understanding of customers' needs and limits is essential." Mark observes that not all market segments buy in the same fashion. "Small companies purchase smaller items but spend more time shopping and comparing. These buyers tend to be less informed and work more tightly within budget constraints. On the other hand, the big companies often buy in line with their particular needs and interests," he states.

Mark strongly supports the importance of gaining a relationship with the customer because most purchasing decisions are emotional, although the buyer may justify the decision logically. "The relationship with my customer must undoubtedly be a strong one. Customers must be able to rely on me as their copier professional. Overall, their trust, respect, and confidence in me are most important in building strong, lasting relationships," he says.

- The buying process is relaxed and nonthreatening, and the customer is an equal participant in the exchange process.
- Personal rewards are great and the growth process may continue over an entire career cycle. Thus, turnover is low because the salesperson has the opportunity to grow and develop.

The next three sections will provide a framework for using the needs-satisfaction theory to build a relational selling presentation, which is described in Chapter 2 as an extension of the consultative selling process. Table 12.1 reviews the development of a relational presentation model.

Managing the Interaction

A relationship-oriented selling philosophy is fundamental to the relational selling process. Table 12.2 provides a checklist for reexamining the four

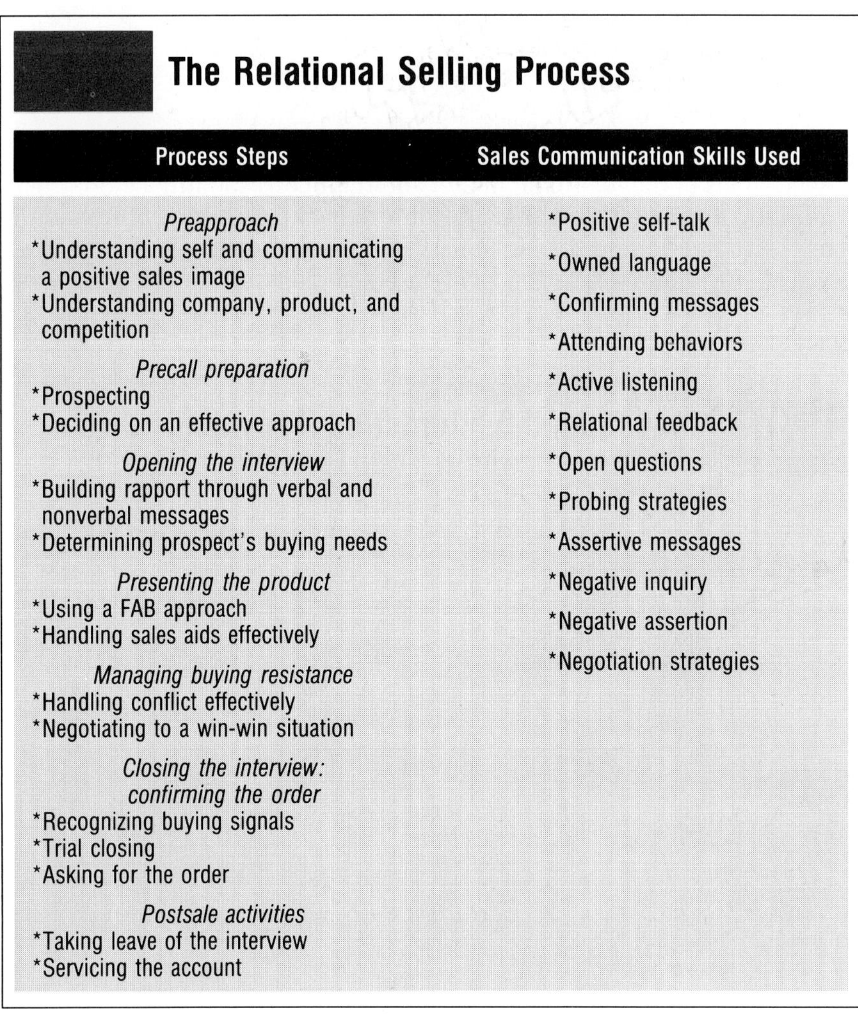

Table 12.1

The Relational Selling Process

Process Steps	Sales Communication Skills Used
Preapproach *Understanding self and communicating a positive sales image *Understanding company, product, and competition	*Positive self-talk *Owned language *Confirming messages *Attending behaviors
Precall preparation *Prospecting *Deciding on an effective approach	*Active listening *Relational feedback
Opening the interview *Building rapport through verbal and nonverbal messages *Determining prospect's buying needs	*Open questions *Probing strategies *Assertive messages
Presenting the product *Using a FAB approach *Handling sales aids effectively	*Negative inquiry *Negative assertion *Negotiation strategies
Managing buying resistance *Handling conflict effectively *Negotiating to a win-win situation	
Closing the interview: confirming the order *Recognizing buying signals *Trial closing *Asking for the order	
Postsale activities *Taking leave of the interview *Servicing the account	

Table 12.2

Relational Selling Philosophy—A Review

Strategy	Philosophy
*Personal selling philosophy	☐ Marketing-oriented ☐ Positive sales image ☐ Relationship-driven
*Customer-driven philosophy	☐ Who is the prospect? ☐ How does the customer buy? ☐ How can the customer be reached?
*Strategic product philosophy	☐ Competitive differential advantage analysis ☐ Features-advantages-benefits analysis ☐ Benefit presentation emphasis
*Relationship-driven philosophy	☐ Mutual exchange process ☐ Maintaining a positive buying climate ☐ Win-win attitude

strategic areas of the relational model and their corresponding guidelines. In addition to reviewing the philosophy checklist, salespeople should focus their attention on the four phases of managing the sales interaction described in Figure 12.1. The next three sections are devoted to these

Figure 12.1

Managing the Interaction (Providing Information about Your Product or Service)

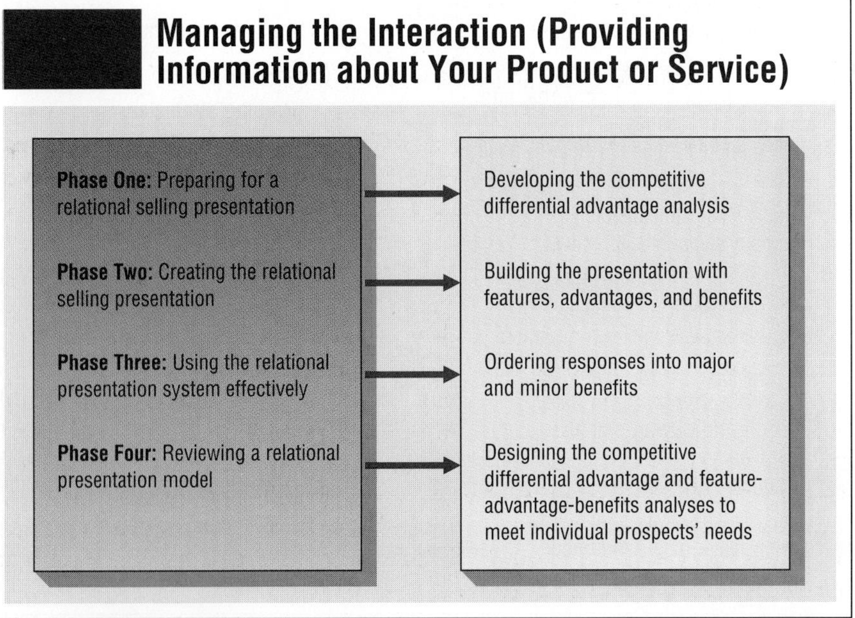

Phase One: Preparing for a relational selling presentation
Developing the competitive differential advantage analysis
Phase Two: Creating the relational selling presentation
Building the presentation with features, advantages, and benefits
Phase Three: Using the relational presentation system effectively
Ordering responses into major and minor benefits
Phase Four: Reviewing a relational presentation model
Designing the competitive differential advantage and feature-advantage-benefits analyses to meet individual prospects' needs

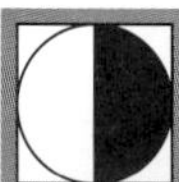

On the Ethical Side Soliciting Valuable Information

After the salesperson has determined what information is needed to prepare for a sales presentation, the next step is to find it. Valuable information might include such materials as the setting of specifications, bid solicitation, supplier selection, and rules governing the behavior of decision makers (for example, with regard to free lunches and gifts). Further insights might include information about competitors the prospect has previously purchased from.

Salespeople should not ignore influential members of a prospective organization. Salespeople who want to become acquainted with the purchasing procedures used by the prospective buyer might make headway by first learning who the influential people in the purchase decision are. Sometimes, cultivating friendly relations and using the "personal touch" with influential people may prove valuable.

Other valuable sources are salespeople or even competitors who may have failed to sell to the prospect. Secretaries or receptionists may also have helpful hints. The salesperson's attitude and approach should be demonstrated carefully and sincerely; information of a confidential nature should never be requested or divulged.

Preparation for a sales call is usually enhanced by learning as much as possible about the organization and the practices of a prospect or an industry. However, is using the "personal touch" approach with influential and insightful people to gain valuable information considered ethical?

four relational selling phases: planning, creating, using, and reviewing the relational presentation model.

Gathering Precall Information

Planning a sales call or interview includes gathering information about the prospect or customer, analyzing this information to establish objectives for the call, and outlining a presentation that will fit the prescribed objectives. As we have discussed, planning is the most critical element in preparing for the sales interview. Often the difference between making and not making the sale is the quality and quantity of background research done by the salesperson *before* making the visit.

Precisely how much information is appropriate to collect on a customer and the customer's organization varies. One guideline would be to weigh the costs involved in collecting information. A cost-benefit analysis can be performed to determine at what point the time and effort involved in gathering information outweigh the benefits derived. Table 12.3 provides a presentation checklist that a salesperson can use in the planning process, and Table 12.4 is a sales call analysis form to help structure the planning process.

Table 12.3

Presentation Checklist

Listed below are six areas of sales presentation planning suitable for industrial, consumer, and service salespeople.

1. **Review Account Profile**
   (Review Chapter 6 on prospecting)

2. **Review Customer's Product/Service Line**
   - What are the products/services?
   - What is the quality of products/services?
   - What manufacturing processes are used?
   - What are the applications/uses of the product?

3. **Review the Customer's Market Situation**
   - Who are the competitors?
   - How do they share this business?
   - What new products are being developed?

4. **Review Sales Situation**
   - What is the immediate problem?
   - How will my product or service overcome this problem?
   - Do I know the customer's agenda, so that I can help him reach his goals?
   - Have I thought of all the possible resistance that the customer may raise, and set my strategies to overcome them?
   - What has gone on before?
   - Where does the project now stand?
   - What did we agree to do in the interim?
   - Has it been done? If not, why not?
   - What has to be done now?
   - Do I have a simple and logical sales plan?
   - Is there an unusual approach that I can make here?
   - What do I have to do now to increase my business here?

5. **Personal**
   - Is my appearance in good taste?
   - Do I have an appointment?
   - Am I on time?
   - Am I in the proper frame of mind?
   - Do I have a positive sales image?

6. **Materials**
   - Do I have a complete sample line?
   - Do I have sales literature and catalogs?
   - Do I have graphics or photos showing the application of our product?
   - Do I have the necessary agreements and paperwork?

Developing the Competitive Differential Advantage Analysis

In Chapter 2 sales competence is described as a function of knowledge and skills. Chapter 5 provides guidelines that can help salespeople

Table 12.4

Sales Call Preparation

The form below is designed to help the salesperson monitor the sales call activities—before, during, and after.

Sales Call Analysis

Salesperson ____________ Date ____________

Name: ____________
Title: ____________
Company: ____________
Division: ____________
City: ____________
State/Zip: ____________
Telephone: ____________

Activity:
☐ Telephone
☐ Meeting
☐ Other

If New Contact: (Source)
☐ Cold Call
☐ Ad Lead
☐ Customer Request
☐ Referral

Meeting Information:

Objective: | People Present at Meeting:

Needs Expressed: | Benefits Accepted:

Resistance/Answers: | Outcome Action Planned:

Action items:
☐ Telephone ☐ Letter ☐ Sales Call

Comments:

understand their company, product, and competition; and Chapter 6 provides direction for qualifying and understanding prospects. This section is geared toward assisting salespeople in taking an in-depth look at their products, firm, and competition so that they can reach the level of confidence (knowledge) that will free them to develop the communication skills needed to reach sales competence. The vehicle through which they may acquire this knowledge is a competitive differential advantage (CDA) analysis. A CDA analysis is an analytical tool for researching a salesperson's company and the competition at four levels, to determine where the salesperson's company is superior and where the competition may have the competitive edge. These four levels involve product, source, people, and service. Figure 12.2 identifies the categories of information that may be collected for each level. Exhibit 12.1 (at the end of this chapter) illustrates how a salesperson for a company that makes office and reprographic equipment might complete a CDA analysis for a copy machine. Note that each category would be expanded as the complexity of the product or service increases.

1. *Product*—The product level applies to all tangible and intangible goods, as well as services. It includes such characteristics as composition, structure, and function. Specific categories may

Figure 12.2

Competitive Differential Advantage (CDA) Analysis

Product

1. Versatility
2. Efficiency
3. Storage
4. Handling
5. Appearance
6. Design
7. Mobility
8. Packaging
9. Life expectancy
10. Adaptability

Service

1. Delivery
2. Inventory
3. Credit
4. Training
5. Merchandising
6. Installation
7. Advertising
8. Financial
9. Maintenance
10. Guarantees

Source

1. Time established
2. Industry standing
3. Marketplace reputation
4. Community image
5. Location
6. Labor relations
7. Size
8. Source of supplies
9. Financial soundness
10. Policies and practices

People

1. Personal knowledge and skill
2. Knowledge and skill of support personnel
3. Integrity and character
4. Availability for emergencies
5. Sophistication on the prospect's industry
6. Standing in the community
7. Flexibility of call schedule
8. Mutual friends
9. Interpersonal skills
10. Cooperation

include versatility, efficiency, storage, handling, appearance, design, mobility, packaging, life expectancy, and adaptability.

2. *Source*—Source is a continuation of the product description and includes such areas as time established, industry standing, marketplace reputation, community image, location, labor relations, size, source of supplies, financial soundness, and policies and practices.
3. *People*—Because of the intense competition between business and industry and because of the multitude of "me-too" products on the market today, it may be that the *only* category in which one has the competitive differential advantage is the area of people. Sales representatives, support and service personnel, and the company's image and reputation for excellence are included in this area. More specifically, this category includes the salesperson's knowledge and skill; the knowledge and skill of support personnel; integrity and character; availability for emergencies; how the salesperson's organization is perceived in the marketplace, especially in terms of a prospect's industry; standing in the community; flexibility of call schedule; association with others in the industry; interpersonal skills; and cooperation.
4. *Service*—Service includes all activities that provide customers with appropriate and effective use of the product or service. Such activities may include delivery, inventory, credit, training, merchandising, installation, advertising, price, maintenance, and guarantees.

When examining the 40 areas listed in the CDA analysis in Figure 12.2, it is critical to salespeople's pursuit of sales competence that they identify each item in specific, factual terms. "Good," "excellent," "great," or "superior" are evaluative terms that have no meaning to the customer unless they are supported with features in specific, operational terms. A salesperson who has completed a CDA analysis will be ready for the next phase of managing the interaction by transferring the facts and features onto a FAB analysis. Preparing this form is the focus of the next section.

Building the Presentation with the FAB Approach

> To be able to answer the customer's universally implied question, "What will it do for me?" you don't have to know much about how a product is designed, manufactured, or developed. What salespeople must know is what it has done for other customers. That's the product knowledge that sells.[6]

As long ago as 1972, V. R. Buzzota and Robert E. Lefton, clinical psychologists and consultants to business and industry, subscribed to the notion that consumers were motivated to make buying decisions based on more than just features or facts about the product. In the book they coauthored with Manuel Sherberg, *Effective Selling through Psychology:*

Try This 12.1 Preparing a Competitive Differential Advantage (CDA) Analysis

Product	Your Co.	Competition	*Service*	Your Co.	Competition
Versatility			Delivery		
Efficiency			Inventory		
Storage			Credit		
Handling			Training		
Appearance			Merchandising		
Design			Installation		
Mobility			Advertising		
Packaging			Financial		
Life expectancy			Maintenance		
Adaptability			Guarantees		
Source			*People*		
Time established			Personal knowledge and skill		
Industry standing			Knowledge and skill of support personnel		
Marketplace reputation			Integrity and character		
Community image			Availability for emergencies		
Location			Perception in the prospect's industry		
Labor relations			Standing in the community		
Size			Flexibility of call schedule		
Source of supplies			Mutual friends		
Financial soundness			Interpersonal skills		
Policies and practices			Cooperation		

Using the categories described under each of the levels above, select a product or service with which you are familiar and prepare a CDA analysis for your company and its principal competitor.

Dimensional Sales and Sales Management Strategies, they suggest that to be effective, a salesperson must present the product or service in three dimensions: features, advantages, and benefits. They defined these terms as follows:

- Feature—a *property* or *attribute* of the product or service (facts)
- Advantage—what the features *does;* describes the *purpose* or *function* of a feature (performance characteristics)
- Benefit—the value or worth that the user derives from a product or service (satisfaction derived)[7]

From these definitions, they built a foundation from which has evolved the present emphasis on benefits, as used in the consultative process. More specifically, Buzzota, Lefton, and Sherberg state:

> While a feature describes the product itself, and an advantage tells what the feature does, a benefit relates all of this to the *user*. Unless features and advantages have been related to the *user* and his needs, no benefit has been shown. This correlation, this connecting of features and advantages to the user's *needs*, is the critical *link* that many salesmen fail to make. They stop short of this point. Because they do, they are unable to take the next step and demonstrate net gain,* thereby giving the customer a *reason to buy*.[8]

In this section, the focus moves beyond the concept of feature-advantage selling to another level called the benefit, which salespeople use in relational selling, the core of the feature relationship process.

Feature

As described in Chapter 11, and as it is applied in this selling system, a feature is a fact about the product or service. It is a characteristic or trait that is an integral part of the product or service. Features tell something about the product or service itself. In the CDA analysis illustrated in Exhibit 12.1, every point is a feature of the product, source, people, or service area. For example, a feature of our copy machine is that it has versatile paper sizes—from $5\frac{1}{2}$ inches × $8\frac{1}{2}$ inches to 11 inches × 17 inches.

Advantage

An advantage is the performance characteristic that is derived from a particular feature or fact. An advantage describes the value or worth (which is usually measurable) that the customer will receive from each feature. For example, in the illustration of our copy machine's feature of versatile paper size, the advantages of this feature are faster production (up 14 percent) and reduced waste (down 9 percent).

Benefit

A benefit is the satisfaction derived or the emotional and rational responses that a buyer may have to the advantage that is realized as a result of the feature. The benefit is the motivator, on a conscious or subconscious level, that stimulates the customer into making a buying decision. To continue with the example of the copy machine, benefits of the feature of versatile paper size are saving money and greater efficiency.

**Net gain* refers to the extent to which a product or service not only will do something for the customer, but will do something that is not now being done or will do it better.

Using Benefits Effectively

Most salespeople are naturally inclined to emphasize features, especially after completing product training or seminars where a new product has been introduced. This method has worked successfully for years. In the relational process, however, where the emphasis is on the customer, an effective alternative is to reverse the procedure and talk about the benefit first. The three dimensions can be linked in this way:

Feature	*Advantage*	*Benefit*
Versatile paper sizes from $5\frac{1}{2} \times 8\frac{1}{2}$ inches to 11×17 inches	Speeds up production and reduces waste	Saves money and offers greater efficiency

Using the same copy machine example, a salesperson might say:

"Ms. Lee, at the end of just one day you'll appreciate the (1) improved efficiency of your duplicating procedures that resulted in (2) reducing waste because you now have (3) versatile paper sizes that you didn't have before."

The shift from talking about features first to discussing benefits first puts the emphasis on the customer and focuses the customer's thinking and feeling at the motivational level. The customer begins to take psychological possession of the product or service when imagining how it will fill that rational and emotional need. Exhibit 12.2 (at the end of this chapter) illustrates a completed FAB analysis based on the information described for your company in the CDA analysis.

Guidelines for Using the Relational Selling Model

Ordering Responses into Major and Minor Buying Points

The salesperson must be able to select information that is important and appropriate for each prospect and then translate that information into major and minor buying points. Major and minor buying points may surface under any or all of the six buying decision categories.

Try This 12.2 Preparing a FAB Analysis

Features (Facts)	Advantages (Performance Characteristics)	Benefits (Satisfaction Derived)

1. Using the information from the CDA analysis (Exhibit 12.1), prepare a FAB analysis following the above format.
2. Select a partner to play the role of the customer. Practice the benefits-advantages-features sequence using the communication skills you have learned so far.

A *major buying point* is a reason for buying that the salesperson perceives to be among the prospect's most important concerns. For one person major buying motives may be economy and efficiency while another prospect may value comfort and image. In any event, major buying motives become the focus of the presentation and are introduced as initial statements to address the customer's reasons for buying.

A *minor buying point* is a reason for buying that a salesperson perceives to be of secondary importance to the prospect. Minor buying points help the prospect make decisions on less significant concerns that eventually lead to the final buying decision. Salespeople may gain commitment on a minor point as they discuss major benefits.

There are five steps involved in using this relational sales presentation format:

1. Preparing a CDA analysis
2. Transferring information from the CDA analysis to a FAB analysis form
3. Using open-ended questions, probing strategies, and active listening to ascertain the prospect's rational and emotional reasons for buying
4. Noting whether the prospect's responses identify major or minor buying points
5. Focusing on major buying points in the presentation while using minor buying points to help the prospect make decisions on lesser concerns

The Skill Builder for this chapter is a schematic drawing of the process. The dialogue that follows the outline demonstrates how a salesperson analyzes the prospect's conversation to determine which buying points are major and which are minor for that specific customer. Notice that the salesperson uses questioning, probing, and active listening skills.

Using Persuasive Communication

Building and maintaining a positive buying climate is a prerequisite for developing a persuasive presentation. Persuasion is the process of attempting to bring about changes in the prospect's beliefs, attitudes, or behavior that lead to a favorable buying decision. The relational selling system is a natural setting for persuasiveness because it makes use of assertive communication skills and behaviors.

There are three basic styles of communication behavior: assertiveness, nonassertiveness, and aggression. For the salesperson, *assertiveness* is the ability to share the entire range of one's thoughts and emotions with confidence and skill.[9] An assertive style is revealed when salespeople:

- Allow customers to finish their thoughts before speaking
- Stand up for the position that matches their feelings or evidence
- Make their own decisions and recommendations based on what they think is right

Skill Builder 12.1 The Relational Sales Presentation Format

Sample FAB Analysis for RAD Tires, Inc.

Features (Facts)	Advantages (Performance Characteristics)	Benefits (Satisfaction Derived—Emotional/Rational Reason)	Major (1) or Minor (2) Buying Point	
			Customer A (Flanigan)	*Customer B (Wellington)*
More rubber-to-the-road contact	Better handling and improved cornering	Safety, thrill of speed	1	
Radial	Smoother ride and increased gas mileage	Pleasure, comfort, economy	1	
Raised white letters	Cosmetically appealing	Pride, ego	2	
Four ply	Thicker rubber	Reliability, safety	1	
Used by winning race car drivers	Testimonial of performance	Status, image	2	
Lifetime warranty	Company backed	Dependability, peace of mind	1	
White or black wall	Cosmetic options	Pride, esteem	2	
Steel belted	Virtually puncture-proof	Safety, dependability, economy	1	

Sample Sales Presentation Based on FAB Analysis of Major and Minor Buying Points
S = Salesperson, P = Prospect

S: Good morning and welcome to RAD Tires. My name is John. What's yours?

P. I'm Ann Flanigan.

S: I see that you're looking at our new F2000. What kind of car are you driving?

P: Yes, I am. Oh, I'm driving a 1989 Ford mini-van that is desperately in need of a set of tires.

S: How many miles do you have on your car, Mrs. Flanigan [looking at her wedding band]?

P: Around 100,000, and we want to keep it for hopefully another 50,000 miles.

S: I heard you say "we." Who drives your van besides you?

P: Well, I shudder to say that my son, Alfred, who is 17, also drives it. But that's not all. Betty is almost 16 and Freddie is 14, so that poor ol' car really takes a beating.

S: I can imagine, Mrs. Flanigan. What kind of driving do you do? Freeway? Surface streets?

P: I spend *hours* on both—plus we use it for the mountains and frequently pull

Continued

our boat to the river. I'm afraid to ask my son where he drives. [She shakes her head from side to side.]

S: What price range do you have in mind?

P: I'm not sure. My husband sent me here and suggested that we invest in something that would last the life of the car, so here I am.

At this point, based on Mrs. Flanigan's responses, the salesperson can order the selling points into major and minor buying motives. See the FAB schematic under Customer A.

Now follow the dialogue as the salesperson presents the F2000 model:

S: Mrs. Flanigan, early in our conversation I recall hearing you say that your 17-year-old son, Alfred, drives your minivan. Is that right?

P: I'm afraid so.

S: Then you'll feel some *safety* [benefit] in knowing that he'll have *better handling* [advantage] at the wheel because the F2000 has *more rubber-to-the-road contact* [feature]. [*major buying point*]

P: Well, that's encouraging.

S: I also recall hearing you say that you spend hours behind the wheel and I'm suggesting that you deserve to pamper yourself. You'll find increased *comfort* [benefit] from the *smoother ride* [advantage] that you'll experience riding on a *radial* [feature]. [*major buying point*] And, incidentally, would you prefer the black or white wall [feature], Mrs. Flanigan? [*minor buying point*]

P: Oh, I don't care. I'll take the black.

S: And would you like four or five tires? [*minor buying point*]

P: I'm not sure. When you check the size, look at the spare and see if we can salvage a tire to use as the spare.

S: Fine. Then may I rack your car?

P: Well, not just yet. I'm not absolutely sure that the one you're describing will last as long as we hope the car will.

S: That's a good point. I failed to mention that you'll have *confidence* [benefit] in knowing that RAD Tires takes pride in its *company-backed* [advantage] *lifetime-warranty* [feature], and the F2000 carries a 50,000 mile warranty. [*major buying point*]

And so the dialogue continues with the salesperson working major and minor benefits together until Mrs. Flanigan has made her final buying decision.

For Practice:

1. Have a classmate or associate play the role of Customer B, Mr. Wellington. Using the same information provided in the first FAB analysis, probe to determine his buying needs. Construct your open questions around the six buying-decision categories of need, product, price, service, timing, and company.
2. When you feel you have gathered enough information from Mr. Wellington to select a particular model for his car, stop and rank your perception of his responses into major (1) and minor (2) buying points.
3. Next, discuss the tires with Mr. Wellington, using the FAB relational format. Be sure to talk from "right to left," from benefit to advantage to feature.
4. Remember to use the communication skills we have covered so far: confirming messages, active listening, questioning, probing, and giving relational feedback.

- Consider the customer relationship as an opportunity to learn more about themselves
- Enter into conversations spontaneously and naturally using moderate volume and tone of voice
- Try to understand the customer's feelings before describing their own
- Try to avoid harm and inconvenience by discussing problems with the customer before they occur, or finding a rational means for coping with unavoidable harm or inconvenience
- Face problems and decisions squarely
- Consider themselves strong and capable but generally equal to most of their customers
- Act responsibly with respect to their situation, needs, and rights[10]

Nonassertive behavior is found at the extreme end of the assertiveness continuum and is defined as "the inability or unwillingness to express thoughts or feelings when necessary."[11] This behavior may result from a lack of confidence or not knowing how to express oneself more directly. Nonassertive people usually avoid conflicts and would rather leave things as they are than face a problem directly and try to solve it. This type of behavior can prove disastrous for the salesperson. The continual frustration and loss of self-respect that accompany nonassertiveness in salespeople may damage rather than enhance the relationship process.

Aggressive behavior is essentially the complete opposite of the nonassertive style. Aggressive people often try to accomplish their goals at the expense of others. These mannerisms usually reveal aggression in salespeople:

- Interrupting while the customer is speaking
- Trying to impose a position on the customer
- Using and abusing the relationship
- Speaking loudly and otherwise calling attention to themselves
- Blaming, accusing, and finding fault with others without regard for their feelings
- Distorting the facts or misrepresenting the truth to get their solutions accepted quickly (for instance, forcing the buying decision)[12]

Assertiveness is a key ingredient of a persuasive sales presentation. Assertive salespeople communicate in an open, direct, honest, and appropriate manner. When the communication skills presented in this text are used in a competent manner, then persuasion is not seen as coercion from the buyer's perspective. Instead, persuasion stresses the satisfaction that a buyer will receive as a result of the purchase.

Using a Persuasive Vocabulary

As pointed out in Chapter 10, the body communicates about 65 percent of the total social meaning of a message, and the words used transmit the

Try This 12.3 Communication Styles

1. Develop a brief description of a product or service.
2. Using the same verbal description, explain the product or service to a partner in a manner that is:
   a. Assertive
   b. Nonassertive
   c. Aggressive
3. Discuss what changes occur with each explanation.

remaining 35 percent. Furthermore, only 7 percent of the emotional impact of a message is communicated by the words spoken. Thus, it is important that salespeople use a vocabulary that has impact and meaning. The Dartnell Corporation, a widely known organization that produces sales training literature and programs, provides a list of "power words" that exert a special influence on the customer (Figure 12.3).

The Dirty Dozen: Management's Suggestions about Presentations

1. No excuses—give me action!
2. Don't tell me what I already know—tell me what I don't know and need to know.
3. Whatever the form—make it short and to the point.
4. Don't waste my time—be prepared and organized.
5. Give me information in a presentable form so that I can pass it along "as is" to others and don't have to spend my time doing it over.
6. Don't brag how smart you are.
7. Tell me how I'll benefit from this presentation—tell me what's in it for me, not just what's in it for you.
8. Let me know that you're keeping on top of things.
9. Let some of your personal qualities come out—be natural.
10. Don't bore me with facts and statistics—hold my interest.
11. Keep me aware of the action on a regular basis.
12. Show me you can handle the assignment.[13]

A Sample Relational Sales Dialogue

Kellogg West Center for Continuing Education is located on the campus of California State Polytechnic University in Pomona. Besides serving as a training facility for a nationally recognized hotel, restaurant, and travel management program, Kellogg West is also available to the public as a conference center with food service and lodging. It has 87

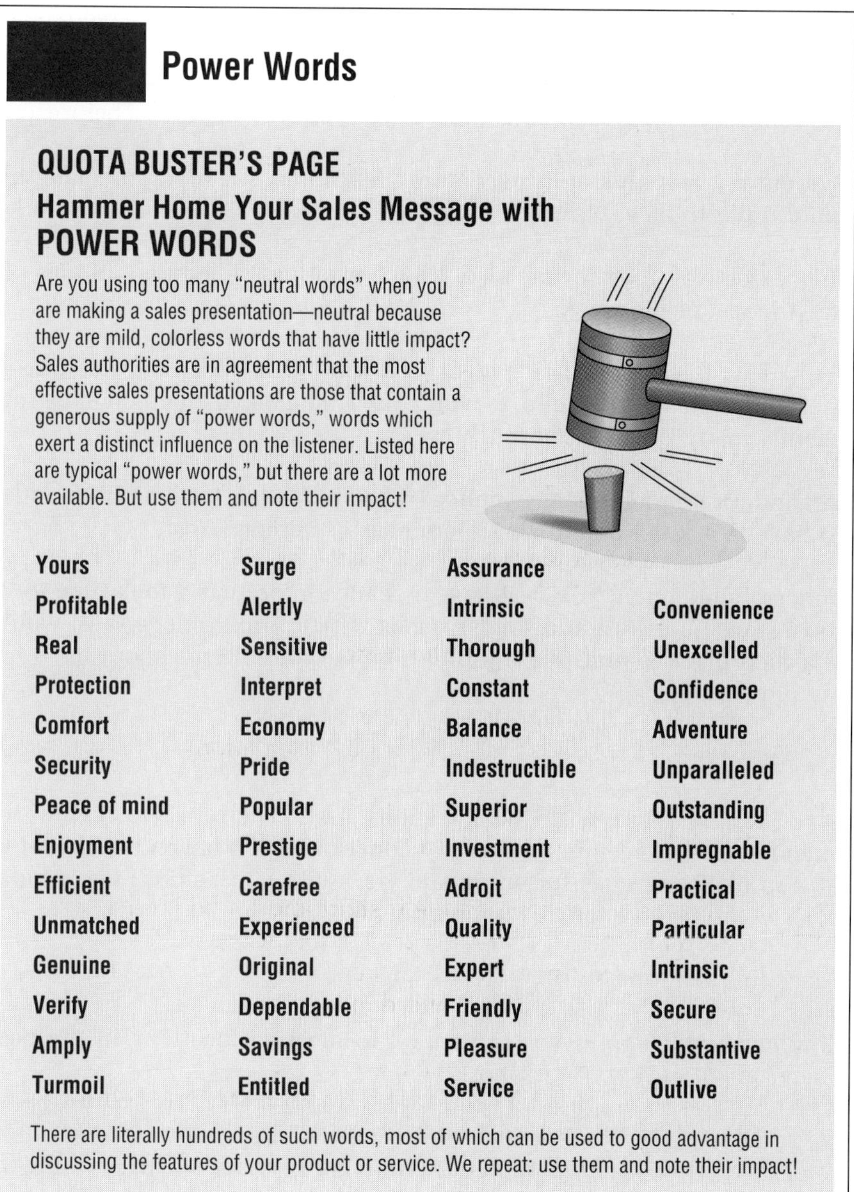

Power Words

QUOTA BUSTER'S PAGE

Hammer Home Your Sales Message with POWER WORDS

Are you using too many "neutral words" when you are making a sales presentation—neutral because they are mild, colorless words that have little impact? Sales authorities are in agreement that the most effective sales presentations are those that contain a generous supply of "power words," words which exert a distinct influence on the listener. Listed here are typical "power words," but there are a lot more available. But use them and note their impact!

Yours	**Surge**	**Assurance**	
Profitable	**Alertly**	**Intrinsic**	**Convenience**
Real	**Sensitive**	**Thorough**	**Unexcelled**
Protection	**Interpret**	**Constant**	**Confidence**
Comfort	**Economy**	**Balance**	**Adventure**
Security	**Pride**	**Indestructible**	**Unparalleled**
Peace of mind	**Popular**	**Superior**	**Outstanding**
Enjoyment	**Prestige**	**Investment**	**Impregnable**
Efficient	**Carefree**	**Adroit**	**Practical**
Unmatched	**Experienced**	**Quality**	**Particular**
Genuine	**Original**	**Expert**	**Intrinsic**
Verify	**Dependable**	**Friendly**	**Secure**
Amply	**Savings**	**Pleasure**	**Substantive**
Turmoil	**Entitled**	**Service**	**Outlive**

There are literally hundreds of such words, most of which can be used to good advantage in discussing the features of your product or service. We repeat: use them and note their impact!

Figure 12.3

rooms, 43 of which are guest rooms. Meeting capacity at the conference center ranges from ten people to a maximum of 300.

Donna Dannon, acting as events coordinator, recorded the following interview that she had with Tracy Fong, a meeting planner for Southern Dynamics, an aerospace firm headquartered in the Los Angeles area.

Donna: Good morning, Ms. Fong. I'm Donna Dannon from Kellogg West [*extending hand and smiling*].

Tracy: Good morning, Donna, come in, and please call me Tracy.

Donna: Thank you. You have such an attractive [*compliment*] and large facility here. How many employees work here? [*level five*]

Tracy: Oh, about 2,500. It's easy to get lost if you haven't been here before.

Donna: I got out my map this morning before I left home. I really appreciate this opportunity to meet with you today.

Tracy: The timing was good for me also. I have meetings scheduled all day—in fact, the rest of the week.

Donna: Tracy, I've discovered that we have a mutual friend. Lori Rushing at Rockwell said to say hello to you. She and I have planned meetings together many times [*level four*].

Tracy: Lori and I were roommates in college. I haven't talked with her in months. I'll have to ask her about her experiences at Kellogg West.

Donna: I sincerely hope that you will have a chance to do that. I took time to jot down some questions and some reasons why I think Kellogg West would be a good place to hold the training seminar you told me about the other day [*level three*].

Tracy: Oh, you have?

Donna: Yes. Shall we start with the questions first? Then, as we review the benefits together, you can raise any concerns that I haven't anticipated. I'd also like to arrange for an on-site visit with you before I leave today [*sales call objective for this appointment*].

Tracy: That's fine with me.

Donna: How have your employees responded to meeting locations in the past, Tracy? [*open question: need*]

Tracy: We've always held our annual conferences and special events at major hotels and encouraged them to make it a family affair. We tried doing the same with training meetings, but many employees complained that they were distracted by the traffic, noise, and general commotion one finds in a large hotel.

Donna: Then having a quiet atmosphere in a relatively secluded area would have appeal? [*active listening*]

Tracy: Yes, I think it would. Our training seminars are intense and exhaustive [*free information*], so it's important that they have a chance to let off steam.

Donna: Specifically, what did you have in mind as activities for them to "let off steam"? [*probe: request for clarification and elaboration*]

Tracy: Well, a variety of things—everything from recreational facilities to the arts.

Donna: Then you'll be pleased to know that they'll be able to enjoy [*benefit*] our recreational facilities, which include a swimming pool, tennis club, full gym, golf course, track, and volleyball, racquetball, and handball courts. They can also unwind [*benefit*] over a game of croquet. For those who would rather rest quietly and be entertained [*benefits*], we offer horse shows, the theater, or convenient [*benefit*] in-room movies. [*level two*]

Tracy: That sounds more than adequate—in fact, very appealing!

Donna: Good. When you come on site for a visit, we'll add these areas to our tour. Would that be something you'd like to include? [*follow-up question*]

Tracy: Yes, it would, assuming that the use of those facilities fits within our budget.

Donna: Speaking of budget, Tracy, what type of budget are your conferees on? [*open question: price*]

Tracy: Hmmmm . . . I can't give you specific figures yet, except to say that they'll have a per diem or travel allowance.

Donna: I noticed that you paused. I wonder if you feel hesitant about whether flexibility can be achieved in budgeting for the upcoming training sessions [*active listening*].

Tracy: Only to the degree that it will fall under next fiscal year's training allocation, and that is being decided this month.

Donna: Well, then, I want to assure you that because Kellogg West is a conference center and not a commercial hotel, you'll experience considerable savings [*benefit*] in all your required services.

Tracy: You've mentioned services—how inclusive are they?

Donna: When we spoke over the phone last week, I recall your mentioning [*highlighting*] that you wanted available a fax machine, copier, camcorder, and monitor. I'm pleased to report that for your quick access [*benefit*] I have arranged to have them at the center during your sessions.

Of course, this interview has only begun. The salesperson would continue probing until buying motives have been uncovered and addressed under each of the buying-decision areas of need, product, price, service, company, and timing. Note that, as Donna responds to Tracy, she uses the FAB analysis by placing the benefit first when describing the facilities and what they have to offer. Also note that the list of communication skills reviewed in Table 12.1 are used spontaneously throughout the dialogue. Remember that sales competence is contingent upon using these skills effectively and appropriately.

Summary

Three major selling systems are currently in use: the stimulus-response model, the formula model, and the needs-satisfaction model. Each model has advantages and disadvantages, but the needs-satisfaction model is of particular interest to sales professionals committed to the customer- or relationship-driven approach because it is the forerunner of relational selling.

In the relational selling process, there are four phases for managing the sales interaction: planning, creating, using, and reviewing the relational presentation model. In the first of these, planning, the salesperson gathers information about the prospect, analyzes the information gathered to establish objectives for a sales call, and outlines a presentation to meet the objectives. Creating, within the context of this chapter, is the function by which the salesperson sets goals and objectives; the competitive differential advantage (CDA) is a useful analytical tool dealing with product, source, people, and service. The features-advantages-benefits (FAB) analysis is also an important tool in this regard. Using these functions (or phases) requires that the salesperson analyze responses of the prospect and categorize those responses as either major or minor buying points; major points are obviously important concerns of the prospect, while minor buying points are those of secondary importance. As the salesperson reviews these points, approaches to meet the prospect's needs are put in proper perspective, enabling the salesperson to enter into a proper relational situation with the prospect.

The basic steps involved in using the relational sales presentation format advocated in this chapter are: (1) preparing a CDA analysis; (2) transfering information from the CDA analysis to a FAB analysis form; (3) using open-ended questions, probing strategies, and active listening to ascertain the prospect's rational and emotional reasons for buying; (4) noting whether the prospect's responses are major or minor buying points to help the prospect make decisions about lesser concerns.

Assertive communication, or the ability to share the entire range of one's thoughts and emotions with confidence and skill, is a key part in persuasive selling. Learning to use the sales tools in this chapter, along with the communications skills presented in earlier chapters, can lead to the comfortable use of assertive communication in relational selling situations.

Exhibit 12.1

Competitive Differential Advantage Analysis

Item	Your Company	No. 1 Competitor
Product		
Versatility		
Paper size	$5\frac{1}{2}'' \times 8\frac{1}{2}''$ to $11'' \times 17''$	$5\frac{1}{2}'' \times 8\frac{1}{2}''$ to $10'' \times 14''$
Reduction capability	75% and 64%	Same
Two-sided copies	25% of copies can be two-sided	15% of copies can be two-sided
Copy ability	Copies onto anything that can go through machine (labels, etc.)	Same
Efficiency	Maximum of 30 copies per min., minimum of 11 copies per min.; 1–99 electronic display	Maximum of 40 copies per min., minimum of 10 copies per min.; 1–99 auto-countdown
Storage	60–90°F environment; (955)21.5W × 19.7D × 17H	Same; (SF-755) 17W × 16.5D × 10.25H
Handling	132–189 pounds	61.7 pounds
Electrical system	120v AC	Same
Appearance	Dark brown and ivory	Cocoa brown
Life expectancy	7-10 years	7 years
Adaptability	Tellurium-tested selenium drum picks up "blues"	Cannot pick up "blues"
	Automatic document feed and sorter add-ons	Same
Dependability	Straighter paper path keeps paper moving and minimizes chance of misfeeds and down time	Paper must make turns through the system
Paper capacity	250 sheets per cassette	Same
Toner system	Single-element dry toner	Same
Design	Flat motor drive eliminates chains, sprockets, clutches, and belts that require continual adjustment	Standard motor coupled with chains, belts, and pulleys that require adjustment
	Built-in dehumidifier	Same

Continued

Exhibit 12.2

FAB Analysis

Features (Facts)	Advantages (Performance Characteristics)	Benefits (Satisfaction Derived)
Product		
Versatile paper sizes—from $5\frac{1}{2}'' \times 8\frac{1}{2}''$ to $11'' \times 17''$	Speeds up production; no waste	Economy and efficiency
Reduction capabilities	Less paper use, gives professional appearance and provides necessary reduction for certain requirements	Saves money; pride
Produces double-sided copies	Saves paper use and makes project look more professional	Economy; a socially responsible company
Copies onto overhead transparencies and address labels	Saves time and money in making trips to professional printers	Economy, convenience, efficiency
Electronic display from 1 to 99	No dials to break and get dirty; for longer runs, no need to stay with machine—just set in number desired	Status, economy, trust, and efficiency
Speed of 20–50 copies per minute	Less employee time spent at copier	Economy and efficiency
Weighs 132–189 pounds	Will not be knocked off table accidentally—sturdy; difficult to carry off (theft reduction)	Security and peace of mind; trust
120v AC	No unusual wiring required	Economy, peace of mind, and safety
Source		
In business since 1884, in copy industry since 1957	Community and marketplace see A.B. Dick as a stable, dependable organization	Dependability, trust, confidence, and peace of mind
Over 1,000 copier service stations worldwide	Wherever you are, we are nearby	Security, assurance, and peace of mind

Exhibit 12.2
Continued

Features (Facts)	Advantages (Performance Characteristics)	Benefits (Satisfaction Derived)
Source		
Subsidiary of General Electric Co., London, England—73rd largest company outside the U.S., with sales of $7 billion per year	Strong financial base—won't disappear on you	Security, confidence, and longevity
Service		
No additional charge for delivery on small units	Reduces initial expenditure	Cost-in-use
Large on-hand inventory	Receive supplies and equipment immediately	Security and efficiency
Factory-trained technical support	Less equipment down time	Peace of mind and reliability
Key operators trained by sales representative	Employees are trained to use and fix equipment	Trust, confidence, peace of mind, and dependability
Purchase, lease, or rent equipment	Financial arrangements available to fit your budget	Affordable
Guarantee	90-day unconditional guarantee	Security, trust, and confidence
Each copier checked for optimal performance before delivery	Product testing and quality control	Peace of mind, security, trust, confidence, and dependability
Service call response is a maximum of 4 hours	We respond quickly to your needs—you will experience little down time	Security, trust, confidence, and dependability
People		
Sales reps receive intensive 2-week training at headquarters in Chicago and a 2-month ongoing training program at the branch office	You deal with people who have skill and knowledge	Trust, confidence, and respect
In-house training of all technical personnel	Repair work performed by skilled employees	Security, trust, and confidence

Continued

Exhibit 12.2
Continued

Features (Facts)	Advantages (Performance Characteristics)	Benefits (Satisfaction Derived)
People		
Call schedule is flexible	Respond quickly to your needs	Assurance, flexibility, and dependability
Member of chamber of commerce and support the general community by contributing to United Way	By buying from us, you are furthering our financial participation in civic affairs	Altruism, social responsibility, pride of ownership
Employees develop a strong dedication to the company	Strong cooperation between employees; you know there will always be someone around to take care of your needs	Security and confidence, satisfaction

Key Terms

Aggressive Behavior Seeking to establish one's own ego as uppermost in a situation

Assertiveness Ability to share the entire range of thoughts and emotions with confidence and skill

Competitive Differential Advantage (CDA) Analysis An analytical tool used to determine which of two or more products or services is superior

Features-Advantages-Benefits (FAB) Analysis An analytical tool based on the information gathered in a CDA analysis; it links features, advantages, and benefits in a hierarchical, comparative fashion

Formula Model A structured or preordered plan for achieving a buying decision

Major Buying Points A prospect's most important buying concerns, those points that have the most influence on the buying decision

Minor Buying Points Peripheral or secondary concerns that must be dealt with after the prospect's major buying concerns have been addressed

Needs-Satisfaction Model A system by which a product is analyzed in relation to customer needs

Stimulus-Response Model A model in which external stimulus (such as product beauty or description of benefits) excites the sensations of the prospect

Review Questions

1. Identify and explain the three selling systems.
2. Use the AIDA selling model to explain a formula approach to selling.
3. Explain the purpose and levels of a CDA analysis.
4. Name and define the components of the FAB analysis.
5. Distinguish between a major and a minor buying point. Give examples of each for the same product or service.
6. Define assertiveness and explain how this skill might apply to presenting a specific product or service.

Discussion Questions

1. Discuss in what ways the needs-satisfaction model is the foundation for the emergence of the consultative selling process.
2. Compare the advantages and disadvantages of the three dominant selling systems.
3. Select a product or service and discuss how the FAB analysis would apply to it.
4. Discuss in what selling situations it might be appropriate to behave assertively, nonassertively, and aggressively.
5. Discuss ways in which the CDA analysis helps to prepare the salesperson for the presentation.

Case 12.1

Getting Prepared for the Presentation

Rob Davis represents a distributor that sells a wide range of supplies to retailers in the pool and spa business. He was recently assigned the entire territory consisting of the midwestern and southern states. At a recent trade show he was informed of the tremendous growth of the spa and pool retail business in his territory. One particular company, Blue Waters, Inc., was noted for opening up 11 new facilities in one state alone.

Rob was already familiar with Blue Waters but never realized its potential. He has jumped at this opportunity and has ventured to seek out more information on this company. His list of information to find out about Blue Waters consists of the following:

- Has any other salesperson in his company ever dealt with it?
- Is there much background information on the company from sources such as trade publications, directories, and manufacturers who may have dealt with it?
- Can he get information about Blue Waters directly from the company?

In 3 weeks Rob had gathered much preliminary information on Blue Waters. He has yet to gather information on the purchasing agent and other people in the company who may be influential in decision making.

Rob is getting prepared to present information about his company to Blue Waters, which would include:

- Its reputation in the industry
- Years in business
- Service support provisions

1. Is Rob's preparation adequate?
2. What additional information does Rob need to know about Blue Waters, and how should he go about acquiring it?
3. Discuss how Rob should approach Blue Waters for an appointment. What additional information about his company should he present?

Case 12.2

Adapting the Presentation to a New Market

When sales declined in the construction industry because of an economic downturn, many wholesale suppliers decided to diversify into selling direct to household users. A large wholesaler selling high-quality merchandise set the opening pace with the household user. They also stocked precision tools designed for the trade.

The responsibility of the salespeople was becoming more than maintaining relationships with the construction firms and industrial buyers, basically just filling their orders in line with trends and keeping

Case 12.2
Continued

them happy. More "selling" was now emphasized, which required extensively educating and informing the user.

One of the sales representatives, Pete Wilson, was given the job of selling bathroom fixtures. In preparing for the sales presentation, Pete justifies the considerably higher price and the excellent quality based simply on the manufacturer's reputation and customers' reactions. As far as he is concerned, everything the buyer needs to know is listed on the package, with clear and understandable explanations.

Pete Wilson has the impression that household users do not understand efficiency concerns, much less installation procedures, because they hired plumbers to do the work. "The technical aspects would only confuse and discourage them," Pete stated.

1. Do you feel that Pete's preparation is adequate? What information about the household users would improve Pete's approach?
2. How could Pete gain more information about the household users?
3. What suggestions about product benefits would you suggest to Pete that should be given priority in the sales presentation?

Notes

1. Joseph Thompson, *Selling—A Managerial and Behavioral Science Analysis*, 2nd ed. (New York: McGraw-Hill Book Company, 1973), p. 146.
2. *Webster's New World Dictionary*, 3rd College Ed., (New York: Simon & Schuster, Inc.), 1988, p. 1317.
3. Thompson, *Selling*, p. 152.
4. E. K. Strong, Jr., *The Psychology of Selling and Advertising* (New York: McGraw-Hill Book Company, 1925).
5. Thompson, *Selling*, p. 155.
6. Jack Falvey, "Let Customers Teach the Troops about Products," *Sales & Marketing Management*, September 1989, p. 94.
7. V. R. Buzzota, R. E. Lefton, and Manuel Sherberg, *Effective Selling through Psychology: Dimensional Sales and Sales Management Strategies* (New York: Wiley-Interscience, 1972), pp. 188–189.
8. Ibid., p. 189.
9. Richard L. Weaver II, *Understanding Interpersonal Communication*, 5th ed. (Glenview, IL: Scott, Foresman/Little, Brown Higher Education, 1990), p. 296.
10. Ibid., p. 303.
11. Ronald B. Adler, Laurence B. Rosenfeld, and Neil Towne, *Interplay*, 4th ed. (Orlando, FL: Holt, Rinehart and Winston, Inc., 1989), p. 296.
12. Weaver, *Understanding Interpersonal Communication*, p. 302.
13. Caryl Winter, *Present Yourself with Impact* (New York: Ballantine Books, 1983), p. 4.

CHAPTER 13

Delivering the Sales Presentation

Knowledge Objectives

In this chapter, you will learn:

1. To use supporting materials to reinforce claims about product features, advantages, and benefits
2. To use sales aids to offer proof and show support
3. Guidelines for using various media to present sales aids effectively
4. Criteria for selecting the most appropriate sales aid
5. A procedure for introducing, presenting, and explaining support materials
6. The power and influence of negotiation in an effective presentation and demonstration

Consider This

The ability to communicate to audiences is becoming increasingly a measure of organizational effectiveness. *Fortune* magazine reports that business is searching for what it labels "interpersonal communication consultants," people who teach clients how to give talks and how to project a forceful, convincing manner. The reason[s] people go to these consultants . . . are to sound more confident and persuasive, to dress more effectively, and to attract favorable attention by engaging in outside activities such as presentations.

Michael Kenny*

**Presenting Yourself* (New York: John Wiley & Sons, Inc., 1982), p. 10.

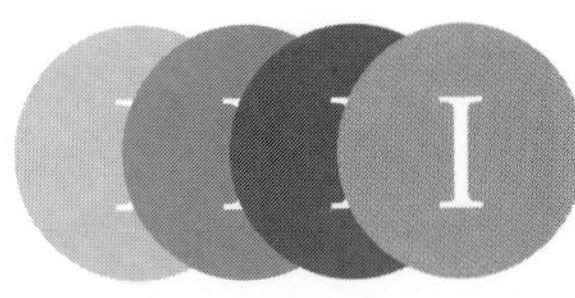

In Chapter 12, we identified the three major types of selling systems in use today: the stimulus-response method, the AIDA or formula approach, and the needs-satisfaction model. While our emphasis is on the development of the needs-satisfaction model, it is important to understand that all three systems have merit in the appropriate buying situation. Competent sales professionals will search for ways in which the strengths of each method can be used to best advantage by analyzing and improving their sales presentations through effective demonstrations. To provide information in a meaningful way to the prospect or customer, the salesperson's presentation mix should include the elements illustrated in Figure 13.1. The focus of this chapter is on the dynamics of a powerful demonstration and how to use sales aids and sales support materials to enhance verbal and nonverbal messages.

This chapter is divided into five sections: (1) the importance of giving an effective demonstration, (2) selecting and using sales support materials,

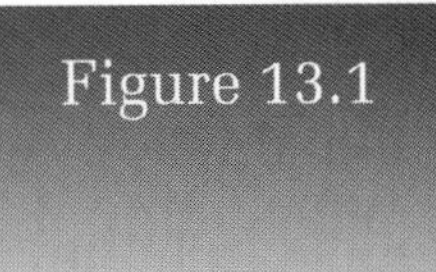

Figure 13.1

The Salesperson's Presentation Mix

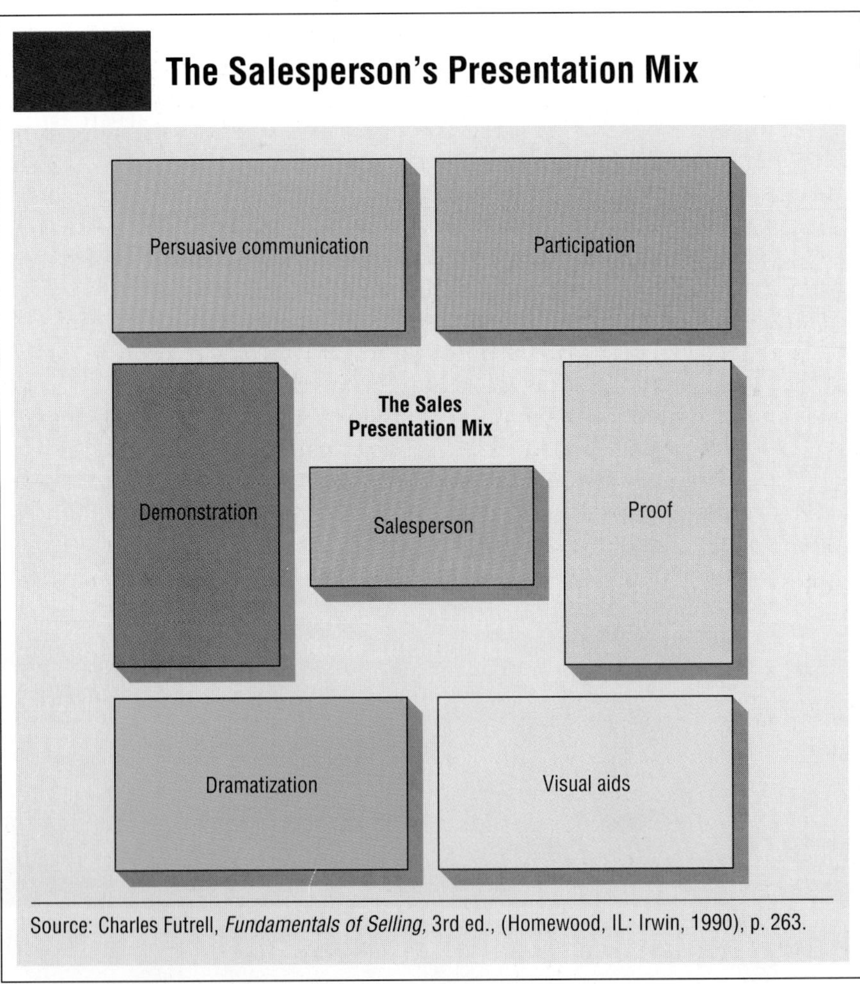

Source: Charles Futrell, *Fundamentals of Selling,* 3rd ed., (Homewood, IL: Irwin, 1990), p. 263.

(3) types of presentations and related sales aids, (4) using the SPESS sequence to practice the demonstration, and (5) negotiation during the presentation.

Importance of an Effective Demonstration

Three particularly important reasons for the salesperson to give an effective demonstration are: (1) to give the customer psychological possession, (2) to improve the buyer's retention, and (3) to show proof of customer benefits.

Gaining Psychological Possession

An important objective for all salespeople should be to assist the buyer in gaining psychological possession as early and as frequently as possible during the presentation. *Psychological possession* occurs in the mind of the buyer before any verbal confirmation to purchase is made. It refers to that state of intense desire when the prospect experiences that "I can't live without it" feeling—the feeling that one's quality of life will be enhanced through ownership, including a conscious or unconscious awareness that value or utility exceeds price. Psychological possession occurs more quickly and more often if the buyer's senses are actively involved in the sales presentation.

The skills presented in this text are vehicles by which both salesperson and customer can be involved in the selling process. For instance, active listening not only requires attention from the salesperson by using nonverbal attending behaviors; it also invites customer participation through open questions that draw out the customer's thoughts. Probing techniques work in conjunction with open questions to draw out the customer at the deepest level of emotional and rational needs. The FAB system is designed to reach the buyer at the emotional and rational (feeling and thinking) levels that are evident in the risk-trust relational cycle.

Improving the Buyer's Retention

In addition to enhancing the exchange process of sales communication, a strong demonstration improves the buyer's retention. Paul J. Micali, president of the Lacy Institute in Sarasota, Florida, reports that when a salesperson shows and tells at the same time, a customer's retention is likely to remain as high as 65 percent after 3 days, compared to only 10 percent if only a verbal message is given (Table 13.1).

Table 13.1

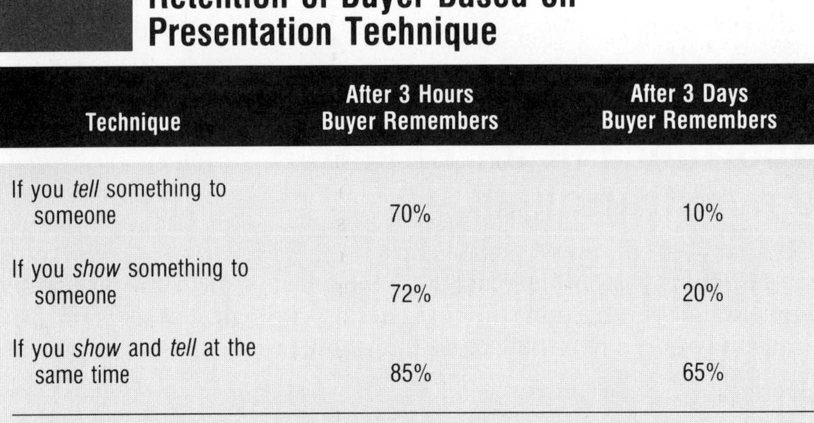

Retention of Buyer Based on Presentation Technique

Technique	After 3 Hours Buyer Remembers	After 3 Days Buyer Remembers
If you *tell* something to someone	70%	10%
If you *show* something to someone	72%	20%
If you *show* and *tell* at the same time	85%	65%

Source: Paul J. Micali, quoted in Gerald L. Manning and Barry L. Reece, *Selling Today—A Personal Approach*, 4th ed. (Needham Heights, ME: Allyn & Bacon, 1990), p. 333.

The flip side of retention is recall. Barbara Pletcher, president of Creative Sales Careers, Inc., and a consultant for corporate recruitment of women in sales and marketing, reinforces the importance of involving the buyer's five senses during a demonstration:

> You must maintain the buyer's interest. You can maintain interest more effectively if you appeal to more than one of the buyer's five senses. . . . If you can see, hear, feel, smell and taste something, it makes a greater impression on you.[1]

The sense of smell, for instance, can trigger an individual's memory, recalling pleasant or unpleasant memories. No one knows this better than the people in the fragrance industry. In 1990 Allan Mottus, a well-known cosmetics industry consultant, decided to "cash in on the Old West craze by selling products that recreate the frontier."[2] While researching the West, he discovered that coyote motifs were popular and that Indian folklore values the mischievous coyote. Says Mottus: "Just letting out a howl when the moon is full is something a self-assured woman in the Southwest can relate to."[3] These "coyote fantasies" would, at least, have regional appeal.

Showing Proof of Customer Benefits

A third reason for presenting an effective demonstration is to show proof of customer benefits. This is particularly true if the salesperson's product is dramatically superior to the competition's. For example, differences in the quality of pictures produced by camcorders may be demonstrated

Try This 13.1 Identifying the Importance of an Effective Demonstration

At the spring 1990 Consumer Electronics Show, one useful tool that got a lot of coverage was the Road Whiz Electronic Interstate Travel Guide ($79). About the size of a calculator, it contains over 30,000 entries for services and points of interest at over 13,700 highway exits. Using the Road Whiz, an individual can pinpoint proximity to gas stations, restaurants, lodging, campgrounds, hospitals, landmarks, and even highway patrol posts.*

As a salesperson for the Road Whiz, prepare a plan to effectively demonstrate your product by identifying how you would:

1. Improve communication with your customer
2. Improve your customer's retention
3. Create a feeling of ownership

*"Short Takes," *Sales & Marketing Management*, July 1990, p. 37.

easily to show superiority. The development of compact discs with virtually no deterioration in quality over long-term use has rendered the record market almost obsolete. High-definition television, still in the experimental stage, is dramatically superior in picture sharpness, with twice the resolution of standard television sets (Mike Shanley, technical services coordinator, Orange Coast College, Costa Mesa, Calif., interview, July 11, 1990).

Selecting and Using Sales Support Materials

The FAB analysis identified in Chapter 11 provides salespeople with important claims they can make about their products or services. These claims are usually not enough, however, to maintain the buyer's interest or persuade the buyer to make a purchase. Salespeople also need to provide support materials that reinforce and prove the claims they are making about the features, advantages, and benefits of the product or service.

Support material is information that captures and maintains customer interest, provides clarification, increases the retention of information, and provides proof. There are five different types of verbal support and various types of sales aids that can provide visual support for claims made about the product.

Sales Professional Spotlight

Charlie Okamoto is a sales representative for the Copy Products Division of Eastman Kodak. Initially, as an intern with IBM, he gained great insight into the career path that he wanted to follow and eventually became a marketing support assistant for IBM before his division was acquired by Kodak.

Charlie stayed with Kodak because of the diverse career opportunities and training the organization offers, and the reputation of the company and the caliber of its people. He also felt that the training provided by Kodak would offer potential for greater mobility in the field of sales. Kodak has always supported its salespeople who want to excel in the profession.

The company continually provides training and sales courses to update and strengthen the sales staff. Charlie comments that his sales training at Kodak is substantially better than that offered by most other companies: "As sales representatives of Kodak, we are initially trained in acquiring selling skills and making presentations. Also, as part of the ongoing process to keep in tune with the significant technological changes and advances, we are required to return to the corporate headquarters in New York for updated training. New product introductions have strengthened our customers' perceptions of Kodak in the electronic imaging marketplace."

In his current sales position with Kodak, Charlie handles a geographic territory that consists of every imaginable type of account. He cites the challenges and diversities he faces with his accounts, which demand adaptation of his presentation. "You certainly would not give the same presentation to an Air Force captain and a legal administrator. Often I must redesign my sales presentation to be most effective in distinguishing Kodak as the vendor of choice," he says.

A crucial step in the selling process is delivering an effective sales presentation. "I get prepared with my 'sales kit,' consisting of such things as pamphlets, full-color brochures, free samples, storyboards, transparencies, reference lists, and benefit listings. Most important, I practice my presentation extensively before I interact with the prospect."

Charlie cites additional information required to make a successful presentation: "Who are the vital people involved in the buying decision? What are their roles? What will motivate them to buy our product over the competitor's? You must stay on top of your competition at all times." He stresses the vital requirement of understanding the buyer's motives.

"I must be able to cover all the features and benefits of the product and give prospects the information they need to help them make a buying decision. Financial analysis information is important to all buyers. My presentation is best when I am able to answer all questions. Product knowledge enables me to tackle all questions. If you are unable to answer all questions, at least know where you can get the answers," he says.

The most important thing to do during the presentation is to reflect confidence. Charlie advises that professional salespeople must do their homework and know their limits. "The presentation should be smooth and relaxed; never be intimidated by tough questions or objections," he says. His success in delivering the presentation has come from being flexible, keeping his commitment to serving customers with current developments, and fostering the right atmosphere.

Five Types of Verbal Support

Of the different types of support material, the five that salespeople will find most useful in providing support for the features, advantages, and benefits they describe are examples, anecdotes, comparisons, statistics, and testimony. Using a variety of support materials will help the presentation to be more interesting and persuasive.[4]

Examples

An example is a brief, specific instance that is used to illustrate a product's features and benefits. Examples can be either real or hypothetical. A real example describes a factual occurrence. For instance, a salesperson for a golf equipment manufacturer might say to a prospective retailer: "Since adding Ping clubs to his line 6 months ago, Tim Saunders over at Whole-In-One has increased his sales 23 percent."

In a hypothetical example, the customer must imagine something. For instance, a salesperson who is selling compact discs might say to a customer, "Imagine listening to this same album while wearing earmuffs." Or, while talking about building an investment program with a client, a financial planner might say, "Imagine what would happen to a family if the head of the household died, leaving a spouse and three children to care for themselves."

Examples are typically combined with other forms of support. Because examples are isolated instances, they provide explanation but not necessarily proof of the claims the salesperson is making. To provide proof, more than one or a few isolated examples must be provided.

Anecdotes

Examples are most effective when they include anecdotes. An anecdote is an example in story form that clarifies or illustrates a product's features, advantages, or benefits. Anecdotes are more detailed than examples and may or may not be based on personal experience. For example, a salesperson for the laptop line of Micro Ease Computer, Inc., might relate the following anecdote to a prospect (for instance, a sales manager) whom he is trying to persuade to automate his sales force:

> It's been my experience that when a company starts buying laptops, it usually gets just one. It's a new toy, and the company wants to see how it works. Press its buttons. Put it through a few paces. Take it to some prospects. See if it can help close some deals. Immediately the company likes it and orders five more. Then the budget is approved for ten, then ten a month. It's an ongoing process; as the company hires new salespeople, it buys laptops. It's part of the start-up cost of a new employee.
>
> A good feature is the ability to carry this little laptop around that you can plug into an external monitor—a color monitor, if need be—to show off your product. A lot of salespeople do that. It gives you a great sense of confidence to know that you can control what happens on a call because everything you need is right here in your hands.

As with examples, anecdotes capture attention and interest by breaking the monotony and relieving tension. They also clarify and increase retention of information, but do not usually offer proof.

As a salesperson, follow these four guidelines when using anecdotes in a sales presentation:

1. Use anecdotes only if they provide support for a particular point about the product's features, advantages, or benefits. If no support is provided, anecdotes become tangential and are likely to irritate and distract the customer.
2. Use anecdotes that are appropriate to the customer, the product or service, and the image that is desired. Clearly relate the point of the story to the context of the sales presentation.
3. The anecdote should last no more than about 1 minute and should make a point quickly. It should support the presentation, not be the center of attention.
4. Rehearse the anecdote in advance so that it can be told smoothly. If you have difficulty telling or remembering stories, the anecdote's effectiveness will be diminished.

Comparisons

A comparison is a statement of support that shows similarities between two points. Both figurative and literal comparisons can be used in a sales presentation.

A figurative comparison explains one thing in terms of an analogous thing. Comparisons frequently involve words such as "like" or "as." For example, salespeople are using a figurative comparison when they claim that "listening to this stereo system is like having a symphony orchestra in your living room" or that "driving a Mercedes Benz is like floating on a cloud." Such comparisons create a vivid picture of product features, advantages, and benefits while increasing customer interest and attention.

A literal comparison identifies actual similarities that exist between the customer's reasons for buying and the product's features, advantages, and benefits. For example:

> Brown and Brown purchased this copier from us last year, and the company's reprographic costs dropped by 35 percent within 10 months [*feature*]. Four other firms whose paper consumption was the same as Brown and Brown's also realized an average cost decrease of 35 percent in their first 12 months of operation using model TX1700. Because you've demonstrated similar consumption patterns, I'm confident that this model will do the same for you [*benefit*].

A salesperson using a literal comparison might say, "The feeling of safety that you experience [*benefit*] when you drive this Buick is at least equal to what you'll feel when you drive any other domestic or imported car on the road today."

Figurative and literal comparisons provide interest, add clarity, and increase customer retention. Literal comparisons can also help salespeople substantiate the claims they are making about their product or service, especially when these comparisons also include statistics and testimony that describe features, advantages, and benefits. As with anecdotes, the strength of this proof depends on how clearly the comparison can show similarities between different products and customers.

Statistics

A statistic is a number that expresses information about a group of examples. Because statistics provide information about more than isolated examples, they can be used as proof for the claims salespeople make about their products. Statistics are typically used in sales presentations to show the size of market segments, sales trends, decreasing or increasing profits, and changes in costs. For example, "The median-priced single-family home in Orange County, California, is over $255,000. This is compared to San Francisco, Honolulu, and Los Angeles, where median-priced homes range from $190,000 to $228,000."

As a salesperson, you will want to remember the following guidelines for using statistics in a sales presentation:

- Do not use so many statistics that the customer is overwhelmed with a barrage of numbers. Instead, provide only the most important numbers that will help support your claim. Additional statistical information can be provided in brochures and other documents.
- In most sales presentations it is permissible to round a figure to the nearest whole number. For example, 64.7 percent can be rounded to 65 percent or "almost two-thirds." It would be dishonest, however, to say that 65 percent is "nearly 70 percent."
- It is often useful to link numbers to concrete images that are more interesting and more easily understood by the customer. Exhibits 13.1 and 13.2 illustrate this technique. Statistics may be too technical for some customers. The use of concrete images gives the customer another perspective from which to understand technical information.

Exhibit 13.1

Presentation Using Statistics

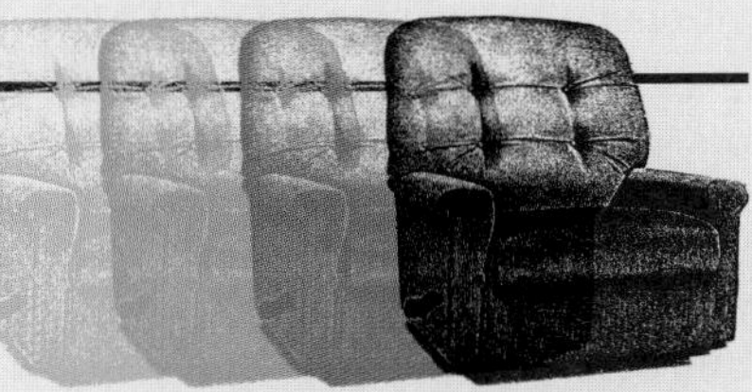

The Mind of the Mover

An important type of mover for the housing industry is the trade-up homebuyer. There are four kinds of trade-up buyers, according to a profile of this market produced by American LIVES of San Francisco, California. The four types are "Conventional Heartland," "Suburban Conservatives," "Winners with Heart," and "Person Centered."

CONVENTIONAL HEARTLAND buyers account for 23 percent of the trade-up market. Their median age is 48, and 54 percent have household incomes above $50,000. Conventional Heartlanders stress safety and security, not homes that show off. Life revolves around the family room, breakfast area, and kitchen.

WINNERS WITH HEART account for 20 percent of trade-up buyers, according to the survey. Their age media is 38, and fully 61 percent have household incomes in excess of $50,000. The most ambitious and upwardly mobile of the four types. But they've traded some of their ambition for concern about spending time with the children.

PERSON-CENTERED homebuyers account for 26 percent of the trade-up market. Demographically they are close to the other types. Person-Centered people are more concerned with being unique than in owning what is unique. Formal areas in a Person-Centered home are separated from private family spaces.

SUBURBAN CONSERVATIVES account for the largest share (31 percent) of trade-up buyers. Their median age is 38, and half have incomes over $50,000. A Suburban Conservative's master suite is on a different floor from the children's rooms.

Adapted from: Larry Long, " Americans on the Move," American Demographics, June 1990, p. 49.

- Charts, graphs, and other sales aids may be helpful when using statistics. Because statistics can be confusing and take a long time for some people to understand, graphics can provide visual support for the numbers being described verbally. (The use of various sales aids will be discussed in the next section of this chapter.)

Testimony

Testimony is a statement from an expert. By using the opinions of people who have special expertise, the salesperson can make a claim about a product more convincing. Statements might be used to add interest, clarify, or provide proof for the claims a salesperson makes:

- "The American Fireman's Association has endorsed the use of the Trenholm Fire Extinguisher."
- "Four out of every five dentists belonging to the American Dental Association recommend the use of 'Floss-a-Dent' at least once each day."

Exhibit 13.2

Sample Graphic Presentation

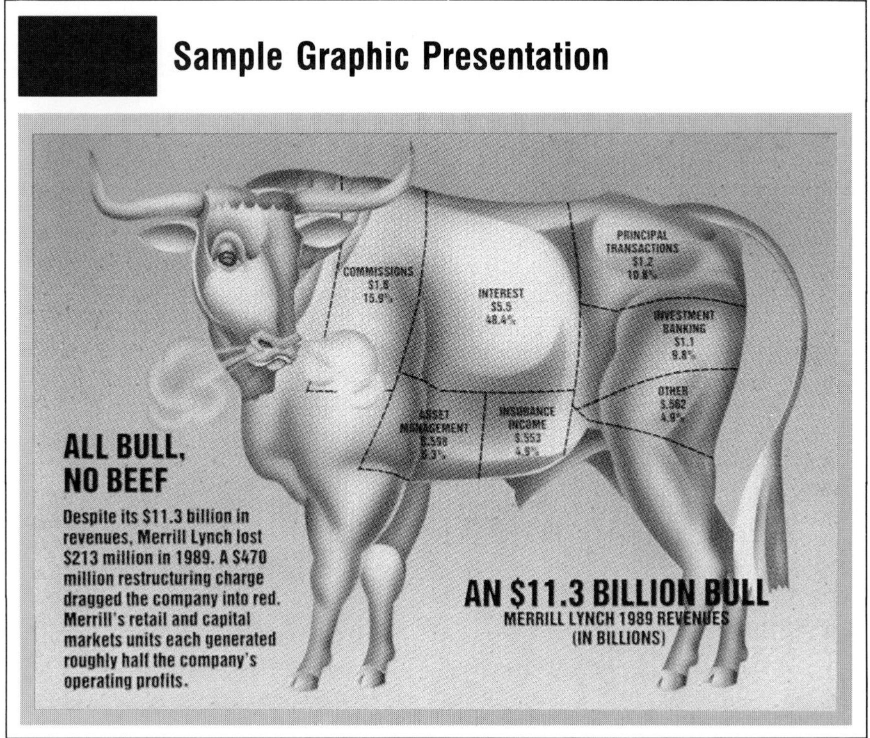

- "In December 1991, *Home-Office Computing* magazine chose the year's 'Best and Brightest' office products—their 'Editors' Picks' for 1991. From the hundreds of products they reviewed all year, they selected one fax for this special recognition—the *dex 150 PowerFax* from Fujitsu."

Salespeople should cite the sources of testimony used in their presentations. It is also important to identify the individual, association, or agency that originally made the statement, including what qualifies the person as an expert. For example:

> Samuel Wheaton, president of the Electronics Industries Association/Consumer Electronics Group, says that "the *dex 150 PowerFax* is packed with an impressive array of basic and advanced features like FaxForwarding, autodialing, voice request, delayed transmission and broadcast." He particularly recommends it for heavy-user global transmission.

Types of Sales Aids

A sales aid is a device used in a presentation to involve one or more of the buyer's senses and illustrate or support information about a product's features and benefits. Sales aids, when used appropriately, move the

Try This 13.2 Identifying Verbal Support Materials

Identify support materials that you could use to make claims about a product's features, advantages, and benefits. Complete the following:

1. Product you are selling: ____________

2. Potential buyer: ____________

3. Identify one important feature, advantage, and benefit for this customer:

   (F) ____________

   (A) ____________

   (B) ____________

Now provide:

A. *Example* to support this FAB ____________

B. *Anecdote* to support this FAB ____________

C. *Comparison* to support this FAB ____________

D. *Statistic* to support this FAB ____________

E. *Testimony* to support this FAB ____________

buyer toward a purchasing decision. The most significant reasons for this result are listed in Table 13.2.

A wide variety of sales aids are available to assist a salesperson in dramatizing and enhancing the impact of the presentation. Major conglomerates such as Procter & Gamble nearly bury their sales force with sample kits, schematic diagrams, printed materials, and point-of-purchase display materials. The salesperson must remember to select the sales aids that are most effective for the product or service being represented and the buying situation in which the presentation is being given.

Regardless of which sales aids are used, explanations and interpretations are required. This section provides a brief overview of some of the most widely used sales tools.

The Product Itself or Product Samples

The product itself is a dynamic aid because it provides the customer with an opportunity for hands-on experience. A product demonstration shows the customer how something functions or how to complete a specific procedure. There are three guidelines for the salesperson to follow when planning a product demonstration:

1. The product's appearance should be neat and clean and its operation flawless. The salesperson should not have to apologize for its appearance or performance.

Table 13.2

Reasons for Using Sales Aids

1. Sales aids meet customer demands for visual and auditory support. Just as consumers expect state-of-the-art technology at home and in the office, they have come to expect lifelike color pictures, wide screens, and Dolby sound tracks in sales presentations.

2. Sales aids generally provide concise information about the product. They allow the salesperson to present more detailed information in significantly less time without sacrificing customer comprehension.

3. Sales aids significantly increase the likelihood that the salesperson will explain the information clearly and that the customer will understand the information. This is especially true when the data being presented are complex, technical, or statistical.

4. Sales aids make presentations more interesting and persuasive. Well-prepared charts, diagrams, and graphs, for example, add variety to information that might otherwise be dull. Product demonstrations help establish product quality or operating ease, especially when they increase customer involvement.

5. Sales aids increase the customer's retention of the information the salesperson presents.

6. Sales aids can be used to enhance the person's sales image and increase the customer's perception of the salesperson's professionalism. When they are well prepared and used effectively, the salesperson is perceived as a credible and polished professional.

2. The salesperson should know how to skillfully demonstrate the product and should practice with the product in advance and anticipate any problems that may arise with its performance. The salesperson should also bring backup equipment or replacement parts in case of a product malfunction during the demonstration.
3. Products should be used that can be set up and removed easily. Companies such as Kodak, Xerox, and IBM have demonstration rooms in their regional facilities because of the complexity, size, and time involved in setting up their copy machine lines. The customer is invited for an on-site demonstration where everything is ready to be shown.

Samples are another effective way to demonstrate a product. A sample is a small amount of the product that the customer can use. Samples are typically used in the food, cleaning, carpeting, toiletry, and pharmaceutical industries. When working with samples, it is important that they be presented gracefully, as if the customer were a guest in the salesperson's home. It is equally important to have the customer's permission before demonstrating samples. Some people are allergic to certain chemicals, fragrances, foods, and fabrics. Customers should always be asked if they would like to try the sample before a demonstration is begun.

Models

It may not always be possible for the customer to experience the product directly. For example, it may be impractical to demonstrate a product because of its weight or size. In these instances, a salesperson may use a model, a scaled representation or mock-up of the product that the salesperson is demonstrating. Models are often used in the real estate management, aerospace engineering, electronics, interior design, medical, and dental fields.

Printed Materials

Printed materials that may be used in a sales presentation include brochures and pamphlets, catalogues, reprints, research reports, guarantees and warranties, and testimonial letters. When using printed materials in a presentation, a salesperson should follow these general guidelines:

1. Because printed materials (like all sales aids) are an extension of the salesperson and the firm, they must always be reproduced clearly and produced on high-quality materials.
2. It is often best to draw the customer's attention to the sections of the printed material that are most important by highlighting these sections with a marking pen.
3. The printed material should be placed directly in front of the customer. If someone must read the material upside-down, it should always be the salesperson and not the customer.
4. Use a pen as a pointer to direct the customer's attention to specific sections of the printed material.
5. When leaving printed materials with the buyer, the salesperson's name, address, and telephone number should be printed clearly on the front. A business card may be stapled to the front for easy reference.

Photographs and Drawings

Photographs and drawings can provide a representation of the product, especially if the actual product or a model cannot be shown conveniently. In fact, they might be used for several reasons: to show a complete line of products, to show several uses or applications of the same product, and to provide a way for the customer to visualize the benefits of the product's use.

One type of artwork that may be useful in a sales presentation is a diagram, a line drawing that shows the most important properties or functions of the product. A diagram does not depict everything about the product, only the most important points the customer needs to know. Examples of diagrams include floor plans (such as Exhibit 13.4), maps, blueprints, circuitry charts, and organizationsl charts. A diagram is most useful when it simplifies a complex product and makes it more easily understandable to the customer. Diagrams are an excellent way to communicate information about the product's size, shape, structure, and

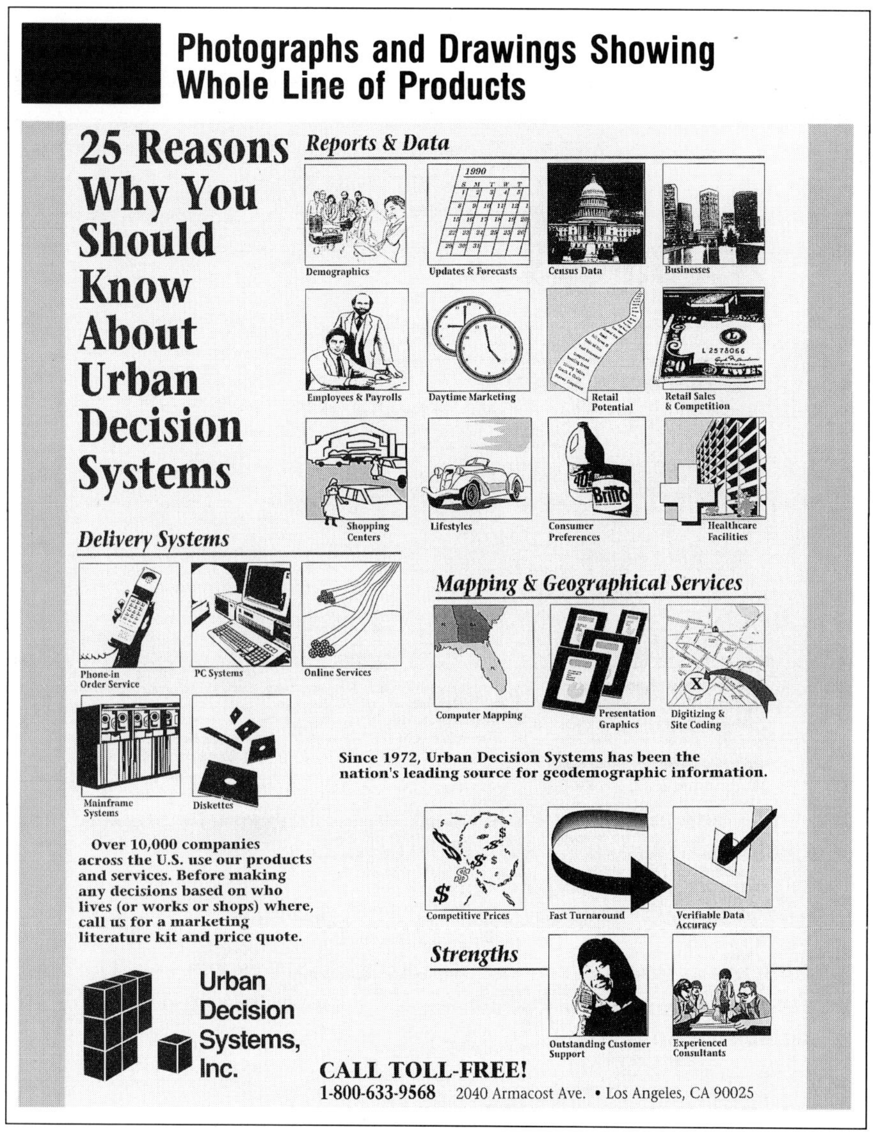

Exhibit 13.3

Photographs and Drawings Showing Whole Line of Products

function. As with other sales aids, diagrams should be simple and include only the most essential elements so that they can be understood quickly and easily.

Pie Charts

A pie chart is a circular diagram with wedge-shaped sections showing how the circle is divided (see Exhibit 13.5). Pie charts provide a visual representation of percentages that add up to 100. The section of the pie that is largest usually begins at the 12 o'clock position, followed by the next largest section of the pie, and so on to the smallest. Each section of the pie should include a percentage and label, either inside or outside

Exhibit 13.4

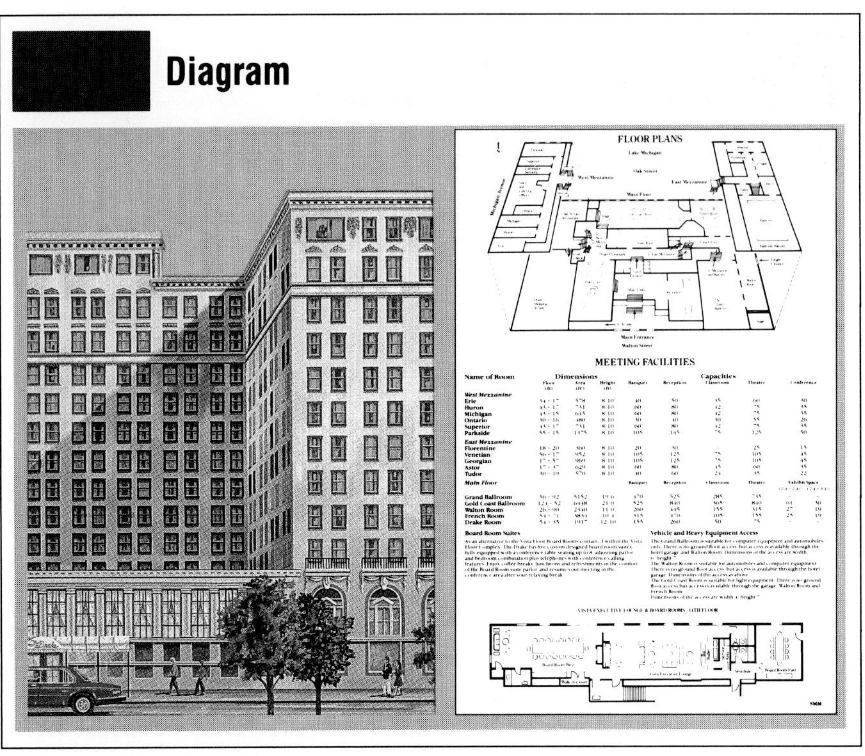

the wedge. For example, a pie chart might be used to diagram how investment money is spent and how it is being invested.

Graphs

Several types of graphs can be used in sales presentations. The most common of these are bar and column graphs, line graphs, and pictographs.

Bar and column graphs compare several items. Bar graphs compare items by using horizontal bars, while column charts use vertical bars. Both types of charts can be used to reflect changes in a single product or multiple items over time. A salesperson who is designing bar or column graphs, or selecting from previously prepared ones, should remember the following guidelines:

1. Time should always be represented on the horizontal axis of the chart.
2. Numerical values must be clearly represented. Label and assign numerical values to each bar inside or adjacent to the bars on the chart.
3. Do not use vertical printing; it is difficult to read.
4. Bars on the chart can be organized from high to low, low to high, in alphabetical order, or in order of importance.

Line graphs can also show changes over time. Single-line graphs may depict trends, such as the growth or decline of one factor over time.

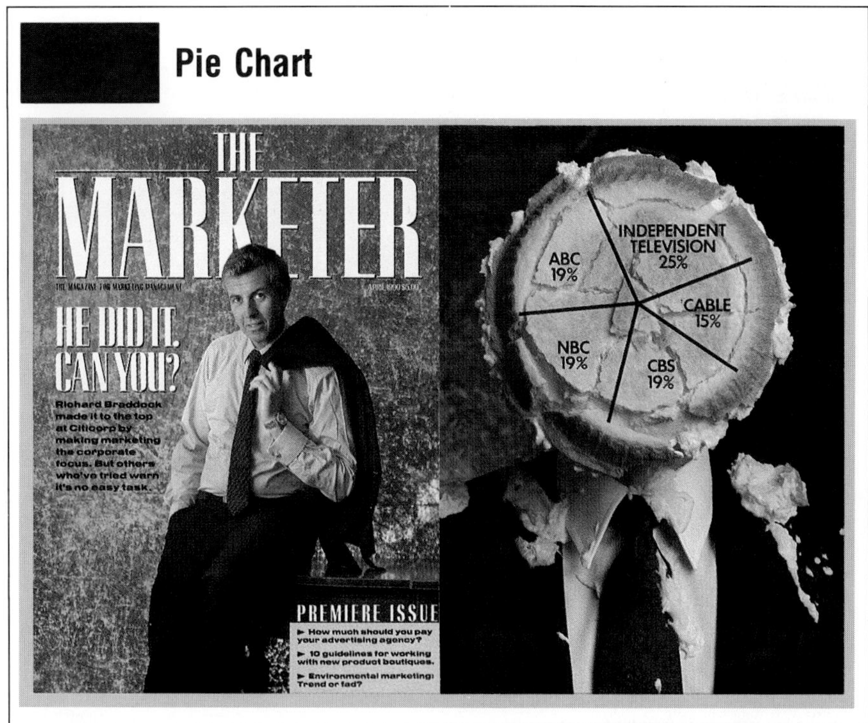

Exhibit 13.5

Pie Chart

Multiple-line graphs show relationships among two or more trends. As with bar and column graphs, line graphs should indicate time on the horizontal axis. Each line should be clearly labeled in a different color or a distinct pattern for maximal clarity. Limit the number of lines to three and use gridlines sparingly. Use a scale that reports the data without distortion.

A pictograph is a modified bar graph that makes the information being presented more interesting by using a drawing or picture to represent a unit of the item being measured. Because it is not as exact mathematically as a bar or column graph, a pictograph is best suited for customers requiring less technical or less precise information about a product.

Preparing printed materials, diagrams, word and number charts, line graphs, and pictographs is much easier since the advent of personal and computer graphics software. During the last few years, sophisticated but relatively inexpensive software packages have enabled people to create professional-quality visual aids, even if they have little artistic training or talent. With the appropriate computer software and hardware, color charts, graphs, and diagrams can be created quickly and inexpensively.

Image Management

Image management or image processing is the wave of the future for those companies that can afford expensive computer software. BIS CAP International in Norwell, Massachusetts, projects a market growth from

Exhibit 13.6

Computer Graphics—From Realistic . . .

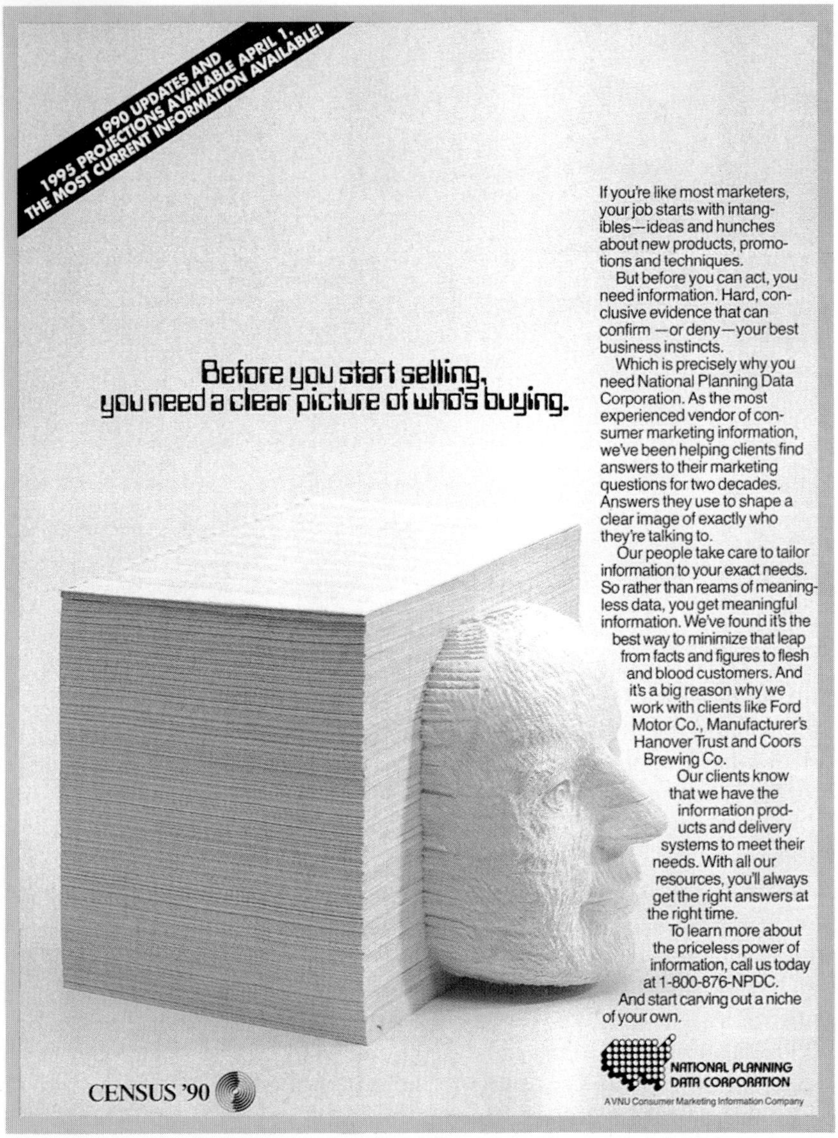

1990 UPDATES AND 1995 PROJECTIONS AVAILABLE APRIL 1. THE MOST CURRENT INFORMATION AVAILABLE!

Before you start selling, you need a clear picture of who's buying.

If you're like most marketers, your job starts with intangibles—ideas and hunches about new products, promotions and techniques.

But before you can act, you need information. Hard, conclusive evidence that can confirm —or deny—your best business instincts.

Which is precisely why you need National Planning Data Corporation. As the most experienced vendor of consumer marketing information, we've been helping clients find answers to their marketing questions for two decades. Answers they use to shape a clear image of exactly who they're talking to.

Our people take care to tailor information to your exact needs. So rather than reams of meaningless data, you get meaningful information. We've found it's the best way to minimize that leap from facts and figures to flesh and blood customers. And it's a big reason why we work with clients like Ford Motor Co., Manufacturer's Hanover Trust and Coors Brewing Co.

Our clients know that we have the information products and delivery systems to meet their needs. With all our resources, you'll always get the right answers at the right time.

To learn more about the priceless power of information, call us today at 1-800-876-NPDC.

And start carving out a niche of your own.

CENSUS '90

NATIONAL PLANNING DATA CORPORATION

A VNU Consumer Marketing Information Company

$359.9 million in 1989 to $1,963.6 billion by 1993, through the use of image management.[5] Image management systems allow companies to store mechanical designs, financial reports and accounts, blueprints, and procedure manuals on ordinary personal computers.

In demonstrating the system to a client, a salesperson might reproduce a copy of Leonardo da Vinci's Mona Lisa (Exhibit 13.8) while saying, "Imagine using a chainsaw on the Mona Lisa, numbering each piece, and trusting her storage and reassembly to a PC."[6]

. . . to Theoretical

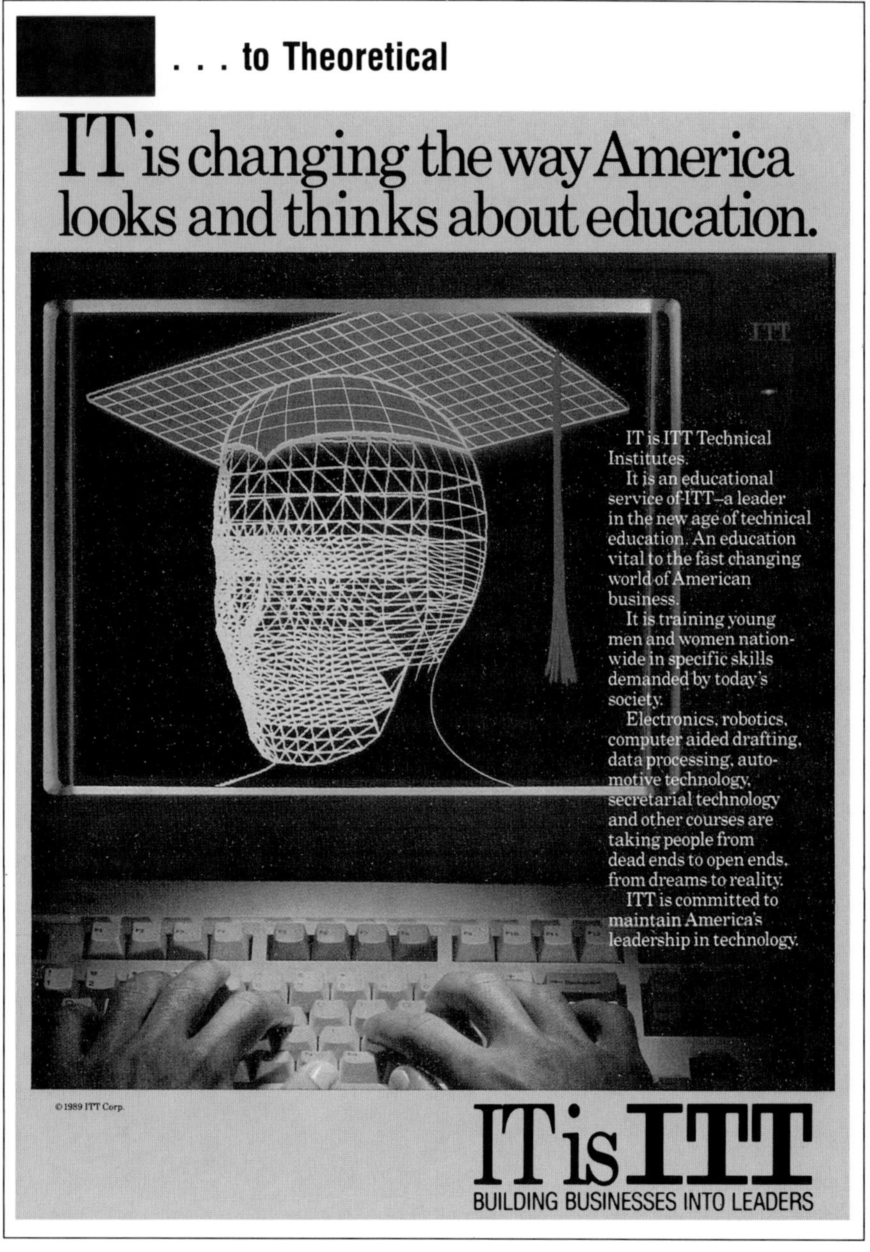

IT is changing the way America looks and thinks about education.
IT is ITT Technical Institutes.
It is an educational service of ITT—a leader in the new age of technical education. An education vital to the fast changing world of American business.
It is training young men and women nationwide in specific skills demanded by today's society.
Electronics, robotics, computer aided drafting, data processing, automotive technology, secretarial technology and other courses are taking people from dead ends to open ends, from dreams to reality.
ITT is committed to maintain America's leadership in technology.
©1989 ITT Corp.
IT is ITT
BUILDING BUSINESSES INTO LEADERS

Exhibit 13.7

This type of nonverbal and verbal message is a powerful way to build value for an expensive item.

Chalkboards or Polymer Writing Surfaces

A polymer board has a white surface that is written on with special colored markers. It is neater than a chalkboard because the chalk dust is eliminated. The surface is easily wiped clean with a cloth or sponge.

Exhibit 13.8

Image Processing

Viewstar's $300,000 Software

by Kathleen Doler

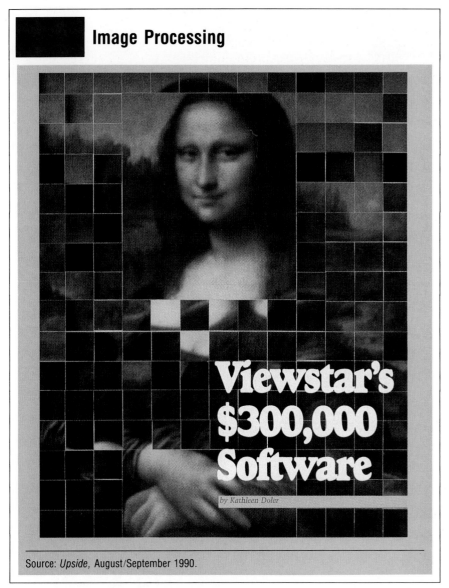

Source: *Upside*, August/September 1990.

Perhaps the greatest advantages to using these aids are the spontaneity and flexibility they provide the salesperson. One can create diagrams, charts, and graphs instantly. For those salespeople with artistic talent, creative and humorous illustrations may help to demonstrate a point.

Transparencies and Overhead Projectors

A transparency is a clear sheet of plastic on which a graphic is printed. An overhead projector uses transparencies to project the graphic on a screen. An overhead projector is effective when making a sales presentation to a large group where it would be difficult to see a flip chart or a small monitor.

Transparencies are relatively easy and inexpensive to create. The graphic to be projected is reproduced in a copying machine onto a plastic sheet. Graphics can also be drawn directly on the plastic transparency. When creating transparencies, the guidelines reviewed earlier for preparing word and number charts apply. Highlight only important features, advantages, and benefits. Use key words, numbers, or phrases, not complete sentences. Use large, bold print.

When using overhead transparencies, a salesperson should remember these simple guidelines:

- Keep the overhead lights on; prospects will be more likely to concentrate on what you are saying.
- Shut off the projector when not using it. Project graphics onto the screen only when they are being discussed.
- Cover a transparency with a blank sheet of paper if the customer is not to read information that has not yet been discussed.
- Keep shoulders oriented toward the customer as speech and eye contact are made. Don't talk to the screen or the projector.
- Use a pointer, if needed, to direct the customer's attention to the projected image.

Types of Presentations and Related Sales Aids

The audiences for a salesperson's presentations will vary in size from one person to a small group. Prospects are generally potential buyers from an industrial firm, retail store, government agency, or service industry. These people are typically professional buyers accustomed to evaluating the products and proposals of many salespeople.

The motivation of these buyers is uncomplicated—they want to collect the information they need to make prudent buying decisions. They are usually impressed by a no-nonsense, fact-filled presentation that gives them features, advantages, benefits, prices, and other related information in a concise and logical manner.

Choosing Appropriate Presentation Aids

What sales aid to use is determined by the type of presentation being given: salesperson to person or salesperson to small group, point of purchase, general sales meeting, or exhibit or trade show.[7]

Salesperson to Person or Small Group

The purpose of this type of presentation is to persuade an individual or a small group to buy a product or service, or to review other proposals and demonstrations that will lead to a buying decision. The prospects are typically professional buyers accustomed to evaluating numerous products and proposals.

This type of sales presentation usually occurs in the buyer's office or a small conference room, which often is not equipped for major audiovisual demonstrations. The most practical equipment for salespeople to use is a self-contained, desktop projector that plugs into a single outlet. The sophistication of these units is as varied as the salesperson's budget will allow.

Because this type of presentation is intended to reinforce or supplement the salesperson's oral presentation, a rule of thumb is to limit the presentation to 10 minutes. Furthermore, many buyers will be pressed for time, and they may terminate the interview if the salesperson lacks sensitivity for their schedules.

Point-of-Purchase Selling

In this presentation the salesperson attempts to persuade the customer to purchase the product being demonstrated. In a point-of-purchase presentation, the theme must be stated quickly and emphatically to attract and keep the prospect's attention. Prospects are usually retail consumers, whose purchases are determined by the desire to gain health, time, popularity, praise, prestige, success, comfort, leisure, and security.[8]

Often the demonstration area serves as the focal point of a larger product display. Customers are usually people in a hurry who will watch a presentation "on impulse." Effective presentations of this type should be given within 1–3 minutes.

General Sales Meeting

Michael Kenny, who designed a presentation manual for Eastman Kodak Company, identifies two specific sales-meeting audiences with slightly different purposes. If the meeting is aimed at sales representatives, then its purposes are to inform them of new products and services, including pricing schedules, sales, and advertising plans; build enthusiasm for the new products and developments; and motivate them to increase sales. If the meeting is aimed at customers, the purposes of the meeting are to stimulate interest in the presenter's products and lay the groundwork for a subsequent call by a sales representative.

General sales meetings often require seating for up to several hundred people. When selecting sales aids, Kenny suggests that equipment be divided into three groups:

> (1) projection equipment—one or more projectors (slide, motion picture or video), dissolve controls, a programmer; (2) audio equipment—tape playback unit, amplifiers, speakers, microphones; and (3) screens—screen or screens capable of producing a sharp, bright image to viewers throughout the seating area.

For those salespeople who have a large enough budget, equipment may include spotlights, laser displays, turntable stages, fountains, and specialized microphones for singers, orchestras, and bands.

Exhibit or Trade Show

A trade show exhibit is sometimes referred to as a "presentation within a presentation." The larger presentation is the booth or display. Within this is usually another presentation given by a salesperson, who is supported by audiovisual material as well as the product. Exhibits may be open to the general public, as with the consumer electronics show held in Las Vegas, Nevada, or they may be limited to a specific trade group or association.

Because these shows are held in large exhibit halls, preparations must be made to minimize the distractions surrounding the presentation. Equipment selections will reflect sales objectives. Presentations within the exhibit, where the emphasis is on person-to-person selling, may use compact, desktop projectors.

The purposes of these presentations are to stimulate interest, spark interesting questions, uncover prospects' problems, and offer solutions within the exhibit area. Presentations of this type are usually no longer than 5 minutes, while those held in theater-like settings usually run 10–15 minutes.

Using the SPESS Sequence to Practice the Demonstration

Michael Kenny has said, "To be a successful presenter, you must first set well-defined communications objectives." Salespeople must do more than just *think* their way to a successful sale—they must *act* their way there through effective planning and rehearsing for the presentation. The key to acting is to set a target goal and then achieve it.

The analysis and planning that go into establishing a target will define what the salesperson wants to accomplish and will suggest the most effective means of reaching that goal. Figure 13.2 summarizes the activities necessary to give an effective demonstration.

Try This 13.3 Selecting the Most Appropriate Sales Aids

Locate at least five different sales aids that you can use to demonstrate the product of your choice. Look for advertisements, photographs, and illustrations of the product in use; brochures and pamphlets; reprints of magazine articles (such as from *Consumer Reports*); charts, diagrams, and test results; product guarantees, warranties, and so on. Make a loose-leaf notebook or file for these materials.

Invite at least two classmates to join you and share these materials with them. Describe to classmates how each sales aid could be used in the presentation. Ask them for feedback about their perceptions of the effectiveness of these materials.

Figure 13.2

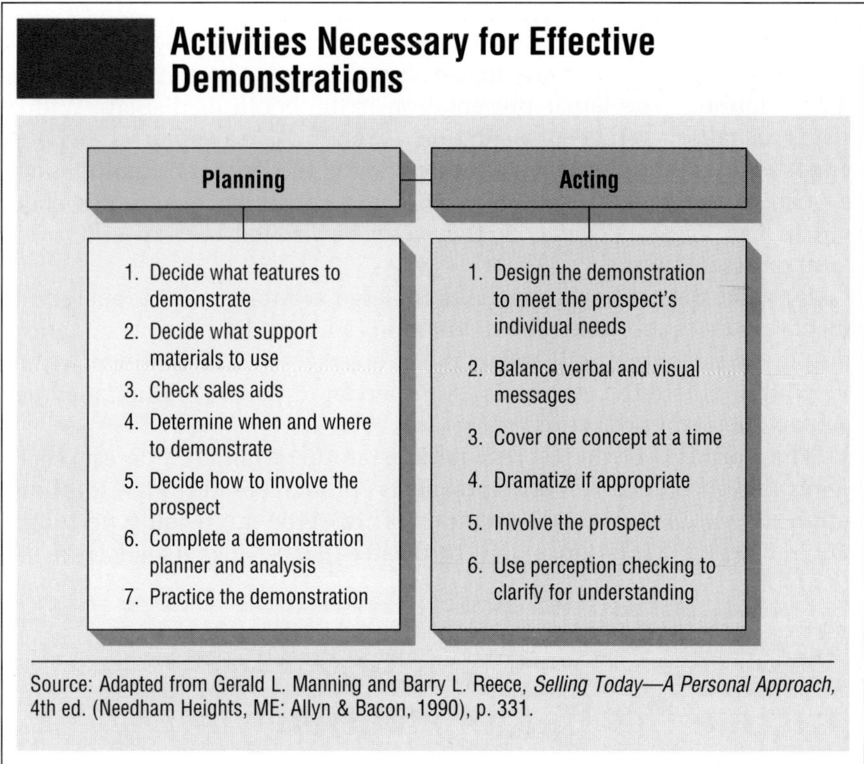

Activities Necessary for Effective Demonstrations
Planning
Acting
1. Decide what features to demonstrate
2. Decide what support materials to use
3. Check sales aids
4. Determine when and where to demonstrate
5. Decide how to involve the prospect
6. Complete a demonstration planner and analysis
7. Practice the demonstration
1. Design the demonstration to meet the prospect's individual needs
2. Balance verbal and visual messages
3. Cover one concept at a time
4. Dramatize if appropriate
5. Involve the prospect
6. Use perception checking to clarify for understanding

Source: Adapted from Gerald L. Manning and Barry L. Reece, *Selling Today—A Personal Approach*, 4th ed. (Needham Heights, ME: Allyn & Bacon, 1990), p. 331.

In the relational sales process there are two objectives that must be developed in setting a target. The first is to ascertain the statements of response that one wants to produce in the customer. These may be referred to as communication objectives. The second type of objective involves production values—making decisions that relate to the use of visual aids, such as the types of visual aids to be used, the length of the presentation, and the most appropriate setting for the presentation. Figures 13.3 and 13.4 provide sample planning and analysis forms that salespeople may use to facilitate their preparation.

Following the planning and analysis stages of the presentation, the final step before "taking the show on the road" is rehearsal. Rehearsing involves practicing what will be said as well as what will be done. For example, when rehearsing the use of sales aids in making product claims, a salesperson should practice the SPESS sequence:

- ***S****tate product claim and introduce the sales aid.* This means stating the product's or service's features, advantages, or benefits and then introducing the sales aid—for instance, "To demonstrate this benefit [or advantage or feature], I'd like you to take a look at this video" or "This graph summarizes the increased savings you'll experience when you purchase a ZKC180." This type of statement tells the customer that aural as well as visual attention is required.

Figure 13.3

Demonstration Planner

A. Name of Company
B. Individual and Title
C. Major Decision Maker and Title
D. Type of Company
E. Products/Services
F. Estimated Annual Sales (gross)
G. Communications Objective (what is to be gained from this presentation)
H. Audience Analysis (general background)

Prospect/customer's Age: ________
Sex: ________
Education/training ________
Other relevant information ________

I. Identifying Verbal Support Materials/ What I will say:

1. ❑ *Example* to support feature/benefit ________
2. ❑ *Anecdote* to support feature/benefit ________
3. ❑ *Comparison* to support feature/benefit ________
4. ❑ *Statistic* to support feature/benefit ________
5. ❑ *Testimony* to support feature/benefit ________

J. Selecting the Appropriate Sales Aids

1. ❑ The product itself
2. ❑ Models
3. ❑ Photographs and illustrations
4. ❑ Reprints
5. ❑ Schematic diagrams
6. ❑ Portfolio
7. ❑ Graphs and test results
8. ❑ Written testimonials
9. ❑ Samples
10. ❑ Interactive video
11. ❑ Audiovisual equipment—overhead, slides, etc.
12. ❑ Computer-assisted media

- *Present the sales aid.* This involves presenting the sales aid to the customer and allowing a few moments for examination before saying anything. For example, when using printed materials, place the material directly in front of the customer and allow it to be reviewed briefly in silence. When using slides or transparencies, give the customer a few seconds to review the information being projected before starting to talk. The customer should be interested in the sales aid; allow a moment for the customer to satisfy natural curiosity.

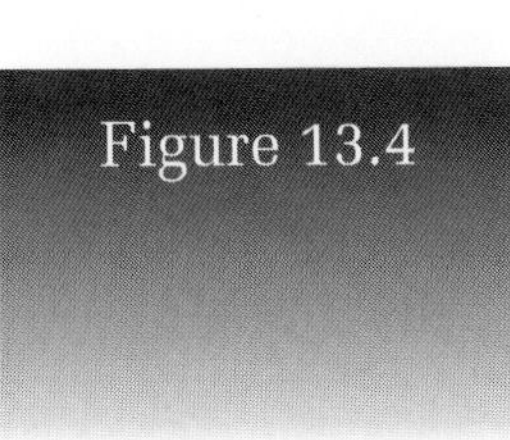

Figure 13.4

Demonstration Analysis

Major Benefits	Feature to Be Demonstrated	Media Used to Demonstrate

Minor Benefits	Feature to Be Demonstrated	Media Used to Demonstrate

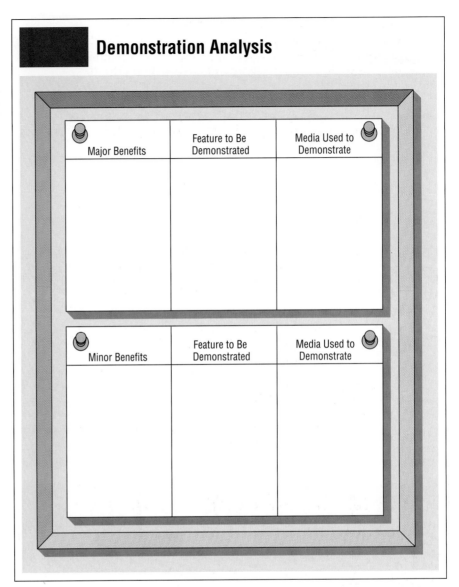

- ***E****xplain the sales aid.* No matter how carefully a sales aid is prepared, it will not be completely obvious. The customer will not necessarily understand the significance of the product demonstration unless you also offer a brief explanation. The printed materials, charts, or graphs that are used require some description. In fact, you will probably want to explain the significance of every sales aid that is used.
- ***S****upport the explanation.* Use examples, comparisons, statistics, and testimony to support your explanation of the sales aid. The support materials should explain the significance of the sales aid to the customer.
- ***S****ummarize.* When you finish explaining the significance of the sales aid, summarize briefly what was said and then remove the

sales aid. As you make additional claims about the features, advantages, or benefits of the product or service, the customer may be distracted by sales aids you have already used. Thus, remove each sales aid when you are finished with it.

In addition to the SPESS sequence, sales professionals use several additional guidelines in preparing for the product demonstration. Table 13.3 provides a straightforward checklist to ensure that the presentation is well thought out and effective.

Table 13.3

A Checklist for Preparing and Rendering Effective Demonstrations

1. Has the product been checked to see that it is working correctly before the customer visit? Have *all* the functions that will be demonstrated been checked?

2. When was the last preventive maintenance check? Do you have back-up parts for components that might need replacing, such as batteries and bulbs?

3. If the demonstration will occur on the customer's premises, will any special conditions be required (lighting, power sources, and so on) and are they already available at the customer's site?

4. Do you know whether or not there will be anyone present who has had any experience using your product? If so, do you know what his or her reactions were? If generally positive, could that person help you demonstrate the effectiveness of your product? If generally negative, how does your product overcome the problems that were experienced earlier?

5. If the product performs a range of functions, which functions will be of most interest to those at the demonstration?

6. Do you plan to have the customer use the product during the demonstration? If so, will it be used in a group? Are there some people who are more skilled who can participate in the demonstration? Is anyone likely to be present whose ineptitude or lack or knowledge might cause embarrassment?

7. As you explain how the product works, avoid jargon unless you know the others understand it.

8. Do you know whether a competitor has preceded you in demonstrating his or her product? If so, what were the features he or she emphasized?

9. If you are going to leave the product with the customer for a trial period, have you, in addition to demonstrating the product, provided the users with hands-on experience? Have you left names and telephone numbers the customers can call to get help after you leave the product with them?

10. If your product requires a warm-up period before it will work to its best advantage, will the customer permit you to set up your demonstration before the presentation begins? This will save the customer's time and ensure that the product is functioning smoothly.

Source: John Coppett and William A. Staples, *Professional Selling: A Relationship Management Process* (Cincinnati, OH: South-Western Publishing Co., 1990), p. 191.

Negotiation during the Presentation

Too often when people think of negotiation, they think of what Michael Schatzki, a professional negotiator, refers to as the "collective bargaining model; namely the acrimonious table-pounding battles between labor and management." The truth is that negotiating in our daily life is virtually limitless.

> Usually negotiations are part of an ongoing relationship—and maintaining that relationship is just as important as getting what you want. If you trick or bully a client, for instance, she probably won't want to do business with you again. And neither will anyone else who hears about your unsavory tactics. . . .
>
> To arrive at the best solution, you first need to discuss the issues and alternatives. The aim isn't a winner-take-all solution; it's to win enough so that everyone's needs are met and people want to do business with you in the future.[9]

In *Negotiating to Yes*, Roger Fisher, a professor of law and negotiation at Harvard Law School, and William Ury, a consultant and lecturer on negotiation and mediation, write:

> Any method of negotiation may be fairly judged by three criteria: It should be a wise agreement if agreement is possible. It should be efficient. And it should improve or at least not damage the relationship between the parties. (A wise agreement can be defined as one which meets the legitimate interests of each side to the extent possible, resolves conflicting interests fairly, is durable, and takes community interests into account.)[10]

Table 13.4 reflects some of the situations in which salespeople negotiate.

In the relational selling model, negotiation is not only expected, it is invited. This philosophy is reflected in our definition of negotiation as a discussion between a buyer and seller of specific proposals for seeking a mutually acceptable solution to a problem or set of needs. It naturally follows that a win-win approach is used to reach the desired outcome. While a win-win outcome is an integral part of the relational selling model, its application here involves eight basic steps.[11]

1. *Identify the problem.* If there is conflict, this involves describing for the prospect or customer the problem the salesperson is having, the salesperson's interpretations and feelings, and the effect the problem has on the salesperson and the relationship to the buyer.

   For example, Bob Smith is a computer technician in the computer center at a college in his hometown. On the side, he builds and sells computer systems that are IBM compatible. To expand his business, he is enrolled in a professional selling course on the campus where he works. His instructor is seeking

Table 13.4

Situations in Which Salespeople Negotiate

Company Selling Situations	Customer Selling Situations
Salesman/Sales Manager Situations Assignment or realignment of territory Account assignment Quota establishment Forecast acceptance Price leverage Product modification request Allocation policy variance New-customer establishment Old-customer discontinuation Key-account concentration Staff support availability Order expediting Performance evaluation Salary review and commission rate establishment *Salesman/Corporate Staff Situations* Customer credit terms or extension from credit manager Customer price reduction from price and contract manager Product modification from engineering, manufacturing, product, or brand managers Customer service from customer service manager	*Complaints* Price exceeds perceived value Product fails to perform according to promise Policy must be defended *Requests* Product specifications must be customer tailored Credit must be extended Service must be applied Unsold merchandise or discontinued models must be returned Advertising and sales promotion support must be provided Market research support must be provided Price concession must be granted Nearby inventory must be established Claims must be settled Product application education must be provided *Innovations* New product must be introduced Product must be put on allocation Delivery must be speeded up or delayed Price increase must be justified Leasing terms must be set Competitive threat must be counteracted Self-manufacture must be discouraged Contract must be renegotiated with a new negotiator Customer policies or objectives change Customer's market grows, shrinks, or changes needs

Source: Reprinted, by permission of the publisher, from *Sales Negotiation Strategies*, by Mack Hanan et al., pp. 9, 10. © 1977 AMACOM, a division of American Management Associations, New York. All rights reserved.

to purchase her first complete system and has asked Bob for his assistance. Bob is concerned because the faculty member has a limited budget, and her office is located in the computer center. While he wants the sale, he is afraid that if he gives her a special price break on equipment and services, other faculty members will expect the same. He also is not comfortable being in the same facility because he does not want to be bombarded with questions after the sale. Furthermore, he is apprehensive about how this transaction might influence his grade.

Not all negotiation involves conflict, however. Suppose this same faculty member approaches Bob and says, "Bob, I have $2,500 to spend on my first computer system, including the printer and software. I've shopped around and am really confused about what to buy. How do your systems compare to the systems and services that I've researched? What are you willing to do for me?" In this case, the relationship is unencumbered and the focus may be on a modified value analysis. A value analysis is "the organized, systematic study of the function of a material, part, component, or system, to identify areas of unnecessary costs that can be eliminated without impairing the capacity of the item to satisfy its objective."[12] Purchasing agents or industrial buyers must work closely with engineers, production managers, and materials handling managers to secure the best product at the least cost. Subsequently, they are more likely to use value analysis extensively.

2. *Describe your needs.* If problems are defined prematurely in terms of solutions rather than in terms of needs, hostility or defensiveness may result. If both the salesperson and the buyer define the problem in terms of their needs, the result is more likely to satisfy both of them.
3. *Confirm the buyer's understanding of problems and needs.* This can be done by asking the buyer to restate what has been said. This step ensures that the buyer has understood the salesperson's statement of needs as well.
4. *Ask for a description of the buyer's needs.* This gives the buyer an opportunity to identify goals and, in so doing, helps to create a more open and cooperative sales communication climate. The probing skills introduced in Chapter 11 and the active listening skills from Chapter 10 are basic skills to use here.
5. *Confirm what is understood about the buyer.* This may be done by paraphrasing the buyer's needs and goals and asking for feedback about the accuracy of the paraphrase. In this step, the salesperson demonstrates that the buyer's needs are clearly understood. A powerful communication tool that may be used here is perception checking. The Skill Builder describes and demonstrates perception checking.
6. *Brainstorm solutions to the problem.* Brainstorming is the unrestrained effort by both the buyer and the salesperson to seek as many different solutions to the problem as they can. It may be helpful to write these ideas down, even if they seem far-fetched or impractical. The key to the success of this step is to generate as many ideas as possible without criticizing any of the ideas until the list is completed.
7. *Evaluate the alternative solutions.* In this step, the customer and the salesperson discuss each of the solutions they have listed in the previous step and decide which ones will and will not work.

Skill Builder 13.1 Perception Checking

Perception is the process of collecting information through your senses and interpreting the data that you collect. In sales communication, the senses of sight and hearing are mainly involved in data collection. The meanings you assign to the observations you make are your interpretations.

There are many ways to perceive what a customer says and does. For example, you may notice a gold chain with a cross and assume that the customer is religious. You may observe a customer looking down rather than directly toward you and think that he or she may not be telling the truth. People usually assume their interpretations about others are accurate, if not factual. However, the assumptions you make may be incorrect and quite different from how customers interpret their own behavior.

A skill to help salespeople clarify their observations and interpretations of their customers and the interaction that takes place between them is perception checking. *Perception checking* is a three-part skill. First, you provide a behavior description, which includes a report of what you see and hear your customer do and say. The second step includes a statement of your interpretation, what the customer's behavior means to you. Finally, you ask the customer to respond about how accurate your interpretations are. For example:

Maureen Faren is a sales representative for International Technologies and Systems Corporation, which distributes the PCW and 800-Portable Barcode Reader. In a conversation with a prospect, the potential buyer says, "I don't think your barcode reader has the capacity to fulfill our inventory needs."

Salesperson: I'm a little confused, Derrick. When you tell me that you don't think our barcoder can handle the size of your inventory [*behavior description*], I'm unsure if you're referring to the reader's ability to handle data or to how well the reader will work in your warehouse [*two interpretations*]. Please clarify this for me [*request for a response*].

As another example:

Bill Mason is a financial services/products representative for The New England, formerly New England Mutual Life Insurance Company. During a recent sales call on one of his prospects, Bill makes the following perception check:

Prospect: Retirement is too far away (big sigh). I'll plan for it someday; besides, I think my employees should take care of it themselves—it's just too much trouble (continued sigh with shaking of head).

Bill: Rich, let me check something. As I hear you speak of planning for retirement someday, I notice a heavy sigh in your voice [*behavior description*], as if your mind is on something else.

It seems as though you'd like to deal with it at some point, but that maybe other needs are more pressing [*interpretation*], or maybe you've got concerns about service and upkeep [*interpretation*].

What more can you tell me? I'd like to understand.

Continued

Notice that the salesperson reports observations of the customer's behavior by describing what was heard and seen ("*I'm* understanding," "*I'm* hearing"). The salesperson does not tell the customer what the customer said or did ("*You* said," "*You're* sighing"). The salespeople's use of "I" to report perceptions helps them to take responsibility for their observations. Similarly, they report their interpretations with "I think," which allows them to assume ownership of their views. As you learned in Chapter 9, the use of "I" to take responsibility for your observations and interpretations is referred to as using owned language.

Through the use of the perception-checking skill in the sample dialogue, the salesperson has not made a judgment about the customer's change of feeling. Rather, the salesperson has used tentative, responsible statements that are likely to contribute to a supportive climate, thereby encouraging the customer to respond more openly and honestly.

The perception-checking skill, like all verbal communication skills, has a nonverbal component. It may be useful for you to review Chapter 11 on the nonverbal means of establishing rapport. Your tone of voice, facial expression, stance, gestures, and other nonverbal communication should match, or be congruent with, the supportive verbal components of this skill.

Respond to another person's description by:

1. Reporting at least one example of the customer's behavior
2. Stating at least two interpretations of the customer's behavior
3. Using an open question to request a response from the customer about the accuracy of your observations
4. Using owned language to take responsibility for your observations and interpretations

---

Exhibit 13.9

Ten Ways to Come Out of Negotiations a Winner

Let's face it, no one goes into a negotiation hoping to lose. The objective of professional negotiations is to achieve a win-win situation where salesperson and buyer come to a mutually beneficial agreement. The following ten concession strategies can help you come out of sales negotiations feeling like a winner.

1. Start negotiations with your highest expectations in price and conditions.
2. Don't assume you have to match the customer's concessions one to one.
3. Don't give a concession away for nothing.
4. Make sure the buyer understands the value of your concession.
5. Make concessions in small amounts.
6. Don't advertise your willingness to make concessions.
7. Don't jump at the "Let's split the difference" offer.
8. Handle the *ridiculous* offer with care.
9. Understand all the requirements before you start making concessions.
10. Before making a concession, get the commitment to buy.

Source: Bob E. Couch, Ph.D., *Personal Selling Power*, July/August 1990, p. 18.

On the International Front

Presentations to foreign buyers make use of visual sales aids, including pictures of the product, its workmanship, and the manufacturing facilities. This is a common practice aimed at getting the buyer to ask questions. In countries with high levels of illiteracy, visual methods of communication are usually used.

Many more demonstrations are often required when presenting to foreign buyers than when dealing with American customers. In most Asian countries, an average of five demonstrations is required, and in the Philippines up to 20 demonstrations may be required to make a sale. More demonstrations means more time and higher costs.

IBM Europe uses video discs linked to touch-screen televisions to sell personal computers through its European dealers. The sales/training message is interactive, allowing the viewer to call up various programs. Demonstrations are now conducted at a uniformly high level in all European countries, in English, Spanish, German, French, Italian, Danish, and Dutch.

Translators or interpreters are sometimes used to help salespeople communicate. A capable translator who has the ability to use the language, idiomatic expressions, and slang of a particular country can be an asset because a salesperson translating a thought or idea into a foreign language risks the possibility that a totally different message will be heard by the prospect.

It is often advisable to avoid using certain technical terms. An example is the use of large numbers—it is possible to mistranslate any number over 10,000. For example, in the United States "a billion" contains nine zeros; however, in Europe it contains 12 zeros. Also, a translated statement or message may require more words than the original.

According to Robert T. Moran, director of the program for cross-cultural communication at the American Graduate School of International Management, "It is most often the intercultural relations that fail, not technical business considerations." Safe rules of thumb in international presentations are:

- When in doubt, overpunctuate.
- Keep ideas separate, making only one point at a time.
- Confirm discussions in writing.
- Write down all figures using the style of the person you are talking to.
- Adjust your English to the level of your foreign counterpart.
- Use visual aids whenever possible.
- Avoid technical, sports, and business jargon.

Sources: Robert T. Moran, "How to Understand Your Partner's Cultural Baggage," *International Management*, September 1983, p. 230; and Vern Terpstra and Ravi Sarathy, *International Marketing* (Ft. Worth, TX: The Dryden Press, 1991), pp. 499, 519.

It is especially important for the salesperson to be honest about solutions because their goal is to find one that both will consider satisfactory.

8. *Decide on the best solution.* The salesperson and the buyer together should choose the solution that best fits both parties' needs. The decision should be discussed thoroughly so that both the buyer and the seller understand it clearly. If the solution involves obtaining approval from other individuals or depart-

ments, clearance should be obtained before implementing the decision.

The preceding steps are a process for dealing with differences between a buyer and a seller. Professional negotiators Roger Fisher and William Ury acknowledge that:

> To be better, the process must, of course, produce good substantive results; winning on the merits may not be the only goal, but certainly losing is not the answer. Both theory and experience suggest that the method of principled negotiation will produce over the long run substantive outcomes as good or better than you are likely to obtain using any other negotiation strategy. In addition, it should prove more efficient and less costly to human relationships.[13]

Summary

There are five important components in the delivery of a sales presentation. Focusing on these components should make us aware of (1) the importance of giving an effective demonstration, (2) the use of sales support materials, (3) the types of presentations and related sales aids, (4) the use of the SPESS sequence to practice the demonstration, and (5) the use of the negotiation process in selling.

In an effective demonstration, the salesperson helps the buyer to achieve psychological possession, or ownership, of the product or service. If the demonstration is effective, the buyer can imagine being the owner of the product or service, experience enhanced retention of features, and understand proof of benefits resulting from the purchase.

Sales support material is an invaluable resource for an effective sales presentation. This material captures and maintains customer interest, provides clarification, increases the retention of information, and provides proof of benefits. Five types of verbal support material are examples (real and hypothetical), anecdotes, comparisons (figurative and literal), statistics, and testimony.

Related to sales support materials are sales aids, which are devices used to involve one or more physical senses in an illustration of product features and benefits. Sales aids include product information, samples, models, photographs and drawings, word and number charts, and pie charts. Guidelines for the use of sales aids in presentations fall under four specific situations: (1) salesperson to person or small group, (2) point-of-purchase selling, (3) general sales meeting, and (4) exhibit or trade show. These guidelines are followed by analysis and planning, by which the salesperson may realize two objectives: (1) ascertaining what responses the salesperson wishes to obtain from the customer and (2) deciding what visual aids should be used, how long the presentation should be, and what is the most appropriate setting for the presentation to obtain these responses.

The SPESS sequence is a planning tool. It consists of (1) **s**tarting the product claim and introducing the sales aid, (2) **p**resenting the sales aid, (3) **e**xplaining the sales aid, (4) **s**upporting the sales aid, and (5) **s**ummarizing.

Negotiation, a discussion of specific proposals between buyer and seller for the purpose of seeking a mutually acceptable solution to a problem or a set of needs, is presented as an essential component of the win-win approach that is intrinsic to the relational setting model. Eight basic steps are identified and explained: (1) identifying the problem, (2) describing one's needs, (3) confirming the buyer's understanding of the salesperson's problems and needs, (4) asking for a description of the buyer's needs, (5) confirming the salesperson's understanding of what the buyer is saying, (6) brainstorming solutions to the problem, (7) evaluating the alternative solutions, and (8) deciding on the best solution.

Studying the material in this chapter will give the professional salesperson a mental advantage in the entire sales approach. This is the point at which concept and application converge.

Key Terms

Anecdote A story that provides a specific incident to clarify or illustrate a product's features, advantages, or benefits; a detailed example

Comparison A form of presentation support that shows similarities between two points

Example The recounting of a brief, specific instance to illustrate a product's features and benefits

Image Management Computer processing of images (art, designs, and photos.)

Review Questions

1. Identify and explain the three reasons for making an effective sales presentation.
2. Define sales support materials. Identify the five types, and give an example of how each might be used in a sales demonstration for a specific product or service.
3. Explain the six reasons for using a sales aid and describe at least three types of aids that might be used in making a specific sales presentation. How do these fulfill the reasons for using aids?
4. Compare and contrast the four types of situations in which sales presentations are typically made. What effect does each have on the choices a salesperson must make to prepare an effective sales presentation?
5. Explain the two objectives a salesperson must consider in setting the target for a sales presentation.
6. Explain how the negotiation process can be an effective component of the sales presentation.
7. Explain the eight steps of the win-win approach to negotiation.
8. Explain the concept of a value analysis.

Figure 13.5

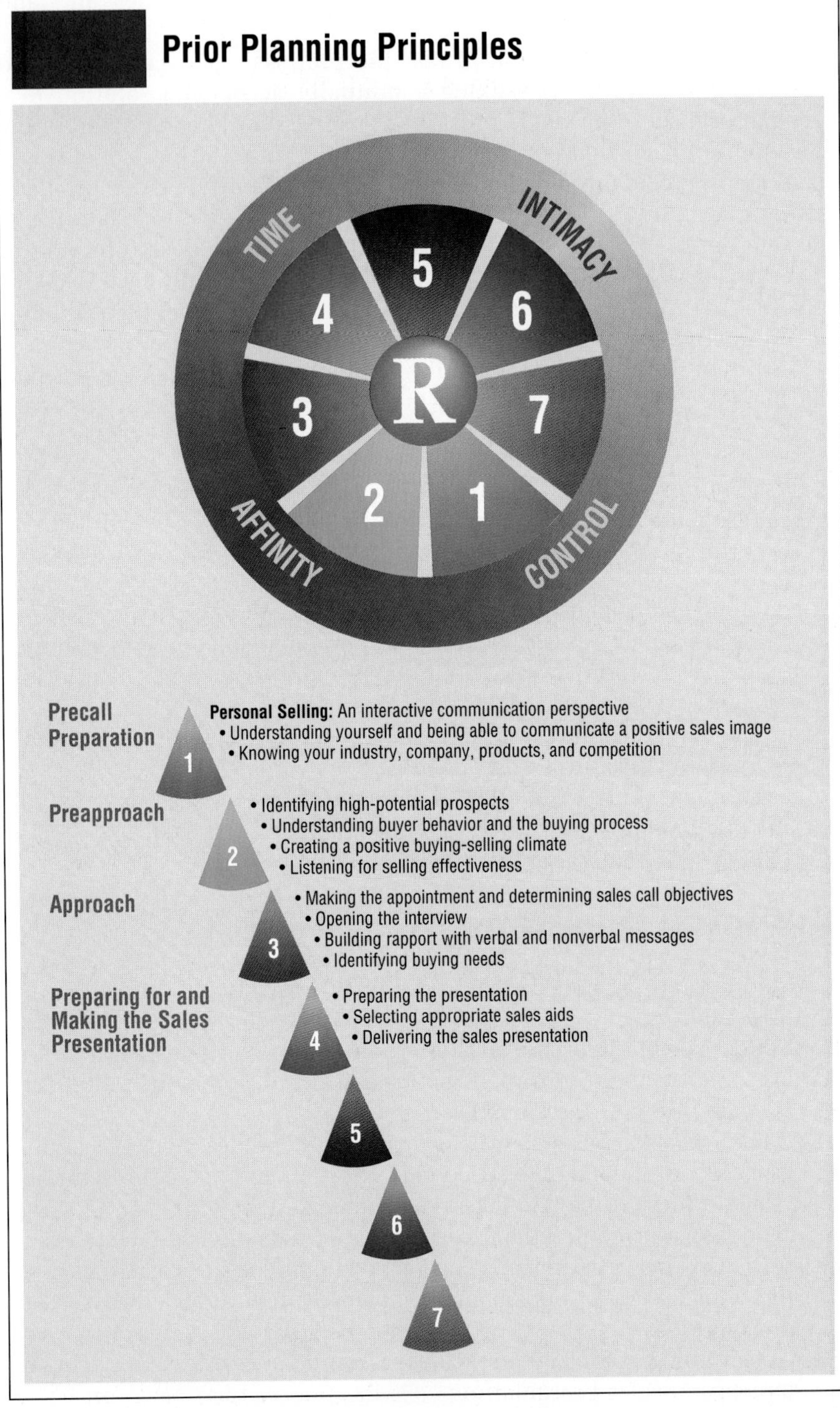
Prior Planning Principles
TIME
INTIMACY
AFFINITY
CONTROL
R
1
2
3
4
5
6
7
Precall Preparation
Personal Selling: An interactive communication perspective
• Understanding yourself and being able to communicate a positive sales image
• Knowing your industry, company, products, and competition
Preapproach
• Identifying high-potential prospects
• Understanding buyer behavior and the buying process
• Creating a positive buying-selling climate
• Listening for selling effectiveness
Approach
• Making the appointment and determining sales call objectives
• Opening the interview
• Building rapport with verbal and nonverbal messages
• Identifying buying needs
Preparing for and Making the Sales Presentation
• Preparing the presentation
• Selecting appropriate sales aids
• Delivering the sales presentation

Discussion Questions

1. What is meant by assisting the buyer in achieving psychological possession or ownership of a product or service? Discuss ways this can be achieved. Discuss ethical and cross-cultural implications.
2. Discuss the characteristics of the five types of sales support materials. Specifically, for what uses can each type be incorporated most effectively?
3. Discuss the advantages and disadvantages of using the types of sales aids described in this chapter. Select a specific product or service and explain what sales aids you might use in a specific setting and what purposes they would serve.
4. Discuss how each of the following selling situations can affect the type of sales aid and sales support material you might use: (1) salesperson to person, (2) point of purchase, (3) general sales meeting, and (4) exhibit or trade show.
5. Identify a product or service. Using the SPESS sequence, role-play a presentation to a small group of four or five classmates. Discuss the outcome.
6. Discuss the concept of negotiation and when it might occur during a sales presentation. In what ways is the negotiation process an essential component of the relational selling model?

Rushing through the Presentation to Avoid Interruption

Case 13.1

Kathy Young accepted a sales position with a well-known sporting goods distributor that has sold equipment for several sports and parts to repair the equipment. Selling in this competitive industry demanded much technical background knowledge and experience, especially for demonstration purposes. Furthermore, the purchasing agents in the sporting industry have developed network systems and deal mostly with affiliates with whom they have developed strong relationships.

Kathy, an athlete herself for many years, accepted the job offer under the pretense that she knew all about the mechanical aspects of the equipment. Although Kathy felt some personal reservation about having adequate preparation, she studied hard during the initial 2 months of training and was given the opportunity to immediately start field sales on her own. She didn't believe the 2 months of training would help much anyway because the trends and technological advancements were constantly changing among most of the products this distributor carried.

An important observation was that the purchasing agents expected their suppliers to be extremely knowledgeable. Kathy felt that many of these prospective buyers would try to test her abilities by asking her difficult questions. Because of her limitations, Kathy was determined to sound knowledgeable and act credible to her prospective buyers.

Case 13.1
Continued

Thinking through her concerns, Kathy developed and memorized a sales presentation covering all aspects of the products that she knew. Because she lacked confidence, her tactic was to start into the sales presentation and move through it swiftly without giving the respondent a chance to interrupt her. In this manner, she would avoid the possibility of being asked questions that she could not answer, which would put her in an awkward position that could result in embarrassment and loss of credibility.

1. Do you agree with Kathy's method and tactic to avoid confrontation?
2. Reacting to Kathy's communication behavior, what advice would you offer her?
3. Is feedback necessary in this sales presentation?

Case 13.2

The Inexperienced Buyer

Michelle Banks sells women's business suits and high-fashion wear for a leading clothing manufacturer in New York. Michelle's territory includes the east coast and several southern states. She has a reputation for having outstanding knowledge of trends and styles in this ever-changing industry.

Michelle is well liked by all of her buyers. She extends a personal touch to each of them and knows many of them personally, to the extent of being considered a close friend. She has also worked closely with many, assisting them with ways to improve their sales and operations through better use of displays and store layout in general.

On occasion she interacts with new buyers who have limited experience. Michelle's recent challenge is with a new chain of stores opening in the South. Upon contacting Mary, the buyer, Michelle learned that Mary had recently been promoted from sales representative to this position and lacked knowledge of the styles and trends in business suits.

Mary seemed to lack confidence as a buyer although she had been successful as a sales representative. She felt the pressures of her new job and having to meet schedules and budget demands. Overall, she was placed in this decision-making capacity, which required undertaking new responsibilities, without adequate preparation.

"I am not ready to order for the upcoming winter season, and I don't even know what is available from other suppliers," Mary said. Realizing this frustration, Michelle developed a presentation around Mary's needs.

Michelle first presented the company's new line of winter wear designed for special occasions. She then offered substantial discounts depending on the quantity purchased. She stressed the refund program and guaranteed customer satisfaction. Finally, she presented merchandising suggestions and ways to display sale items that would attract consumers to the store.

Concerned with the size of the order that was required to get the best prices, Michelle then presented an ordering program that included exceptional financing. Mary then proceeded to place an order, after expressing much satisfaction and appreciation for Michelle's kind assistance.

Case 13.2
Continued

1. Did Michelle take advantage of the inexperienced buyer?
2. Suggest additional benefits that Michelle could have included in her selling presentation.
3. How could Michelle better use her experience in strengthening the buyer's belief in her knowledge and advice? Discuss.

Notes

1. Barbara Pletcher, *Saleswoman* (New York: Pocket Books/Simon and Schuster, 1978), p. 157.
2. Rebecca A. Farnin, "What's That Strange Smell?," *The Marketer*, April 1990, p. 10.
3. Ibid.
4. R. B. Adler and G. Rodman, *Understanding Human Communication*, 3rd ed. (New York: Holt, Rinehart and Winston, 1988).
5. Kathleen Doler, "Viewstar's $300,000 Software," *Upside*, August/September 1990, p. 61.
6. Ibid., p. 59.
7. Michael Kenny, *Presenting Yourself* (New York: John Wiley & Sons, 1982), pp. 19–51.
8. Ibid., p. 32.
9. Ellen J. Belzer, "The Negotiator's Art: You *Can* Always Get What You Want," *Working Woman*, April 1990, pp. 98, 131.
10. Roger Fisher and William Ury, *Negotiating to Yes* (New York: Penguin Books, 1987), p. 4.
11. Sharon A. Ratliffe and David D. Hudson, *Skill Building for Interpersonal Competence* (New York: Holt, Rinehart and Winston, 1988), pp. 337–338.
12. J. J. Westing, I. V. Fine, and Gary J. Zenz, *Purchasing Management* (Santa Barbara, CA: John Wiley & Sons, 1976), p. 234.
13. Roger Fisher and William Ury, *Negotiating to Yes*, p. 154.

CHAPTER

14

Managing Buying Resistance

Knowledge Objectives

In this chapter, you will learn:

1. The nature of buying resistance and how to handle it relationally
2. How the concepts of overcoming sales objections and managing buying resistance differ
3. How buying resistance can be transformed into opportunities to increase sales and customer satisfaction
4. Traditional methods for handling resistance effectively
5. How to merge communication skills with traditional methods for acknowledging and resolving resistance
6. How to respond to criticism and other defense-producing messages in nondefensive ways

Consider This

People resist making decisions. Decision making is risk taking. Openly stating a decision is a commitment; it may be viewed as a turning point from which there is no retreat. A decision is always followed by consequences that may be either good or bad, and that are visible to others. If those consequences prove bad, the result may affect not only the buyer but also any number of other people in the company or the family. The buyer is risking money, the inconvenience of struggling with a product that is unsatisfactory, and the possible loss of others' respect.

David J. Lill*

**Selling: The Profession* (New York: Macmillan Publishing Company, 1989), p. 366.

- *"perceived scarce rewards"*—Time and money are two rewards that are often perceived to be in limited supply. Struggles over how to use time and money effectively are often the source of conflict. When salespeople have facilitated long-term relationships with customers in such a way that the customer believes they are a team working to solve problems in the customer's environment, the two of them can honestly, openly, and creatively manage resources such as time and money in ways that allow immediate and long-range goals to be effectively met. The key to using this approach is the ability for both the salesperson and the customer to perceive time, money, and other resources as tools in their *mutual* problem-solving process, rather than as "mine versus yours."
- *"interference from the other parties"*—When seemingly incompatible goals and scarce rewards are expressed openly and honestly between salespeople and their customers, then the likelihood that either party will perceive the other as interfering is dramatically reduced. Interference is also reduced when both parties are able to examine their struggles in the framework of immediate and long-range planning. In fact, they can then welcome conflict as a test of the solutions to problems that they derive together.

To facilitate the constructive management of conflict in the

Try This 14.1 Intra-/Interpersonal Conflict Inventory

Every day we encounter numerous conflict situations. A natural response is to blame others for the conflict we find in ourselves. Most often, however, a combination of outside factors and our own personality, thoughts, or feelings are the cause of our problem. To increase your awareness of intra- and interpersonal conflict, conduct a self-inventory by answering the following questions:

1. Do you consider your thoughts to be more important than those of others (customers, peers, parents)?
2. Do you feel conflict about how you relate to other people?
3. Are your feelings more positive than those of others with whom you associate?
4. Are you in conflict over how you spend your time?
5. Do you speak with authority?
6. Are you in conflict over your lifetime goals?
7. Are you able to listen to others (such as customers or clients) when you are annoyed by them?
8. Are you highly tolerant of other people's negative feelings?
9. Do you believe that your principles are superior to those of your customers?
10. Do you believe in saying exactly what you feel in dealing with others?
11. Do you care for the people with whom you talk?

Source: Adapted from Richard L. Weaver II, *Understanding Interpersonal Communication*, 5th ed. (Glenview, IL: Scott, Foresman/Little, Brown Higher Education, 1990), pp. 328, 339.

sales relationship, it is important to address conflict in this context as "managing buying resistance" or "acknowledging and resolving resistance," rather than as "overcoming sales objections."

Reasons for Adopting the Buying Resistance Concept

The value of viewing conflict as a useful and necessary tool in reaching favorable buying decisions seems obvious from the extended definition of conflict as it applies to the sales relationship. In contrast, the notion of "overcoming sales objections" creates a win-lose relationship and implies a communication style on the salesperson's part that is likely to encourage aggressive or defense-arousing behavior. In other words, in a win-lose situation, someone is going to lose. Most people do not want to be losers, and salespeople and their customers are no exception. Therefore, they enter into a competition, with the salesperson defeating any objections the customer may raise. Strategies for winning are developed and used by both people as if they were opponents in a poker game. They no longer view themselves as a team working for mutual goals; consequently, ideas and feelings are withheld from each other. Stress levels increase.

When this description characterizes a sales relationship, then conflict is usually harmful, resulting in emotions that are debilitative for both parties. Consequently, the relationship is weakened. This approach to conflict—viewing it as a need to "overcome sales objections"—can best be described as dysfunctional. In contrast, when salespeople are willing to approach conflict in a sales relationship as the need to "manage buying resistance," then conflict can become more functional, as the relationship-driven concept implies.

One mechanism salespeople may use to aspire toward functional ends in managing conflict is using *assertive messages*. Sales professionals use assertive messages when they express their ideas, feelings, and wants clearly and directly to their customers in such a way that they stand up for their own rights while at the same time demonstrating respect for the customer's rights.

Where aggressive behavior overpowers the customer by calling for judgments and demands, the use of assertive messages contributes to a supportive buying climate while requesting a change in the customer's behavior. Chapter 12 provides additional information on aggressive, assertive, and nonassertive behaviors. Skill Builder 14.1 introduces and demonstrates how to use assertive messages effectively and appropriately. With this understanding of the nature of buying resistance and the need to adopt the viewpoint of "managing buying resistance" in the relational approach to sales communication, we are ready to examine the types of buying resistance and the skills for managing them.

Types of Buying Resistance

Resistance occurs at two levels: attitudinal and behavioral. Salespeople can only guess what is happening at the attitudinal level unless customers

Skill Builder 14.1 Using Assertive Messages

An assertive message expresses the salesperson's thoughts, feelings, and needs directly and clearly to the customer without judging or demanding and in a way that respects the customer's rights.

There are six basic components to an assertive message:

1. *Identify the topic of your concern.* In this first step, the salesperson reports the customer's behavior that he or she would like to discuss and inquires as to whether the time is right for the discussion. For example:

   "Mark, I'd like to talk with you about some observations I have of the manner in which you handled the rebates on our last shipment of merchandise to you. Is this a good time?"

2. *Describe the behavior you would like the customer to change.* Once the customer acknowledges a willingness to discuss the topic, then the salesperson can use behavior description to report observations of the customer's behavior in specific and nonjudgmental language. Interpretations are excluded from this step. For example:

   "Four weeks ago, when you placed your order with us, I understood you to agree to sending the rebate certificates on sold goods directly to me so that I could personally handle your credit with the accounting department because I had made an exception and offered you an additional 7 percent return as a preferred customer. Yesterday, the manager of the accounting department called me in and showed me the certificates she had received from you. She denied your extra 7 percent because I had not cleared it with her first."

3. *Offer at least two different interpretations.* The salesperson should then offer at least two possible reasons for the customer's behavior using nonjudgmental and owned language. This step suggests to the customer that the salesperson believes there are at least two logical explanations for the behavior. For example:

   "I started to think that maybe you'd forgotten about our agreement to have me walk the papers through the process. I also wondered if maybe you intentionally decided to circumvent the procedures we had agreed to."

4. *Report your feelings as they relate to the behavior you are describing.* When salespeople report their interpretations with their emotions, they clearly and directly state for discussion purposes the resistance that they feel toward their customers' behavior. It is important to use owned language when reporting one's feelings. "You [it] make[s] me feel . . ." is disowned because the responsibility for the salesperson's feeling is displaced onto the customer or the events that have transpired. For example:

   "Mark, I feel let down and a little angry because it appears that you didn't follow through on our plans as I thought we had agreed."

   Notice that the salesperson states the context for the feelings in a tentative and owned manner by using "it appears" and "as I thought."

5. *Explain the tangible effects of the customer's behavior on you.* This statement is based on the principle that for every action there is a reac-

tion. The tangible effects on the salesperson refer to how the customer's behavior (action) directly affects the salesperson's own behavior (reaction). Tangible effects do not include the reactions one may have at the idea or feeling levels; they are behaviors. The effectiveness of the salesperson's assertive message will be increased if the customer clearly understands how his or her behavior has consequences for the salesperson. Tangible effects relate to money, time, extra work, hindrance in completing a task, harm to one's possessions, risk to one's safety, and any other concrete, observable consequences of the customer's behavior on the salesperson. For example:

"As a result, Mark, I gave up my commission to fulfill my commitment with you."

6. *State your wants or intentions.* A salesperson may describe wants in one of two general ways. The first method is to invite the customer to discuss how to prevent similar behavior or actions from occurring in the future. This problem-solving approach enables the customer to view himself or herself as part of the solution, thereby contributing to a supportive climate while confirming the worth of the customer. For example:

"Mark, I'd like to sit down and talk with you about how we can avoid this breakdown in communication another time. Would you be willing to discuss this with me?"

A second method of stating the salesperson's wants or intentions involves prescribing the alternative behavior he or she would like the customer to use in the future. This method places the salesperson in a superior position of indicating the behavior desired from the customer. Depending on how the customer views the specific request, prescribing wants can contribute to increased resistance and other forms of defensive behavior. However, the salesperson does have the right to request specific behavior, just as the customer has the right to refuse compliance. For example:

"In the future, Mark, I'm willing to continue providing special financial benefits to you. In return, I'd like you to follow through according to our initial agreement. I'd really like to know how you respond to this, Mark."

At the same time as the salesperson uses an assertive message to directly report to the customer behaviors that are not satisfactory, the salesperson is also directly reporting degrees of resistance that he or she feels in the sales relationship.

1. Select a situation that involves a customer with whom you have a long-term relationship.
2. Develop a dialogue for that situation using the six steps in an assertive message:
   a. Identify the topic of your concern.
   b. Describe the behavior you would like the customer to change.
   c. Offer at least two interpretations.
   d. Report your feelings as they relate to the behavior you are describing.
   e. Explain the tangible effect of the customer's behavior on you.
   f. State your wants or intentions.
3. Select a partner who will act as your customer, and deliver your assertive statements. Practice using your assertive message until you feel comfortable with your dialogue.

specifically talk about their attitudes. Similarly, when salespeople feel resistance toward requests made by a customer, unless they communicate their attitude of resistance the customer can only guess about it. The consequence is a guessing game.

When salespeople are trained to manage buying resistance, they are responsible for openly stating their attitudes of resistance, as well as observing and listening to the customer so that they can supportively assist the customer to state attitudes of resistance directly. One must be observant of both verbal and nonverbal cues that may signal various types of resistance:

- no perceived need
- uncertainty about the product
- price resistance
- service dissatisfaction
- timing issues
- company resistance
- resistance to the salesperson

In Chapter 11, five types of resistance are shown to coincide with the focal points of customer buying decisions. Therefore, managing buying resistance directly involves creating an awareness of resistance in these areas and then working with the customer to manage it.

Below are brief explanations of each type of resistance, with sample customer statements and behaviors.

No Perceived Need

The customer may be unaware of a need, uninformed about the product or service, or content with the present situation. This type of resistance is likely to occur before or during the first step in the problem-solving process—need identification, which was the subject of Chapter 11. As is true with all seven types of resistance, however, the lack of a perceived need may cause resistance at any time during the sales interview and relationship. For example: While walking toward the door, the customer says, "We still have plenty in stock," or "We've been ordering from Dow Industries for the past 10 years. I don't see any reason to change to your company as our source for this particular item."

Product Uncertainty

The product or service may be tangible or intangible. It includes such characteristics as composition, structure, and function. The customer's uncertainty may center on anything from the color to the design of an entire system. For example: "I want a copier that will give me two-sided copies; yours won't," or "I feel as though I'm being pressured into buying a system that I know will be obsolete within 2 years" (shakes head and sighs).

Price Resistance

Price includes such functions as billing, financing, credit terms, discounts, and markups. For example: "It's hard to believe that I'm going to receive this kind of service for free" (frowns while making this statement). Or the customer walks away while saying, "Adding another line will cost me a bundle. I'm already satisfied with the discount and terms that S & R gives us."

Service Dissatisfaction

Service includes delivery, follow-up, warranties, guarantees, repair, maintenance, installation, and training. For example: "I'm fed up with hospitals not communicating with me about the status of my injured employees" (shakes head and tosses pen on the desk). Or "I've heard horror stories from some of my associates about your slow turnaround time for repairs."

Timing Issues

Timing involves such areas as premature pressure or haste to buy, as well as procrastination. For example: "Really, I'm busy right now. I don't even have time to think about it." Or, while moving to dial the phone, the customer says, "I'll have to wait and talk with Jack before I make a decision."

Company Resistance

Resistance to the company may involve such concerns as the age, size, financial standing, market share, and rate of growth of the firm, its affiliation with other well-known firms, the status of existing customers, patents held, sound labor relations, and efficiency of operation. For example: The customer sighs, yawns, and says, "I'd feel more comfortable dealing with a nationally known firm," or "You're too small to accommodate the volume we'll need."

Salesperson Resistance

Resistance to the salesperson may include references to such issues as personal weaknesses, rude manners, and unfriendly feelings. For example: The customer waves the salesperson out the door, saying, "Get me another rep down here! I don't like dealing with an arrogant rookie!" or "Do you have the audacity to sit here and tell me how to run my business?"

These seven types of buying resistance may arise at any level of intensity and at any time during the sales call or the relationship. Once the nature of the resistance is understood, however, the salesperson may transform it into opportunity.

Try This 14.2 Identifying Types of Buying Resistance

1. Review the section in this chapter on identifying the seven types of buying resistance: need, product, price, service, timing, company, and salesperson.
2. Select either an industrial product, a consumer good, or a service.
3. Relate the types of buying resistance to your product or service that you would most likely encounter during your sales call. Write two statements, using both verbal and nonverbal messages, for each of the seven types. For example:

   Timing
   a. "Right now, I don't have any available shelf space."
   b. "Next Friday is not a good day for me to receive delivery."

4. Using a format similar to the one below, write 14 statements that relate the seven types of buying resistance:

Need
a. ______
b. ______

Product
a. ______
b. ______

Price
a. ______
b. ______

Service
a. ______
b. ______

Timing
a. ______
b. ______

Company
a. ______
b. ______

Salesperson
a. ______
b. ______

Transforming Resistance into Opportunity: Traditional Methods for Managing Buying Resistance

Five traditional methods for managing buying resistance have been used successfully throughout the years. We refer to these strategies as traditional because they have endured throughout the evolution of selling from product-driven to sales-driven and then to customer-driven systems. These methods are direct denial, indirect denial, boomerang, superior benefit, and trial offer.

Direct Denial

To use direct denial, the salesperson must refute what the customer has said. This method must be used with extreme caution because, although this type of resistance is often caused by the customer having incomplete or inaccurate information, people do not like to be told that they are wrong. A salesperson should consider using this only when the facts are adequate to clearly support the denial. For example:

Prospect: We've always wanted to have a house on or near the ocean, but the property taxes are so high that we'll just have to be satisfied living inland. I guess that means looking in Orange or Tustin or Santa Ana as opposed to Newport Beach or Corona del Mar.

Salesperson: I can appreciate your concern. Orange County has a reputation for high taxes. What surprised me—and I'm confident it will you, also—is that in the last quarter's county assessor's property tax guide [which is shown to the customer], both Huntington Beach and Dana Point have a considerably lower tax base than either Tustin or Orange.

Indirect Denial

The indirect denial method is also referred to as the "agree and counter" or "yes-but" method. In this case, the salesperson appears to agree with the prospect and then counters with a qualifying statement. Perhaps because it is important for people to feel their views are valuable or worthwhile, this method is one of the most widely accepted. It may also be popular because the salesperson has an opportunity to clarify misinformation or inaccuracies in the buyer's perception. For example:

Prospect: A 15-percent increase in packaging costs seems rather high.

Salesperson: Yes, that is substantial, but would a 22-percent increase in sales compensate for the difference?

or

Prospect: Your networks cost more than your competitors'.

Salesperson: Yes, we do cost a little bit more than our competitors, but the 32Com network systems are differentiated from the competition in some very important ways. We offer networks with *open* architecture. This ensures application developers and system integrators with compatibility for today's popular DOS and OS/2 standards. With our single-vendor solution we offer integrated, network-optimized systems and components that provide better price/performance ratios.

Boomerang

The boomerang method takes the prospect's resistance and gives it back to the prospect as a reason for buying. It is used effectively when the reason for the resistance is partially true or when the prospect makes excuses for not wanting to listen to the presentation. For example:

Prospect: You are such a young realtor, you probably haven't been practicing very long.

Salesperson: No, I haven't, as a matter of fact. But this only motivates me more to help find the right home for you.

Superior Benefit

Sometimes referred to as the compensation method, this method is designed to present a benefit that will outweigh the prospect's particular concern. As with indirect denial, the salesperson may use "yes-but" when stating a superior benefit or compensation. For example:

Prospect: Your offices seem outdated and badly in need of refurbishing.

Salesperson: Yes, I know. My boss has also observed this but feels that both his and my time are best spent helping people find homes.

or

Prospect: I sure wish zoning would allow horses.

Salesperson: Just 5 minutes away is a boarding stable with a very good reputation. Cleaning and feeding are done automatically, so that you may spend more of your time riding.

Trial Offer

The trial offer is used for those buyers who may resist because they haven't used either the salesperson's product or services or a competitor's product or service. It offers them the opportunity to use the product without making a buying commitment. This method is especially effective for the person who is apprehensive because, if the product or service is satisfactory, the buying resistance is likely to disappear. For example:

Prospect: I'm sure you have good copy machines, but we are happy with the ones we are using now.

Salesperson: I can understand your reluctance to change. And for that very reason I'd like to have your permission to deliver our ZOOM-200 at no charge to you so that you and your staff may compare yours with ours during the next month.

Merging Communication Skills with Traditional Selling Methods

In Chapter 2 we emphasized that a competent sales professional who operates within the framework of the relational selling model has more

Try This 14.3 Using Traditional Methods to Manage Buying Resistance

1. Select one statement from each of the types of resistance that you identified in "Try This" exercise 14.2.
2. For each of those statements, select one of the traditional methods for managing buying resistance discussed in this chapter and write your response using that method. Use a format similar to the one below.
   a. **Direct Denial**
      Customer: __________
      Salesperson: __________
   b. **Indirect Denial**
      Customer: __________
      Salesperson: __________
   c. **Boomerang**
      Customer: __________
      Salesperson: __________
   d. **Compensation or Superior Benefit**
      Customer: __________
      Salesperson: __________
   e. **Trial Offer**
      Customer: __________
      Salesperson: __________
3. Select a partner who will act as your customer, and deliver your statements and responses. Practice using these methods until you feel comfortable with your dialogue.

flexibility and spontaneity than one who is limited to working within only one of the other three selling systems. A major criterion for developing sales competence is the mastery of communication skills that match the appropriate step and situation in the selling process. In this section we will review those skills and show how they can be merged with traditional selling methods to help the salesperson develop competence in managing buying resistance. The tools we will discuss are active listening, probing with open and closed questions, perception checking, and assertive messages. Note that any of the traditional methods may be incorporated into the sales communication skills. This linking or interfacing is analogous to merging traditional methods for opening the interview with the five levels of communication for building rapport, which we presented in Chapter 10.

By using these skills to manage buying resistance, salespeople model techniques that the customer also may begin to use. The result is a strengthened relationship in which both the buyer's and seller's goals are satisfied.

Active Listening

Active listening skills include three components: attending behavior, a paraphrase of the customer's ideas and feelings, and a verification question to determine the accuracy of the salesperson's paraphrase. Because resistance is usually both mental and emotional, a salesperson's paraphrase of a customer's ideas and feelings can achieve several important goals in managing buying resistance:

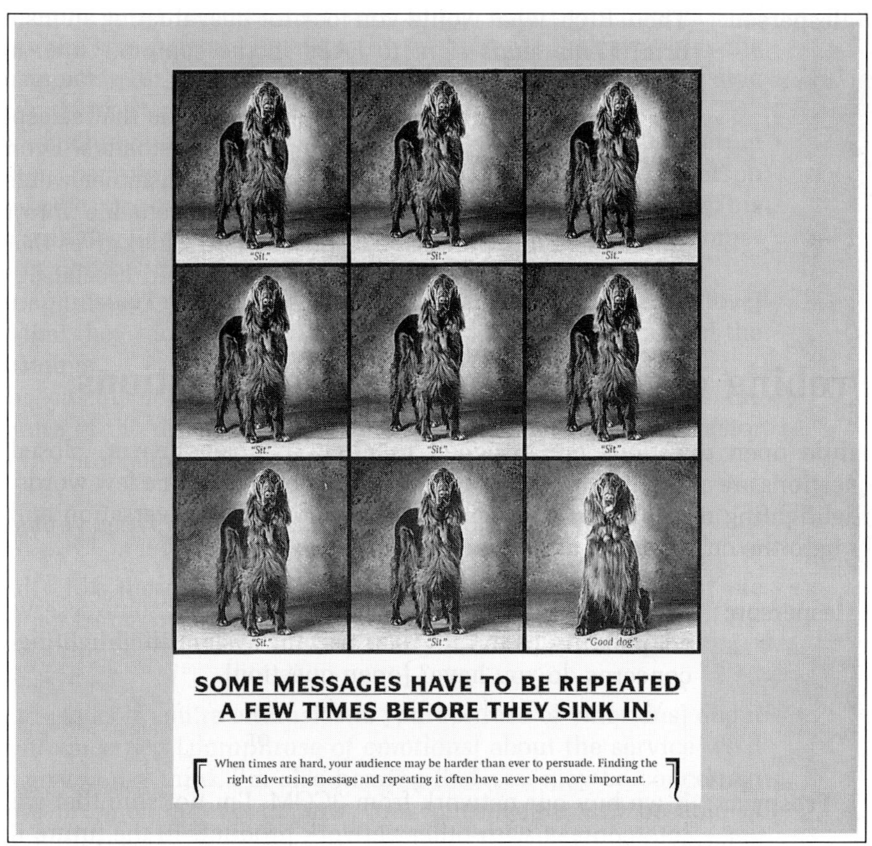

"Sit."
"Sit."
"Sit."
"Sit."
"Sit."
"Sit."
"Sit."
"Sit."
"Good dog."
SOME MESSAGES HAVE TO BE REPEATED
A FEW TIMES BEFORE THEY SINK IN.
When times are hard, your audience may be harder than ever to persuade. Finding the right advertising message and repeating it often have never been more important.

Remember that perception checking is a three-part skill. The first step is for the salesperson to provide a behavior description, which includes a report of what the salesperson sees the customer do and say. The second step is a statement of the salesperson's interpretation of what the customer's behavior means. Finally, the salesperson asks the customer to respond about how accurate the interpretations are. For example:

Prospect: I do everything myself, and it all seems to work out okay.

Salesperson: I understand that doing the payroll yourself is a viable option, yet I'm also noticing that it's just "okay"—not great [*behavior description*]. I'm thinking that your payroll system could be better in some way [*interpretation*]. How accurate am I? [*request for response*]

or

Prospect: It all sounds nice but too complicated.

Salesperson: It sounds as if you like our system but are hesitant about the details [*behavior description*]. It seems as though you're unsure about some of our procedures [*interpretation*]. Is this correct? [*request for response*] or

Prospect: Your company is awfully new and there are only three of you. We can't afford any delays in parts or services.

Salesperson: Let me check something with you, Ron [*request for response*]. By the hesitation in your voice and your raised eyebrows, I'm sensing that you are apprehensive about working with a startup company like ours [*behavior description*]. I'm wondering if you have had some unpleasant experience in the past or if you are associating quality of service with the size and age of the company [*interpretations*].

Assertive Messages

Assertive messages were introduced in Skill Builder 14.1; this is a good point at which to review that discussion. Consider an additional application of this skill:

In an earlier chapter we used a dialogue in which Donna Dannon, the event coordinator for Kellogg West Center for Continuing Education at California Polytechnic University in Pomona, was trying to initiate an account with Tracy Fong, meeting planner for Southern Dynamics. Since then, Donna has worked on a regular basis with Tracy.

In the early summer they spent time together planning a series of meetings for the fall quarter. Tracy "fell in love" with the new restaurant at the Center for Hospitality Management and asked that Donna work with the student advisors to plan special dinners for her groups. This arrangement would allow her conferees a unique experience and keep them on site.

Tracy was to approve the formal agreement in August and confirm all dates and group sizes. When Donna contacted Tracy according to their prearranged schedule, Tracy said that she had made other plans at a local restaurant for their dinners and refused to honor their agreement. Donna addresses the situation with an assertive message:

Hi, Tracy. I'd like to talk with you about the way you handled the reservations for your groups' dinner plans. Is this a good time?

Identify topic of concern

In early summer you expressed a desire for a unique dining experience for your conferees. I made special arrangements with the CHM advisors to plan their class assignments around your groups. Now, when it is time to sign a formal contract, you tell me that you have made other arrangements for your dinners.

Describe the behavior I would like to change

I started to think that you had forgotten our agreement and how far in advance our class assignments must be finalized. I also wondered if you were uncomfortable with our arrangement and purposely did not communicate your feelings to me.

Offer at least two interpretations

Tracy, I feel betrayed and disappointed because you did not honor our verbal agreement.

Report my feelings as they relate to the behavior I am describing

As a result, Tracy, the faculty advisors to the restaurant are reluctant to reserve space for other Kellogg West groups in the future.

Explain tangible effects of customer's behavior on me

Try This 14.4 Using Communication Skills to Manage Buying Resistance

1. Select one statement from each of the resistance types that you identified in "Try This" exercise 14.2.
2. For each of those statements in each of the seven categories of buying resistance, select the communication skills that would best fit that statement. Write your response using a format similar to the one below. You may want to refer to the examples in this chapter to review the steps and components of each skill.
   a. **Active Listening**
   Customer: __________
   Salesperson: __________
   b. **Probing with Open and Closed Questions**
   Customer: __________
   Salesperson: __________
   c. **Perception Checking**
   Customer: __________
   Salesperson: __________
   d. **Assertive Messages**
   Customer: __________
   Salesperson: __________
3. Select a partner who will act as your customer, and deliver your responses. Practice using these skills until you feel comfortable with your dialogue.

State wants or intentions

Tracy, I'd like to sit down and talk with you about how this change in plans without my knowledge could be avoided in the future. Would you be willing to talk with me about this situation?

Responding to Criticism and Other Defense-Arousing Messages

As described in Skill Builder 14.1, using assertive messages allows salespeople to provide constructive criticism to their customers while also allowing the customers to feel supported. At times, however, a salesperson will receive criticism that the customer may not express in a supportive manner.

George Bernard Shaw said, "The test of a man or woman's breeding is how they behave in a quarrel." Regardless of whether the customer's use of defense-arousing messages is caused by a lack of communication skill or other reasons, it is in the best interest of the relationship that the salesperson respond to defense-arousing messages in a nondefensive manner. This can be accomplished by genuinely requesting more information from, or by agreeing with, the customer.

Requesting Additional Information from the Customer

When a customer uses judgmental language, assumes a sense of superiority, or uses other defense-arousing behaviors to criticize the salesperson, the salesperson must communicate in a way that will stop the defensive spiral. One way that the salesperson can transform defensiveness into supportiveness is to request additional information from the customer. A request for information will help the salesperson understand the criticism more fully while serving to reduce its intensity.

Asking for more information requires listening with an open mind and making a genuine effort to understand the criticism. When the customer provides additional information, it is helpful for the salesperson to check perceptions and actively listen to verify an understanding of the new information. The salesperson need not agree with the criticism. Once the salesperson has listened carefully to the criticism, however, that person will be in a better position to explain the behavior or disagree with the criticism. The salesperson may also discover from the additional information that some of the criticism is valid.

Responding to criticism by asking for more information is typically referred to as *negative inquiry*.[2] In the following dialogue, the customer uses evaluative language, and the salesperson has every right to respond defensively. Instead, however, we have provided some nondefensive inquiries for additional information. For example:

Customer: What good is our recent investment in the IDC monitor if we have to buy special tools to run it? I don't want to be pressured into buying any more cheap gadgets!

Salesperson: What exactly don't you like about the tools? In what ways do you feel pressured? I'd really like to know more about what you mean by "cheap gadgets."

The salesperson must remember to request additional information in a calm, steady tone of voice and with a pleasant facial expression. Questions intended to be supportive can become aggressive when paired with incongruent nonverbal signals.

Agreeing with the Customer

As an alternative to negative inquiry or after using that skill, a salesperson may want to use negative assertion. *Negative assertion* involves either agreeing with the content of the criticism or acknowledging the customer's right to perceive the situation from that perspective.[3] If the salesperson has made a mistake or if agreements made with the customer have not worked out as planned, the salesperson should agree with the content of the criticism: for example, denying that an order has been lost when in fact it has may weaken the relationship because it is dishonest. Similarly, if one agrees to deliver an order by a specified date and it does not arrive, there is little to be gained by denying the truth.

If the criticism seems in error or unjust, the salesperson can agree with the customer by simply acknowledging that person's right to perceive the situation without taking a stand on the content of the criticism itself. For example:

Customer: Your delivery record with our company is not very impressive. I'm really angry with you for messing things up!

Salesperson: Mike, I just don't understand why you're mad. As far as I know, both those deliveries were for next week's schedule. What can you tell me about this? [*negative inquiry*]

Customer: I wanted them here by yesterday.

Salesperson: I can understand why having the parts in your inventory readily accessible to you is important [*negative assertion—acknowledging the customer's perceptions*]. It was my understanding that you really didn't need them until next week. Was I wrong?

Customer: Because we received a large order from one of our major accounts 2 days ago, we'll need to start production immediately.

Salesperson: I see. Let me see if I understand. What I'm hearing is that our delivery is on schedule but an unexpected order from one of your important accounts makes it urgent that you receive the delivery earlier than we agreed. In fact, I'm hearing that you would have liked the order to be here yesterday [*paraphrase*]. Is that about it? [*verification question*]

Customer: That's it in a nutshell!

Salesperson: Let me call the office right now and put a next-day rush on your order.

This response uses negative assertion to agree with the customer's right to perceive things, even though the salesperson does not share the customer's viewpoint. By remaining calm and genuinely interested in understanding and meeting the customer's needs through the combined use of negative assertion, negative inquiry, and active listening, this salesperson strengthened the relationship with the customer and used a functional approach to managing buying resistance.

Summary

This chapter focuses on sales resistance and is based on the premise that conflict is an inevitable and desirable component of the relational selling approach. Conflict, viewed as sales resistance, can be used to strengthen the sales relationship and the effectiveness of the exchange between salesperson and customer.

Seven points are covered in this chapter to assist the student in acquiring and practicing the skills to manage sales resistance supportively and productively. The seven topics are: (1) the nature of buying resistance and how to handle it relationally, (2) how the concepts of overcoming sales objections and managing buying resistance differ, (3) reasons for adopting the concept of buying resistance, (4) types of buying resistance,

Try This 14.5 Using Negative Inquiry and Negative Assertion to Manage Buying Resistance

1. Select one or more statements from each of the types of buying resistance that you identified in "Try This" exercise 14.2, or create a new situation to fit this exercise.

2. For each of the situations in each of the seven types of buying resistance, write a response that uses negative inquiry. Repeat the process using negative assertion.

Negative Inquiry

a. Need
Customer: ____
Salesperson: ____

b. Product
Customer: ____
Salesperson: ____

c. Price
Customer: ____
Salesperson: ____

d. Service
Customer: ____
Salesperson: ____

e. Timing
Customer: ____
Salesperson: ____

f. Company
Customer: ____
Salesperson: ____

g. Salesperson
Customer: ____
Salesperson: ____

Negative Assertion

a. Need
Customer: ____
Salesperson: ____

b. Product
Customer: ____
Salesperson: ____

c. Price
Customer: ____
Salesperson: ____

d. Service
Customer: ____
Salesperson: ____

e. Timing
Customer: ____
Salesperson: ____

f. Company
Customer: ____
Salesperson: ____

g. Salesperson
Customer: ____
Salesperson: ____

3. Select a partner who will act as your customer, and deliver your statements and responses. Practice using these skills until you feel comfortable with your dialogue.

(5) traditional methods for managing buying resistance, (6) merging communication skills with these traditional methods, and (7) responding to criticism and other defense-arousing messages. A careful study of these topics is essential to learning how to handle sales resistance.

The nature of buying resistance is described in terms of the five characteristics of a typical conflict: an expressed struggle between two interdependent parties who perceive incompatible goals with perceived scarce rewards and expected interference from other parties. All five components must be present for conflict, or sales resistance, to exist.

On the International Front

Negotiations between buyer and seller are quite common in many countries. For example, when buyers walk through shopping districts in Hong Kong or Taiwan, they have opportunities to do business with vendors selling everything from toys to high-priced clothing. These vendors quote a price, but it is expected and acceptable for the buyer to propose a lower price, going back and forth with price offers until a price is attained that is acceptable for both parties. When negotiating, the people work out a price that is acceptable to both, rather than relying on a listed price.

The following are insights for negotiating internationally in industrial settings:

- Know about the country and culture of your business counterpart.
- Contracts represent different things to different people.
- The travelling negotiator is always under enormous pressure not to return home empty-handed. As a result, the travelling negotiator is more anxious to make the deal than if the same work were being negotiated at home.
- It is a great advantage to negotiate in your own country.
- "Salami tactics" refers to demanding just a little more or taking back small slices at the end of the negotiations, just before the opponent leaves for the airport. Keep in mind that your opponent is often testing you by doing this.
- Concession-making techniques vary greatly from country to country.
- Cultures also differ in the importance negotiators attach to being viewed as likeable, reasonable, and fair and in their inclination to create goodwill with their opponent.
- Japanese, Middle Eastern, and Latin American negotiators generally build in a great deal of fat between their opening stance and their planned target. Overreaching is not just part of their game; they do it to give themselves ample room to maneuver.
- In many Western countries, issues are negotiated. Parties try to reach agreement on one issue before moving on to the next one. The final agreement is the sum total of all the subagreements on separate issues.
- Try not to hamstring yourself or your business counterpart with departure dates. Do not give your business counterpart the impression that your departure date is an absolute deadline for you.

Source: Adapted from Cynthia Barnum and Natasha Wolniansky, "Why Americans Fail at Overseas Negotiations," *Management Review*, December 1989.

The concept of buying resistance is contrasted with the notion of overcoming sales objections. The latter concept stimulates a win-lose, defensive style of communication on the part of the salesperson. Assertive messages—the expression of ideas, feelings, and wants clearly and directly to a customer in such a way that the salesperson's rights are protected while demonstrating respect for the customer's rights—are a tool assisting salespeople to aspire toward a functional approach to managing buying

Figure 14.A

Prior Planning Principles

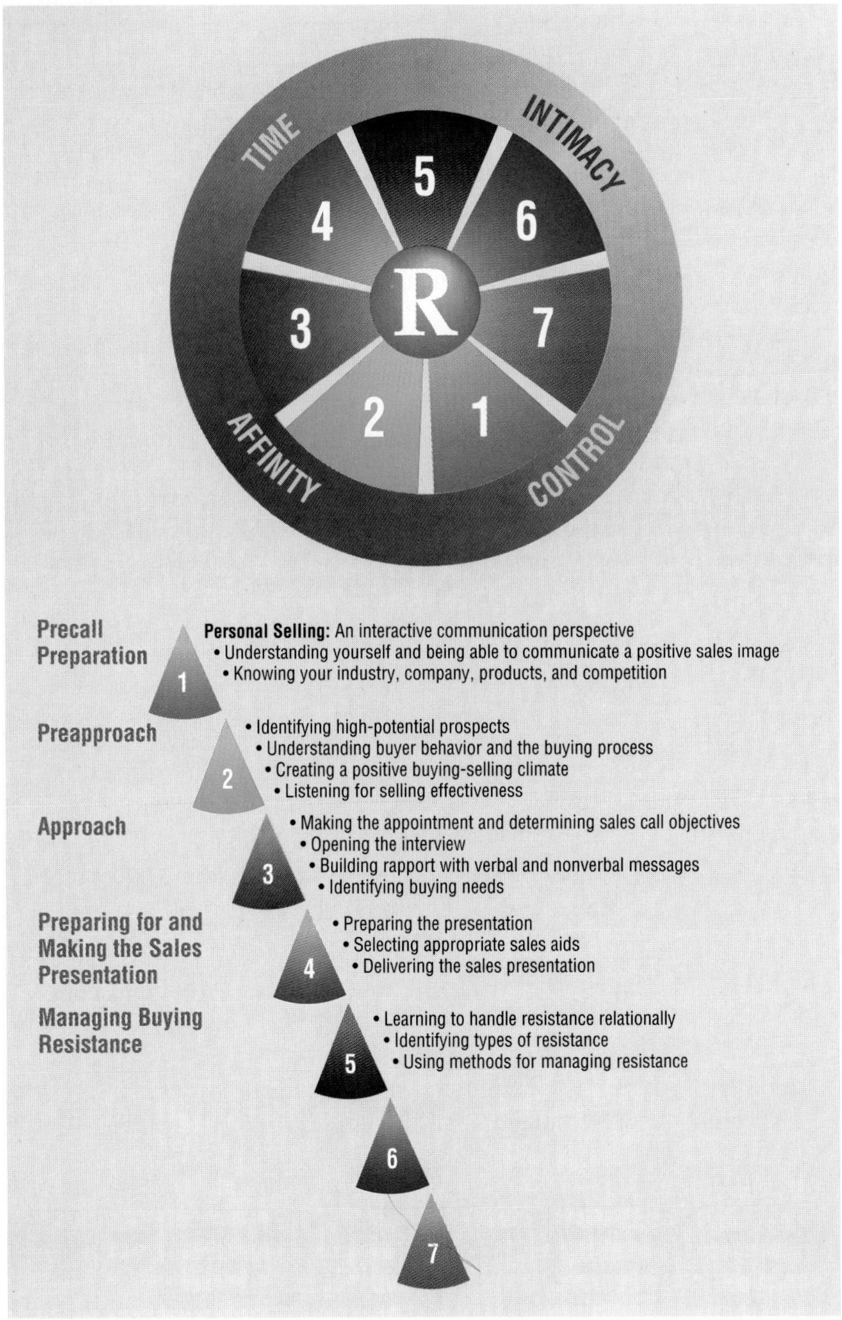

TIME
INTIMACY
AFFINITY
CONTROL
R
1 2 3 4 5 6 7

Precall Preparation (1)

Personal Selling: An interactive communication perspective
- Understanding yourself and being able to communicate a positive sales image
- Knowing your industry, company, products, and competition

Preapproach (2)
- Identifying high-potential prospects
- Understanding buyer behavior and the buying process
- Creating a positive buying-selling climate
- Listening for selling effectiveness

Approach (3)
- Making the appointment and determining sales call objectives
- Opening the interview
- Building rapport with verbal and nonverbal messages
- Identifying buying needs

Preparing for and Making the Sales Presentation (4)
- Preparing the presentation
- Selecting appropriate sales aids
- Delivering the sales presentation

Managing Buying Resistance (5)
- Learning to handle resistance relationally
- Identifying types of resistance
- Using methods for managing resistance

6

7

resistance. Another section deals with how the concepts of overcoming sales objections and managing buying resistance differ, especially as they pertain to the relational process.

Types of buying resistance are discussed at both attitudinal and behavioral levels. Five types of verbal and nonverbal clues to the presence of buying resistance are brought out in this section.

Traditional methods can be used to manage buying resistance in ways that transform resistance into opportunity. Five methods are discussed because they have been effective throughout the evolution of all selling systems, whether product-driven, sales-driven, or customer-driven. These methods are the direct denial, indirect denial, boomerang, superior benefit, and trial offer approaches.

Communication skills can be merged with traditional methods of managing buying resistance. The salesperson can integrate the skills of active listening, probing with open and closed questions, perception checking, and using assertive messages with the traditional methods to manage buying resistance effectively.

Responding to criticism and other defense-arousing messages in nondefensive ways is the seventh topic. Negative inquiry, or requesting additional information from the customer, and negative assertion, either agreeing with the content of the criticism or acknowledging the customer's right to perceive the situation from a different perspective, are discussed as methods for managing criticism nondefensively.

Review Questions

1. Identify and explain the five characteristics of conflict as described by Frost and Wilmot.
2. Distinguish between the concepts of buying resistance and overcoming objectives. Explain the consequences that may occur when a salesperson operates from each perspective.
3. Distinguish between functional and dysfunctional conflict. Give an example of each. Describe the eight pairs of alternatives that can be used to distinguish between functional and dysfunctional conflict.
4. Identify and explain the seven types of buying resistance that might be signaled by either verbal or nonverbal cues.
5. Identify and explain the five traditional methods for managing buying resistance that have survived throughout the evolution of the product-driven, sales-driven, and customer-driven selling systems.
6. Explain how active listening, perception checking, or using assertive messages might be combined with one or more of the traditional methods for managing buying resistance in a selling situation. Be specific by providing a real or hypothetical example.
7. Distinguish between negative inquiry and negative assertion. Give an example of how each might be used to manage criticism in a win-win manner.

Discussion Questions

1. Discuss the characteristics of conflict as presented by Frost and Wilmot by giving an example of a conflict you have recently experienced and identifying their five characteristics. If all five were not present, what may this mean?
2. Identify a real or hypothetical sales-related conflict situation. Using the seven sets of descriptors that distinguish functional from dysfunctional conflict along a continuum, give a specific example and contrast how the functional and dysfunctional alternatives along each continuum might be recognized in the specific situation. It may be useful to hold this discussion in a small group.
3. Discuss the types of buying resistance and situation. It may be useful to hold this discussion in a small group.
4. In a small group, discuss the types of buying resistance, select a product or service, and then role-play a salesperson using traditional methods of managing buying resistance.
5. In a small group, role-play the use of active listening, perception checking, and assertive messages to negotiate buying resistance.
6. In a small group, role-play situations in which the salesperson receives criticism from the buyer. Take turns using negative inquiry and negative assertion, along with active listening and perception checking, to manage the criticism in a win-win manner. Afterward, discuss how congruent the salesperson's verbal and nonverbal cues were and what the effect is of this degree of congruence on maintaining a win-win situation.

Case 14.1

Uncovering Resistance

John Webb, the salesman for Kerns Wood Company, was disappointed when he learned that he had lost the flooring contract for a housing project of 150 condominiums. This was the third time that a contract in his community had been given to an out-of-town firm.

Kerns Wood Company is a large firm with a reputation of providing excellent workmanship for over 20 years. Its relationship with past customers is good and it has received many letters of commendation. Kerns is large and well equipped enough to handle contracts of this magnitude. Also, it has always been extremely price competitive, using the finest quality materials and including good guarantees. There appears to be nothing in Kerns' background and performance history that would indicate any source of resistance.

John attempted to find out the price of the winning contract and was informed that it was not a part of procedure to publicly announce this information. He did find out the contractor's name and was stunned that it was the same firm that had been awarded two previous contracts for which Kerns Wood Company had submitted bids.

This particular contractor has often been awarded contracts despite higher bids and equivalent quality. Furthermore, John's curiosity grew when he realized that the winning contractor was a small firm that would seem to have difficulty meeting the production levels and time schedules.

John was repeatedly shunned when he asked for an explanation. The purchasing agent refused to discuss the decision and commented, "They came in with a much better proposal at the right price and I am afraid your bid exceeded the limits of our budget. There's nothing I can do about it now."

1. Discuss the nature of the resistance as illustrated in this case. What type of resistance is illustrated?
2. What questions might John ask if he does not agree with the purchasing agent's comments?
3. What would you do in this situation? Why?

Your Price Is Too High!

Case 14.2

Judith Owens, a computer service specialist, was halfway through her presentation to CGS, Inc., when suddenly, the purchasing agent interrupted and asked, "What's your price?" Judith stated that she would prefer to quote a price after presenting the entire proposal, which was designed specifically for CGS.

Near the end of the presentation, the purchasing agent insisted on knowing the price. At that time Judith quoted a standard price and the purchasing agent immediately reacted unfavorably, saying, "I can't afford this and I know I can get comparable equipment and design for a better price from a competitive firm. I think we will just stick with our present system."

The purchasing agent at CGS then raised the following objections regarding the installation of a new system:

1. The company will not get any bigger for 2 years, so why change now?
2. The company tried getting its workers excited about changing to an updated system, but morale was too low to propose any changes at this time.
3. The company doesn't want to spend a lot of money at this time and find itself strapped financially later.
4. A friend told the purchasing agent that the company would run into all kinds of problems, such as continuous breakdowns and productivity delays, when adapting to a new system.

Judith attempted to probe her prospect to uncover areas of possible dissatisfaction with the present system. She reviewed several situations about the system that appeared to reflect inefficiency.

"I will think about your input on my system and call you in about a month," was the purchasing agent's response. "In the meantime I want to check around for other bids," he added.

1. What is the best way to react when the price resistance is raised early in the presentation?
2. Prepare answers to the resistance that was raised to the use of the present system.
3. How do you think the information Judith gathered could be used to counter possible price resistance?

Notes

1. J. H. Frost and H. H. Wilmot, *Interpersonal Conflict*, 2nd ed. (Dubuque, IA: W. C. Brown, 1985), pp. 22–29.
2. Manuel J. Smith, *When I Say No, I Feel Guilty* (New York: Bantam Books, 1975), p. 120.
3. Ibid., pp. 100–119.

CHAPTER

15

Closing the Sale and Taking Leave of the Interview

Knowledge Objectives

In this chapter, you will learn:

1. The importance of a positive attitude toward closing the sale
2. To recognize both verbal and nonverbal buying signals
3. The distinction between trial and formal closing attempts
4. The various types of closing vehicles
5. How to use these closing vehicles effectively
6. How to ask for the order using supportive language

Consider This

Samuel Clemens (aka Mark Twain) once told of going to a missionary meeting and becoming terribly impressed with the speaker's religious zeal. At first, he decided to donate five dollars at collection time, instead of his usual donation of one dollar. As the preacher spoke on, Clemens became even more enthusiastic and decided to write a large check to the missionary's charity. But instead of shutting up and passing the plate, the preacher got carried away with the sound of his own voice. And the longer he spoke, the more irritated Clemens became at the man's lack of good judgment. Finally, when the preacher passed the plate, Clemens was so steamed that instead of making a contribution, he took out a dime.

It's all too common for salespeople to spend a half hour selling their services and two hours buying them back. There's a time to talk, a time to listen, and a time to close. And those who succeed at winning and keeping customers know how to recognize, respond to, and reward those moments of truth when the customer gives buying signals. Whenever you recognize that a customer is giving definite buying signals, that's your cue to do three things in the following order:

- **Reinforce the buying signal**
- **Make it easy to buy**
- **Ask for the business**

Michael LeBoeuf*

**How to Win Customers and Keep Them for Life* (New York: G. P. Putnam's Sons, 1987), pp. 116–117.

Developing a Positive Attitude toward Closing

The relationship process has been advanced by using such skills as determining buying needs through open-ended questions and active listening; presenting the product by emphasizing benefits and advantages; managing buying resistance with perception checking, negative inquiry, negative assertion, and assertive messages; and creating a supportive climate for the exchange-relationship process.

Because consultative selling and communication are dynamic, skills and methods have been provided that may be used to build and maintain the spontaneity found in a mutually satisfying relationship. While these skills are presented in a structured and logical order, it is important to

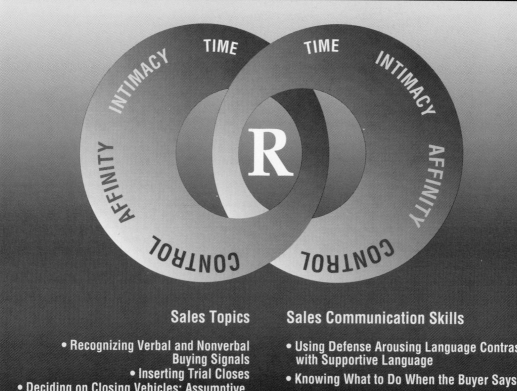

Step 6 | Closing the Sale and Taking Leave of the Interview

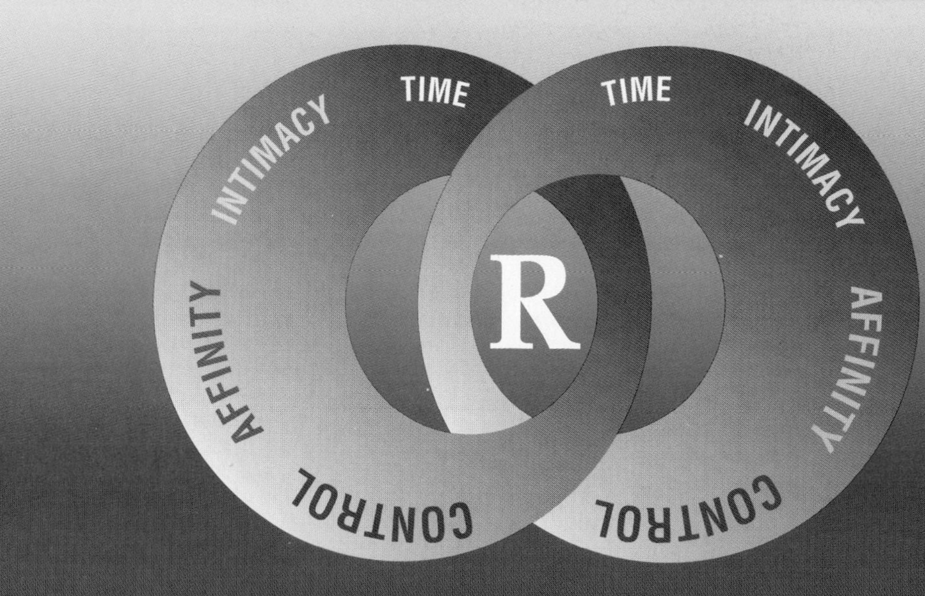

Sales Topics

- Recognizing Verbal and Nonverbal Buying Signals
- Inserting Trial Closes
- Deciding on Closing Vehicles: Assumptive, Alternative Choice, Summary of Benefits, Balance Sheet, Concession, Direct Appeal, and Narrative
- Ending and Closing the Interview

Sales Communication Skills

- Using Defense Arousing Language Contrasted with Supportive Language
- Knowing What to Do When the Buyer Says "Yes"
- Knowing What to Do When the Buyer Says "No"
- Taking Leave of the Interview: Formalizing, Summarizing, Supporting, and Showing Continuance

realize that all the parts are synergistic in both theory and application. For example, a salesperson actually starts to close the sale by what is said at the beginning of the interview, and the creation of a supportive climate is begun through the congruence between the salesperson's verbal and nonverbal mannerisms.

This chapter will tie all of the parts together in an approach that will enable the salesperson to confirm the order while using time effectively. We will focus on four specific areas: identifying buying signals, inserting trial closes throughout the presentation, asking for the final commitment, and using relational terms appropriate to ending and taking leave of the interview.

Identifying Buying Signals

In a University of Notre Dame survey on closing attempts made by salespeople, it was found that 46 percent of salespeople asked for the order once and then quit, 24 percent asked for the order twice, 14 percent asked for the order three times, and 12 percent asked for the order four or more times. The results showed that 60 percent of positive customer responses came on the fifth attempt.[1]

In a study conducted by McGraw-Hill Research Department, 1,155 sales executives were asked, "Approximately how many calls does it take to close a sale?" The average response was 5.5 calls per sale.[2]

Numerous articles have been published on the number of attempts required to close a sale. While the numbers range from five to nine, it is appropriate to follow the axiom called the "ABCs of closing"—**A**lways **B**e **C**losing.

Confirming the order requires the salesperson to use skills acquired through constant repetition and practice. Asking for the order is not a passive activity; it requires assertive behavior and a constant awareness of the dynamics between the customer and the salesperson. These dynamics are frequently referred to as buying signals or closing clues. A *buying signal* is an indication that the prospect is interested in the product or service and is preparing to make a buying decision. Buying signals may be either verbal or nonverbal.

Try This 15.1 Developing a Positive Closing Attitude

1. Select a product and write your responses to the following questions:
   a. Why are so many people reluctant to ask for the order?
   b. What are your fears, if any, in asking for the order?
   c. How does a salesperson know when to close?
   d. Discuss the statement, "There is no need for closing."
   e. Are there techniques for creating opportunities to close?
   f. How does one develop a positive attitude toward closing?
2. Select a partner and exchange your views on the above questions.

Verbal Buying Signals

Verbal buying signals can be divided into three categories: questions, confirmations, and conditions.

- *Questions*—Questions from the prospect, either open or closed, are probably the most obvious kind of verbal buying signal. For example:

  "You say that this software is compatible with my current system?" (need)

  "Do you have colors that match our existing decor?" (product)

  "What kind of financing do you offer?" (price)

  "How soon can you deliver?" (service)

  "Can you have the system up and running by the end of the week?" (timing)

  "What kind of support training do you provide to our staff upon installation?" (company)

  "Will you be personally responsible for training our staff?" (salesperson)

- *Confirmations*—Confirmations are positive statements made by the prospect about the salesperson's product or service or about some aspect of the sale. For example:

  "We certainly have the patient flow to justify a new cardiac scanner." (need)

  "Your cellular phone seems to have less static than others I've examined." (product)

  "I really like the idea of the deferred payment option available to me at this time." (price)

  "Your extended warranty package is certainly a unique benefit." (service)

  "I'd like to have this up and running before we are visited by the regional manager next month." (timing)

  "One thing that impresses me about your firm is that you've maintained a 60-percent market share throughout the current recession." (company)

- *Conditions*—A prospect may state a requirement that must be met before the salesperson's product or service can be purchased. For example:

  "I have to reduce my current inventory before I add any new stock." (need)

  "My new copier will have to have two-sided copy and four-color reproductive capabilities." (product)

  "Price flexibility is important for us to maintain our competitiveness." (price)

  "We have to have a guarantee that your staff will train our employees to use the equipment." (service)

"It's critical that the plumbing be installed before next week because the electricians are scheduled for the following week." (timing)

"A company image built on trust and reliability is necessary to keep our high-volume customers satisfied." (company)

Nonverbal Buying Signals

The prospect may provide verbal questions or statements that are obvious buying signals; on the other hand, those signals may be obscure. Observation of a prospect's facial expressions, body movement, and vocal expression will help the salesperson detect more subtle, nonverbal buying signals. For example, a prospect may:

- Smile and nod while the salesperson is describing a major benefit
- Pick up the agreement and begin to read it
- Walk closer to the area where the product would be installed and take an imaginary measurement of the space
- Lean forward and increase volume and rate of speech while responding to a question
- Reach for the product and start to examine it

The SOFTENS technique introduced in Chapter 8 will help the salesperson recognize the nonverbal buying signals a prospect may use. Table 15.1 provides an additional list of verbal and nonverbal buying signals.

Once the salesperson recognizes verbal and nonverbal buying signals in the prospect's behavior, the next step is to follow up with a trial close.

Try This 15.2 Recognizing Buying Signals

1. Which of the following verbal and nonverbal messages represent buying signals?
   a. "That's awesome!"
   b. A purchasing agent sits in his chair with his arms and legs crossed, shaking his head up and down.
   c. "Uh, may I get back to you on this?"
   d. "How does your financing plan work?"
   e. "When do you deliver?"
   f. The buyer interrupts by picking up the phone and dialing the engineering department.
   g. "What's your turn-around time on repairs?"
2. Select a product or service. Prepare a list of verbal and nonverbal buying signals you might recognize from a prospect.
3. Select a partner and discuss your lists. Brainstorm with each other to make the list as complete as possible.

Table 15.1

How to Recognize and Reinforce Buying Signals

In general, a buying signal is anything that a customer says or does that indicates enthusiasm or excitement about what you're offering. More specifically, below are some of the more common verbal and nonverbal buying signals.

Verbal Buying Signals

- The customer asks such questions as, "Could I see that again?" "Would you go over that one more time?" "How soon can you get one for me?" "What other colors does it come in?"
- He agrees with what you're saying.
- He talks positively about what it would be like to own what you're offering.
- He answers your questions easily and positively.
- He wants more information, such as how much down payment is required or whether financing can be arranged.

Nonverbal Buying Signals

- The customer leans slightly forward.
- He looks at you more.
- His eyes open up and twinkle or the pupils dilate slightly.
- He smiles and his brow is relaxed and unfurrowed.
- He nods in agreement with what you say.
- His lips are relaxed and open, rather than tight and drawn.
- His arms are relaxed and open and the palms of his hands are open toward you.
- His legs are uncrossed, or crossed facing toward you.
- He rests his hands on his chin or cheek or rubs his hands together.
- He handles or studies order forms or sales materials.
- He unconsciously reaches for his checkbook, wallet, or purse.
- He makes calculations on paper.
- He reaches for the sales contract.

Source: Michael LeBoeuf, Ph.D., *How to Win Customers and Keep Them for Life* (New York: G.P. Putnam's Sons, 1987), pp. 116–117.

Using Trial Closes Effectively

Probably the most misunderstood and misused part of the selling process involves knowing the difference between a trial and formal close. A *formal* or *final close* is a request that the prospect make a decision or commitment of payment in exchange for the product or service. It is the final buying decision. In contrast, a *trial close* often involves asking a prospect to make a decision on a minor point. Because the selling system presented in this textbook is based on spontaneity rather than on memorized presentations that lead to predetermined responses, the salesperson must be able to distinguish what is of major or minor benefit to the buyer before using the different skills required for trial and formal closes. Reviewing the section on probing skills in Chapter 11 will help develop the ability to make this distinction. The section will focus on the

Sales Professional Spotlight

Marc Crockett is a California-based sales representative for McKinley Equipment Corporation, a small, family-owned supplier of material handling equipment that represents various nationally known manufacturers. Marc went to work for the company in 1986, after earning a bachelor's degree in business administration.

Marc thought out the approach to his new selling job carefully. When asked how he got started with McKinley, he replied: "I was intrigued by careers in industrial sales, especially the small, growing companies. I was particularly attracted to the material handling industry because of the array of opportunities, variety, and income potential. I also felt that working for a company with an excellent reputation was the best bet for launching a career in sales."

Like McKinley, Marc has a philosophy of steady growth and improvement. He remarks about the learning curve of 2–5 years in this industry and admits that the field of selling has occasional moments of frustration, posing the need to be patient. His job demands prioritizing. He handles 50–80 prospects at a time, from which he is likely to get 10–15 orders. Project cycles can take from a week to 2 years, with selling prices ranging from several hundred dollars to $1 million.

Being a commissioned sales representative, Marc sometimes wonders where his next paycheck will come from. "I compare what I do to a board game. Rolling the dice is analogous to a point of contact. If the presentation is productive and positive, I gauge the progress and move forward toward the end of the game—an order," he says.

In closing the sale, he stresses the importance of getting the prospect to agree early in the presentation that there are three, four, five, even ten important reasons for purchasing this type of equipment. This approach defines the parameters of the decision criteria. He proceeds to emphasize these reasons in the presentation and gets the prospect to agree.

A clear, concise presentation works best for Marc. He introduces conceptual ideas and develops a trusting relationship with the prospect. "Tentative closes throughout each presentation enable me to check my progress. It is very important to control the interview and feel confident that I will get the order," he says.

When asked what he likes most about his sales position, Marc comments on the thrill of helping customers by proposing solutions to their problems. Buying decisions in the material handling industry are usually well thought out. Marc claims, "If prospects believe in me and my solution is backed with credibility, then getting the order is made much easier. My objective is always to make the prospects look like heroes and expose them to as little risk as possible. Believing in me at this point means giving me the order."

skills involved in using trial closes to bring about the sale by building confirmations and affirmations throughout the interview toward the buying decision.

A trial close is a barometer measuring the climate between the customer and the salesperson; it measures where the customer is in relation to making a final buying decision.

> Test closes are special questions. When answered, they show that the prospect has reached a high level of interest, and that they're happy and excited and ready to go further. When you ask a test question, you're looking for an answer that gives you positive stimulus.[3]

The more affirmations the customer makes about the product or service during the interview, the easier and more appropriate the final closing becomes. Trial closes are a sign that problems are being solved throughout the interview.

There are four points along the buying continuum at which a trial close may be appropriate:

1. After an initial benefit statement
2. After recognizing a buying signal
3. After handling resistance
4. Anytime the prospect shows significant interest in the product or service

Figure 15.1 identifies other times during the presentation when closing attempts may occur.

A trial close may take the form of a question or a paraphrase that focuses the interaction. Prospects may respond to a trial close in one of two ways. They may take a step toward the final buying decision. For example, in response to an alternative choice questions, such as, "Would you prefer a four-drawer file or a three-drawer file configuration?" the customer might respond, "I need to save space, so let's go with the four-drawer file system to use less floor space." In contrast, the prospect may respond with confusion by saying, "I'm not sure." This response is a form of resistance that impedes the buying decision until the salesperson provides the prospect with information that eliminates the confusion. Once the resistance has been identified and managed, then the salesperson may insert another trial close, such as, "Now that we've measured the available floor space, I understand that the four-drawer file system is the option you'd prefer. Is that right?"

By combining the use of questions and paraphrasing to assist the prospect in making decisions, the salesperson manages the problem-solving process. Trial closes test the alternative solutions to the prospect's needs by narrowing the process toward the final buying decision. The more trial closes a salesperson includes throughout the sales interview, the easier the final buying decision becomes and the more confident the prospect is in having made the appropriate decision.

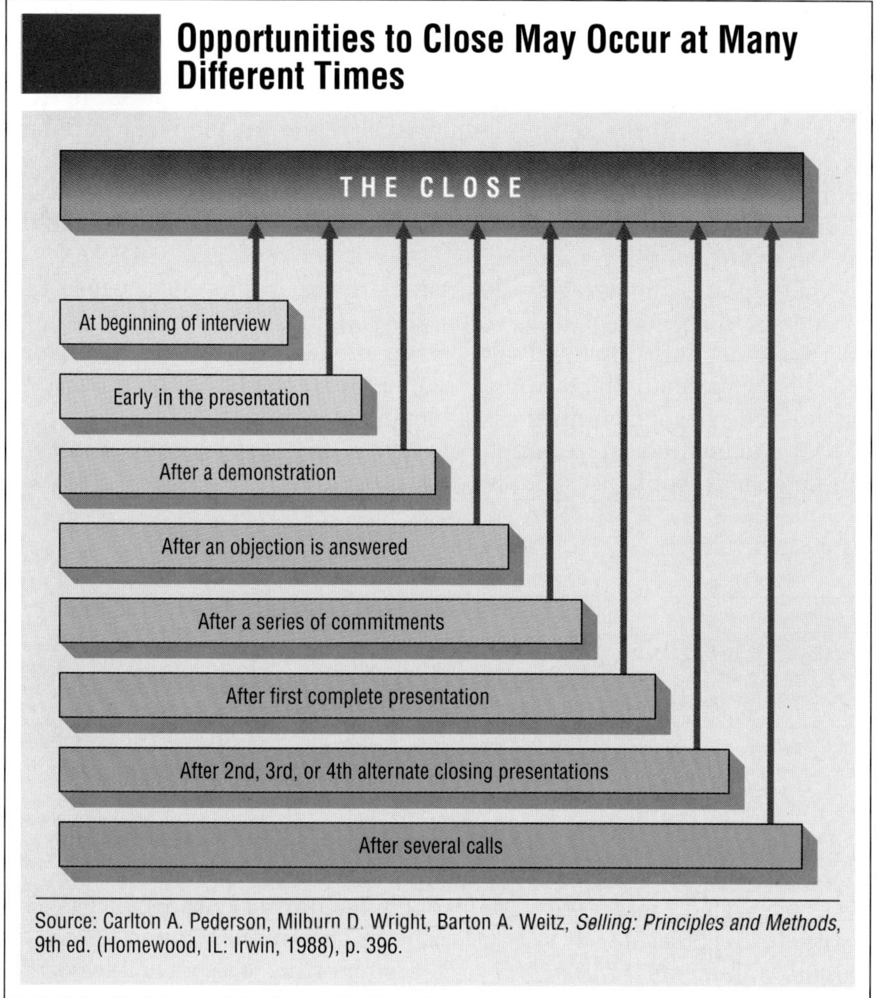

Source: Carlton A. Pederson, Milburn D. Wright, Barton A. Weitz, *Selling: Principles and Methods*, 9th ed. (Homewood, IL: Irwin, 1988), p. 396.

Figure 15.1

The novice salesperson may make the mistake of using formal closes instead of trial closes. For example, the salesperson might prematurely attempt a formal close by saying, "So you're confused. If I can show you how to maximize your space by using the four-drawer file system, will you buy it now?" A misplaced formal close may increase the prospect's resistance because the prospect may feel forced into making a decision not yet appropriate, since the major buying criteria have not been satisfied. As a result, the salesperson may have generated a defensive rather than a supportive climate by forcing the prospect into an intractable position from which there can be no deviation. The purpose of the trial close is to focus on a problem-solving discussion by seeking mutual clarification and identifying and managing resistance without defense-arousing communication. When trial closes are managed in this way, the formal close becomes a logical, spontaneous part of the process.

Types of Closing Vehicles

There are literally hundreds of methods for confirming the order. In this section we present the seven methods that represent the most popular, current, and easily adaptable techniques for use with the consultative selling style. In conjunction with attending behaviors, active listening, relational feedback, and perception-checking skills, these methods facilitate the relational selling process.

Sales professionals agree that sales are lost primarily because the salesperson does not ask for the order. Asking for the order is a two-step, assertive procedure. First, the salesperson must identify a *closing vehicle*, or a closing method, that is appropriate to the dynamics of the interview. Second, the salesperson must ask a closing question.

An explanation and example of each of the seven closing vehicles will help salespeople use this two-part procedure.

On the Ethical Side

Charles Larson, author of the book *Persuasion*, offers some guidelines and ethical criteria:

- Do not use false, fabricated, misrepresented, distorted, or irrelevant evidence to support arguments or claims.
- Do not intentionally use specious, unsupported, or illogical reasoning.
- Do not represent yourself as informed or as an expert on a subject if you are not.
- Do not use irrelevant appeals to divert attention or scrutiny from the issue at hand.
- Do not ask your audience to link your idea or proposal to emotion-laden values, motives, or goals to which it actually is not related.
- Do not deceive your audience by concealing your real purpose, your self-interest, the group you represent, or your position as an advocate of a viewpoint.
- Do not distort, hide, or misrepresent the number, scope, or intensity of undesirable features or consequences.
- Do not use emotional appeals that lack a supporting base of evidence or reasoning or that would not be acceptable if the audience had time and opportunity to examine the subject itself.
- Do not oversimplify complex situations.

The salesperson must also provide supportive information to reduce postpurchase anxieties, reinforcing the buyer's belief that a wise purchase decision was made. The salesperson is expected to support the buyer's choice and expectations. Handling postpurchase feelings professionally will build a favorable relationship for future sales.

Assumptive Close

The assumptive close uses the tentative assumption that the sale will be consummated. The attitude behind this close is an ongoing posturing by the salesperson that is used in describing and probing with the buyer about the product or service. For example, instead of saying "*If* you decide" the salesperson says "*When* you decide" or "*As you're making* your decision." By using this language, the salesperson creates a positive momentum that focuses on the eventuality of reaching a solution.

In addition to using optimistic language, the salesperson can facilitate the order by using nonverbal cues that invite the prospect to take action. For instance, the salesperson may hand the buying agreement to the prospect while stating, "With your approval, I can process the paperwork as soon as I leave today [*assumptive vehicle*]. May I have your authorization? [*closing question*]"

Alternative Choice Close

The alternative choice close asks the prospect to select from two options. For example, "We have two financing methods available—30-day open credit or 1-year, long-term financing [*alternative choice*]. Which one do you prefer? [*closing question*]" When all six buying decisions have purportedly been satisfied and the salesperson senses that pricing is the major concern, this vehicle may help the prospect focus on the options available to meet the concern.

Summary of Benefits Close

In using a summary of benefits close, the salesperson reviews the major benefits that the prospect has agreed with. When technical information or quantitative data have been involved in the presentation, this vehicle is especially useful to help the prospect see the entire picture. For example:

Prospect: Well, I think I understand what's involved. Where do we go from here?

Salesperson: John, I'd like to clarify what we have gone over today. We will begin shipping the Imatron system in January. That will include the work stations for two operators as well as the Data General optical disk drives. The software package will be the recently updated version, and you won't be needing another image formatter. It looks like we can bring you in at just under $1.4 million on this system, saving you nearly $75,000 compared to the competitor's quote [*summary of benefits*]. If that sounds correct to you, then may I start processing the paperwork? [*closing question*]

Balance Sheet Close

The balance sheet close involves listing all of the reasons for and against acting now. This close facilitates the problem-solving process and uses a problem-orientation approach to maintain a supportive climate. There is a risk, however, that a reason for inaction will outweigh the reasons for taking action, and the work that has been completed may come to an abrupt juncture: In that case, either the discussion must revert to an earlier stage in the problem-solving process or the sale will fall through. For example:

Salesperson: Greg, we have discussed the pros and cons of starting this project right away. Whenever I have a tough decision to make, I take out a sheet of paper and actually list reasons for moving forward with the decision and reasons for waiting [*balance sheet*]. Let's do it together.

Reasons for Acting Now	Reasons for Not Acting Now
1.	1.
2.	2.
3.	3.
4.	4.

Salesperson: Weighing each of the columns you've made, it appears to me that your decision is clear.

Prospect: I think you're right. There really doesn't seem to be any strong reason for waiting.

Salesperson: Then with you're approval, we can get started right away. Is that agreeable with you? [*closing question*]

Concession/Inducement Close

The concession/inducement close offers the prospect something extra for acting immediately. The concession or inducement may be a deferred payment plan, an introductory offer, special training seminars at no additional cost, or another added benefit that was not anticipated by the prospect. To maintain a supportive buying climate by using spontaneous communication with a prospect instead of promoting a defensive climate, however, the extra benefit must emerge genuinely out of the dynamics of the interaction. If the salesperson withholds a benefit as a strategy to induce the buying decision, a defensive climate may be evoked. For example:

Prospect: I'm still concerned about the individual unit price compared to what I've been offered by another rep.

Salesperson: Joan, I'm unable to go below the unit price I've quoted you for 20 phones. If you're willing to purchase 25 phones, however, you'll qualify for the corporate rate, which will save you 10 percent. In addition, under this rate, you will receive a 2-year rather than a 1-year unconditional guarantee. It may be worth your while to project the growth of your sales staff over the 2-year period and buy phones for additional staff now [*concession/inducement close*]. How about it? [*closing question*]

Direct Appeal Close

Asking for the order in a straightforward manner is the essence of a direct appeal close. Prospects who make decisions quickly and decisively usually appreciate this vehicle. This vehicle is best used when the prospect has displayed a definite interest in the product or service. It is also important that rapport has been clearly established in the relationship between the prospect and the salesperson before using this vehicle. For example:

Prospect: Will it take long to upgrade the memory capacity of the barcode readers?

Salesperson: It will take our technical staff an extra day maximum to upgrade your barcode readers. If we send the order in today, you'll have the barcode readers in your warehouses within 4 days, with plenty of time to train employees efficiently before you take your next inventory count. With your help, Melissa, I'd like to arrange our terms for the first order and those for the following orders [*direct appeal close*]. May I have it? [*closing question*]

Narrative Close

A narrative close involves telling a brief, true story that illustrates how acting immediately is appropriate. This vehicle frequently involves a third-party reference or an anecdote about another customer. For example:

> When the people at the Reno site originally decided to replace their existing 9000 GE, they fully intended to move to the 9800 quickly, until they started to look at the advantages of our product. Since installation last year, they have increased their productivity by 29 percent and they have joined the elite ranks of the top research facilities in the country: San Francisco, Mayo Clinic, and Loma Linda. Melissa, I'm sharing this information with you because I see your situation as paralleling theirs and I'd very much like to have you take the proposal we worked on to the buying committee for final approval [*narrative close*]. Will you do it? [*closing question*]

Using Closing Vehicles Effectively

The way salespeople communicate the various closing vehicles will determine whether they maintain a supportive climate or initiate a defensive climate with the prospect. Inappropriate language can result in the prospect feeling pressured, which often leads to the feeling of being coerced into making a decision. A review of Gibbs' categories of supportive

Try This 15.3 Practicing Using Closing Vehicles

1. For each of the closing vehicles listed below, write an example that includes these three elements: (a) what the prospect might say or do to offer a buying signal, (b) what closing vehicle would be appropriate, and (c) what you will say or do to demonstrate that you know how to use the vehicle.

   EXAMPLE:

   Prospect: Well, Kerry, I think I understand everything. Where do we go from here?

   Closing Vehicle: Summary of benefits

   Salesperson: John, I'd like to clarify what we have discussed today. The EXACTO system will start shipping in March. That will include the work stations for two operators as well as the data optical disk drives. The software package will be the recently updated version, and you won't be needing another image formatter. It looks like we can bring you in at just under $1.4 million on this system. Does that sound covered to you? Then may I start processing the necessary paperwork so that all promised delivery dates will be met?

   Use a similar format.

   a. Prospect:
      Closing Vehicle: Assumptive
      Salesperson:
   b. Prospect:
      Closing Vehicle: Alternative choice
      Salesperson:
   c. Prospect:
      Closing Vehicle: Summary of benefits
      Salesperson:
   d. Prospect:
      Closing Vehicle: Balance sheet
      Salesperson:
   e. Prospect:
      Closing Vehicle: Concession/inducement
      Salesperson:
   f. Prospect:
      Closing Vehicle: Direct appeal
      Salesperson:
   g. Prospect:
      Closing Vehicle: Narrative
      Salesperson:

2. Select a partner and exchange responses. Practice using these closing skills until you feel comfortable.

and defensive climates in Chapter 4 will help identify supportive and confirming language. Salespeople should practice putting these closing vehicles into language that is supportive. Here are some examples of defense-arousing language contrasted with more supportive language:

Defense-Arousing Language	*Supportive Language*
"I can give you a *good deal* on . . ."	"I'm prepared to offer you . . ."
"What I *need* you to do is . . ."	"I would like you to consider . . ."
"Just *sign* here . . ."	"Would you authorize . . ." or "May I have your permission . . ." or "May I have your approval . . ." or ". . . OK . . ."
"If you'll go ahead and *sign* this *contract* . . ."	"If you'll authorize this agreement . . ."
"Let me give you a *pitch* on the rest of this little demo . . ."	"I'd like you to participate in the remainder of my presentation . . ."
"The product is *cheap* compared to . . ."	"This is an inexpensive product . . ."
"You're getting a real *bargain* . . ."	"You're receiving an excellent value . . ."
"Since you're an *old* account . . ."	"Because you're an established account . . ."
"I'll send you a *reminder* of the *deal* we *cut* today . . ."	"I'll send you a confirmation of the agreement we reached today . . ."
"What you're *spending* on this . . ."	"What you're investing in this . . ."
"I *can't* do that, but I can *substitute* . . ."	"In lieu of this, you have another option . . ."

In addition to using supportive language, a competent salesperson uses nonverbal messages that are congruent with the verbal statements being made and that reflect the SOFTENS technique described in Chapter 8.

What to Do When the Buyer Says "No"

Sometimes the fear of rejection creates emotional paralysis, causing the salesperson to "freeze" when it is time to ask the buyer to make a commitment. Subsequently, the buyer either says "no" or remains uncommitted to what the salesperson is offering. At other times, no matter how well structured or eloquent the salesperson's closing attempts are, the prospect refuses to buy. As Tom Hopkins aptly puts it, "The number of failures salespeople have is not important. What counts is the number of times they succeed, and this is directly related to the number of times they fail and keep trying."[4]

In either case, the weak salesperson will never experience failure because no attempt will be made to ask for the order. The average or mediocre salesperson will pack up and leave when the prospect says "no." The sales professional will diplomatically and assertively seek to find out why the buyer is hesitating or resisting.

If there is no hidden agenda on the buyer's part, then the sales professional should gracefully terminate the interview and leave. In this case, the goal of the salesperson should be to maintain a positive rapport with the prospect and leave the door open for future contact. Table 15.2 provides a self-inventory for reviewing the selling situation. Honest responses to these questions may provide a springboard for preventing repetition of faulty practices and for encouraging professional growth.

What to Do When the Buyer Says "Yes"

When each step in the relational sales process is handled competently, the close is the natural conclusion to a successful sales interview. Paradoxically, the sale begins when the deal is made. This statement is an axiom among sales professionals because future sales often depend on the salesperson's effectiveness in departure and follow-up activities.

The next section will focus on how to take leave of the interview in a way that encourages continuance and development of the relationship. In Chapter 16 we will discuss appropriate and effective ways of developing competence in servicing the account.

Taking Leave of the Interview

In taking leave of the interview, it is important for the salesperson to tie up any loose ends, both in terms of the agreement regarding the product or service presented and the outcome, and in terms of the salesperson-customer relationship. We recommend using a combination of four direct skills: (1) formalizing the intent to leave, (2) summarizing the content of the interview, (3) indicating support and acceptance, and (4) expressing a desire to continue the relationship.

1. *Formalizing the intent to leave*—Often no one takes the initiative to end the interview directly. There is a point at which continuing the interaction is counterproductive. When a salesperson believes the business is completed, initiative should be taken to conclude the interview. For example, "I see that we've completed all the necessary paperwork to get started, so I'll be leaving now."
2. *Summarizing the content of the interview*—In leaving, it usually is helpful for the salesperson to briefly restate perceptions of what conclusions have been reached and then verify them with the prospect. For example, "Before I go, I'd like to check once more with you what we've agreed to do. You'll be checking with Donnell for the additional funding and warehousing facilities

Postcall Inventory

Table 15.2

1. Company: Date:
   Prospect: No. of Calls:
2. Review Customer's Product/Service Line
   * Did I know what products/services they manufacture, distribute, or sell?
   * Did I know what quality their products/services are?
   * Did I know what manufacturing processes are/were used?
   * Did I understand the applications/uses of the product?
3. Review Customer's Market Situation
   * Who are their competitors?
   * How do they share this business?
   * What new products are they developing?
   * What new products are being developed?
4. Review Sales Situation
   * Did I identify their immediate problem?
   * Did I know how my product/service will solve this problem?
   * Did I know the customer's agenda and needs so that I could help reach those goals?
   * Did I think of all the possible resistance the prospect might raise and select my strategies for managing the resistance?
   * Did I have a simple and logical sales plan?
   * Did I know what had happened previously and where the project now stands?
   * Was there a better approach that I could have made here?
   * What buying signals were given by the prospect?
   * When and how often did I trial close?
   * Did I assertively ask for the order?
5. Personal
   * Was my appearance in good taste?
   * Did I arrive on time for my appointment?
   * Did I have a positive sales image?
   * What did I learn from this experience?
   * What can I do to change and improve the next time?
6. Materials
   * Did I have a complete sample line?
   * Did I have the appropriate literature, catalogs, and so on?
   * Did I have the appropriate sales aids and equipment aids in smooth working order?
   * Did I have the necessary legal documents, order forms, and paperwork immediately available?
7. What are my perceptions of why I lost this sale?

   ____
   ____
   ____
   ____
   ____

before Wednesday. I'll get back to you in the morning with the exact dimensions and price breakdown. And I'll set up the tentative delivery date for Friday, assuming you get the funding. Is that how you understand it?"

3. *Indicating support*—At this point, the salesperson may wish to make a genuine statement of feelings about the relationship with the prospect, especially as it has been advanced during the present interview. For example, "I'm excited about having the equipment you need and I personally feel very appreciative of your willingness to approach Donnell for increased funding. I see that as an extra effort on your part, and I want you to know I'm committed to having this order work out as my first priority."
4. *Expressing a desire for continuance*—This is primarily a relationship issue and involves a genuine, direct disclosure of the salesperson's desire for continuance. For instance, "I'm really looking forward to our meeting at the beginning of your fiscal year to explore how we can incorporate this line as part of your permanent inventory. I'll be calling you by 9 in the morning."

Even though the salesperson may have a continuing relationship with the customer, it is important to end every interview *directly*, using data from that interview to complete the discussion regarding both the product or service and the buyer-seller relationship. Skill Builder 15.1 provides further review and practice.

Skill Builder 15.1 Leave-Taking Skills

The leave-taking skills presented here are geared to help salespeople tie up loose ends and leave in a graceful and professional manner that models the relational process. This exercise will help the salesperson exit the interview smoothly and efficiently by developing a dialogue that includes four components: (1) formalizing the intent to leave, (2) summarizing the content of the interview, (3) indicating support and acceptance, and (4) expressing a desire for continuance of the relationship. The following examples illustrate the appropriate leave-taking skills.

A. *Salesperson for West Coast Air Devices, an Industrial Product*

Formalizing:
Terry, I see that we have covered everything. I want to get back to the office and start on the follow-up paperwork.

Summarizing:
Before I leave, I would like to summarize what we discussed. You'll get the paperwork going on your end to get us qualified, and I'm going to okay everything with my manager and get back to you by this Friday. Right?

Supporting:
I look forward to working with you and Aerojet. I have a keen interest in some of the projects you are doing, and I am personally committed to making sure that all your fastener needs will be taken care of.

Expressing a Desire
for Continuance:
I'm really looking forward to you coming to our facilities for the inspection. I'll be calling you tomorrow with the quote for the requisitions you gave me today and to confirm an on-site visitation date with you.

B. *Salesperson for AT&T Local Area Networks, A Commercial Product*

Formalizing:
Asif, I see everything has been completed. I'll be going back to the office to discuss the final price breakdown with the credit department so that we can speed things up.

Summarizing:
May I take a moment to summarize what we've agreed to? Your order will be placed today and will be received and installed within 3 weeks, after the financing has been approved.

Supporting:
I'd like to thank you for the patience you've exhibited as this large packet has been put together. I hope you've felt the support I've given you in return.

Expressing a Desire
for Continuance:
I look forward to seeing you in 3 weeks when we implement the system and periodically after that to check for updates or concerns.

1. Select a product or service. Prepare a dialogue that includes the four elements for effective leave taking as outlined above. You may want to review this chapter for additional examples of each component.
2. Select a partner who will act as your customer and deliver your leave-taking dialogue. Practice using this skill until you become comfortable with your dialogue.
3. Have your partner observe and comment on how you:
   a. Formalized your intent to leave the interview
   b. Summarized the content of the interview
   c. Indicated support in an appropriate manner
   d. Expressed a desire to continue the relationship
   e. Used owned language consistently
   f. Used effective attending behavior by applying the SOFTENS technique

---

Summary

Verbal buying signals may be divided into three categories: questions, confirmations, and conditions. Questions and skills at paraphrasing customer responses are methods of discovering verbal and nonverbal buying signals and can tell the salesperson when it is appropriate to begin closing the sale. The salesperson can use trial closes, if they are necessary, and then move on to the formal (or final) close when the time comes.

Trial closes become good selling strategy at three points in the sales presentation: after an initial benefit statement, after recognizing a buying

On the International Front

Buyers in foreign settings are known to spend more time making the decision to buy or not to buy compared to their counterparts in the United States. When it comes time to act, however, the reverse is true, as in the case of the Japanese, who are known to respond more quickly when acting on a decision.

Minimizing risk and avoiding confrontation are also philosophies of the Japanese. Japanese buyers will choose to do nothing when it is safe to do so and will act only when events pressure them into some kind of action. Furthermore, Japanese buyers avoid making decisions on their own because the group rather than the individual exercises the decision-making function. As stated by Ryushi Iwata, a renowned consultant on the Japanese system, priority is put on accomplishing the task assigned to the work force rather than on the individual employee who is performing the job. This structural mechanism is consistent with characteristic features of the Japanese attitude toward responsibility—namely, the vague nature of individual responsibility, the idea of joint group responsibility, and the strong sense of responsibility toward the small, close group.

Furthermore, international management consultant William Newman states that in certain cultures, "today's commitment may be superseded by a conflicting request received tomorrow, especially if that request comes from a highly influential person. Agreements merely signify intention and have little relation to the capacity to perform."

Furthermore, a prospect's "no" rarely means a complete turndown in foreign countries. A simple "yes" or "no" answer can mean "maybe" or even the opposite response. Listen and watch for the sales clues, which include the prospect's personality, facial expression, and word reactions. Arabs, for example, like expressiveness and periodic displays of emotion. Although they can easily become outraged, these displays are not serious.

Consequently, patience is a prerequisite when closing the sale in many cultural settings. In dealing with many foreign buyers it is advisable not to rush at the point of closing because people in a hurry may be viewed with suspicion and distrust.

Sources: Ryushi Iwata, *Japanese-Style Management: Its Foundations and Prospects* (Tokyo: Asian Productivity Organization, 1982), p. 5; William H. Newman, "Cultural Assumptions Underlying U.S. Management Concepts," in Joseph L. Massie and Jan Luytjes, eds. *Management in an International Context,* (New York: Harper & Row, 1982), p. 331; and Sak Onkvisit and John J. Shaw, *International Marketing* (Columbus, OH: Merrill Publishing Company, 1989), p. 249.

signal, and after handling resistance. Formal closes are closing vehicles when coupled with a formal question. There are seven types of formal closes: assumptive, alternative choice, summary of benefits, balance sheet, concession/inducement, direct appeal, and narrative.

Four direct communication skills that help the salesperson solidify the relationship with the customer and increase the likelihood of future sales are formalizing the intent to leave, summarizing the content of the

Exhibit 15.1

He Kept Right on Talking

His arguments were well received.
His point had, clearly, been achieved,
And his sincerity had quelled
All reservations that I held.
I would have signed the order then,
If he had just produced the pen,
But he kept right on talking.

Couldn't he see he'd raised my hopes,
That I was hanging on the ropes?
He had me sold and, man alive,
The time to close had now arrived.
I wanted desperately to sign
If he would just point out the line,
But he kept right on talking.

And then my mind began to stray
To pressing matters of the day.
His voice, now growing ever higher
In the enthusiastic fire,
Became distraction, then a bore.
I couldn't take it any more.
But he kept right on talking.

I stood, to bring it to an end,
"My time is limited, my friend,"
"But, sir, I thought . . . ," he numbly said.
"You thought that I was interested?
Perhaps I was, but not today."
I didn't have the heart to say
He'd killed his sale by talking.

It is a paradox, but true
Though talk can bring success to you,
Oh, what a tragic thing to see
The source of failure it can be.
So if you want the winner's cup
You'll make your point, then SHUT UP,
And not keep right on talking.

Source: *Sales & Marketing Management,* February 14, 1974, p. 1.

interview, indicating support, and expressing a desire for continuance of the relationship. If there is an element of riskiness in the purchasing decision, it is vital to follow up the sale to reassure the buyer and keep the relationship solid.

Figure 15.2

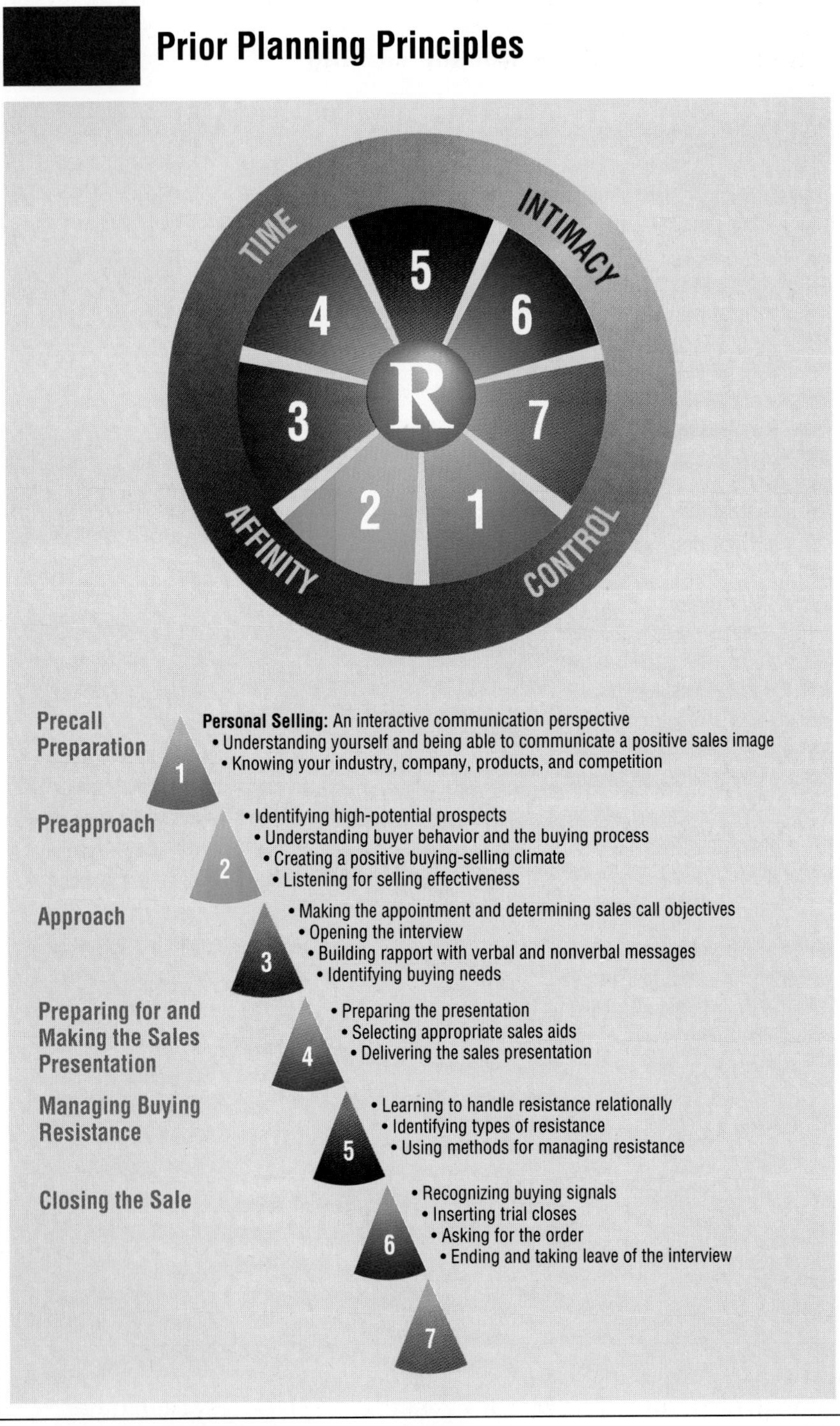
Prior Planning Principles
TIME
INTIMACY
AFFINITY
CONTROL
R
1
2
3
4
5
6
7
Precall Preparation
Personal Selling: An interactive communication perspective
• Understanding yourself and being able to communicate a positive sales image
• Knowing your industry, company, products, and competition
Preapproach
• Identifying high-potential prospects
• Understanding buyer behavior and the buying process
• Creating a positive buying-selling climate
• Listening for selling effectiveness
Approach
• Making the appointment and determining sales call objectives
• Opening the interview
• Building rapport with verbal and nonverbal messages
• Identifying buying needs
Preparing for and Making the Sales Presentation
• Preparing the presentation
• Selecting appropriate sales aids
• Delivering the sales presentation
Managing Buying Resistance
• Learning to handle resistance relationally
• Identifying types of resistance
• Using methods for managing resistance
Closing the Sale
• Recognizing buying signals
• Inserting trial closes
• Asking for the order
• Ending and taking leave of the interview

The salesperson needs to be alert to the customer's time constraints and leave at the appropriate time; otherwise, the sale may be nullified by a customer whose patience has worn too thin.

Key Terms

Buying Signal An indication that the prospect is interested in the product or service and is preparing to make a buying decision

Closing Vehicle Also **closing method;** one of seven methods—assumptive, alternative choice, summary of benefits, balance sheet, concession/inducement, direct appeal, and narrative—by which the salesperson obtains the customer's commitment to buy

Formal Close Also **final close;** a request that the prospect make a decision or commitment of payment in exchange for the product or service

Trial Close A buyer's commitment on a minor point that eventually leads to a formal close

Review Questions

1. Define a buying signal and give examples of both verbal and nonverbal types.
2. Distinguish between a trial close and a formal close.
3. Identify and explain the four points in the sales presentation when a trial close is most likely to be appropriate.
4. Explain how salespeople may make the mistake of using a formal close instead of a trial close. Explain the possible consequences and how this error might be corrected.
5. Identify and explain the two steps in assertively closing the order.
6. Identify, explain, and give examples of the seven closing vehicles described in this chapter.
7. Identify four skills recommended for taking leave of the interview.

Discussion Questions

1. Discuss verbal and nonverbal types of buying signals. In a group, role-play a sales interview using the three types of verbal buying signals, and practice recognizing and responding to them.
2. Discuss the four points when trial closes are most likely to be appropriate. Give examples of possible closes at each time.
3. Discuss ways a salesperson may respond when a trial close is met with resistance. Role-play responses using a variety of communication skills.
4. Discuss the appropriateness of each of the seven closing vehicles in the situation presented in the previous question. What might be the advantages and disadvantages of using each?

5. Discuss ways of responding to a buyer who gives a negative response to a final close.
6. Discuss how the salesperson would deal with doubt and postpurchase feelings to reinforce the buyer's belief that a wise purchase decision was made.

Case 15.1

Getting the Order

Steven Dean has been a sales representative for a major vendor of communications supplies for over 3 years. He has always enjoyed selling and is proud of the honest, straightforward approach he takes with his clients. One of his key prospects is Peter Gorski, the purchasing agent for XYZ Corporation.

After meeting with Gorski on several occasions to discuss the needs of XYZ Corporation, Steven was able to put together an outstanding package at a competitive price. For Steven, XYZ Corporation would be a major new account that would reflect well on his sales productivity. He realizes that the communications supply contract with this firm would total approximately $60,000 annually, and this account would exceed his quota for the year, resulting in a substantial year-end bonus.

The time has come to close the sale. Although all of their meetings have gone well, there is a sudden turn of events when Gorski tells Steven that, given the size of the order, he would expect some type of gift in return. Gorski mentions that he is very interested in a new television set. According to him, the cost of the TV is approximately $500.

Steven Dean is determined to get this order. The situation and request for such an expensive gift, however, makes him uncomfortable, as he is aware that his firm does not encourage extending gifts of more than a nominal value. Steven is confused as to Gorski's expectation of receiving a new television and does not know what to do.

1. Can it be argued that this expectation of gift giving is ethical and customary?
2. What would you advise Steven Dean to do about the situation he is confronting?
3. Would a less valuable gift be considered acceptable in this instance?

Asking for the Order

Case 15.2

Gourmet Kitchens, a large chain of restaurants, contacted Crown Bakeries requesting information on its baked goods. The company specifically inquired about Crown's pastries, cakes, croissants, cookies, and Danish sweet rolls.

Crown's sales representative, Bill Harris, started out the presentation to Gourmet Kitchens' purchasing agent, Betty Hollis, by reviewing his observations from having visited several of Gourmet's restaurants. He made reference to the merchandising of baked goods and explained the benefits of selling Crown's products.

During the presentation Bill discussed Crown's many years of baking experience. He also presented several testimonials and a list of satisfied customers that have continued to do business with Crown throughout the years. He attributed this customer loyalty to the friendly, reliable service, freshness, and consistently good taste of the company's products.

Bill further discussed the training of Crown's bakers and the dedication and pride they take in preparing the goods, especially the French pastries. He listened to Betty's concern regarding freshness and informed her that Crown could serve Gourmet on a daily delivery schedule. She appeared very interested and did not object to price because the competitive nature of the business forces Crown to offer low prices.

Bill is nearing the end of the presentation, and it is time to close the sale. He feels good about the presentation and discussion because he has addressed everything he could think of.

1. Comment on Bill's sales presentation. How can he improve in this area?
2. Suggest different ways that Bill could ask for the order.
3. If you were Betty, what plan of action would you follow before deciding on Crown as a supplier of baked goods?

Notes

1. Gerald L. Manning and Barry L. Reece, *Selling Today: A Personal Approach*, 4th ed. (Needham Heights, MA: Allyn & Bacon, 1990), p. 393.
2. "5.5 Calls to Close," *Personal Selling Power*, November 1984, p. 5.
3. Tom Hopkins, *How to Master the Art of Selling*, 2nd ed. (Scottsdale, AZ: Warner Books, 1982), p. 201.
4. Tom Hopkins, *The American Salesman*, Vol. 27, No. 6 (March 25, 1984), p. 2.

CHAPTER

16

Servicing the Account

Knowledge Objectives

In this chapter, you will learn:

1. The nature of relationship management and how to increase profits through customer satisfaction
2. The purposes for and tasks involved in postsale activities
3. Techniques and guidelines for building customer goodwill
4. What customers want and expect from customer service
5. How to use the win-win method of problem solving to handle complaints fairly
6. How to communicate with customers who behave in deceptive and argumentative ways

Consider This

Everyone in our company—people in sales, telemarketing, research and development and training—must keep our customers in mind on a daily basis. They must keep in mind the three C's of management: customer satisfaction at all costs, caring about other people at Lanier, and consistency in decisions and actions. Our objectives should always be to do it right the first time. . . .

- **68 percent of customers seek a new vendor because they feel they are being treated with indifference by their current suppliers;**
- **It takes 12 positive service incidents to make up for one negative incident;**
- **Dissatisfied customers will tell an average of eight people about their problems with a particular vendor. But on a more upbeat note, 70 percent of complaining customers will return if their complaint is resolved.**

Lance Herrin
*Executive Vice President and Manager of the Copying System Division, Lanier Worldwide, Inc.**

*Quoted by Jane Ammeson, "Customer Vision Means Service and Quality at Lanier," *Compass Readings* (Northwest Airlines), August 1990, p. 24.

Sales Professional Spotlight

Donna Baum is a sales representative for Harcourt Brace Jovanovich Publishing Company, one of the nation's largest since its merger with The Dryden Press and W. B. Saunders Publishing. Recognized for her outstanding performance over 17 years, Donna has progressed to senior sales representative and manages a territory consisting of the largest and best schools in the Boston area.

The publishing business has been almost a lifelong career for Donna. Her first job after graduating from college was with Prentice-Hall Publishers. This sales position, serving a small territory of 20 schools in the New York area, allowed her to gain sales experience that she felt would be valuable for any business career she might ultimately undertake. "The job was a challenge because I was the manager of my territory, which included sales and editorial work," she says.

"It has been my choice to stay in the publishing field because I really like being the manager of my own territory. Boston is a great opportunity for me, in terms of both sales potential and author potential," she says. Donna emphasizes the challenge of striving to increase sales year after year and the occasional difficulty of getting professors to select a specific text.

An essential part of the sales representative's job is to provide high-quality service. Donna describes the most rewarding aspect of her job as providing top-quality service to the instructor, who in most cases is the decision maker in textbook selection. "I have been very successful in providing quality service to the college professors I call on, as well as the bookstores. Spending time communicating with professors is vital to understanding their needs, concerns, frustrations, and problems. I am always prepared to help professors resolve the dilemma in selecting an appropriate text for their classes.

"I have learned that it is a lot easier to keep a satisfied customer than to start from the beginning with a new one. Keeping the professors informed about such things as new editions of texts, the competition, any problems with availability of texts, and other information regarding textbooks is a valuable service I provide. It is even more important that I continually provide support, being accessible to them in any way I can." Once Donna has demonstrated an ability to serve professors, they rely on her service and try very hard to select another text published by the same company if a change is necessary.

For Donna, developing a personal relationship with a professor may take 2 years. "Thereafter, the professor tends to rely on me for advice and service support. My role becomes that of a consultant," she says. She advises that building a long-term personal relationship through consultancy selling is a key element in professional selling.

Try This 16.2 Using the Win-Win Method of Negotiation to Manage Complaints Fairly

1. Identify a complaint that you have had as a customer or have received from a customer.
2. Meet with two classmates to negotiate a win-win solution. Invite one of your classmates to role-play the person in your situation. During the role play, you will:
   A. Describe the problem, including both persons' unmet needs
   B. Brainstorm at least five possible solutions
   C. Evaluate these alternative solutions
   D. Decide on the best solution
3. After each person in your group has had an opportunity to develop a win-win solution to a problem, discuss the following summary questions:

   How does the win-win method of negotiation compare to the way you typically manage interpersonal conflicts in general? When communicating with salespersons? When you are the salesperson?

8. *Decide on the best solution.* Select the solution that seems most beneficial to both the salesperson and the customer. For example, the salesperson and Mrs. Ott may decide that she will have the movers bring the large furniture to the garage on Monday, leaving smaller items that require less care and are not breakable in her present home. After the carpet is installed a week later, then the carpet company will use its truck to transport the smaller items for Mrs. Ott at no charge.

Communicating with Customers Who Behave in Deceptive and Argumentative Ways

Customers with complaints may respond defensively to such a degree that using the win-win method of problem solving is not a realistic option. At this point, the skills to communicate with customers for the purpose of transforming a defensive climate into a more supportive one become essential. Realistically, it may only be possible to stop the defensive climate from spiraling to a more intense level by not responding to defense-arousing behaviors with defensive responses.

The fundamental principle in such a situation is to assume the best motives of the customer. It is impossible to observe the motives of customers. Characteristics such as deceitfulness are nearly impossible to verify. Argumentative behavior is more readily observable, but, in any case, the primary concern of the salesperson is to focus on understanding the customer's needs and feelings while avoiding any form of accusation or defensive response. Therefore, the skill with which to begin managing deceitfulness and argument is active listening.

If a customer wants to evoke a confrontation, the use of active listening by the salesperson will begin to reverse the defensive spiral by demonstrating that the customer's thoughts and emotions are heard and understood. Active listening provides responses that both surprise and support the irritated customer, serving to slow down and reduce the amount of energy present in the interaction. It is important to respond with active listening to each disclosure made by the customer. Regardless of how irate the customer becomes, without active listening the interaction probably would have deteriorated to an even less productive level.

Using active listening as the basic skill, the salesperson should integrate additional skills, including negative inquiry and negative assertion, as practiced in Chapter 14. These skills will assist in drawing more information from a customer to gain an understanding of the basis for the behavior while taking every opportunity to agree with the customer's criticism when there is truth in it.

Try This 16.3 Using Assertive Messages to Communicate with Customers Who Behave in Deceptive and Argumentative Ways

This exercise will help you use sales communication skills—including active listening, negative inquiry, and negative assertion—to communicate with customers who behave in deceptive and argumentative ways.

1. Invite two classmates to join you.
2. Brainstorm a list of situations in which you have observed or worked with customers who behave in deceitful or argumentative ways.
3. Assign yourselves the following roles:
   A. The salesperson, who will use active listening, negative inquiry, and negative assertion
   B. The customer, who will behave in deceptive and argumentative ways
   C. The processor, who will monitor the behavior of the salesperson by placing a hand on the salesperson's arm whenever the salesperson's voice or attending behavior becomes defensive and whenever the salesperson does not provide an active listening response before making a statement to the customer
4. Take turns playing each role in different situations.

Customer Satisfaction Response Systems

How well salespeople perform their postsale activities and manage or service their accounts depends to some degree (in some cases to a large degree) on their company's attitude toward determining its customers' level of satisfaction. For years, competition in the retail and wholesale industries grew increasingly intense; as target marketing became the force behind successful marketers in the 1980s, Procter & Gamble followed suit. As we move forward in the 1990s, Procter & Gamble once again emerges as a champion of total quality and commitment to customer satisfaction. Early in 1990 Procter & Gamble's top executives met with eight senior executives of Wal-Mart, one of the largest buyers of Procter & Gamble's products. The conference was a "part of P & G's ongoing effort to focus all of its business relationships on satisfying the ultimate consumer—the person who buys and uses P & G products."[13] The two groups discovered that each company had its own strategy to reach the ultimate consumer, built on what each perceived to be the wants and needs of customers who buy Procter & Gamble products from Wal-Mart's shelves. They also learned why their strategies were sometimes incompatible. For example, Procter & Gamble assumed that most shoppers look for bargains. Thus, the company emphasized discounts and sales promotions. Wal-Mart, on the other hand, assumed that its shoppers value steady, predictable pricing. Consequently, its strategy was to offer low everyday prices.

Through this discovery, the executive teams worked together to define the ultimate consumer requirements, needs, and preferences in a way that both companies could share and profit from. They also needed to define customer preference criteria that could guide them through a process called *backwardation*. The term is borrowed from the finance community and refers to a form of analysis used particularly in the commodities market. Backwardation allows the individual to examine the process backward from the point at which it touches the ultimate consumer.

Victor Rosansky, senior vice president of Organizational Dynamics, Inc., who led the conference, reported his views about the backwardation process:

> With each step backwards, we'd stop and ask, "Is this part of our process really geared to the ultimate customer's needs? How could it be modified to better serve the ultimate consumer?"
>
> Backwardation does several things. It gives you a clear picture of where you are now and how you arrived there. It reinforces the fact that *all* parts of the work process impact ultimate customer satisfaction. And it subjects each part of the process to a consistent, rational test of customer focus.
>
> Backwardation usually turns up wasteful redundancies and procedures that are being followed without any really good reason. It also opens up a lot of opportunities for innovation, since the whole idea is to question whether the current process is performing as it should.[14]

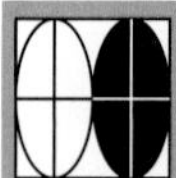

On the International Front

Service Support as a Competitive Tool

A competive edge can be gained by providing service capabilities for certain technical products available in a foreign country. So important is the need for service in the automobile industry, for example, that many multinational corporations have increased the amount of their support, resulting in increased sales and profits. The following examples illustrate the point:

- To improve service support to its 1,350 European dealers, General Motors (GM) set up an automated communications network with a computer at each dealership. Once established, it provided numerous benefits to GM, the dealers, and their customers. Among other benefits, ordering errors were eliminated and processing time was shortened.
- Japanese automobile manufacturers have also realized the importance of service support. They develop training facilities in areas that offer sales and profit potential. The Middle East, for example, is an area where automobile mechanic training has been provided. In one venture Toyota, Nissan, and Honda joined to set up service shops in 44 Libyan towns. The benefits of such a plan are to gain income potential from the service itself and to boost car sales. Buyers tend to select a new car that can be repaired locally.
- Borg-Warner Transmission Products Group established over 20 service centers around the world, in areas where it has important customers but no subsidiary. These centers enable the company to guarantee quick service to customers who are not near a plant facility.

Salespeople need to be attentive to the provision of high-quality service when pursuing sales opportunities in foreign countries. Service obligations must also encompass any warranties and guarantees promised to the buyer. These efforts must be supplemented with regional service centers and skilled staff.

Many companies set up service facilities to support their product sales as soon as they begin selling their products. Where the manufacturer relies on an independent foreign dealer to provide this service support, however, quality control measures must be put in place. If finding a reliable service provider proves difficult, the manufacturer should take on the responsibility of providing the dealer's service support personnel with special training. The relationship works best when high quality, reliable service, and adequate facilities are all present.

Source: Adapted from *Business International*, August 30, 1985, p. 274.

Good Service—What Customers Want

When determining buyers' needs, sales professionals are generally attuned to the individual's perceived needs. Likewise, when top salespeople service their individual accounts, they are sensitive to what their buyers' expectations of good-quality service and servicing are. According to

Cynthia Webster, associate professor of marketing at Mississippi State University, "Whether people are satisfied with service depends on their expectations. . . . And expectations are shaped by many factors, including age, sex, race, and income."[15]

In a survey of service expectations of 300 residents of a large southwestern city, Webster reported these observations in a recent article in the *Journal of Services Marketing:*

- Age is especially important among consumers of professional services such as physicians', attorneys', and dentists' services.
- Adults aged 35 to 64 years care more than younger people about the areas of courtesy, security, a company's name, reputation, confidentiality, and how well a professional knows the client.
- Middle-aged service customers care more about competence, reliability, and accessibility—that is, wanting the service available at convenient hours and accessible by phone.
- Age was not a difference in consumers' attitudes toward nonprofessional services such as banking, laundry, dry cleaning, and automobile-related businesses.[16]

According to Impact Resources in Columbus, Ohio, older consumers are more likely than their younger counterparts to identify service as a reason for selecting a particular place to shop. In studies conducted among shoppers in 35 major metropolitan markets between 1986 and February 1989, it found that "27 percent of 18- to 24-year-olds see service as the main reason for picking a food store, compared with 35 percent of those aged 55 to 64."[17]

Campbell Soup Company also found that age influences customers' expectations. "People 35 and older want the recipe," reports Anthony

Adams, vice president of marketing research for Campbell. "Younger shoppers (under 35) wanted a 1-2-3 product."[18] To attract and please the younger group, Campbell is working to streamline its selection of soups so that people can find them more easily. "After about 45 seconds, we find that consumers just give up," Adams says.

Judith Langer, president of Langer Associates of New York City, has conducted research that points out that devising one service strategy for all older people is a mistake:

> When we look at other age groups, we tend to look in four-year increment. . . . Suddenly, it's 50 to infinity. An affluent 50-year-old in good health with a good job has different service needs than a 75-year-old retiree with limited income in poor health. . . . The old myth was that no one over 50 has money. The new myth is that everyone does.[19]

Impact Resources reports that race also affects a person's service expectations. African Americans are the racial group most likely to be concerned about service, followed by whites and Hispanics. Only 16 percent of Asians considered service important in choosing a place to shop for children's clothing, compared with 18 percent of Hispanics, 20 percent of whites, and 21 percent of African Americans.

Gender influences a person's perception of service as well. In Webster's study, women typically had higher expectations of the quality of professional services than men. Specifically, women were more likely than men to have high expectations about accuracy in billing, convenient hours of operation, and compentence of personnel.

Finally, Import Resources' study found that people with annual household incomes of $50,000 or more are harder to characterize. Affluent customers are actually less concerned about service when they shop for health, beauty aids, and children's clothing. On the other hand, 32 percent of those interviewed cited service as a reason for choosing where to shop when buying men's clothing.[20]

Regardless of the type of sales job a person may enter, the challenge for the sales professional is to offer customers service that is based on the customer's expectations, not the salesperson's or the company's perceived notions. This practice is fully compatible with the relational process. Furthermore, the endless supply of research data available offers assistance to the sales professional in building sales communication competence.

Other Customer Satisfaction Instruments to Help the Salesperson

Surveys

Customer satisfaction surveys give credence to a salesperson's claims. A firm's budget may dictate the extent of the survey. Regardless of the size of the budget, however, it is possible to design a customer satisfaction

A Sample Customer Satisfaction Survey

Figure 16.2

Customer Satisfaction Survey

Customer's Name: ____________ Title: ____________

Company's Name: ____________ Phone: ____________

Address of Company: ____________

Sales Rep: ____________ Company: ____________

1. On a scale of 1–10, please rate your sales representative on the basis of service you received after the sale. Please include in your rating follow-ups for the past 30 days.

Poor	Average	Above Ave.	Excellent
1 2 3	4 5	6 7 8	9 10

If you would like to expand on your numerical rating, please use this space: ____________

2. How many times has our representative called on you in the last thirty days? ____________

3. If you received service calls, what was the average response time? ____________

4. What was the reason for these service calls? ____________

5. In the case of service calls, how effective do you think our sales representative was as a mediator between your company and our service department? ____________

6. What do you think of our product? Please circle one rating.

Poor Average Above Ave. Excellent

7. When you are considering purchasing other products, would you consider doing business with us in the future? ____________

Thank you for your time in filling out this questionnaire, which we hope will help us in improving our service to you. We have enclosed an envelope for your use in returning it to us.

Customer signature: ____________

survey that is customized and effective. Three basic components of such a survey should be questions that focus on how the customer feels about the product, the service, and the company and its representatives. Figure 16.2 is a sample customer satisfaction survey.

Because this form is given to the customer by the salesperson, it must be easy to fill out. The salesperson can help ensure that the customer will return it by following these four guidelines:

1. Make the survey only one page long.
2. Fill out the customer's name and address.
3. Use mostly multiple-choice questions.
4. Include a self-addressed stamped envelope.[21]

Video Feedback

Video booths offer customer service feedback in industries such as the airlines and travel industries. For example, as a part of a test, American Airlines set up a booth in the baggage area of the Nashville Metropolitan Airport to tape customers' observations on the carrier. Travelers were invited to spend at least a minute describing their posttravel complaints or praise. The tapes were then evaluated, and measures were taken to improve customer service in response to the customers' concerns.[22]

Focus Groups

Focus groups are a popular way of gathering qualitative research that may offer determinants of customer satisfaction. A focus group brings together eight to 12 people in a conversational setting and asks them to talk freely about the product or subject. A trained facilitator moves the discussion along, ensuring that the marketer's questions get addressed, while also giving the group members freedom to express their opinions. These sessions typically last 1–2 hours, and the respondents usually receive some form of compensation.

Summary

Servicing the account is an area of relational selling that deserves special attention because it is a prime consideration in customer satisfaction. The foundation of proper account servicing is the establishment of an open, trusting relationship between the customer and the salesperson, with both parties of the relationship defining their own needs and seeking methods to reach a mutually satisfactory, win-win understanding.

This chapter identifies five postsale activities that the salesperson may employ to strengthen and build such a relationship. These activities are showing appreciation, processing the order, account penetration, after-sale support directly involving the service or product sold, and training users and customers' salespeople in maintaining open communication channels.

The salesperson should possess communication skills sufficient for handling complaints. Methods of analyzing reasons for complaints, and of managing them, are discussed, as are several customer satisfaction response systems.

Prior Planning Principles

Figure 16.3

TIME
INTIMACY
AFFINITY
CONTROL
R
1 2 3 4 5 6 7

Precall Preparation (1)

Personal Selling: An interactive communication perspective
- Understanding yourself and being able to communicate a positive sales image
- Knowing your industry, company, products, and competition

Preapproach (2)

- Identifying high-potential prospects
- Understanding buyer behavior and the buying process
- Creating a positive buying-selling climate
- Listening for selling effectiveness

Approach (3)

- Making the appointment and determining sales call objectives
- Opening the interview
- Building rapport with verbal and nonverbal messages
- Identifying buying needs

Preparing for and Making the Sales Presentation (4)

- Preparing the presentation
- Selecting appropriate sales aids
- Delivering the sales presentation

Managing Buying Resistance (5)

- Learning to handle resistance relationally
- Identifying types of resistance
- Using methods for managing resistance

Closing the Sale (6)

- Recognizing buying signals
- Inserting trial closes
- Asking for the order
- Ending and taking leave of the interview

Postsale Activities (7)

- Continuing to manage the relationship
- Building customer goodwill
- Using ethical practices in servicing the account

Exhibit 16.3

An Outline for Developing a Sales Presentation

A. Step One: Precall Preparation
   1. Sales topics
      a. Understanding yourself and communicating a positive sales image.
      b. Knowing your industry, company, products, and competition
   2. Sales communication skills
      a. Learning to use active listening
      b. Using attending behaviors: the SOFTENS Technique
      c. Learning positive self-talk
      d. Making "I" statements
      e. Changing disconfirming into confirming messages
      f. Identifying sales communication styles

B. Step Two: Preapproach
   1. Sales topics
      a. Identifying high-potential prospects
      b. Understanding buyer behavior and the buying process
      c. Creating a positive buying climate
      d, Listening
   2. Sales communication skills
      a. Using relational feedback
      b. Identifying emotional triggers in listening
      c. Listening interpersonally
      d. Identifying response styles

C. Step Three: Approach
   1. Sales topics
      a. Making an appointment
      b. Setting sales call objectives
      c. Opening the interview
      d. Developing verbal and nonverbal rapport
      e. Determining buying needs
   2. Sales communication skills
      a. Using levels of communication to open the interview
      b. Writing probes to encourage buyer to share
      c. Developing supportive climates
      d. Using free information
      e. Using nonverbal messages
      f. Developing open questions
      g. Uncovering emotional and rational motives
      h. Revising loaded and leading questions into neutral questions

D. Step Four: Preparing for and Delivering the Sales Presentation
   1. Sales topics
      a. Deciding on a presentation model
      b. Preparing a competitive differential advantage analysis

Exhibit 16.3
Continued

c. Preparing a features-advantages-benefits analysis
d. Selecting and using sales support materials
e. Managing the interaction
2. Sales communication skills
a. Using perception checking
b. Using the FAB system to present benefits
c. Using persuasive communication
d. Developing nonverbal congruence and body language
e. Using win-win negotiation

E. Step Five: Managing Buying Resistance
1. Sales topics
a. Handling resistance relationally
b. Identifying types of resistance by need, price, service, company, and timing
c. Selecting traditional methods for handling resistance
2. Sales communication skills
a. Using assertive messages
b. Probing with open and closed questions
c. Using active listening
d. Using perception checking
e. Working with criticism through negative inquiry and negative assertion

F. Step Six: Getting Commitment (Closing the Sale)
1. Sales topics
a. Recognizing buying signals: verbal and nonverbal
b. Inserting trial closes
c. Deciding on closing vehicles: assumptive, alternative choice, summary of benefits, balance sheet, concession, direct appeal, and narrative
d. Ending and closing the interview
2. Sales communication skills
a. Using defense-arousing language contrasted with supportive language
b. Knowing what to do when the buyer says "yes"
c. Knowing what to do when the buyer says "no"
d. Taking leave of the interview: formalizing, summarizing, supporting, and showing continuance

G. Step Seven: Postsale Activities
1. Sales topics
a. Developing a relationship management program
b. Techniques and guidelines for building customer goodwill
2. Sales communication skills
a. Using win-win methods in negotiating to "yes"
b. Using a win-win method of negotiating for handling complaints fairly
c. Communicating with customers who behave in deceptive and argumentative ways

Key Terms

Account Penetration Matching the size of the order to fit the customer's buying situation

Backwardation A form of analysis that allows the company to examine the company's marketing efforts backwards from the point at which they touch the ultimate consumer.

Cognitive Dissonance Doubt that the customer experiences after the buying decision has been reached

Focus Group A group of people brought together and asked to talk freely about a product or subject

Goodwill The sum total or value of all the positive feelings that a customer has toward the salesperson and the company

Negotiation Discussion of specific proposals among two or more people to find a mutually acceptable solution to a problem

Relationship Management Tactful, sincere communication that nurtures a close connection between salesperson and customer

Video Feedback Videotapes of customers' responses to a product or service; lasts 1 minute or more

Review Questions

1. Explain the time element in relationship management. Include a specific example to clarify your explanation.
2. Explain cognitive dissonance as it applies to consummating a sale.
3. Identify and explain five postsale activities.
4. Identify and give examples of each of the five causes of customer complaints listed in this chapter.
5. Identify and explain the eight steps in the win-win method of handling a complaint.
6. Explain and provide an example of the process of backwardation.
7. identify and explain three types of customer satisfaction instruments available to salespeople.

Discussion Questions

1. Discuss how consummating the sale is only the beginning of a salesperson/customer relationship.
2. Discuss how each of the five postsale activities can help solidify the relationship.
3. Discuss and role-play the win-win method of handling complaints.
4. Discuss the communication skills particularly useful in determining and maintaining customer satisfaction.

Taking No Chances with Quality Service

Case 16.1

Mike Thomas was a new salesperson for the Olympic Shoe Company. In addition to soliciting new accounts, Mike was assigned a list of existing accounts to service. The salesman who had dealt with these accounts had recently been fired because of many complaints from customers.

Mike spent the first month on the job visiting these assigned accounts, introducing himself as Olympic's new sales representative. One of these accounts was Southern Illinois University. Upon entering the athletic director's office he immediately knew he was in trouble.

"It's about time you came. What excuses do you have about the complaint about the running shoes I sent in to your company 2 weeks ago? Is Olympic slipping in their commitment to providing customer satisfaction?" snapped Coach Brown.

"What problems with this last shipment of running shoes are you referring to?" Mike remarked. "That's strange because this is the first time I've heard anything about problems with your last order. The previous salesman who handled your account is no longer with Olympic, and no one was notified of such problems. Tell me more about your complaint."

Coach Brown cited several cases of poor quality and his request that four new pairs be forwarded before the competition the previous weekend. "Since we never heard from Olympic, the track coach was forced to contact Helms International Shoe Company for a rush order, which was shipped overnight to arrive on the day of the championship," Brown abruptly stated.

Mike promised that he would check with the quality control department as soon as he returned to the office, and that he would attempt to find out what went wrong with this particular shipment and why the problem was not rectified immediately. Mike also promised to take up this quality concern with manufacturing, insisting that this problem would be avoided in the future.

In closing, he reminded Coach Brown that because the basketball season was drawing near, Olympic was calling for orders. And, as the new representative in this territory, he would make sure that the account is handled professionally in the future.

"I have decided to give my business to Helms for all athletic supplies," stated Coach Brown. "We cannot take the chance of a problem like the running shoes recurring!"

1. Where did the previous sales representative at Olympic Shoe Company go wrong?
2. What did Mike Thomas fail to do at the time that Coach Brown informed him of the problem?
3. What actions on the part of Mike Thomas would be appropriate in preventing Coach Brown to switch suppliers? What assurance could Mike now give him to ensure customer satisfaction?

Case 16.2

The Importance of Servicing the Account

Lynn Brooks was thrilled with her new position as sales representative with Miles Paper Supplies, Inc. Her potential for earnings was encouraging because she was assigned a sales territory extending to the east coast.

After 4 weeks of training, Lynn was ready to take on the responsibility of meeting the customers in her territory and improving Miles' image, which had become somewhat distorted over the last 4 years. A major problem was the lack of attention to vendors. In several instances Miles had neglected some areas in the territory.

Problems at Miles escalated further when many salespeople were fired for poor sales performance and left no documentation in the files regarding the status of the accounts. After contacting her first ten customers, Lynn concluded that the salespeople at Miles never realized the importance of supporting the sale and following up with the customer to seek repeat orders. They thought that the customers would call if they had complaints with their order or needed any more supplies. Some of the buyers still had obsolete supplies on hand.

Lynn's encounters with vendors were discouraging because of the hostility and distrust developed during the vendors' dealings with the former salespeople at Miles. "I have no interest in doing any business with Miles Paper Company. I was promised service when I ventured into business with you and once the agreement was signed I never saw a salesman again," one prospect exclaimed. "The competition is too keen in this industry for me to take any chances with a company that fails to realize the importance of servicing an account. I eventually gave the business to one of your competitors who has tried to get my business for over a year," another vendor remarked.

The difficulties and obstacles did not cease as her meetings with vendors continued to be laced with comments about lack of service support and inattentiveness to customers. Lynn began to question her decision to be affiliated with Miles Paper Supplies and undertake such a difficult assignment.

1. What should Lynn do to improve the image and eventually the sales in her territory?
2. How much time should she allocate to improving relations with the prospects, if this is even possible?
3. What had the previous salespeople done or failed to do that angered the customers?

Notes

1. Theodore Levitt, *The Marketing Imagination* (New York: The Free Press, 1983), pp. 111–112.
2. Ibid., p. 113.
3. Ibid., p. 114.
4. R. F. Wendel and W. Gorman, *Selling: Personal Preparation, Persuasion, and Strategy*, 3rd ed. (New York: Random House, Inc., 1988), p. 418.
5. Ibid., p. 445.
6. T. C. Taylor, "G.E. Posts a Sentry to Give Customers Better Service," *Sales & Marketing Management*, December 6, 1982, p. 46.
7. Milind M. Lele, "The Four Fundamentals of Customer Satisfaction," *Business Marketing*, June 1988, pp. 80–94.
8. M. Daniel Rosen, "Expanding Your Sales Operation? Just Dial 1-800 . . . ," *Sales & Marketing Management*, July 1990, p. 82.
9. Lele, "The Four Fundamentals of Customer Satisfaction," *Annual Editions: Marketing, 1989–90*, Article 7, p. 48.
10. Ibid., p. 51.
11. Jim Domonski, "7 S.P.E.C.I.A.L. STEPS to Better Listening, *TeleProfessional*, Fall 1989, p. 21.
12. Levitt, *The Marketing Imagination*, p. 119.
13. "Procter & Gamble's Superordinate Goal: Satisfy the Ultimate Consumer," *ODI Newsbrief* (Burlington, MA: Organizational Dynamics, Inc., 1990), p. 8.
14. Ibid., p. 10.
15. Patricia Braus, "What Is Good Service?" *American Demographics*, July 1990, p. 36.
16. Ibid., p. 38.
17. Ibid.
18. Ibid.
19. Ibid.
20. Ibid.
21. Ibid.
22. Barry J. Farber, "Increase Your Sales with Customer Satisfaction Surveys," *Personal Selling Power*, January/February 1990, p. 50.

PART 5

Staying Alive—Methods of Maintaining a Professional Sales Career

Sales Topics

- Telemarketing, Technology, and Communication Systems
- Integrating Computers into the Sales Operation
- Sales Management's Role in Recruiting, Selecting, Training, and Performance Evaluation of its Salesforce
- Career Management

Sales Communication Skills

- Using Communication Skills to Develop a Telemarketing Program
- Using the Telephone Effectively
- Managing Self, Time, Territory, and Career
- Making Affirmations

CHAPTER

17

Telemarketing, Technology, and Communication Systems

Knowledge Objectives

In this chapter, you will learn:

1. How telemarketing can be used to conduct selling activities effectively and efficiently
2. How to establish a telemarketing center
3. Communication skills for using the telephone effectively
4. How technologically based methods can be incorporated into the company's sales system
5. How to integrate computers and other communication efforts into the company's sales operation

The last ten years have seen more and more promises of the potential of information technology—computers plus workstations plus data micros. Managers have been offered the Cashless Society, the Information Age, the Paperless Office, and above all, Productivity.

Peter G. W. Keen, Ph.D.
Executive director of the International Center for Information Technologies*

*Competing in Time (Cambridge, MA: Ballinger Publishing Co., 1988), p. 2.

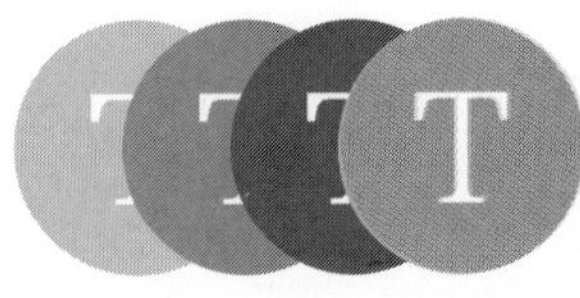

Two topics that emerge frequently in the popular press are the exponential rate at which the amount of information available to us is growing and the rapid innovation of technological advances to help us assimilate and manage the information relevant to our daily lives. Certainly, both the information age and state-of-the-art technology to manage it have arrived in the field of sales.

Less than 20 years ago, obtaining a loan to buy a home meant that the customer visited several financial institutions to find the best loan and then to qualify for it. Today, loan brokers with laptop computers visit a prospective buyer's home. After a brief exchange to determine the customer's needs, the loan broker punches up the characteristics of a loan that may suit the buyer's needs and then places it alongside several others on the tiny screen so the buyer can complete a comparative analysis on several dimensions in a relatively brief time. Once the loan broker leaves the customer's home, little or no record keeping is required in the broker's office—all the information is stored in the computer. In addition, the salesperson leaves a printout of what has been discussed with the customer. When the customer decides on a loan, the transaction can be completed in the customer's home. For both the customer and the salesperson, time, energy, and stress are managed effectively.

This chapter is about using state-of-the-art technology as a support system to manage time efficiently for both salespeople and their customers, resulting in increased and more accurate service. Proper use of such technology may shift the balance in their workload to less paperwork, possibly less travel time, and more selling time. The first section of this chapter focuses on the development of a sales communication system with telemarketing at the center. Hence, effective use of the telephone becomes an important sales skill. Electronic communication systems are emphasized in the second section, including teleconferencing and other modes of telecommunication. Finally, the integration of computers into the sales communication system is dealt with in the third section.

Telemarketing

The importance of interaction and flexibility in the presentation is emphasized by Dennis Morgan, vice president of Creative Marketing Concepts:

> Never ask a complete stranger, "How are you doing today?" You really don't care. They know you don't care. You know they know you don't care. And they know that you know that they know you don't care.[1]

A few years ago, a telemarketer at General Electric received a phone call about a cogeneration system. Using a scripted guideline, he qualified the inquiry and passed the information along to the company sales engineers. The result was a $100-million sale.

Sales Professional Spotlight

With all his responsibility at the Saudi American Bank in Saudi Arabia, Abdulrehman Algheriri is extremely sensitive about efficiency in providing information to advise customers on investment issues. He emphasizes that advanced communications systems enable him to guide customers through immediate decisions that are affected by worldwide economic conditions.

Abdulrehman believes that all salespeople will soon be armed with modern technologies to enhance their selling jobs in many different ways. Functions of the bank's treasury customer division in Riyadh include processing investment decisions and providing customer service. "Accuracy and speed are at the heart of our service orientation. The system at the treasury is designed to expedite results, especially at times when customers expect responses with accuracy and speed," he says.

According to Abdulrehman, handling and managing accounts is also improved through efficient coordination with other departments using computers. "Electronic equipment, such as board and mail, enables the delivery of information to keep our staff in tune with all changes and developments at all times that might be crucial to a customer's portfolio." He also stresses the importance of salespeople assimilating and managing information relevant to their daily activities, giving them the time to concentrate on serving clients with accuracy of services.

From the standpoint of the Saudi American Bank's international activities, efficiency has increased the use of telecommunications technology and computer networks. "Delivery of documents and follow-up activities can now be immediate. Furthermore, our sales staff can offer advice involving stock and bond purchases, and monetary conversion rate information, in a most timely manner, giving the client an added advantage to increase investment potential," he states.

Abdulrehman also admits to the benefits of electronic advances in communications, serving as an economical alternative to flying the bank's salespeople around the world. Nonetheless, he clearly emphasizes that "the professional salesperson must be attentive to the personal contact that may be required at times in maintaining and strengthening good working relationships with clients."

Abdulrehman recalls the unsettling feelings and resistance he once had toward computers when undergoing his training in the United States. He advises students not to be discouraged by the growing role of computers. "If you really work hard at it you will eventually become skilled and disciplined, and gain that competitive edge in meeting the challenges in the sales profession."

A telemarketer at W. N. Taylor, a $7-million industrial distributor in Allentown, Pennsylvania, opened an account with the U.S. Navy. Two years later, without the help of an outside salesperson, she received a $134,000 order.[2]

Are these reports unusual? Not really. In 1987, *The Annual Guide to Telemarketing* reported that more than $115 billion of industrial products, ranging from steel fasteners to computer service contracts, were marketed by telephone.[3] And yet, many businesses are apprehensive about telemarketing.

Marketing products and services through telephone contacts is known as *telemarketing*. Many telemarketing programs fail because they try to focus on key products rather than on the company's entire product line and they are unable to hire the right people for the job.

On the Ethical Side

Most people who telemarket for sales are legitimate, but there are some whose ethics are suspect. Law enforcement officials are cracking down on unscrupulous telemarketing practices. The following precautions are suggested to avoid becoming a victim:

1. Allow only an authorized purchasing agent to order, receive, and pay for supplies. Refer all calls to that person.
2. Use written purchase orders.
3. Inform all employees about your company's purchasing, receiving, and payment systems.
4. Put a notice or caution sticker on all copiers.
5. Don't buy from new suppliers without first confirming their existence and reliability.
6. Always ask toner representatives for their name, company name, and telephone number. If they're vague, hang up.
7. Don't answer questions about copiers, including inquiries about model or serial number.
8. Be suspicious of a hard sell, name dropping, rudeness, and other inappropriate sales behavior.
9. Verify the product and price offered before agreeing to anything.
10. Don't accept delivery if suppliers or invoices are unfamiliar, and don't pay without being sure the order was authorized.
11. Don't accept COD shipments.
12. When in doubt, check with the local Better Business Bureau or refer to the Federal Trade Commission pamphlet "Buying by Phone."

Xerox and other reputable companies are seeking ways to combat this fraudulent action. The Silent Witness hotline is available, whereby callers can anonymously report telemarketers whom they suspect of fraud.

Source: Adapted from Kate Bertrand, Toner Phoner Con Artists Ringing Up More Victims," *Business Marketing*, September 1990, p. 18.

Finding the right person for a telemarketing position is frequently the most difficult part of starting a program. Often a company may try to convince the customer service staff to do the selling or bring an outside salesperson in from the field. Both may prove ineffective, for two reasons. First, salespeople often do not enjoy handling details or being confined to a desk; they may lack the necessary patience for a telemarketing position. Second, customer service people are frequently afraid to make that first call. One answer to finding the most suitable person is to recruit telemarketers from the sales support staff or salespeople tired of being on the road.

Regardless of a company's attitudes about telemarketing, the high cost of personal selling has forced firms to integrate the telephone into the activities of every field sales representative's day. To reinforce this point, McGraw-Hill's Laboratory for Advertising Performance now separates telephone contact from face-to-face selling in its research. For instance, in 1977, face-to-face selling took up 39 percent of sales time; in 1986, face-to-face selling took up 25 percent and telephone selling 17 percent.

Thus, the primary objectives of most telemarketing systems are to reduce the high cost of personal selling, by reducing the number of personal-contact calls required to close a sale, and to avoid overappropriation of time to small accounts. Sales efforts are maximized when a greater proportion of in-person contact is directed toward larger and more profitable accounts. Findings reveal that it costs less than one-sixth as much to sell by phone as through a personal contact.[4] Dow Chemical, for example, determined that it would be uneconomical for its sales force to visit accounts representing less than $50,000 in revenue. These accounts are sold and managed by phone.[5]

In Chapter 1 we showed a breakdown of the median cost per in-person call by industry for 1990[6]:

Consumer products	=	$210.34
Industrial products	=	$250.54
Services	=	$222.66

In contrast, the cost of a sales call by telephone averages $5–10. Furthermore, according to Steve Franzmeier, "Just as many sales are closed with five phone calls as with five personal sales calls."[7] Even if one were to extend the cost of a telemarketing call to $20, the total of five calls would be only $100 compared with over $1,000 for five face-to-face calls.

Jim Winkelspect, an industrial distributor for W. H. Taylor of Allentown, Pennsylvania, reported that his vice president of sales turned over approximately $600,000 worth of small accounts to the company's two telemarketers. He estimated that sales calls cost $20 per contact using the telemarketers, compared to $250 for a visit by one of his nine salespeople. After nearly 6 years in operation, his telemarketing program "now contributes $1.6 million to the company's $7 million in annual sales."[8]

This section will show how salespeople can set up a telemarketing program without the assistance of expensive consultants. The discussion will be centered on four topics: (1) examining precall planning and organization as they apply to marketing by telephone; (2) explaining nonverbal and verbal communication skills for telephone use; (3) outlining techniques for prospecting, setting appointments, and making sales presentations by phone; and (4) describing high-tech telemarketing systems, of which the telephone is a central part.

Precall Planning and Organization

When implemented correctly, a telemarketing program is an effective way to increase sales, manage accounts, and increase the productivity of the outside selling force. The cost of a telemarketing program will vary according to job market, products sold, location, and how large an operation is planned. The salary for a telemarketing salesperson will usually range from hourly wages to about 80 percent of an outside salesperson's salary.

Community colleges and job fairs are good places to recruit beginning telemarketers. Unless all calls are local, plan on a monthly phone bill of $300–400 per person. Other operational fees may include $2,000 for a computer and software, an office, a desk, and a phone; if you use an outside trainer or consultant, plan on $500–1,500 per day for that person's time.[9]

The background required for a competent sales telemarketer depends on the responsibilities to be performed and the products being sold. For example, at Lotus Development in Cambridge, Massachusetts (annual sales of $282.6 million), all telemarketers have either college degrees or technical training.[10] Other companies may match the qualifications to responsibilities only. For example, in a company that uses telemarketing to sell highly technical products, the telemarketer may be required to have a degree in engineering. If the telemarketer is doing more basic work, such as lead generation or qualifying, however, then technical training will suffice. In either case, effective verbal and nonverbal communication skills are mandatory.

The local phone company is a good place to obtain advice on starting a telemarketing program. Such advice is part of the phone company's service. Many operations use specially designed long-distance services to reach their target markets. Wide-Area Telecommunications Service (WATS) lines are available on an incoming, toll-free basis and for outgoing calls made to both interstate and intrastate destinations. Each WATS line covers a defined area, which should encompass the firm's target area. Outgoing WATS lines enable businesses to contact prospects at a rate that may be 30–50 percent below listed long-distance rates. Incoming WATS (800) lines provide prospects and customers with toll-free access. Prospects are more likely to pick up the phone if they can call free to obtain advice or information on the company's products or services. The 800 number is also a complement to the firm's direct marketing effort, which may be conducted by mail or by sales support personnel.[11]

The use of enhanced 800 and 900 numbers for marketing is changing the way people communicate. The rapid growth of this telemedia industry reflects its effectiveness. Programs that have mass appeal with minimal labor intensity use 900 numbers. Sweepstakes and contests are popular examples. Thomas L. Kenny, chairman of Communications Management and Information, Inc., in Atlanta, Georgia, notes, "There were fewer than 250 900-programs in 1988, compared with 14,100 in 1990. By 1992, 900-numbers are projected to generate more than $2 billion in revenue."[12]

The effectiveness of a telemarketing program depends on sound management planning. The salesperson may find these five guidelines helpful in developing a telemarketing program:

1. Segment and identify the particular market intended.
2. If possible, identify specific subsets of those segments most likely to have an interest in the product. (Refer to *Sales & Marketing Management's Annual Survey of Buying Power* for assistance.)
3. Develop or tailor a selling approach to meet the needs of each segment—that is, an approach focusing on price, product, company, service, source, or timing.
4. Vary the approaches to find which one produces the most sales in which segment.
5. Remove any stigma that may prescribe a need for elaborate marketing sophistication. Stay focused on the fact that telemarketing is "simply an organized method for reaching customers and prospects."[13]

One task involved in precall planning as discussed in Chapter 6 is to organize the territory by A-B-C account volume or potential. This procedure may be helpful for organizing the prospects and customers in a telemarketing operation as well. Peter Peltier, an executive at Permag, a Chicago electronics and magnetic material distributor with annual sales of $34 million, used a version of the A-B-C account analysis in his successful telemarketing operation:

> The company started with its 12,000-name company list with the intention of finding out where they stood with their customers. The first step Peltier took was to compile a list of the firm's dormant accounts from five years back. Then Peltier had two telemarketers call the accounts to find out their status, their sales history, and why they had stopped purchasing from the company. Peltier estimated that 2% of key accounts were not called and another 30% were eliminated, either because they had gone out of business or had changed companies.
>
> They then placed the remaining accounts on a priority list. "A" accounts were marginal buyers (less than $1,000 annually); "B" accounts hadn't made a purchase in the last 12 months; and "C" accounts hadn't placed an order in 3 years but still showed interest. According to Peltier, the results were well worth the effort. "We generated a lot of five-figure orders from accounts that we would never have gotten business from otherwise. It was a nice bonus."[14]

Nonverbal and Verbal Communication Skills

As we have seen in earlier chapters, rapport is established when mutual feelings of trust and respect exist between the salesperson and the customer. Chapter 10 introduces skills and techniques that help build rapport nonverbally. Also described is the impact of a message: 55 percent of the message is communicated by our bodies while 38 percent is communicated by our voices and only 7 percent by the words we speak. Realizing this heavy emphasis on nonverbal behavior, salespeople must apply the same principles used for communicating nonverbally in a face-to-face selling situation to the telephone context, in which a "cable" is the only connecting link.

The SOFTENS technique can be adapted to successful telemarketing:

- *Smiling*—Your facial expression will affect the tone of your voice. Imagine that the prospect or customer is sitting across the room. If necessary, place a photo of someone whose face prompts a smile where it is in full view while you are on the telephone.
- *Open posture*—Keep feet flat on the floor as opposed to propped up on a chair or wrapped around the chair legs. Clear the desk of as much clutter as possible so that there will be no distractions and you can give your undivided attention to the person you are talking with.
- *Forward lean*—Often, you will be taking notes during the conversation or referring to product or company literature. Leaning toward the desk or placing your arms on the desk, as in a writing position, will help maintain a forward lean. Sitting erect and leaning slightly forward will help you actively listen and concentrate on what is being said.
- *Touching by shaking hands*—Obviously, physical touching is impossible, but warmth and interest can be expressed through a warm and caring tone of voice. Women often must learn to lower the pitch of their voice when talking on the phone, and men may have to concentrate on vocal variety so as not to fall into a monotone. "Reach out and touch someone" is a well-conceived slogan designed by Pacific Bell that demonstrates the impact of touching in building and maintaining rapport, goodwill, and the dynamics of a relationship.
- *Eye contact*—One way to maintain a visual image of a person sitting across the room is to put a mirror directly over the desk and look into it as you talk with the customer. This also facilitates an awareness of facial expressions and can help increase the effectiveness of using the SOFTENS technique on the telephone.
- *Nodding*—Use the same facial expressions on the phone as in person, including nodding when appropriate to indicate that you are attentive to what the prospect is saying.
- *Space*—Act as if you are sitting about 4–5 feet from the customer rather than miles apart. State-of-the-art phone equipment provides

the clarity and distortion-free connection that gives the customer the feeling of being in the same room with you.

In addition to using the SOFTENS technique, the salesperson should also focus on vocal behavior during the conversation with the customer. Particular attention should be given to volume, emphasis, pitch, and disfluencies. It is also important that the salesperson concentrate on pronouncing words clearly and maintaining a moderate speaking rate and volume to enable the prospect or customer to fully understand what is being said. The customer ordinarily watches the salesperson's expression, particularly the lips; the message may take longer to process through the customer's ears alone.

Techniques for Prospecting, Making Appointments, and Giving Sales Presentations

As discussed in Chapter 6, one of the most commonly used methods for prospecting in the consumer products industry is the use of direct mail with a follow-up phone call to respondents. Another way of qualifying prospects is to secure an appointment by telephone because prospects who grant an appointment either are interested in the salesperson's product or have little buying resistance.

Most telemarketers use a well-planned script. All scripts should be simple, brief, and to the point. They should perform four functions:

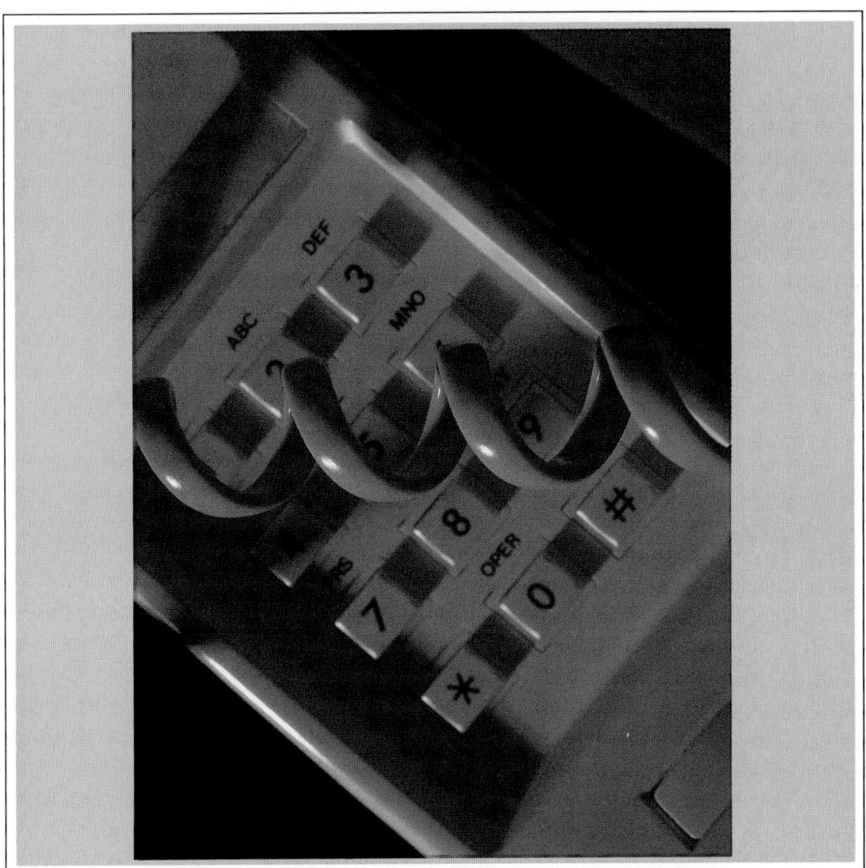

(1) gain attention and credibility, (2) probe and involve the prospect, (3) describe benefits and pertinent facts, and (4) urge the customer to take action.

Three basic scripting styles are used in a telemarketing program. The least personal style is a verbatim script that is electronically recorded and used as part of a direct selling system. This is strictly an information-giving device; the prospect has no opportunity to ask questions or offer resistance.

A slightly more personal type of verbatim script is a canned written pitch, which the salesperson must follow word for word, even replying to resistance with preconceived responses. There may be a limited amount of unscripted dialogue between the salesperson and the prospect; for the most part, however, the salesperson is instructed to adhere to the exact wording of the script.

A third, more personalized approach to effective telephone selling is the conceptual script, in which two-way communication and prospect participation are encouraged. It is flexible and allows the individual salesperson to construct the presentation format. The conceptual script also provides the framework by which the consultative sales presentation and the relational process can be developed.

This outline may help the competent sales communicator to build an effective telemarketing presentation:

1. Establish your identity and that of your company, as well as the purpose of the call.
2. Clarify that the prospect is either the key account buying influence, the decision maker, or the person with authority to set an appointment, if that is the desired outcome (qualify the prospect).
3. Establish rapport to reduce defensive reactions to the call, using the five levels for establishing verbal rapport discussed in Chapter 6:
   A. Make a friendly or caring remark (level five).
   B. Mention something that you and the prospect may have in common (level four).
   C. Make a statement about the seller's concerns at an idea level (level three).
   D. Report a fact about the seller's concerns at a feeling level (level two).
   E. Request a response at both the thinking and feeling levels (level one potential).
4. Build a customer profile.
   A. Use open and neutral questions.
   B. Develop questions around the six buying decisions—need, company, product, price, service, and timing.
5. Prepare a sales message.
   A. Stress features, advantages, and benefits.
   B. Match FABs to the major concerns identified by the customer.
6. Manage resistance by using:
   A. Paraphrasing.
   B. Perception checking.
   C. Negative inquiry.
   D. Negative assertion.
7. Request that the prospect take action by:
   A. Asking for the order.
   B. Setting an appointment for a personal visit.
   C. Scheduling another telephone call.
8. Optional actions to consider:
   A. Follow up on the call within 48 hours.
   B. Request referrals.

Once the salesperson has a plan, it is important to determine the best time to call. Industries may be receptive to vendors' calls at different times. Some companies may even dictate specific hours and days on which a salesperson can see a prospect. Table 17.1 offers guidelines for appropriate hours when a salesperson will increase the opportunity to make a favorable phone contact.

To integrate the steps in this outline as a workable tool for building a telemarketing program, practice Skill Builder 17.1.

Table 17.1

Suggested Telephoning Times

Profession	When to Call
Accountants	Usually not between January 1 and April 15. Otherwise, anytime during the day.
Bankers and stockbrokers	Before 10:00 A.M. and after 5:00 P.M.
Chemists and engineers	Between 1:00 P.M. and 3:00 P.M.
Clergymen	Between Monday and Friday
Contractors and builders	Before 9:00 A.M. and after 5:00 P.M.
Dentists	Before 9:30 A.M.
Druggists and grocers	Between 1:00 P.M. and 3:00 P.M.
Executives, merchants, store managers, and department heads	After 10:30 A.M.
Lawyers	Between 11:00 A.M. and 2:00 P.M.
Physicians and surgeons	Between 8:30 A.M. and 10:00 A.M. and after 4:00 P.M.
Professors and teachers	Between 7:00 P.M. and 8:00 P.M.
Publishers and printers	After 3:00 P.M.
Salaried employees	At home in the evening.

Source: Reprinted courtesy of Northwestern Mutual Life Insurance Co.

Establishing a Telemarketing Center

The telemarketing center is established to support field sales. It is designed to provide information and reports to other departments within the company. Figure 17.1 depicts a typical telemarketing center performing such functions as order processing, sales support, account management, and customer service. Coordination is vital in strenghtening the working relationship among departments.

Several examples describe companies that use telemarketing centers to support common functions of sales support, order processing, account management, and customer service (Figure 17.2).

B. F. Goodrich Chemical Group uses a telemarketing center for order taking, customer service, and information dissemination. When customers call, a center specialist brings up the customer's file on a computer screen, records the order, checks inventory, and, when necessary, talks with production and shipping to schedule shipment. Field sales personnel are then provided current inventory data and estimated arrival times. High-volume accounts are scheduled for field visits, thus increasing the number and quality of contacts between B. F. Goodrich and its best customers.[16]

How important can a telemarketing center be to a multibillion-dollar computer manufacturer such as Digital Equipment Corporation (DEC)? According to a report in *TeleProfessional*, a monthly trade publication:

> It is critical because 70% of the annual orders come in via direct marketing channels (including the telephone and on-line Electronic Store). . . . Every

Skill Builder 17.1 Using the Telephone Effectively

This exercise is designed to give you practice in developing a conceptual telemarketing script. It will help you to organize your telephone presentation into the following categories:

A. Identifying self and company
B. Giving a reason for calling
C. Qualifying the prospect
D. Establishing rapport
E. Building a customer profile
F. Preparing a sales message
G. Managing buying resistance
H. Requesting appropriate action

Instructions:

1. Using a company in which you have an interest, describe a situation in which you would use the telephone as a part of your selling process (such as for prospecting, setting an appointment, making a sales presentation, or a combination of the three).
2. Using the conceptual script format, write a script that corresponds to your objective. Follow the outline below.

Format

Your situation ______

Script:

A. Identification
   1. Name ______
   2. Company ______
   3. Reason for call ______

B. Qualifying the prospect
   1. Authority to buy (name) ______
   2. Buying decision influence ______
   3. Secretary/receptionist (name) ______

C. Establishing rapport
   1. Level 5 ______
   2. Level 4 ______
   3. Level 3 ______
   4. Level 2 ______
   5. Level 1 ______

D. Building a customer profile using open, neutral questions
   1. Need ______
   2. Company ______
   3. Price ______
   4. Service ______
   5. Product ______
   6. Timing ______

E. Preparing a sales message
   1. Identify buyer's major areas of concern ______
   2. Relate FABs to major needs ______

F. Preparing responses to possible resistance (use two)
   1. Active listening ______
   2. Perception checking ______
   3. Negative inquiry ______
   4. Negative assertion ______

G. Requesting action
   1. Ask for the order ______
   2. Set an appointment or call-back ______

Figure 17.1

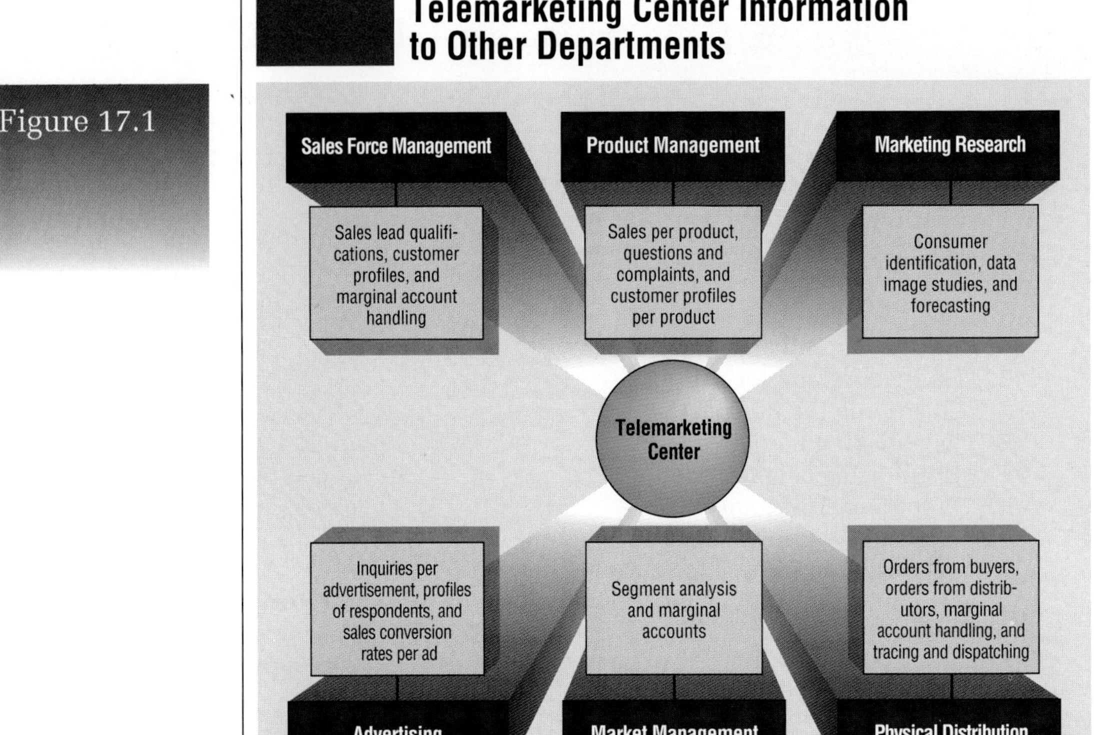

Source: John I. Coppett and Roy Dale Voorhees, "Telemarketing," *Industrial Marketing Management*, 1983, p. 81.

> product from the largest mainframe to the smallest accessory is supported by DECdirect, the group responsible for implementing direct marketing activities for the company.
>
> DEC started using direct marketing tools in 1978 when they centralized the order-taking function within a telemarketing facility for low-end items. This allowed the field sales force to perform their expected role as sales engineers rather than order takers. . . .
>
> In 1983 DEC introduced the Electronic Store. This system provided a service that would allow prospects and customers to dial in and obtain product information, including technical details, demonstrate software and order products and services.[17]

By 1991 all sales channels and support systems were completely integrated. *TeleProfessional* publishers Carol and Ross Scovotti summarize the role that telemarketing plays at DEC:

> Before the sale, prospects may call and consult with technical representatives about anything from configurations to engineering specifications. They may request catalogs or other literature. They may check the Electronic Store for demonstrations, product information or pricing.

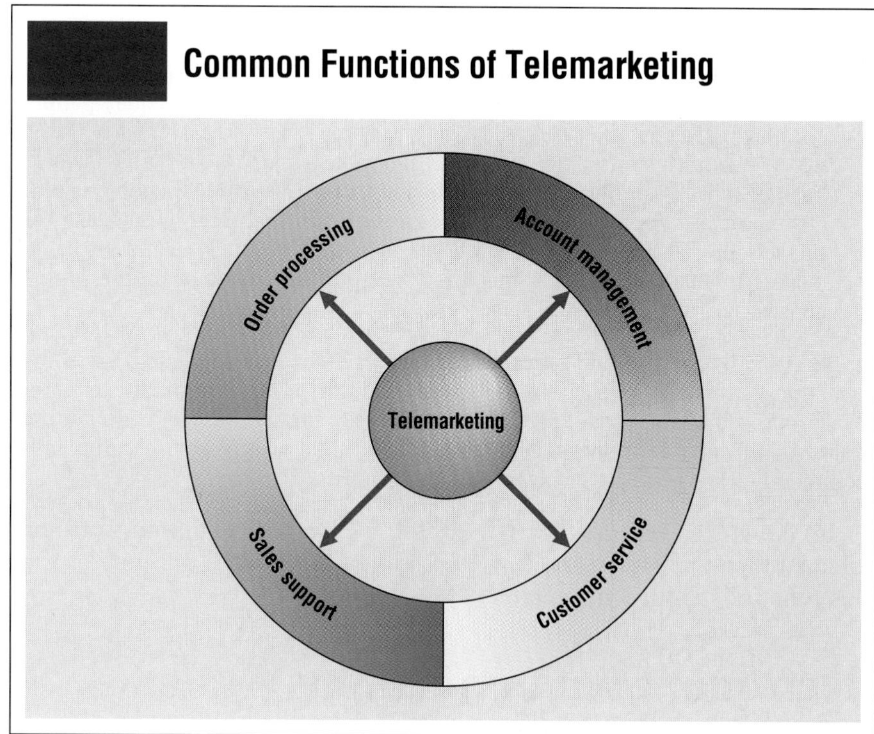

Figure 17.2

> When it's time to order, they may call the order center, deal directly with their local sales representative or place it through the Electronic Store. Whichever channel is used, the transaction is entered into the database and the Account Manager receives credit for the sale.
>
> After the order, telemarketing support continues with technical assistance, customer satisfaction surveys and outbound telemarketing.[18]

Overall, customer service is at the heart of the telemarketing center. Extending customer service is a way to achieve that competitive advantage, especially at times when customers expect a quick and accurate response. One group committed to improving customer service through the use of the telephone is the IBM National Telemarketing Center. With annual sales of $69 billion, IBM operates the 125-person center in Rochester, Minnesota. These 125 people are responsible for lead generation, prospect qualification, and postsale customer satisfaction surveys for IBM's Application System/400 (AS/400) line of computers. In 1991, the company's efforts earned it one of the most prestigious awards given for customer service, the Malcolm Baldridge Quality Award.[19]

Historically, customer service has been considered a postsale function. It follows, then, if the purpose is to improve satisfaction, that respondents would already be customers and subsequently would be considered as a cost to the salesperson's company. This view is changing, however, as both large and small companies find that customer service is a revenue generator. One of the most widely known customer service operations is the GE Consumer Answer Center in Louisville, Kentucky. Known as the largest consumer-information service in the world, it employes 220 call people who are available 24 hours a day, 7 days a week to serve the needs of both present and future customers.[20]

N. Powell Taylor, former manager of the GE Consumer Answer Center, reports:

> Today's market is changing and everyone is looking for that competitive edge. As quality becomes more equal, and price becomes more equal, people are turning to customer service to get the competitive edge.
>
> We handle some 3,000,000 calls per year, some 70,000 calls a week. Each of these is an opportunity to increase brand loyalty. All contacts with customers are opportunities. . . . The dealers like the program because we pre-sell the customer on the product. In fact, 15% of our calls are from dealers themselves. Many times, they will put the customer on the phone and we will help close the sale.[21]

Because all inquiries and referrals are logged, GE has been able to draw some interesting estimates for account potential (Exhibit 17.1). Although customer service representatives do not sell, they can be extremely effective in upgrading accounts and cross-selling—"recognizing the unfilled needs of the caller and recommending new or better ways to fill those needs."[22]

In the next section, we will examine electronic communications systems other than telemarketing that add to the overall support of the sales functions and requirements.

Electronic Communications Systems

This section will focus on two specific areas: teleconferencing and integrating computers into sales support systems through telecommunication systems.

Exhibit 17.1

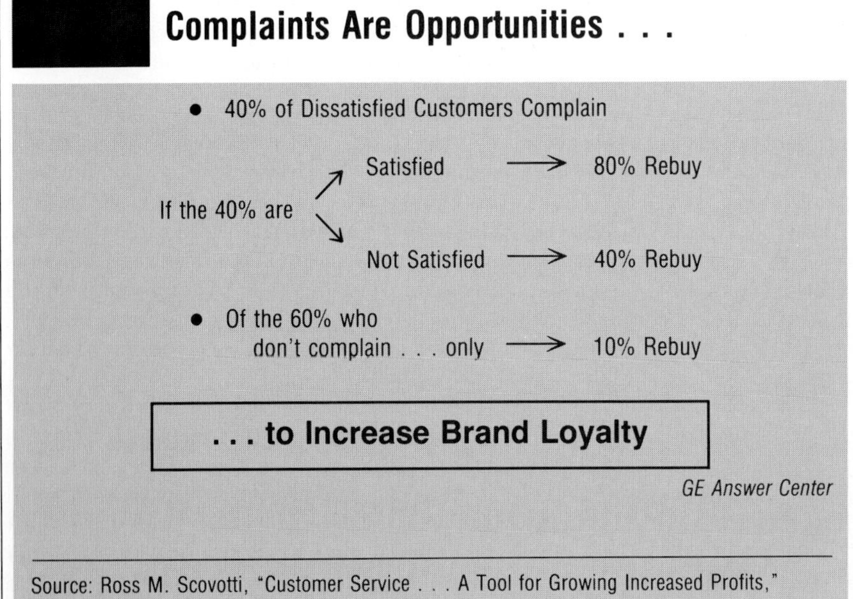

Complaints Are Opportunities . . .
• 40% of Dissatisfied Customers Complain
If the 40% are
Satisfied → 80% Rebuy
Not Satisfied → 40% Rebuy
• Of the 60% who don't complain . . . only → 10% Rebuy
. . . to Increase Brand Loyalty
GE Answer Center

Source: Ross M. Scovotti, "Customer Service . . . A Tool for Growing Increased Profits," *TeleProfessional*, 1991, p. 24.

On the International Front

International Focus: Increasing Productivity in International Sales

Telemarketing is now international. Service 800 S.A. is a firm that offers toll-free dialing in more than 40 countries on five continents, much like firms using 800 numbers for telemarketing in the United States. The firm has over 600 clients, and service is available in over 110 cities around the world. Financial services account for 40 percent of clients, and many others are in the travel industry. Firms such as DuPont, Digital Equipment, and Lee's Jeans are among the 60 American clients. Many firms use this service as an intermediate step before establishing a sales office in a country.

Other technology used in automating an international sales force includes the use of software and hardware to link the home office with salespeople on the road in foreign lands. It is essential in a competitive international arena to have access to data communications that provide instant contact with customers and the sales force.

Despite the many benefits of sales automation, salespeople must be aware of potential problems when conducting sales internationally:

- Phone systems in many countries are unreliable.
- Software of current lists, such as foreign addresses, is often either unavailable or incompatible.
- Customs offices in many countries frown on travelers entering with laptop computers. Having a laptop confiscated at the airport can be a major drawback for the salesperson.
- Answers to technical questions may not be readily available in a foreign country.

Sources: Eric J. Adams, "Stalking the Global Sale," *World Trade*, June/July 1991, pp. 34–36; and Vern Terpstra and Ravi Sarathy, *International Marketing* (Ft. Worth, TX. The Dryden Press, 1991), pp. 518–519.

Teleconferencing

According to communication specialists Sigband and Bell, each year "American business spends billions of dollars in expenses related to flying business bodies around the world. In most cases only business *minds* need to travel."[23] One of the advances made in electronic communications to facilitate this approach while reducing costs is teleconferencing. A *teleconference* is a visual phone call, in which cameras and microphones in one meeting room transmit visual and auditory signals by satellite or telephone line to a similarly equipped meeting room in another part of the city, region, country, or world.

There are several advantages to teleconferencing rather than traveling. Salespeople can avoid the stress of travel, including time away from family and friends. Sales aids that could not fit on a plane—such as charts, models, prototypes, and other visual support—can now be used for display. Personnel, such as technical sales support staff, who were unavailable to travel with the salesperson can participate in a teleconference.

The two main disadvantages to teleconferencing are the limitation of using equipment that is available in the customer's facility and the lack of training for participation in a teleconference. Salespeople may have difficulty trusting important negotiations to teleconferences because of several unknown quantities: What do I look like on camera? What will the camera focus on? How will I know when to speak, or when someone on the other end wants to speak? How will I make eye contact with decision makers in the group? These concerns can be resolved only by training salespeople to adapt their sales communication skills to the teleconferencing context.

Another teleconferencing application is computer conferencing. This technique involves people sitting at their computer terminals and talking with one another electronically, without calling a formal meeting. This equipment is especially useful when the salesperson wants to communicate with the engineering and production departments on matters related to the product. It saves time and money, particularly when they are located in different sites throughout the building.

Telecommunications

According to information technologist Peter G. W. Keen:

> Telecommunications eliminates barriers of geography and time on service and coordination. It has redefined the base level of customer service in entire industries, changed the economics of market innovation in others, and allowed major companies to reposition themselves. It is a significant product differentiator, especially in mature markets.[24]

Investing in telecommunications technology is expensive, and the technology itself is rapidly changing and complex. The risks increase as traditional marketplaces are changed by electronic delivery systems, new markets open up, and some marketing-oriented firms use communications to reposition their businesses. The most popular technologies are cellular phones, modems, electronic bulletin boards, voice messaging and voice mail, electronic mail (E-Mail), facsimile (fax) machines, and videotex systems.

Cellular Phones

Cellular phone systems enable salespeople to conduct transactions by phone from almost anyplace. They can use the phone to make appointments, call in orders, and work while in their cars.

The mobile or cellular telephone also gives salespeople greater flexibility in communicating with customers and the home office. The next step is the cellular briefcase telephone, which is completely portable and personal, allowing the salesperson to call anytime and from anyplace.

A similar electronic development is the computerized road map. In one version, a screen installed in the car displays a road map and indicates the location of the car with a symbol. The destination is marked with a star, and the map rotates around the car symbol as one drives. The driver may, if desired, zoom in on any mapped area for a closer look.[25]

Modem

The modem converts data into a form that can be transmitted over telephone lines. This enables one computer to "talk" to another, thus allowing salespeople to interact with the computer at the office from another facility.

Electronic Bulletin Board

An electronic bulletin board enables messages to be sent throughout an office, keeping employees attuned to any developments or changes taking place.

Voice Messaging and Voice Mail

Voice messaging acts as a complex phone answering machine, giving out prerecorded messages and taking messages. Voice mail is a means for salespeople to have their phones answered automatically if they are away from the office or car.

Today's voice messaging technology has become interactive; information is routed from a touchtone phone via an interactive voice response system to a host computer-digitized voice. This procedure often eliminates the need for human operator intervention. In sum, the caller interacts with an external database to retrieve information unique to the caller or the situation; the interactive voice response system acts as the salesperson.[26] Figure 17.3 describes the marketing applications that are possible using interactive voice messaging.

Facsimile Machine

Imagine putting an order into a copy machine and having the copy turn up in an office in another country. Fax machines enable the salesperson to send a letter or longer document to a customer or supplier and have the addressee receive it almost immediately. PayFAX machines, phone stations that hang on the wall, will soon be available worldwide. Exhibit 17.2 describes fax applications being used by sales force personnel.

Videotex

The videotex system allows members of the general public to gain access to a central computer that provides a variety of services, such as sales messages, shopping tips, and other information. It enables consumers to purchase goods and services by providing them with the type of information vital to decision making.

Exhibit 17.2

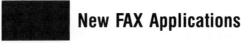

New FAX Applications

PC Fax Boards

by Larry Fromm

It is no secret that facsimile machines have augmented telephones as a valuable business communications tool. What is less well known, however, is the variety of ways fax devices can be used to complement traditional sales and marketing methods.

Many of the new fax applications have been spurred by PC-based fax hardware and software. But the latest innovation in fax, and one of today's most talked about technologies, is integrated voice, which combines voice processing and fax processing.

Integrating Voice and Fax

By adding a voice interface to a fax system, interacting with PC Fax systems is simplified, making them easier to use and more functional. As a result, fax boards are now being designed to integrate with the same voice processing components that are used to build voice mail and voice response systems. One such product is Dialogic Corporation's (Parsippany, NJ) FAX/120, a 12-line fax board that works with Dialogic's D/120 12-line store and forward board.

Integrated voice and fax processing allows users to take advantage of a variety of applications, including fax response, fax broadcast, and fax messaging. The following are some application examples of how integrated voice and fax can be used.

Fax Response

Fax response applications supplement voice response applications by being able to supply printed information in addition to spoken information. Fax response is currently used at several magazines for article requests. Readers can call, listen to voice prompts describing the documents, then use the telephone keypad to select documents and enter the fax number where information is to be sent.

Fax response can also be used when placing orders by phone. Customers place their orders by selecting from a variety of voice prompts, entering commands using the telephone keypad, and receive printed confirmation of their order, without speaking to a live person.

Fax Broadcasting

Fax broadcasting applications enable a single document to be delivered to multiple individuals. For example, fax broadcasting allows companies to quickly distribute new product or pricing information to all of their sales offices. Faxing large documents is easier because it doesn't require someone physically checking for paper jams.

Perhaps your company is running a special product promotion that requires that pricing updates be announced to all branch offices. Fax broadcasting can also simplify the distribution of press announcements. By programming the fax numbers on your list just once, subsequent mailings can be sent by fax.

Fax Messaging

Voice messaging and fax messaging can be integrated to provide a single mailbox, allowing the sending and receiving of both voice and fax messages. Analogous to voice messaging, fax messaging enables documents to be stored and delivered at a later point in time.

Exhibit 17.2
Continued

Sales forces can take advantage of fax store and forward when traveling. When arriving at a new location the salesperson can check his fax mailbox and, selecting from a series of voice prompts, instruct where the faxes be sent. Like voice messaging, fax messaging is confidential, allowing information to be accessed only by user I.D. number. Fax messaging also provides fast response. Documents can be retrieved quicker than those sent through the mail.

Fax Service Bureaus

Integrated voice and fax systems are now available from several voice processing and fax processing companies. For companies who cannot yet justify the purchase of an integrated voice and fax system, service bureaus are cost-effective alternatives. For about $50 per month, a fax service bureau provides users with the capability to test the many applications of integrated voice and fax processing.

As the demand for fax processing systems grows, integrated voice and fax has the potential to become a major market of its own. The benefits of integrated voice and fax to sales and marketing organizations will ultimately create a new productivity and communications tool. ■

Source: Larry Fromm, "New FAX Applications," *TeleProfessional,* June 1991, pp. 40–41.

Figure 17.3

Marketing Applications Enabled by Interactive Voice Response

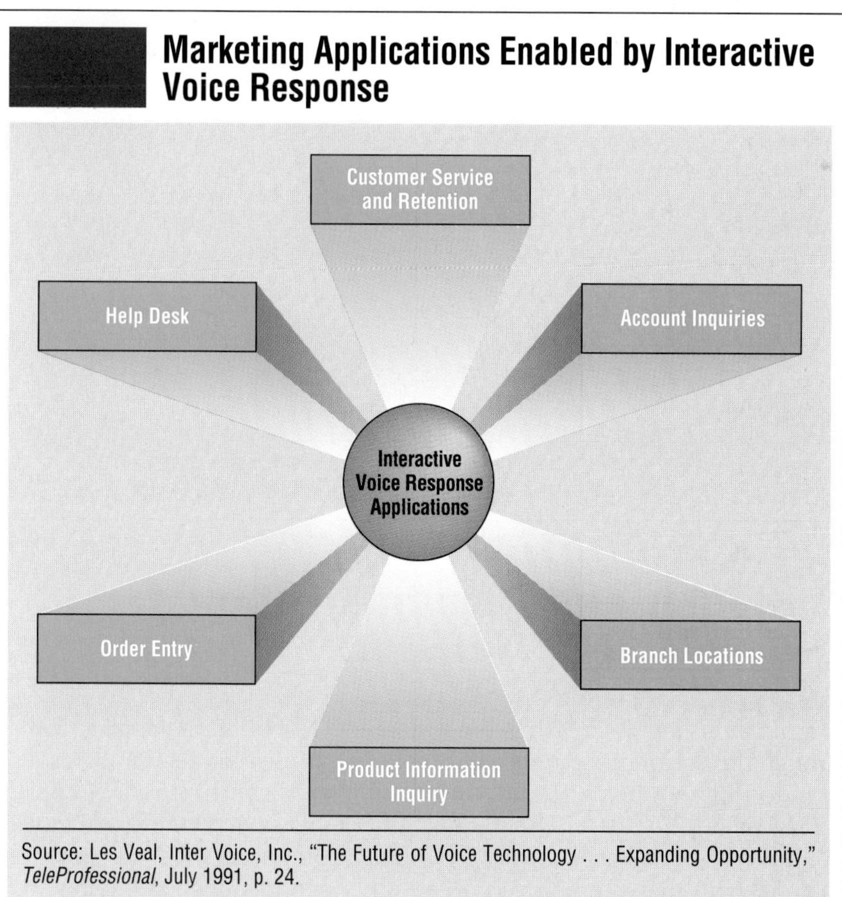

Source: Les Veal, Inter Voice, Inc., "The Future of Voice Technology . . . Expanding Opportunity," *TeleProfessional,* July 1991, p. 24.

Exhibit 17.3

Sales Rep Usage of Computers

		Use Computer at Work					
	All Workers	Total	%	Word Processing	Spread-sheet	E-mail	Communi-cations
Sales occupations	13,272	4,665	34.9%	10.0%	7.0%	4.9%	8.9%
	6,947	2,770	39.9	12.3	9.7	6.0	11.1
	6,425	1,895	29.5	7.5	4.0	3.7	6.4
Supervisors, proprietors	3,918	1,477	37.7	10.0	8.9	5.9	10.8
	2,566	1,042	40.6	10.4	10.9	6.3	12.0
	1,352	435	32.2	9.2	5.0	5.0	8.6
Sales reps, finance & business services	2,289	1,364	59.6	24.4	14.0	9.9	20.4
	1,315	734	55.8	24.9	15.7	9.8	19.6
	974	630	64.7	23.7	11.8	10.1	21.5
Sales reps, commodities, except retail	1,656	662	40.0	14.2	10.9	5.9	10.5
	1,294	494	38.2	13.2	10.7	6.0	10.6
	362	168	46.4	17.7	11.6	6.9	5.5
Sales workers, retail & personal services	5,443	1,159	21.3	2.8	1.5	1.9	2.2
	1,755	498	28.4	5.1	2.9	3.0	3.9
	3,688	661	17.9	1.7	0.9	1.4	1.4
Sales-related occupations	66	3	NA	NA	NA	NA	NA
	17	2	NA	NA	NA	NA	NA
	49	1	NA	NA	NA	NA	NA

Both Sexes □ **Male** □ **Female** □

NA: Not available; base less than 75,000 persons.

Source: Census Bureau, *Computer Use in the United States: 1989 (Series P-23, No. 171).*

Computer and Communication Technologies

Organizations are increasing the efficiency levels of their sales forces through the use of computers and other communication technologies that include video support and portable computers. According to a U.S. census bureau report, *Computer Use in the United States*, by 1989 the percentage of employees in sales occupations who use computers (34.9 percent) was on a par with that of employees in all other occupations (34.8 percent).[27] The figures reported in Exhibit 17.3 debunk the widely held belief that sales professionals trail in computer use. In fact, personal computer penetration becomes remarkable when the various categories of sales professionals are considered.

The census bureau report also underscores the computer's pervasive presence in all aspects of our lives. For example, during 1984–1989, the percentage of households with a personal computer almost doubled. The Electronic Industries Association's consumer electronics group estimated that 28 percent of all households had computers as of January 1991.[28]

According to Robert Jurik, a sales automation consultant for Modatech Systems, Inc., in Uniondale, New York, 85 percent of the sales forces in the United States will be automated to some degree by 1995. Considering the percentage of sales forces that were automated in 1991, that significant increase sends a strong message to companies looking for a competitive edge. Jurik also reports:

> Automation emphasizes the real issues involved in the sales process: getting information to the prospect and servicing the customer. By automating your sales force correctly, you can dispense with all the inefficiencies that have plagued the sales process and decreased salespeople's potential.[29]

Today's laptop computers give the salesperson a portable office on the road; tomorrow's will also provide portable studios for creating more effective sales presentations. Small, light, notebook-type laptop models appear to be growing in popularity and have dramatically improved screen displays. The competitive need to maximize the limited time spent in front of the buyer means that salespeople are increasingly relying on computer-based visual aids that can be customized easily and that give the sales presenter more control and flexibility.

Another example of customer-oriented computer creativity is the handheld computer or portable data recorder (PDR). The PDR is widely used to conduct inventories and count shelf displays in retail stores. Another version of a handheld computer is the integrated PDR, which has contact or laser scanners, either with or without keyboards.[30]

Additional data on personal computer applications by sales force size are reported in Exhibit 17.4. Most companies believe that sales automation is proving its worth. Of the firms interviewed for the data presented in the exhibit, 78 percent reported that personal computers helped salespeople become more productive.[31]

Exhibit 17.5 may clear up some of the confusion that sales managers and salespeople experience when trying to determine what hardware will best fit their selling needs.

The examples that follow illustrate typical applications of the computer as a sales support tool:

- Salespeople for the womenswear division of Wrangler use laptop portable computers in the customer's office to confirm stock availability and enter the order directly, expediting delivery.[32]
- At Rockwell International's heavy vehicle components division, sales representatives were given personal computers to help sell automatic slack adjusters. Programs contained the cost data to compute what fleet operators were spending on brake adjustments. These figures were then compared with the cost of Rockwell's

Exhibit 17.4

Computer Applications by Sales Force Size

Applications	Total	Small	Medium	Large
Word processing	78%	79%	79%	75%
Account management	60	52	68	65
Proposal preparation	55	54	55	60
Call reports	53	53	50	65
Account/prospect profile	52	52	52	50
Spreadsheets	52	44	58	60
Lead tracking	42	46	42	30
Sales presentations	41	41	41	45
Call planning	41	41	42	35
Sales forecasts	40	35	47	35
Sales analysis	38	33	41	45
Direct marketing	34	30	39	30
Territory management	33	25	39	40
E-mail	32	23	33	60
Graphics	27	25	27	35
Telemarketing	26	25	29	15
Order entry	25	23	21	45
Inventory/ship. status	19	13	20	45
Market analysis	19	17	21	25
Budgeting	18	17	23	10
Mapping	9	9	6	15

Source: *Sales & Marketing Management's* fifth annual PC survey, July 1991, p. 69.

slack adjusters to show the savings to the customer from using this equipment.[33]

- Ryder Rental Trucks developed a computer model that helps salespeople illustrate the cost trade-off between leasing and purchasing trucks. The salesperson asks the customer questions concerning estimated mileage driven and the type of truck needed, enters the answers into the portable computer, hits a single key, and reviews the printout with the customer.[34]

Overall, the maximum benefit of computers is achieved when the computer is linked to the total communication system. Moreover, the system must involve the customers, suppliers, and other parts of the selling process, both internal and external. Thus, it is important to consult with these other facets to make the system as compatible as possible. The goal is to become more competitive in serving customers by communicating more quickly and expediting sales transactions more efficiently.

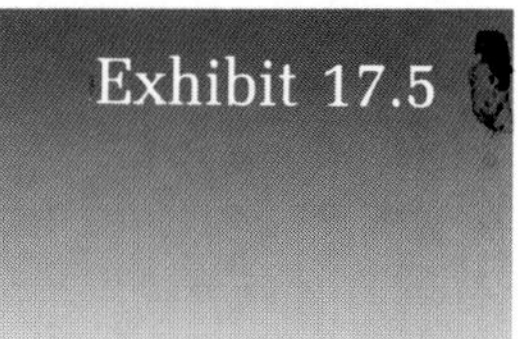
Exhibit 17.5

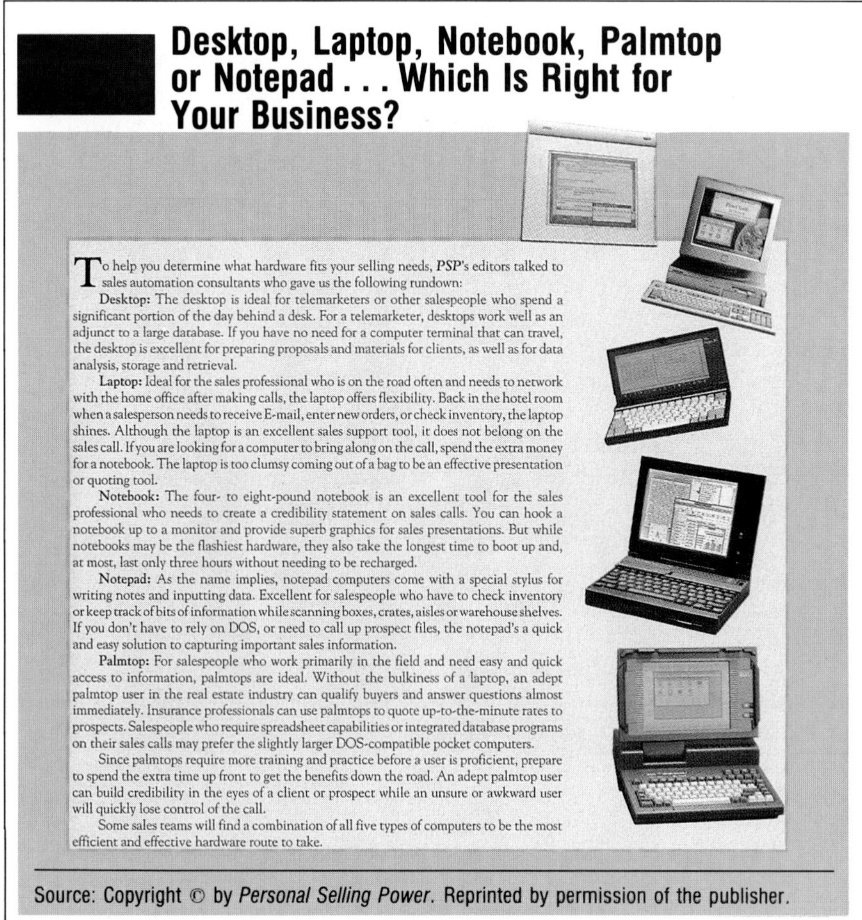
Desktop, Laptop, Notebook, Palmtop or Notepad . . . Which Is Right for Your Business?

To help you determine what hardware fits your selling needs, *PSP*'s editors talked to sales automation consultants who gave us the following rundown:

Desktop: The desktop is ideal for telemarketers or other salespeople who spend a significant portion of the day behind a desk. For a telemarketer, desktops work well as an adjunct to a large database. If you have no need for a computer terminal that can travel, the desktop is excellent for preparing proposals and materials for clients, as well as for data analysis, storage and retrieval.

Laptop: Ideal for the sales professional who is on the road often and needs to network with the home office after making calls, the laptop offers flexibility. Back in the hotel room when a salesperson needs to receive E-mail, enter new orders, or check inventory, the laptop shines. Although the laptop is an excellent sales support tool, it does not belong on the sales call. If you are looking for a computer to bring along on the call, spend the extra money for a notebook. The laptop is too clumsy coming out of a bag to be an effective presentation or quoting tool.

Notebook: The four- to eight-pound notebook is an excellent tool for the sales professional who needs to create a credibility statement on sales calls. You can hook a notebook up to a monitor and provide superb graphics for sales presentations. But while notebooks may be the flashiest hardware, they also take the longest time to boot up and, at most, last only three hours without needing to be recharged.

Notepad: As the name implies, notepad computers come with a special stylus for writing notes and inputting data. Excellent for salespeople who have to check inventory or keep track of bits of information while scanning boxes, crates, aisles or warehouse shelves. If you don't have to rely on DOS, or need to call up prospect files, the notepad's a quick and easy solution to capturing important sales information.

Palmtop: For salespeople who work primarily in the field and need easy and quick access to information, palmtops are ideal. Without the bulkiness of a laptop, an adept palmtop user in the real estate industry can qualify buyers and answer questions almost immediately. Insurance professionals can use palmtops to quote up-to-the-minute rates to prospects. Salespeople who require spreadsheet capabilities or integrated database programs on their sales calls may prefer the slightly larger DOS-compatible pocket computers.

Since palmtops require more training and practice before a user is proficient, prepare to spend the extra time up front to get the benefits down the road. An adept palmtop user can build credibility in the eyes of a client or prospect while an unsure or awkward user will quickly lose control of the call.

Some sales teams will find a combination of all five types of computers to be the most efficient and effective hardware route to take.

Source: Copyright © by *Personal Selling Power*. Reprinted by permission of the publisher.

Summary

In this chapter, telemarketing is presented as an increasingly important component of strategic marketing and sales management. Specific attention is given to how marketing activities can be used effectively and efficiently to enhance sales through the development of a carefully executed telemarketing program. The sales communication skills that are described throughout this text are adapted for use in telemarketing.

Teleconferencing is a way to create face-to-face communications settings over long distances. Numerous high-tech telecommunications systems are rapidly becoming an inherent part of the salesperson's electronic sales-support environment. These include cellular phones, modems, electronic bulletin boards, voice messaging and voice mail, fax machines, and videotex.

The integration of computers and computer technologies for sales efficiency is also explored. Laptops are described as portable studios for creating effective sales presentations. The portable data recorder, used for inventories, was described. Computers can be most beneficial when they are linked to the total communication system.

Key Terms

Cellular Phone Phone that can be used from anyplace; "wireless" phone

Electronic Bulletin Board Message board normally hung in a particular place; message on the board can be updated or changed via a remote keyboard

Facsimile (Fax) Machine Machine that transmits copy of a document via telephone line

Modem Converts data into a form that can be sent over telephone lines, enabling computers to "talk" to each other

Portable Data Recorder (PDR) Used to conduct inventories and count shelf displays in retail stores

SOFTENS Technique Acronym for **S**miling, **O**pen posture, **F**orward lean, **T**ouching by shaking hands, **E**ye contact, **N**odding, and **S**pace; technique for open, relational communication

Teleconference A visual phone call, in which cameras and microphones in one meeting room transmit visual and auditory signals (via satellite or telephone line) to another, similarly equipped room anywhere else in the world

Videotex A central computer available to the general public for services ranging from sales messages to shopping tips

Voice Mail Complex telephone answering machine capable of giving prerecorded messages and receiving incoming messages

Wide-Area Telecommunication Service (WATS) Line Telephone service by which long-distance incoming and outgoing calls can be made at no charge or at a reduced rate

Review Questions

1. How does telephone selling differ from face-to-face selling?
2. What are the advantages of telephone rather than face-to-face interactions?
3. Telecommunications equipment allows data and information to be transmitted over telephone lines or through satellite communication systems. List five types of telecommunications technology beneficial for domestic operations; list two types suitable for international sales.
4. Give two benefits of using a toll-free 800 number.
5. What is a telemarketing center?
6. When would be the best time to call a person's home? A lawyer's office? A college professor?
7. Why is the cost per sales call rising?
8. How does computer-to-computer ordering work? What are its benefits?
9. Show two applications of the laptop computer in selling.
10. When does the issue of ethics come into play when using electronic networks?

Discussion Questions

1. The high costs of personal selling have forced industrial salespeople to seek ways of controlling those costs without impairing sales productivity. Explain how telemarketing may be used to accomplish these ends.
2. You have contacted a prospect by telephone who remarks, "You inconsiderate jerk, don't call here trying to push a product on me. I don't believe one word you have said." As a professional salesperson, how would you respond to such comments?
3. How would the use of telemarketing differ in its application to sales support versus account management? Also compare its application to order processing versus customer service.
4. The area of customer service is becoming more important in selling. Discuss.
5. What kind of products lend themselves best to communication via incoming WATS lines? Via outgoing WATS lines?
6. Under what conditions is telemarketing most likely to be associated with invasion of privacy?
7. Discuss the coordination required among departments in the successful operation of a company's telemarketing center.
8. Discuss at least two ways in which the computer has had an impact on professional selling.
9. Will modern telecommunication systems replace salespeople? Discuss.
10. What are the trends in sales organizations today that make knowledge of computers and communications technology more important?

Handling Increased Demands without Compromising Service

Case 17.1

Mike Friske, sales manager of West Imports Bicycle Distributor, is a successful operator in the midst of the booming bicycle industry. This exclusive U.S. distributor supplies Japanese bicycle parts throughout the western United States.

West Imports has become the largest distributor in the United States representing ten leading Japanese manufacturers of bicycle parts. West Imports' success is attributed to the excellent customer service extended by its sales representatives.

The two segments of the market served by West Imports are competitive racers and touring or recreational enthusiasts. The company's salespeople have become specialists, acquiring the necessary training and preparation to serve the company's nearly 165 wholesalers. The sales staff regularly visits dealers to acquire orders, support sales, and provide product information.

Because of increased expectations and trends in the marketplace, new products are constantly being introduced by West Imports that require extensive technical knowledge and dealer support. Additional efforts to increase exposure of its new product entries include conducting seminars and participating in trade shows. At the same time, West Imports has to deal with severe competitive interaction. This condition forces the company to develop competitive pricing strategies without compromising personalized customer service.

Although West Imports Bicycle Distributor is doing an outstanding sales job, Mr. Friske is concerned that pressures are mounting as demand levels of orders escalate. He is also aware of the importance of maintaining good customer relations and service provisions.

1. Based on the current situation of West Imports, what new selling methods would you recommend to Mr. Friske?
2. How might telemarketing be used to deal with increasing demands?
3. Offer suggestions regarding the company's customer service requirements.

Case 17.2

Selling by Phone

Ken Gordon works for Inland Security Systems, selling over the telephone to homeowners. Ken has a good telephone voice, and he is polite and enthusiastic. Here is his sales pitch:

> Good morning, Mr./Ms. ____________________. This is Ken Gordon with Inland Security Systems, Inc. We thought you would like to know that our service technicians will be in your neighborhood this week, and we would like to come by and present a proposal on the installation of a security system. For the next 2 weeks we are offering reduced rates to new sign-ups in this community. When would be a good time?

Often when Ken gets to this point in asking for the appointment, the prospect says, "I am not interested," "I already have a security system," or "give me your phone number and I'll call if I become interested" or simply hangs up.

If the prospect does not hang up, Ken might interject: "Are you aware of the increase in crime in ________ County?" After briefly citing the statistics, he then suggests, "For peace of mind, isn't it worth taking precautions?"

At this time, Ken again requests an opportunity to make a presentation and hopes that the prospect agrees to an appointment.

1. How can Ken improve his presentation to gain the prospect's interest?
2. Is he giving the prospect enough information from which to make a decision about potential installation and security measures?
3. If you were Ken, how would you appeal to the prospect to commit to a time for a presentation?

Notes

1. Dennis L. Morgan, "Why Most Telemarketing Scripts Don't Work . . . and What to Do about It," *TeleProfessional*, July 1991, p. 39.
2. B. Kelley, "Is There *Anything* That Can't Be Sold by Phone?," *Sales & Marketing Management*, April 1989, pp. 60–63.
3. Ibid.
4. "Reps' Fears of Telemarketing Present Management Hurdle," *Marketing News*, April 25, 1986, p. 8.
5. "Dow Corning Blends Inquiry Handling with Telemarketing," *Business Marketing*, October 1983, p. 116.
6. "Cost per Call," *Sales & Marketing Management: Sales Manager's Budget Planner*, June 17, 1991, p. 72.
7. S. Franzmeier, "Dailing for Dollars," *Airport Business Journal*, February 1989, p. 8.
8. Kelley, "Is There *Anything* . . . ," pp. 60–63.
9. Ibid.
10. Ibid.
11. Franzmeier, "Dialing for Dollars."
12. Ibid.
13. Franzmeier, "Dialing for Dollars."
14. Kelley, "Is There *Anything* . . . ," p. 62.
15. G. L. Manning and B. L. Reece, *Selling Today—A Personal Approach*, 3rd ed. (Needham Heights, MA: William C. Brown, 1987), p. 476.
16. Roy Voorhees and John Coppett, "Telemarketing in Distribution Channels," *Industrial Marketing Management*, 12(1983), p. 105.
17. Ross Scovotti and Carol Scovotti, "Marketing Technology . . . Practicing What They Preach," *TeleProfessional*, June 1991, p. 28.
18. Ibid., p. 30.
19. Ibid.
20. Ross M. Scovotti, "Customer Service . . . A Tool for Growing Increased Profits," *TeleProfessional*, September 1991, p. 22.
21. Ibid., pp. 22–24.
22. Ibid., p. 27.
23. N. B. Sigband and A. H. Bell, *Communication for Management and Business*, 4th ed. (Chicago, IL: Scott, Foresman, and Co., 1986), p. 110.
24. Peter G. W. Keen, *Competing in Time—Using Telecommunications for Competitive Advantage* (New York: Ballinger Publishing Co., 1988), p. 3.
25. Beverly Reach, "Just for the Record," *Sales & Marketing Management*, October 7, 1985, p. 103.
26. Les Veal, "The Future of Voice Technology . . . Expanding Opportunities," *TeleProfessional*, July 1991, p. 24.
27. Thayer C. Taylor, "Computers," *Sales & Marketing Management*, June 1991, p. 121.
28. Ibid.
29. Malcolm K. Fleschner II, "How to Automate Your Sales Force," *Personal Selling Power*, September 1991, p. 42.
30. Taylor, "Computers," p. 123.
31. Ibid., p. 68.
32. Thayer C. Taylor, "The Wrangler Lap-Top Experiment," *Sales & Marketing Management*, May 13, 1985, pp. 54–56.
33. Norman Weiner, "Software Unlocks the PC's Power," *Sales & Marketing Management*, March 12, 1984, p. 55.
34. Terry Kennedy, "Boost Productivity with Computer Enhanced Selling," *Marketing News*, November 9, 1984, pp. 20–21.

CHAPTER 18

Managing Self, Time, and Territory

Knowledge Objectives

In this chapter, you will learn:

1. How selling efficiency can be increased through self-management
2. The principles of self-management
3. Patterns that lead to self-sabotage
4. To avoid sales career pitfalls
5. The value of time and how to manage selling activities as a means of controlling time use
6. The steps in developing a routing and scheduling plan
7. The importance of doing paperwork as a tool for improving selling efficiency

Consider This

It has been my personal experience that the time I spent deciding exactly what I wanted to accomplish and what I was going to say from the beginning of the sales interview was a key to my success. One manages time and gets more customer contact time through advanced preparation. Too many salespeople don't think about what they are going to do until they shake hands with the prospect. This is not managing their time.

H. Reed Muller, Professor
The Franklin P. Perdue School of Business,
Salisbury State University,
Salisbury, Maryland

Selling efficiency can be described in many ways. One company may think of selling efficiency in terms of net profit per sales call. Another firm may use the annual cost-per-sales-call statistics published by McGraw-Hill Research Department. Whichever method is used, the bottom line translates to the number of dollars of profitable sales obtained from a specified level of time and money spent on the sales effort.

There are two fundamental ways to increase selling efficiency: (1) increase the dollars of profitable sales from a certain level of selling effort, and (2) reduce the amount of time and money spent to obtain each dollar of profitable sales. To achieve the first goal, a salesperson must increase the effectiveness of those critical moments spent actually selling. To accomplish the second goal, a salesperson must minimize selling costs.

Personal selling activities can be managed like any other business activity. To address the topic of selling efficiency, this chapter is divided into three sections: self-management, time management, and territory management. The first section focuses on self-management from the perspectives of handling stress and self-sabotaging success. The second section explores the value of time and some of the time management techniques used to plan selling activities. The final section offers directions to the salesperson in managing the territory. These activities include routing, scheduling, and handling paperwork.

On the Ethical Side — Priority Based on Profit Potential and Power

Imagine that a salesperson for a major supplier is evaluating the potential of a customer or territory. A particular company is evaluated as being "small" based on size and resource strength. Would these factors have any bearing on the salesperson's selection criteria? Was the small company fairly evaluated?

Many small companies are viewed as limited and inadequate, sometimes restricting the availability of reasonable terms and commitments from larger entities. A small company's growth potential and overall managerial strength are often not considered. In some situations, large borrowers can even obtain more desirable credit terms because of their security base and strength in the industry. This reduced cost of capital gives the larger company leverage to outcompete the smaller company. It is also a known fact in business that the big company, the one with greater proven financial ability, gets paid before the small one, despite the fact that the small company is usually more in need of the funds.

Priority is usually given to the company that is needed the most by the supplier. All links in the business system have a common goal: to generate the highest sales revenue. Is giving priority to the big company unethical if maximizing profit potential and minimizing risks and costs are normally prime objectives in sales?

Sales Professional Spotlight

Lawrence Ellman has worked for 4 years with Burke Commercial Real Estate as an industrial property specialist in California's north Orange County area. Shortly after obtaining a B.S. degree in business administration in real estate from the University of Southern California, Lawrence secured a 9-month apprenticeship with this regional brokerage firm. Larry had a long-term interest in real estate development and decided to begin his career in the brokerage sector to gain an understanding of the real estate arena and its users, as well as to gain the financial rewards of professional selling. He had a strong feeling that this sales experience and education in the "people" side of the business would help to build a solid foundation for his future.

In 1990 Larry earned the "top producer" award for highest sales at Burke's regional office. Larry attributes his success to his educational background and training program as well as his strong self-motivation and time management skills.

"I believe that two of the most important elements needed to succeed in the brokerage business are a strong awareness of the value of time and the ability to maximize its usage. One can be technically advanced in every aspect of real estate and be highly skilled in selling but fail miserably from an inability to manage time efficiently," he says. He further reveals that the commercial real estate business involves hundreds of actions and steps that must be performed, from securing the listing to closing the transaction. Other activities, such as administrative duties, should be delegated to support staff.

Delegation has played a major role in Larry's sales career. During an active market 2 years ago, he found himself overworked and without enough time to service his existing business. He spent a lot of time performing basic support tasks. He immediately hired an assistant to perform those administrative tasks and prospecting duties. This resulted in a more relaxed state of mind, enhanced concentration, and more effective preparation. The decision to delegate was critical to his selling career.

"Once it is realized that our time is effectively spent dealing with prospects and clients, it is even more important that we do a good job at qualifying the prospects. On the average, I pursue one out of every five leads I acquire. I must do a good job at screening. I rate prospects in terms of their need in relation to my product, geographic specialty, and size standards, their urgency, motivation, expectations, resources, authority to make decisions, and perceived loyalty. I only pursue those that I believe will provide a solid opportunity to use my time profitably." Larry has saved a tremendous amount of time by turning down less qualified prospects.

Larry further emphasizes that you must become subconsciously aware of the value of time before you can manage it successfully. "In the commercial brokerage business, where our product is literally our market knowledge and our service, we essentially act in a consultative capacity. It is extremely important to understand, however, that we make our living as commission salespeople. Salespeople must realize that their income is directly related to certain productive actions, such as cold calling, setting appointments, making presentations, and performing demonstrations. Furthermore, the sheer number of possible actions in a given period is limited only by time. The more efficiently we use our time to produce these actions, the greater our income will be. Only after accepting this concept will one be able to implement time management skills with self-discipline."

Of primary importance to implementing successful time management skills is the ability to plan and set objectives, both short and long term, and to prioritize these objectives. To succeed in Larry's area of sales, one must establish goals and then follow them up with an action plan within a designated time frame to produce the desired results. Indeed, time management skills such as these are critical in every sales position, regardless of the specific field.

Self-Management

Whether a salesperson is trying to increase the effectiveness of selling time or reduce the cost of selling, self-management is the key to selling efficiency. *Self-management* is the control and effort that salespeople exert in handling their activities so that they match personal objectives to company goals. Thus, self-management is valuable to salespeople for several reasons:

1. Field salespeople have much individual freedom and little direct supervision.
2. The growth and success of sales professionals is due largely to their individual efforts.
3. Effective self-management provides them with the tools to develop those all-encompassing success traits of self-discipline and self-motivation.

Self-management also is important to the company for several reasons:

1. The company's overall sales performance is upgraded as it hires or develops more competent and efficient sales professionals.
2. Opportunities for incentives other than the traditional financial rewards are greatly enhanced.
3. The continually spiraling costs of supporting a salesperson in the field (travel expenses, lodging, food, and entertainment) can be partially offset by the competence and efficiency of the sales force.[1]

In sum, salespeople must value being their own bosses most of the time. Moreover, they must commit themselves to self-discipline and self-motivation in making their goals compatible with their firm's goals. These efforts often involve pressure to perform and other stress-related situations. Thus, it is important to examine stress and ways of managing it.

Managing Stress

Jackie Joyner Kersee's
CHAMPIONSHIP MANAGEMENT STRATEGIES
MANAGE YOUR TIME: use the time you have away from your areas of professional pursuit to develop yourself as a person, to enlarge your interests, to think creatively, to plan for reaching your goals.
1
MANAGE YOUR BODY: eat healthy foods, get enough rest, take time for yourself, exercise regularly. By maintaining a healthy physical standard you build in a high resistance to stress, a can-do feeling that carries you through the tough times.
2
MANAGE YOUR THOUGHT PATTERNS: feed your mind with useful information. Use thoughts as active facilitators to engage your body in activities that will further or enhance your goals. Use your thoughts for positive reinforcement and powerful expectations.
3
MANAGE YOUR COMMITMENTS: realize that you can't be all things to all people all the time. Mark out blocks of time for your own commitments to yourself. Follow a predictable pattern of activities outside of your stated goals.
4

Stress is inevitable and universal. We cannot be alive and not experience it. Hans Selye, M.D., professor and director of the Institute of Experimental Medicine and Surgery at the University of Montreal, is best known for his work on the body's physiological response to stress. He defines stress as "the nonspecific response of the body to any demand made upon it."[2] To understand the definition, we must understand what is meant by *nonspecific*. According to Selye:

> Each demand made upon our body is in a sense unique, that is, *specific*. . . . [I]n addition to their specific actions, all agents to which we are exposed also produce a nonspecific increase in the need to perform adaptive functions and thereby to re-establish normalcy. This is independent of the activity that caused a rise in the requirements. The nonspecific demand for activity as such is the essence of stress.[3]

For example, when we are exposed to heat, we sweat because the evaporation of perspiration from the surface of the skin has a cooling effect. When we eat too much sugar and the blood sugar level rises above normal, we excrete some of it and burn up the rest so that the blood sugar returns to normal.[4]

While there are numerous definitions of stress, most authorities define *stressors* as the source of all stress. A stressor is "anything that causes your body to react physiologically of psychologically."[5] By itself, a stressor is neither positive nor negative. How an individual reacts to stressors determines whether stress becomes negative or positive.[6]

In sales, negative stress arises from social, psychological, or physical situations that salespeople believe are beyond their control. This kind of stress produces undesired and often unintended results. In short, salespeople may lose the ability to cope. Tensions often build in pressures that may overwhelm a person. Continued negative stress may eventually diminish the salesperson's resistance to other stressors, causing a "snowball effect."

Self-discipline is necessary in dealing with the stress that results from daily sales activities, such as being late for an appointment, prospecting, having a conflict with a customer, or meeting a sales quota. Because a salesperson's work requires dealing with a variety of people with different needs and expectations, stress is extremely likely to occur in a sales job.

The following behavior patterns in several areas may indicate that a salesperson is suffering from negative stress:

- Renewal—requiring longer periods of time to renew or recharge oneself
- Concentration—losing concentration or being easily distracted
- Memory—forgetting the key information that was easily remembered in the past
- Sleep—sleeping too much or too little
- Appetite—overeating or losing appetite
- Patience—becoming impatient, often to the point of outright anger
- Motivation—lacking drive, energy, or desire to perform the job
- Mood—feeling depressed, sad, hopeless, or hyperactive
- Relating—being unable to relate to others, as indicated by withdrawal, hostility, or rudeness[7]

Because salespeople are constantly exposed to stressful situations, they must be concerned about the effects of stress on their productivity. Thus, paying attention to a potential source of stress and handling it properly is one way to turn stress into an advantage. Positive stress can result from the same situations that might have caused negative stress. For example, a sales manager screaming at the sales representative for not making a quota does not have to upset the salesperson; the situation can be processed as a challenge and even seen as a motivation for achieving greater success.[8]

A leading psychiatrist at the Presbyterian Medical Center in Philadelphia, Pennsylvania, David O. Burns, M.D., describes additional symptoms of anxiety as shown in the inventory in Table 18.1. Dr. Burns suggests that anxiety can often be treated effectively without drugs. In his experience, people who follow his treatment are often free of symptoms within a short period of time.[9]

A variety of personal solutions can help to reduce stress. Regular exercise and fitness are certainly healthy ways for a salesperson to cope with stress. It is also helpful if the salesperson goes to work relaxed and well rested. Fatigue will reduce one's level of tolerance. Other positive tools that salespeople may use include:

- Building relaxation time into the day
- Seeking spiritual nourishment
- Meditating
- Delegating work
- Maintaining a sense of humor
- Establishing a routine
- Practicing imaging
- Releasing anger appropriately
- Choosing options that are realistic
- Seeking opportunity from crisis
- Leaving time for the unexpected[10]

Table 18.1

The Dr. Burns Anxiety Inventory

The following is a list of symptoms people may experience during the course of a week.

Anxious Feelings

- Anxiety, nervousness, worry, or fear
- Feeling that things around you are strange, unreal, or foggy
- Feeling detached from all or part of your body
- Sudden unexpected panic spells
- Apprehension of a sense of impending doom
- Feeling tense, stressed, "uptight," or on edge

Anxious Thoughts

- Difficulty concentrating
- Racing thoughts or having your mind jump from one thing to the next
- Frightening fantasies or daydreams
- Feeling that you're on the verge of losing control
- Fears of cracking up or going crazy
- Fears of fainting or passing out
- Fears of physical illness or heart attacks or dying
- Concerns about looking foolish or inadequate in front of others
- Fears of being alone, isolated, or abandoned
- Fears of criticism or disapproval
- Fears that something terrible is about to happen

Physical Symptoms

- Skipping, racing, or pounding of the heart
- Pain, pressure, or tightness in the chest
- Tingling or numbness in the toes or fingers
- Butterflies in the stomach
- Constipation or diarrhea
- Restlessness or jumpiness
- Tight, tense muscles
- Sweating not brought on by heat
- A lump in the throat
- Trembling or shaking
- Rubbery or "jelly" legs
- Feeling dizzy, lightheaded, or off balance
- Choking or smothering sensations or difficulty breathing
- Headaches or pains in the neck or back
- Hot flushes or cold chills
- Feeling tired, weak, or easily exhausted

Source: David D. Burns, M.D., *The Feeling Good Handbook: Using the New Mood Therapy in Everyday Life* (William Morrow & Company, Inc., 1989).

Fundamentally, successful self-management means turning stress into positive energy. Peter G. Hanson, M.D., author of *Stress for Success*, believes that stress can be full of joy. The following passage is his prescription for helping an individual to experience positive stress:

> Recognize your most important job of all, and run your Department of One as if your life depended on it because, in truth, it does. Treat those who work for you with patience and guidance. Treat those who work with you with honesty and commitment. Treat those who love you with more time. And even more importantly, treat yourself with respect, humor, good food, mental and physical exercise, relaxation, adventure, daydreams and memories. Never retire from at least some kind of work, and never try to hide from a challenge.[11]

Art Mortell, a former IBM sales representative, is now on the lecture circuit and suggests that salespeople follow these techniques for managing stress:

- *Competition*—Possible goals might be prospecting for new accounts, increasing present account size, or introducing a new product to an established account. A salesperson might select another individual within the company who is selling more or doing better, and challenge this person to a 1-month sales contest with the loser buying dinner. Most important, the competition should be friendly and not too intense.
- *Be a Leader*—A salesperson can help others accomplish what needs to be achieved. After deciding where in the job there is inconsistency, the salesperson might invite another person to join in on the calls, whether listening while the salesperson is on the telephone or traveling along in the field. This can help a person stay productive as well as sharpen skills.
- *The Buddy System*—A salesperson might select someone to meet with once a week for breakfast or lunch, or while working out, to share feelings and exchange ideas. Sharing successes, expressing disappointments, and exploring solutions can help keep an individual on track.[12]

Mortell is a firm believer in self-management and self-discipline:

> Throughout the selling process, salespeople have a constant need to manage themselves. One of the sources of stress among sales professionals is that a large percentage of people are unable to function effectively in an unstructured environment. Therefore, to succeed in selling often requires the ability to create structure, just to keep ourselves on target.[13]

Self-Sabotage

For many individuals, a subconscious fear of success can undermine their dreams of personal achievement. Consider these two scenarios:

Linda S., a real estate agent who specializes in residential property, has earned around $50,000 a year for the past 7 years. Even during an economic recession, Linda managed to maintain her average annual earnings.

Two years ago the economy started to recover and, although real estate sales soared, Linda ended up those years with an average of $51,000 each year. She would like to do better but finds herself psychologically trapped by the $50,000 ceiling she seems to have built over her head.

Each new fiscal year she will start with intense enthusiasm, hard work, and commitment—often earning 80 percent of her income within the first 6 months. Then she starts hanging around her home or her office more, slowing down her attempt to obtain new listings, or taking mini-vacations to reward herself for all the hard work she had done over those first 6 months. By the end of the year she has sold only 20 percent of what she did during the first half. She has no new listings and no new prospects.

Bill T. is a sales manager for a *Fortune* 500 company. He recently convinced his boss of a brilliant plan that had the potential for reversing the company's rapidly declining financial position. His boss was so impressed with the idea that he gave Bill his full support and named him head of the team to design and implement the new program.

Bill started out with great enthusiasm and eagerness, but by the end of the month, he lost his interest and momentum in the program. His boss tried everything from pep talks to threats but to no avail. Finally, he got together with the vice president of marketing to study Bill's track record. What they found after reviewing his performance appraisals during the past 3 years was that "most of his initially successful spurts with new projects had eventually ground to a halt and were followed by long periods of indecisiveness and procrastination."

The following Monday, Bill was called into his boss's office and, after a brief confrontation, was terminated. Amazingly enough, Bill appeared not only relieved, but almost joyful.

What Linda and Bill have in common is a basic ambivalence about succeeding. This is not uncommon among salespeople. Clinical psychologist Eugene Raudsepp, president of Princeton Creative Research, Inc., in New Jersey, designed a self-test to help determine to what extent a person may be afraid of success (see Exhibit 18.1). Here is Raudsepp's interpretation of the score:

> A score of 30 to 54 indicates that you have no problem with "fear of success." You are strongly achievement-oriented, and you like to come up a winner. You are able to make commitments and persevere with your projects until a successful outcome is assured. You take pride in your skills and talents, and you have full confidence in yourself. Although independent-minded and assertive, your relationships with others are trustful and open.
>
> If you scored 6 to 29, you have a tendency to occasionally set unrealistically high standards, and you're not always satisfied with your achievements. You prefer win/win rather than win/lose situations. You're concerned about what other people think of you, and you want to be universally liked. Because of fluctuating self-esteem, you periodically lapse into self-critical ruminations about your ability to succeed. You have some trouble making decisions and then sticking with them. The limelight is certainly not for you, and you regard those who want to be the life of the party with scorn. Because you have a moderate fear of success, you're not living up to your success potential.

Exhibit 18.1

Are You Afraid of Success?

Instructions: Answer each question with A (agree), B (agree somewhat, or don't know), or C (disagree). The scoring key is at the bottom of this exhibit; the interpretation of scores is in the text.

1. When things seem to be going really well for me, I get uneasy because I know it won't last.
2. Most of the time I find that I measure up to the standards I've set for myself.
3. I find it difficult to tell my friends that I excel at something.
4. I feel uncomfortable when I have to break a date or an appointment.
5. I like it when someone makes a fuss over me.
6. It is important for me to be liked by people with positions of higher status and power than mine.
7. When I win a competitive game, I feel a bit sorry for the other player.
8. When I have to ask others for help, I feel that I'm imposing on them.
9. Although I may sometimes experience difficulty doing so, I generally finish essential tasks.
10. When I think I've been too forceful in making a point to someone, I worry about having made that person feel unfriendly toward me.
11. When people compliment me on my work, I feel that they are being insincere.
12. When I complete an important piece of work, I am usually satisfied with the result.
13. When engaged in competitive games, I make more mistakes near the end than at the beginning.
14. When my boss praises my work, I wonder whether I can live up to his expectations in the future.
15. At times, I believe that I have gotten this far in my career because of good luck and not because I deserve it.
16. It is just as important to win a game as to merely enjoy it.
17. I feel self-conscious when people are watching me play a game.
18. I often daydream about doing something that no one else has ever done before.
19. I like being the center of attention at a social gathering.
20. Most people are secretly pleased when I get into trouble.

A score of −25 to 5 indicates that you want to win but frequently end up losing in the end. You tend to be passive and withdrawn and prefer to take a back seat in competitive situations. Because of your excessive need to be liked, you refrain from arguments and contests of will. You lack self-confidence and seldom give yourself the credit you deserve for your accomplishments. You tend to be somewhat distrustful of other people's motives and feel that they cannot always be relied on. Fear of success definitely hampers your accomplishments.

Exhibit 18.1
Continued

21. I'm pretty skillful at most things I try.
22. When I make a decision, I usually stick with it.
23. I often get excited when I start working on a new project, but it gets stale rather quickly.
24. I often feel let down after completing an important project.
25. At times, my accomplishments amaze me because I feel that I rarely put in the effort that I could.
26. When I hear about the accomplishments of my friends or acquaintances, I tend to think how little I have accomplished.
27. Once I have completed a project, it no longer interests me.
28. When I reach the winning point in a game, I often get distracted or think of other things.
29. I'm not influenced one way or another by persuasive people.
30. When a project seems to be going well, I often get scared that I'll do something to botch it.

To compute your score on the test, assign the following values to each of the 30 statements, and then figure the total.

	A	B	C		A	B	C
1.	A = −1,	B = 0,	C = 2	16.	A = 2,	B = 1,	C = −1
2.	A = 2,	B = 0,	C = −1	17.	A = −1,	B = 0,	C = 1
3.	A = −1,	B = 0,	C = 1	18.	A = 3,	B = 0,	C = −2
4.	A = −1,	B = 0,	C = 1	19.	A = 2,	B = 1,	C = −1
5.	A = 2,	B = 1,	C = 0	20.	A = −1,	B = 0,	C = 1
6.	A = −1,	B = 0,	C = 1	21.	A = 2,	B = 1,	C = −1
7.	A = 1,	B = 0,	C = −1	22.	A = 3,	B = 0,	C = −2
8.	A = −2,	B = 1,	C = 2	23.	A = −2,	B = 1,	C = 2
9.	A = 3,	B = 0,	C = −2	24.	A = −1,	B = 0,	C = 1
10.	A = −2,	B = 1,	C = 2	25.	A = −1,	B = 0,	C = 1
11.	A = −1,	B = 0,	C = 1	26.	A = −2,	B = 0,	C = 2
12.	A = 2,	B = 0,	C = −1	27.	A = −1,	B = 0,	C = 1
13.	A = −2,	B = 0,	C = 2	28.	A = −1,	B = 0,	C = 2
14.	A = −2,	B = 0,	C = 2	29.	A = 3,	B = 1,	C = −2
15.	A = −2,	B = 1,	C = 2	30.	A = −1,	B = 0,	C = 2

Source: Eugene Raudsepp, "Self-Sabotage," *Success*, March 1984, pp. 18–20.

A score of −40 to −26 means that fear of success is a definite problem for you. You're very nonassertive and self-effacing and consider modesty a virtue. You're never satisfied with your achievements and frequently manage to snatch defeat from victory. Doubtful about whether you have any luck at all, you tend to worry about the future most of the time. Because you're too concerned about others' opinions of you, you frequently act like a doormat, although you don't enjoy it. You don't like to give or receive compliments.[14]

Raudsepp suggests that three characteristics stand out about people who fear success:

1. These individuals have a high ambivalence and vacillation about success. They are driven both to succeed and not to succeed.
2. There is a fear of success in their adult lives because of suppressed childhood experiences. Many of the old scripts are still being played over and over in their subconscious minds.
3. People who fear success use numerous defense mechanisms and rationalizations as protection from the intense anxiety created both by their initial self-enhancing drives and by later self-defeating manuevers.[15]

Salespeople who fear success may actually deny any internal desire to succeed. When they are successful in spite of themselves, they tend to "attribute it to luck, or others' help or even stupidity, rather than to their own ability and effort."[16] Thus, Raudsepp concludes that by discrediting their own competence, individuals also rob themselves of any real enjoyment of the successes that do occur. They almost never realize a solid feeling of self-fulfillment.

The good news for salespeople who experience fear of success is that they can change through positive self-management. Similar to the skill of positive self-talk, which was discussed in Chapter 4, is another communication skill called *affirmation*. An affirmation is a statement of fact or belief that is written out in a personal, positive, present-tense form, as though the goal were already accomplished. Skill Builder 18.1 offers guidelines for writing affirmations.

Managing Time

The second component of achieving selling efficiency is a cost-oriented focus based on making the best possible use of time and effort. Alan Lakein, a time planning and life goals consultant to major companies around the world, considers himself an "effectiveness expert," not an efficiency expert. Regarding time mangement, he makes this distinction:

> Effectiveness means selecting the best tasks to do from all the possibilities available and then doing it the best way. Making the right choices about how you'll use your time is more important than doing efficiently whatever job happens to be around. Efficiency is fine in its place, but to my mind effectiveness is a much more important goal.[17]

This section will examine how salespeople can manage their time effectively by: (1) looking at how they spend their time, (2) analyzing their sales call activities and setting priorities, (3) planning for sales calls, and (4) using sales quotas as performance measures.

Skill Builder 18.1 Making Affirmations

An affirmation is a statement of belief that is written out in a positive, personal, present-tense form, as though the goal being set has already been accomplished.

Guidelines for Writing Affirmations

Personal	Use an "I" statement. You can only affirm for yourself.
Positive	Write out your affirmation in a positive sentence structure: "I am eager and highly energetic."
Present tense	Write in the present tense—this is the only time frame that the subconscious mind operates in.
Indicate achievement	Write statements like "I have" and "I am." By viewing your goal as completed, you reduce some of the stress associated with trying to achieve your goal.
Use action words	Describe the activity you are affirming in terms that create pictures of you performing in an easy and anxiety-free manner: "I easily," "I thrive on," "I enjoy," "I eagerly," "I quickly."
Accuracy	Affirm yourself only as "high" as you can truly (honestly) imagine yourself becoming or performing.
Examples	"I enjoy taking calculated risks to ask for the order."
	"I have an excellent memory with clear and easy recall."
	"The pressure of making quota is exciting and stimulating to me, and I do an even better job when I am under pressure."
	"I have a positive expectation of performing well on cold calls and can cope with any challenge that arises."

Instructions

Write two affirmations pertaining to three goals that you have set for yourself, either as a salesperson or as a student:

Goal 1: __________
Affirmation A: __________
Affirmation B: __________

Goal 2: __________
Affirmation A: __________
Affirmation B: __________

Goal 3: __________
Affirmation A: __________
Affirmation B: __________

How Salespeople Spend Their Time

In the *26th Survey of Sales Force Compensation, 1990*, Dartnell Corporation reported that sales representatives spent 30 percent of their time in face-to-face selling, 23 percent in waiting and traveling, 20 percent in telephone selling, 14 percent in administrative tasks, and 13 percent in service calls (see Figure 18.1). Compare those numbers with the percentages shown in Figure 18.2 from the previous year, and a shift can be seen in the way salespeople are spending their time. Note that while the percentage given for face-to-face contact is decreasing, the time spent traveling and waiting is on the rise. As traffic continues to become more congested in high-density sales territories, technology is allowing the salesperson to use waiting and traveling time by making available such tools as electronic notebooks, laptop computers, and cellular phones. The increased time spent in waiting and traveling, together with the increased

On the International Front Setting Appointments

Although time and schedules are important in the United States, making appointments to the minute is unheard of in many countries. Often, even setting appointments to the hour is not proper. Differences in cultural settings with reference to attitudes about punctuality are important to international salespeople.

In general, a lack of punctuality is typical in Asia and Africa, and it is not uncommon to be half an hour or an hour late for an appointment. Chinese businesspeople observe strict punctuality for appointments, however, and it is essential to arrive early in Hong Kong. In Africa, lateness in beginning meetings is a part of life, although when dealing with foreigners, Africans try to be on time.

Europeans and Japanese generally observe strict punctuality for appointments. The Japanese consider it rude to be late for a business meeting, but it is acceptable to be late for a social occasion. Latin American countries, on the other hand, have a more relaxed attitude toward time and are often late, although they expect Americans to be on time.

In the Middle East, long waits for appointments are typical, and usually no excuse is offered. One incident involved an American banker who waited 2 days for an Arab sheik in London, only to be told to fly to Riyadh, Saudi Arabia, to meet him. After 3 days of anxious waiting there, discussions finally began, resulting in a positive relationship. Sometimes, lack of punctuality may imply importance and status. Saudi Arabia is interesting because appointments are made for the intervals between the five daily prayer times.

The flexibility of time planning in most countries suggests a need for the salesperson to be patient and understanding. Many cultures do not see the need for a sales situation to be urgent; people come first, not time.

Sources: M. Katherine Glover, "Do's & Taboos: Cultural Aspects of International Business," *Business America*, August 13, 1990, pp. 3–4; Sak Onkvisit and John J. Shaw, *International Marketing* (Columbus, OH: Merrill Publishing Company, 1989), p. 232; and Robert Moran, "How to Understand Your Partner's Cultural Baggage," *International Management*, September 1983, pp. 50–51.

Figure 18.1

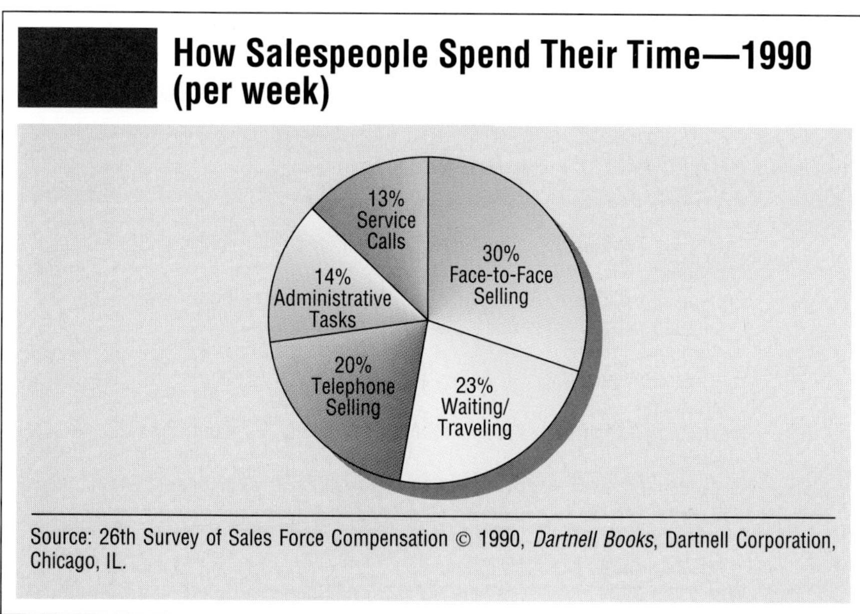

cost of personal sales calls, may well influence the increase in the percentage of time spent on telephone selling.

It is important to note that the use of sales time varies by company and industry. Table 18.2 indicates the average length of a salesperson's day in various industries and the amount of time spent in each in face-to-face selling.

Although spending a third of each day in face-to-face selling may not sound impressive, the impact on sales efficiency and effectiveness can be

Figure 18.2

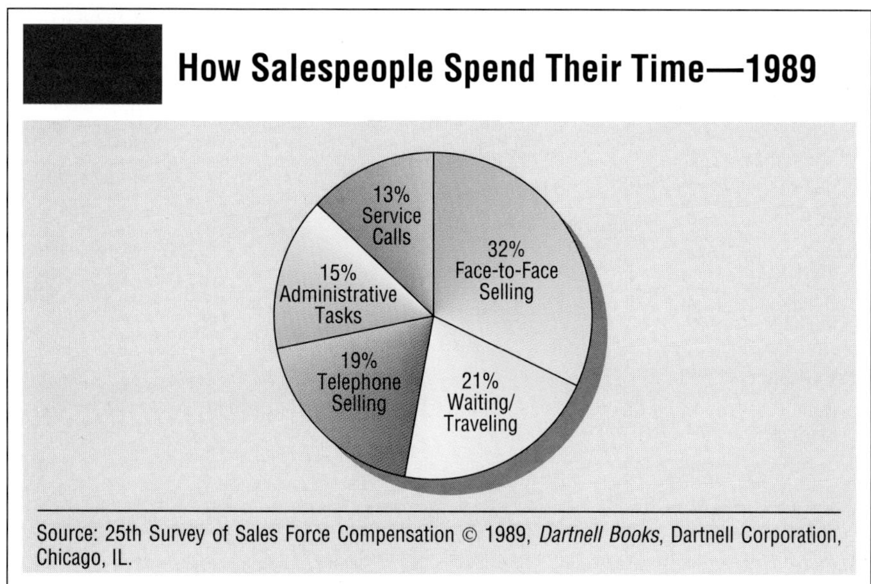

Table 18.2

Length of a Salesperson's Day in Total and Amount of Time Spent in Face-to-Face Selling

SIC Number*	Industry	Average Length of Day	Time Spent in Face-to-Face Selling
28	Chemicals and allied products	9 hours and 4 minutes	3 hours and 6 minutes
30	Rubber and miscellaneous plastic products	9 hours and 21 minutes	2 hours and 9 minutes
34	Fabricated metal products	8 hours and 43 minutes	2 hours and 13 minutes
35	Machinery, except electrical	8 hours and 53 minutes	2 hours and 23 minutes
36	Electrical and electronic products	8 hours and 36 minutes	1 hour and 31 minutes
38	Instruments and related products	8 hours and 41 minutes	1 hour and 24 minutes
50	Wholesale trade, durable goods	9 hours and 29 minutes	2 hours and 32 minutes
	Average	8 hours and 49 minutes	2 hours and 12 minutes

* Standard Industrial Classification code.
Source: "Involvement of Salespeople in Different Daily Activities Varies by Industry," *Report 7023.3 Laboratory of Advertising Performance* (New York: McGraw-Hill Research, 1987).

Table 18.3

Sales Call Costs by Industry per Year in the Field

Industry	Calls per Territory per Day		Est. Days in Field per Year	Calls per Territory per Year	
	A	*B*		*A*	*B*
Consumer					
Range	3–6	2–4	187	561–1,122	374–748
Median	4.5	3		841.5	561
Industrial					
Range	3–5	2–4	187	561–935	374–748
Median	4	3		748	561
Service					
Range	4–8	2–5	187	748–1,496	374–935
Median	6	3.5		1,122	654.5

Source: Adapted from "1991 Sales Manager's Budget Planner," *Sales & Marketing Management*, June 17, 1991, pp. 6, 72.

significant. Table 18.3 offers a broad picture of the cost to companies by industry for all the face-to-face calls a salesperson makes in a year. The following explanation is presented by the staff of *Sales & Marketing Management*, which publishes the widely used annual "Sales Manager's Budget Planner":

> In this table, *A Territory* is defined as a metro area where customers and prospects are heavily concentrated and a salesperson can easily make multiple calls, or a selling philosophy that emphasizes a high call quota. *B Territory* reflects a territory where customers are widely dispersed, and more time is spent traveling between calls. The *Estimated Days in the Field per Year* is based on 4 days × 52 weeks per year, less 6 holidays and 15 days vacation and/or sick leave, resulting in a figure of 187 days. The *Calls per Territory per Year* reflects *Calls per Territory per Day* ranges and/or medians multiplied by this figure, the median being the midpoint in each set of ranges.[18]

The median cost per call was determined by the magazine staff, using another formula that involved direct sales costs, which are limited to compensation and field expenses for midlevel and top-level salespeople. To emphasize the importance of effective time management, we have extended the table to show approximately how much a company could spend on field sales calls per person in 1 year.

In another study conducted by the McGraw-Hill Research Department, the average industrial salesperson was found to spend only 25 percent of

	Median Cost per Sales Call 1990		Cost of Sales Calls per Territory per Year	
			A	B
×	210.34	=	118,000.74–236,001.84 117,001.11	78,667.16–157,334.32 118,000.74
×	250.54	=	140,552.94–234,254.90 187,403.92	93,701.95–187,403.92 140,552.94
×	222.66	=	166,549.68–333,099.36 249,824.52	83,274.84–208,187.10 145,730.97

time actually selling and 25 percent traveling and waiting for interviews.[19] Estimating that an industrial salesperson works 240 days per year for a total of 2,117 hours, this person has only 529 hours per year to actually sell. If the salesperson's desired annual income is $50,000, selling time is worth $94.52 per hour to that salesperson. Waiting in an office for an hour or driving around needlessly for an hour costs that person $94.52 in lost earnings. Table 18.4 shows that, as the desired income goes up, so does the value of the salesperson's time. A salesperson who aspires to earn $75,000 per year can value an hour at over $140.[20]

Furthermore, the value of selling time and the time allocated to making sales calls may increase if more sales calls are made. "You've got to make extra calls," claims Shelby Carter, Xerox's former vice president of sales for U.S. field operations, "because *one* more call a day is *five* a week, 20 a month, and 240 calls a year. If you close 10 percent of the people you contact, you have an extra 24 sales a year. You have to be tough on yourself to make that extra call."[21]

Spending more time in selling activities by making more sales calls means spending less time performing nonproductive activities. Therefore, it seems appropriate to analyze sales call activities.

Analysis of Sales Call Activities and Setting Priorities

Sales professionals handle the frequent demands on their time by taking a daily inventory of necessary duties followed by specific actions to avoid

Table 18.4

Value of an Hour's Time to a Salesperson

Salesperson's Desired Annual Income	Value of 1 Hour of Salesperson's Time
30,000	$ 56.71
35,000	66.16
40,000	75.61
45,000	85.07
50,000	94.52
55,000	103.97
60,000	113.42
65,000	122.87
70,000	132.33
75,000	141.78
80,000	151.23
85,000	160.68
90,000	170.13
95,000	179.58
100,000	189.04

Source: Robert W. Haas, *Industrial Marketing Management*, 4th ed. (MA: PWS-Kent, 1989), p. 313.

the emotional paralysis that often occurs as a result of too many demands. A simple self-check or inventory may start with three questions:

1. What were some of the unexpected demands that interfered with my daily plan?
2. Were they directly connected with my selling time or were they of a personal nature?
3. What did I fail to do, and what was the reason?

Rigorous answers to these questions may be encouraged by taking two simple steps:

1. Set aside a specific time each day to analyze how that day's time has been spent.
2. Identify what has been accomplished and what was not accomplished by assigning tasks an A-B-C value of importance, with
   A = highest priority
   B = medium priority
   C = lowest priority

Sales professionals often respond to self-analysis with the following actions:

1. List the possible activities for achieving each A-rated goal.
2. Set priorities to select the most effective activity that can be done *now*.
3. Stay loose—be flexible—to accommodate unexpected happenings.[22]

Table 18.5 lists tips that will help salespeople perform a regular analysis of their daily sales activities.

Sales Call Planning

Sales call planning is a process used to set the course of action for the week as well as for each day. Planning is the most important element of managing both time and territory. This section will focus on three areas: (1) making an appointment calendar, (2) classifying accounts, and (3) preparing a sales call plan and result sheet.

Making an Appointment Calendar

The reasons for preparing and keeping an appointment calendar are to save time and avoid scheduling problems. The design of the calendar will vary according to the type of selling position. Whether a salesperson plans a week in advance or on a daily basis, most of the person's working time should be spent in essential sales activities.

Table 18.5

Steps to Better Use of Time

In the Field

- Decide how many hours are to be spent in the field on a daily basis.
- Determine the maximum number of hours per week to spend in front of prospects; then do it every week.
- Realize that good sales interviews can vary in length, usually from approximately 20 minutes to an hour and a half. Allow one and a half hours for each interview.
- Plan minimum travel time based on good geographical planning.
- Establish a time when you will leave your house every morning and a time before which you will not arrive home in the evening.
- Do any personal business before or after working time.
- Always carry additional prospect cards for cold calls on people in the area in case of canceled appointments, shortened interviews, or other time gaps.
- Avoid long coffee breaks.

In the Office

- Give priority to items directly related to selling, such as telephoning for appointments, preparing sales presentations, and personal organization.
- Handle all paper items such as correspondence and filing on a daily basis if possible.
- Place in an "Action" file all matters requiring prompt action.
- Place in a "Later" file all other matters.
- Do required reading at home after hours.
- Avoid idle chats with other salespeople or staff.
- Avoid long coffee breaks.

Source: Frank Brennan, *Personal Selling: A Professional Approach* (Chicago: SRA, 1983), pp. 311–312.

When preparing a daily or weekly appointment calendar, salespeople should follow these guidelines:

- Decide which accounts to call on, remembering to allocate at least 65 percent of face-to-face selling time to A-level accounts.
- Distribute time among present customers, potential customers, and service calls.
- Allocate time appropriately between actual selling and nonselling activities, such as paperwork and meetings.
- Schedule extra time to be spent with overly demanding customers or prospects.
- Plan for traffic snags if working in a heavily populated metropolitan area, such as New York, Chicago, or Los Angeles.
- Allocate phone calls to the time of day when the customer or prospect will be most receptive to receiving calls from salespeople.
- Allow time in each day and week to handle unforeseen or emergency situations.

Try This 18.1 Making an Appointment Calendar

1. Examine the weekly appointment schedule provided in Table 18.6.
2. How would you reschedule this person's week?
3. Using the guidelines presented in this chapter, redesign the calendar to meet the suggested criteria.

For the most part, salespeople will want to schedule their selling activities first. Table 18.6 provides a sample schedule. Time that cannot be spent selling should be devoted to such activities as servicing accounts, filling out reports, and making telephone calls to schedule appointments or report to the home office.

Classifying Accounts

Salespeople often use account profile cards to classify customers. Establishing a "tickler file" as described in Chapter 6 is one way to achieve this. A rule of thumb is that 80 percent of the sales in a given territory come from 20 percent of the customers. Therefore, when gathering information for the account card, it is important to determine and record what the sales volume or sales potential is for each account.

In Chapter 6, customers were classified into A-B-C account priorities. Using this ranking, the salesperson can determine the frequency or priority of sales calls. For example, prospecting should be directed primarily toward A accounts. As time permits, B and C accounts may be developed systematically.

A classification system of this type can help the new salesperson overcome the tendency to concentrate on congenial customers. Many times new salespeople spend most of their time on the customers with whom they feel most comfortable. Buyers for large accounts can seem impersonal and abrupt, while small-volume customers are perceived as willing to converse all day. Efficient time management, however, requires that larger and more profitable accounts receive more of the salesperson's time.

Preparing a Sales Call Plan and Result Sheet

Figure 18.3 provides a sales call plan and result sheet that salespeople can use to establish priorities for prospects and customer calls. After determining sales call frequency and account classification, the salesperson should concentrate planning efforts on key accounts. For each key account, a set of goals and objectives should be established. The salesperson needs to identify the specific activities required to achieve each goal.

Table 18.6

Weekly Calendar

Time	Monday	Tuesday
7:00–8:00	Paperwork, mail, etc.	Gather sales aids for morning's calls
8:00–9:00	Arrange next week's appointments	See Cust. B account
9:00–10:00	See Cust. A account	See Cust. C account
10:00–11:00	See Cust. B account	See Cust. A account
11:00–12:00		See Cust. A account
12:00–1:00	Take Cust. A account to lunch	Lunch alone to follow up on morning calls
1:00–2:00		Back to office to cold call customers via telephone
2:00–3:00	Drive back to office	
3:00–4:00	Office tele. follow up	Meet with sales manager
4:00–5:00	Reports, direct mail	
5:00–6:00	Arrange demo's for Tuesday's appointments	See Cust. B account
6:00–7:00	Home?!	Home after B account paperwork on call
7:00–8:00	Dinner, TV, bed . . .	Set up Wednesday's calls Dinner, etc. . . .

Total weekly calls = 16
A accounts = 10 (62%)
B accounts = 4 (25%)
C accounts = 2 (13%)
16 (100%)

Sales Quotas as Performance Measures

Sales quotas, which are derived from sales forecasts, are used as quantitative measures for evaluating a salesperson's performance. They are normally stated in terms of unit or dollar volume. Sales managers rely heavily on sales quotas to evaluate the performance of individual salespeople. Superachievers frequently use sales quotas as an incentive for improving their performance and productivity. If their company does not assign quotas, they often establish their own quotas for performance measures in their respective territories.

Wednesday	Thursday	Friday
Go through mail, etc., prepare for calls	Office, paperwork	Read paper, mail, etc., at the office
See Cust. A account	Cold calling	Confirm Monday's appointments
	Cold calling	
	Cold calling	Telephone followup on the week's calls
	Cold calling	
See Cust. A account	Cold calling	See Cust. A account
	Cold calling	
Office: paperwork, etc. . . .	Lunch alone after cold calling all morning	See Cust. A account
Lunch with Cust. B account, massage acct	See Cust. A account	Lunch with Key Account
See Cust. C account	See Cust. B account	
Prospecting from office, confirm important appointment on Friday	See Cust. A account	Office; reports, follow up on lunch date, and others
Telephone confirm other appointments, paperwork followup	See Cust. A account	Home early on Friday
misc. . .	Follow up on day's calls back at the office, reports, etc.	Travel
Home?		
Etc. . . .	Home?!	

Territory Management

The third component of selling efficiency is territory management. In viewing salespeople's responsibilities for territory management, it is helpful to think of salespeople as "managers of valuable assets, the most valuable of which is the customer base, which could represent millions of dollars in actual and potential sales."[23] Salespeople are expected to provide a return on the investment their companies have made in them—salaries, bonuses, fringe benefits, and so forth. Effective territory

Figure 18.3

Sales Call Plan and Results

Sales Call Plan and Results

Date of preparation: Year:________ Month:________

Salesperson:________ Territory:________

Planned days:________ Days of month:________

Actual days:________ Days of month:________

Planned Calls	**Calls Completed**
Telephone calls	
Sales calls	
Presentations	
Demonstrations	
Customer service calls	

Coverage of All Accounts

Planned (% or #)	**Completed (% or #)**
A accounts	A accounts
B accounts	B accounts
C accounts	C accounts

Specific Account Information

Company	No. of People Contacted	Location (City/State)	Contact Purpose	Time Spent on Call	Travel Time (Miles)	Call Results

management can help to maximize this return by making efficient use of selling time.

Most salespeople have territories assigned to them. Territories are geographical areas in which salespeople often live and usually spend most of their working time and energy. There are many reasons why companies divide their markets into territories[24]:

- *To improve market coverage*—Territories make it easy to pinpoint customers and prospects and decide who should call on them.
- *To establish responsibility*—Territories allow the company to keep track of who is to call on which customer and who has primary responsibility for representing it in each area.
- *To improve communications*—Messages, complaints, orders, and similar communications can be handled in depth, improving the marketing intelligence available from each territory.

It All Begins with You . . .

Exhibit 18.2

Both management and the sales force are keenly interested in improving customer satisfaction after the sale. As a result, they cast about for ways to accomplish that goal, often spending money on "gimmicks" that offer little genuine pleasure for the customer. The fact is, the major resource for true customer satisfaction is already in place in most companies, since true customer satisfaction can only be made possible by an attitude of concern offered by all the company's personnel.

Getting started begins with you. You must commit yourself to making sure your customers know you're interested in their problems, and then you must do all in your power to get your fellow employees to commit to that same spirit. That shouldn't be too hard, since the self-satisfaction that comes with providing customer satisfaction is infectious. You may be surprised to see that your attitude toward customer care will motivate others throughout your company.

Source: Adapted from *Advertisement, Sales & Marketing Management,* March 1991, p. 65.

- *To specialize company capabilities*—Hiring and training salespeople for the needs of specific customer groups within a territory improves the match between customer and company and provides better service.
- *To decrease costs*—Because coverage will be more intense if territories are designed around the locations of customers, this

should be less costly than if salespeople were to "roam at will." Also, there is less likelihood of duplication that could result if territories overlapped.

Routing Techniques

Territory management is organized by routing techniques. *Routing* refers to listing calls for a given day or trip in an orderly and efficient manner. The salesperson's routing plan should be customer-oriented (that is, built around specific customers with specific needs at specific locations). Five popular routing plans are the straight-line, skip-stop, leapfrog, cloverleaf, and circular techniques.[25]

1. *Straight line*—The salesperson travels in a straight line to the first cluster, calls on each account in that cluster, and then travels in a straight line to the next cluster. Figure 18.4 illustrates straight-line routing.
2. *Skip-stop*—In this plan, the salesperson routes the itinerary through all the accounts during one sales trip. Note in Figure 18.5 that on the next sales trip the salesperson should skip those accounts that are less profitable, perhaps calling only on A or B accounts.
3. *Leapfrog*—In this approach, the salesperson travels to a distant point in the territory, then works back to the office, making calls

Figure 18.4

Straight-Line Approach to Routing

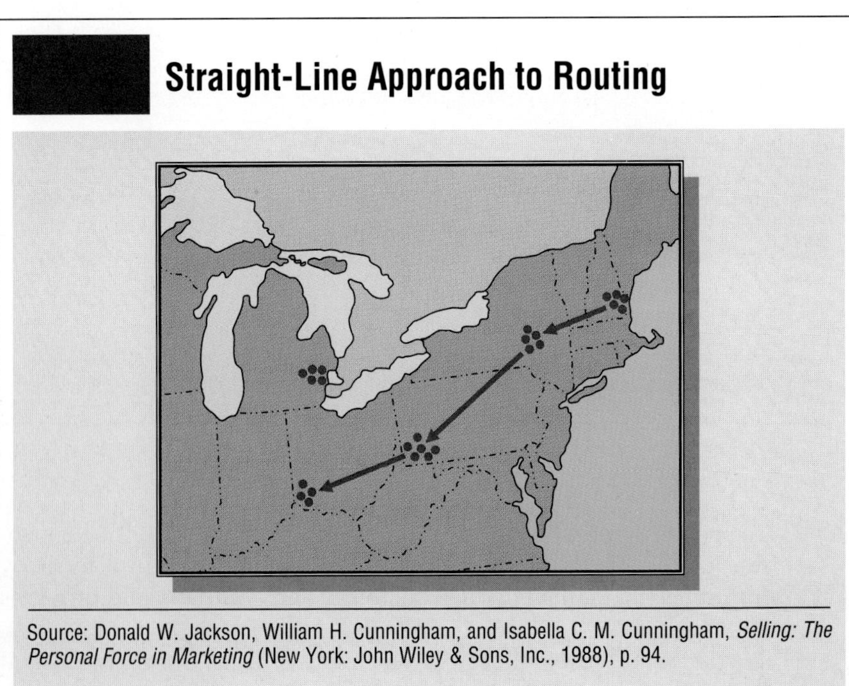

Source: Donald W. Jackson, William H. Cunningham, and Isabella C. M. Cunningham, *Selling: The Personal Force in Marketing* (New York: John Wiley & Sons, Inc., 1988), p. 94.

Skip-Stop Approach to Routing

Figure 18.5

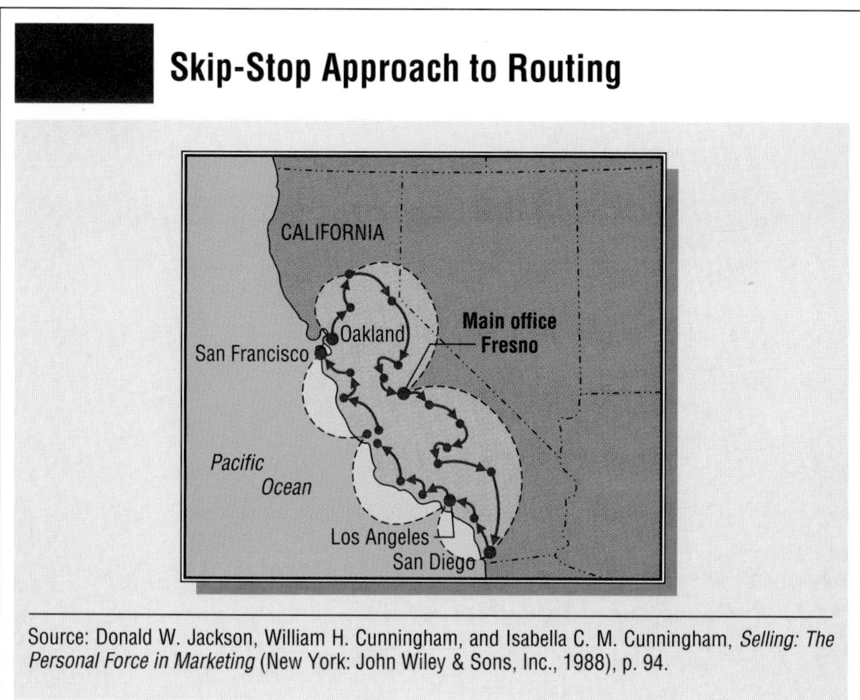

Source: Donald W. Jackson, William H. Cunningham, and Isabella C. M. Cunningham, *Selling: The Personal Force in Marketing* (New York: John Wiley & Sons, Inc., 1988), p. 94.

en route. The main point with this approach is that because the salesperson has started at the most distant point, if there is not enough time to call on all accounts before returning home, the accounts not visited can be called on later because they are close to the office and will be less expensive to return to later (see Figure 18.6).

4. *Cloverleaf*—A cloverleaf approach is especially effective when there is a heavy concentration of accounts in certain parts of the salesperson's territory. A focal point is chosen in each area, and calls are then made in loops. It is useful to remember that alternate sales calls and any calls made less frequently are also placed in the loop (Figure 18.7).
5. *Circular*—When accessibility and frequency of calls are about the same for each account, the circular approach works well. Figure 18.8 demonstrates how this approach is used by drawing concentric circles around the accounts. The salesperson then begins calling on those accounts closest to the office and works out around the circle until each account has been seen. The edge of the outer circle can also become the starting place, and the salesperson can spiral back to the office.

Scheduling is the process of prioritizing sales calls based on appointments. Routing and scheduling may require periodic adjustments. Salespeople must be prepared to respond quickly to customer requests and to

Figure 18.6

Leapfrog Approach to Routing

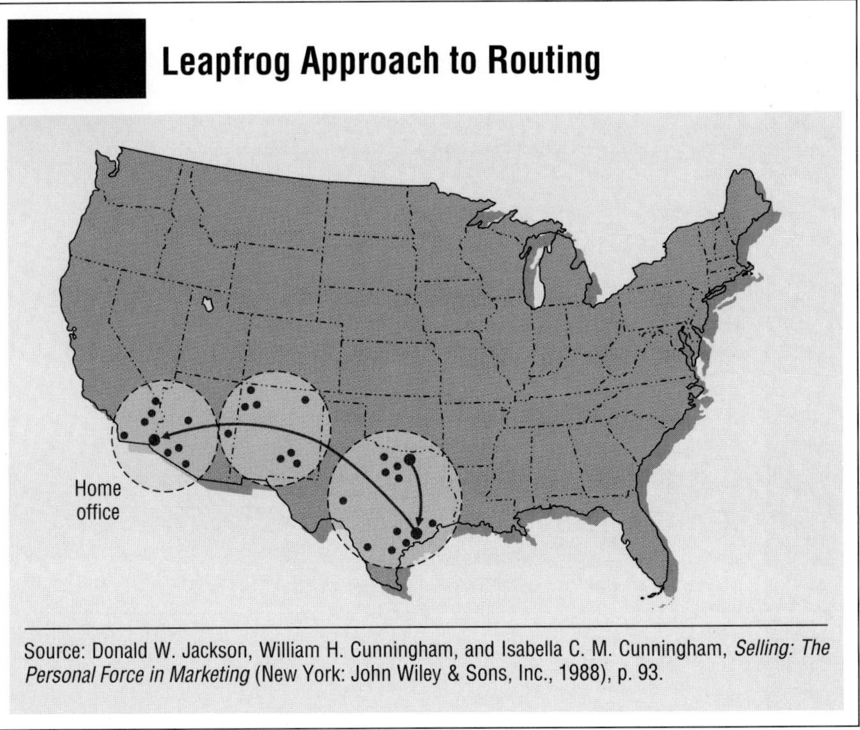

Source: Donald W. Jackson, William H. Cunningham, and Isabella C. M. Cunningham, *Selling: The Personal Force in Marketing* (New York: John Wiley & Sons, Inc., 1988), p. 93.

Figure 18.7

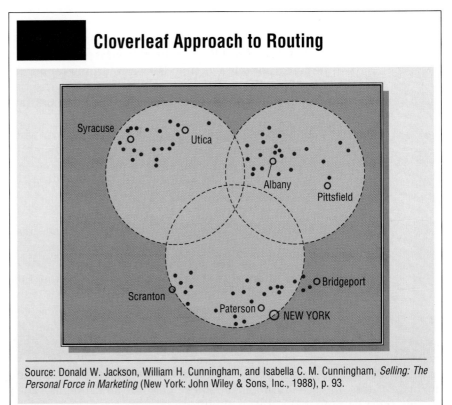

Cloverleaf Approach to Routing

Syracuse

Utica

Albany

Pittsfield

Scranton

Bridgeport

Paterson

NEW YORK

Source: Donald W. Jackson, William H. Cunningham, and Isabella C. M. Cunningham, *Selling: The Personal Force in Marketing* (New York: John Wiley & Sons, Inc., 1988), p. 93.

Figure 18.8

Circular Approach to Routing

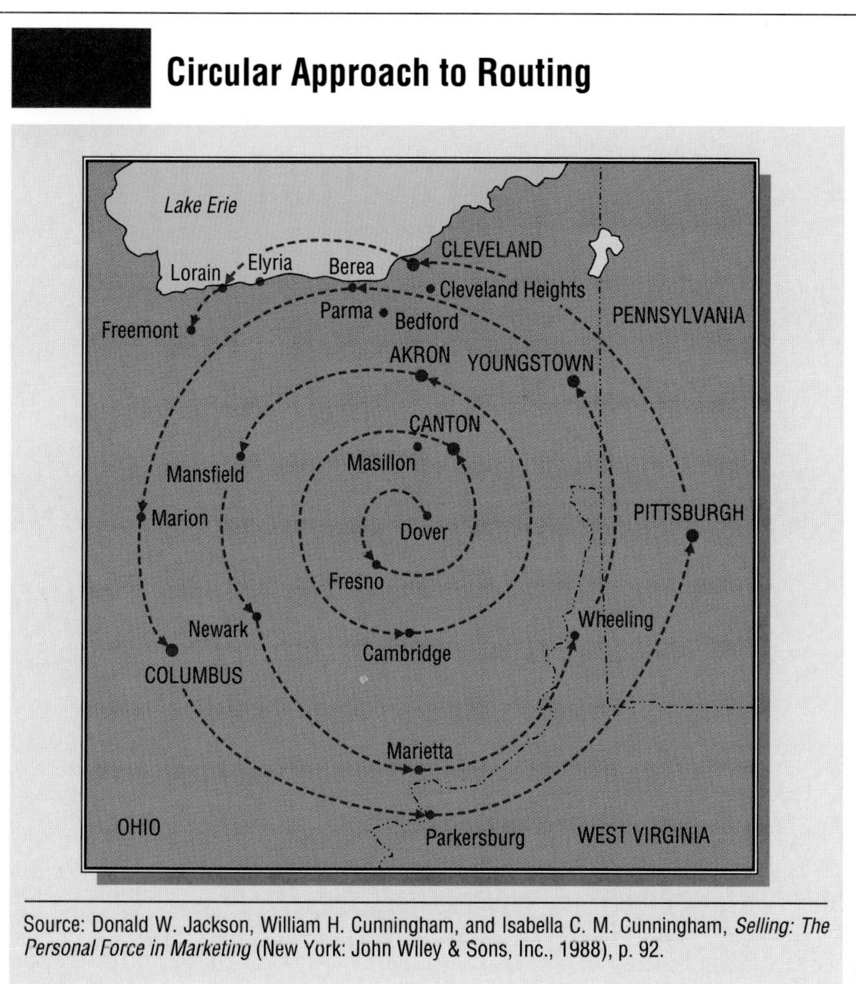

Source: Donald W. Jackson, William H. Cunningham, and Isabella C. M. Cunningham, *Selling: The Personal Force in Marketing* (New York: John Wiley & Sons, Inc., 1988), p. 92.

competitive actions. These six guidelines may be used in developing a routing and scheduling plan:

1. Locate all customers on a map. Customers are often located near one another in clusters.
2. Estimate the travel time between customers.
3. Determine what time of day calls should be made that are a long distance from home or city.
4. Determine whether expected sales justify travel costs and time away from the area.
5. When mapping calls, start working the outlying areas first and plan to finish in the home area. Typically, the home area is the largest account-volume location. Furthermore, if an emergency recalls the salesperson to the home area, it will not be necessary to travel as far to get back on track.

6. When covering a city or a small territory within a 2-hour radius of the home area, the territory should be divided into zones. Work the zones one at a time. Use the same princicples of starting with the outermost customers first.

Managing Paperwork and Reports

We live in a paper-intensive society. All of our high-tech electronic equipment augments the rate at which we can collect, process, and accumulate reams of "hard copy" data. With all this sophistication, paperwork is still an essential part of the salesperson's job. While paperwork may be classified as a nonselling activity, it is still important and should be done *thoroughly* in the least possible time.

Salespeople are expected to complete a variety of types of reports:

- A daily work plan—A listing of all customers the sales representative plans to see and what is to be accomplished
- Daily call report—An outline of activities and results
- Weekly reports—A summary of the activities and results of the week; sometimes replaces the daily call report
- Monthly expense reports—A list of expenses incurred by the salesperson for the month, such as travel and entertainment costs
- Miscellaneous reports—Reports on topics such as the status of large accounts, future accounts, lost accounts, dealer inventories, expense statements, and competitive activities

A salesperson who wants to improve selling efficiency in managing paperwork should follow these five suggestions:

1. Do not allow paperwork to accumulate. Complete routine reports daily.
2. Think positively about the paperwork. It then becomes easier to do.
3. Make notes of things to do and points to remember throughout the day. Keep a notebook or clipboard in the car. Be sure to date and record the time on all notes so that they can be placed in a correct time sequence when the report is written.
4. Set aside a block of time to do paperwork. This will help avoid interruptions.
5. Use whatever electronic technology is available to facilitate smart record keeping and report writing.

Summary

Managing self, time, and territory are the keys to wise selling practices. Fundamental to good management of these areas are methods of increasing profitable sales dollars and reducing the time and money spent in generating each dollar of profit.

Managing the self depends largely on the control and effort salespeople exert as they handle their activities so that personal objectives and company goals coincide. Becoming adept at self-management involves a good deal of stress, and nine behavior patterns outlined in the chapter may indicate to the salesperson that stress is present. These are balanced with a variety of tools for coping with stress. Nevertheless, some people have an unconscious fear of success, sometimes so strong that it results in self-sabotage of the person's goals or career. The Skill Builder introduces a technique aimed at reducing the fear of success by achieving positive self-management through the use of affirmations.

Managing one's time properly can be a tool for achieving selling efficiency. Examples are given of how salespeople spend their time, how to analyze sales call activities and set priorities, how to plan sales calls, and how to use sales quotas as performance measures. A self-check inventory is provided for analyzing sales call activities and setting priorities. This is a particularly helpful tool because salespeople use such planning not only for detailing each day's work effort, but for planning the entire week as well. Suggestions for improving sales planning include making an appointment calendar, classifying accounts, and preparing sales call plans and keeping track of results.

Finally, managing one's territory is the third component of selling efficiency. In explaining territory divisions as rational and workable, the chapter addresses why a company will divide its market into territories, popular routing plans, guidelines for prioritizing sales calls within the routing and scheduling plan framework, and typical required reports along with suggestions for the efficient management of paperwork.

Key Terms

Affirmation A statement of fact or belief that is written out in a personal, positive, present-tense form, as though the goal were already accomplished

Self-Management The control and effort salespeople exert by handling their activities in ways that match their personal objectives to their company's goals

Self-Sabotage Destruction of one's goals or career because of an unconscious fear of success

Stress The nonspecific response of the body to any demand made on it

Stressors Anything that causes the body to react physiologically or psychologically, or causes stress

Review Questions

1. What does the phrase "time is money" mean to the salesperson?
2. Why is personal organization so important in selling?
3. What is involved in making efficient use of time?
4. What activities should be included in your daily schedule?

5. Why is territory management important in selling?
6. Explain why companies assign salespeople to territories.
7. How can the time needed for travel in the sale territory be kept to a minimum?
8. Explain how a computer can be used to help design sales territories.

Discussion Questions

1. Is there a relationship between self-management and nonperformance? Explain.
2. What is wrong with long lunch breaks?
3. What is sales call planning and why is it necessary?
4. Discuss the various personal organizational tools available to salespeople.
5. Discuss why salespeople should strive to be in the presence of prospective buyers at least a certain number of hours each week.
6. Are quotas important to a salesperson? Provide several reasons.
7. How might an insurance salesperson increase the number of calls made per day?
8. Considerable emphasis has been placed on the use of computers and other communication systems in the selling field. List two types of systems that might be useful in managing territories.
9. You have a chance to play golf with a member of a school board whose district will soon decide on a contract that could mean a lot of business for your company in the future. Playing golf would necessitate giving up most of your day at a busy time of the month. Choose the alternative that best fits your selling priorities:
   a. Take the opportunity to play golf with this person, who may be able to offer help in acquiring future contracts.
   b. Find out how important this board member is. If the person is directly or indirectly involved in the board's purchasing decisions, you play golf; if he is not, then cancel the game but keep the door open.
   c. What other alternative would you consider?
10. You have spent most of the morning waiting to see an important prospect. At 10:30 a.m. the secretary comes out to the waiting room and asks you to come back at 2:30 p.m., which is a more convenient time for the purchasing agent to see you. Choose the alternative that best fits your selling priorities:
    a. Ask the secretary if you can see the customer for a few minutes now because coming back will waste a lot of your time.
    b. Go to a nearby restaurant and take care of a lot of needed paperwork, and then return at 2:30 p.m.
    c. Tell the secretary that you will phone at 2:00 p.m. and indicate if coming back is convenient for you.
    d. What other alternative would you consider?

Scheduling Sales Calls

Case 18.1

Frank Adams, an experienced salesman, discusses his procedure for scheduling sales calls as he directs young people pursuing a career in sales.

His many years of experience in industrial sales have taught him that the timing of a sales call is vital in gaining a favorable response. Mr. Adams claims that it is important to reach buyers when they are in the right mood and when they are not overburdened with other tasks. He explains that is is difficult to deal with most buyers on Fridays, early Monday mornings, or on the day before a long holiday weekend.

He also reveals that certain buyers may have administrative commitments at specific times and on certain days of the week. When contacting them before those meetings, it may be difficult to hold their attention because they are concentrating on the meeting's agenda. If contact is made at an inopportune time, he would immediately suggest rescheduling. Mr. Adams made it a point to learn particularly difficult times and days from reliable sources, such as secretaries within the firm.

Mr. Adams' strongest advice is to learn everything you can about your prospects and customers, and pay close attention to scheduling appointments when they would be most receptive to a sales call.

1. Do you think the advice given by Mr. Adams is good advice?
2. How can a professional salesperson determine whether the timing of a call is accurate or desirable?
3. What other information should salespeople know about their prospects and customers to help them schedule sales calls?

The Disorganized Salesman

Peter Marks is a real estate salesman in Miami, Florida. After 5 years of representing a leading sales agency, he has become one of the top salespeople among a staff of about 20.

One of Peter's weaknesses has been his poor organizational ability. He has a hard time keeping files in order and never puts them back where they belong. This disorganization makes it difficult for Peter to find documents when he needs them. It takes him twice as long to complete any task involving paperwork because he spends so much time looking for what he needs.

Peter finally decided that he needed to do something about this problem, so he decided that once a month on the weekend he would make a concerted effort to commit himself to a 2-hour venture devoted to organizing his office. This monthly clean-up time proved beneficial in helping Peter complete his paperwork in a more timely manner.

Peter has recently begun to neglect this assignment, however, due to the numerous calls from booming potential sales activity and weekend visits from clients and prospective buyers. The constant interruptions make it impossible to do anything but interact with office personnel and clients.

Although Peter recognizes the importance of being accessible to incoming calls and his colleagues, he is instructing the operator that all calls be held for at least 2 hours once a week on Saturdays. Peter isn't sure that this idea is a good one, however. By denying all contact at a regularly assigned time, Peter could lose sales.

Peter is also thinking about finding some other time during the week for desk work. Peter's problem is that he must block out a time and stick with it, or disorganization will persist.

1. Peter has proved himself capable of operating under his present, disorganized system. What should he do?
2. Suggest any alternatives to assist Peter in getting organized.
3. Could Peter develop a method to avoid losing the incoming calls and at the same time prevent interruption during an assigned "organizing" time? Discuss.

Notes

1. David L. Kurtz, H. Robert Dodge, and Jay E. Klompmaker, *Professional Selling*, 5th ed. (Texas: Business Publications, Inc., 1988), p. 255.
2. Hans Selye, M.D., *Stress without Distress* (New York: Signet Books, 1974), p. 14.
3. Ibid., p. 15.
4. Ibid., p. 14.
5. Andrew E. Slaby, M.D., Ph.D., M.P.H., *60 Ways to Make Stress Work for You* (New York: Bantam Books, 1991), p. 27.
6. Ibid.
7. Michael E. Cavanagh, "What You Don't Know about Stress," *Personnel Journal*, July 1988, p. 55.
8. Slaby, *60 Ways to Make Stress Work for You*, p. 28.
9. Gerhard Gschwandtner, "Lower Your Anxiety and Boost Your Sales," *Personal Selling Power*, March 1992, p. 16.
10. Ibid., pp. 47–114.
11. Peter G. Hanson, MD, *Stress for Success* (New York: Ballantine Books, 1989), p. 258.
12. Art Mortell, "The Value of Stress," *Sales & Marketing Management*, October 1991, p. 56.
13. Ibid., pp. 56, 58.
14. Eugene Raudsepp, "Self-Sabotage," *Success*, March 1984, p. 20.
15. Ibid.
16. Ibid.
17. Alan Lakein, *How to Get Control of Your Time and Life* (New York: Penguin Books, 1974), p. 11.
18. "1991 Sales Manager's Budget Planner," *Sales & Marketing Management*, June 17, 1991, p. 6.
19. William J. Tobin, "How to Find More Time to Sell in 1983," *Agency Sales Magazine*, January 1983, p. 21.
20. Robert W. Haas, *Industrial Marketing Management*, 4th ed. (MA: PWS-Kent, 1989), p. 313.
21. Robert L. Shook, *The Greatest Salespersons* (New York: Harper & Row, 1978), p. 79.
22. Lakein, *How to Get Control of Your Time and Life*, pp. 37-51.
23. Thomas N. Ingram and Raymond W. LaForge, *Sales Management: Analysis and Decision Making* (Hinsdale, IL: The Dryden Press, 1989), p. 50.
24. Ronald Balsley and E. Patricia Birsner, *Selling: Marketing Personified* (Hinsdale, IL: The Dryden Press, 1987), p. 364.
25. Donald W. Jackson, Jr., William H. Cunningham, and Isabella C. M. Cunningham, *Selling: The Personal Force in Marketing* (New York: John Wiley & Sons, Inc., 1988), pp. 91–94.

CHAPTER 19

Sales Management

Knowledge Objectives

In this chapter, you will learn:

1. The nature of sales management and the functions of a sales manager
2. What qualities are necessary to become a competent sales manager
3. How the sales organization is structured
4. Management's role in the recruiting, selecting, training, and performance evaluation of its sales force

Consider This

Our goal is to deploy the best sales force in the industry. For us, that means fielding the best quality people at the lowest cost and at the highest levels of customer satisfaction.

Manuel Diaz, Director
of Sales and Marketing for
the U.S., Canada, and
Latin America,
Hewlett-Packard*

* "Excellence," *Sales & Marketing Management*, September 1991, p. 48.

As described in Chapter 1, the route to a career in either sales management or personal selling often begins at the sales trainee level. The opportunities are good for a person who performs successfully in a selling situation to be considered for a sales management position. This chapter will provide insights into the managerial framework of a sales organization. Our discussion is limited, however, to activities involved with managing field sales professionals.

This chapter is organized into five sections. The first describes the nature of the sales manager's job and the qualities found in a competent sales manager. In addition, six position titles are identified and explained. The second section concentrates on organizing the sales force by studying five basic kinds of sales organizations: geographic, product, market, functional, and hybrid. Next we will examine the recruitment and selection of a sales force, along with the types of compensation plans awarded salespeople. The cost and length of sales training and developing a training program are the focus of the fourth section. The final section looks at guidelines for developing appropriate performance appraisal instruments.

An Overview of Sales Management

The following passage is taken from a Procter & Gamble recruiting brochure used between 1986 and 1989:

> What It Takes to Be a Sales Manager at Procter & Gamble
>
> Sales managers have to be effective managers of people, good decision makers, creative problem solvers, and outstanding communicators. They must also work closely with other disciplines as part of the overall marketing team, helping to coordinate and focus the efforts of Product Development, Manufacturing, Market Research, and Advertising. For example, sales managers must jointly develop national marketing objectives and strategy with Advertising, and then tailor these plans to suit regional differences, the competitive environment, consumer preferences, and so on. The sales manager is also responsible for "making it happen" in the marketplace. In addition, sales managers use consumer data from Market Research to demonstrate the benefits of P & G products to their accounts, helping create strong brand support. And, they make recommendations to Product Development, based on responses from accounts, which may result in an improved product or better packaging.
>
> To be happy in Sales Management, you have to love challenges because you'll be getting them every day. You have to be tough enough to cope with a customer who turns you down, creative enough to solve problems for your accounts, motivated enough to set lofty goals for yourself and then strive to exceed them. And you have to love working with people, because it's the essence of the job.
>
> Because P & G sales managers' responsibilities require working with all disciplines in the Company, a career in Sales Management

Sales Professional Spotlight

Janis Dietz is the national accounts manager for two divisions at Masco, a *Fortune* 200 company and leader in the home and building industry. Formerly employed at General Electric, she was the recipient of the Sector Service Award for her outstanding sales efforts in establishing relationships with her customers. She has also written several articles in *Top Performance* magazine on choices and integrity as a sales tool.

With over 20 years of sales experience in retail and industrial sales, Janis has been affiliated with large companies such as Johnson & Johnson and Masco. Her experiences also include sales training in the field of banking. Janis is active in Capital Associates, a sales training organization that sponsors public and private seminars.

Her sales management experience has included positions at regional and national levels. Her assignments have ranged from managing a regional factory sales force of 13 to managing as many as 45 manufacturers' representatives. Some of her responsibilities include training, counseling, forecasting, goal setting, and recruiting.

She emphasizes training as an ongoing process that demands constant updating of skills and knowledge. "I am sensitive to the differences of desires and motivations important to my salespeople, and offer guidance and support. Feedback from my salespeople is vital in making adjustments to changing conditions, and when planning for the future. Importantly, goals are set on a yearly basis, with regular updating and modification," she says. Acquiring a top-quality sales force is very high on Janis's priority list.

Janis credits her success as a sales manager to developing lasting relationships based on strong customer service, enthusiasm, and integrity. She believes strongly that the sales process requires listening, caring, follow-through, and honesty in dealing with customers. "The industry really does not matter because these issues transcend products. A salesperson can listen to customers anywhere, determine their needs in any industry, and follow through with the sale in any country," she says.

Janis advises students going into a sales career to be flexible and able to take rejection. "Not taking problems personally is an important way for salespeople to grow and a good way to remain objective about upcoming challenges." The increasing number of women in the sales field has produced some special challenges for Janis. She serves as a role model for women succeeding in a male-dominated industry, having been on several occasions the only woman in a company's national sales force.

When lecturing at universities on the topic of sales management, she encourages students to recognize the tremendous opportunities in the field of selling. "Selling is not only one of the most highly paid professions, but it offers people a chance to be creative and make their mark on the world," she says.

provides the kind of broad experience important to assuming a general management responsibility.

Sales management is the planning, implementation, and control of the personal selling component of the promotional variable in the marketing mix. Simply stated, sales management is "management of an organization's personal selling function."[1] Figure 19.1 presents a model of the personal selling functions for which the sales manager is responsible. Note that the first three boxes are all parts of the planning element, while the fourth box covers implementation. The last box shows the control component that is demonstrated through methods used to determine sales-force effectiveness and performance.

Professional selling success, as presented throughout this text, depends on the relationship process facilitated by a competent salesperson who has mastered interpersonal communication skills. In contrast, sales

Figure 19.1

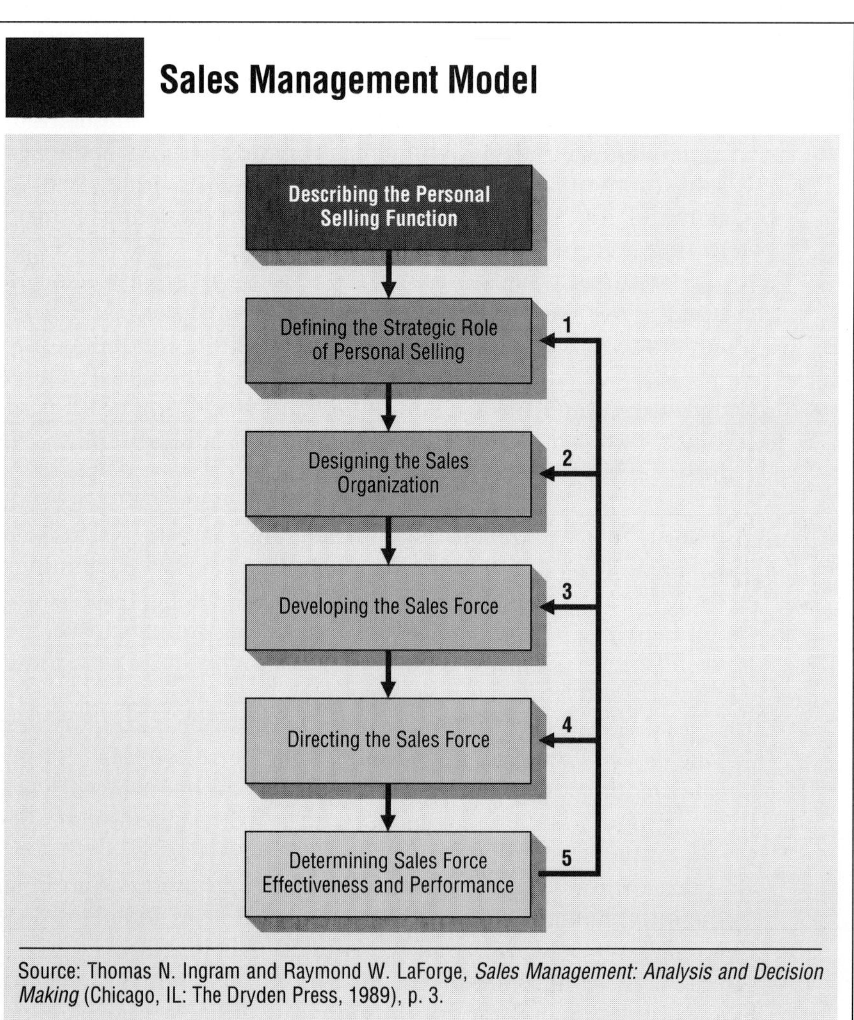

Source: Thomas N. Ingram and Raymond W. LaForge, *Sales Management: Analysis and Decision Making* (Chicago, IL: The Dryden Press, 1989), p. 3.

management success demands a mastery of administrative skills such as organizing, directing, controlling, and evaluating the activities of all sales and support personnel.

The primary goal of the sales manager is to achieve the levels of sales volume, profit, and growth desired by higher levels of management. Thus, sales managers are responsible for generating sales levels that meet corporate goals.[2] The determining factor in achieving these goals is the sales manager's ability to work with people in personal selling functions and other relevant areas in the organization, and with individuals outside the organization, especially customers. Furthermore, a person who has mastered communication skills and integrated them into the selling process will have substantially increased chances of executing the administrative tasks of a sales manager.

Qualities and Functions of the Competent Sales Manager

A classified ad for the 1990s sales manager might read:

> WANTED: Need an individual that can plan, direct, and control the personal selling activities of a rapidly growing firm. Qualified applicant must be a sales forecaster, market analyst, strategic planner, student of buyer behavior, opportunity manager, intelligence gatherer, scarce-product allocator, accounts receivable collector, cost and profit analyst, budget manager, leader and master communicator (both verbal and nonverbal). Duties will be performed in an environment characterized by high buyer expertise, high customer expectations, intense foreign competition, revolutionary changes in communications technology, and an influx of women and minorities into personal selling jobs.[3]

A sales manager is a person who plans, directs, and controls the personal selling activities of a business, including recruiting, selecting, training, equipping, assigning, routing, supervising, paying, and motivating salespeople.[4] In carrying out these duties, the sales manager will more specifically be responsible for:

- Preparing sales plans and budgets
- Setting sales force goals and objectives
- Estimating demand and forecasting sales
- Determining the size and structure of the sales force organization
- Recruiting, selecting, and training salespeople
- Designing sales territories, setting sales quotas, and defining performance standards
- Compensating, motivating, and leading the sales force
- Conducting sales volume, cost, and profit analyses
- Evaluating sales performance
- Monitoring the ethical and social conduct of the sales force[5]

On the Ethical Side How Should Sales Managers Deal with Ethical Problems?

Corporations across the United States are addressing ethics in their sales training programs, and more and more business schools are offering courses in ethics. Beyond these training programs and courses, however, are the sales managers who must deal with ethical questions in today's workplace.

How do sales managers deal with ethical problems? In general, there are two main steps: Recognize the problem, and then apply the appropriate set of ethical standards to the situation. Of course, this is not always easy.

Not all ethical problems in sales are easy to identify. Some problems are obvious; the people involved know they shouldn't be doing what they are doing. The less obvious situations require increased vigilance on the part of management. These can occur in industries where the rules of doing business are changing or where competition is keen enough to make people want to cut corners.

After a problem is recognized, a clear and consistent ethical standard can help sales managers decide what to do about it. Common ethical maxims like "Do unto others as you would have them do unto you" serve most cases well, but some situations are more difficult to deal with.

Professor Thomas W. Dunfee of the Wharton School recommends that managers act to avoid even the appearance of a conflict of interest. Other experts advocate acting so that other people's freedoms and life-styles are respected.

The ultimate way to deal with ethical problems is to prevent them from happening. Formal codes of ethics are common, but they are probably not as effective as an atmosphere in which people are encouraged to think about ethics and to express ethical concerns before problems arise. If sales managers set the example and follow through on their values, their employees will know that their ethics mean business.

Sources: Amanda Bennett, "Ethics Codes Spread Despite Skepticism," *The Wall Street Journal*, July 15, 1988, p. 13; Walter Kiechel III, "Unfuzzing Ethics for Managers," *Fortune*, November 23, 1987, pp. 229–234.

A sales manager's responsibilities vary from company to company. One way to identify functions of the sales manager is to review position titles and the duties associated with them. The following list identifies the most commonly used position titles[6]:

1. *Top-Level Sales Executives*
   A. *Vice President of Sales*—Typically reports to the vice president of marketing or company president and is usually involved in top-level planning and long-term sales strategies
   B. *National Sales Manager*—The link between the highest level of company planning and line sales managers; provides overall direction to the sales force and renders top-level decisions on sales operations to regional sales managers

2. *Middle-Level Line Managers*
   A. *Regional, Divisional, or Zone Sales Manager*—Zone sales manager reports to division sales manager, who in turn reports to regional sales manager; responsible for sales activities of subdivisions of company sales operations
3. *First-Level Sales Managers*
   A. *District, Branch, or Field Sales Manager*—Usually responsible for successively smaller territorial duties that involve handling day-to-day activities of salespeople
   B. *Sales Supervisor*—Responsible for providing guidance and advice to a few salespeople in a given branch or field territory
4. *Key Salespeople*
   A. *National Account Manager, National Account Salesperson, Account Executive, or Key Account Salesperson*—Top-performing salespeople who work with a few major accounts, such as large national or regional chains in various consumer fields
5. *Salespeople*
   A. *Marketing Representative, Territory Manager, Account Representative, Account Manager, Sales Representative, Sales Engineer, Salesperson, or Sales Associate*—Various industrial, consumer, and service sales personnel
6. *Sales Management Staff*
   A. *Assistant to the Sales Manager, Sales Analyst, and Sales Training Director or Manager*—Staff positions need to support the line and function of sales, usually responsible for assisting in the performance of related functions at different levels in the sales organization (such as sales planning, promotion, recruiting, training, and analyses)

Although this list deals with the sales manager's responsibilities individually, they are not necessarily handled sequentially. In fact, often these responsibilities are carried out concurrently. Additionally, the sales manager is charged with carrying out duties within the larger framework of organizational objectives and marketing strategies, which include all target markets and marketing mix variables.

Figure 19.2 illustrates that as individuals ascend the managerial staircase, the required skills shift from selling to supervisory, to managerial, to administrative and leadership. At all levels, however, interpersonal skills provide the vital link between the sales force and higher levels of management.[7]

Organizing the Sales Force

One way in which sales management titles can be differentiated is by their categorization as line or staff positions. *Line* sales management positions are part of the direct management hierarchy within the firm. In

Figure 19.2

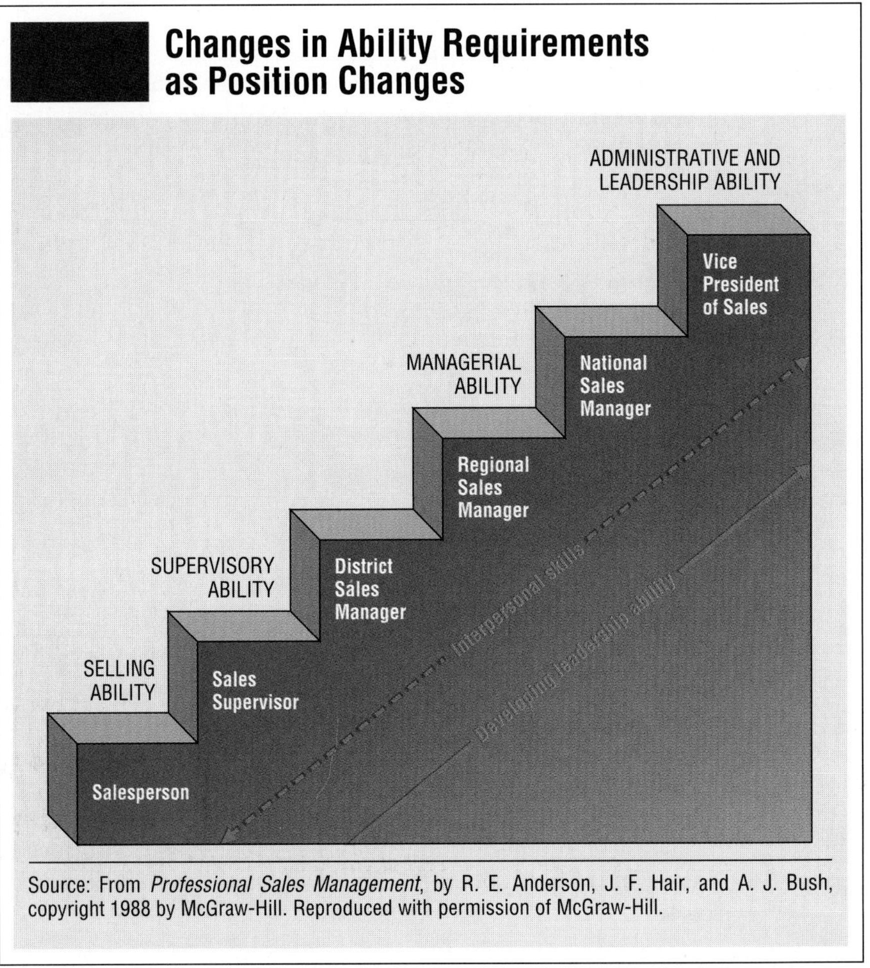

Source: From *Professional Sales Management*, by R. E. Anderson, J. F. Hair, and A. J. Bush, copyright 1988 by McGraw-Hill. Reproduced with permission of McGraw-Hill.

other words, managers in these positions report directly to the next level within the organization. Line management is often a feature of small firms that have few managers who exercise authority over specific functional areas of the business, such as production, finance, distribution, and sales. This system works effectively until the organization expands, at which time managers become burdened with too many activities and duties to perform. In that case, *staff* positions may be added that also have management status within the organization. Staff sales managers do not directly manage people, but they are responsible for certain functions, such as recruiting, selecting, and training.

Figure 19.3 shows a simple line and staff structure that creates more functional areas and adds staff assistants to accomplish support activities, including such areas as sales forecasting and market research. In this type of organization, line managers have direct authority to carry out the operations of the firm; staff managers are able only to make recommendations and assist line managers. In other words, staff managers serve in an advisory capacity.[8]

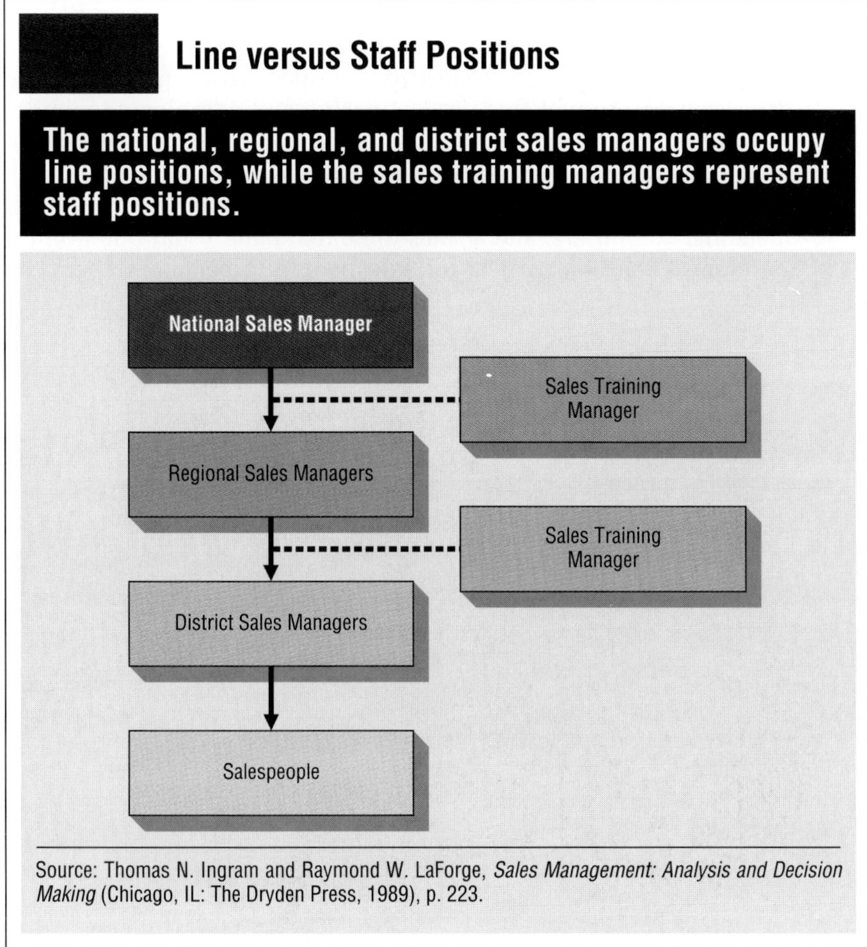

Source: Thomas N. Ingram and Raymond W. LaForge, *Sales Management: Analysis and Decision Making* (Chicago, IL: The Dryden Press, 1989), p. 223.

Figure 19.3

Every sales organization centers its efforts around products, markets, and functions, which are blended together to match the specific industry's overall company objectives. Sales departments are typically organized into four categories: geographic, product, market, and functional. Recently, a combination of the four types has developed, called a hybrid sales organization.

- *Geographic Sales Organization*—In a geographic sales organization, the sales manager usually has total authority over a specific geographic area. Several salespeople who are assigned specific parts of the territory report directly to the manager. Sales managers may be called regional, divisional, or district sales managers.

  Most sales forces have some type of geographic specialization. This is the least specialized, most generalized type of sales force. Examples are banks with suburban branches, magazine publishers with regional editions, hotel chains with regional divisions, and companies with international and domestic sales divisions. Figure 19.4 illustrates a geographic sales organization.

- *Product Sales Organization*—Product specialization is found in firms where product lines are extensive and complex enough to warrant individualized attention. IBM makes extensive use of this structure. The company has separate sales forces that sell mainframe computers and peripherals, another group selling personal computers, and a sales force that handles all other office products. The objective is for salespeople to become experts in

Figure 19.4

Geographic Sales Organization

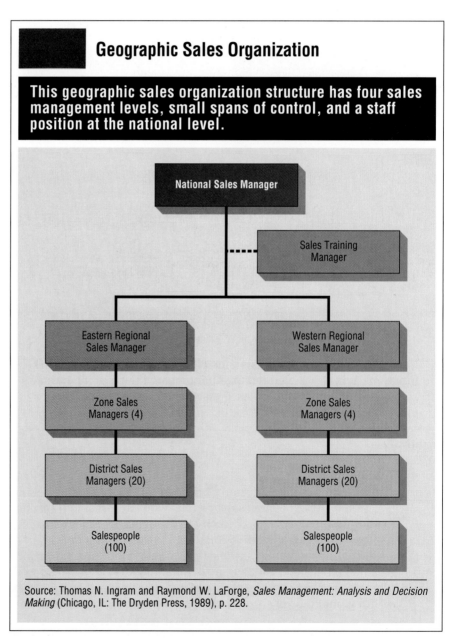

This geographic sales organization structure has four sales management levels, small spans of control, and a staff position at the national level.

National Sales Manager
Sales Training Manager
Eastern Regional Sales Manager
Western Regional Sales Manager
Zone Sales Managers (4)
Zone Sales Managers (4)
District Sales Managers (20)
District Sales Managers (20)
Salespeople (100)
Salespeople (100)

Source: Thomas N. Ingram and Raymond W. LaForge, *Sales Management: Analysis and Decision Making* (Chicago, IL: The Dryden Press, 1989), p. 228.

their assigned product category. Figure 19.5 provides an illustration of a product sales organization.

- *Market Sales Organization*—The market sales structure may be found when the company's products are purchased in multiple combinations by a variety of customer categories with a unique set of needs. In a market specialization, salespeople are assigned specific types of customers and are expected to satisfy all their needs.

  Example of the structure described in Figure 19.6 are firms such as Beckman Instruments, Hughes Aircraft, and utility companies that separate their markets into industrial, commercial, and customer accounts. A utilities company may also divide its business into commercial and residential accounts.
- *Functional Sales Organization*—This kind of organizational structure is categorized by major functions, such as the development of new accounts and maintenance of current customers. This format offers specialization and efficiency in performing selling

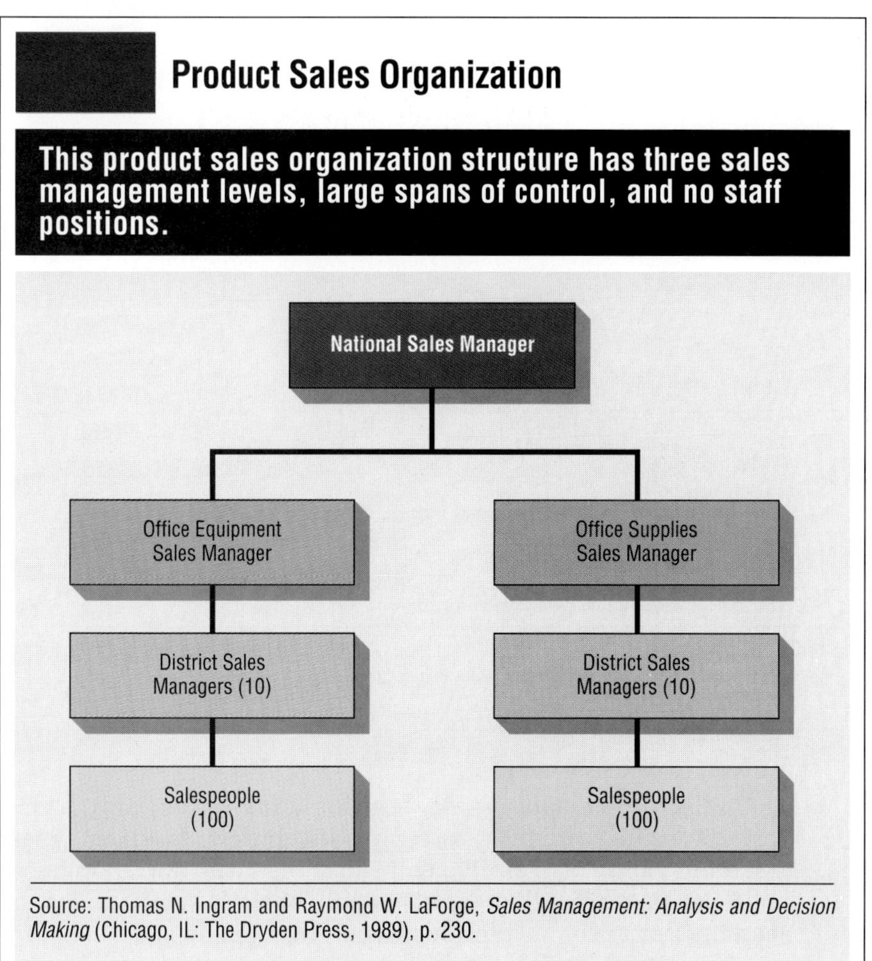

Source: Thomas N. Ingram and Raymond W. LaForge, *Sales Management: Analysis and Decision Making* (Chicago, IL: The Dryden Press, 1989), p. 230.

Figure 19.5

Figure 19.6

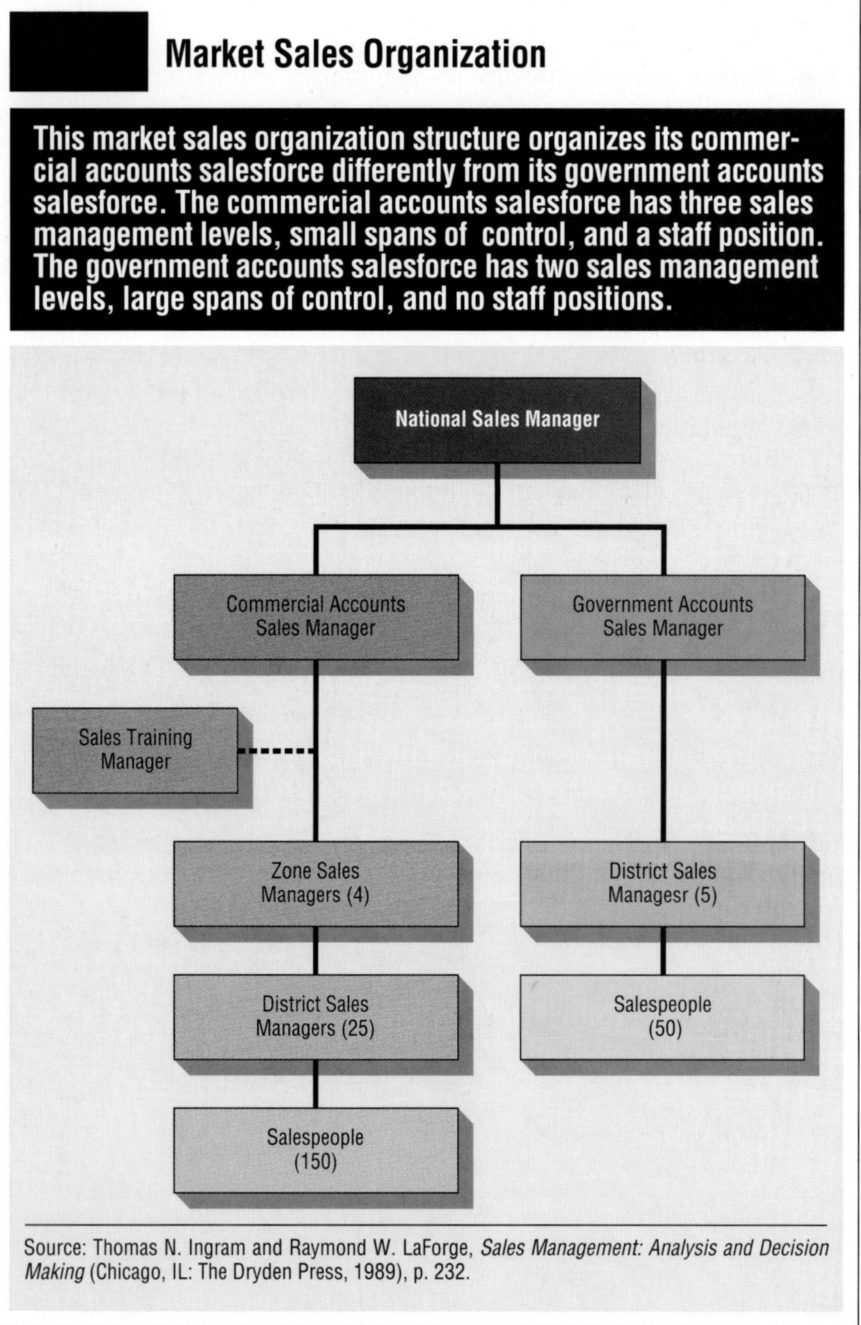

Market Sales Organization

This market sales organization structure organizes its commercial accounts salesforce differently from its government accounts salesforce. The commercial accounts salesforce has three sales management levels, small spans of control, and a staff position. The government accounts salesforce has two sales management levels, large spans of control, and no staff positions.

Source: Thomas N. Ingram and Raymond W. LaForge, *Sales Management: Analysis and Decision Making* (Chicago, IL: The Dryden Press, 1989), p. 232.

activities. It generally works best for firms selling only a few or very similar products to comparatively few customer types. Medium- and large-sized companies that can afford to have salespeople restrict their efforts to only one or a small number of activities can use this type of system. An example of a functional organizational structure is presented in Figure 19.7.

Figure 19.7

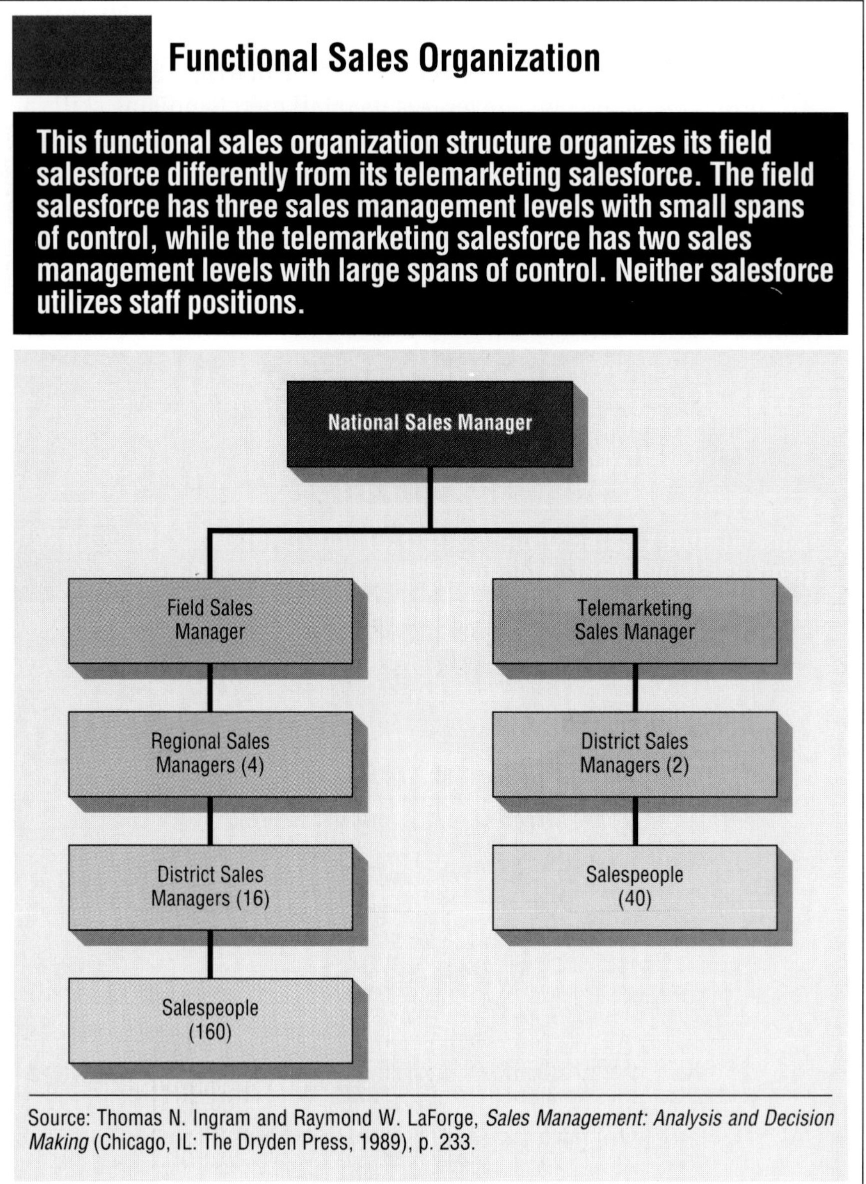
Functional Sales Organization
This functional sales organization structure organizes its field salesforce differently from its telemarketing salesforce. The field salesforce has three sales management levels with small spans of control, while the telemarketing salesforce has two sales management levels with large spans of control. Neither salesforce utilizes staff positions.
National Sales Manager
Field Sales Manager
Telemarketing Sales Manager
Regional Sales Managers (4)
District Sales Managers (2)
District Sales Managers (16)
Salespeople (40)
Salespeople (160)

Source: Thomas N. Ingram and Raymond W. LaForge, *Sales Management: Analysis and Decision Making* (Chicago, IL: The Dryden Press, 1989), p. 233.

- *Hybrid Sales Organization*—In a hybrid sales organization, salespeople are trained to sell systems of interrelated products and services in a consultative manner. Having market knowledge, rather than product expertise, is considered the salesperson's principal resource in helping customers improve profits. An example of such collaborative marketing is Pizza Hut packaging its coupons inside "Teenage Mutant Ninja Turtles" videocassettes. The producers of the videotapes increased their sales by building in more value, and Pizza Hut gained distribution into eight million households, which in turn boosted its restaurant and take-out volume.[9]

Figure 19.8 illustrates a complex form of hybrid sales organization. Life Savers, Inc., leverages its retail merchandising skills and sales force account coverage to sell Tums on behalf of Revlon's Norcliffe Thayer subsidiary. And Nestle sells General Mills' Cheerios brand in markets outside North America. In still another situation, K. Hattori, the distribution partner for Seiko watches in Japan, markets Schick razors there. As a result, Schick has the

Figure 19.8

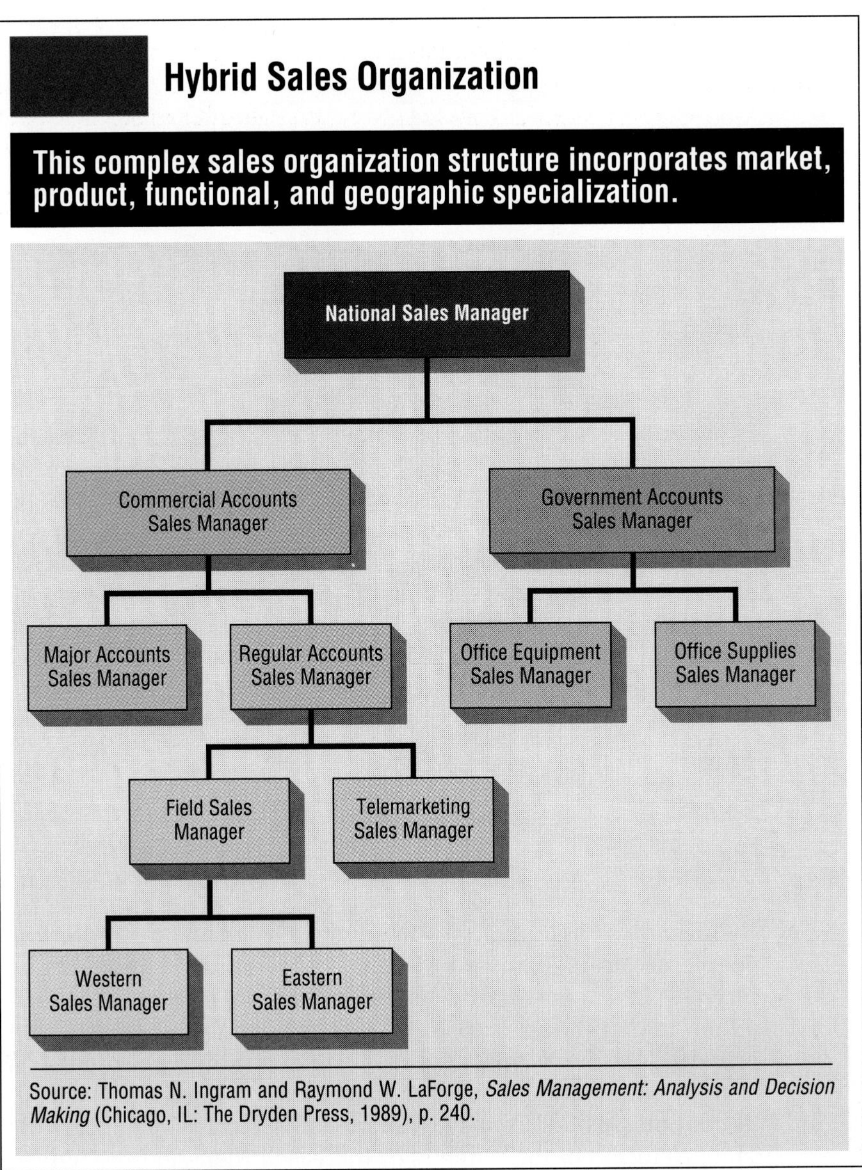

Source: Thomas N. Ingram and Raymond W. LaForge, *Sales Management: Analysis and Decision Making* (Chicago, IL: The Dryden Press, 1989), p. 240.

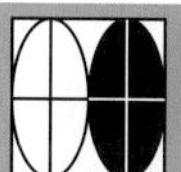 **On the International Front**

Finding an International Sales Manager

International sales pursuits have given rise to the position of international sales manager. Although many sales managers have learned the ropes the hard way, by making mistakes, successful companies have basic guidelines for selecting a good international sales manager.

Spalding, with international sales of about $200 million annually, lists the following guidelines in selecting an international sales manager:

- Look for someone with experience inside the company, or provide a thorough training program.
- Choose someone in a senior position, or provide a high-level contact in upper management.
- Pick a person with a flexible personality.
- Look for someone with extensive international knowledge or someone willing to gain it.

As proposed by international consultant Stephen Simurda, the first choice should be an inside person who knows the company. If the company has to select from among outsiders, then thorough training is essential. An important requirement for the outsider is knowledge of the industry and the trade channels. The person chosen must be able to closely coordinate those functions that have bearing on the sales potential.

The sales manager's base should depend on the size of the international operation and the distribution network. The choice of location will also depend on the relationship with a potential overseas distributor. If a good relationship already exists, then someone need not be assigned to the overseas location until the extent of business justifies the need for a sales manager. These positions are sometimes filled by expatriates, people living outside their own country.

Overall, an international sales manager must be comfortable with cultural diversity, quick to find opportunities in unfamiliar settings, and able to marshal many conflicting forces for the benefit of sales opportunities. Sometimes the company may prefer to select an international sales manager who is presently active in one of its other markets and knows the situation and cultural context of the new market. An essential aspect of the success of the international sales manager is ample experience working with foreign condition, customers, and markets.

Sources: Andrew Kupfer, "How to Be a Global Manager," *Fortune*, March 14, 1988, pp. 52–58; and Stephen Simurda, "Finding an International Sales Manager," *Northeast International Business*, September 1988, pp. 15–16.

leading market share in Japan despite Gillette's leading market strength in most other international markets.[10]

There are many ways to structure a sales organization. Some structures are more suitable to a particular selling situation than others. Table 19.1 summarizes the four basic types of sales organizations by comparing the advantage and disadvantages of each structure.

Table 19.1

Comparison of Sales Organization Structures

Organization Structure	Advantages	Disadvantages
Geographic	■ Low cost ■ No geographic duplication ■ No customer duplication ■ Fewer management levels	■ Limited specialization ■ Lack of management control over product or customer emphasis
Product	■ Salespeople become experts in product attributes and applications ■ Management control over selling effort allocated to products	■ High cost ■ Geographic duplication ■ Customer duplication
Market	■ Salespeople develop better understanding of unique customer needs ■ Management control over selling effort allocated to different markets	■ High cost ■ Geographic duplication
Functional	■ Efficiency in performing selling activities	■ Geographic duplication ■ Customer duplication ■ Need for coordination

Source: Thomas N. Ingram and Raymond W. LaForge, *Sales Management: Analysis and Decision Making* (Chicago, IL: The Dryden Press, 1989), p. 239.

Recruiting and Selecting the Sales Force

Selected Compensation Plans

A compensation plan is the method by which a salesperson is rewarded for performing the duties outlined in the job description. Compensation is composed of direct and indirect monetary remuneration. There are three basic methods of direct monetary compensation: straight salary; commission only; and salary plus incentive, in the form of a commission or bonus or both. Table 19.2 shows the percentages of companies using each type of financial compensation plan.

Straight salary involves a fixed or predetermined amount of money paid at predetermined intervals, such as weekly or monthly. Commission only is either a percentage or a specific dollar amount assigned to the results achieved by the salesperson, tied either to sales or profits. Salary plus incentive offers a combination: either salary and commission, salary

Table 19.2

Types of Financial Compensation for Salespeople

Description	Percentage of Companies Using
Salary and bonus (combination plan)	45.9%
Salary and commission (combination plan)	45.9%
Commission only (straight commission)	3.5%
Salary only (straight salary)	4.7%

Source: Thomas N. Ingram and Raymond W. LaForge, *Sales Management: Analysis and Decision Making* (Chicago, IL: The Dryden Press, 1989), p. 490.

and bonus, or salary and commission plus bonus. Figure 19.9 outlines the three methods of direct monetary compensation by industry group.

Indirect monetary compensation may also be thought of as psychological compensation. Examples are recognition and opportunities for growth. Other indirect financial remuneration involves incentives and fringe benefits. Some worthwhile fringe benefits are special parking; company stock options; day-care service; country club membership; health club membership; spouse traveling on company business; executive vacations; pension plans; additional insurance coverage; loans and mortgages; financial counseling; sabbaticals; use of the company yacht, airplane, or apartment; and personal legal services.

It is virtually impossible to develop a compensation plan that satisfies all salespeople in an industry. Table 19.3 provides a summary of the advantages, disadvantages, and common uses of the three basic plans that may help the sales manager reach a decision.

Recruitment and Selection of Sales Personnel

Recruitment is the process of seeking potential applicants, discussing the company with them, and encouraging them to apply for the sales position. While it is not within the scope of this chapter to discuss all the activities that are critical to successful recruitment, the following three areas deserve attention: planning, locating, and selecting sales personnel. Figure 19.10 presents a model of the recruitment and selection process.

Planning for Recruitment and Selection

The first step in the planning process involves specific procedures such as conducting job analyses, establishing job qualification, writing a job description, setting recruitment and selection objectives, and developing a recruitment and selection strategy.[11]

Figure 19.9

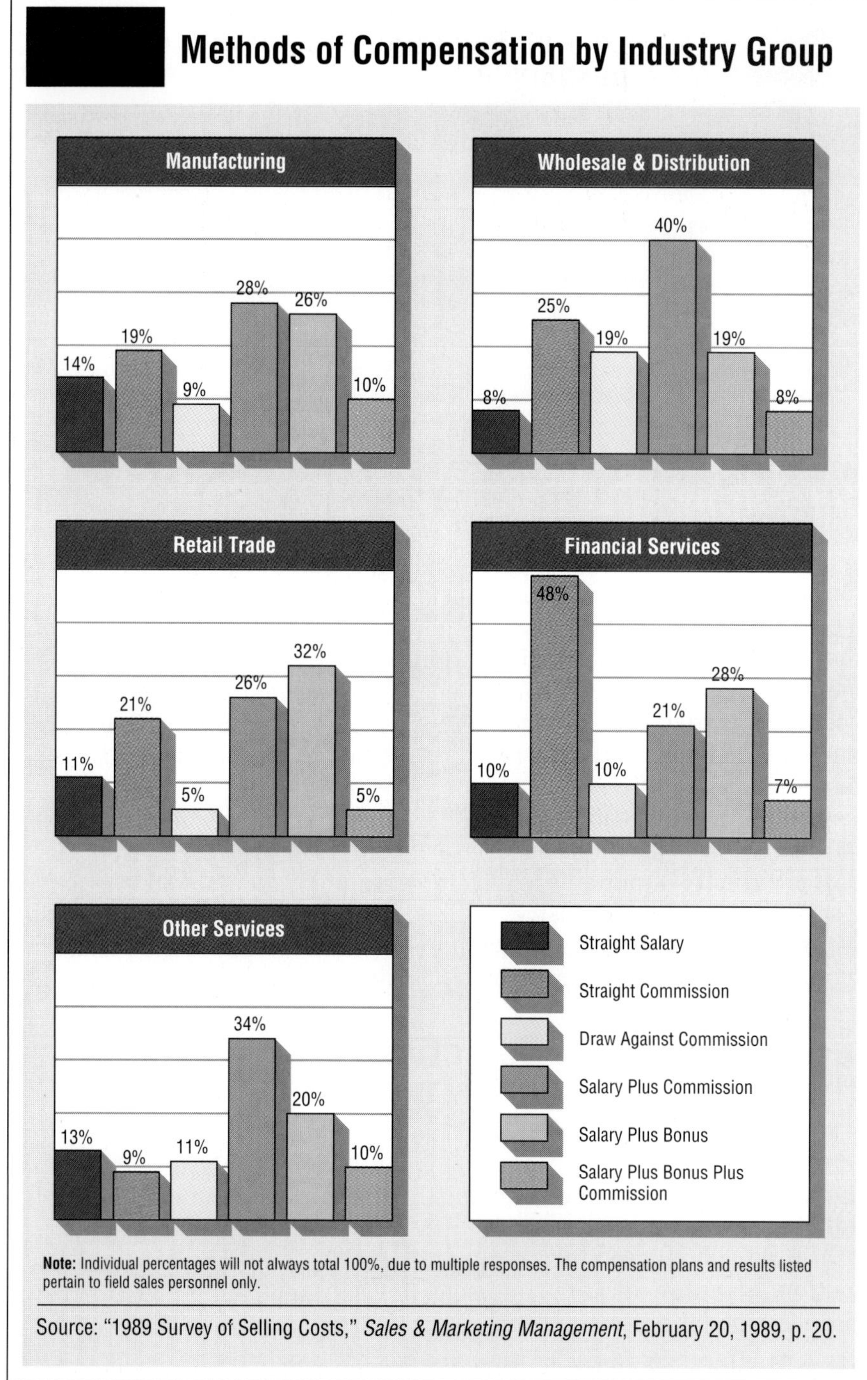
Methods of Compensation by Industry Group
Manufacturing
14%
19%
9%
28%
26%
10%
Wholesale & Distribution
8%
25%
19%
40%
19%
8%
Retail Trade
11%
21%
5%
26%
32%
5%
Financial Services
10%
48%
10%
21%
28%
7%
Other Services
13%
9%
11%
34%
20%
10%
Straight Salary
Straight Commission
Draw Against Commission
Salary Plus Commission
Salary Plus Bonus
Salary Plus Bonus Plus Commission
Note: Individual percentages will not always total 100%, due to multiple responses. The compensation plans and results listed pertain to field sales personnel only.
Source: "1989 Survey of Selling Costs," Sales & Marketing Management, February 20, 1989, p. 20.

Table 19.3

Summary of Financial-Compensation Plans

Type of Plan	Advantages	Disadvantages	Common Uses
Salary	Simple to administer; planned earnings facilitates budgeting and recruiting; customer loyalty enhanced; more control of nonselling activities	No financial incentive to improve performance; pay often based on seniority, not merit; salaries may be a burden to new firms or to those in declining industries	Sales trainees; team selling; sales support; seasonal sales
Commission	Income linked to results; strong financial incentive to improve results; costs reduced during slow sales periods; less operating capital required	Difficult to build loyalty of salesforce to company; less control of nonselling activities	Real estate; insurance; wholesaling; securities; automobiles
Combination	Flexibility allows frequent reward of desired behavior; may attract high-potential but unproven recruits	Complex to administer; may encourage crisis-oriented objectives	Widely used—most popular type of financial pay plan

Source: Thomas N. Ingram and Raymond W. LaForge, *Sales Management: Analysis and Decision Making* (Chicago, IL: The Dryden Press, 1989), p. 491.

Recruitment—Locating Prospective Candidates

The second step refers to the procedures the sales manager takes to attract and locate a pool of qualified prospective job applicants. Both internal and external sources are used:

1. *Internal*—people from other departments within the company, such as production or accounting, or people from other nonselling areas of the sales department who are already familiar with company policies and the technical aspects of the product itself.
2. *External*—people from a competing firm who are trained and have experience selling similar products to similar markets. Noncompeting companies are productive sources because they usually have selling experience and require less training than new salespeople, particularly if they are working with similar

Figure 19.10

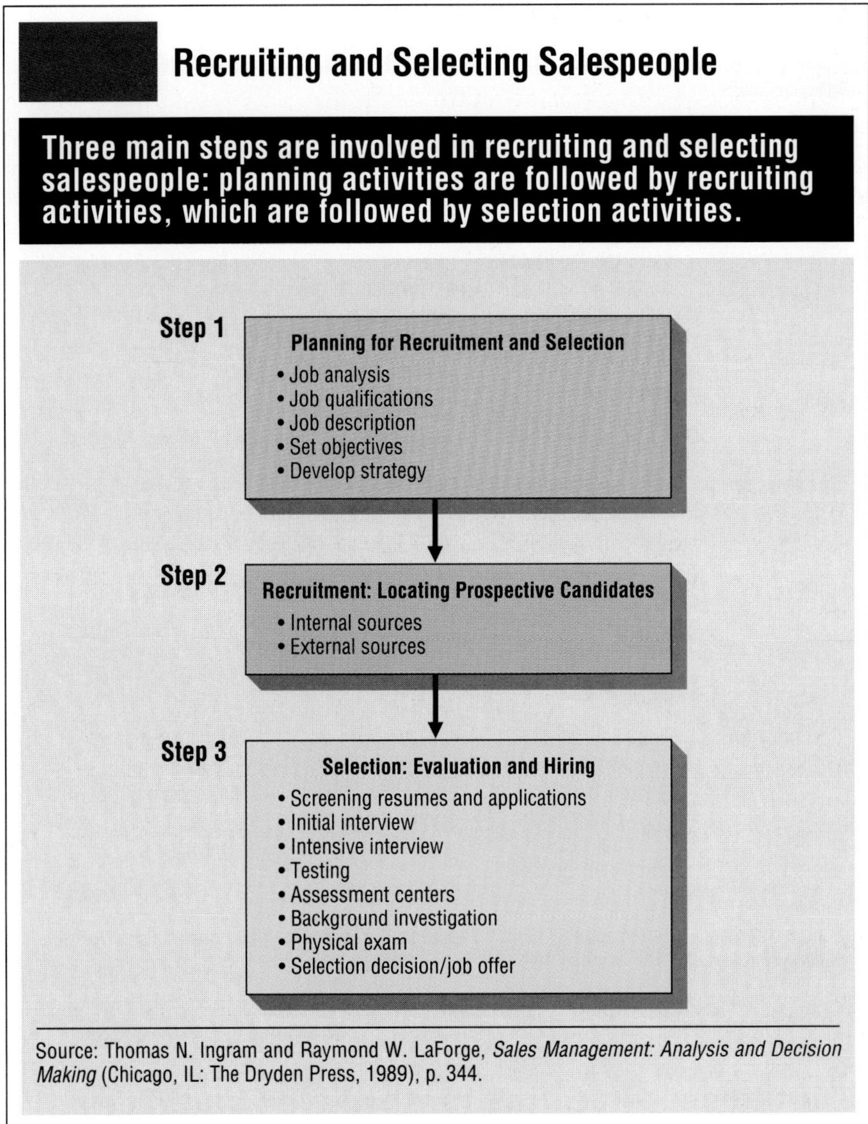

Source: Thomas N. Ingram and Raymond W. LaForge, *Sales Management: Analysis and Decision Making* (Chicago, IL: The Dryden Press, 1989), p. 344.

products or selling to the same market. Educational institutions are an excellent pool of talent: high schools, continuing education classes, business schools, vocational and technical schools, community colleges, state colleges, and universities. Advertisements are useful for recruiting high-caliber sales and sales management people when placed in publications such as *The Wall Street Journal* and *Sales & Marketing Management*. In addition, employment agencies can provide a useful service to the sales manager by screening candidates so that the recruiter can spend more time with qualified prospects for the job.

Selection—Evaluation and Hiring

Selection is the process of choosing which candidates have the best qualifications and the greatest aptitude for the job. In this third step, a variety of screening and evaluation methods are used: resumes and job application forms, interviews, tests, assessment centers, background investigations, and physical examinations. For example, an interviewing guide such as the one in Exhibit 19.1 can be used by an interviewing panel, with each member investigating one or more of the seven categories of information about the candidate.[12]

Training the Sales Force

In sales-driven companies, training is generally not regarded by top-level management as an important element in the selling function. The view that "good salespeople are born, not made" prompts the attitude that the organization should recruit and select top sales producers. Training consists of product familiarization with little or no attention given to building interpersonal skills that form the foundation for long-term relationships.

Today, companies that are customer-driven and relationship-driven are recognizing the importance of developing specifically designed training programs for their sales forces. Exhibit 19.2 provides a checklist for firms that focus on the relational process and charge their sales managers with the responsibility for developing and implementing a training program.

Cost and Length of Training

The cost of training can vary anywhere from $1,000 to $50,000 per year per person. Figure 19.11 shows an average cost of sales training per salesperson by product type, as well as the average length of the training period for a sales trainee. Figure 19.12 breaks down the average training period in months by industry group.

Keep in mind that a formal training program is really not a cost to the company. Instead, it should be considered an investment, for the long-term gains will be recognized by top performance and long-term profits through customer satisfaction.

Developing a Training Program

Most firms have a need for some type of sales training. One estimate puts American annual corporate spending at over $30 billion dollars on 17.6 million training courses.[13] Of all those millions of training programs and courses offered, Figure 19.13 identifies the various instructional methods that are used.

Exhibit 19.1

Interview Guide

Meeting the Candidate

At the outset, act friendly but avoid prolonged small talk—interviewing time costs money.

- Introduce yourself by using your name and title.
- Mention casually that you will make notes. (You don't mind if I make notes, do you?)
- Assure candidate that all information will be treated in confidence.

Questions

- Ask questions in a conversational tone. Make them both concise and clear.
- Avoid loaded and/or negative questions. Ask open ended questions which will force complete answers: "Why do you say that?" (Who, what, where, when, how?)
- Don't ask direct questions that can be answered "Yes" or "No."

Analyzing

- Attempt to determine the candidate's goals. Try to draw the candidate out, but let him/her do most of the talking. Don't sell—interview.
- Try to avoid snap judgments.

Interviewer Instructions:

You will find two columns of questions on the following pages. The left hand column contains questions to ask yourself about the candidate. The right hand column suggests questions to ask the candidate.

During the interview it is suggested that you continually ask yourself "what is this person telling me about himself or herself? What kind of person is he/she?" In other parts of the interview you can cover education, previous experience and other matters relating to specific qualifications.

Ask Yourself

I. Attitude

- Can compete without irritation?
- Can bounce back easily?
- Can balance interest of both company and self?
- What is important to him/her?
- Is he/she loyal?
- Takes pride in doing a good job?
- Is he/she cooperative team player?

Ask the Candidate

1. Ever lose in competition? Feelings?
2. Ever uncertain about providing for your family?
3. How can the American way of business be improved?
4. Do you feel you've made a success of life to date?
5. Who was your best boss? Describe the person.
6. How do you handle customer complaints?

Exhibit 19.1
Continued

II. Motivation

• Is settled in choice of work? • Works from necessity, or choice? • Makes day-to-day and long-range plans? • Uses some leisure for self-improvement? • Is willing to work for what he/she wants in face of opposition?	1. How does your spouse (or others) feel about a selling career? 2. When and how did you first develop an interest in selling? 3. What mortgages, debts, etc., press you now? 4. How will this job help you get what you want? 5. What obstacles are most likely to trip you up?

III. Initiative

• Is he or she a self-starter? • Completes own tasks? • Follows through on assigned tasks? • Works in assigned manner without leaving own "trademark"? • Can work independently?	1. How (or why) did you get into (or want) sales? 2. Do you prefer to work alone or with others? 3. What do you like most, like least about selling? 4. Which supervisors let you work alone? How did you feel about this? 5. When have you felt like giving up on a task? Tell me about it.

IV. Stability

• Is he or she excitable or even-tempered? • Impatient or understanding? • Does candidate use words that show strong feelings? • Is candidate poised or impulsive; controlled or erratic? • Will he or she broaden or flatten under pressure? • Is candidate enthusiastic about job?	1. What things disturb you most? 2. How do you get along with customers (people) you dislike? 3. What buyers' actions irritate you? 4. What were your most unpleasant sales (work) experiences? 5. Most pleasant sales (work) experiences? 6. What do you most admire about your friends? 7. What things do some customers do that are irritating to other people?

V. Planning

• Ability to plan and follow through? Or will he depend on supervisor for planning? • Ability to coordinate work of others? • Ability to think of ways of improving methods? • Ability to fit into company methods? • Will he or she see the whole job or get caught up in details?	1. What part of your work (selling) do you like best? Like least? 2. What part is the most difficult for you? 3. Give me an idea of how you spend a typical day. 4. Where do you want to be five years from today? 5. If you were Manager, how would you run your present job? 6. What are the differences between planned and unplanned work?

Continued

Exhibit 19.1
Continued

Ask Yourself	Ask the Candidate
VI. Insight	
• Realistic in appraising self? • Desire for self-improvement? • Interested in problems of others? • Interested in reaction of others to self? • Will he or she take constructive action on weaknesses? • How does he/she take criticism?	1. Tell me about your strengths/ weaknesses. 2. Are your weaknesses important enough to do something about them? Why or why not? 3. How do you feel about those weaknesses? 4. How would you size up your last employer? 5. Most useful criticism received? From whom? Tell me about it. Most useless? 6. How do you handle fault finders?
VII. Social Skills	
• Is he/she a leader or follower? • Interested in new ways of dealing with people? • Can get along best with what types of people? • Will wear well over the long term? • Can make friends easily?	1. What do you like to do in your spare time? 2. Have you ever organized a group? Tell me about it. 3. What methods are effective in dealing with people? What methods are ineffective? 4. What kind of customers (people) do you get along with best? 5. Do you prefer making new friends or keeping old ones? Why? 6. How would you go about making a friend? Developing a customer? 7. What must a person do to be liked by others?

Source: "Interviewing the Candidate." Sales Consultants International, Inc., Cleveland, Ohio. Cited in Thomas N. Ingram and Raymond W. LaForge, *Sales Management: Analysis and Decision Making* (Chicago, IL: The Dryden Press, 1989), p. 357–358.

Because training needs vary from one sales organization to the next, so do sales objectives. By setting objectives for sales training, the manager avoids the "wasteful practice of training for training's sake."[14] Sales management authors Thomas Ingram and Raymond LaForge suggest that one or more of the following objectives should be included in all sales training programs[15]:

- Increase sales or profits.
- Create positive attitudes and improve sales force morale.
- Assist in sales force socialization.
- Reduce role conflict and ambiguity.
- Introduce new products, markets, and promotional programs.

Checklist for Developing Sales Training Programs

Exhibit 19.2

Needs Analysis

Who needs to be trained?
What can't they do?
Why can't they do it?
How can the deficiency be corrected?
When should the training be done?
Where should the training be done?

Education Evaluation

Who do we send?
How do we determine the outcome?
What benefits can we expect?
What kind of follow-up is expected?

Sales Training Objectives

What role will sales training play in the organization?
Can we define the objectives of the sales training department?
Will the sales training development solve our existing problems?
Who will we find to run the sales training department?

Sales Training Program Content

List a profile of salespeople who will be trained.
List qualifications of training staff.
Will outside speakers be necessary?
Can demonstrations be used?
Can measurements for training performance be developed?

Location of Training

What will be the class size?
Do we have the available space?
What will be the cost per individual?
How long will the training program last?
How flexible can the program be to the different types of salespeople who will attend?

Source: Adapted from Mary E. Boylen, "The ABC's of Training," *Data Management*, December 1980, pp. 32–35. Cited in R. E. Anderson, J. F. Hair, Jr., and A. J. Bush, *Professional Sales Management* (New York: McGraw-Hill Book Co, 1988), p. 260.

- Develop salespeople to take future management positions.
- Ensure awareness of ethical and legal responsibilities.
- Teach administrative procedures such as expense accounts and call reports.
- Ensure competence in the use of sales and support tools such as portable computers.
- Minimize sales force turnover rate.
- Prepare new salespeople for assignment to a sales territory.

Figure 19.11

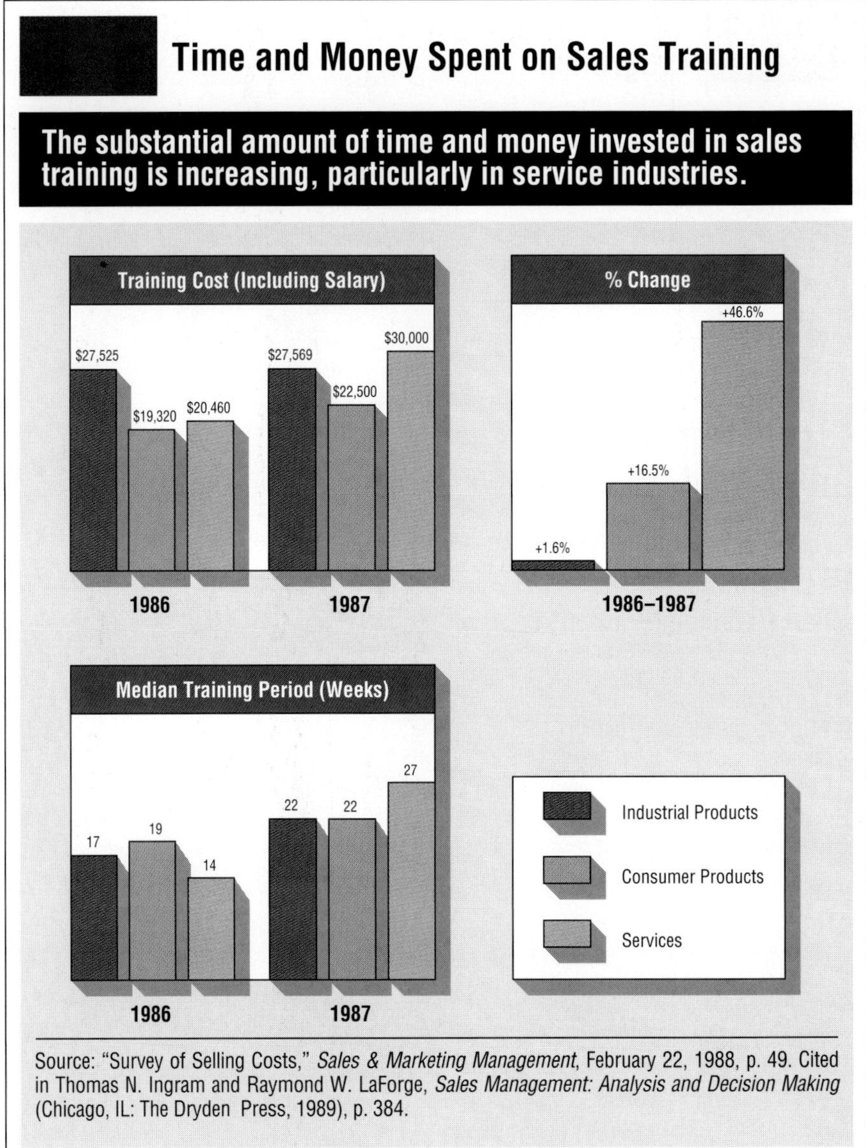

Source: "Survey of Selling Costs," *Sales & Marketing Management*, February 22, 1988, p. 49. Cited in Thomas N. Ingram and Raymond W. LaForge, *Sales Management: Analysis and Decision Making* (Chicago, IL: The Dryden Press, 1989), p. 384.

Sales training should focus on skill enhancement. Training should instruct people how to do their jobs better, faster, and more efficiently. The result should be a sales force of *competent* sales professionals who have a range of skills that they can use *effectively* and *appropriately*. (Refer to Chapter 2 for a review of communciation competence.)

To determine if a training program is a good investment and economically sound, a sales manager should have a predetermined plan for evaluation, keeping in mind four criteria: reactions, learning, behavior, and on-the-job results.[16]

Length of Sales Training by Industry

Figure 19.12

TRAINING

Industry Group	Average Training Period (Months)
Agriculture	5.7
Amusement/Recreation Services	2.0
Business Services	4.1
Chemicals	4.5
Communications	4.2
Construction	5.0
Electronic Components	1.5
Electronics	3.4
Fabricated Metals	3.5
Food Products	2.8
Instruments	2.7
Insurance	5.5
Lumber/Wood Products	2.7
Machinery	5.6
Manufacturing	3.3
Office Equipment	2.8
Paper/Allied Products	6.0
Primary Metal Products	4.5
Printing/Publishing	5.5
Rubber/Plastics	6.5
Wholesale (Consumer)	1.5
Wholesale (Industrial)	3.9
Average	**4.0**

Note: Industry Groups reflected categories selected and reported by Dartnell Corporation. The overall average has been calculated by *Sales & Marketing Management* based on data from the 22 industries listed.

Source: "1991 Sales Manager's Budget Planner," *Sales & Marketing Management*, June 17, 1991, p. 77.

Reactions

The sales manager should answer several questions about participants' reactions to a training program:

- What did participants say about the program?
- Was it what they expected?
- Was it worthwhile?

Figure 19.13

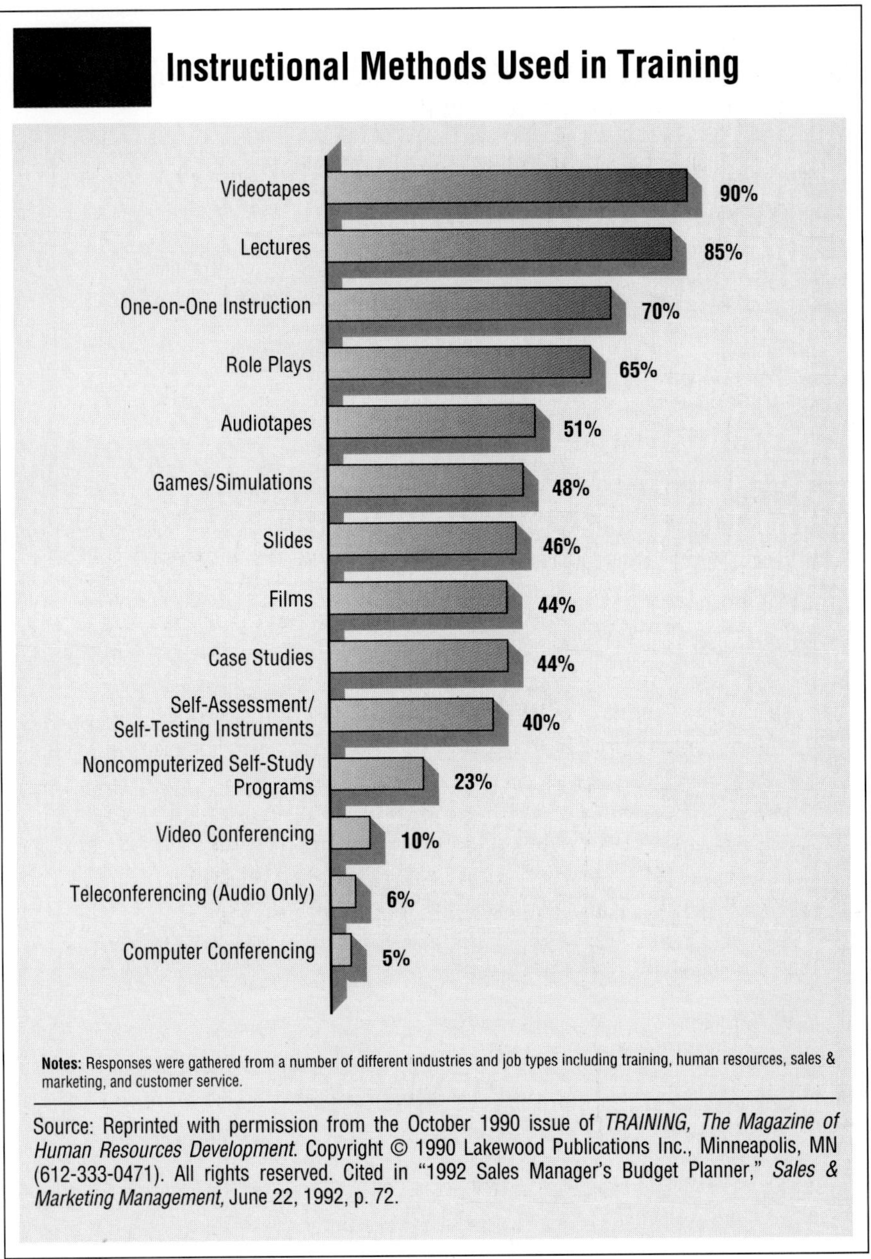

Source: Reprinted with permission from the October 1990 issue of *TRAINING, The Magazine of Human Resources Development.* Copyright © 1990 Lakewood Publications Inc., Minneapolis, MN (612-333-0471). All rights reserved. Cited in "1992 Sales Manager's Budget Planner," *Sales & Marketing Management,* June 22, 1992, p. 72.

- Would they do it again?
- Would they recommend that others participate in it if given a chance?

When salespeople have positive feelings about their experiences, they feel better about their skills and come away more prepared and motivated to do their jobs better. This kind of motivation helps build self-confidence and a positive sales image.

Learning

How well participants learn from a training program should be an important consideration in evaluating its effectiveness:

- Do the participants know more about the subject than they did before the training program?
- Did their attitudes change?
- Did their interpersonal skills improve?
- Was the training relevant?

A sales training director should consider that the presentation is aimed at both auditory and visual learners. Therefore, a mix of both presentation methods will achieve the best results.

Behavior

Salespeople's behavior can provide an indication of the program's efficacy:

- Is there a noticeable difference in the way the participants are now selling?
- Are they more efficient and more competent?
- Do they waste less time and do their jobs more effectively?
- Have negative behaviors been replaced by more positive ones?

To determine if behaviors in the salespeople have changed, the training director or manager must first decide what behavioral modifications to expect. For example, if a salesperson is having difficulty managing resistance, the training program should develop skill in conflict resolution and negotiation. Customer service and customer relations training should result in fewer customer complaints.

On-the-Job Results

Results in job situations should be a strong consideration in selecting a beneficial training program:

- Are the participants selling more now than they did before?
- Are they selling enough more now to warrant the cost of the training?
- What is the rate of return coming from the training?

It is natural to expect that training value will show up on the bottom line. Some noticeable increases might include more sales closed, more calls made, fewer complaints, fewer problems with completing reports on time, and more effective use of time and self-management. It is equally important to remember that a before-and-after measurement of results from the training program may not show immediate results.

Sales managers must take into consideration the cumulative effects of training. For example, a salesperson who closes only a few more sales a year after training may not look impressive in the short run. But a few more sales each year over a 10- or 15-year career with the firm can amount to impressive payoffs.

Evaluation of Sales Performance

One of the most difficult and important tasks required of sales managers is the evaluation of their sales forces' performance. Exhibit 19.3 provides a flowchart for measuring and evaluating sales force performance. It is the ultimate responsibility of the sales manager to provide a systematic procedure by which the sales organization's goals and objectives can be measured effectively and efficiently. "EFFECTIVENESS is results-oriented and deals with whether or not the organization's objectives are being achieved. EFFICIENCY focuses on costs and the economical use of resources."[17]

Some sales managers use a performance appraisal form such as that shown in Exhibit 19.4 to evaluate sales performance. If a printed form is not available, the sales manager should consider the criteria presented in Table 19.4 and develop an appropriate performance appraisal.

When faced with performance issues, it is natural for a sales manager to assume that everything will sort itself out eventually. Some managers even expect problems to somehow correct themselves. Unfortunately, they probably will not. It is up to the sales manager to identify the problem and solve it. For example, salespeople, like professional athletes, have slumps from time to time. Without being intrusive, the sales manager needs to know how the salespeople are doing and what they are thinking. A well-seasoned sales manager will probably be able to recognize the issue and begin the dialogue needed to get the salesperson back on track.

By using various methods to evaluate the behavioral development, results, and profitability of salespeople, the sales manager can collect important information about the sales force's performance. The critical task is to use this information to improve the individual salesperson's performance and the overall operations of the sales organization. Once the "absolute" and "relative" performance of each salesperson are determined, these determinants provide the basis for reward disbursements, special recognition, and promotions.[18]

Summary

Sales management is a many-faceted area of expertise. The sales manager plans, directs, and controls the personal selling activities of a given business; this includes recruiting, selecting, training, equipping, assigning, routing, supervising, paying, and motivating salespeople. Sales managers fall under various designations, depending on their companies' preference and, in some cases, their rank. A few of these are vice president of sales; national sales manager; regional, divisional, or zone sales manager;

Exhibit 19.3

Sales Force Performance Measurement and Evaluation System

Planning
Execution
Control
Establish sales force objectives and goals.
Develop sales plan.
Set performance standards.
Allocate resources and sales force efforts in implementing the sales plan.
Measure sales force performance against standards.
Are standards being met?
Yes
No
Revise standards.
Revise standards.
Revise objectives and goals.
Determine deviation from standards.
Implement corrective action.
Are standards being met?
Yes
No
Take new action.
Are standards being met now?
Yes
No

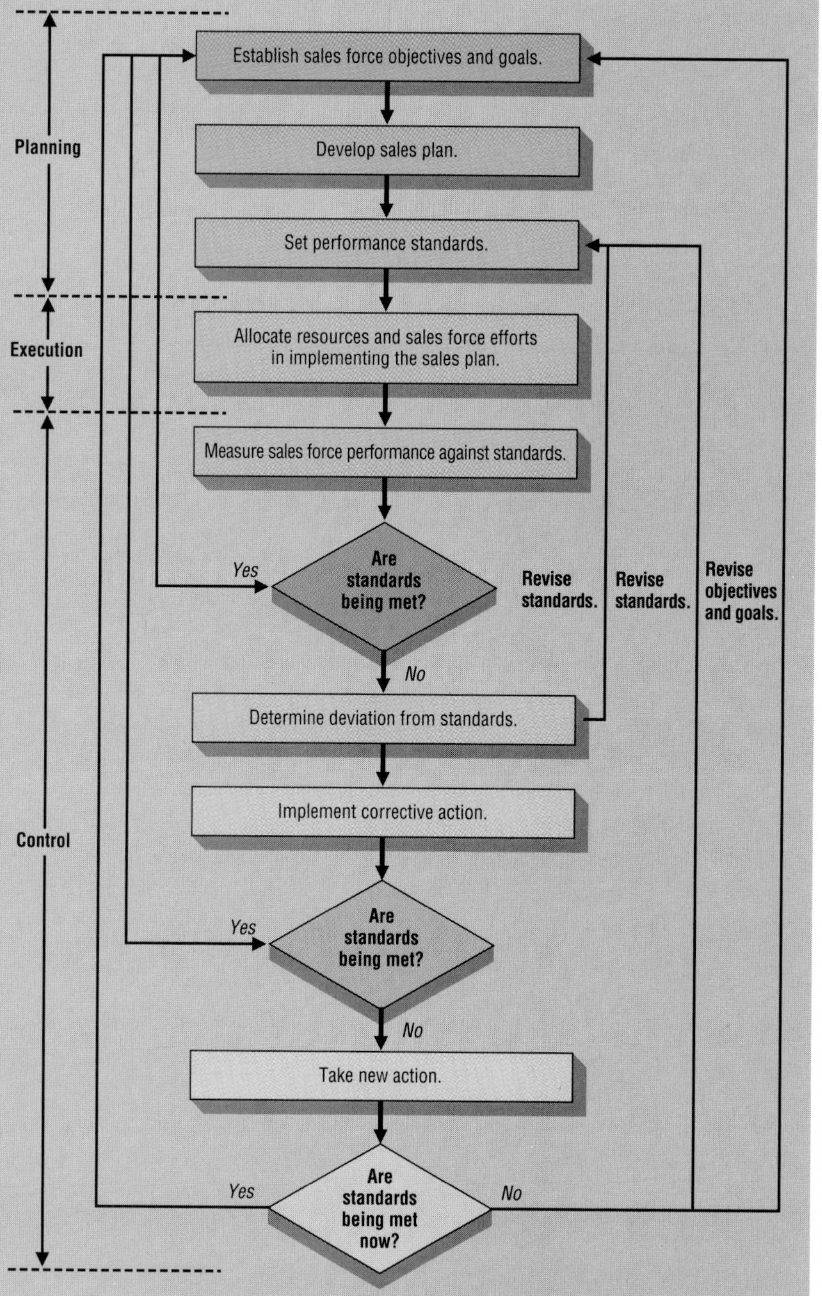

Source: Adapted from *Professional Sales Management*, by R. E. Anderson, J. F. Hair, and A. J. Bush, copyright 1988 by McGraw-Hill. Reproduced with permission of McGraw-Hill.

Exhibit 19.4

Example of a District Sales Manager's Yearly Appraisal

Name: Ray Adams

Name of Rep.: Jim Zamanek　　Territory: 014

Skills	Outstanding	Satisfactory	Unsatisfactory
Product Knowledge			
1. Company products	[ ]	[×]	[ ]
2. Competitive	[ ]	[×]	[ ]
3. Technical vocabulary	[ ]	[ ]	[×]
Overall Planning			
1. Planning sales presentation	[ ]	[×]	[ ]
2. Customer call programs	[ ]	[×]	[ ]
3. Call backs	[ ]	[×]	[ ]
4. Use of daily written plan	[ ]	[×]	[ ]
Overall Sales Skills			
1. Listening skills	[ ]	[×]	[ ]
2. Ability to sell without pressure	[ ]	[×]	[ ]
3. Ability to overcome objections	[ ]	[×]	[ ]
4. Ability to ask for the business	[ ]	[×]	[ ]
5. Clear, well-developed presentation	[×]	[ ]	[ ]
Retail Calls			
1. Planning	[ ]	[×]	[ ]
2. Rapport	[ ]	[×]	[ ]
3. Knows people	[ ]	[×]	[ ]
4. Checks, rotates stock	[ ]	[×]	[ ]
5. Aggressively sells deals	[ ]	[×]	[ ]
6. Good shelf space	[ ]	[×]	[ ]
7. Obtains promotions	[×]	[ ]	[ ]
Personal Traits			
1. Attitude	[ ]	[×]	[ ]
2. Ego	[ ]	[×]	[ ]
3. Empathy	[ ]	[×]	[ ]
4. Appearance	[×]	[ ]	[ ]
5. Conference participation	[ ]	[×]	[ ]
6. Self-improvement	[ ]	[×]	[ ]
7. Human relations	[ ]	[×]	[ ]
8. Management potential	[ ]	[×]	[ ]
9. Paperwork	[ ]	[ ]	[×]

Sales

1. Sales potential: [×] Growing [ ] Static [ ] Losing
2. Actual sales: $ 1,352,00 This year; $ 1,202,000 Last year
3. Percentage improvement: 11 % This year; 8 % Last year
4. Meeting individual product quota: 83 No. Quota: 81 No. Met

General

1. Is the person working at potential: × Yes ___ No Why? See attached
2. Is the person devoting time necessary to maintain and improve sales territory? × Yes ___ No Why? See attached

Source: Charles Futrell, *Sales Management* (Chicago, IL: The Dryden Press, 1988), p. 703.

district, branch, or field sales manager; sales supervisor; and key salesperson.

The organization of a sales force can be viewed from five perspectives: geographic organization, product organization, market organization, functional organization, and hybrid organization. Recruiting and selecting salespeople for each type of organization is an important sales management function, as is matching the proper method of compensation—straight salary, straight commission, or salary plus incentive program—with the proper recruit within each of these organizational formats.

The sales manager's involvement in training is generally dictated by three criteria: the cost of the training, the average length of the training period within a given industry, and the type of training program to be developed. Training itself is a high-cost item in the sales management budget of a company. Providing the most effective training program for the dollar is thus an area of primary concern for the sales manager. Sales managers should use tools such as appraisal forms and a list of performance criteria to gauge the performance of their sales forces.

Key Terms

Compensation Plan Method by which a salesperson is rewarded

Efficiency Focus on costs and economical use of resources

Effectiveness Results-oriented assessment of whether the organization's objectives are achieved

Management The planning, implementation, and control of the personal selling component of the promotional variable in the marketing mix

Recruitment The process of seeking out potential applicants, discussing the company with them, and encouraging them to apply for a sales position

Sales Manager A person who plans, directs, and controls the personal selling activities of a business; duties include recruiting, selecting, training, equipping, assigning, routing, supervising, paying, and motivating salespeople

Selection The process of choosing which candidates have the best qualifications and the greatest aptitude for a particular job

Review Questions

1. Identify the characteristics of an effective sales manager.
2. What are the basic responsibilities of a sales manager?
3. Compare the qualities needed for selling with those needed for managing.
4. How has the role of the sales manager changed in the last decade?
5. What can a sales manager do to motivate salespeople?
6. Contrast the advantages and disadvantages of straight salary, straight commission, and combination compensation plans.

Table 19.4

Sales Force Performance Evaluation

Quantitative Measures

Sales Results

Orders:
Number of orders obtained
Average order size (units or dollars)
Batting average (orders ÷ sales calls)
Number of orders canceled by customers

Sales volume:
Dollar sales volume
Unit sales volume
By customer type
By product category
Translated into market share
Percent of sales quota achieved

Margins:
Gross margin
Net profit
By customer type
By product category

Customer accounts:
Number of new accounts
Number of lost accounts
Percent of accounts sold
Number of overdue accounts
Dollar amount of accounts receivable
Collections made of accounts receivable

Sales Efforts

Sales calls:
Number made on current customers
Number made on potential new accounts
Average time spent per call
Number of sales presentations
Selling time versus nonselling time
Call frequency ratio per customer type

Selling expenses:
Average per sales call
As percent of sales volume
As percent of sales quota
By customer type
By product category
Direct selling expense ratios
Indirect selling expense ratios

Customer service:
Number of service calls
Displays set up
Delivery cost per unit sold
Months of inventory held by customer type
Number of customer complaints
Percent of goods returned

Qualitative Measures

Sales-related activities:
Territory management: sales call preparation, scheduling, routing, and time utilization
Marketing intelligence: new-product ideas, competitive activities, new customer preferences
Follow-ups: use of promotional brochures and correspondence with current and potential accounts
Customer relations
Report preparation and timely submission

Selling skills:
Knowing the company and its policies
Knowing competitors' products and sales strategies
Use of marketing and technical backup teams
Understanding of selling techniques
Customer feedback (positive and negative)
Product knowledge
Customer knowledge
Execution of selling techniques
Quality of sales presentations
Communication skills

Table 19.4
Continued

Personal characteristics:
Cooperation, human relations, enthusiasm, motivation, judgment, care of company property, appearance, self-improvement efforts, patience, punctuality, initiative, resourcefulness, health, sales management potential, ethical and moral behavior

Source: R. E. Anderson, J. F. Hair, and A. J. Bush, *Professional Sales Management* (New York: McGraw-Hill Book Co., 1988), p. 519.

7. What are perks?
8. What is the value of sales training?
9. List some common sources for obtaining sales recruits.

Discussion Questions

1. A good salesperson does not always make a good sales manager. Discuss some of the changes and prerequisites needed to make the adjustment.
2. What extent of planning is conducted at each level of sales management?
3. "Sales management in international markets is the same as it is in the United States." Explain whether you think this statement is right or wrong.
4. Give examples of why a company might organize around a functional specialization, a geographical specialization, a product specialization, or a customer specialization.
5. Why do sales managers feel that they, rather than the personnel department, should select the salespeople? Are there any reasons why a firm might put the personnel department in charge of hiring salespeople or even sales managers?
6. Discuss why salespeople's performance should be evaluated.
7. Discuss the proper procedures for evaluating performance. Assuming that you are sales manager, how often would you plan to conduct a performance evaluation of each of your salespeople?
8. Discuss what you consider to be the most important incentives sales managers should provide to increase productivity.
9. Discuss two key functions of a sales manager.

Case 19.1

A New Method of Compensating Employees

Peter Howell, vice president of sales, is eager to design a new compensation plan for the salespeople in his company because of the many complaints and concerns over inequity in remuneration. Three salespeople have left the company, declaring the compensation quite unfair and discouraging.

The curent compensation system is a combination of straight salary and commission. As an added incentive, this system also provides for standardized reimbursement of a limited amount of expenses. Each salesperson is given the same allowance each month to cover such expenses as travel and entertainment. Expenses exceeding this amount become the responsibility of the salesperson.

A recent occurrence brought to the attention of upper management was when the highest producer for the quarter gained an increase in individual expenses, receiving full reimbursement for excessive expenditures as an additional reward. Many of the other salespeople felt denied, especially when they were serving smaller territories of less potential or were in the process of becoming established. Although the successful salespeople have realized promising long-term returns for the company, it had never been a company policy to provide full reimbursement under particular circumstances.

In light of the high turnover rate of top salespeople, the sales manager decided that redesigning the compensation system to provide fairness and equity was essential to revitalize morale among the sales staff.

1. How do you evaluate the manner in which the company deals with the reimbursement of expenses?
2. What changes in the reimbursement of salespeople's expenses would you recommend to the sales manager?
3. What types of incentives could be offered to improve employee morale?

Case 19.2

A Coordinated Effort

Mike Douglas, a sales representative for a major pharmaceutical and cosmetics firm, has complained to upper management that some of the other departments have too much power and influence over the sales force. According to Mike, they constantly make demands on the salespeople and other upper-level executives to participate in job assignments that are not related to sales.

The marketing research department is requiring that the sales force conduct research on the competition and provide feedback as often as once a month. More specifically, the researchers want the salespeople to talk to the buyers on a regular basis and allocate time in their daily schedule to identify problem areas and document findings for review.

Case 19.2
Continued

Mike strongly disagrees with these demands and feels that it is their job to be in tune with changing market conditions and serve in an advisory capacity, offering suggestions for change and improvement. Furthermore, he has expressed concern for the time allocation needed for such an assignment in addition to conducting their selling function.

The sales manager has discussed the positions and job assignments with the sales force and has encouraged the salespeople to work together and coordinate research efforts toward serving customers' needs to the utmost. According to the sales manager, input is vital from all perspectives and levels as the organization strives to maintain a leadership position in the marketplace.

1. Is it important that the sales department be involved in research?
2. The situation calls for clarification of job assignments. Discuss some of the activities to be conducted with each function.
3. Discuss the importance of coordination among departments in response to serving customers' needs.

Notes

1. Thomas N. Ingram and Raymond W. LaForge, *Sales Management: Analysis and Decision Making* (Chicago, IL: The Dryden Press, 1989), p. 2.
2. Charles Futrelly, *Sales Management*, 2nd ed. (Chicago, IL: The Dryden Press, 1988), p. 16.
3. Ingram and LaForge, *Sales Management* . . . , p. 1. The job characteristics and environmental situations are adapted from Rolph E. Anderson and Bert Rosenbloom, "Eclectic Sales Management: Strategic Response to Trends in the Eighties," *Journal of Personal Selling and Sales Management*, November 1982, pp. 41–46; and Bert Rosenbloom and Rolph E. Anderson, "The Sales Manager: Tomorrow's Super Marketer," *Business Horizons*, March/April 1984, pp. 50–56.
4. American Marketing Association, 1990.
5. R. E. Anderson, J. F. Hair, and A. J. Bush, *Professional Sales Management* (New York: McGraw-Hill Book Company, 1988), p. 4.
6. Ibid., p. 6.
7. Ibid., p. 21.
8. Ibid., p. 159.
9. Allan J. Magrath, "Collaborative Marketing Comes of Age—Again," *Sales & Marketing Management*, September 1991, p. 61.
10. Ibid.
11. Ingram and LaForge, *Sales Management* . . . , p. 343.
12. Ibid., pp. 356, 359.
13. John Hafer, Ph.D., "Do You Get Back the Investment on Your Training Dollars?," *Personal Selling Power*, September 1991, p. 24.
14. Ingram and LaForge, *Sales Management* . . . , p. 394.
15. Ibid.
16. Hafer, "Do You Get Back the Investment . . . ," p. 24.
17. Anderson et al., *Professional Sales Management*, pp. 510–511.
18. Ingram and LaForge, *Sales Management* . . . , p. 651.

CHAPTER

20

Career Management

Knowledge Objectives

In this chapter, you will learn:

1. The nature of career management in preparing for a professional selling career
2. What to consider when setting career goals and selecting an employer and working environment
3. What components are necessary in preparing an effective résumé and cover letter
4. How to prepare for and successfully complete a job interview

Consider This

No career is a single buggy ride anymore. The one-company experience that marked our parents' generation is as mythical today as the corporate loyalty that nurtured it. Career paths must be self-cobbled, using a variety of vehicles to gain the experiences necessary for long-term success. Companies are in business to make money, not executives. The responsibility lies with you to develop the management skills that can earn the salary and life-style you wish to become accustomed to.

Roxanne Farmanfarmaian
Contributing editor of
*Working Woman**

*"How to Manage Your Career for Lifelong Success," *Working Woman*, October 1989, pp. 101–102.

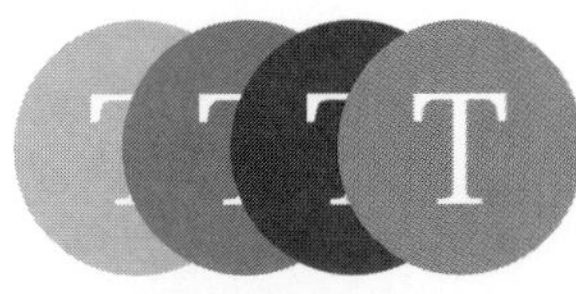

he purpose of this chapter is to provide assistance in preparing for a career in sales. This chapter is divided into four sections. First, we will focus on planning and researching a selling career with emphasis in two areas: researching and realistically assessing yourself, and finding a sales position. Looking for an employer and a working environment that come as close as possible to meeting your career goal is the subject of the second section. Next, we offer assistance in developing a résumé and preparing a persuasive cover letter. The fourth section examines the job interview from six perspectives: (1) critical skills that stimulate interest in the candidate; (2) types of interviews; (3) questions commonly asked by recruiters; (4) questions to ask a recruiter; (5) interviewing predictors of rejection; and (6) letters pertaining to the interview process.

Planning and Researching a Sales Career

Facing Up to a Recruiter

One of these days, you'll be tapped on the shoulder by a recruiter scouting around for new management or sales talent. Or you may decide to initiate the process yourself. Either way, over the course of your career, one, or possibly several of these corporate gatekeepers may enter your life and come to know you in ways that people who ordinarily cross your path rarely do. How you prepare yourself for the experience—or ordeal, as some characterize it—could make the difference between moving the next step up in your career or finding yourself at a professional standstill because you've been written off as an unsuitable candidate.

Recruiters base their judgments on a number of considerations above and beyond the hard-core statistics of job skills, experience, education, and knowledge of an industry. They delve into your successes and failures; your capacity for leadership, team play, and independent action; your creative and intuitive skills; your energy level; the psychological factors that drive you to excel and compete (or be a plodder); and your ability to get along with people. They may also explore the quality of your family life and try to find out if you have any addictions that prevent you from performing optimally.[1]

Researching and Realistically Assessing Yourself

Imagine what it would be like to be a corporate recruiter whose job is to travel from campus to campus in search of outstanding students. Imagine what it must be like to see hundreds of students on a regular basis who are impeccably groomed, well rehearsed, and enthusiastic—in short, almost programmed to look alike. The following are examples of the most commonly heard statements from recruiters expressing their frustrations:

- "Sometimes I can't see any differences in candidates at all. It's as if someone has cloned them."
- "The hardest work I do is trying to distinguish one A student from another. They look alike, they think alike, they talk alike. It's almost frightening at some schools. I look forward to meeting the occasional eccentric just because he or she will be memorable."[2]

Of course, recruiters do not believe that students actually are all the same. When interviewed privately, however, recruiters admit that many graduates make no attempt to be memorable. Some students, however, have an ability to integrate communication and sales skills in ways that most college graduates cannot; the following guidelines will help you be more memorable and more appealing, so that you can gain the competitive edge that will lead to the desired sales position[3]:

1. *Examine your goals and objectives, and decide what you want to do and where you want to do it.* As an applicant, you must sell your way into a job that meets your career goals and objectives. This can be a source of motivation and satisfaction.
2. *Review all your work experience (part time, summer, and volunteer), extracurriculur activities, hobbies, and awards.* Describe each in terms of the job title or function, responsibilities, skills learned or used, areas of satisfaction or frustration, special likes and dislikes, areas of growth, contributions made, and personal achievements and accomplishments. Look for patterns and trends throughout your job history and identify the skills you most enjoy using.
3. *Assess yourself in terms of creativity, leadership qualities, communication skills, interpersonal skills, technical skills, and so forth.* You must recognize the value of your contribution to the job as well as to the organizations to which you belong. Do not downplay or exaggerate what you have done. Instead of saying, "I handed out advertising flyers that I designed when I worked for a tiny sportswear shop—it was no big deal," think about the experience in this manner: "When I worked for a sports apparel shop, I created and distributed advertising flyers that brought the store an average of $800 a month in increased sales for a 3-month period. In addition to the $2,400 of additional revenue generated, I saved them another $500 over a year's period by devising a procedure to distribute the flyers that increased both coverage and expediency."
4. *Analyze your strengths, weaknesses, personal aspirations, work values, attitudes, and expectations.* In assessing these areas, consider the impact you have made in your jobs, classes, professional or social organizations, and influence on others. Specifically, how did you make a difference? What common threads or

Sales Professional Spotlight

Is professional selling a good career choice for a hard-working person who wants to gain personal satisfaction and financial security? If you were to ask Mike Assumma, his answer would be "Yes."

When asked how he got started in sales, Mike replied: "I always wanted to be in marketing, ever since I was attending community college. And after selling at the retail level and enjoying it, I felt strongly about pursuing a career in sales. Realizing that my interest was not in retail selling, I ventured to seek industrial sales experience with several companies over the last 6 years."

Mike finally launched a sales career with Climet Industrial Instruments in southern California. "I was really impressed with Climet and felt it was a strong, growing company to work for, on both domestic and international levels." Climet is a leading manufacturer of particle counters and semiconductors, selling to a variety of industries throughout the world.

Mike recalls his first days with Climet and the excitement of his first big sale. "That same personal satisfaction is still felt even in my most recent sale," he states. Sales success is based on performance. "I strive to keep my performance at the highest level by constantly setting attainable and measurable objectives for myself and my salespeople." His work with Climet also involves managing resources, which includes providing leadership for, motivating, and evaluating the sales representatives. He stresses the importance of interacting with other departments, particularly engineering, to gain a competitive edge by coordinating internal strengths.

To be successful in selling, a salesperson must have a strong working relationship with customers after developing a climate of trust. Also, it is important to be an outstanding communicator. "I spend a lot of time interacting with the decision makers and buyers who use our products," he says. He views salespeople as VIPs, performing a very important function as problem solvers. Mike works hard to maintain customer satisfaction, offering suggestions for improving efficiency and enhancing profits by using specific products. He advises his customers on where to allocate funds for maximum gain.

Persistence and mental and physical strength are the qualities Mike finds most important for successful salespeople. His top performers work harder, study more, and are generally self-driven. Sometimes salespeople face situations with little training and expose themselves to "hard knocks." Successful salespeople know how to deal with rejection and have learned to bounce back in difficult situations. Financial gain may also be important to some salespeople; however, he finds that the need for achievement seems to be a more prominent motivation among most successful salespeople.

Finally, Mike offers advice to students pursuing a sales career. "You must first understand who you are, then choose an industry that you are excited about and comfortable with, since each industry requires different assignments and preparation. There are many techniques and methods to professional selling, but you must develop your own style. A career in selling is not all glamour; it entails hard work and dedication." He stresses the importance of a good education. "Although it is not a prerequisite to have a graduate degree, it has helped me tremendously in acquiring a solid foundation."

patterns can you see among these experiences? What impact are you making in your current life situation?

Think about some of the people you admire and use as models for your behavior. Ask yourself: What is it about these individuals that I respect or emulate? What do I have in common with them? Who are my mentors? What personal qualities are part of my self-image? What do I like about myself? If I were to change one thing about myself, what would it be?

Review the skills learned in this textbook and include them in your analysis of strengths and weaknesses, always focusing on what short- and long-term goals you have set for yourself to turn sales communication weaknesses into strengths. An ability to use sales communication skills to acquire a sales position is the first major step in setting yourself apart from other applicants and placing yourself on the cutting edge.

5. *Review your educational background (classes taken, projects, major and minor areas of study).* Match your course strengths to a sales position and the company's needs. For instance, if you are an engineering major with a marketing minor, you should describe how the skills you have learned in a professional selling course have prepared you for a position in technical sales.

Self-assessment is a process of self-examination that hopefully will be repeated throughout your life. When you use self-assessment as a positive tool by incorporating the skills learned in Chapter 4, you will discover that the process helps you continue to develop sales competence in four ways[4]:

1. *Increase your confidence level, particularly during the job search.* Nurturing yourself by reviewing your strengths will help you remain balanced, centered, and confident.
2. *Polish your skills.* Learning and maintaining effective sales communication skills involves both continual use and periodic reassessment of how well your interpersonal and sales skills are integrated. You will want to take refresher courses while on the job to update and renew your sales communication competence.

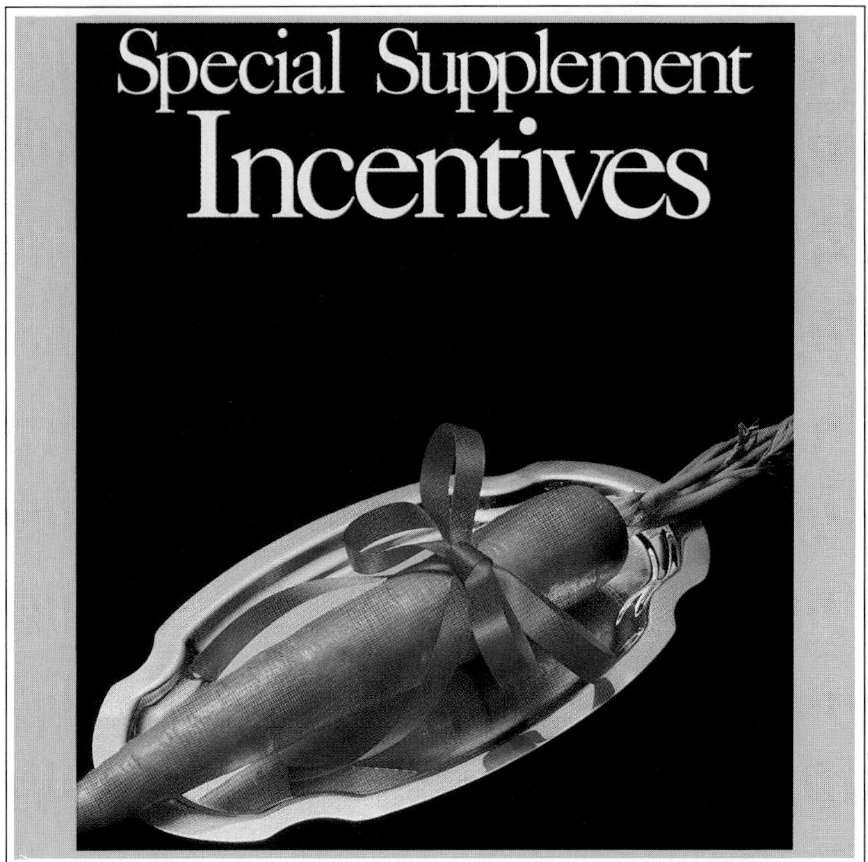

3. *Stay in touch with your changing self, especially with your maturing goals, values, and interests.* As you progress in your career, your life-style will undoubtedly change. Timely, periodic reassessment will help you make such changes. For example, if you plan to buy a house, you may want to change territories to be closer to where you live. If you plan to start a family, you may want predictable hours or scheduling flexibility.
4. *Make sound employment decisions and job changes.* You may be ready to move on, and reassessment can help you realize that you want to change jobs. If this is the case, then you can pinpoint likes and dislikes about your current job and what expectations you have for future positions. You can establish criteria for evaluating the organizations you are considering and each job offer you receive.

Finding Sales Jobs

There are six major sources for finding a sales position: college placement offices and career centers, executive search firms, employment agencies and placement services, professional associations, informal networks, and advertisements. We will consider the benefits and purposes of each.

College Placement Offices and Career Centers

Few agencies are as effective, well prepared, and inexpensive as placement offices on college campuses. College placement officers are generally experienced in various phases of personnel testing, counseling, and evaluation. Therefore, they are capable of recommending job opportunities that may not have been considered by the applicant. The placement officer's primary function is to match employers' needs with students' abilities.

Career centers usually host corporate recruiters who visit campuses in search of field sales personnel. The placement office or career center will schedule prospective applicants for interviews. Usually, the recruiter will interview a student once or twice on campus. Students who are considered appropriate prospects are invited to continue the interviewing process at the company offices.

The astute student will take advantage of the services offered by campus placement offices and career centers. Interviewing with as many recruiters as possible will help build confidence and refine communication skills.

Executive Search Firms

Executive search firms specialize in specific jobs or administrative levels and frequently handle placements and transfers for positions that pay in the six-figure range. Individuals who have several years of experience, who are trying to improve their position, or who are unemployed are the most frequent users of executive search firms. Placement fees are usually high.

Employment Agencies and Placement Services

Employment agencies frequently specialize in specific technical areas, such as sales, engineering, or computers. They also charge a fee for their services, which is usually based on the new employee's first-year salary. Employment agencies also act as intermediaries in matching the prospective employee with interested firms.

Professional Associations

A person who is about to enter the job market should consider joining a professional association at the local, state, regional, or national level. Not only do such organizations provide an excellent opportunity to network with one's colleagues, they also frequently have résumé exchanges at their annual conferences and conventions.

Advertisements

The classified ad sections of newspapers are the most common source of entry-level positions. Many opportunities also are advertised in professional journals, trade magazines, and trade papers such as *The Wall Street Journal*.

Selecting an Employer and Working Environment

Perhaps the most important factor in seeking a professional selling career or in making a career change is to approach the task optimistically and systematically. The first step in selecting an employer involves idealizing the kind of sales position you prefer. More specifically, you should describe your fantasies about preferences, including details about the kind of organization and work environment; the type of people; ideal salary, compensation, and fringe benefit package; travel possibilities; and any other areas that pertain to your perception of your ideal job.

Once you have created the ideal job profile, according to Karen Dowd, director of placement for the Darden Graduate School of Business at the University of Virginia in Charlottesville, the next step is to answer these questions before seeking an employer:

- What motivates you to do more—and better—work?
- What keeps you going?
- How important are feedback and praise? Status and prestige?
- Do you look for the thrill in meeting new challenges?
- Are you spurred on by money?
- How important is job security?
- How would you prioritize the promise of financial independence, retirement benefits, promotions, and opportunities for advancement and recognition?
- What kind of selling philosophy are you most comfortable with?
- Do you crave intellectual stimulation and having opportunities for learning additional skills?
- Are you excited about implementing new ideas, having new experiences, or being your own boss?[5]

The third step involves looking for an employer and a working environment that come as close as possible to meeting these career goals. Dowd suggests that a person consider the following factors:

On Selecting a Company

- Annual growth rate
- Number of employees
- Size of sales force and sales support staff
- Amount of sales revenue by territory
- Industry standing
- Type of industry—manufacturing, service, growth-oriented, stability of corporate philosophy and mission
- Training programs and ongoing training programs
- Major challenges and future directions
- Location
- Relocation benefits, such as salary, bonus, health insurance, daycare facilities, spouse relocation, and tuition reimbursement
- Management style

On Describing Your Ideal Work Environment

- Importance of flexible time
- Mobility to come and go
- Camaraderie among fellow employees
- Office appearance and decor
- Your own secretary or assistant
- Working alone or as part of a team
- High security or high-risk challenges
- Supervising or being supervised
- Low or high pressure
- Size of organization—"mom-and-pop" size or corporate giant
- Attitude of company toward sales department

Developing a Résumé and a Cover Letter

The Résumé

A *résumé* is a concise summary of a person's qualifications. When prepared properly, it conveys a positive message about the individual's skills and accomplishments that relates to or matches the job being sought. The purpose of the résumé is to secure an interview.

Employers often skim rather than read résumés. Therefore, it is vital that information be focused, organized, and well written. An effective résumé and cover letter communicate who the individual is and what that person wants. Before you actually write the résumé, a thorough inventory of skills and experience should be compiled. Sandra Grundfest, former assistant director of career services at Princeton University and now a private career and educational consultant, suggests that you develop an inventory in the following manner[6]:

1. List all activities in which you have been involved during your college years (do not highlight high school interests unless they were pursued in college).
2. Include work experience, mentioning both unpaid internships and paid jobs; extracurricular activities; and community service.
3. Using a separate sheet of paper for each experience, record the following information:
   A. Name of organization and city and state in which it is located, if not your campus
   B. Your title and position, dates, and length of time involved
   C. Functions and activities you performed, including both assigned and volunteer tasks
   D. Day-to-day as well as special assignments

   After making a specific list of your activities and accomplishments for each experience, cross out those you would prefer to avoid in a future job, either because you did not like them or because you felt that you were not competent to perform them. Place a star beside the activities you enjoyed most and in which you felt the most pride. These are the activities you should stress in your résumé.

Before writing a résumé, it will help to understand general guidelines, possible formats, and components.

General Guidelines

The Career Center at California State Polytechnic University in Pomona, California, offers these general guidelines for writing a résumé:

A résumé should be:

- Accurate—Up-to-date and true
- Correct—Appropriate grammar, spelling, and punctuation
- Pertinent—All information should relate to job objective
- Positive—Show your best side; don't be negative
- Active—Describe duties and skills using verbs such as those listed in Table 20.1
- Organized—Key information should be easy to find
- Neat—Clean, unwrinkled, and free of stray marks
- Concise—Short and to the point
- Consistent—Set up a format in each section; follow it diligently
- Personalized—Select the best format for you

Do not use:

- First-person pronouns (*I, me, my*)
- Slang or little-known buzz words
- Trite expressions
- Too many numbers and dates
- Negative words
- Abbreviations

For a person just entering a profession, a one-page résumé is preferable. If the applicant has extensive work experience or abilities and credentials related to the job objective, a two-page résumé may be necessary.

Choosing a Format

The three most commonly used résumé formats are the chronological, functional, and targeted types. Any of these types may be altered to fit an individual's specific needs. A person should remember to include only information pertinent to the job objective.

Chronological résumé. A chronological résumé is the most frequently used format, in which a person arranges qualifications by category in reverse chronological order (the most recent activity listed first). An

Table 20.1

Action Words

Accomplish	Contracted	Expanded	Monitored	Restored
Accounted for	Contributed	Expedited	Motivated	Revamped
Accumulated	Controlled	Experienced	Navigated	Reviewed
Achieved	Cooperated	Financed	Negotiated	Revised
Acquired	Coordinated	Fixed	Notified	Routed
Activated	Corrected	Forecasted	Obtained	Scheduled
Adapted	Correlated	Formed	Operated	Screened
Administered	Corresponded	Formulated	Ordered	Secured
Advanced	Counseled	Founded	Organized	Selected
Advertised	Created	Gathered	Originated	Served
Advised	Criticized	Generated	Overcame	Set up
Allocated	Debugged	Guided	Oversaw	Showed
Analyzed	Decreased	Handled	Participated	Simplified
Appraised	Defined	Headed	Performed	Sold
Approved	Delegated	Identified	Persuaded	Solved
Arbitrated	Deleted	Implemented	Pinpointed	Sorted
Arranged	Delivered	Improved	Pioneered	Sparked
Assembled	Demonstrated	Increased	Planned	Specified
Assessed	Designed	Informed	Prepared	Speeded
Assisted	Detailed	Initialized	Presented	Sponsored
Assumed	Determined	Initiated	Processed	Stimulated
Assured	Developed	Innovated	Procured	Streamlined
Attended	Devised	Inspected	Produced	Strengthened
Audited	Diagnosed	Inspired	Programmed	Structured
Augmented	Directed	Installed	Promoted	Studied
Authorized	Discovered	Instituted	Proposed	Submitted
Automated	Dispensed	Instructed	Protected	Succeeded
Built	Disproved	Integrated	Proved	Summarized
Calculated	Distributed	Interfaced	Provided	Supervised
Changed	Documented	Interpreted	Publicized	Supplied
Charted	Doubled	Interviewed	Purchased	Supported
Clarified	Drafted	Invented	Qualified	Surveyed
Coded	Drew up	Investigated	Raised	Tailored
Collected	Earned	Involved	Realized	Taught
Communicated	Edited	Issued	Received	Tested
Compared	Educated	Justified	Recommended	Tracked
Compiled	Effected	Keynoted	Reconciled	Trained
Completed	Eliminated	Launched	Reconstructed	Transformed
Composed	Employed	Lectured	Recruited	Translated
Compounded	Engaged	Led	Reduced	Tripled
Computed	Engineered	Logged	Referred	Troubleshot
Conceived	Enhanced	Made	Refined	United
Conducted	Enlarged	Maintained	Rendered	Updated
Configured	Enriched	Managed	Reorganized	Upgraded
Conserved	Equipped	Marketed	Reported	Utilized
Considered	Established	Mastered	Represented	Validated
Consolidated	Evaluated	Measured	Requested	Verified
Constructed	Examined	Mediated	Required	Won
Consulted	Executed	Modified	Researched	Wrote

Source: "Action Words," *Résumé Writing Guide* (Pomona, CA: The Career Center, California Polytechnic University, Spring 1989), p. 14.

objective can be included but is not required. This type of résumé is generally appropriate for recent college graduates with limited job experience or with a progressive job history related to their career goal. Exhibit 20.1 is a chronological résumé.

Exhibit 20.1

Sample Chronological Résumé

JOHN MARTIN

Campus Address (until 12/18/92)	Home Address
1212 Treadaway, Apt. 12	1422 Fairmount Avenue
Abilene, Texas 79602	Fort Worth, Texas 76104
(915) 873-2642	(817) 924-0601

EDUCATION — McMURRY COLLEGE, Abilene, Texas: B.A. expected December 1992
Major in English with a broad range of business, including statistics, economics, marketing, and management
GPA: 3.5 in major
Marjorie Daw award for best prose article, spring 1992

CAMPUS ACTIVITIES — President Sigma Tau Delta (English Club), 1991-1992
Vice president, Student Council, 1990-1991
Assistant intramurals coordinator, 1990-1992

WORK EXPERIENCE — WALL STREET JOURNAL, Dallas, Texas
Research Assistant, Summer 1992
* Researched general business news items
* Researched information in information data bases on assignment from editors

JUICYBURGER, INC., Butternut St. Store, Abilene,Texas
Assistant Store Manager, summer 1991 to summer 1992
* Supervised and trained sales staff members
* Maintained store inventory, purchased necessary supplies
* Handled night audits of daily sales

BERT'S AUTO SUPPLY, Fort Worth, Texas
Counter Salesperson, summer 1990
* Filled customer orders
* Maintained inventory of parts
* Stocked parts
* Maintained customer relations in person and over telephone

PERSONAL INTERESTS — Reading, playing racquetball, travel in England and Germany, listening to music, playing the guitar

REFERENCES — Available upon request

Advantages:

- Highlights most recent experience
- Employers are comfortable with it
- Most widely used of three styles
- Easy to write and read
- Achievements can be displayed regardless whether a job objective is stated

Disadvantages:

- Highlights lack of experience
- Calls attention to time gaps
- Stresses recent experience, which may be a hindrance if changing job or careers

Functional résumé. A functional résumé emphasizes an individual's qualifications by skill areas, allowing accomplishments, strengths, interests, and abilities to be grouped by functional job tasks. This type of résumé is especially valuable for people who are changing careers or integrating skills from a wide variety of life experiences, which would not be evident in a chronological résumé. The functional résumé usually begins with a skills section and ends with a work history. Exhibit 20.2 is a functional résumé.

Advantages:

- Draws attention to a person's accomplishments rather than when and where the achievements were made
- Deemphasizes time gaps in work history
- Allows greater flexibility in organizing and presenting skills gained through personal experience (such as spending a year studying abroad)
- Particularly useful for entry-level or reentry applicants whose employment is brief or scattered

Disadvantages:

- If not organized and developed properly, may appear confusing and lengthy
- Employers may prefer to see dates and employer names
- Some employers may be suspicious of this format because they think the résumé may be hiding gaps in the person's background

Targeted résumé. The targeted résumé emphasizes a specific position or job objective, the target. It focuses on the individual's capabilities and accomplishments that support his job target and removes all unrelated data. Exhibit 20.3 is a targeted résumé.

Exhibit 20.2

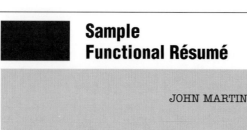

Sample Functional Résumé

JOHN MARTIN

Campus Address (until 12/18/92)	Home Address
1212 Treadaway, Apt. 12 Abilene, Texas 79602 (915) 873-2642	1422 Fairmount Avenue Fort Worth, Texas 76104 (817) 924-0601

JOB OBJECTIVE	An entry-level position in marketing, with special interest in market research and product planning
EDUCATION	McMURRY COLLEGE, Abilene, Texas: B.A. expected December 1992 Major in English with a broad range of business courses, including statistics, economics, marketing, and management GPA: 3.5 in major Marjorie Daw award for best prose article, spring 1992
SALES AND CUSTOMER RELATIONS	* Successfully turned unhappy shoppers into satisfied customers * Increased volume of sales an average of twenty percent in two unrelated retail businesses
RESEARCH AND PLANNING	* Drafted reports for market research publisher * Researched business data for national publishing company * Assisted in planning and projecting sales for a new retail outlet * Directed planning for various projects for student government while in college
LEADERSHIP AND TIME MANAGEMENT	* Maintained high grades while working 15-20 hours per week and being involved in campus activities and athletics * Trained and supervised sales staff * Organized and directed committees involved in campus projects.
WORK HISTORY	WALL STREET JOURNAL, Dallas, Texas Research Assistant, summer 1992 JUICYBURGER, Abilene, Texas Assistant Manager, summer 1991 to summer 1992 BERT'S AUTO SUPPLY, Fort Worth, Texas Counter Salesperson, summer 1990
CAMPUS ACTIVITIES	Vice president, Student Council President, Sigma Tau Delta Assistant intramurals coordinator
REFERENCES	Available upon request

Advantages:

- Can be impressive and powerful if a person has done the necessary research
- Can make an individual look like a natural candidate for the job

Sample Targeted Résumé

Exhibit 20.3

JOHN MARTIN

Campus Address (until 12/18/92)	Home Address
1212 Treadaway, Apt. 12	1422 Fairmount Avenue
Abilene, Texas 79602	Fort Worth, Texas 76104
(915) 873-2642	(817) 924-0601

JOB TARGET A marketing position in a consumer goods firm

EDUCATION McMURRY COLLEGE, Abilene, Texas: B.A. expected December 1992
Major: English

CAPABILITIES
* Research and analyze merchandising trends
* Judge consumer needs
* Plan services and products to satisfy customer needs
* Develop new personnel
* Mollify unhappy shoppers
* Gauge and implement marketing and advertising plans
* Use statistics as a tool to forecast sales

ACHIEVEMENTS
* Opened, marketed, and advertised a new retail store
* Turned unhappy shoppers into satisfied customers
* Increased sales at two different retail locations by an average of twenty percent
* Maintained a 3.5 GPA in major field while working15-20 hours per week and being involved in campus activities and athletics
* Researched business stories for a nationwide publication

WORK HISTORY
WALL STREET JOURNAL, Dallas, Texas
Research Assistant, summer 1992

JUICYBURGER, INC., Abilene, Texas
Assistant Store Manager, summer 1991-summer 1992

BERT'S AUTO SUPPLY, Fort Worth, Texas
Counter Salesperson, summer 1990

CAMPUS ACTIVITIES President of Sigma Tau Delta; vice president of the Student Council; assistant intramurals coordinator

REFERENCES Available upon request

- Projects one's abilities even though that person may not have directly related experience
- Allows a person to prepare a different résumé for each position applied for

Disadvantages:

- A person may not have enough experience to justify the achievements cited
- There is a tendency to embellish capabilities and achievements
- Descriptions may not match job target

Résumé Components

There are several parts to a résumé. Whichever format is used, the essential information needs to be included. A chronological résumé usually includes seven components in this order: (1) identification (personal data, including name, address, and phone number); (2) job objective, which is optional; (3) education; (4) campus activities; (5) work experience; (6) personal interests and skills; and (7) references or reference line. In a functional or targeted résumé, seven categories are usually included in the following order: (1) identification; (2) job objective or job target; (3) education; (4) skills, capabilities, and achievements; (5) work history; (6) campus activities (optional); and (7) reference line.

The Cover Letter

Without exception, directors of human resources and recruiters expect the résumés and letters of college graduates to be free of errors. One employment recruiter made this observation:

> There are few more important letters an individual will ever write than the job application letter. It should be perfect. We can understand when a letter from a shop supervisor exhibits an error or two, but not when the message comes from a college-trained man or woman. After all, if he or she is careless in a letter, what can we expect of his or her handling of our ledgers?[7]

An individual's letter needs to be accurate, concise, and complete.

The *cover letter* is a person's opportunity to articulate the relationship-driven philosophy and demonstrate a mastery of sales communication skills to obtain the first sales interview. You should think of a cover letter as the first contact with the potential employer, and think of the employer as a prospect who is waiting to buy. All six buying decisions must be affirmed, and it is up to you to match your ability (the product) with the potential employer's buying needs (the job position).

The cover letter is an extension of an individual's ability to communicate and persuade in a written context. The following guidelines may help you develop an effective cover letter:

1. The cover letter should be changed according to the advertisement being answered and the position for which the individual is applying.
2. If "excellent interpersonal skills" are part of the job description, then emphasize these skills in the letter.

3. The letter should arouse interest, reflect enthusiasm, and motivate the reader to read the résumé.
4. You should be customer- or relationship-driven in matching your letter to the reader's point of view. Match advantages and benefits to the reader's needs.
5. State the position being applied for and relate your qualifications to that position. You may refer to the résumé but should not repeat its contents.
6. Only a typewritten original letter should be sent with the résumé. Do not use a form, photocopied, or handwritten letter. Unless a high-quality laser printer is available, the applicant should not send a letter produced by a computer printer.
7. The letter should be addressed to a specific individual if possible. Otherwise, indicate a specific job title, such as Regional Sales Manager, rather than Personnel Officer or Director of Human Resources.
8. Unlike a sales letter to a customer, it is not necessary to state your intention to follow up after a certain period of time. This is particularly true if travel or long-distance telephone expenses are involved. It would be wise, however, to call or follow up if no reply has been received within 2 weeks from a local company or within 3 weeks from a national firm to which a résumé has been submitted.
9. Stationery and résumé paper should match in terms of weight, size, and shade. Using $8\frac{1}{2}'' \times 11''$ paper in white, off-white, ivory, or light gray is acceptable.

Exhibit 20.4 offers an example of an effective cover letter to accompany the chronological, functional, and targeted résumés provided in Exhibits 20.1, 20.2, and 20.3.

A persuasive cover letter usually has at least five paragraphs, each of which focuses on a specific objective.[8] An example of each paragraph is provided here:

First Paragraph

Function: Summarizes the applicant's major attributes and how that person can help the organization

Example:

Your very attractive advertisement in yesterday's *Wall Street Journal* seemed made to order for me . . . and I for the job. Your need is for an assistant manager for your Vienna subsidiary. The individual you want should have "thorough background in financial management, good marketing skills, and some fluency in German." I believe that I score at the top in all three areas.

Second Paragraph

Function: Emphasizes the individual's key attribute or selling point

Example:

My experience and educational background have given me excellent training in financial management and marketing. For two years, as an employee of a well-

Exhibit 20.4

Sample Cover Letter

1212 Treadaway, Apt. 12
Abilene, Texas 79682
(915) 873-2642

June 24, 1992

George Tyron
Director of Marketing Training
Wallace Publications Group, Inc.
1439 Santa Monica Boulevard
Los Angeles, California 90029

Dear Mr. Tyron:

In researching companies in the Directory of Training Programs, I discovered that your company seems to offer the type of marketing approach that I am hoping to become familiar with after I receive my degree from McMurry College this December. Having also been exposed to some of your publications, I am intrigued with your program's emphasis on market research, product planning, and the implementation of catalog sales. I believe that I am well-qualified for your program and hope that you will consider this packet as my application for it.

Even though my major is English, marketing has been a major focus of my college and work experience . I have a strong foundation in psychology, business, and quantitative methods. I have used this foundation in my work in retail stores and in my association with The Wall Street Journal.

I have considerable experience in merchandising through my summer jobs in retailing and have experienced first-hand customer frustration and anxiety. My ability to turn dissatisfied shoppers into satisfied customers has placed me in good standing with my previous employers.

I have enclosed my resume as a part of this packet. It provides specific information about my academic background and activities. I have been a contributing member of my campus community and expect to bring that same commitment and high energy level to my place of employment after graduation.

I would have liked to have discussed my opportunities with your company with one of your representatives on campus, but Wallace Publications was not represented on our campus this year. I hope I can arrange an interview with your firm toward the end of August, when I will be in the Los Angeles area before beginning my final semester in school. Please call me at the number indicated above so that we may arrange a time for an interview that is convenient with you.

Sincerely,
(Signature)
John Martin

known public relations firm, I was involved primarily in marketing entertainers. Financial management was my MBA area of concentration.

Third Paragraph

Function: Gives the applicant's second-level selling point; this might include experience, personal attributes, or education

Example:

My German is first-rate. For two years I attended graduate classes at the University of Heidelberg. From 1990 to the present I have compiled, summarized, and translated materials from German into English for researchers at the well-known research institute The Rand Corporation.

Fourth Paragraph

Function: Gives some indication of the applicant's personality, goals, and aspirations
Example:

In addition to this, I have served as a lecturer in the School of Business at the University of Southern California. In this capacity, I was in daily contact with dozens of individuals and found that I related very well with all of them. This ability, plus my complete understanding of German work habits, culture, and values, will permit me to do an outstanding job for your organization.

Fifth Paragraph

Function: Frequently referred to as an action paragraph; intended to secure a response
Example:

The enclosed résumé will provide some facts for you. However, I'm sure you want to learn more about me as an individual. I certainly want to know more about your organization. Please call me at (213) 394-2163 so that we may arrange a time for an interview to be held at your convenience.

Exhibit 20.5 shows the cover letter in complete form.

The Job Interview

When a positive response is received from the cover letter and résumé, the individual should be ready to succeed in the job interview. This section provides information about six facets of the job interview: (1) critical skills that stimulate interest in the candidate, (2) types of interviews, (3) questions commonly asked by recruiters, (4) questions to ask the recruiter, (5) interviewing predictors of rejection, and (6) letters pertaining to the interview process.

Critical Skills That Stimulate Interest in You as a Candidate

The skills involved in creating verbal and nonverbal rapport that were discussed in Chapter 10 are just as fundamental to succeeding in a job interview as they are in a sales interview. Reviewing those skills before the job interview will give an individual self-confidence and refresh the memory about the importance of rapport when meeting new people,

Exhibit 20.5

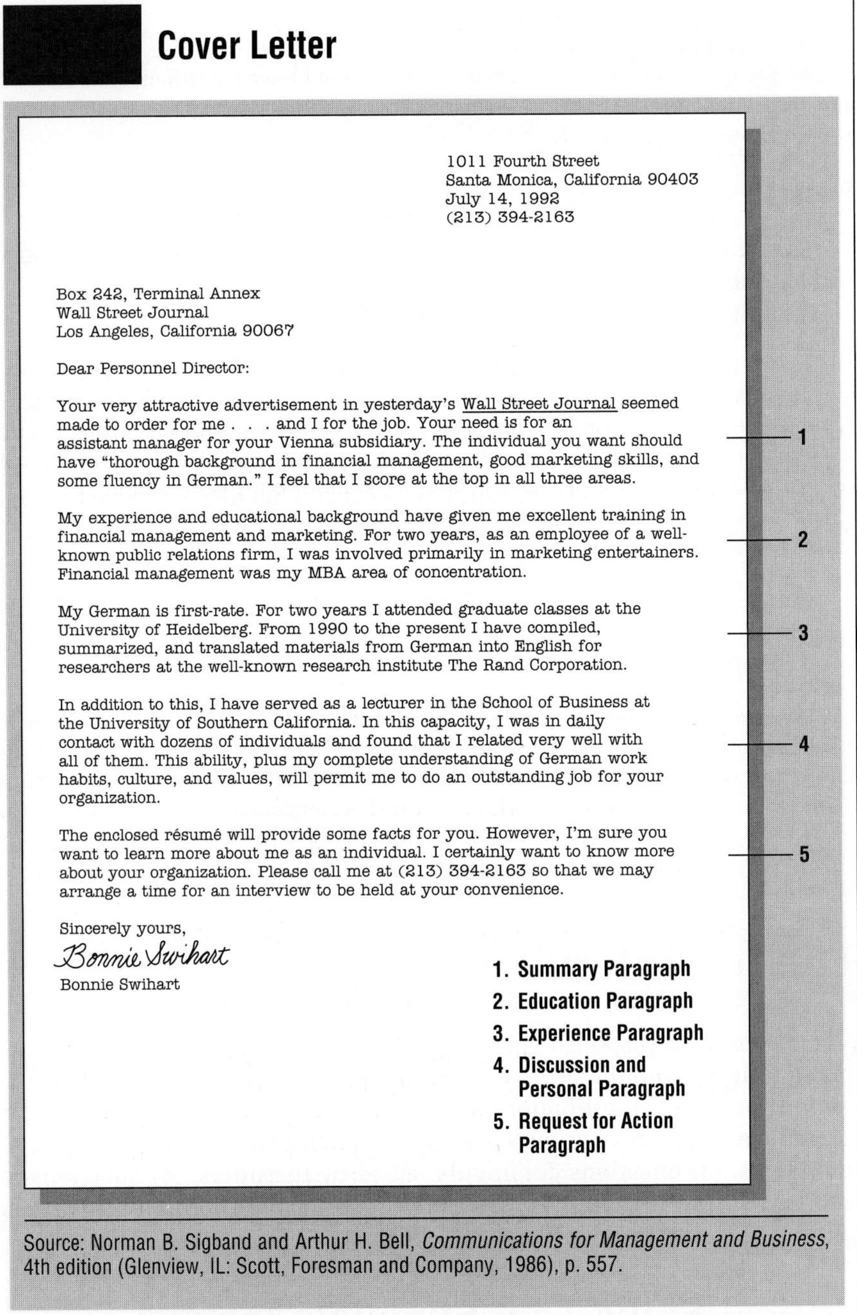

Cover Letter

1011 Fourth Street
Santa Monica, California 90403
July 14, 1992
(213) 394-2163

Box 242, Terminal Annex
Wall Street Journal
Los Angeles, California 90067

Dear Personnel Director:

Your very attractive advertisement in yesterday's Wall Street Journal seemed made to order for me . . . and I for the job. Your need is for an assistant manager for your Vienna subsidiary. The individual you want should have "thorough background in financial management, good marketing skills, and some fluency in German." I feel that I score at the top in all three areas. — 1

My experience and educational background have given me excellent training in financial management and marketing. For two years, as an employee of a well-known public relations firm, I was involved primarily in marketing entertainers. Financial management was my MBA area of concentration. — 2

My German is first-rate. For two years I attended graduate classes at the University of Heidelberg. From 1990 to the present I have compiled, summarized, and translated materials from German into English for researchers at the well-known research institute The Rand Corporation. — 3

In addition to this, I have served as a lecturer in the School of Business at the University of Southern California. In this capacity, I was in daily contact with dozens of individuals and found that I related very well with all of them. This ability, plus my complete understanding of German work habits, culture, and values, will permit me to do an outstanding job for your organization. — 4

The enclosed résumé will provide some facts for you. However, I'm sure you want to learn more about me as an individual. I certainly want to know more about your organization. Please call me at (213) 394-2163 so that we may arrange a time for an interview to be held at your convenience. — 5

Sincerely yours,

Bonnie Swihart

Bonnie Swihart

1. **Summary Paragraph**
2. **Education Paragraph**
3. **Experience Paragraph**
4. **Discussion and Personal Paragraph**
5. **Request for Action Paragraph**

Source: Norman B. Sigband and Arthur H. Bell, *Communications for Management and Business*, 4th edition (Glenview, IL: Scott, Foresman and Company, 1986), p. 557.

especially a recruiter who will assess communication skills. Tony Lee, senior editor of *The Wall Street Journal*, lists eight critical skills that excite recruiters about a candidate[9]:

1. Written communication skills
2. Decision-making skills

3. Positive attitude toward the work ethic
4. Oral communication skills
5. Judgment skills
6. Maturity
7. Well-developed work habits
8. Interpersonal skills

In the paragraphs that follow, some of the nation's top recruiters discuss each of these categories.[10]

Written Communication Skills

Wayne Davis, corporate staffing representative of Baxter Healthcare Corporation in Deerfield, Illinois, says: "There seems to be a marked decline in written communication skills among managers, and many companies are hoping to stop that descent by hiring students who can write." Robert Conner at Transamerica adds: "One of the saddest things we've seen of late among new graduates is an inability to write. We ask for writing samples and give writing tests . . . when students are invited to an on-site interview."

Decision-Making Skills

Irv C. Pfeiffer, IBM Corporation's Chicago-based college relations manager for the west and midwest, reports: "Knowing why a student decided on a certain major, college, or course work can communicate a sophisticated pattern of life-planning. . . . Be prepared to explain how and why you made those decisions as they relate to attaining your desired goals." Tami Simmons, assistant employment manager at Campbell Soup Company in Camden, New Jersey, recalls: "I say to students, 'Describe the last critical decision you made; what was your thought process and the outcome?' "

Positive Attitude toward the Work Ethic

Kersten Dwyer, recruiting manager at Oracle Group, a Belmont, California, software maker, has this to say: "Graduates we hire should be brilliant and pleasant to work with, but they should also be compulsive. In our intense environment, we need hard workers who can grow with the company. . . . People here need to be innovative. It's important for us to stay on the cutting edge." Another common characteristic that emerges among recruiters is a need for people who are self-starters, who strive for perfection, and who do more than what is required.

Oral Communication Skills

Finding a balance between the applicant who mumbles and the one who rambles and does not know when to stop talking is a critical factor for all recruiters. Other top considerations are an ability to think on one's feet, organize one's thoughts, and then present a logical argument that is easily understood. Again, Irv Pfeiffer at IBM responds: "A solid track record is the best guarantee of interview success, but only if you can articulate that record to recruiters. Excellence in oral communications often is the tie-breaker between top candidates."

Judgment Skills

This area is evaluated in many ways. Frequently students are asked to give illustrations of something they have identified as a potential problem and how they sought help from others to reach a solution. Ray Chapman at J. C. Penney reports that he assesses judgment skills by asking why a student chose one elective course over another. Tami Simmons at Campbell Soup indicates that a student shows a clear lack of judgment if "anyone asks about starting salaries early on or downgrades past jobs."

Maturity

Maturity is a difficult trait to identify in a 30- to 45-minute meeting and is usually appraised from a student's demeanor. At Baxter Healthcare, Wayne Davis says: "I see it in the depth of student answers when asked about career goals. . . . Are their responses thoughtfully considered before spoken?"

Well-Developed Work Habits

The area of work habits refers to specific techniques and aptitudes developed by students in past jobs. Wayne Davis asks: "Are they well organized? Do they use a daily to-do list? Do they have an impact on others through their presence?" Kathy Brumitt, college relations supervisor at Anheuser-Busch Company in St. Louis, wants to know: "Have they accomplished past work objectives, and how much did they have to stretch themselves?"

Interpersonal Skills

"People who are monosyllabic and can't present themselves well won't fit in anywhere," says M. Alana Demers at New Hampshire Public Service. Again, Wayne Davis asserts: "Our surveys show that executives who have advanced the fastest here have strong interpersonal skills." The student who can relate to all levels in the business world is the one, recruiters say, who is rewarded later with promotions and large paychecks.

Types of Interviews

Besides one-on-one interviews, there are many other types of interviews in which a candidate may participate. Some general types are the preliminary or screening interview, a panel interview, a group interview, and a conversational or informal interview.[11] A description of each type follows.

Preliminary or Screening Interview

A preliminary interview is used to determine whether or not the individual meets the minimum requirements for the position. It is also used to verify facts, fill in gaps, and probe into areas not mentioned in a person's cover letter or résumé.

Panel Interview

The panel interview is conducted with two or more interviewers. One person may ask all the questions, however. It is important for the individual to direct answers to all panel members by giving direct eye contact and acknowledging each person's presence. Using the SOFTENS technique described in Chapter 8 to make nonverbal contact with all panel members, regardless of how many are actually questioning the candidate, is an effective tool.

Group Interview

The group interview is used to disseminate information to a large number of candidates and sometimes to distinguish natural leaders. Because several candidates are interviewed at the same time, it is important to be memorable. Use verbal communication skills that were presented in Chapter 10 to establish contact and rapport with the interviewers, as well as the other candidates when appropriate.

Conversational or Informal Interview

When an individual's qualifications are clearly expressed in the résumé and cover letter, the recruiter may use an informal interview to determine communication skills, attitudes, interests, poise, and values. Usually the candidate will be encouraged to talk about anything except the job (such as hobbies, interests, vacations, or the weather).

Questions Commonly Asked by Recruiters

When preparing for an interview, it is important to consider answers to questions that may be asked. Usually, questions will cover such categories as personal goals, personal assessment, work attitudes, evaluation of the applicant's education, and career expectations. While the interviewer may ask questions from some or all of these categories, the applicant should be ready to respond to each question on this list (reprinted by permission of The Career Center at California State Polytechnic University, Pomona).

Typical Questions Asked College Seniors by Recruiters

A. *Personal Assessment*
   1. What are your short-range and long-range goals and objectives and how are you preparing to achieve them? (career related)
   2. What goals have you established for yourself in the next 5 years, 10 years? (noncareer related)
   3. What do you really want to do in life?
   4. What do you see yourself doing in the future?

5. What rewards are the most important to you in your chosen career?
6. What were your motivations in choosing the career for which you are prepared/preparing?
7. What salary expectations do you have—now, 5 years, 10 years from now?
8. What do you consider to be your strengths and weaknesses?
9. How would you describe yourself?
10. How do you think other people who know you describe you?
11. What motivates you to put forth your greatest effort? Why?
12. What supervisory or leadership roles have you held?
13. What are your hobbies or recreational activities?
14. Why should I hire you?

B. *Evaluation of Applicant's Education*
1. Why did you select your college or university?
2. What motivated you to choose your major?
3. What college subjects have you liked and why? What college subjects have you disliked and why? Tell me about your senior project.
4. If you could do so, how would you plan your academic studies differently? Why?
5. What changes would you make in your college or university?
6. Do you think your grades are a good indication of your academic achievement? Explain.
7. Describe your most rewarding college experience.
8. Describe your most unrewarding college experience.
9. If you were hiring a recent college graduate for this position, what qualities would you look for?
10. Have you been involved in extracurricular activities? Explain what you have learned from this type of participation.
11. Do you have plans for continued study or an advanced degree?

C. *Evaluation of Applicant's Work Experience*
1. Tell me about some of your work experiences. What have you liked most about a work experience and why? What have you liked least about a work experience and why?
2. How would you describe the ideal job for you following graduation?
3. What two or three factors are most important to you in your job?
4. How do you work under pressure?
5. In what kind of work environment are you most comfortable and why?
6. Describe the type of relationship that should exist between a supervisor and subordinates.
7. What qualities do you have that you think would make you successful in your chosen career?
8. How do you determine or evaluate success for you?

9. What do you think it takes to be successful in our organization?
10. In what significant ways do you think you can make a contribution to our organization?
11. Why did you leave your previous employer?

D. *Knowledge of the Employer*
   1. Why did you decide to seek a position with this organization?
   2. What do you know about our organization?
   3. What criteria are you using to evaluate the organization for which you want to work?
   4. What are your short-range and long-range career goals?
   5. Are you seeking employment in a particular organization? What type?
   6. Do you have a geographical preference? Why?
   7. Will you relocate? Does relocation bother you?
   8. Are you willing to travel?
   9. What salary level do you expect? Why?
   10. How is your previous experience applicable to what we do here?
   11. Are you applying to other organizations?
   12. Is there someone we can contact who is familiar with your activities?

Questions to Ask a Recruiter

Job interviews involve two-way communication, just as sales interviews do. When you are asked if you have any questions, take the opportunity to ask relevant, focused questions. The interviewers are probably assessing the type of questions you ask. Do not respond to the opportunity to ask questions by indicating that you have none.

If this is your first interview with a company, questions about paid vacations, holidays, sick leave, salary, and any benefits that allow a person to get away from work—such as "What kind of maternity leave do you offer?"—should be avoided. Questions that you might consider asking, as they apply to the specific situation, might include:

1. What are the major responsibilities of this position?
2. How would you describe a typical day in the life of a person holding this position?
3. What type of characteristics are you seeking most in the person who fills this position?
4. How would you describe your organizational structure, and to whom would I report?
5. What is your company's philosophy concerning upward mobility?
6. What is the typical career path in this field? How long is the average time it takes to get to ______ level?

7. What kind of training do you offer, specifically product and sales training? How do these two types of training differ?
8. What is the typical size of the territory I am expected to cover?
9. How much travel is normally expected? Do you provide a car?
10. What does your relocation policy include?
11. How many people have held this position? Why have they left?
12. What have you personally liked most about your company? What have you liked least about it?
13. How many people am I competing with for this position?
14. When do you expect to make a decision?
15. Where do we go from here?

Notice that all of these questions are open and neutral, enabling the applicant to elicit extended responses and details from the interviewer while at the same time demonstrating interest in the position in a supportive manner.

Employer's Expectations during the Interview

People have certain expectations that they would like to have met when they apply for jobs. The same is true for employers. The employer is looking for, or expecting, certain behaviors and responses during the interview process. It is on these expectations that the individual's performance will be judged.

A study of various employers has shown that there are a number of expectations to be met. There are three clusters of expectations that employers consider to be most important:

- *Cluster 1: Appearance*
  - Do you look like you belong in the job?
  - Is your appearance neat and clean?
  - Is the paperwork you present (applications, résumé, work samples) neat and clean?

- *Cluster 2: Attendance and Punctuality*
  - Are you on time daily and stay for the full day?
  - Are you back from breaks on time?

  Reliability
  - Will you do the work appropriately?
  - Are you a trustworthy employee?
  - Can you admit mistakes and accept criticism and instructions?

  Dependability
  - Can the employer depend on you to help in tight spots, such as when overtime is required?
  - Are you a regularly attending employee?
  - Are you willing to make sacrifices for improved business performance?

- *Cluster 3: Skills*
  - The things you can do immediately to help the employer meet the needs of the business

  Abilities
  - Transferable skills; things that you can learn to do without much training time—if you can type, you can probably learn to work other machines that require manual dexterity

Interviewing Predictors of Rejection

Exhibit 20.6 identifies factors during the interview that frequently lead to rejection. If a person can convert these factors into positive statements and behaviors, then interviewing success can be predicted.

Letters Pertaining to the Interview Process

"You never have a second chance to make a first impression." This axiom is as true for correspondence as it is for face-to-face selling and job interviews. Letters are statements of what and who you are. Therefore, your work should be autographed with excellence.

Letters used throughout the job search and interviewing process typically fall into three categories: letters of application, letters of inquiry, and responses to employer communication.

Letters of Application

Letters of application include responses to an advertised position, applications to a company when there is no advertised position, or attempts to introduce oneself to a company as an interested applicant. This type of letter usually contains three or four paragraphs that explain the reason for sending the letter, expand on the individual's interest in the position or company and provides one's qualifications, and indicate a follow-up response.

Letters of Inquiry

Letters of inquiry include requests for information about a company or about positions or openings in a particular field. These letters should be brief, concisely stating the information the applicant would like to receive, reasons that prompted the inquiry, and the address to which the information can be mailed.

Responses to Employer Communication

Response letters include confirmation of an appointment, letters of appreciation, and letters declining a job offer. These letters are different from the other types in that the individual is responding to specific action taken by the company. Exhibit 20.7 provides examples of the various

Exhibit 20.6

Factors Identified during the Employment Interview That Frequently Lead to Rejection

- Poor appearance
- Overbearing, overaggressive, conceited attitude
- Inability to express self clearly; poor voice, diction, grammar
- Lack of career planning; no purpose or goals
- Lack of interest and enthusiasm; a passive, indifferent manner
- Lack of confidence and poise; nervousness
- Failure to participate in extracurricular activities
- Overemphasis on money, interest in "best dollar" offer
- Poor scholastic record
- Unwillingness to start at the bottom; the expectation of too much too soon
- Evasiveness; failure to be clear about unfavorable factors in record
- Lack of tact
- Lack of maturity
- Lack of courtesy
- Condemnation of past employers
- Lack of social understanding
- Marked dislike for schoolwork
- Lack of vitality
- Failure to look interviewer in the eye
- Limp, fishy handshake
- Indecision
- Unhappy married life
- Friction with parents
- Little sense of humor
- Sloppy, poorly prepared application
- Evidence of merely shopping around for a job
- Desires job for short time only
- Lack of knowledge in field of specialization
- No interest in company or industry
- Emphasis on whom the applicant knows
- Unwillingness to go where company may want to send him
- Cynical attitude
- Low moral standards
- Laziness
- Intolerance; strong prejudice
- Narrow interests
- Evidence of wasted time
- Poor handling of personal finances
- No interest in community activities
- Inability to take criticism
- Lack of appreciation of the value of experience
- Radical ideas
- Tardiness (to interview) without good reason
- Failure to express appreciation for interviewer's time
- Failure to ask questions about the job
- Indefinite responses to questions

Source: R. E. Anderson, J. F. Hair, and A. J. Bush, *Professional Sales Management* (New York: McGraw-Hill Book Co., 1988), p. 231. Adapted from *The Northwestern Endicott Report*, published by The Placement Center, Northwestern University, Evanston, Illinois.

kinds of letters an individual might write in response to communication initiated by an employer. Regardless of the situation, it is important to focus on the purpose of the message and write with the clarity, openness, directness, and tact one would use in a face-to-face contact.

Sample Responses to Employers

Exhibit 20.7a & b

1212 Treadaway
Abilene, Texas 79682
June 30, 1992

George Tyron
Director of Marketing Training
Wallace Publications Group, Inc.
1439 Santa Monica Boulevard
Los Angeles, California 90029

Dear Mr. Tyron:

This note is to confirm our appointment for 10:00 a.m. on Monday, August 24, 1992. I look forward to meeting with you.

Sincerely,
(Signature)
John Martin

[A letter to confirm an appointment exhibits an applicant's enthusiasm, as well as an efficient, business-like approach.]

1212 Treadaway, Apt. 12
Abilene, Texas 79682
(915)873-2642

August 28, 1992

George Tyron
Director of Marketing Training
Wallace Publishing Group, Inc.
1439 Santa Monica Boulevard
Los Angeles, California 90029

Dear Mr. Tyron:

This note is meant as a "Thank You" for the interview we had on Monday. I enjoyed very much having the opportunity to meet you and discuss your—and I hope eventually, my—organization.

You have proved to me that Wallace Publishing is a dynamic and diversified firm, one that I feel positively about joining. I believe my educational background and work experience will facilitate the transition into your department.

Should you have any additional questions, feel free to call. I look forward to our next meeting in November, and I do thank you for scheduling it at a time when I can get away from school.

Sincerely,
(Signature)
John Martin

[A "Thank You" letter after the first interview is a must. It exhibits not only courtesy, but provides an opportunity for reinforcing one's qualifications in the mind of the interviewer. When time is short between first and second interviews, a FAX or other quick-forward communique may be appropriate.]

Exhibit 20.7c & d

Sample Responses to Employers

1212 Treadaway, Apt. 12
Abilene, Texas 79682
(915)873-2642

November 30, 1992

George Tyron
Wallace Publishing Group, Inc.
1439 Santa Monica Boulevard
Los Angeles, California 90029

Dear Mr. Tyron:

I really enjoyed our meeting Friday. Finding out that my research and public relations efforts in my previous employment closely parallels your departmental requirements confirmed my basic instinct that these are important aspects of business. I feel even more sure than ever that I can make a contribution to your company.

I look forward to the opportunity to visit with you and Mr. Royal on December 20. I have some ideas that I believe will interest you.

Thanks again for your time and the interesting and informative meeting.

Sincerely,
(Signature)
John Martin

[A thank you letter after a second interview is always appropriate.]

1212 Treadaway, Apt. 12
Abilene, Texas 79682
(915)873-2642

January 15, 1993

George Tyron
Director of Marketing Training
Wallace Publishing Group, Inc.
1439 Santa Monica Boulevard
Los Angeles, California 90029

Dear Mr. Tyron:

I just wanted to say that I am very sorry I did not meet all the criteria necessary for my employment with your company. However, I do want you to know that I enjoyed meeting you, and that I thank you for all the time you invested in trying to match my qualifications with your open position. Your advice about my future is invaluable to me.

Should you hear of any other positions that become available for which you think I might be suited, I would appreciate very much you contacting me. Again, thanks very much for your interest.

Sincerely,
(Signature)
John Martin

[A follow-up letter when the job went to someone else is a wise investment for the future; one never knows when another position will open up within that company, or when the contact may run across a position elsewhere that you would be imminently qualified for.]

In an article in the *New York Times*, Harris L. Sussman of Digital Equipment Corporation was quoted: "As a career counselor, I tell people that everybody is ultimately self-employed. And if you don't think that way, then you've given up control over the decisions in your life to somebody else. There are dozens and dozens of paths to follow."[12]

On the International Front

As international sales opportunities and foreign competition increase, companies are giving special attention to selecting professional salespeople qualified to sell in the international arena. The overall challenge to the international sales manager is to identify the right kind of person, matching certain personal qualities to the functional requirements of a specific selling situation.

A question often raised is whether there is one set of characteristics that makes up the ideal international salesperson. Although the tasks and skills vary from country to country, the successful international salesperson must possess certain key characteristics and attributes. According to Warren Keegan, international professor and consultant, these attributes are self-sufficiency, aggressiveness, and patience:

- *Self-sufficiency*—Salespeople must be secure in themselves, competent in the field, and self-confident, because traveling will not allow immediate counsel from their domestic counterparts.
- *Aggressiveness*—Salespeople must have determination, persistence, perseverance, and dedication. The doors to the international market do not always open as easily as they do domestically.
- *Patience*—Salespeople must have the ability to put up with unexpected delays and nonproductive periods.

The international salesperson must also possess personality dynamics and attitude traits such as interest, tact, emotional stability, consideration, trainability, and the ability to make decisions. Locating individuals with the characteristics and abilities to be adaptable and responsive is important, as is recognizing that the job will not be exactly the same in all markets.

As market conditions vary from country to country, so do the cultural perspectives and influences. The task of adapting to cultural dynamics is perhaps the most challenging one confronting the international salesperson. Thus, the international salesperson must be able to operate in many different climates and customs, requiring flexibility and sensitivity to strange surroundings and the irregularities of foreign situations.

The international salesperson proceeds with increased preparation, maturity, and occasional deep understanding. Lack of understanding may hinder adaptation and adjustment to differences, leading to frustration and insecurity. Overall, the salesperson must be imaginative to observe and adopt new approaches with an international orientation, to accomplish objectives in the light of these international market opportunities.

Sources: Warren J. Keegan, *Multinational Marketing Management* (Englewood Cliffs, NJ: Prentice-Hall, Inc., 1990); and Vernon R. Stauble, *International Center Newsletter* (Pomona, CA: California State University, Pomona, Spring 1987), p. 11.

Regardless of the path chosen, by using the marketing principles and sales communication skills presented in this book, the applicant will prepare for the future and achieve goals. By following the suggestions offered in this chapter, you can become a "career entrepreneur."[13] Furthermore, you will have achieved the ultimate job seeker's skill—marketing yourself.

Summary

Success in selling a product or service for a company must be preceded by an individual's ability to sell oneself in getting the job. This chapter helps the individual to become a career entrepreneur by understanding the nature of career management in preparing for a professional selling career.

Planning and researching a selling career are as vital as having the skills to do the job. One must consider carefully the desired qualities of an employer and the daily working environment. After these have been decided, the applicant must develop an effective résumé and cover letter and prepare well for the job interview. An effective way of selling oneself is through appropriate, well-written letters that impress the employer with the applicant's ability to communicate graciously and that stress the applicant's true interest in the job itself.

Key Terms

Chronological Résumé A résumé in which qualifications are arranged by category, in reverse chronological order

Cover Letter Letter written by the applicant to accompany a résumé; stresses the applicant's unique abilities for the job; its major aim is to secure an interview with the employer

Functional Résumé A résumé that emphasizes an individual's qualifications by skill areas

Interviewing Predictors of Rejection Factors during the interview that lead to rejection

Résumé A concise summary of a person's job qualifications

Targeted Résumé A résumé that emphasizes a specific position or job objective, or target

Review Questions

1. Explain the five guidelines that can help college graduates achieve their desired sales position.
2. Explain the four ways self-assessment may help you continue to develop your sales competence.
3. List and describe the six major sources for finding a position in sales.

4. Explain the three steps in selecting an employer and working environment.
5. List and explain the guidelines to use in assessing the appropriateness of a résumé.
6. List and explain the three most commonly used formats for résumés. Describe the advantages and disadvantages of each.
7. Explain the function of a cover letter and list the nine guidelines to follow when writing one.
8. List the eight critical skills that excite recruiters about candidates.
9. List and describe the four types of interviews.
10. In what four general areas do the common questions asked by recruiters fall? Give examples in each category.

Discussion Questions

1. Imagine yourself in the role of a corporate recruiter coming to your campus to interview students for positions in the career of your choice. Discuss your strengths and weaknesses. Discuss how you would prepare to talk with the recruiter.
2. Discuss the six sources for finding positions in sales. Identify those most pertinent to the type of position in which you are interested.
3. In teams of two, participate in a role-playing exercise in which you interview an employer. Follow the steps for selecting an employer and working environment.
4. Prepare a résumé. In small groups, critique the participants' résumés using the guidelines provided in this chapter.
5. In teams of two, practice job interviewing techniques by role-playing an employer and an applicant.
6. Discuss factors that lead to success, and contrast these with factors that may lead to rejection in a job search.

Changing Careers

Case 20.1

At age 24, Jennifer Sheridan is a sports nutritionist who works as a spokesperson for a leading public relations firm in Chicago, Illinois. Jennifer joined Action Health after she graduated from college, where she earned a certificate as a registered dietician. She went into this profession because she enjoyed being associated with health clubs and stores, sports medicine clinics, and sports-oriented people in general.

Jennifer's assignments consist of visiting clients to support the many lines of health products Action represents, and introducing new products and their uses. She also attends sports events, creating widespread exposure by presenting a good image of the firm. Her main responsibility, however, is to handle customer problems to maintain good relations with buyers.

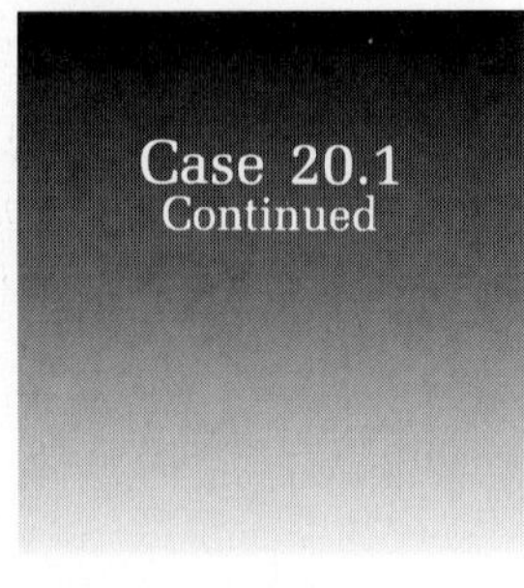

Jennifer has had 5 years of experience in her present position, currently earns $35,000 a year, and is eligible for a raise in 9 months. Although there is nothing wrong with her present position, she is starting to have some doubt about her career path. She is career-oriented and considers herself to be upwardly mobile and ambitious. Promotion opportunities to the managerial level become available perhaps every 3–4 years.

As Jennifer became more acquainted with the large pharmaceutical companies that sell drugs and medical equipment, she began to realize the potential opportunities for growth in a variety of domestic and international positions. She has recently been offered a sales position with a nationally known pharmaceutical firm selling medical equipment.

The starting salary of this sales position is $42,000 a year plus commission and a modest quarterly bonus depending on performance. In addition to the salary plus commission and bonus, she will receive an all-expense-paid automobile and an attractive health benefit package.

One of Jennifer's concerns is that she will have to relocate to southern California. The more Jennifer looks at the competitive nature of the industry and the cost of living in California, the more uncertain she becomes about giving up her secure job with Action Health. A major concern is that she has never really sold anything before. Her responsibility has been to simply discuss the products' benefits and present a favorable image of the company. She has never had to take an order, much less ask for one.

1. What should Jennifer evaluate about her present position as she tries to reach a decision?
2. What factors posing opportunity for advancement seem to be influential in encouraging Jennifer to accept this new offer?
3. What would you advise Jennifer to do in her efforts to manage a career change?

Case 20.2

A Career Decision

John Hall is facing a career-change dilemma. He has been with American Household Products for almost 4 years, representing the company's line of products in 14 states. His career ambition is to be in management someday and reduce the tremendous amount of traveling he does. He is undergoing pressure at home because he has to be on the road at least twice a week.

American has an outstanding management internship program. This program involves management training for 4 months and then an assignment as a management trainee for an additional 4 months. The requirements for selection consideration are outstanding performance and loyalty and 6 years with the firm. John has an excellent performance record and has shown extreme loyalty to the firm, placing him at the top of the list for consideration to be admitted into the program. The obstacle is that no one has ever been selected with less than 4 years of service to the firm.

Case 20.2
Continued

John is committed to becoming a sales manager and is confident of his ability to undertake management training and do a good job as a manager. Because of his disappointment with American at this time, he has become encouraged by an offer from a competitive firm, since he is not eligible for consideration in the internship program for two more years. American did, however, offer him a 15-percent pay increase to continue serving in the capacity of sales representative, and in 2 years he would qualify for the management internship program.

The job offer is a sales management position with little training for an entirely new territory. The decision is difficult because John is happy working for American and committed to his clientele. He knows his territory well, and the pay is attractive. He is unsure of taking on management responsibility without adequate training, and he worries about the time required to get acquainted with a new company, territory, and clientele.

1. Evaluate John's career-path decision.
2. Would John's decision to accept a position with a competitive firm be considered unethical?
3. Do you agree with the 6 years of service commitment that American requires before a salesperson can be considered for management training?

Notes

1. Alice Shane, "Facing Up to a Recruiter," *Sales & Marketing Management*, May 1989, p. 38.
2. M. M. Kennedy, "Selling Yourself on Your Skills," in *Business Week's Guide to Careers*, "How to Get a Job Guide," 1986 edition, p. 29.
3. K. O. Dowd, "How to Realistically Assess Yourself," in *Business Week's Guide to Careers*, "How to Get a Job Guide," 1986 edition, pp. 6–7.
4. Kennedy, "Selling Yourself on Your Skills."
5. Dowd, "How to Realistically Assess Yourself."
6. S. Grundfest, "A Cover Letter and Resume Guide," in *Business Week's Guide to Careers*, "How to Get a Job Guide," 1986 edition, pp. 8–9.
7. N. B. Sigband and A. Bell, *Communication for Management and Business*, 4th ed. (Chicago, IL: Scott, Foresman and Company, 1986).
8. Ibid.
9. Tony Lee, "Making an Impression," in *Managing Your Career, The Wall Street Journal*, the college edition of the National Business Employment Weekly, Spring. 1989, pp. 30–31.
10. Ibid., p. 31.
11. "Preparing for the Interview," (Pomona, CA: The Career Center, California State Polytechnic University, 1989).
12. Dorothy Leeds, *Marketing Yourself—The Ultimate Job Seeker's Guide* (New York: Harper Collins Publishers, 1991), p. 7.
13. Ibid.

Glossary

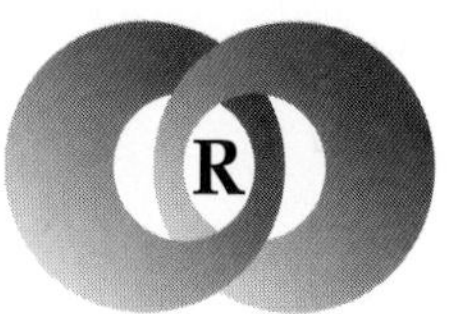

Account Penetration Matching the size of the order to fit the customer's buying situation

Advantage A term used to describe the function of a feature

Advertising Any paid form of nonpersonal communication of ideas, goods, or services used by individuals, business firms, and nonprofit organizations, the purpose of which is to inform and persuade members of a particular audience

Affinity The degree to which salespeople and their customers like or appreciate each other

Affirmation A statement of fact or belief that is written out in a personal, positive, present-tense form, as though the goal were already accomplished

Aggressive Behavior Seeking to establish one's own ego as uppermost in a situation

Anecdote A story that provides a specific incident to clarify or illustrate a product's features, advantages, or benefits: a detailed example

Assertiveness Ability to share the entire range of thoughts and emotions with confidence and skill

Attitude A person's feelings, tendencies, or point of view

Backwardation A form of analysis that allows the company to examine the company's marketing efforts backwards from the point at which they touch the ultimate consumer.

Belief A person's opinion or thought on a particular subject

Benefit Satisfaction the buyer derives from a particular advantage or feature

Buying Signal An indication that the prospect is interested in the product or service and is preparing to make a buying decision

"Buzz" Words Words that are popular in a culture, but have lost their precise meanings through overuse: jargon

Cellular Phone Phone that can be used from anyplace: "wireless" phone

Center of Influence Influential person in the community who is in a position to, and willing to, provide referred leads

Chronological Résumé A résumé in which qualifications are arranged by category, in reverse chronological order

Closing Vehicle Also **closing method;** one of seven methods—assumptive, alternative choice, summary of benefits, balance sheet, concession/inducement, direct appeal, and narrative—by which the salesperson obtains the customer's commitment to buy

Cognitive Dissonance Doubt that the customer experiences after the buying decision has been reached

Common Ground Area of mutual interest between salesperson and customer

Comparison A form of presentation support that shows similarities between two points

Compensation Plan Method by which a salesperson is rewarded

Competitive Differential Advantage (CDA) Analysis An analytical tool used to determine which of two or more products or services is superior

Complementary Relationship A relationship in which one person's behavior complements (or reciprocates) the other's

Confirming Message A message that expresses feelings of value toward others

Congruence When verbal statements and nonverbal behavior are perceived to reinforce or emphasize what one is saying

Consultative Selling Model Selling strategies that are customer-driven

Context of Communication The time and place in which the communication takes place

Control Refers to who makes decisions in the relationship

Cooling-off Law Provides buyers in certain states with a specified period within which to void sales contracts; applies particularly to door-to-door and high-pressure sales

Cover Letter Letter written by the applicant to accompany a résumé; stresses the applicant's unique abilities for the job; its major aim is to secure an interview with the employer

Culture Shared language, beliefs, events, symbols, rituals, and value systems of a group of people; organizational culture evolves from past members' behavior and is reconfirmed by current members

Customer-driven One of two extensions of the market-oriented system; implies a process in which the focus is on identifying and satisfying buyers' needs and building a relationship that results in repeat business

Debilitative Emotions Emotions of extreme intensity and duration, to the point that they prevent salespeople from functioning as they would like

Decoding The process of making order and sense from the words and actions of another communicator

Defensive Climate Climate established by response styles that generate an atmosphere where participants feel they are being attacked

Disconfirming Message A message that expresses feelings of lack of value toward others

Disfluency Use of stalling words or sounds, such as "uh" or "ah," while thinking

Drive Strong internal structure that induces action to fulfill needs

Effectiveness Results-oriented assessment of whether the organization's objectives are achieved

Efficiency Focus on costs and economical use of resources

Electronic Bulletin Board Message board normally hung in a particular place; messages on the board can be updated or changed via a remote keyboard

Emotion Consists of four components that directly influence a positive sales image: physiological changes, nonverbal manifestations, cognitive interpretations, and verbal expressions

Encoding The process of putting ideas and feelings into words and actions

Endless Chain Prospecting concept based on the idea that the salesperson will obtain names of additional prospects at each interview for future sales calls

Entertainment Providing meals, shows, or other pleasurable benefits in the hope that the prospective customer will be kindly disposed to do business with the host salesperson's company

Environmental Noise Disruptive elements outside the receiver that make hearing and understanding difficult

Ethics Principles of conduct governing an individual or group: a set of moral principles or values

Example The recounting of a brief, specific instance to illustrate a product's features and benefits

Extended Family The nuclear family and other relatives

Facilitative Emotions Those emotions, regardless of intensity or duration, that contribute to one's effective performance

Facsimile (Fax) Machine Machine that transmits a copy of a document via telephone line

Family A group of two or more persons related by blood, marriage, or adoption

Feature A benefit fact related to a product or service

Features-Advantages-Benefits (FAB) Analysis An analytical tool based on the information gathered in a CDA analysis; it links features, advantages, and benefits in a hierarchical, comparative fashion

Feedback Receiver's response to another person's verbal and nonverbal communication

Feeling Statement An expression of empathy by one person to another

Focus Group A group of people brought together and asked to talk freely about a product or subject

Foreign Corrupt Practices Act Limits payment of fees for obtaining foreign contracts

Formal Close Also **final close;** a request that the prospect make a decision or commitment of payment in exchange for the product or service

Formula Model A structured or preordered plan for achieving a buying decision

Free Information Information that goes beyond or is outside the focus of the sales interview and that the salesperson can appropriate and use advantageously

Functional Résumé A résumé that emphasizes an individual's qualifications by skill areas

Goodwill The sum total or value of all the positive feelings that a customer has toward the salesperson and the company

Gratuity A gift that rewards and is of personal benefit to the customer; to qualify as a gratuity, the gift must not unduly influence or corrupt the buyer

Highlighting Referring to something said earlier

Household All persons, related or not, who occupy a housing unit

Image Management Computer processing of images (art, designs, and photos.)

Inciting Words Emotionally active words that may evoke a defensive or guarded stance on the part of the listener

Incongruence When nonverbal behavior is perceived as contradicting one's verbal statements

Inferential Message A message that is assumed, but may not be based on fact

Interpersonal Listening Listening to others

Interviewing Predictors of Rejection Factors during the interview that lead to rejection

Intimacy The closeness of one's contact with another person on intellectual, emotional, and physical levels

Intrapersonal Listening Listening to one's own inner voice

Irrational Thinking Thinking that is muddled, leads to illogical conclusions, and promotes debilitative emotions

Jargon Specialized vocabulary and idioms used by members of a certain profession

Johari Window A grid by which one can chart the dynamics of any conversation between people

Lead Person or organization that could benefit from buying a particular product or service

Libel Unfair or untrue statements about a company or an individual communicated in writing to a third party

Major Buying Points A prospect's most important buying concerns, those points that have the most influence on the buying decision

Management The planning, implementation, and control of the personal selling component of the promotional variable in the marketing mix

Minor Buying Points Peripheral or secondary concerns that must be dealt with after the prospect's major buying concerns have been addressed

Misrepresentation Providing loosely interpreted or false data for the purpose of obtaining business

Modem Converts data into a form that can be sent over telephone lines, enabling computers to "talk" to each other

Motive A drive directed toward a specific goal

Need The result of a deficit condition or a lack of something desirable

Needs-Satisfaction Model A system by which a product is analyzed in relation to customer needs

Negotiation Discussion of specific proposals among two or more people to find a mutually acceptable solution to a problem

Networking Process of making and using contacts

Nonverbal Message Body language and other physical actions intended for communication

Nuclear Family The immediate group of father, mother, and children living together

Operationalize Verbal language that breaks into distinct steps what others say and do.

Organizational Climate Human environment in which employees accomplish their tasks

Parallel Relationship A combination of complementary and symmetrical relationships

Perception Interpreted data about a particular thing

Personal Observation Recognizing and singling out leads in any circumstance or situation

Portable Data Recorder (PDR) Used to conduct inventories and count shelf displays in retail stores

Power Ability to influence another person to accomplish the preferred results

Profitability Earning and increasing profits by generating revenue through goods and services

Prospect A *qualified* potential buyer who has the means and authority to complete the transaction

Psychic Income A measure of one's degree of satisfaction relative to having made someone else's life better, as well as improving one's own growth and development

Publicity Any unpaid form of personal communication that stimulates demand for a person, product, organization, or cause

Qualifying Act of identifying legitimate buyers

Qualitative Determinants Derived from the nature of the relationship between the customer and the salesperson, and gauged by how well their needs are mutually satisfied

Quantitative Determinants Assigning a numerical or dollar value to everything a salesperson does

Rational Thinking Thinking that results in logical conclusions and promotes facilitative emotions

Reciprocity The practice of doing business with prospects to convince them to do the same in return

Recruitment The process of seeking out potential applicants, discussing the company with them, and encouraging them to apply for a sales position

Referral Any identification of a suspect by a third party

Relationship Determinants The eight factors by which one establishes an interpersonal relationship: appearance, similarity, complementarity, reciprocity, competence, disclosure, proximity, and exchange

Relationship-driven A reciprocal process between customer and salesperson that enables them to meet each other's needs

Relationship Management Tactful, sincere communication that nurtures a close connection between salesperson and customer

Résumé A concise summary of a person's job qualifications

Sales Manager A person who plans, directs, and controls the personal selling activities of a business; duties include recruiting, selecting, training, equipping, assigning, routing, supervising, paying, and motivating salespeople

Sales-driven Implies a unilateral process in which the salesperson acts as the chief authority, almost coercing the customer into a buying decision

Selection The process of choosing which candidates have the best qualifications and the greatest aptitude for a particular job

Self-Acceptance The degree to which a person likes and is satisfied with self in the role of salesperson

Self-Actualization The process of selecting specific aspects of one's sales image that need changing, setting personal goals, and devising a plan to accomplish them

Self-Awareness The process of bringing all the information about self that is associated with one's sales image to a conscious level

Self-Disclosure Verbally communicating information about oneself to another

Self-Management The control and effort salespeople exert by handling their activities in ways that match their personal objectives to their company's goals

Self-Sabotage Destruction of one's goals or career because of an unconscious fear of success

Selling The process of defining needs and persuading potential customers to respond favorably to an idea that will result in mutual satisfaction for both buyer and seller

Slander Unfair or untrue oral statements made about another (for instance, a competitor) to a third party (such as a customer) that damage the business or personal reputation of that company or a person within that company

SOFTENS Technique Acronym for **S**miling, **O**pen posture, **F**orward lean, **T**ouching by shaking hands, **E**ye contact, **N**odding, and **S**pace: technique for open, relational communication

Standard Industrial Classification (SIC) Codes Codes developed by the U.S. government to group industries according to types of economic activities

Stimulus-Response Model A model in which external stimulus (such as product beauty or description of benefits) excites the sensations of the prospect

Stress The nonspecific response of the body to any demand made on it

Stressors Anything that causes the body to react physiologically or psychologically, or causes stress

Structure Arrangement or interrelation of all parts of an organization

Subculture A group of people within a culture who hold values, interests, and experiences in common

Supportive Climate Climate established by response styles that generate an atmosphere of acceptance

Suspect Each person within a target market for a product or service

Symmetrical Relationship A balanced relationship in which both buyers and sellers contribute to the relationship

Targeted Résumé A résumé that emphasizes a specific position or job objective, or target

Teleconference A visual phone call, in which cameras and microphones in one meeting room transmit visual and auditory signals (via satellite or telephone line) to another, similarly equipped room anywhere else in the world

Telemarketing Person-to-person interaction between salesperson and suspect via telecommunications systems

Traditional Selling Model Selling strategies that are product- or sales-driven

Trial Close A buyer's commitment on a minor point that eventually leads to a formal close

Uniform Commercial Code (UCC) Governs such aspects of selling as the need for written contracts, warranties, delivery agreements, and commissions

Values and Lifestyles (VALS) Program Consumer typology as categorized by psychographic research

Verbal Message Any verbal utterance intended for the purpose of communication

Video Feedback Videotapes of customers' responses to a product or service; lasts 1 minute or more

Videotex A central computer available to the general public for services ranging from sales messages to shopping tips

Vocalics The manner in which people say words, as opposed to the actual words being spoken

Voice Mail Complex telephone answering machine capable of giving prerecorded messages and receiving incoming messages

Want Learned needs

Wide-Area Telecommunication Service (WATS) Line Telephone service by which long-distance incoming and outgoing calls can be made at no charge or at a reduced rate

Index

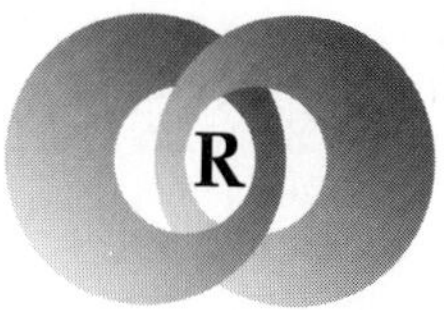

Credits

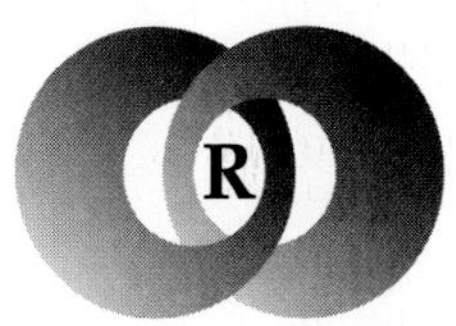

Color Photos

P. 19 Reprinted with permission from *Entrepreneural Woman* Magazine November, 1991.

P. 33 Photo by Al Ferreira, Courtesy of The Stanley Works.

P. 58 Robert Krist, Photographer. Courtesy of Merck & Co., Inc.

P. 64 © 1986 Gary Gladstone

P. 114 Courtesy of Metropolitan Life Insurance Co., NY, NY.

P. 124 John Segal

P. 156 Courtesy of Frito-Lay, Inc.

P. 177 Westlight © Adamsmith

P. 245 Courtesy of Lakeway Inn, A Conference Resort.

P. 300 Stephen Sweny

P. 303 © Chris Andrews/Stock Boston

P. 325 From The Soft Sell, Tim Connor, CSp, Training Associates International, Ann Arbor, MI 48106.

P. 384 Illustration: Steve Attoe

P. 462 Courtesy of Dow Jones and Co. /*The Wall Street Journal*/ J. Walter Thompson.

P. 515 The Clorox Company

P. 521 Photo compliments of Campbell Soup Co.

P. 540 Courtesy of NASA

P. 543 © Robert Rathe/Stock Boston

P. 544 © Comstock

P. 569 © Mark Hanauer/Onyx

P. 644 Photo copyright © Alastair Finlay.

Chapter 1

Figure 1.1 Reprinted by permission of *Sales & Marketing Management*. Copyright: March 1991.

Figure 1.2 Reprinted by permission of *Sales & Marketing Management*. Copyright: March 1991.

Figure 1.3 Material from "A job hunter's crystal ball." Copyright © 1989, *The Los Angeles Times*. Chart reprinted by permission. All rights reserved.

P. 17 Reprinted with permission from The Forum Corporation.

Pp. 6–7 F. A. Russell, et al, Excerpt from *Selling Principles and Practices*, 11e. Copyright © 1982 by and reprinted by permission of McGraw-Hill, Inc.

Table 1.1 From *Sales & Marketing Management*, February 20, 1989, pp. 24, 26. Reprinted by permission of *Sales & Marketing Management*. Copyright: Survey of Selling Costs, February 20, 1989.

Chapter 2

Pp. 57–58 Paul Hershey, "A Look at Situational Selling in Action" by Paul Hershey, *Selling: A Behavioral Science Approach*, © 1988, pp. 120–124. Adapted by permission of Prentice Hall, Englewood Cliffs, New Jersey.

Chapter 3

P. 94 Illustration: Joel Spector.

P. 96 Reprinted from *TeleProfessional Magazine*, Waterloo, Iowa, April 1991.

P. 100 Reprinted from *TeleProfessional Magazine*, Waterloo, Iowa, Winter 1989.

Exhibit 3.1 Reprinted by permission of Avon Products, Inc.

Exhibit 3.2 "AMA Adopts New Code of Ethics" from *Marketing News*, September 11, 1987, pp. 1, 10. Reprinted by permission of The American Marketing Association.

Exhibit 3.7 Chart of "Five Rules for Women in International Sales" from *Going International* by Lennie Copeland and Lewis Briggs. Copyright © 1985 by Lennie Copeland and Lewis Briggs. Reprinted by permission of Random House, Inc.

Chapter 5

Figure 5.1 Courtesy of MacGregor Golf Co.

Table 5.2 Chart of "Topics Covered in Sales Training Programs" from *Training The Sales Force: A Progress Report* by David S. Hopkins. Copyright © 1984 by and reprinted by permission of The Conference Board.

Exhibit 5.3 "EC '92: A Guide for the Small Company" from *Sales & Marketing Management* by Daniel M. Rosen. Reprinted by permission of *Sales & Marketing Management*. Copyright: September 1990.

Exhibit 5.8 Excerpted from *Marketing Problem Solver* by Cochrance Chase and Kenneth L. Barasch. Copyright 1977 by the author. Reprinted with the permission of the publisher, CHILTON BOOK COMPANY, Radnor, PA.

Chapter 6

Exhibit 6.2 © Yellow Pages Publishers Association.

Exhibit 6.4 Agency: The Campbell Group, Baltimore, MD. Client: Inter-Continental Hotels.

Exhibit 6.5 Figure from *Market Research: Methodological Foundations*, Fifth Edition, by Gilbert A. Churchill, Jr., copyright © 1991 by The Dryden Press, reproduced by permission of the publisher.

Chapter 7

Figure 7.1 Figure from *Consumer Behavior*, Sixth Edition, by James F. Engel, Roger D. Blackwell, and Paul W. Miniard, copyright © 1990 by The Dryden Press, reproduced by permission of the publisher.

Exhibit 7.2 Reprinted with permission © *American Demographics*, August 1990, p. 37.

Exhibit 7.3 Reprinted with permission © *American Demographics*, June 1990, p. 32.

Figure 7.3 Reprinted with permission © *American Demographics*, July 1990, p. 30.

Table 7.1 Chart of "Diagnosing The Consumer Decision-Making Process" excerpted from *Consumer Behavior*, Sixth Edition by James F. Engle, Roger D. Blackwell, and Paul W. Miniard, copyright © 1990 The Dryden Press, reprinted by permission of the publisher.

Table 7.2 Chart of "Characteristics of The Consumer Decision-Making Process" excerpted from *Consumer Behavior*, Sixth Edition by James F. Engle, Roger D. Blackwell, and Paul W. Miniard, copyright © 1990 The Dryden Press, reprinted by permission of the publisher.

Table 7.3 Chart of "A Summary of American Cultural Values" by Leon G. Schiffman/Leslie Lazar Kanuk, *Consumer Behavior*, 4e, © 1991, p. 424. Adapted by permission of Prentice Hall, Englewood, New Jersey.

Exhibit 7.4 "National Presidents Show Concern" from *The Kappa Alpha Theta Magazine*, Summer 1991. Copyright © 1991 by and reprinted by permission of *The Kappa Alpha Theta Magazine* & The National Panhellenic Conference.

Chapter 8

Pp. 238–239 Barbara Sanfilippo, "Thirteen Steps to Develop Your Own Sales Culture" from *Personal Selling Power* by Barbara Sanfilippo. Copyright © 1986 by Personal Selling Power. Reprinted by permission of the publisher.

Table 8.2 Chart of "How Sales People Relate Themselves & Other People" from *Effective Selling Through Psychology* by V.R. Buzzota, R.I. Lefton, & M. Shergerg. Copyright © 1972 by V.R. Buzzaota, R.I. Lefton, & M. Shergerg. Reprinted by permission of HarperCollins Publishers.

Figure 8.2 Chart of "Dimensional Model of Sales Behavior" from *Effective Selling Through Psychology* by V.R. Buzzota, R.I. Lefton, and M. Shergerg. Copyright © 1972 by V.R. Buzzota, R.I. Lefton, and M. Shergerg. Reprinted by permission of HarperCollins Publishers.

Chapter 9

Exhibit 9.1 Excerpt from "Turning Salespeople into Partners" from *Sales & Marketing Management*, by Arthur Bragg. Reprinted by permission of *Sales & Marketing Management*. Copyright: August 1986.

Exhibit 9.2 Excerpt from *Listening a Response Technique* by Loretta Girzaitis. Copyright © 1972 by and reprinted by permission of Loretta Girzaitis, Author, Speaker, Director of Victories Spirit Enterprises.

Table 9.1 Chart of "Review of Guidelines to Good Listening" by Anthony J. Alessandra, *Non-Manipulative Selling*, © 1979, pp. 77–79. Adapted by permission of Prentice Hall, Englewood Cliffs, New Jersey.

Chapter 10

Table 10.2 Chart of "Determining Your Sales Call Objective," excerpt from *Role Playing: The Principles of Selling* by David Sellars III, copyright © 1987 by The Dryden Press, reprinted by permission of the publisher.

Skill Builder 10.1 Excerpt from "Write a Dialogue For Your Product or Service Moving Through Five Levels" by William C. Mason from Marketing 435, November 29, 1989, pp. 14–15. Reprinted by permission of the author.

Table 10.4 Excerpt from "Rapport Building for Salespeople: A Neuro-Linguistic Approach" from *The Journal of Personal Selling & Sales Management* by William G. Nickles, Robert F. Everett, & Ronald Klein. Copyright © 1983 by and reprinted by permission of Pi Sigma Epsilon.

Chapter 11

Table 11.2 Chart of "Major Purposes of Questioning" excerpted from *Selling: Marketing Personified* by Donald D. Balsley and E. Patricia Birsner, copyright © 1990 by The Dryden Press, reprinted by permission of the publisher.

Exhibit 11.1 Chart of "Types, Purposes, and Uses of Questions" excerpted from *Selling: Marketing Personified* by Ronald D. Balsley and E. Patricia Birsner, copyright © 1990 by The Dryden Press, reprinted by permission of the publisher.

Chapter 12

Figure 12.3 Reprinted with permission of Dartnell Corporation, Chicago, Illinois.

Chapter 13

Figure 13.1 Figure from *Fundamentals of Selling*, third edition, by Charles Futrell, copyright © 1990 by Richard D. Irwin, Inc. Reprinted by permission of the publisher.

Exhibit 13.2 From *The Marketer* April 1990. NTC Publishing Group.

Exhibit 13.3 Urban Decision Systems, Inc., A Blackburn Group Company.

Exhibit 13.4 Compliments of The Drake Hotel.

Exhibit 13.5 From *The Marketer* April 1990. NTC Publishing Group.

Exhibit 13.6 Artwork courtesy of Claritas/NPDC (formerly Claritas Corporation and National Planning Data Corporation), The Leader in Precision Marketing ™.

Exhibit 13.7 Courtesy ITT Corporation

Chapter 15

Figure 15.1 Figure from *Selling: Principles and Methods*, ninth edition, by Carlton A. Pederson, Milburn D. Wright, and Barton A. Weitz, copyright © 1988 by Richard D. Irwin, Inc. Reprinted by permission of the publisher.

Chapter 17

Figure 17.1 Reprinted by permission of the publisher from "Telemarketing," by John I. Coppett and Roy Dale Voorhees, *Industrial Marketing Management*, 1983, p. 81. Copyright 1983 by Elsevier Science Publishing Co., Inc.

Chapter 18

Figure 18.4 "Straight-line approach to routing," from *Selling: The Personal Force in Marketing* by Donald W. Jackson, William H. Cunningham, and Isabella C.M. Cunningham, 1988, p. 94. Reprinted by permission of John Wiley & Sons, Inc.

Figure 18.5 "Skip-stop approach to routing," from *Selling: The Personal Force in Marketing* by Donald W. Jackson, William H. Cunningham, and Isabella C.M. Cunningham, 1988, p. 94. Reprinted by permission of John Wiley & Sons, Inc.

Figure 18.6 "Leapfrog approach to routing," from *Selling: The Personal Force in Marketing* by Donald W. Jackson, William H. Cunningham, and Isabella C.M. Cunningham, 1988, p. 93. Reprinted by permission of John Wiley & Sons, Inc.

Figure 18.7 "Cloverleaf approach to routing," from *Selling: The Personal Force in Marketing* by Donald W. Jackson, William H. Cunningham, and Isabella C.M. Cunningham, 1988, p. 93. Reprinted by permission of John Wiley & Sons, Inc.

Figure 18.8 "Circular approach to routing," from *Selling: The Personal Force in Marketing* by Donald W. Jackson, William H. Cunningham, and Isabella C.M. Cunningham, 1988, p. 92. Reprinted by permission of John Wiley & Sons, Inc.

Exhibit 18.2 © Comstock

Chapter 19

Figure 19.1, 19.3, 19.4, 19.5, 19.6, 19.7, 19.8, 19.10, 19.11 Figures from *Sales Management: Analysis and Decision Making* by Thomas N. Ingram and Raymond W. LaForge, copyright © 1989 by The Dryden Press, reprinted by permission of the publisher.

Figure 19.9 Reprinted by permission of *Sales & Marketing Management*. Copyright: *Survey of Selling Costs*, February 20, 1989.

Figure 19.12 26th Survey of Sales Force Compensation, © 1990 Dartnell Books, Dartnell Corporation, Chicago, IL.

Table 19.1 Chart of "Comparison of Sales Organization Structures," excerpt from *Sales Management: Analysis and Decision Making* by Thomas N. Ingram and Raymond LaForge, copyright 1989 by The Dryden Press. Reprinted by permission of the publisher.

Table 19.2 Chart of "Summary of Financial-Compensation Plans," excerpt from *Sales Management: Analysis and Decision Making* by Thomas N. Ingram and Raymond LaForge, copyright 1989 by The Dryden Press. Reprinted by permission of the publisher.

Exhibit 19.4 Chart of "Checklist for Developing Sales Training Programs" from *Professional Sales Management* by Ralph Anderson, Joseph Hair, Jr., and Alan Bush. Copyright © 1988 by and reprinted by permission of McGraw-Hill, Inc.

Exhibit 19.5 Chart of "Example of a District Sales Manager's Yearly Appraisal," Figure from *Sales Management*, Second Edition by Charles M. Futrell, copyright © 1988 by The Dryden Press, reproduced by permission of the publisher.

Table 19.4 Chart of "Sales Performance Evaluation" from *Professional Sales Management* by R.E. Anderson, J.F. Hair, and A.J. Bush. Copyright © 1988 by and reprinted by permission of McGraw-Hill, Inc.